24th Italian Symposium on Advanced Database Systems (SEBD 2016)

Ugento, Italy
19 – 22 June 2016

Editors:

Mario A. Bochicchio
Giansalvatore Mecca

ISBN: 978-1-5108-3690-7

Printed from e-media with permission by:

Curran Associates, Inc.
57 Morehouse Lane
Red Hook, NY 12571

Some format issues inherent in the e-media version may also appear in this print version.

Printed by Curran Associates, Inc. (2017)

For permission requests, please contact Matematicamente.It
at the address below.

Matematicamente.It
Corso Umberto, 39
73010 San Donato (Lecce)
Italy

info@matematicamente.it

Additional copies of this publication are available from:

Curran Associates, Inc.
57 Morehouse Lane
Red Hook, NY 12571 USA
Phone: 845-758-0400
Fax: 845-758-2633
Email: curran@proceedings.com
Web: www.proceedings.com

Volume Editors

Mario A. Bochicchio
Dipartimento di Ingegneria dell'Innovazione
Università del Salento
Via per Monteroni
73100 Lecce, Italy
mario.bochicchio@unisalento.it

Giansalvatore Mecca
Dipartimento di Matematica, Informatica ed Economia
Università della Basilicata
C.da Macchia Romana
85100 Potenza, Italy
giansalvatore.mecca@unibas.it

Preface

The Italian Symposium on Advanced Database Systems (SEBD) is the major annual event of the Italian database research community. The twenty-fourth edition of SEBD is organized by the Universities of Salento, in Ugento (LE) from June 19th to June 22nd 2016.

The symposium program includes invited keynote talks by Alon Halevy on structured data in Web search results, by Shamkant B. Navathe on challenges and opportunities of data mining and predictive modeling applications for clinical healthcare data and by Michael Franklin on human-in-the-loop analytics.

It also includes tutorials by Michelangelo Ceci on Big Data analytics, by Ernesto Damiani on techniques, technologies and models for Big Data as a service and by Antonella Longo on service level aware contract management: data management models and methods.

The research track involves presentations of 6 research papers and 35 discussion papers. The latter are shorter papers mainly devoted to presentations of preliminary and ongoing work, system and application descriptions and new ideas of interest to the SEBD audience. Discussion papers include also extended abstracts of recent publications of the authors. The papers cover several research topics, such as query answering, data modeling, data integration and interoperability, Big Data and NoSQL systems, ontologies and the Semantic Web, process and service management, data mining, knowledge discovery, data clustering, logic programming and data warehousing.

This year the symposium also hosts a Panel on Big Data: perspective & opportunities which includes talks by senior members of the community: Fosca Giannotti (CNR Pisa), Sonia Bergamaschi (Università di Modena e Reggio Emilia) and Donato Malerba (Università degli Studi di Bari) and Mauro Draoli (AGID).

We would like to thank the invited keynote speakers and presenters of the tutorials, all authors who submitted papers to the symposium, the members of the SEBD Steering Committee for their valuable support in the various decisions that had to be taken during the event organization, the members of the Program Committee and the additional reviewers for their efforts to produce fair and thorough evaluations of the submitted papers, the local organization committee headed by Mario Bochicchio, the general chair Paolo Paolini and the publicity chair Antonella Longo.

We are grateful to the sponsors for their generous support: Dipartimento di Ingegneria dell'Innovazione dell'Università del Salento, Dipartimento di Informatica dell'Università di Bari, Fondazione Politecnico di Milano and l'Università della Calabria. Finally, we would like to thank the organizing agency Matematicamente.it for supporting and making effective the symposium.

Lecce, June 2016

Mario A. Bochicchio
Giansalvatore Mecca

Organization

The 2016 edition of the SEBD is organized by the University of Salento (DII Department)

General Chair

Paolo Paolini	Politecnico di Milano

Program Chairs

Mario A. Bochicchio	Università del Salento
Giansalvatore Mecca	Università della Basilicata

Local Chair

Antonella Longo	Università del Salento

Organizing Committee

Barbara Livieri	Università del Salento
Massimo Marra	Università del Salento
Donato Tarantino	Università del Salento
Lucia Vaira	Università del Salento
Marco Zappatore	Università del Salento

Program Committee

Giuseppe Amato	NEMIS
Maurizio Atzori	Università di Cagliari
Francesco Buccafurri	Università di Reggio Calabria
Andrea Calì	University of Oxford
Barbara Catania	Università di Genova
Michelangelo Ceci	Università di Bari
Silvia Chiusano	Politecnico di Torino
Nicola Ferro	Università di Padova
Matteo Interlandi	University of California, Los Angeles
Davide Martinenghi	Politecnico di Milano
Elio Masciari	ICAR-CNR
Michele Melchiori	Università di Brescia
Stefano Montanelli	Università di Milano
Paolo Papotti	Arizona State University
Marco Patella	Università di Bologna
Domenico Potena	Università Politecnica delle Marche

Andrea Pugliese	Università della Calabria
Elisa Quintarelli	Politecnico di Milano
Salvatore Rinzivillo	KDD Lab
Riccardo Rosati	Università La Sapienza di Roma
Salvatore Ruggieri	Università di Pisa
Maria Luisa Sapino	Università di Torino
Laura Tarantino	Università dell'Aquila
Sergio Tessaris	Libera Università di Bozen - Bolzano
Riccardo Torlone	Università Roma Tre
Pierangelo Veltri	Università di Catanzaro
Gianluigi Viscusi	École Polytechnique Fédérale de Lausanne, EPFL

Steering Committee

Maristella Agosti	Università di Padova
Antonio Albano	Università di Pisa
Paolo Atzeni	Roma Tre Università
Sonia Bergamaschi	Università di Modena e Reggio Emilia
Valeria De Antonellis	Università di Brescia
Maurizio Lenzerini	Università La Sapienza di Roma
Domenico Saccà	Università della Calabria
Fabio Schreiber	Politecnico di Milano
Letizia Tanca	Politecnico di Milano
Paolo Tiberio	Università di Modena e Reggio Emilia

External Reviewers

Filippo Benvenuti	Università Politecnica delle Marche
Marcello Buoncristiano	Università della Basilicata
Antonio Giuzio	Università della Basilicata
Pietro Hiram Guzzi	Università di Catanzaro
Mirjana Mazuran	Politecnico di Milano
Alex Mircoli	Università Politecnica delle Marche
Serena Nicolazzo	Università di Reggio Calabria
Giulio Rossetti	KDD Lab
Donatello Santoro	Università della Basilicata
Cinzia Incoronata Spina	Università di Padova
Emanuele Storti	Università Politecnica delle Marche
Giuseppe Tradigo	Università di Catanzaro
Lucia Vaira	Università del Salento
Enzo Veltri	Università della Basilicata
Marco Zappatore	Università del Salento

Patronage & Sponsors

UNIVERSITÀ DEL SALENTO
DIPARTIMENTO DI INGEGNERIA DELL'INNOVAZIONE

UNIVERSITÀ DEGLI STUDI DI BARI ALDO MORO

Fondazione Politecnico di Milano

UNIVERSITÀ DELLA CALABRIA
DIPARTIMENTO DI INGEGNERIA INFORMATICA, MODELLISTICA, ELETTRONICA E SISTEMISTICA
DIMES

Contents

1 Tutorials

2 Keynote Talks

3 Research Papers

4 Discussion Papers

Big Data Analytics

Michelangelo Ceci, University of Bari

michelangelo.ceci@uniba.it

Big data is a broad term that indicates data sets so large or complex that make traditional data processing applications inadequate. Challenges include analysis, data capture, data curation, search, sharing, storage, transfer, visualization, querying and information privacy. Among them, we will consider the extremely challenging task of big data analysis whose goal is to turn an ocean of messy data into knowledge and wisdom. In this task, four concepts are typically considered: i) Use as much data as possible, following the principle that "even noisy Big Data could be more valuable than tiny samples" (Agrawal et al., 2011). ii) Take care about correlation rather than causation: Figuring out what causes what is hard, whereas figuring out what is correlated with what is much cheaper and easier. iii) Consider the (possible) combination of models (and methods) of different kind that can complement each other and can therefore better exploit the variety and complexity of information usually carried by Big Data. iv) Consider the (possible) streaming nature of the data: analyzing this kind of data might require to develop analytical models that take into account the concept drift phenomenon. All these aspects are orthogonal to scalability which has to be considered by means of distributed approaches: Data mining/machine learning algorithms should be redefined through a distributed paradigm which exploits the natural distribution of (big) data. All these aspects will be considered in the tutorial, where also applicative scenarios will be described.

Techniques, Technologies and Models for Big Data as a service

Ernesto Damiani, University of Milano

ernesto.damiani@unimi.it

In the past few years, many organizations in all domains have discovered that to become - or remain- competitive they have to deal with business cases where the volume of data reaches terabytes and even petabytes. As the volume of data keeps growing, the data types to be considered have also become much richer than before. Many technologies have been developed to support data intensive applications, and practitioners propose to their customers mix of solutions including NoSQL ("notonlySQL") databases like Cassandra or HBase, data preparation utilities like Paxata, and distributed/parallel computing systems like Hadoop or Stark. As a result, Big Data application developers and users have devoted little attention to master abstract representations and models of the computational paradigms underlying these tools. Even traditional data modelling, which focused on representing relationships among schema-enabled data, has been often neglected as no longer relevant to Big Data scenarios. The tutorial will first analyze existing Big Data technologies and solutions, focusing on the ones that can be relevant for Big-Data-as-a-Service. It will then introduce a model-driven approach for designing big data pipelines, including data, processes, and security models, and corresponding model transformations for producing procedural models that specify how to execute analytics. Simple model transformations will be used to go from platform independent, technology agnostic representation of Big Data pipelines to platform dependent ones that instantiate the technologies introduced in the tutorial and that are deployable on-premises as well as on public clouds.

Service Level Aware Contract Management: Data Management Models and Methods

Antonella Longo, University of Salento

antonella.longo@unisalento.it

Digital services are driving business and public organizations towards a Digital Transformation which demands a deep change in how organizations perform their business functions and interact with their customers. Several factors hinder this path: complexity in digital service provisioning, inherent challenges of traditional, paper-based, natural-language service contracts, with corresponding ambiguity about contractual terms, and informational (and business) asymmetries across the contracting parties. Service contracts can play a pivotal role in Digital Transformation, since they are the actual tools formalizing the relationship between service-clients and providers, primarily through the management of service levels. The tutorial will first analyze existing scholar approaches and industrial solutions in data management of service level, with specific attention to cloud computing and business process outsourcing scenarios. It will then introduce and discuss several model-driven methods and approaches, along with multiple use cases where the proposed solutions have been applied by the authors.

Structured Data in Web Search Results

Alon Halevy, Recruit Institute of Technology

alon@recruit.ai

In recent years, the main search engines have started displaying answers from structured data sources in response to Web search queries. These answers are based on vast knowledge bases about notable entities in the world, their properties and relationships between them. These answers focus on head queries, are required to be of very high accuracy and must be non-controversial. In this talk I will describe a few efforts to expand the breadth of answers from structured data. In the first, I will describe recent results about the WebTables Project in which we mine a corpus of HTML tables on the Web that contain high-quality data about long-tail content and present them in response to relevant queries. In the second, I describe the Biperpedia Project, which aims to considerably expand the schema on which the Google Knowledge Graph is based. Biperpedia mines attribute names from the query stream and from Web text and contains the long and heavy tail of attributes that are of interest to users. This unique collection of attribute names presents new opportunities to understand the space of queries concerning structured data. Finally, I describe the Surveyor System that discovers high-confidence subjective facts about properties of entities. Surveyor uses a probabilistic model about content generation on the Web to analyze the content of Web documents and decide whether there is a dominant opinion about such subjective facts.

Challenges and opportunities of data mining and predictive modeling applications for clinical healthcare data

Shamkant B. Navathe, College of Computing, Georgia Institute of Technology

sham@cc.gatech.edu

The vast amount of data in healthcare and the possibility of clinicians and healthcare practitioners using decision support systems for better treatment is on the rise and stands to benefit from the area of predictive analytics. The overarching goals in healthcare are personalized medicine, cost reduction and quality monitoring. In this talk we will outline the nature of a number of interesting problems that can be attempted by applying data mining approaches to historical clinical data and summarize some studies we have participated in. The data mainly comes in the form of EHR (Electronic Health Records) containing disease and treatment histories and claims with insurance and Medicare etc. In using treatment data we have introduced a non-conventional graph approach to make it easier to mine significant sequences by including multiple edge types and considering the overlap of medications. We have used these techniques on treatment recommendation for Glioblastoma (GBM- brain tumor) patients with the goal of improving longevity. We have used clinical as well as genomic data and even treatment patterns as features in building predictive models for GBM. We developed a model for predicting readmission of patients by an NLP analysis of textual data in the form of physician notes which typically goes largely unaccounted for and showed better results with just structured clinical information. We have analyzed claims data in heart disease, breast cancer and autism to observe prevalence of different patterns of treatment within regions of the U.S. In another study, we are developing predictive models for 16 anti-epileptic drugs by a pharma company to determine stable vs. unstable therapies. By applying current "big-data" technologies and some semantic web techniques we are attempting to make our models scalable and effective.

Human-in-the-loop Analytics

Michael Franklin, CS Division at UC Berkeley

franklin@berkeley.edu

The "P" in AMPLab stands for "People" and an important research thrust in the lab has been on integrating human processing into analytics pipelines. Starting with the CrowdDB project and continuing into the more recent SampleClean and AMPCrowd/Clamshell projects, we have been investigating ways to maximize the benefit that can be obtained through involving people in data collection, cleaning and query answering.

Crowdclustering Digital Resources

Silvana Castano[1], Alfio Ferrara[1], and Stefano Montanelli[1]

Università degli Studi di Milano
DI - Via Comelico, 39 - 20135 Milano
{silvana.castano,alfio.ferrara,stefano.montanelli}@unimi.it

Abstract. Crowdclustering has been recently proposed to engage humans in automated categorization tasks and it shows to be effective especially when digital resources are involved, with complex features to be abstracted for an automated procedure, like images or multimedia resources. In this paper, we propose the HC^2 crowdclustering approach for unsupervised classification of digital resources, by allowing the classification categories to dynamically emerge from the crowd. In HC^2, crowd workers actively participate to clustering activities i) by resolving tasks in which they are asked to visually recognize groups of similar resources and ii) by labeling recognized clusters with prominent keywords. To increase flexibility, HC^2 can be interactively configured to dynamically set the balance between human engagement and automated procedures in cluster formation, according to the kind and nature of resources to be classified as it will be discussed in the experimental evaluation.

Keywords: crowdclustering, cluster similarity evaluation, consensus-based crowdsourcing

1 Introduction

Resource categorization is one of the most popular application domains where crowdsourcing is nowadays employed since classification results provided by a crowd of humans are widely recognized to be more accurate than those produced by fully-automated approaches [5]. This is true for instance when categorization is invoked on a dataset of multimedia resources like images and videos for which automated labeling and content recognition functionalities are not completely satisfying [6, 7]. Recently, the so-called *crowdclustering* approaches have been proposed to show how to combine human work and automated procedures to address categorization tasks in a more effective way [9, 11]. Crowdclustering extends the role of crowdsourcing by introducing similarity tasks where workers are asked to decide whether a pair of resources is similar and can be placed in the same cluster by an algorithm. An open issue in crowdclustering is the capability to actively engage workers in the clustering process, by asking not only the evaluation of pairwise resource similarity, but also the cluster formation and suitable cluster labeling activity.

In this paper, we go in this direction and we propose HC^2, a crowdclustering approach for unsupervised classification of digital resources. HC^2 is characterized by two main distinguishing features. First, crowd workers actively participate to clustering activities by resolving tasks in which they are asked to visually recognize groups of similar resources. In addition, workers are asked to associate featuring keywords with the recognized groups (crowd-labeling task), by allowing the classification categories to dynamically emerge. Second, HC^2 provides an interactive configuration mechanism to dynamically set the balance between classification accuracy and crowdsourcing costs to be afforded, by specifying the task-size (i.e., the number of resources to be analyzed in a task) and the minimum degree of similarity (similarity threshold) that must hold for human-formed clusters to be re-assigned in tasks for another crowdclustering round of work. For experimentation and evaluation, the HC^2 approach has been deployed on the Argo platform providing crowdsourcing techniques for consensus-based task execution [4].

The paper is organized as follows. Section 2 discusses work related to crowd-based resource categorization and crowdclustering. The HC^2 approach and related crowdclustering techniques are presented in Section 3 and 4, respectively. In Section 5, we illustrate experimental results and main considerations on the proposed approach based on evaluation results achieved. Concluding remarks are finally provided in Section 6.

2 Related work

The idea of exploiting a human crowd for supporting resource classification has been recently emerging in the literature to improve the effectiveness of state-of-the-art clustering algorithms. Usually, the crowd is employed in the so-called *re-representation* tasks, where workers are invoked to extract salient labels from available descriptions about the resources to classify. In particular, labeling can be enforced by asking workers to insert free keywords, thus fostering the crowd feeling to emerge [2]. Otherwise, label specification through folksonomy-based and/or vocabulary-controlled constraints can be also supported [5]. By relying on crowdsourced labels, resource classification is then performed through conventional clustering algorithms [5, 10]. In some recent work, the crowd is directly involved in *validation* tasks for collecting human feedback on results of automated algorithms. In [10], workers are invoked for disambiguation purposes and for deciding the most appropriate cluster for a certain resource given two or more options determined by the algorithm. Outlier identification is another possible crowd involvement to enforce classification refinement and to support training of automated SVM classifiers [6]. Crowdclustering approaches shift the role of the crowd by proposing to involve workers also in the evaluation of the similarity between pairs of objects and in determining whether they must be placed in a same category (*must-link*) or they should be split in two different categories (*cannot-link*). In [9], each worker is involved in the execution of HITs (Human Intelligent Tasks) where the goal is to generate a *local cluster-set*, namely a set of clusters where a (small) number of resources have been grouped according to their similarity. The local cluster-sets provided by different crowd workers are characterized by possible *rumors* that are incoherent resource classifications due to the fact that workers rely on different perceptions of similarity. A bayesian method is proposed in [9] to generate a global cluster-set on the basis of the different (and possibly incoherent) local cluster-sets.

Original paper contribution. In the state-of-the-art about crowdclustering, the crowd is either involved in i) activities that are preparatory to automated clustering procedures (i.e., re-representation, similarity evaluation) or ii) activities that are devoted to validate results produced by automated clustering procedures (i.e, disambiguation, outlier identification). The key contribution of our work is that we propose a crowdclustering approach to perform digital resource classification: i) by relying on the human classification capability as much as possible, in that a worker is asked to actively recognize and cluster similar resources and to properly label resulting resource cluster(s) on the basis of her own skill/perception/judgment; and ii) by consolidating the classification perception of single workers as much as possible, in that a consensus mechanism is put in action to achieve a shared agreement on resulting similarity clusters.

3 The HC^2 approach

Consider a dataset $R = \{r_1, \ldots, r_n\}$ of digital resources to cluster like web pages, images, multimedia resources, microdata, or social data. HC^2 enforces a hierarchical crowdclustering approach for progressively aggregating the resources R into similarity clusters. The approach is based on the execution of iterative *crowdclustering sessions* characterized by a combination of *human clustering* techniques and *automated similarity* techniques. The final result of HC^2 is a cluster-set $CL^p = \{cl_1, \ldots, cl_s\}$ where p is the number of executed crowdclustering sessions and s is the number of resulting clusters. A cluster $cl_i \in CL^p$ is a group of similar resources and it is associated with a representative label l_i providing a synthetic and prominent description of the cluster resources.

The HC^2 process is shown in Figure 1. For initialization, the **singleton-cluster generation** step is executed to create the initial cluster-set $CL^0 = \{cl_1, \ldots, cl_n\}$ where each resource $r_j \in R$ is placed in a singleton cluster $cl_j = \{r_j\}$. In CL^0, clusters are not labeled ($l_j = NULL,\ \forall j \in [1 \ldots n]$). Crowdclustering sessions are then iteratively executed to progressively transform CL^0 into the final cluster-set CL^p.

A **crowdclustering session** $CS^i = \langle CL^{i-1}, CL^i, T^i, C^i \rangle$ ($i \in [1 \ldots p]$) transforms an input cluster-set CL^{i-1} into an output cluster-set CL^i through a set T^i of clustering tasks executed by the crowd. Automated techniques for cluster similarity evaluation are then invoked over CL^i for deciding whether to activate a new crowdclustering session. If similar clusters are detected in CL^i, a new session is activated to ask the crowd to execute clustering tasks over them. Otherwise, the cluster-set CL^i is considered as the final result and it is returned as

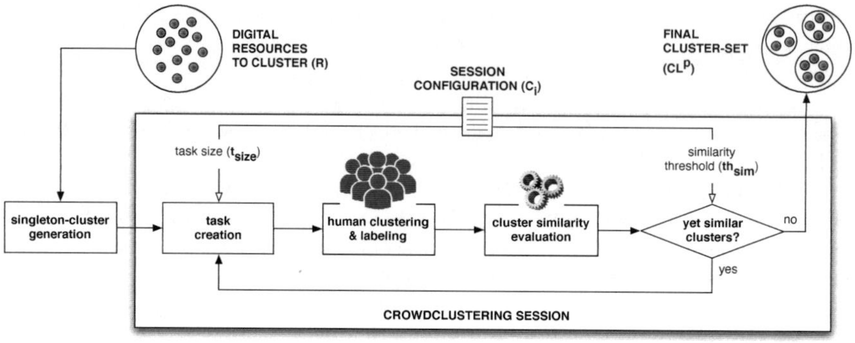

Fig. 1. The HC^2 process

the output of HC^2. A *session configuration* tuple $C^i = \langle t_{size}, th_{sim} \rangle$ is defined to enable the flexible customization of the crowdclustering session execution. The *task-size* t_{size} sets the maximum number of resource clusters contained in each clustering task $t \in T^i$ to control the complexity of the crowdsourcing tasks demanded to workers. The *similarity threshold* th_{sim} sets the minimum degree of similarity required between pairs of clusters in an output cluster-set CL^i to be considered similar, and thus to trigger the activation of a new crowdclustering session.

4 Crowdclustering techniques

For a crowdclustering session CS^i, the set of clustering tasks T^i is generated through a partitioning mechanism of the input cluster-set CL^{i-1} by which each cluster $cl \in CL^{i-1}$ is inserted in exactly one task $t \in T^i$ (i.e., task creation step). A clustering task $t_j = \langle d, RCL^i_j, RCL^{i+1}_j, L^{i+1}_j \rangle$ is characterized by a *task description* d providing a short summary of the task goal, a set of *input resource-clusters* RCL^i_j, a set of *output resource-clusters* RCL^{i+1}_j, and a set of *cluster labels* L^{i+1}_j one-to-one associated with each output resource-cluster. In the first crowdclustering session, a random partitioning mechanism is employed to distribute the singleton clusters of CL^0 into $|T^1| = \left\lceil \frac{n}{t_{size}} \right\rceil$ tasks. In subsequent sessions, a task can contain a number $|RCL^i_j| \leq t_{size}$ of either singleton and non-singleton resource clusters, depending on the clustering actions performed by workers in previous crowdclustering sessions.

4.1 Human clustering & labeling

Human clustering techniques enforce resource classification through the clustering tasks T^i to be executed by crowd workers (i.e., human clustering & labeling step). An example of clustering task $t_j \in T^i$ containing web images is shown in Figure 2. In t_j, the description d and the set of input resource-clusters RCL_j^i are

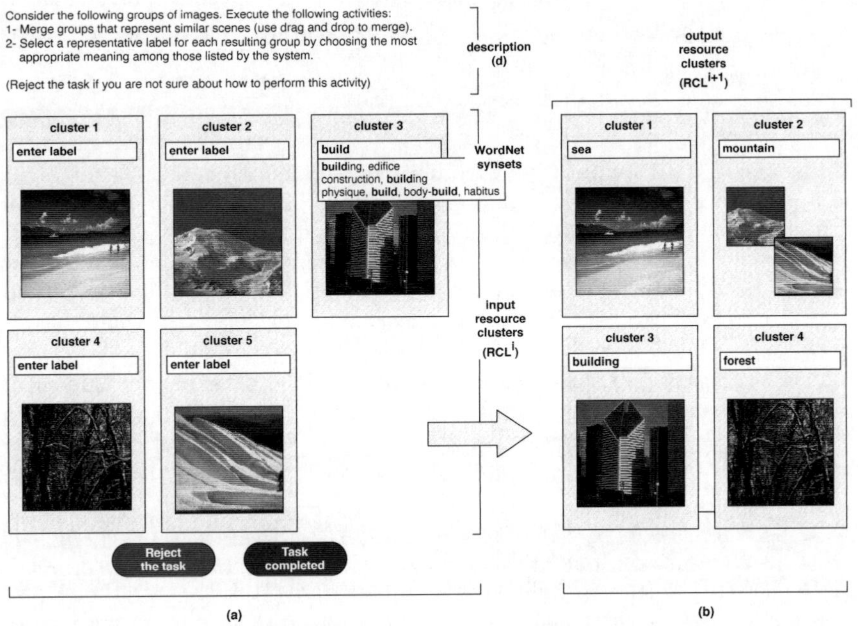

Fig. 2. Example of clustering task (a) before execution, and (b) after execution by a worker W_1

provided. Receiving the task, a worker is asked to execute the following sequence of actions:

1. Drag and drop input resource-clusters to perform pairwise cluster merge, until all the similar resources are grouped.
2. Select a featuring label (i.e., WordNet synset) for each output cluster.

As argued in [2], we enforce a "concept-based" labeling strategy and we choose to rely on WordNet for providing a standardized common vocabulary in HC^2 cluster descriptions[1]. Given a label l inserted by the worker, the choice of the most appropriate WordNet synset is "tool-supported", meaning that the list of synsets containing l is shown. The worker has to select the most prominent

[1] Depending on the domain of the considered resources, the WordNet lexical system can be replaced by other kinds of support knowledge-bases like folksonomies, shared vocabularies, and domain ontologies.

synset according to the perceived meaning and content of cluster resources to be labeled (see the labeling example of cluster 3 in Figure 2).

When the task execution is completed (i.e., the worker clicks on the "task completed" button), the resulting clusters RCL_j^{i+1} and the corresponding labels L_j^{i+1} become the task output. The result of executing all the tasks T^i of the session CS^i is the output cluster-set $CL^i = \bigcup_{t_j \in T^i} RCL_j^{i+1}$.

Consensus-based evaluation of clustering tasks. By assigning each task to a single worker, the risk is that possible lacks of worker comprehension or expertise generate inaccurate clustering results as discussed in the crowdsourcing literature (e.g., [3]). In HC^2, we address this problem by consolidating the results of clustering tasks through *multi-worker task assignment* and *consensus evaluation techniques* by relying on our experience and research results in this field [4]. In particular, each task $t_j \in T^i$ is assigned to a group of workers G_j.

The consensus on a clustering task result is defined as an answer agreement among the members of the group that received the task for execution. Given a clustering task $t_j \in T^i$ assigned to a group G_j, two workers $W_k, W_h \in G_j$ agree on the task answer when they apply the same clustering operations over the input resource-clusters RCL_j^i, thus providing the same output resource-cluster RCL_j^{i+1}. For consensus evaluation, we employ a *weighted-voting mechanism* called **supermajority** where the answer of a worker W has a weight corresponding to her trustworthiness/reliability[2]. Supermajority verifies that the answer that obtained the highest degree of consensus within the group G_j constitutes a majority of workers with enough weight (i.e., trustworthiness) for satisfying a given quorum $q \in [0.51, 1]$ [4]. A task is committed when the supermajority constraints are satisfied (i.e., consensus is verified) and we call *consensus-majority* the set of workers that contributed to commit the task. The output cluster-set RCL_j^{i+1} of a committed clustering task is the answer provided by the workers in the consensus-majority. On the opposite, when supermajority constraints are not satisfied, the task remains uncommitted. In this case, the clustering operations applied by crowd workers in the execution of the task t_j are rollbacked and the final task result corresponds to the input cluster-set RCL_j^i.

Example. Consider the task t_j shown in Figure 2. The task is assigned to a group of workers $\mathsf{G}_j = \{\mathsf{W}_1, \ldots, \mathsf{W}_6\}$ and it is committed on the output cluster-set RCL_j^{i+1} = {{cluster 1}, {cluster 2, cluster 5}, {cluster 3}, {cluster 4}}. The workers in the consensus-majority are {W_1, W_3, W_4, W_5}. The corresponding set of labels is L_j^{i+1} = { {sea}, {mountain}, {building}, {forest}}.

[2] The worker trustworthiness is set on the basis of task answers provided by the worker. It is increased when the worker answer contributes to reach the consensus and it is decreased otherwise. See [4] for further details about worker trustworthiness specification.

4.2 Automated similarity evaluation

Consider the cluster-set CL^i resulting from the human clustering and labeling step of a crowdclustering session CS^i. The clusters in CL^i are submitted to pairwise comparisons and a cluster similarity matrix SM^i is created whose entry (x, y) denotes the similarity value σ_{xy} of clusters $cl_x, cl_y \in CL^i$ based on labels assigned to clusters by worker (i.e., cluster similarity evaluation step). Given two clusters $cl_x, cl_y \in CL^i$ and the corresponding labels l_x and l_y, their similarity value $\sigma_{xy} = wup(l_x, l_y)$ corresponds to the result of the *Wu & Palmer* (wup) similarity function over the label synset of WordNet [14]. The idea of wup is to consider WordNet as a taxonomy where synsets are nodes and WordNet lexical relationships (e.g., synonymy, hypernymy, meronymy) are directed edges. Given two label synsets l_x and l_y, the similarity value $wup(l_x, l_y)$ is based on the depth of the Least Common Subsumer (i.e., most specific ancestor node) between l_x and l_y normalized on the depth of the two synsets l_x and l_y in the overall WordNet taxonomy. The higher is $wup(l_x, l_y)$, the higher is the similarity value σ_{xy} [14].

Triggering a new crowdclustering session. Consider a cluster-set CL^i, the cluster similarity matrix SM^i, and the similarity threshold $th_{sim} \in C^i$ of the HC^2 configuration. A new crowdclustering session CS^{i+1} is activated when at least one pair of clusters exists in CL^i whose similarity is higher than or equal to $th_{sim} \in (0, 1]$[3], that is:

$$\overline{CL} = \{cl_x \mid cl_x \in CL^i \wedge \exists \sigma_{xy} \geq th_{sim} \wedge \sigma_{xy} \in SM^i \wedge x \neq y\} \neq \emptyset$$

only the clusters in $\overline{CL}$ are exploited for generating the set of clustering tasks T^{i+1} to be assigned to workers in the next session CS^{i+1}. The clusters in $CL^i \setminus \overline{CL}$ are considered as definitive and they are inserted in the final HC^2 cluster-set.

Defining the set of clustering tasks to execute. Consider a set of similar clusters $\overline{CL}$, the cluster similarity matrix SM^i, and the task-size $t_{size} \in C^i$ of the HC^2 configuration. The goal is to define the set of clustering tasks T^{i+1} to be executed in the next session CS^{i+1}, where the following constraints must be satisfied:

- a minimum number of tasks must be created;
- clusters are placed into tasks according to their similarity value, so that the higher is the similarity value σ_{xy}, the higher is the likelihood that the corresponding clusters cl_x and cl_y are inserted in the same task;
- for each clustering task, the number of input resource-clusters is lower than the task-size t_{size} specified in the configuration tuple;

According to these constraints, the specification of the set of clustering tasks T^{i+1} can be considered as a *clique cover problem* [13]. Build a graph $\mathcal{G} = \langle V, E \rangle$

[3] The value of th_{sim} is determined experimentally. Since cluster labeling is based on a common vocabulary, the choice of a high value of similarity threshold is recommended. In our experimentation, we set $th_{sim} = 0.8$.

where a vertex $v \in V$ is a cluster of $\overline{CL}$, and an edge $e \in E$ is a similarity value $\sigma_{xy} \geq th_{sim}$ connecting the vertex of $cl_x, cl_y \in \overline{CL}$. The set of tasks T^{i+1} coincides with the cliques of size $\leq t_{size}$ that are contained in the graph $\mathcal{G}$. The clique cover problem is NP-hard. For this reason, we choose to determine the set of clustering tasks T^{i+1} by employing the heuristic approach to the clique cover problem proposed in Crowder [13]. The approach splits the vertices of the graph $\mathcal{G}$ in two different components called i) *large connected components* ($LCCs$) having more than t_{size} vertices, and ii) *small connected components* ($SCCs$) having t_{size} vertices or fewer. The set of tasks T^{i+1} is obtained by applying a *partition-packing* technique. Partition is used on LCCs to reduce the size of the connected components until they are compatible with t_{size}. To further reduce the number of tasks in T^{i+1}, packing is used on SCCs to increase the size of the connected components (within the limit of t_{size}) [13].

Example. Consider the clusters cluster A, cluster B, and cluster C with corresponding labels l_A =building, l_B =tower, and l_C =bedroom assigned by crowd workers. According to the wup similarity function, the cluster similarity values $\sigma_{AB} = 0.85$, $\sigma_{AC} = 0.75$, and $\sigma_{BC} = 0.75$ are inserted in the matrix SM^i. Given a similarity threshold $th_{sim} = 0.8$, the cluster-set $\overline{CL}$ is composed by the cluster A and the cluster B.

5 Experimental results and considerations

For preliminary experimentation of the proposed approach, we compare HC^2 results against those obtained using a conventional crowdsourcing approach which consists in taking resources labeled by the crowd and submit them to an automated clustering algorithm to produce the final cluster-set.

We consider a resource dataset of 130 web images representing different scenes and subjects. The dataset is taken from [7] where images have been categorized and validated into thirteen classes like for example highway, building, street, forest, kitchen, living room. This categorization will be exploited as ground-truth for evaluation of the resulting clusters. We first exploited the crowd for labeling each image with one or more labels describing its subject content. Then, the labeled images have been submitted to two independent clustering processes.

In the first process, clustering has been executed by the crowd according to the HC^2 approach. In particular, we executed three crowdclustering sessions, by saving the cluster-set obtained after each session (named crowd-1, crowd-2, crowd-3), in order to observe the evolution of the clustering results along the different sessions. The HC^2 session execution has been implemented in the Argo crowdsourcing platform [4].

In the second process, clustering has been executed automatically, by exploiting a hierarchical agglomerative clustering algorithm [8] with the wup similarity function. In hierarchical clustering, two merging strategies are possible. When

[4] `http://island.ricerca.di.unimi.it/projects/argo/` (Italian language).

a single-link strategy is adopted, σ_{cl} represents the maximum similarity value between any pair of resources belonging to a cluster cl. When a complete-link strategy is adopted, σ_{cl} denotes the minimum similarity value holding between any pair of resources in cl. In our evaluation, we executed the automated hierarchical clustering with both the single- and the complete-link strategy, obtaining two different cluster-sets named h-single and h-complete, respectively.

As a final result of the experiment, we compared all the five cluster-sets, namely crowd-1, crowd-2, and crowd-3 (produced by the HC[2] approach) and h-single, h-complete (produced by the hierarchical algorithm) against the ground-truth. A descriptive overview of the cluster-sets in terms of number of clusters and average cluster size is given in Table 1[5].

Table 1. Dimension and average cluster size of the evaluation cluster-sets

	ground-truth	crowd-1	crowd-2	crowd-3	h-single	h-complete
# of clusters	13	95	54	35	36	41
avg. size	10	1.37	2.41	3.71	3.61	3.17

5.1 Evaluation measures

To analyze clustering results against the ground-truth, we use three well-known measures for clustering comparison, namely *Purity* [15] and *F-measure* [12]. Purity is a measure of accuracy based on the frequency of correspondence between the most common category and each cluster [1]. Given a cluster-set C, the category set L, and the number of clustered resources N, purity is defined as follows:

$$Purity(L, C) = \sum_i \frac{|C_i|}{N} max_j\{Precision(L_j, C_i)\}$$

where precision is defined as:

$$Precision(L_j, C_i) = \frac{|L_j \cap C_i|}{|C_i|}$$

Purity is basically a redesign of the classical Information Retrieval precision measure for the purpose of cluster-sets comparison. Purity measures the level of correspondence between a cluster-set generated by the experiment and the ground-truth.

[5] In hierarchical clustering, a similarity threshold th_{sim} is used to cut the tree at the desired level of depth and to define the final cluster-set out of the similarity tree. In our experimentation, we tested different similarity thresholds and we finally set $th_{sim} = 0.7$ for both h-single and h-complete strategies, that is the threshold value providing the best clustering results with respect to the ground truth.

F-measure complements purity in that it takes into account not only the precision of cluster-sets but also their recall, namely the capability of a cluster-set to cover all the categories of the ground-truth. F-measure is defined as follows:

$$F = \sum_i \frac{|L_i|}{N} max_j\{Fm(L_i, C_j)\}$$

where:

$$F(L_i, C_j) = \frac{2 \cdot Recall(L_i, C_j) \cdot Precision(L_i, C_j)}{Recall(L_i, C_j) + Precision(L_i, C_j)}$$

$$Recall(L_i, C_j) = \frac{|L_i \cap C_j|}{|L_i|}$$

5.2 Evaluation results

The results of our evaluation using the Purity and F-measure are shown in Figure 3. As a first consideration, we note an increasing quality in terms of

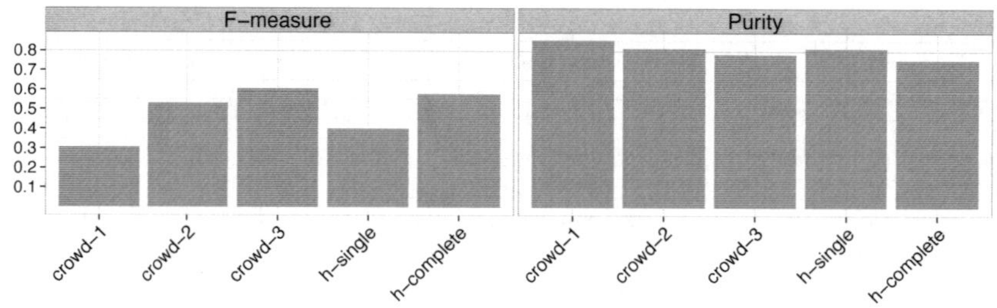

Fig. 3. Evaluation results

F-measure going from the first to the last HC^2 sessions, meaning that session after session, the crowd defines cluster-sets which are closer to the ground-truth. This is an expected result, but it is interesting to note that the Purity decrease is marginal if compared with he increment of the F-measure. This is mainly due to the fact that session after session the crowd aggregates more and more resources in larger clusters. As a consequence, the number of singleton clusters decreases, which is obviously good in terms of precision but not in terms of recall. In comparison with hierarchical clustering, we note that the F-measure of HC^2 becomes higher than h-single after the second session and it is definitively higher then both h-single and h-complete after the third session. This means that only few sessions of HC^2 are needed to achieve results comparable or even better than the automated approach.

5.3 Considerations

The results of Figure 3 show that HC^2 achieves a good quality of clustering in a limited number of sessions when compared with a fully automated approach based on the hierarchical agglomerative algorithm. In addition to this, HC^2 provides two main advantages with respect to an automated clustering process.

Labeling. Having synthetic and representative labels describing the content of each cluster (i.e., the cluster centroid) is generally considered as an important and desirable feature. However, automated clustering algorithms do not provide any mechanism for automatically labeling clusters. The only labels involved in the process are those provided by the crowd at the beginning of the process. These labels are used to calculate the resource similarity, but, after that, they are no more used by the algorithm for clustering. As a consequence, the resulting clusters are merely groups of images. To label clusters, a further procedure of cluster analysis is required. In HC^2 instead, labeling is intrinsically part of a crowdclustering session. This means that the final clusters are naturally associated with labels and also that session after session workers have the chance to revise and re-assign the labels associated with clusters, to adapt them to the new cluster contents deriving from merge operations. This way, labels are continuously refined by the crowd and are really representative for cluster contents.

Insight. HC^2 places more than two clusters in a single task (i.e., task-size $t_{size} \gg 2$). This positively affects the quality of work, since observing more resources at a time gives to the workers the opportunity to gain more insight from the task context. Of course, there is a tradeoff on the number of clusters to place in a task. On the one side, according to the common crowdsourcing recommendations, it is better to deal with small and simple tasks. On the other side, larger tasks provide workers a wider context for similarity evaluation. HC^2 provides a flexible configuration for tuning the task-size in order to achieve the desired balance.

6 Concluding remarks

In this paper, we presented the HC^2 approach and related techniques for crowdclustering digital resources. Evaluation results are promising. Ongoing research activity is about the HC^2 application to larger resource datasets (e.g., thousands of images). For example, an issue that affects the quality of work of the involved workers is the number of items shown per single cluster within a task. The visualization of the full-set of cluster items provides an effective insight of the cluster contents to the worker. However, this choice can be hard to manage through a visual task interface when clusters of large size are considered (e.g., number of cluster items higher than few units). A possible solution under investigation is to limit the cluster visualization to a small subset of cluster items selected through a relevance-based criterion (e.g., top-similar items).

Acknowledgements. The authors would like to thank M.Sc. Riccardo Corbella for the fruitful contribution to the HC^2 specification and experimentation.

References

1. Amigó, E., Gonzalo, J., Artiles, J., Verdejo, F.: A Comparison of Extrinsic Clustering Evaluation Metrics based on Formal Constraints. Information retrieval 12(4) (2009)
2. André, P., Kittur, A., Dow, S.P.: Crowd Synthesis: Extracting Categories and Clusters from Complex Data. In: Proc. of the 17th ACM Conference on Computer Supported Cooperative Work. Baltimore, MD, USA (2014)
3. Barowy, D.W., Curtsinger, C., Berger, E.D., McGregor, A.: AutoMan: A Platform For Integrating Human-Based and Digital Computation. In: Proc. of the 27th Annual ACM SIGPLAN OOPSLA Conference. Tucson, AZ, USA (2012)
4. Castano, S., Ferrara, A., Genta, L., Montanelli, S.: Combining Crowd Consensus and User Trustworthiness for Managing Collective Tasks. Future Generation Computer Systems 54 (2016)
5. Chae, G., Park, J., Park, J., Yeo, W.S., Shi, C.: Linking and Clustering Artworks using Social Tags: Revitalizing Crowd-sourced Information on Cultural Collections. Journal of the Association for Information Science and Technology (2015)
6. Chen, Q., Wang, G., Tan, C.L.: Web Image Organization and Object Discovery by Actively Creating Visual Clusters through Crowdsourcing. In: Proc. of the 24th Int. Conference on Tools with Artificial Intelligence. Toronto, Canada (2012)
7. Fei-Fei, L., Perona, P.: A Bayesian Hierarchical Model for Learning Natural Scene Categories. In: Proc. of Computer Vision and Pattern Recognition. San Diego, CA, USA (2005)
8. Ferrara, A., Genta, L., Montanelli, S., Castano, S.: Dimensional Clustering of Linked Data: Techniques and Applications. In: Transactions on Large-Scale Data- and Knowledge-Centered Systems XIX, pp. 55–86. Springer (2015)
9. Gomes, R.G., Welinder, P., Krause, A., Perona, P.: Crowdclustering. In: Proc. of the 25th Int. Conference on Neural Information Processing Systems (NIPS). Granada, Spain (2011)
10. Lee, J., Cho, H., Park, J.W., Cha, Y.R., Hwang, S.W., Nie, Z., Wen, J.R.: Hybrid Entity Clustering Using Crowds and Data. The VLDB Journal 22(5) (2013)
11. Ng, A.Y., Jordan, M.I., Weiss, Y.: On Spectral Clustering: Analysis and an Algorithm. In: Proc. of the 15th Int. Conference on Neural Information Processing Systems. Vancouver, British Columbia, Canada (2001)
12. Steinbach, M., Karypis, G., Kumar, V., et al.: A Comparison of Document Clustering Techniques. In: Proc. of the 6th ACM SIGKDD KDD-200 Workshop on Text Mining. Boston, MA, USA (2000)
13. Wang, J., Kraska, T., Franklin, M.J., Feng, J.: Crowder: Crowdsourcing Entity Resolution. Proceedings of the VLDB Endowment 5(11) (2012)
14. Wu, Z., Palmer, M.: Verbs Semantics and Lexical Selection. In: Proc. of the 32nd Annual meeting of the Associations for Computational Linguistics. Las Cruces, New Mexico (1994)
15. Zhao, Y., Karypis, G.: Empirical and Theoretical Comparisons of Selected Criterion Functions for Document Clustering. Machine Learning 55(3), 311–331 (2004)

A model for visual building SPARQL queries

Fabio Benedetti, Sonia Bergamaschi

Dipartimento di Ingegneria "Enzo Ferrari" - Università di Modena e Reggio Emilia - Italy
firstname.lastname@unimore.it

Abstract. LODeX is a Semantic Web tool that, leveraging a summarized representation of a LOD source structure (i.e. Schema Summary), helps users explore and query SPARQL endpoints by hiding the complexity of Semantic Web technologies. By leveraging Schema Summary of a LOD source, LODeX guides the user in composing visual queries that are automatically translated in correct SPARQL queries through a SPARQL compiler. In this work we inspected how LODeX can deal with the high expressivity of SPARQL. In particular, we propose a formal model that allow to define queries over the Schema Summary (i.e. Basic Query) and we analyze how this model can handle different join patterns used in SPARQL queries. Finally, we inspect how LODeX can satisfy real world users necessities by analyzing the query logs contained in the LSQ dataset. We show that LODeX could be able to generate the 77.6% of the 5 million queries contained in LSQ dataset.

1 Introduction

In the last few years, the Linked Data Cloud is growing at dizzying pace, its number of datasets has risen from 294 in the 2009 to 1024 in the 2014 [23], without taking in consideration the huge amount of Semantic data recently embedded in web pages thanks to the RDFa standard [2]. In this context, one of the greatest issue is the complexity of the Semantic Web technologies, indeed, a user for effectively dealing with this kind of data have to master several complex standards: RDF [10], a metadata data model used for defining semantic data according to a graph data model; RDFS [8] and OWL [16], languages for defining ontological constraints and enabling inference upon semantic data; SPARQL [24], a query language used for extracting information from RDF data. Moreover, each data sets is usually described by its own vocabulary, increasing on one hand the flexibility in data representation but raising on the other hand the complexity in data consumption, especially for unskilled users. Writing SPARQL queries is a error-prone and tedious task but today is the only way for extracting information from RDF data.

For supporting the user in the consumption of Linked Data we defined a model, called Schema Summary [5] [7], and a tool, called LODeX [4] [6], both of them finalized in supporting the user in exploring an unknown datasets. Each LOD source is composed by two kind of knowledge: the *intensional knowledge* defines the terminology used in the dataset and it is described in RDFS or OWL; the *extensional knowledge* usually covers most of the datasets and it contains the entities of the real world described in the dataset. The Schema Summary of a LOD source is extracted by analyzing the distribution of the instances within the extensional knowledge and LODeX allows user to build visual queries over this summary. In the paper we want to inspect how much the expressivity of SPARQL is covered by the SPARQL queries that can be generated by LODeX. In particular, we propose the definition of the *Basic query* model used within LODeX and the algorithm of the SPARQL compiler, that allow to generate SPARQL queries starting from the Schema Summary of a LOD source and an instance of Basic Query. Then, we inspect how the Basic Query model can handle different join pattern that can be found in SPARQL. Finally, we evaluate how LODeX can satisfy the real world users requests by using the LQS Dataset [21]. This dataset contains more than 5 million of queries, extracted from logs of 3 different SPARQL endpoints, executed from real users. The analysis that we propose is finalized to verify how many of these query could be generated by LODeX.

The remainder of the paper is structured as follows. We discuss related work in Section 2. We summarize the architecture of LODeX in Section 3. Section 4 illustrates the component of LODeX that manage the formulation and translation of queries, while Section 5 reports the capabilities and limitations of the Basic Query model. Section 6 contains the analysis of the queries contained in LSQ respect to the capabilities of LODeX, and finally, Section 7 sketches the conclusions.

2 Related Works

In the literature, we can find several tools that aim to support users in LOD visualization, browsing and in the definition of complex queries. These tools can be divided in two major groups: tools with the main goal of providing a synthetic overview of the whole structure of an RDF dataset and tools that allow the browsing of a dataset just at instance level.

In the first group, we can find only few examples; the most important two are LOD Visualization and ProLOD; these tools aim to provide to users an high level analysis of a LOD dataset. In particular, LOD Visualization is a prototype based on the Linked Data Visualization Model [9], and it allows to build analysis, transformations and visualizations of Linked Data. Whereas, ProLOD [1] automatically provides a group of statistical analysis regarding the content of a dataset, but it does not foresee any querying possibility.

In the second group we can find tools that provide visual querying functionalities, but their focus is limited to the instance level. A first example is LD Query Wizard [15], a tool that allows to select instances through keyword search and it uses a powerful tabular view that allows users to browse an RDF graph. LODlive and LODmilla [17] provide a visually appealing way to explore information associated with an instance using a graph visualization, but they do not provide any query building functionality. Also gFacet [13, 14] uses the same strategy of exploration (with a graph visualization), but in this case, each node is a class that contains a list of instances and the user can link new nodes (classes) as if he was building a visual query, but it does not produce as output any SPARQL query. SPARKLIS [12] implements a fascinating approach in which a SPARQL query is composed as if the user was composing a natural language request. ISPARQL [18] is one of the most famous tool for building visual SPARQL query and it allows to incrementally build a SPARQL query by extending it step by step; this kind of approach is not very intuitive and a user have to own a good knowledge of SPARQL for being able to use ISPARQL. Moreover, the tool does not provide any guidance to users, indeed, they have to understand the schema of the LOD source before being able to define a SPARQL query.

As reported in [11], the majority of the tools for data visualization requires the user to manually explore the dataset and they are not able to provide a synthetic *schema* representing the structure of the source. LODeX differs from the tools described above since it provides a synthetic representation of LOD source schema and the user can use it to build visual queries. Moreover, LODeX hides to the final user the complexity of the Semantic Web technologies allowing users to build SPARQL query without knowing its syntax. The only tool that provide this characteristic is SPARKLIS which, however, does not provide user a whole picture of the structure of the dataset.

3 Architecture Overview

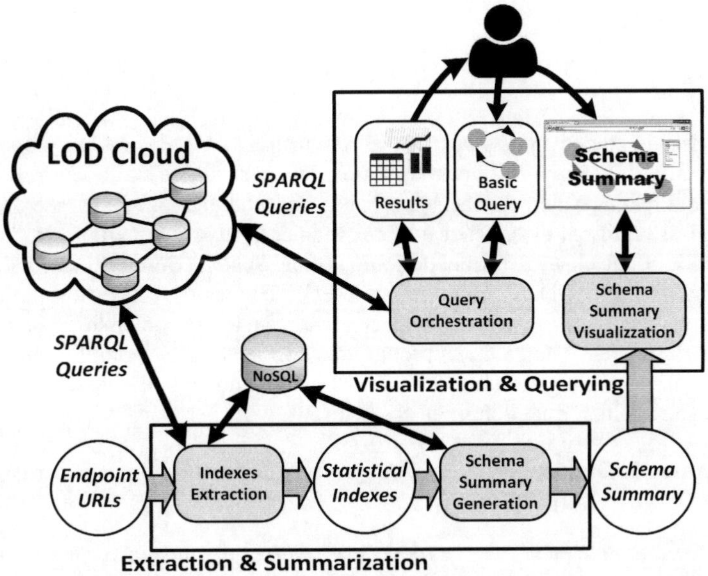

Fig. 1: LODeX architecture

LODeX consists of four distinct components (as illustrated in Figure 1), each responsible for a specific activity:

- **Indexes Extraction**: it takes as input the URL of a SPARQL endpoint and generates a set of queries able to extract a set of indexes from the extensional knowledge (extensional group of Statistical Indexes in [3]).

- **Schema Summary Generation**: it generates the Schema Summary thanks to the indexes extracted in the previous step (see [7] for additional information).
- **Schema Summary Visualization**: the visualization is performed by a web application through which the user can interact for browsing the Schema Summary and build the visual query.
- **Query Orchestration**: it manages the interaction between the GUI and the user in composing the visual query, in the generation of the SPARQL queries and in the submission of it to the remote endpoint.

4 Query Orchestration

The Query Orchestrator is the component that manages the formulation of the visual queries and the translation of these queries in SPARQL ones. These functionalities are available thanks to a model, called *Basic Query*, used for describing the visual query that the user is building. A SPARQL compiler takes in input an instance of a *Basic Query* and the related Schema Summary for producing as output the corresponding SPARQL query.

4.1 Basic Query

The user is guided by LODex in the composition of a Basic Query upon a Schema Summary. A Schema Summary is a pseudo-graph where the nodes are classes connected through properties; each classes is associated to a set of attributes, each attribute of a class represent the existence of a particular datatype property having as subject an instance of this class. A formal definition of the Schema Summary and a description of the interface of LODeX can be found in [7]. The classes, properties and attributes selected by the user in Schema Summary participate to the composition of a Basic Query Q. A Basic Query has a tree structure that overlaps the Schema Summary graph, the nodes of the tree are classes $\in C$, while the leafs can be both classes $\in C$ or attributes $\in A$. Here is its formal definition:

Definition 1 (Basic query) *A basic query Q, defined on a schema summary S, is a tuple Q= (T,m_C,m_E,m_A,o,F), where*

- *T is a directed and labeled tree composed by two kinds of vertices, T = (C',A',E'), where:*
  - *C' is a set of vertices where each vertex refers to a class in the Schema Summary*
  - *A' is a set of vertices where each vertex refers to an attribute in the Schema Summary. This kind of node can appear only as leaf of the tree T*
  - *E' is a set of edges where each edge consist of an ordered pair of vertices e=<n1,n2>, $e \in E'$, $n1 \in C'$, $n2 \in C' \cup A'$*
  - *$r \in C'$ is the root node,*
- $m_C : C' \rightarrow C$ *is a mapping function that links each vertex in C' with a vertex in C(S);*

- m_A: *A'* $\rightarrow$ *A is a mapping function that links each vertex in A' with an edge in A(S);*
- m_E: *E'* $\rightarrow$ *P is a mapping function that links each edge in E' with an edge in P(S);*
- o: *E'* $\rightarrow$ $\{true, false\}$ *is called optionality function.*
- *F contains the filtering conditions associated with the attributes of the query and it is composed by a set of tuple (a,k,v), where a is the attribute* $\in$ *A', k contains the filtering operator (a regular expression, or an arithmetic operator) and v is the value through which to assess the filter expression.*

Graphically, a user starts composing a basic query by selecting the first class in the Schema Summary, then, if the user selects a property for this first class, also the connected class is shown in the query panel and the edge and vertex are added to the tree. The user may also select the attributes of each class: in this case, the tree is further enriched with edges and leafs.

4.2 SPARQL compiler

The Query Orchestrator translates the Basic Query into a SPARQL query through a compiler. The compiler exploits an iterative algorithm that traverses the Basic Query tree for producing the SPARQL query. The Query Orchestrator allows the usage of these SPARQL operators: AND (.), OPTIONAL (also nested), FILTER, ORDER BY, OFFSET and LIMIT. The pseudo-code of the SPARQL compiler is presented in Algorithm 1. For simplicity, I show only the compilation of the body of the query, then, this body will be equipped with the SELECT statement, the pagination condition (LIMIT and OFFSET) and the ORDER condition, if specified. Algorithm 1 takes as input the Schema Summary S and the basic query Q. The output (SQ) of Algorithm 1 contains a SPARQL query. I use some of the algebraic operators defined in [19] to describe the formulation of the query: the triple pattern *(s,p,o)*, in which the elements can also be parameters (in this case we use the function $Par(node)$ for assigning a unique parameter); the operator *AND* that represents the dot (.) in SPARQL; the operator *OPT* (OPTIONAL); the operator *FILTER* (i.e. ?parameter condition value). The compiler is based on a recursive algorithm which is initialized from line 2 to 4, where the the BGPs (i.e. basic graph pattern [20]) related to the root node of the Basic Query are translated. The function m_C, m_A and m_E retrieve the URIs related to classes, attribute and properties from the Schema Summary S. The function $attributes(class, currentquery)$ append to $currentquery$ the statements related to the attributes of the current class. The function $filtCon(a)$ returns the filter statements associated to the current attribute. When the algorithm is initialized, the recursive function $recursivebody(class, currentquery)$ is called (line 4); this function traverse the query tree and it inserts the statements regarding the various nodes. The edges composing the query can refers to properties that exist in the Schema Summary with a revers direction, this case is handled in lines 10 and 11. When the algorithm has traversed all the query tree the SPARQL query is returned.

```
Data: S, Q, F
Result: SQ
Algorithm compiler()
    SQ=(Par(Q.r),rdf:type,m_C(Q.r));
    SQ=attributes(Q.r,SQ);
    SQ=recursivebody(Q.r,SQ);
    return SQ;
Function recursivebody(c,RQ)
    forall the child ch of c do
        CHQ=(Par(ch),rdf:type,m_C(ch));
        if m_E(<c,ch>) is directed from c to ch in S then CHQ=CHQ AND
        (Par(c),m_E(<c,ch>),Par(ch));
        else CHQ=CHQ AND (Par(ch)),m_E(<c,ch>),Par(c);
        CHQ=attributes(ch,CHQ);
        if ch is not a leaf node then recursivebody(ch,CHQ);
        if o(ch) then RQ=RQ OPT ( CHQ );
        else RQ=RQ AND CHQ;
    end
    return RQ ;
Function attributes(c,SQ)
    forall the attribute a connected with c do
        AQ=(Par(c),m_A(<c,a>),Par(a));
        if exist F(a) then AQ=AQ AND filtCon (a);
        if o(a) then SQ=SQ OPT ( AQ );
        else SQ=SQ AND AQ;
    end
    return SQ ;
Function filtCon(a)
    FC=∅;
    forall the fc in Q.F related to a do
        concatenate in FC, using the AND operator, each fc condition as: FILTER
        (Par(a), fc.k fc.v);
    end
    return FC ;
```

Algorithm 1: SPARQL compiler algorithm

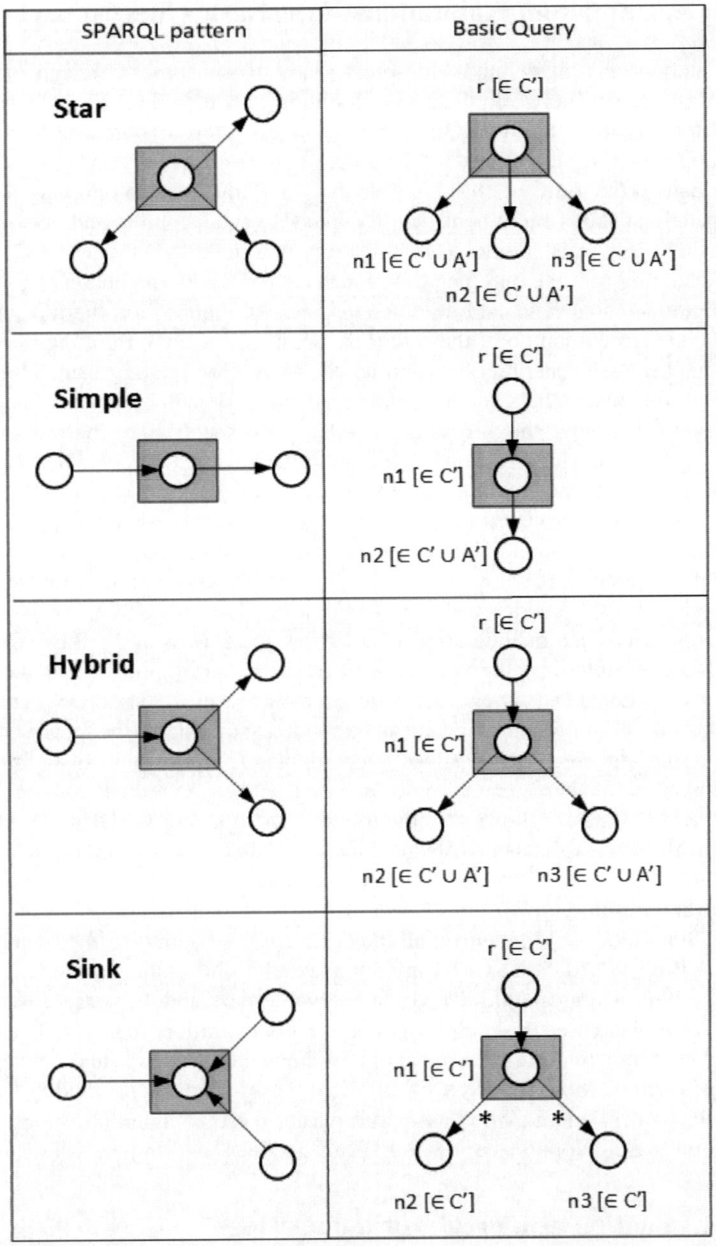

Fig. 2: Kinds of hypergraph patterns and their representation as Basic Query (Legend: *r* root node, *C'* class, *A'* attribute, * the Basic Query is translated in a SPARQL query and the direction of the edge is reversed).

5 Capabilities and limitations of the Basic Query model

The authors in [22] defined 4 different kinds of join types that can be found in a SPARQL query. These join patterns differ in the way the join node is connected within the BGPs forming the SPARQL query. A join node has an *outgoing link* if it appears as subject of a triple pattern and it has an *incoming link* if it appears as object. In a **Star** pattern the join node has multiple incoming links but no outgoing links. A **Simple** pattern contains a join node that has precisely one incoming and one outgoing link. A **Hybrid** pattern is composed by three ore more links and the join node has at least one incoming and one outgoing link. Finally, a **Sink** pattern contains a join node with multiple incoming links and no outgoing ones. In Figure 2 on the left you can see a schematic representation of these four patterns, while on the right their representation through the Basic Query model is proposed. As you can see they can all be represented through the Basic Query model and, even if the *Sink* pattern expects the existence of only incoming links, the SPARQL compiler can translate edges between nodes of the query in the opposite direction, according to the information contained in the Schema Summary. The Basic Query is able to model all the acyclic combinations of these pattern. A tree model is not enough expressive to represent cyclic queries, but this kind of queries are not so common in real use cases (as it will be shown in Section 6).

From the point of view of the SPARQL operators supported, LODeX is able to generate SPARQL queries with a SELECT form. The OPTIONAL pattern is allowed, indeed, the user can include optional attributes and classes in the Basic Query and the SPARQL compiler is able to correctly translate the query; if a class is included in the query as optional, all its child have to be included in the OPTION clause. LODeX supports the FILTER operator that can be applied to attributes (the greatest part FILTER clauses are applied on literal values). In particular, LODeX allow the definition of filter statement on number (greater, minor or equal) and string (equal, contains and regular expression). LODeX allows also the usage of the operator ORDER BY and it can be used with both classes and attributes. Moreover, the operators LIMIT and OFFSET are available, indeed, LODeX automatically paginates the results in order to speed up the retrieval of results.

LODeX does not implement all the SPARQL 1.1 operators; in particular, UNION, GROUP BY, MINUS, EXCEPT are not available. This choice is primarily due to the willing of providing an intuitive visual query interface, and the usage of such operators would have increased the complexity in the query definition. In fact, LODeX aims to be a tool used for exploring the content of an unknown LOD source and for easily building simple queries. Moreover, LODeX allows the user to manually modify the generated SPARQL query and a skilled user, who master these complex operators, can quickly build the skeleton of his query with LODeX and then modify it at will.

6 Evaluation using real world query logs

The LSQ datasets contains SPARQL queries extracted from endpoint logs [1] executed on three public datasets: DBpedia (logs from 30/04/201020/07/2010; a dataset with

[1] The LSQ dataset is available from `http://aksw.github.io/LSQ/`.

232 million triples), Linked Geo Data (LGD) (24/11/2010 06/07/2011; with 1 billion triples), Semantic Web Dog Food (SWDF) (16/05/201412/11/2014; with 300 thousand triples) and the British Museum (BM) (08/11/201401/12/2014; with 1.4 million triples). These queries represent a good sample for evaluating the real usage of SPARQL and we analyzed them for discovering how much the limitations of the Basic Query model would affect a real scenario.

Table 1: Number of queries contained in the LSQ dataset and number of queries involving the intensional or extensional knowledge.

Dataset	Total Queries	Distinct Queries	Correct Queries	Intensional Knowledge	Extensional Knowledge	% Extensional
DBpedia 3.5.1	1728041	1208789	782364	43812	738552	94.4
Linked Geo Data	1656254	311126	297580	4761	292819	98.4
SWDF	1411483	99165	85520	4533	80987	94.7
British Museum	879426	129989	29073	0	29073	100
Total	5675204	1749069	1194537	53106	1141431	**95.55**

The number of queries contained in the dataset is more than 5 million, but, by removing the duplicate queries and the malformed ones the number goes down to 1.2 million (as you can see in the left part of Table 1). The Schema Summary produced by LODeX covers only the extensional knowledge of a LOD source [5]. Thus, we first inspected which portion of the queries contain some BGPs targeting the intensional knowledge. The results are shown in the right part of Table 1; as you can see just the 4.45% of the queries contains some clauses involving the intensional knowledge. This is not a surprising result because only users with a deep knowledge about Semantic Web usually target this kind of data.

Table 2: Percentage of queries containing join nodes and cyclic queries

Dataset	Star	Path	Hybrid	Sink	No Join	Cyclic
DBpedia3.5.1	38.57	8.6	6.79	6.31	61.23	4.26
Linked Geo Data	28.18	9.46	7.57	1.24	72	2.58
SWDF	10.7	11.24	4.01	0.92	84.25	4.11
British Museum	0	0	0	0	100	0
Overall	33.05	8.79	6.62	4.51	66.5	**3.72**

Secondly, we analyzed the queries looking for what kinds of join structure they contain. In Table 2 you can see a summary of the results. The greatest part of the queries have a very basic structure, with no join, or with a single join node. Only the 3.72% of the queries contains a combination of join nodes that forms cycle and they are not compatible with the Basic Query model.

We also analyzed the operators used. In Table 3 the utilization percentage of the principal operators not supported by LODeX is summarized. As you can see in the top Table, advanced features like federation, sub-query and negation are rarely used. Aggregation features (GROUP BY) are a bit more used but they are lower long the 1%. The bottom Table contains others operators: UNION, CONSTRUCT, DESCRIBE and ASK. In this case the impact is a bit higher but two of the operators (DESCRIBE and ASK) are used primarily for exploring a dataset when a user do not know its structure. LODeX do not need these operators because the structure of source is revealed thanks to the Schema Summary. The most impactful operator is UNION that involves the 8% of the queries overall and almost the 33% in the SWDF dataset.

Table 3: Percentage of queries containing unsupported operators.

Dataset	Federation	Sub-Query	Aggregators	Negation
DBpedia3.5.1	0.0005	0.0037	0.0005	0.001
Linked Geo Data	0	0.0074	0.0074	0
SWDF	0.0012	0.0152	2.4053	0.0012
British Museum	0	0	0	0
Total	0.0004	0.0054	0.1744	0.0008

Dataset	UNION	COSNTRUCT	DESRIBE	ASK
DBpedia3.5.1	4.4153	0.8991	0.0977	4.3572
Linked Geo Data	9.6475	2.3115	0.0081	8.3676
SWDF	32.714	0.0493	31.1165	0.0645
British Museum	0	0	0	0
Total	7.6373	1.1684	2.2881	4.9438

In Figure 3 a summary of this analysis is shown. As you can see LODeX could support user in the definition of the greatest part of the unique SPARQL queries contained in LSQ. In particular, the global percentage of executable queries is 77.79%. We obtained the worst results with the SWDF endpoints (56.75% of queries executable) and the main reason is the kind of users that usually queries this dataset. In fact, SWDF is a dataset containing data regarding conferences and articles about the Semantic Web, so, the most probable kind of consumers are academics and Semantic Web experts. The Semantic Web skill of these users is above the average and they are outside the possible range of users that could use LODeX for building their SPARQL queries.

7 Conclusion

The Basic Query model represent an expressive model that can satisfy real world needs in supporting users in formulating SPARQL queries. LODeX, that internally uses this model, represents a powerful tool in supporting users in exploring unknown LOD sources [7]. In this paper we showed that LODeX could be able to support users in the formulation of the 77.6% of the queries contained in LSQ dataset. Some of the limitations of LODeX, like the focus in the extensional knowledge, and of the Basic Query model, like the impossibility of composing cyclic queries, have barely affected this result. However,

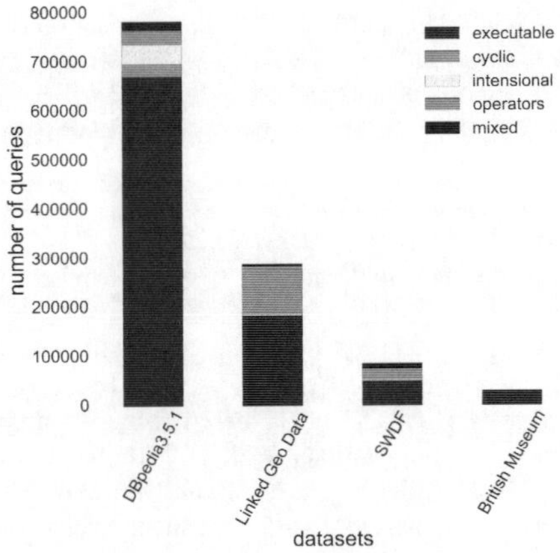

Fig. 3: Summary of the number of unique queries executable or not through LODeX. Legend: *executable*: executable through LODeX; *cyclic*: cyclic query not executable through LODeX; *intensional*: queries not executable through LODeX because they target the intensional knowledge; *operators*: queries containing unsupported SPARQL operators; *mixed*: unsupported queries for more than one specific reason of the latter three.

this analysis allows to delineate future lines of improvement. First of all, we could ulteriorly meet users needs by including the possibility of building UNION queries. Successively, we could focus our effort in extending the Basic Query model for enabling aggregation queries.

References

1. Z. Abedjan, T. Grütze, A. Jentzsch, and F. Naumann. Profiling and mining RDF data with prolod++. In I. F. Cruz, E. Ferrari, Y. Tao, E. Bertino, and G. Trajcevski, editors, *IEEE 30th International Conference on Data Engineering, Chicago, ICDE 2014, IL, USA, March 31 - April 4, 2014*, pages 1198–1201. IEEE, 2014.
2. B. Adida, M. Birbeck, S. McCarron, and S. Pemberton. Rdfa in xhtml: Syntax and processing. *Recommendation, W3C*, 7, 2008.
3. F. Benedetti, S. Bergamaschi, and L. Po. Online index extraction from linked open data sources. *Linked Data for Information Extraction (LD4IE) Workshop held at International Semantic Web Conference*, 2014.
4. F. Benedetti, S. Bergamaschi, and L. Po. A visual summary for linked open data sources. *International Semantic Web Conference (Posters & Demos) 2014*, 2014.
5. F. Benedetti, S. Bergamaschi, and L. Po. Exposing the underlying schema of lod sources. In *Web Intelligence (WI) and Intelligent Agent Technologies (IAT), 2015 IEEE/WIC/ACM International Joint Conferences*, 2015.
6. F. Benedetti, S. Bergamaschi, and L. Po. Lodex: A tool for visual querying linked open data. In *International Semantic Web Conference (ISWC 2015 Posters & Demos)*, CEUR Workshop Proceedings. CEUR-WS.org, 2015.

7. F. Benedetti, S. Bergamaschi, and L. Po. Visual querying lod sources with lodex. In *Proceedings of the 8th International Conference on Knowledge Capture*, K-CAP 2015, pages 12:1–12:8, New York, NY, USA, 2015. ACM.
8. D. Brickley and R. V. Guha. {RDF vocabulary description language 1.0: RDF schema}. 2004.
9. J. M. Brunetti, S. Auer, and R. Garca. The linked data visualization model. In *International Semantic Web Conference (Posters & Demos)*, 2012.
10. R. Cyganiak, D. Wood, and M. Lanthaler. Rdf 1.1 concepts and abstract syntax. *W3C Recommendation*, 25:1–8, 2014.
11. A.-S. Dadzie and M. Rowe. Approaches to visualising linked data: A survey. *Semantic Web*, 2(2):89–124, 2011.
12. S. Ferré. Expressive and scalable query-based faceted search over sparql endpoints. In P. Mika, T. Tudorache, A. Bernstein, C. Welty, C. Knoblock, D. Vrandei, P. Groth, N. Noy, K. Janowicz, and C. Goble, editors, *The Semantic Web ISWC 2014*, volume 8797 of *Lecture Notes in Computer Science*, pages 438–453. Springer International Publishing, 2014.
13. P. Heim, T. Ertl, and J. Ziegler. Facet graphs: Complex semantic querying made easy. In *The Semantic Web: Research and Applications, 7th Extended Semantic Web Conference, ESWC 2010, Heraklion, Crete, Greece, May 30 - June 3, 2010, Proceedings, Part I*, pages 288–302, 2010.
14. P. Heim, J. Ziegler, and S. Lohmann. gfacet: A browser for the web of data. In *Proceedings of the International Workshop on Interacting with Multimedia Content in the Social Semantic Web (IMC-SSW'08) Koblenz, Germany, December 3, 2008.*, 2008.
15. P. Höfler, M. Granitzer, E. E. Veas, and C. Seifert. Linked data query wizard: A novel interface for accessing SPARQL endpoints. In *Proceedings of the Workshop on Linked Data on the Web co-located with the 23rd International World Wide Web Conference (WWW 2014), Seoul, Korea, April 8, 2014.*, 2014.
16. D. L. M. P. F. P.-S. Jie Bao, Elisa F. Kendall. Owl 2 web ontology language quick reference guide, Oct. 2009.
17. C. Kiefer and A. Bernstein. Lodmilla: a linked data browser for all. In *Proceedings of the Posters and Demos Track of 10th International Conference on Semantic Systems*, SEMANTiCS2014, pages 31–34. CEUR-WS.org, 2014.
18. C. Kiefer, A. Bernstein, and M. Stocker. The fundamentals of isparql: A virtual triple approach for similarity-based semantic web tasks. In *Proceedings of the 6th International The Semantic Web and 2Nd Asian Conference on Asian Semantic Web Conference*, ISWC'07/ASWC'07, pages 295–309, Berlin, Heidelberg, 2007. Springer-Verlag.
19. J. Pérez, M. Arenas, and C. Gutierrez. Semantics and complexity of sparql. *ACM Transactions on Database Systems (TODS)*, 34(3):16, 2009.
20. J. Pérez, M. Arenas, and C. Gutierrez. Semantics and complexity of SPARQL. *ACM Transactions on Database Systems*, 34(3):1–45, Aug. 2009.
21. M. Saleem, M. I. Ali, A. Hogan, Q. Mehmood, and A.-C. N. Ngomo. Lsq: The linked sparql queries dataset. In *The Semantic Web-ISWC 2015*, pages 261–269. Springer, 2015.
22. M. Saleem and A.-C. N. Ngomo. Hibiscus: Hypergraph-based source selection for sparql endpoint federation. In *The Semantic Web: Trends and Challenges*, pages 176–191. Springer, 2014.
23. M. Schmachtenberg, C. Bizer, and H. Paulheim. Adoption of the linked data best practices in different topical domains. In *The semantic web–ISWC 2014*, pages 245–260. Springer, 2014.
24. A. S. Steve Harris. Sparql 1.1 query language, Mar. 2013.

Perspectives in Healthcare Data Management with Application to Maternal and Fetal Wellbeing

Lucia Vaira[1], Mario A. Bochicchio[1] and Shamkant B. Navathe[2]

[1]Set-Lab, Department of Engineering for Innovation, University of Salento, Lecce, Italy
{lucia.vaira, mario.bochicchio}@unisalento.it
[2]School of Computer Science, College of Computing, Georgia Institute of Technology, Atlanta
sham@cc.gatech.edu

Abstract:
Medical informatics has been addressing healthcare data management for a variety of applications. While valid and interesting solutions have been proposed and presented, it is quite apparent that the problem is not just of a technical nature. A part of the problem stems from resistance to change, other obstacles are more structural in nature. However, we need to overcome the obstacles from a more complex systemic point of view. The potential of technology to positively impact healthcare management and coordination is evident, but information technology is not so widely adopted by physicians and health systems worldwide and there is a lack of standards even among the EMRs (Electronic Medical Records) systems. Research on areas like virtual reality, robotics, genomics and proteomics has a great potential to benefit healthcare and personalized health. But to realize this benefit, the systemic approach will involve organizational, social, and regulatory transformations keeping in mind privacy protection concerns. In this paper we identify the overriding issues that are the stumbling blocks for the adoption of information technology in healthcare. As a case study we consider the obstetric and gynecological sector, which stands out because of the huge potential for improvement at multiple levels: diagnosis, care planning and treatment. We present our experience with developing a cloud-based system solution for maternal wellbeing and fetal growth monitoring.

Keywords. Healthcare applications, data acquisition, transmission, management and visualization; Personalized health; Patient tracking; Fetal Growth.

1 Introduction and background

We have experienced a decade of progress in digitizing medical records, as pharmaceutical companies and other organizations have aggregated years of research and development data in electronic databases. Moreover, transparency policies have made decades of stored data usable, searchable and actionable by the healthcare sector as a whole [1]. With the so-called "Big data" revolution to address very large Volume of data with high Variability and Volatility (the 3 V's), recent technologic advances have improved their ability to work with such data, by extracting Value (the 4th V) and opportunities [2]. It is hard to underestimate the importance of healthcare information technologies as they have become embedded within the everyday working practices of healthcare clinical staff. However, despite best practice research that identified success factors for health information technology projects, a majority of them still fail [3], [4]. This can happen also to big players. Google Health project, which offered users the opportunity to manage their own health information, did not succeed. Introduced in 2008, and retired with at the start of 2012, Google Health failed to capture widespread adoption and achieved only limited use. Microsoft HealthVault project, started in October of 2007 as a platform to store and maintain healthcare and fitness information, did not succeed either. Many authors analyzed the causes behind these failures [3], [4] the majority of which are the low rate usage due to the fact that these portals were not really designed by determining what type of information would help the patient and the physician; they were just offered as a place to store data. There was a lack of physician involvement and institutions were skeptical about these efforts from the start.

The lack of standards in healthcare in terms of treatment protocols, payment systems etc. as well as different payer-provider-patient relationships around the world were partly instrumental for these failures because these applications could not be leveraged for possible wider applicability similar to the Google Maps, as an example. This amounted to a lack of a business model for generating revenue.

These two big failures show that the problem is not just of technical nature. For healthcare IT initiatives to succeed, physicians, patients and researchers have to work in concert, the healthcare system must undergo some fundamental changes, and a new generation of approaches is required. Normally, a good way to identify the issues behind these and other similar failures of systems, tools and data repositories is to start with the notion of conceptual modeling of applications.

In the information systems field, we use "conceptual modeling" to refer to the activity that elicits and describes the general knowledge a particular information system needs to incorporate [5]. Traditionally, it represents the activity which models data in order to design and build user interfaces such as forms or online menus, with a firm notion of what data must be stored and managed by the system to support an application. When designing practical information systems (for enterprises, including those in healthcare), just the conceptual modeling of the information needed by the application is inadequate because in addition to data it is also necessary to model processes and the scope of the system [6] (e.g. in terms of stakeholders goals and value exchanges [7]). System architectures are needed that will offer modeling tools with a wider reach as well as service levels and metrics, or Key Performance Indicators (KPIs) so that modern applications can be developed not only to solve technical problems but also the overall system problems. Let us specifically consider the healthcare systems in existence today. Majority of healthcare systems are subject to several factors that negatively affect their success and adoption:

- lack of data, one of the major problem in health databases, which can be due to several (technical/social/political/legal) reasons;

- data obsolescence makes reference data less useful due to the variations of patient populations over the years. Without a live source of data, a healthcare system cannot survive;
- population-based studies lose credibility due to the increasing mobility of people. There can be a high degree of variation in evaluated populations from country to country and from region to region within the same country;
- lack of procedures for data integration and communication making it difficult, if not impossible, to easily share data among different hospitals and healthcare providers, partly because of privacy concerns. And even within a single hospital, information often remains confined within one department;
- there is heterogeneity among methods and methodologies used to define reference standards even for the same disease or a related set of disorders;
- lack of standards and protocols for treating similar patients and about the types of data maintained for similar patients based on disease codes;
- different levels of granularity and detail of data maintained for similar patients across health systems and across Electronic Medical Records (EMRs) systems.
- different naming conventions for drugs from generic and branded sources, and for genes in various studies.

Referring to these issues, we observe that in order to achieve a deeper comprehension of medical and clinical phenomena, a global approach taking into account the significant heterogeneity of genotypes, phenotypes and lifestyles characterizing our ethnically mixed society, has to be adopted. To support this, a readily, accessible location (website or server), for storing certified and updated information related to each type of medical phenomenon could allow researchers and health practitioners to coordinate their work and share research results worldwide.

In this paper we discuss the issues and challenges for the adoption of information technology in healthcare and the possibility to solve these problems with a global approach for collecting and analyzing healthcare data. In particular, we discuss about several management, technology, security, and legal issues that have to be addressed. We have been particularly studying the problem of maternal health and wellbeing as well as fetal growth monitoring for the past couple of years in conjunction with a number of national bodies and international experts. We present an application of our cloud-based system approach that can be a step forward for maternal and fetal health. We also show in that case study how we have attempted to address the major stumbling blocks and challenges that we identify in the next two sections.

2 Administrative policies and legal issues

It is well known that Personal Health Records (PHRs) contain extremely sensitive personal information and hence pose strong privacy concerns. Health data management policies differ from country to country. To scale-up healthcare applications at international level, a hierarchical scheme is needed possibly with three levels: global, countrywide, and institution-wide. Country-based laws such as the HIPAA (Health Insurance Portability and Accountability Act) regulation in the U.S. will play a major role; but global privacy regulations and guidelines currently do not exist. Institution-specific guidelines will have to be considered.

The use of cloud computing presents many legal issues such as service contracts, intellectual property rights, data jurisdiction, and privacy [8], [9], [10]. Whereas many health systems would benefit by moving their clinical and administrative data into the cloud, data jurisdiction, confidentiality, secured access, and privacy issues are major concerns. Often, the reluctance to sharing one's own healthcare data is troublesome, but occurs due to our cultural background. In terms of population health studies, anonymous data sets are adequate for performing statistical operations and applying machine learning algorithms. The science of clinical healthcare delivery cannot progress unless patients are willing to "donate" their data anonymously for research; however, potential unethical exploitation of healthcare data should be avoided.

2.1 Concerns on data collection, privacy and security

Lack of data is one of the major problems in health databases and it is due to several reasons - the local nature of traditional data collections, managed by bureaucratic units; the legitimate conflict of interest existing among physicians (practicing defensive medicine), patients and health administrations (focused on costs reduction); and the lack of adoption of proper data gathering techniques. Technological improvements have to go hand-in-hand with a systematic regulatory framework for balancing the involved interests.

Particular attention has to be paid to the data harvesting process, which refers to adopting several strategies concurrently to obtain relevant data from all possible channels directly from the field. In order to preserve privacy and confidentiality in the data gathering process, all involved patients have to receive written and oral information about the study (possible utilization of data) and must give informed consent, which authorizes to store and manage their sensitive personal data.

2.2 Creation of an authoritative Big Data repository

Up to 50% of European adults search online for health information [11]. The need for widespread online access to accurate, updated and relevant information about diseases and therapies, as well as to personal health data, is essential.

Access to a massive quantity of certified authoritative and constantly updated information, which takes into account the social context, and changes (environment, lifestyle, pathologies, drugs, people's mobility, etc.), could help to decrease the level of undue anxiety in patients. It could act as a first-level support to patients and avoid unnecessary and expensive further investigation. The same is true on the research side, where access to a vast quantity of shared healthcare data for scientific purposes could reinforce, support and validate clinical studies to make progress. A Big Data repository, if organized hierarchically by chronic and acute diseases and within those by specific disease codes can offer the capability for real-time and continuous learning and can be useful to increase the ability to generate and test hypotheses that could lead to important insights. Continuous data feeds from hospitals and healthcare systems will be needed to improve statistical validity and some input directly from patients can be incorporated in an anonymized form. The idea of creating a data repository for all diseases sounds like a utopian dream, and would require a buy-in from stakeholders from governmental authorities to individual researchers and practicing physicians. But presently, small examples do exist in the form of the repositories of bone marrow donors and organ donors. There are also university-wide efforts at U.S. universities to create data warehouses by combining aggregated clinical information across multiple hospitals. When these repositories become available, it would be possible to perform analytical studies on vast amounts of data using scalable big data technological solutions [17].

3 Data management and technical problems and solutions

To better understand the technical issues arising when dealing with healthcare data, we present below the main steps throughout its lifecycle: data acquisition, data design and storage, data access and visualization.

3.1 Data acquisition

Data collection: lack of high quality data is one of the major problems arising when collecting healthcare data from different data sources. It arises from a variety of reasons: security regulations for sharing, data ownership issues, human mistakes or faulty equipment (i.e. data incompleteness) or lack of interest by physicians and health systems to share data. In order to collect data from all possible sources directly from the field, new data harvesting techniques have to be adopted:

- form-based input (on Web pages or Apps) to be filled by physicians and patients. This is a time-intensive channel, more appropriate for patients, who generally have a strong motivation to describe in detail and to precisely address their own problems;
- new generation mobile devices, which typically are packed with sensors (e.g. GPS, gyroscopes, accelerometers, touch-sensitive surfaces, microphones and cameras) or have physical interfaces that allow the connection of external modules (e.g., blood pressure cuffs, blood glucose monitoring) to harvest data;
- direct connection to medical equipment (e.g. medical imaging machines, medical ventilators, medical monitors, …) with automatic DICOM metadata decoding and/or signal processing techniques;
- data extraction from medical documents, both printed and digital, provided to patients after medical test or extracted from large digital archives by means of Optical Character Recognition (OCR) techniques;
- smart digital devices (e.g. for weight and height measurement, speech-to-text software, etc.) provided to physicians to simplify data collection at the clinic visit. This is in line with the current evolution of Internet of Things in which smart devices help to transform clinical practice and to improve the delivery of care as in the "connected health";

- data-scraping techniques able to emulate a human agent interacting with the user interface of a non-interoperable software in order to insert/extract relevant data for specific purposes or for massive ingestion.

These techniques allow a direct and automatic data transfer and would improve data ingestion reducing data incompleteness and errors.

Incompleteness can lead to a significant reduction in the quality of data analysis jeopardizing the attempts to achieve meaningful information from available data. As described in [12], the multidimensional analysis of incomplete data can be conducted by implementing additional data structures and functions based on binary data tables and Boolean operations. A pilot implementation of these concepts and some experiments on a real dataset of fetal growth data has demonstrated the effectiveness of the approach and its sustainability in terms of response time and computing power [13].

Data privacy and confidentiality: in order to guarantee privacy and confidentiality, several strategies and techniques can be adopted:

- data suppression: exclusion of specific data elements is the basis of most general restrictions on data use. In this realm, carefully constructed aggregate data or removal of entire records provides the highest level of confidentiality (e.g. K- anonymity [14], L-Diversity, etc.);
- data transformation/perturbation: the idea is to preserve aggregate trends in the original data by removing or altering the actual data; the modifications are irreversible and destroy the original values or correlations but preserve the relationships of interest [15];
- data swapping: values can be swapped to discourage users from matching, since matches may be based on incorrect data;
- data encryption, a widely adopted reversible data transformation;
- physical separation among personal data, clinical data (e.g. medical reports, details on wellness status, lifestyle, etc.) and the adoption of keys derived from cryptographic hash functions for reconciliation purposes;
- random noise addition: numerical data can be protected by adding randomly selected amount (a random draw from a normal distribution with mean equal to zero) either to the observed value or to answer to statistical queries.

3.2 Data design, storage and archiving

Data modeling and integration issues: One of the most serious challenges for healthcare IT systems is the need for integration between different, and sometimes inconsistent, systems. This is a direct result of the different and diverse sources of data in hospitals: patients' data come from one system, their X-rays from another, and their lab results from a third one. Therefore to get all data for a patient all these systems must be integrated together. The EMR systems are alleviating the problem to some extent but they are not compatible among themselves.

Data storage and archiving issues: Cloud Computing makes possible approaches on a global scale and allows the creation of large information resources and the development of significant statistical samples. It can reduce data obsolescence, but opens a wide class of new problems such as those related to data protection and national regulations. In several countries data protection laws require knowledge of where data are stored or even obligate data storage in a specific geographic location (e.g. in France, Spain and Italy). Technological advances have made it easier to clean data and preserve patient privacy: name and personal information can be easily removed and records can be anonymized complying with patient-confidentiality standards. In this way data can be stored, managed and shared securely. Lack of trust in data security and privacy by users, organizational inertia, lack of governance, and provider's lack of compliance represent other critical challenges.

Data warehousing Solutions: In order to collect and integrate data coming from heterogeneous sources, a data warehouse system can be considered, which consists of a source layer (containing multiple data pools), a reconciliation layer and a data warehouse layer (containing both data warehouse and data marts). ETL (Extraction, Transformation and Loading) pipelines can be purposely developed to clean up and integrate the sources of input data to a common standardized form. Moreover, in order to take advantage of the data and to try to apply historically archived data warehouses to a personal level, the concept of Homogeneous Patient Groups [16] can be considered. It is assumed as clusters of patients with similar genetic make-up (ethnicity, familial aspects, etc.) and similar environmental conditions (nutrition, smoking, drugs, etc.).

3.3 Data access for Personalized Treatment

The availability of extended conceptual models, including goals, stakeholders, value exchange, processes, etc. is especially important to define the access layer.

Security and confidentiality: For all stakeholders, the main benefit of a global solution is in an easier and ubiquitous access to health data anytime, anywhere and on any device. Nevertheless, the adoption of cloud platforms causes a whole new class of concerns on security and confidentiality, even in relationship to cloud service providers. Encryption, strong authentication and authorization policies and secure channels, both at data level and communication level, have to be taken into consideration to face these problems.

Run-time computation challenges: Adopting a global approach that takes into account the heterogeneity of genotypes, phenotypes and lifestyles of patients requires a considerable change in the underlying mathematical models (and the related computational load) that would identify at run-time patient clusters (stratified and personalized medicine) characterized by homogeneous responses to treatments and drugs. This would increase the effectiveness of the available diagnostic techniques and would reduce the number of inappropriate treatments and reduce overall cost in healthcare.

The patients' segmentation can be considered from different point of views, each of which responds to specific stakeholders' needs (hospitals, administration, patients, doctors and researchers) – with anonymous data sources, the clusters do not raise specific privacy issues. Generally, it is almost impossible to be able to identify a single patient in such clusters. At the other extreme, there is a definite interest in rare diseases where patients do not mind being singled out as a one-element cluster for the potential benefit of better diagnosis and treatment.

Health intelligence, analytics and KPIs: Health policy makers require updated and trustworthy indicators for their activities and quality improvement like for example life expectancy, infant and maternal mortality rates, incidence counts of pathologies (e.g. diabetes, depressions, obesity, etc.), smoking and alcohol habits and so on.

One of the expected impacts of the EU Program HORIZON 2016-2017, on the area of "Health, demographic change and well-being" [18], is about "turning large amounts of data into actionable information to authorities for planning public health activities".

A global and connected health system would offer a remarkable opportunity to estimate such indicators in near real-time on live data sources as already done in several other fields on the Web.

4 Current status of application to maternal and fetal wellbeing

The obstetric and gynecological sector has a huge potential for improvement at multiple levels: diagnosis, care planning and treatment. This is supported by more than 160 millions of newborns per year worldwide, whose families are very sensitive to all aspects concerning the wellbeing of both mother and fetuses/newborns and are highly motivated to change their lifestyle and their approach to healthcare. In this context, in the last few years we worked on a well-known and worldwide-established diagnostic test: the intrauterine growth tracking. The test, based on the assumption that biometric parameters can be modeled as Gaussian distributions, is used for fetal wellbeing monitoring and early detection of fetal growth restriction; it is essential to estimate the perinatal outcome and promptly treat possible complications.

Currently, the test is performed by comparing the fetal biometric parameters (ultrasound measurements) with "standard growth curves" on which a large debate is reported in literature because of the problems described in Section 2 and 3. No "standard" approaches are used to collect and analyze fetal and maternal data at global level so that the adopted standard curves are practically ineffective "by design". Population-specific fetal growth curves are not the solution to the problem since ethnicity is not the only parameter to take into account and also because fetal biometric parameters are highly variable from country to country and within regions from the same country. Moreover, methods adopted in literature to create population-specific growth curves are not homogeneous (our extensive review is published at http://fpgt.unisalento.it/FPGT/curves/curves.php) and even if suitable for comparisons among populations, they cannot be cumulatively used to extract reference growth curves. In order to face these problems, we developed a new approach based on a more comprehensive mathematical model, like the "Gaussian Mixture", able to estimate the fetal growth, case by case, by taking into account all the relevant parameters (genetics, environment, lifestyle, pathologies, etc.). Indeed, the adoption of the Gaussian Mixture instead of the simple Gaussian distribution permits the identification of homogeneous sub-families, characterized by a lower variance with respect to the variance of the whole population, and consequently increases the diagnostic power of the fetal growth test (see section 3.3).

The new approach, complemented with several elements coming from well-established conceptual modeling techniques (EER [17], E^3 value [7], KAOS [19], BPMN, etc.) has been used to develop a cloud-based prototype able to manage the Italian fetal growth data production (about 0.55 million newborn per year) [20].

The block architecture of the proposed system is represented in Fig. 1. The "*acquisition*" component represents the different "channels" we implemented to gather data in order to solve, at least in part, the data acquisition concerns (see section 3.1). In particular, in order to incorporate as much data as possible, we have tried encouraging both pregnant women and physicians to provide their fetal growth data. The "encouragement" consists in remunerating them with useful/desired services (e.g. the "*daily wellbeing log*" and the "*where is the nearest hospital*" implemented as an App for the pregnant or the "*my personal database*" and "*my customized fetal growth curves*" for the physicians). In more detail, we have implemented 5 main channels: 1) form-based input (manual entries by means of web applications or mobile Apps); 2) direct connection to ultrasound machines; 3) automatic growth-data extraction from printed/digital ultrasound pictures; 4) adoption of smart digital devices able to automatically store data by communicating each other; 5) data-scraping techniques useful to gather data from electronic documents (web pages, electronic forms, etc.), available on non-interoperable systems and mainly based on software techniques able to emulate a human agent interacting with the user interface in order to insert/extract relevant data for specific purposes or for massive ingestion. In order to preserve privacy and confidentiality in our experiments, all involved patients received written and oral information about the study and signed the informed consent authorizing us to store and manage their sensitive personal data (see section 2.1). From a technical point of view, data are stored and managed on three separate instances of MySQL, an instance of Pentaho Business Analytics (a Business Intelligence suite) and a purposely-built Web Application with mobile-enabled features. Privacy and security issues have been addressed by adopting five main techniques: 1) physical separation among personal data, clinical data and reconciliation keys; 2) adoption of keys derived from cryptographic hash functions for reconciliation purposes; 3) strong authentication and authorization policies to define data access/treatment rules; 4) secure channels for communication; 5) record restrictions and anonymization on open data published for statistical and analytical purposes (see sections 2.1, 3.1, 3.3).

The "*design & storage*" component is able to embrace the world production of fetal growth data (Fetal Growth Database, FGDB), which is of the order of Petabytes of data [16] (see section 3.2).

Finally, the "*access*" component represents the front-end that patients and physicians use for customized fetal growth tracking and diagnosis and researchers' use for data analysis. To guarantee secure accesses and record restrictions we have adopted strong authentication and authorization policies defining visibility roles and access/treatment policies (see sections 2.1 and 3.3).

Referring to the data analysis functions, the FGC-B&C block (Fetal Growth Curves Builder & Comparison) is able to evaluate and plot the customized fetal growth curve and to compare it with the available reference curves. The MUDIB block (Multidimensional Builder), instead, allows to interactively build and explore the multidimensional cubes representing the fetal growth data, by exploiting the usual multidimensional operations (e.g. drill-down, roll-up, etc.; see [17]), looking for correlations among the available measures and dimensions.

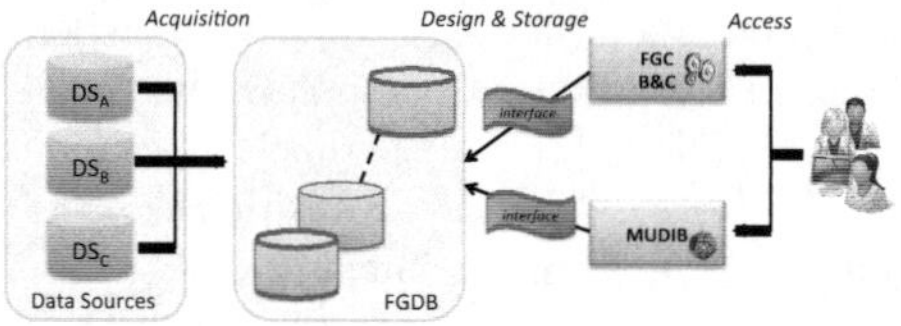

Fig. 1. Block architecture of the proposed system

5 Conclusions and future works

The availability of global and integrated information resources is essential in large organizations (including healthcare providers) for both operational aspects (data transactions) and governance (business intelligence, analytics, decision support systems, and enterprise applications).

In healthcare, while data are often produced and collected at local level for specific aspects, no systematic gathering and integration approaches seem to have gained momentum. The problem is not just technical, because new advanced solutions and standards for integrated healthcare data management and interoperability are emerging rapidly, but are not being widely adopted due to several stumbling blocks. The identification and analysis of these stumbling blocks is essential to model, design and build data management solutions, which are not only technically correct but also practical and effective from a systemic and administrative point of view. For this reason, conceptual data modeling has to be extended and integrated with other modeling techniques (value exchanges, goals, stakeholders, processes, etc.) to involve all stakeholders in the definition of shared and sustainable models in which information (constantly updated and trustworthy data) plays the role of the enabling factor. This will open up opportunities for new global health models leading to new business and research opportunities. The observations and analysis proposed in this paper has been a result of discussions and an agreement with the help of several physicians, public policy makers and ICT experts of two European countries in the context of a recent European call (SC1-PM-18-2016: Big Data supporting Public Health policies); we have also found other European and United States initiatives operating in the same direction. The concepts mentioned above have been applied to the obstetric and gynecological sector because of its huge potential for improvement at multiple levels: diagnosis, care planning and treatment. For this purpose, a cloud-based prototype has been developed for maternal wellbeing tracking and fetal growth monitoring. This permitted the extension of the mathematical model currently adopted for growth monitoring with benefits in terms of better diagnoses, cost reduction and improved patient support. We are encouraged by this pilot effort and are seeking partners from other European countries and elsewhere to join us in the vision outlined in this paper. We fully understand that information and communication technology can only be regarded as an enabler of higher quality, cost-effective and personalized healthcare to patients. More willingness on behalf of health systems and physicians to share data for research purposes and for the development of tools will go a long way in this direction.

References

[1] P. Groves, B. Kayyali, D. Knott, S. Van Kuiken. The big data revolution in healthcare. Accelerating value and innovation, McKinsey&Company, 2007

[2] R.B. Parikh, M. Kakad, D.W. Bates. Integrating Predictive Analytics Into High-Value Care - The Dawn of Precision Delivery. Journal of the American Medical Association. 2016; 315(7):651-652

[3] T. Spil and R. Klein. Personal Health Records Success: Why Google Health Failed and What Does that Mean for Microsoft HealthVault? 47th Hawaii International Conference on System Science, 2014

[4] M. Landeweerd, T. Spil, R. Klein. The Success of Google Search, the Failure of Google Health and the Future of Google Plus. IFIP Advances in Information and Communication Technology Vol 402 pp 221-239

[5] A. Olivé, Conceptual Modeling of Information Systems, Springer, 2007.

[6] C. Batini, S. Ceri, S.B. Navathe: Conceptual Design: An Entity Relationship Approach, Benjamin Cummings, 1992

[7] J. Gordijn and H. Akkermans. E3-value: Design and Evaluation of e-Business Models. In IEEE Intelligent Systems, Vol. 16(4):11-17, 2001

[8] S. Pearson. Taking account of privacy when designing cloud computing services. IEEE ICSE Workshop on Software Engineering Challenges of Cloud Computing 2009, NY

[9] D. Svantesson, R. Clarke. Privacy and consumer risks in cloud computing. Comput Law Secur Rev 2010; 26(4):391-397

[10] C. Kuner. Data protection law and international jurisdiction on the Internet. Int J Law Inf Technol 2010; 18(2): 176-201

[11] European Commission, Digital Single Market. Managing Health Data https://ec.europa.eu/digital-agenda/en/managing-health-data

[12] M.A. Bochicchio and L. Vaira, Using Binary Tables to Manage Incompleteness in Multidimensional Analysis. 22nd Italian Symposium on Advanced Database Systems (SEBD), Gaeta, Italy, 2015.

[13] M.A. Bochicchio, L. Vaira, E. Cicinelli, A. Vimercati. Dealing with incompleteness in multidimensional analysis of health records: An experience on fetal growth. IEEE International Conference on Bioinformatics and Biomedicine 2015 pp 1032-1038

[14] L. Sweeney. K-anonymity: a model for protecting privacy. Int J Uncertainty, Fuzziness Knowledge-Based Syst. 2002; 10:557–570

[15] D.E. Bakken, R. Rarameswaran, D.M. Blough, A.A. Franz, T.J. Palmer. Data obfuscation: anonymity and desensitization of usable data sets. IEEE Secur Privacy. 2004; 2:34–41.

[16] M.A. Bochicchio, L. Vaira, A. Longo, A. Malvasi, A. Tinelli, Multidimensional Analysis of Fetal Growth Curves. BigData In Bioinformatics and Health Care Informatics (BBH), Santa Clara, 2013.

[17] R. Elmasri and S.B. Navathe, Fundamentals of Database Systems, Ed.7, Pearson Publishing, 2015.

[18] SC1-PM-18–2016: Big Data supporting Public Health policies available at http://ec.europa.eu/programmes/horizon2020/sites/horizon2020/files/08.%20SC1-Health%202016-2017_pre-pub.pdf

[19] A. van Lamsweerde, E. Letier. From Object Orientation to Goal Orientation: A Paradigm Shift for Requirements Engineering. Proc. Radical Innovations of Software and Systems Engineering, 2003.

[20] M.A. Bochicchio, A. Longo, L. Vaira, A. Malvasi and A. Tinelli. Creating dynamic and customized fetal growth curves using cloud computing. 13th IEEE International Conference on BioInformatics and BioEngineering (BIBE 2013) pp. 1- 4

The Main Challenges around Integrating Digital Libraries

Antonella Longo, Marco Zappatore, Mario A. Bochicchio

Dept. of Innovation Engineering, Univ. of Salento, via Monteroni sn, 73100 Lecce, Italy
{antonella.longo, marcosalvatore.zappatore,
mario.bochicchio}@unisalento.it

Abstract. The quantity of literary contributions in every scientific domain grows daily and on a global scale. Researchers typically employ a wide range of different publication formats to present and share their work, such as journal papers, technical reports, patents, books and so on. This rainfall of documents brings a real drowning threat to those who have to swim across scientific repositories. Existing Web digital libraries and the ways they can be queried against are useful tools in such a scenario but they usually return overlapping or out of scope results and they behave as proprietary systems exposing heterogeneous query tools and closed data manipulation procedures. Since the availability of consistent, domain-based bibliographic corpora may significantly boost research and collaborations amongst academics, by identifying core authors and core publication targets, we believe that having such resources will be more and more perceived as a need in the near future. From these premises, in this paper we analyze the challenges to create a robust and consistent Web dataset of references within a specific knowledge area. In order to exemplify the topics a use case dealing with the emerging and multi-disciplinary community of Online Laboratories is presented, as well as the semi-automatic content analysis and processing pipeline used to produce the bibliographic dataset.

Keywords: Data Warehouse; Bibliography; Reference Management System; Reference Processing; Data Cleansing.

1 Introduction

Scientific literary production is one of the most consolidated ways to disseminate scholar outcomes, to assess research quality and even to identify promising starting points for new works. Consequently, researchers from any knowledge domain experience the necessity of querying documental sources on a daily basis. Contents for such queries vary depending on several factors, starting from which scientific area a given scholar belongs to, but common search needs can be highlighted. For instance, one can be interested in knowing what publication trends are taking place within her/his area of expertise or which are the core reference authors, independently from the fact she/he is a physician, an IT scientist or an astronomer. For these reasons, scientific Web Digital Libraries (DLs) have become unavoidable landmarks in researchers' everyday life.

They offer large repositories of both research works and bibliographical references. They may refer to specific sectors (such as PubMed[1] in Health Sciences or IEEExplore[2] in engineering), or they may cover broader, multidisciplinary knowledge areas (like Web of Science[3] or Scopus[4]).

The increasing diffusion of DLs has led to some well-established practices in managing research data. DLs expose search forms mimicking Web search engines where scholars submit keyword-based queries (with a query formalism depending on the current DL) and define filtering options (e.g., period of publication, research field, authors' names, publication target, etc.) in order to get a first set of matching references. Results are presented as collection of references and/or number of citations; they can be further refined through the use of facets [1]. References can be used to reach the corresponding full documents, if they are available within that DL. Large-scale DLs exhibit: 1) relatively simple query methods; 2) continuous improvement; 3) cross-domain research.

Nevertheless, scholars who desire to gather a reliable and certified collection of references, which truly wraps the majority of contributions in a given scientific community, cannot benefit from current available tools due to a series of shortcomings. Moreover, it is difficult to create, maintain and update a bibliographic dataset describing a given research community that has to be accessed online by users, since DLs only allows scholars to perform search and store their search results.

Some approaches to overcome these issues are available: federated queries, Reference Management Systems (RMS), specific alert services offered by some DLs that notify scholars when new records satisfying their stored queries are added. However, these solutions do not resolve completely the problems mentioned above: services that submit federated queries to multiple DLs are yet to be largely adopted, RMS lack in effective reporting features about the references they store and DLs exhibit relevant heterogeneities in terms of available datasets, reference formats, query mechanisms and result retrieval methods. These issues severely hinder the possibility to have consistent and certified Web bibliographical collections. These collections would act as open shared staging areas where a scientific community can: a) add new references; b) fully profile its members and the available publication targets; c) gather typical analytics figures, such as the most prolific authors, the most cited ones, and so on. As a result, researchers would gather knowledge about the community, and be supported in profitably sharing their works amongst peers as well as to create or foster scientific collaborations. For example, authors' citation policies could receive a positive effects, since this tool could be easily connected to Google Scholar user profiles, thus improving citation management.

However, this task cannot be achieved easily, since many relevant aspects have to be preliminarily examined. The hindering challenges have to be identified and then tackled effectively by adopting efficient content processing pipelines. For such reasons,

---

1 National Institute of Health, US National Library of Medicine: http://www.ncbi.nlm.nih.gov/pubmed

2 IEEExplore Digital Library: http://ieeexplore.ieee.org/Xplore/home.jsp

3 Thomson Reuters, Web of Science: https://webofknowledge.com/

4 Scopus Database: http://www.scopus.com/home.url

in this paper we propose a web-hosted preliminary collection of bibliographical references pertaining to a specific research domain, obtained through the adoption of a specific pipeline. We refer to an emerging and multi-disciplinary scientific community known as Online Laboratory Research (OLR) for multiple reasons. Firstly, we believe that only by examining a real case study, the challenges and opportunities related to web bibliographic datasets can be assessed. In addition, the OLR community has been chosen since in the past years it has progressively acquired so much relevance to be worthy of being considered as an autonomous research domain [2]. Moreover, being relatively limited in size, this community allow us to perform manually some steps in the pipeline, with the help of data management and domain sector experts, in order to check how the issues mentioned above can be coped with, and how the data processing steps could be subsequently automatized.

The paper is structured as in the following: Section 2 outlines research background and motivation. Section 3 describes the adopted case study and research methodology. The examined dataset as well as data processing steps are described in Section 5. Section 6 discusses findings and results. Section 7 draws conclusions and summarizes the most relevant challenges in DL integration.

2 Background and Motivation

State-of-the-art reviews present large analyses of a given knowledge area. However, because of space and time limitations, even the most comprehensive reviews cannot provide a complete list of bibliographical references about a given topic. In addition, such publications are occasional, thus making real-time analysis quite impossible. Therefore, DLs such as PubMed, IEEExplore, ACM Digital Library[5] or Scopus can be used to perform keyword-based searches on the spot and to make personal collection of bibliographical references but even DLs exhibit a series of issues. Firstly, the significant number of retrieved results, which also varies from DL to DL, may push scholars to produce only partial reviews (and the more active and prolific a scientific community is, the more troublesome this search-and-review process become).

Similarly, retrieved results may not entirely cover a specific knowledge domain, thus representing only a portion of all possible results. DLs may expose limited querying capabilities or too much complicated query formalisms, thus reducing the effectiveness of users' search sessions. Another significant issue is the heterogeneity of query systems, which prevent to submit the same query to multiple DLs at the same time.

To simply sketch how difficult can be the management of query results from a numerical point of view, let us consider a couple of easy, keyword-based queries covering the time span 2008-2013 and referring to title, abstract and keywords only (i.e., the facets on which the queries are executed). The first one searches for the term "NoSQL",

[5] ACM Digital Library: http://dl.acm.org/

while the second one searches for "online laboratory". Both the queries have been submitted against the following DLs: ACM Digital Library, DBLP[6], Google Scholar[7], IEEExplore, Microsoft Academic Search[8], Science Direct[9], Scopus and Web of Science. Due to the issues mentioned above (Table 1), query results are significantly discordant.

Table 1. Number of returned records for different DLs

Digital Library (DL)	Q_1: *"NoSQL"*	Q_2: *"online laboratory"*
ACM Digital Lib.	934	91
DBLP	113	30
Google Scholar	7060	1280
IEEExplore	141	1051
MS Academic Search	74	64
Science Direct	15	520
Scopus	346	176
Web of Science	156	76

A possible solution to query heterogeneity is to query different platforms in sequence, by using each time their specific query language, and proceed to result comparisons, simulating a kind of meta-search engine for Web Scholar Digital Library. This approach usually produces overlapping datasets, sometimes inconsistent, in the sense that by using the same keywords they will get different results, sometimes out of scope. Another possible solution is represented by federated queries or by search engines capable of accessing multiple DLs, like as the Protocol for Metadata Harvesting by Open Archives Initiative (OAI-PMH) [3] which aims at achieving interoperability through metadata exchange across different repositories. However, these approaches still have a limited usage in practice and do not offer a complete coverage to all available DLs.

Once a researcher has found a viable pool of bibliographical sources, she/he may revolve to RMSs, such as Mendeley[10], JabRef[11] or EndNote[12], to manage bibliographies and possibly to share them amongst peers. Indeed, these applications allow users to create their collection of bibliographical references, to extract references from electronic documents (including also webpages) and to handle results obtained from DLs. Although, these solutions may improve reference management and sharing practices across scholars but they do not offer a significant improvement in the overall quality of the datasets they manage. In other words, RMS can be seen as a useful complementary set of applications for those who have to systematically work with scholar references.

Other crucial issues in this scenario refer to DLs, which may have different reference and citation management policies, thus making difficult to export data from one to another and even to compare collected data. Heterogeneous bibliographic formats (e.g.,

6 DBLP Computer Science Bibliography: http://www.informatik.uni-trier.de/~ley/db/
7 Google Scholar: http://scholar.google.com/
8 Microsoft Academic Search: http://academic.research.microsoft.com/
9 Elsevier Science Direct. The full-text Scientific Database: http://www.sciencedirect.com
10 Mendeley: http://www.mendeley.com/
11 JabRef - Reference Manager: http://jabref.sourceforge.net/
12 Thomson Reuters. EndNote X7: http://endnote.com/about/x7

BibTex-based ones, plain text ones and XML-based ones) are employed and very often the same reference stores inhomogeneous amount of metadata which depend from the queried DL. Proprietary query mechanisms make troublesome to submit the same query to different DLs (e.g., some DLs do not allow to use Regular Expressions, RegEx). Thus, users are compelled to make some compromises if they want to compare results from different DLs for the same query. Bibliographic metrics and citation indexes differ as well, depending on which DLs scholars refer to. All these challenges have been already pointed out in some useful research works ([4], [5]) but no unique aligning solutions have yet emerged.

Another challenge is the quality and robustness of the references retrieved from DLs: just a few attempts have been made so far to properly profile and analyze a scientific community and its outputs. An example of this kind of contribution, dealing with these issues, was proposed by the authors of [6] in order to analyze the e-Gov scientific arena. The authors profiled the community, published and commented both the results and the dataset (which is yearly updated) but they do not described the pipeline of tools used to produce them.

At our knowledge, no systematic approach to build and publish online bibliographical datasets for specific scientific domains has been presented so far to help scholars deepening the knowledge about their communities. Therefore, we believe that a processing methodology can be set up to produce reliable and consistent reference datasets and then made accessible on the Web and constantly updated.

The convenience deriving from this proposal is twofold: on the one hand, the issues around integrating several DLs can be pointed out; on the other hand, from the scientific community point of view, important quantitative and qualitative trends can be discovered, such as distribution of authors, leading research topics, reference publication targets and typical publication outcomes. In addition, authors may gain insights about where their scientific communities are moving to.

3 Case Study Description and Research Methodology

The relatively recent OLR scientific sector has been selected as our test case due to its multi-disciplinary scope ([7], [8]) and its relatively limited literary production (in order to proceed with a gradual examination of our approach).

A set of research questions (RQs) has been defined. We borrowed and revised the RQs from a similar case study, presented in [9], where a preliminary analysis of publication trends in OLR was performed.

- **RQ#1**: Which individuals form the core of OLR community and how many are they?
- **RQ#2**: Which topics and which methods do they prefer in their research?
- **RQ#3**: Which publication outlets (e.g., journals, conferences, books, etc.) do the core researchers prefer?
- **RQ#4**: Is the OLR community equivalently expanding both w.r.t. to number of authors and number of publications?
- **RQ#5**: Which is the typical number of coauthors for OLR publications?

A complete and up-to-date bibliographical dataset has been built, named OLR Reference Dataset for Effective Researches 2014 (ORDER2014), for analyzing challenges and opportunities in creating a specialized bibliography and integrating several DLs.

Suitable publication repositories have been selected and queries capable of extracting references to the desired papers formulated (these two starting steps are performed manually, since the contribution of domain experts is fundamental to evaluate query outcomes and to discard unwanted results). A semi-automatic data processing pipeline is then needed, in order to make it possible to answer RQs by performing analysis and reporting against the final reference dataset. The pipeline consists of the reference extraction step, reference cleaning and normalization steps (Fig. 1). The pipeline exploits both the constraints presented in [9] and newly defined ones.

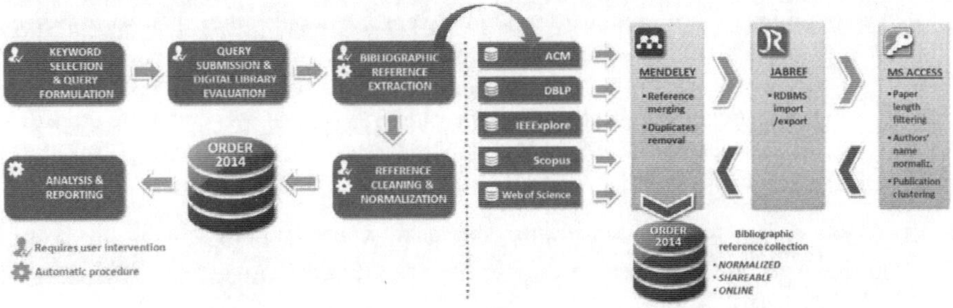

Fig. 1. Bibliographic reference extraction. Overview of processing steps

Firstly, specific queries are needed to gather pertinent papers across online repositories. Keyword-based Boolean queries were adopted as they are not affected by the inherent complexity of natural language queries and since they allow combining relevant terms into complex logical expressions. However, even if extremely accurate, this way of querying does not provide ranking mechanisms, so wrong results are possible. For such reasons, manual filtering is required.

Two keyword subsets (KWSs) have been chosen to widen the scope of our research at most. The first one encompasses terms that are surely relevant within the OLR scientific domain, while the latter collects names of significant projects in that area.

- **KWS_1**: "remote laboratory", "online laboratory", "virtual laboratory", "web laboratory", "online experiment", "remote experiment"
- **KWS_2**: "iLab", "LiLa", "VISIR", "NetLab", "Labshare", "Sahara", "SmartLabs", "Lab2Go"

The resulting Search String (SS) is the inclusive logical disjunction of all the items from KWS_1 and KWS_2. The query has been submitted to all the most relevant scientific publication archives. Moreover, preliminary research tests highlighted that some of the items in KWS2 provide too many false positives to be worth of being considered as valuable keywords if the semantic environment is not previously bordered. This was mainly due to homonymy issues. Keywords generating more false positives than correct results were discarded. The following terms were therefore removed: "Sahara" (homonymy with the corresponding geographical region); "VISIR" (whose acronym also stands for the very large telescope spectrometer imager for the mid-infrared [10]); "LiLa" (that usually indicates Lithium-Lanthanum compounds in chemistry).

As a result, the conclusive version of our query string, where KWS_1 and KWS_2 has been defined previously and T symbolizes the time span for the query (i.e., the years 2008-2013), is given by: $SS = \{KWS_1 \cup \{KWS_2 - \{\text{"Sahara"}, \text{"}VISIR\text{"}, \text{"}LiLa\text{"}\}\}\} \cap T$.

False positives affect KWS_1 as well, especially when keywords are located within abstracts. Indeed, sentences such as "[...] the samples were mailed to a remote laboratory [...]" or "[...] on-line experiments will be carried out as future developments to verify [...]" contain the selected keywords but actually do not deal with OLR-related topics. Therefore, manual filtering is a crucial step in ORDER2014 implementation.

As for query customization level, we selected fully customizable search strings whenever plain text query composition forms were available rather than form-based ones in order to use all the functionalities provided by each search engine.

In order to show the heterogeneity of query formats, two different versions of the Search String (SS) are now presented. The first one (SS_{IEEE}) has been submitted to IEEExplore, whilst the second one (SS_{SD}) to Science Direct (where the operator "tak" addresses the search string to Title, Abstract and Keyword metadata only).

- **SS_{IEEE}:** ((remote OR virtual OR online OR web) AND (labor* OR experim*)) OR (iLab OR NetLab OR Labshare OR SmartLabs OR Lab2Go) AND "Publication-Year":"2008-2013".
- **SS_{SD}:** tak("remote laborator*" OR "online laborator*" OR "virtual laborator*" OR "web laborator*" OR "online experimen*" OR "remote experimen*" OR "iLab" OR "NetLab" OR "Labshare" OR "SmartLabs" OR "Lab2Go") AND pub-date>2007 AND pub-date<2014.

These data sources must be searched for considering the same data fields in order to make the research as uniform as possible. Search strategy has been limited to: title, abstract, keywords. During preliminary search trials, MS Academic Research was discarded because it yielded few results. Google Scholar returned a large quantity of results, affected by an excessive number of false positives (as Science Direct), due to its barely tunable search options (queries can be only ran against the title or the entire body of an article), therefore it was discarded as well. Table 2 summarizes selected search and query features, searched data fields and numerical results for year 2013.

Table 2. Query analysis for year 2013 from examined DLs (gray rows are discarded DLs)

Digital Library (DL)	Search typology	Query type	Searched data fields	Search results	False positives
ACM Digital Lib.	Advanced	Search string	T, A	18	11.1%
DBLP	Complete	Search string	T, A	57	1.75%
Google Scholar	Advanced	Form-based	T	338	48.12%
IEEExplore	Command	Search string	T, A, K	114	9.63%
MS Academic Search	Advanced	Search string	T	1	0%
Science Direct	Expert	Form-based	T, A, K	54	59.86%
Scopus	Advanced	Text-based	T, A, K	426	19.95%
Web of Science	Basic	Text-based	T, A, K	316	37.44%

4 Data Processing Methodology

We decided to adopt RMS as the first data processing layer in our data processing pipeline. Therefore, a careful examination of the available alternatives has been performed. We searched for RMSs that satisfy the following criteria: 1) cross-platform compatibility; 2) import/export capability; 3) RDBMS compatibility; 4) Robustness; 5) Suitability. The following alternatives were evaluated: Mendeley, Zotero[13], JabRef, Endnote X7 and Publish or Perish[14]. After extensive trials and cross-comparisons, by using a small subset of references from OLR area as testbed, Mendeley has emerged as the RMS satisfying the majority of evaluation criteria. However, since only JabRef complies with the RDBMS compatibility (which we deemed as mandatory for our purposes) we decided to include it as well in our data processing pipeline.

As for reference formats, both BibTeX[15] and RIS[16] were selected since they are the most widely used across scientific community and the most largely supported by both RMS and digital libraries.

In order to obtain a unique, stable and sharable dataset (ORDER2014), we modeled a data processing pipeline. At the beginning of this pipeline, lies the Mendeley standalone version, which has been used to merge together datasets coming from different archives and to remove duplicate references. The resulting collection has to be subsequently exported to JabRef and from there into an SQL database, which serves as data source for a VBA-based Microsoft Access application. This application has been designed and implemented by the authors to perform data cleaning and normalization steps before getting ORDER2014 in its final shape.

The very first step cleans the dataset from unwanted results based on data cleansing criteria enlisted in [9]. For instance, only 4-page technical articles and 6-page non-technical articles written in English are evaluated. By doing so, the following types of publication outputs have been considered: full-length scientific papers, books, chapters, thesis, reports, research notes, work-in-progress papers. The following ones have been discarded: short papers, posters, conference (or workshop or symposium) summaries (or introductions), extended abstracts, editorial notes, commentaries, short reviews.

Having preserved only relevant papers, data normalization can be now carried out. Since bibliographic references present the entire list of coauthors for each publication, the initial step is to extract single authors' names from the dataset. Subsequently, these names must be normalized, in order to properly manage duplicate records that are typically due to the following ambiguities: 1) accented characters; 2) abbreviations; 3) multiple names and surnames; 4) wrong exports.
The proposed normalization technique, based upon a proper combination of string manipulation functions and Regular Expression (RegEx) patterns, aligns all authors' full names to the format <Surname, A B>, where the initials of the author's names follow the surname. We used manual filtering to solve few complex cases.

---

[13] Zotero: https://www.zotero.org/

[14] Publish or Perish: http://www.harzing.com/pop.htm

[15] BibTeX: http://www.bibtex.org/

[16] Research Information System (RIS) format: http://www.refman.com/support/risformat_intro.asp

The following step is represented by publication targets clustering in order to remove duplicates as well. Double records in this data field are mainly due to the different ways references are provided, thus the same conference name could come in different versions. For instance, we found "2013 10th Int. Conf. on Remote Engineering and Virtual Instrumentation", "10th Int. Conference on Remote Engineering & Virtual Instrumentation (REV)" or simply "REV 2013" but much more alternative combinations are possible. To tackle such issues, a combination of RegEx patterns and semantic distance computation has been adopted. Manual filtering completes this step. It is worth to say that conference proceedings are more affected by similar issues than journals.

5 Findings and Results

Data cleaning and normalization phases provide the ORDER2014 final version. Before this step, 2389 papers have been collected. By filtering them w.r.t. to paper length, we ended up with a dataset that gathers 1852 scientific papers (i.e. the 77.52% of the papers satisfies the page threshold). These papers have been published between the years 2008 and 2013 and have been collected from 5 different digital libraries. The dataset enlists 4368 different authors, 7050 authorship relations and 4 distinct publication targets (conference proceeding; journal; book or book part; other). The dataset is currently under publication as an openly shareable Mendeley group.

Many interesting insights can be gathered from ORDER2014. The first one refers to the relationship existing between papers and their authorships. By comparing these quantities, it is possible to determine how the OLR community is expanding yearly. Figure 2A summarizes the following elements: papers, distinct authors and authorships (where each authorship accounts for a person who has authored a paper in that year). As we can see, numerical results show a similar increasing trend for each quantity, demonstrating how the OLR domain is expanding quite uniformly. It is worth to mention that the larger is the bias between authors and authorships, the higher is the number of authors having published more than one paper in that year. For instance, at the moment of writing, we have 375 papers published in the year 2013, with 1183 distinct authors and a total of 1500 authorships.

Figure 2B shows the distribution of coauthors per paper within the time span 2008-2013. The majority of papers exhibit a number of coauthors in the range 2-5. We have 410 papers with 2 coauthors (22.16% of the published papers), 470 papers with 3 coauthors (25.41% of the total), 360 papers with 4 coauthors (19.46% of the total) and 205 papers with 5 coauthors (11.08% of the total). This distribution mimics a Gamma distribution with a shape parameter $k = 5.5$ and a scale parameter $\theta = 0.6$.

The distribution of papers per author is crucial as well. Indeed, it allows to ascertain the number of researchers which are occasional authors in comparison with the most prolific ones. Figure 2C illustrates such aspects by comparing authors having published just one paper per year, 2 papers per year, 3 or more papers per year. Each category is presented in percentage format w.r.t. the total number of distinct authors per year. Let us define as Most Prolific Authors (MPAs) those authors having published at least 2 papers per year. As it can be inferred from the graph, MPAs are always below the 20%

of the authors' totality. In other words, we can assert that a considerable slice (always exceeding the 80% threshold) of the authors participating in the OLR community is represented by sporadic contributors.
As for dataset core features, the Core Authors (CAs) category gathers researchers having yearly published at least one paper in the last 5 years. Table 3 describes CAs in terms of average number of papers per year ($\overline{p}$) and average number of coauthors per year ($\overline{ca}$). We believe in the importance of these two parameters. The former one allows us to determine how many CAs belong to the MPA category as well. The latter one quantifies the authorship network of each CA (i.e., how large is her/his collaboration network). This analysis give us a subset of 38 CAs, amongst which 33 can be also considered as MPAs (since they have $\overline{p} > 1.5$). Therefore, the 86% of CAs also belongs to the MPA subset, thus corroborating the fact that those authors effectively represent the OLR community core. In the same way, we identified two core publishers which have the greatest number of publications, with 303 and 354 papers respectively.
The examination of ORDER2014 also allow us to consider bibliographic reference quality, whose impact grows when the starting dataset grows in size as well. Indeed, even the most advanced DLs suffer from incomplete references. This determines a variable lack of information hindering the dataset and requiring manual intervention, thus challenging a complete exploitation of the reference management capabilities.

While authors, titles, publication targets and publication types are usually available, publishers, DOIs and keywords exhibit different missing element percentages. With explanatory purposes, we outlined these aspects in Table 4. As it can be seen, publishers are nearly absent, while keywords were not specified for almost a half of the references. DOIs are missing in a considerable quantity as well. However, DOIs show quite a clear decreasing trend in the amount of missing values. This confirms that the greater grows the interest for indexing procedures in scientific community, the more DOIs become a mandatory part of citation mechanisms, thus compelling digital libraries to include DOIs within their reference repositories.

Table 3. Core Authors (after anonymization)

Core author	$\overline{p}$	$\overline{ca}$	Core author	$\overline{p}$	$\overline{ca}$
Author #1	7.6	30	Author #6	4.8	21.2
Author #2	7.6	21.8	Author #7	4.6	16.2
Author #3	6.6	19.8	Author #8	3.6	8.4
Author #4	6.2	18.4	Author #9	3.4	1.2
Author #5	6.2	27	Author #10	3.4	1.2

Table 4. Percentages of missing elements in evaluated DLs

Year	Publisher	Keywords	DOI
2008	96.42%	65.59%	72.4%
2009	95.88%	66.67%	62.55%
2010	96.43%	48.21%	84.29%
2011	78.83%	46.25%	73.62%
2012	86.63%	33.43%	72.67%
2013	86.4%	59.73%	46.13%

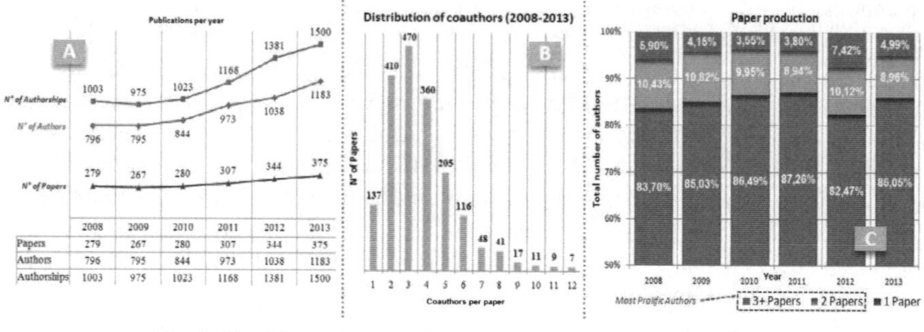

Fig. 2. Significant charts and data distributions about the dataset

6 Conclusions and Future Works

The aim of the paper is to describe the main challenges in creating a repository of scholar bibliographic references for a specific scientific community and to highlight how the integration between several scientific Digital Libraries (DLs) exhibits a series of challenges. The paper presents a processing pipeline, which is fed by query results from DLs, which outputs a consistent reference dataset (called ORDER2014) that can be shared on the Web amongst scholars. The online availability of such dataset represent a useful tool to improve research quality and to promote collaborative research amongst academics.

A concrete case study, dealing with the multi-disciplinary community of Online Laboratory Research has been evaluated. A set of scientific DLs has been examined and then queried, by using keyword-based queries encompassing those terms deemed as the most relevant for the OLR research domain. The proposed data processing pipeline cleans and normalizes references taken from DLs. A thorough analysis and validation of its contents has been performed. Reporting results has been presented as well and a series of challenges have been pointed out: heterogeneity in DLs and bibliographic formats, proprietary and not-straightforward query mechanisms, lack of reporting tools in RMSs, partial completeness of DLs with respect to metadata describing publishers, keywords and DOIs. The most relevant problem concerns how DLs are queried, since heterogeneous DL-related formalisms make difficult to define truly comparable search-strings. In this paper, we proposed a) to identify which are the most effective search techniques to be considered and b) to select a set of significant keywords to orient properly the search, with the help of domain experts.

As for the returned results, numerous issues have arisen due to the lack of normalization: authors' names are typically reported differently depending on the various DLs, thus requiring proper ways to disambiguate them; heterogeneity in reference formats (e.g., BibTeX and RIS); missing (e.g., DOIs, publishers, keywords) and misaligned information (e.g., the same data can be stored differently). As a consequence, the pipeline is useful to identify rigorously the requirements need to develop a proper Extraction Transform and Load (ETL) approach to align different formats, compare records and retrieve them univocally which represents a fundamental step for achieving effective integration across DLs.

Another important aspect elicited thanks to the proposed pipeline allow us to focus on how keywords can be systematized: due to their inhomogeneity, a more formal approach should be advisable. The pipeline, further improved with text-mining capabilities, will contribute to define a taxonomy whose contents can be browsed by the authors. For these reasons, starting from the issues highlighted and from the experience derived from the development of this semi-automatic pipeline, we will improve the pipeline by adopting specific ETL (Extract, Transform and Load) tools in conjunction with document DBMSs. These updates will provide users with more effective and efficient processing platforms. In addition, the adoption of graph DBMSs will be evaluated to improve the creation and examination of authors' networks.

7 Reference

1. Henry, M. J., Hampton, S., Endert, A., Roberts, I., Payne, D.: MultiFacet: a Faceted Interface for Browsing Large Multimedia Collections. In : ISM'13, pp.347-350 (2014)
2. Ma, J., Nickerson, J. V.: Hands-on, Simulated and Remote Laboratories: a Comparative Literature Review. ACM Computing Surveys 38(3), 1-24 (September 2006)
3. Lagoze, C., Van de Sompel, H., Nelson, M., Warner, S. In: The Open Archives Initiative Protocol for Metadata Harvesting.
4. Salisbury, L.: Web of Science and Scopus: a Comparative Review of Content and Searching Capabilities. The Charleston Advisor 11(1), 5-18 (July 2009)
5. Kulkami, A. V., Aziz, B., Shams, I., Busse, J. W.: Comparisons of citations in Web of Science, Scopus and Google Scholar for Articles Published in General Medical Journals. JAMA 302(10), 1092-1096 (Sep. 2009)
6. Erman, N., Todorovski, L.: Co-Authorship Network Analysis in the e-Government Research Field. In : 3rd. Int. Symp. on the Development of PA in South East Europe, , pp.1-11 (2011)
7. Bolaños, ., Contreras, L.: Virtual Laboratory for Supporting Chemistry Learning and Practicing. In : IEEE Education Engineering (EDUCON), pp.1949-1954 (2010)
8. Bean, L., Fridovich-Keil, J., Hegde, M., Rudd, M., Garber, K.: The Virtual Diagnostic Laboratory: a New Way of Teaching Undergraduate Medical Students about Genetic Testing. Genetics in Medicine 13(11), 973-977 (2011)
9. Bochicchio, M., Longo, A.: Profiling the Online Laboratories Research Community and Its Core. In : REV2013, pp.1-5 (2013)
10. Lagage, P., Durand, G., Lyraud, C., Rio, Y., Pel, J., de Haas, J.: Final Design of VISIR. Astronomical Telescopes and Instrumentation, 1120-1131 (2000)

Biconnectivity of Social and Web Graphs*

Giuseppe Chiapparo[1], Umberto Ferraro-Petrillo[2], Donatella Firmani[3], and Luigi Laura[2]

[1] University of Rome "Tor Vergata"
giuseppe.chiapparo.91@gmail.com
[2] Sapienza University of Rome
laura@dis.uniroma1.it, umberto.ferraro@uniroma1.it
[3] Roma Tre University
donatella.firmani@uniroma3.it

Abstract. Network connectivity is a basic notion for big data analysis, with many practical applications. In particular, the analysis of the largest strongly connected component is at the heart of the famous bow-tie structure of the Web. In this paper, we go beyond connected components and characterize the properties of the higher-connectivity components that lie inside real-world networks. We combine and extend recently developed techniques for scaling up to real-world datasets with up to 23.1 billion edges. Our experiments point out a striking difference between structural properties in social and web graphs, and highlight deep properties of social networks which may be helpful in devising theoretical models that can better capture their structure

Keywords: big data analysis, web graphs, social networks.

1 Introduction

Network connectivity is a basic notion having both theoretical and practical importance in big data analysis. Several experimental studies have shown that the largest strongly connected component (in short, lSCC) plays a crucial role in the structure of real-world networks, such as the Web and Twitter graph. First, the topology of the lSCC is at the heart of the famous bow-tie structure of the Web [10, 20] and of social networks, such as the Twitter graph [15]. Second, the lSCC of web graphs and social networks has a remarkable size and most of the user activity happens inside it. Meusel et al. [20] have shown, indeed, that the lSCC of a recent crawl of the web graph contains approximately 51.28% of its vertices, while other vertices are fragmented into smaller components. Gabilekov et al. [15] have shown that the lSCC of the Twitter graph contains about 50.71% of its vertices and accounts for 98.05% of the tweets, which represent a significant sample of the network for many big data applications.

* This paper has been partially supported by MIUR, the Italian Ministry of Education, University and Research, under Project AMANDA (Algorithmics for MAssive and Networked DAta).

For these reasons, there has been extensive work on understanding how the lSCC of a network changes when vertices are deleted; in this scenario, detecting vertices whose removal results in a significant degradation of the connectivity seems to be of practical importance [2]. Depending on the application at hand, those critical nodes may be used to understand, to promote or to mitigate information flows and diffusive processes that are acting upon the underlying network. For instance in social networks, finding vertices whose deletion breaks down some connectivity properties is related to identifying key players whose removal fragments / disrupts the underlying network. In this framework, several vertex-centrality indices attempt to measure how some graph invariant changes when vertices and edges are deleted (see, e.g., [1, 7, 8, 21]). Along those lines, Donato et al. [12] have shown that the lSCC of web graphs can reduce its size to 35-40% when removing less than 1% of the high indegree or outdegree vertices, and Boldi et al. [5] have proposed efficient removal strategies that can disconnect almost all pairs of vertices of a web graph by removing vertices (and their incident edges) until only about 30% of the edges have been removed.

Despite some similarity in the lSCC topology of social networks and web graphs, none of the above strategies is able to disrupt social networks as much as a web graph[4] [5], suggesting that the lSCC in social networks – differently from web graphs – is *robust* in a strong sense, since removing few vertices and edges seems to have no noticeable impact on its underlying structure. Although few proposals to find features that highlight such differences have been presented (see e.g., [22, 5, 11]), to the best of our knowledge no clear-cut results are known.

In this paper, we address this issue by analysing the inner structure of the lSCC of different web graph and social networks with up to 23.1 billion edges. While computing the lSCC can be done efficiently in a big data setting, computing the robust components of the network that cannot be easily disrupted, is much harder. To this end, we build a scalable framework for computing the so-called *biconnected components* inside the lSCC, that are the portions of the networks that cannot be disrupted by removing single vertices (i.e., 2-vertex connected components) and edges (i.e., 2-edge connected components). We show that most social networks have giant biconnected components containing up to 70% of vertices of the whole network (almost completely covering the lSCC), while web graphs have substantially smaller biconnected components (with less than 15% of vertices). For these reasons, we believe that the notion of biconnectivity in directed graphs provides new insights for understanding the structure of social networks, and may help in devising a theoretical model that is able to capture their finer properties and their essential differences with web graphs.

[4] In their analysis [5], Boldi et al. do not consider centrality measures based on distances, such as betweenness centrality [9], because they are computationally too expensive to be computed on large networks with billion edges.

2 Preliminaries

2.1 Basic Terminology

Let $G = (V, E)$ be a directed graph – a *digraph* – with n vertices and m edges. A directed path in G is a sequence of vertices $v_1, v_2, \ldots, v_k$, such that edge $(v_i, v_{i+1}) \in E$ for $i = 1, 2, \ldots, k-1$. G is said to be *strongly connected* if there is a directed path from each vertex in the graph to every other vertex. The *strongly connected components* of G are its maximal strongly connected subgraphs. A vertex $v \in V$ is a *strong articulation point* if its removal increases the number of strongly connected components of G. Similarly, an edge $e \in E$ is a *strong bridge* if its removal increases the number of strongly connected components of G.

Let G be strongly connected. If G does not contain any strong articulation point, or bridge, then it is connected in a even stronger sense: not only every pair of vertices is connected by a directed path, but it also remains connected whatever vertex or edge is removed from the graph. Such robust connectivity is represented by the notion of 2-*connectivity*. Formally, G is said to be:

- 2-*vertex connected* if it has no strong articulation points, i.e., the removal of any vertex leaves G strongly connected;
- 2-*edge connected* if it has no strong bridges, i.e., the removal of any edge leaves G strongly connected.

In other words, strong articulation points are exactly the vertex cuts for 2-vertex connectivity, while strong bridges are exactly the edge cuts for 2-edge connectivity. The 2-*vertex- (resp.,* 2-*edge-) connected components* of G are its maximal 2-vertex- (resp., 2-edge-) connected subgraphs. In the remainder of this paper, we use the notation 2ECC (resp., 2VCC) to denote 2-edge- (resp., 2-vertex-) connected components, and l2ECC (resp., l2VCC) to denote the largest 2-edge- (resp., 2-vertex-) connected component contained in graph.

Figure 1 illustrates the notion of strong articulation points, strong bridges, 2-vertex and 2-edge-connected components on directed graphs. We refer the interested reader to [16, 18] for more definitions and examples.

2.2 Algorithms

The 2-vertex and 2-edge connectivity of a directed graph can be tested very easily, even on very large instances such as web graphs and social networks [18]. Unfortunately, simply testing connectivity gives limited information about the underlying network and computing the 2VCCs and 2ECCs is computationally expensive: the asymptotically faster algorithms run in $O(n^2)$ time [17] and are very sophisticated, thus are likely to have also high implementation constants.

In our experiments we use simpler $O(mn)$ algorithms, which are known to be fast in practice [19]. Furthermore, many real-world graphs are inherently sparse, i.e., m is likely to be always $O(n)$ in practical scenarios: in this setting, $O(mn)$ reduces substantially to $O(n^2)$. We describe these algorithms in the following.

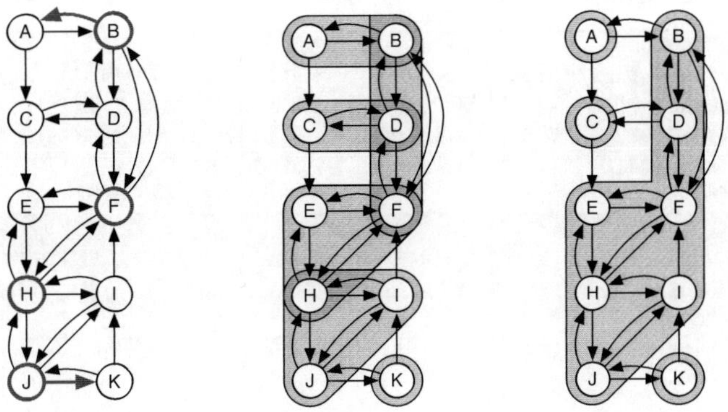

(a) (b) (c)

Fig. 1: (a) A strongly connected graph G, with strong articulation points and strong bridges highlighted in red. (b) The 2-vertex connected components of G. (c) The 2-edge connected components of G. (Better viewed in color).

The algorithm for computing the 2-edge-connected components consists of repeatedly removing all the strong bridges in G, until no strong bridges are left. Since there can be at most $O(n)$ rounds, and all strong bridges of a directed graph can be computed in linear time [18], the total time required by this algorithm is $O(mn)$. The 2-vertex-connected components can be computed with similar high-level ideas, i.e., by removing strong articulation points of G, one at the time, until no further strong articulation points are left. Once again, the algorithm proceeds in rounds: there are $O(n)$ rounds, and each round can be implemented in time $O(m+n)$. Thus the total time required by the algorithm is $O(mn)$. The details of this algorithm are more involved, however, as vertex connectivity cuts are more complicated than edge connectivity cuts. We refer the interest reader to reference [19] for the full details of the method.

3 Experimental Setup and Implementations

3.1 Test Environment

Our experiments were performed on a machine with two CPU Intel Xeon E5-2630 units with 8 cores each, running at 2.4GHz, with 20MB of cache and 512GB RAM. The operating system was Linux CentOS 6, with kernel version 2.6.32, Java Virtual Machine version 1.8.0_45 (64-Bit) and WebGraph library version 3.3.0. We wrote our implementations in Java, in order to exploit the features offered by the WebGraph library [6], which has been designed to deal with large graphs. The algorithms in [19] are implemented in C++, using g++ version 4.6.4 with full optimization (flag -O3) to compile the code.

Graph	Repository	n	m	lSCC	#scc
		Social networks			
amazon-2008	WebGraph	735 K	5.1 M	85%	90.6 K
twitter-higgs-follow	SNAP	456 K	14.8 M	79%	91.6 K
ljournal-2008	WebGraph	5.4 M	79 M	78%	1.1 M
enwiki-2013	WebGraph	4.3 M	101.3 M	89%	449.7 K
twitter-2010	WebGraph	41.6 M	1.5 G	80%	8 M
twitter-2012	[15]	398.8 M	23.1 G	64%	141.6 M
		Web Graphs			
in-2004	WebGraph	1.4 M	17 M	43%	367.7 K
indochina-2004	WebGraph	7.4 M	194.1 M	51%	1.7 M
uk-2002	WebGraph	18.5 M	298.1 M	65%	2.9 M

Table 1: Real-world social networks and web graphs in our experiments.

3.2 Data Sets

In our experiments we considered a number of web graphs and social networks with various sizes and characteristics. Web graphs considered in our experiments are two crawls of the `.in` domain (`in-2004`, `indochina-2004`), and a 2002 crawl of the `.uk` domain (`uk-2002`) [5]. Social networks considered in our experiments are generated by different human activities, such as a co-purchase network[6] (`amazon-2008`), a snapshot of the English part of Wikipedia (`enwiki-2013`), LiveJournal (`ljournal-2008`), and crawls of the Twitter follow network (`twitter-higgs-follow`, `twitter-2010`, `twitter-2012`).

The graphs considered in our experiments, together with information about the repository where the graph was taken, number of vertices (n) and edges (m), number of vertices in the largest strongly connected component expressed as percentage of n (lSCC), and number of strongly connected components (#scc), are listed in Table 1. Graphs taken from the SNAP repository were converted into the WebGraph file format before performing the experiments. Due to its huge size, the graph taken from [15] has been first converted to the WebGraph file format. Next, it has been compressed using the Layered Label Propagation technique [3]. This allowed us to shrink the graph size from about 230 Gigabytes to about 32 Gigabytes. We refer the interested reader to the repositories SNAP [24] and WebGraph [25], and to [15] for more information about those graph datasets.

Implementation details. On the machine used in our experiments, the implementations of the simple $O(mn)$ algorithms in [19] were able to compute the 2-edge-connected and the 2-vertex-connected components of graphs up to 300

[5] We chose to experiment with these graphs because they are well-studied in literature as they have been considered in several previous works in this field

[6] Vertices of a co-purchase graph correspond to products, while edges connect commonly co-purchased products (i.e., there is a directed edge from x to y when users who bought product x also bought product y).

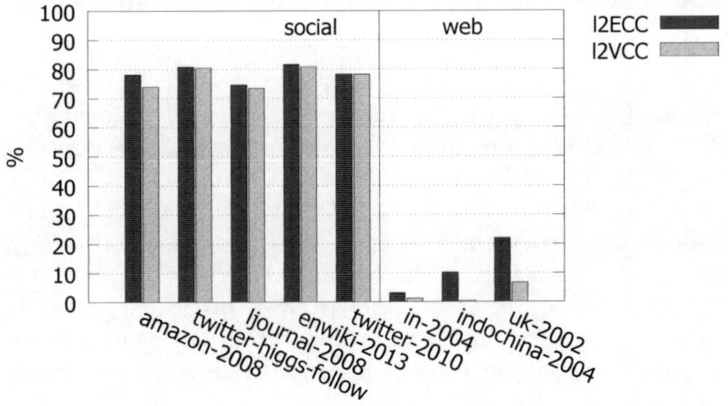

Fig. 2: Number of vertices of the largest 2VCC and 2ECC, expressed as percentage of the vertices in the lSCC.

million edges in our data set in less than half an hour. Unfortunately, when processing the Twitter crawls in our dataset the memory requirements of the implementations in [19] exceeded the resources available. To circumvent this problem, we designed a memory-efficient *heuristic* that allowed us to compute the l2ECC and l2VCC of the largest graphs in our data set within a reasonable time. The main idea of our heuristic is that if the l2VCC is a sizeable fraction of G, is easy to pick uniformly at random one vertex v among those nodes that lie within and then compute only the 2VCCs including v. For lack of space, more details about the heuristic can be found in the full version.

4 Experimental Results

In the following, we report the results of our experiments. We first analyse the biconnected components of social networks `amazon-2008`, `twitter-higgs-follow`, `ljournal-2008`, `enwiki-2013`, and `twitter-2010`, and compare them to web graphs in our dataset. We then investigated the robustness of the social networks and web graphs, comparing how their connectivity changes when some of their vertices or edges are iteratively deleted. Finally, we show the scalability limits of our framework by computing the number of strong articulation points and strong bridges of `twitter-2012`, which is one of the biggest crawls of the Twitter graph to the best of our knowledge. We do not run the biconnected components experiment on `twitter-2012`, because it would make the computation too slow. However, it is reasonable to assume that the biconnected components of `twitter-2012` would be similar to `twitter-2010`.

4.1 Size of Biconnected Components

In this section we compare the sizes of the l2ECC and l2VCC of social networks and web graphs in our dataset. We consider the number of vertices belonging to the l2ECC and l2VCC compared to those in the lSCC. Figure 2 shows for each network the number of vertices in the l2ECC and l2VCC as a fraction of the number of vertices in the lSCC. It can be easily seen that social networks in our dataset have a remarkably larger l2ECC and l2VCC than web graphs. Furthermore, in social networks the l2ECC and the l2VCC are very close to each other, while in the case of web graphs the l2ECC is just a smaller fraction of the l2VCC. In other words, very differently from web graphs, in social networks there is large biconnected subgraph inside the giant strongly connected component (between 70% and 80% of its vertices).

Figure 3 confirms this intuition, showing the size distribution of 2-edge-connected components for each network. Social networks in Figures 3(a–e) have much higher positive skew than web graphs in Figures 3(f–h). All of the 2ECCs of social networks, except for the largest one, are indeed concentrated on the left side of the figure.

4.2 Application to robustness

In this section we investigate the robustness of social networks and web graphs in our dataset. To this end, following the methodology introduced by Boldi et al. [5], we consider a certain ordering of the vertices of a digraph (that is supposed to represent their importance) and remove vertices (and their incident edges) following this order, until 30% of the edges have been deleted.

Vertex removal strategies. We consider a natural vertex removal strategy, based on the vertex cuts for 2-vertex connectivity. We compute all the strong articulation points of a digraph, and remove all such vertices in a random order. Since the removal of a strong articulation point v increases the number of strongly connected components, it disconnects all the pairs which belong to the same SCC of the original digraph and – after v has been deleted – end up in different SCCs of the new graph. Our strategy, that we refer to as *strong articulation point strategy* (in short, SAP strategy), is more principled than previously designed vertex removal strategies and guarantees that the number of reachable pairs strictly decreases after every removal operation.

As frame of comparison, we also consider the *label propagation strategy* (in short, LP strategy) [5], which has been previously shown to be the most effective strategy for both social networks and web graphs. This strategy consists in computing vertex labels using the Label Propagation algorithm [23] for clustering undirected graphs (this requires to make the digraph symmetric by adding the missing edges). Then, the removal strategy picks first, for each cluster in decreasing size order, the vertex with the highest number of neighbors in other clusters. Once we have removed all such vertices, we proceed again, cluster by

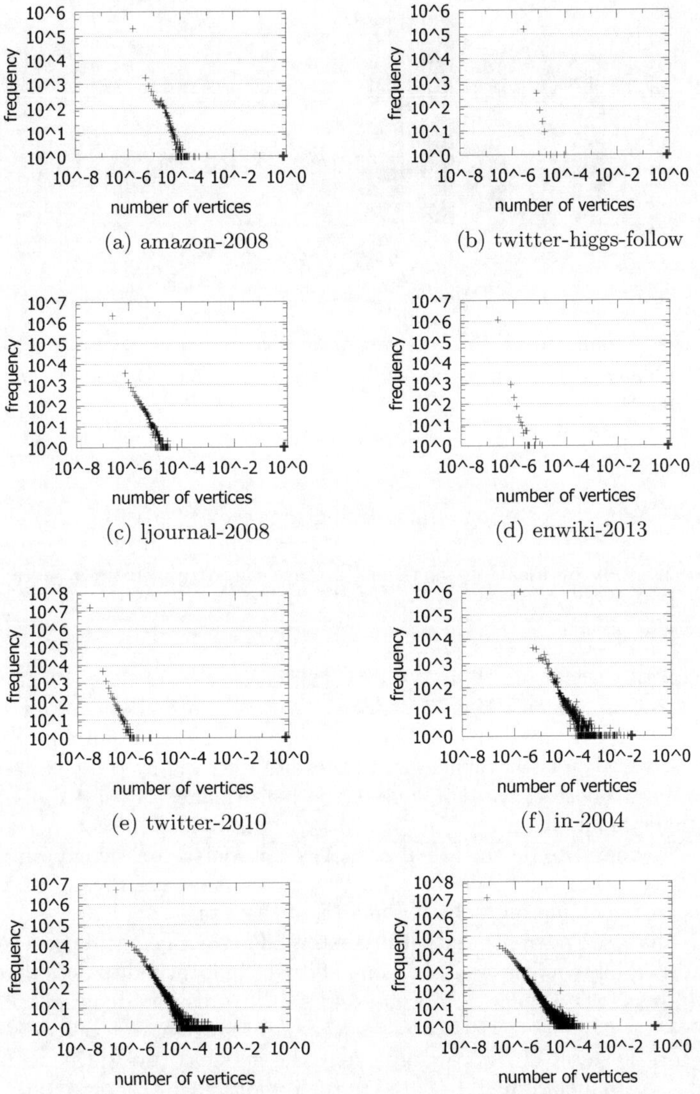

(a) amazon-2008 (b) twitter-higgs-follow

(c) ljournal-2008 (d) enwiki-2013

(e) twitter-2010 (f) in-2004

(g) indochina-2004 (h) uk-2002

Fig. 3: Frequency plot of the 2-edge-connected component size distribution of the networks in our dataset. Size is expressed as percentage of the vertices of the lSCC. The size of the l2ECC is highlighted in red. (Better viewed in color).

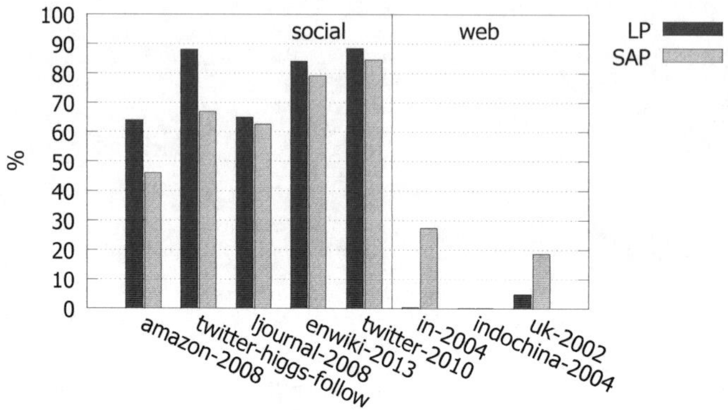

Fig. 4: Reachable pairs upon the removal of 30% of the edges according to LP and SAP strategies, expressed as percentage of the number of reachable pairs in the original network.

cluster, using the same criterion (thus picking the second vertex of each cluster that has more connection towards other clusters), and so on. This strategy is a very effective way of locating vertices that are important from a structural viewpoint [5].

Comparison of strategies. Figure 4 shows for each network the percentage of reachable pairs that are left when 30% of the edges are removed, according to the LP and SAP strategies respectively. As expected, social networks are likely to be less disconnected when their vertices and edges are removed by those strategies. It is interesting to note that, in this case, the performance of the LP strategy are worst than the one exhibited in [5], where it was able to disconnect about half (or less) of the pairs on the social networks considered for the experiments. This is especially the case of the two Twitter datasets, where the LP strategy succeeds in disconnecting only about the 10% of the pairs.

Instead, the SAP strategy outperforms the LP strategy on all considered social networks, thus confirming to be more effective in locating vertices that are more important in the structure of web graphs. In details, in one case (i.e., the `amazon-2008` dataset) the SAP strategy succeeds in lowering the percentage of reachable pairs down the 50%, probably due to the sparse nature of this network. Another case worth mentioning is related to the performance of the SAP strategy on the two Twitter networks (`twitter-higgs-follow` and `twitter-2010`). As it is clearly visible in Figure 4, the SAP strategy appears to be more effective on `twitter-higgs-follow` rather than on `twitter-2010`. This happens despite the fact that the density and the relative size of the biconnected components for these two datasets are very similar (see, respectively, Table 1 and Table 2). This difference can be explained by considering the crawling strategy used to collect

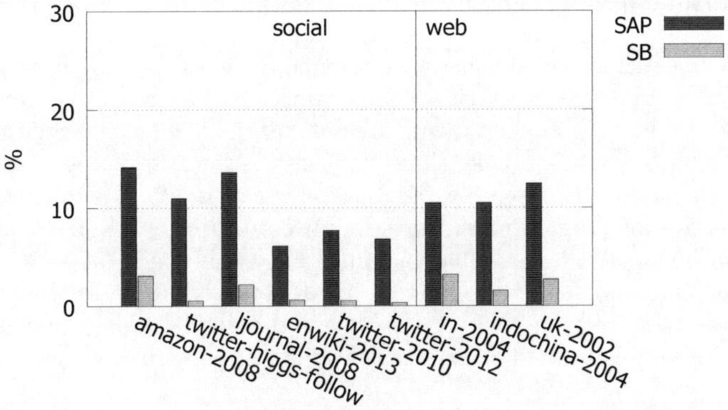

Table 2: Number of strong articulation points and strong bridges for social networks and web graphs in our experiments, expressed as percentage of the total number of vertices and edges respectively.

these two datasets. The `twitter-2010` dataset comes from a complete crawl of the Twitter service whereas the `twitter-higgs-follow` has been obtained by collecting the social relationships existing among all the users that were only sharing a similar activity (i.e., twitting about the Higgs boson). As a result, the `twitter-2010` network shows a more robust and cohesive structure, typical of a social network. On the contrary, the `twitter-higgs-follow` network exhibits a more fragile structure with the presence of vertices (i.e., influential Twitter accounts typically with a large number of followers) acting as hubs in spreading the information about the Higgs boson. Our experimental results seem to suggest that some of these hubs are strong articulation points for the underlying network and so they are the main candidates to be removed by the SAP strategy.

4.3 Strong articulation point and strong bridges

For sake of completeness, Figure 2 shows the number of strong articulation points and strong bridges of the social networks and web graphs in our dataset. We include in this experiment the biggest crawl of the Twitter graph in our dataset, `twitter-2012`. The computation of strong articulation points and strong bridges of `twitter-2012` required less than 48 hours. The fraction of vertices and edges that are respectively strong articulation points and strong bridges respectively in social networks is similar to web graph. In other words, social networks do not contain less vertex and edge cuts than web graph, despite they have much larger 2VCCs and 2ECCs. This suggests that social networks have giant biconnected components because their strong articulation points and strong bridges connects either the largest biconnected components to small ones, or small components together.

5 Conclusions

Our experiments showed a structural difference between social and web graphs. In particular, we showed that most social networks have a giant 2VCC and 2ECC, while in web graphs these components are substantially smaller, suggesting that social networks are more robust than web graphs because, as we observed, a much larger portions of these networks are 2-vertex- and 2-edge- connected and thus the removal of a vertex might have a limited impact on the network. Based on our experiments, we believe that biconnectivity analysis, i.e. 2-vertex- and 2-edge-components, might be a useful tool for understanding better the structure of social networks, and may help in devising a theoretical model that is able to capture these properties and their essential differences with web graphs.

Acknowledgments. We are indebted to Giuseppe F. Italiano for suggesting the problem as well as for his comments on an earlier version of the manuscript, and to William Di Luigi, Loukas Georgiadis, Nikos Parotsidis, and Federico Santaroni for making their code for the algorithms in [13, 14, 18, 19] available to us.

References

1. William Aiello, Anthony Bonato, C. Cooper, Jeannette C. M. Janssen, and Pawel Pralat. A spatial web graph model with local influence regions. In *Proc. of WAW*, pages 96–107, 2007.
2. Réka Albert, Hawoong Jeong, and Albert-László Barabási. Error and attack tolerance of complex networks. *Nature*, 406(6794):378–382, 2000.
3. Paolo Boldi, Marco Rosa, Massimo Santini, and Sebastiano Vigna. Layered label propagation: A multiresolution coordinate-free ordering for compressing social networks. In *Proceedings of the 20th international conference on World Wide Web*, pages 587–596. ACM, 2011.
4. Paolo Boldi, Marco Rosa, and Sebastiano Vigna. HyperANF: Approximating the neighbourhood function of very large graphs on a budget. In *Proceedings of the 20th International Conference on World Wide Web*, WWW '11, pages 625–634, New York, NY, USA, 2011. ACM.
5. Paolo Boldi, Marco Rosa, and Sebastiano Vigna. Robustness of social and web graphs to node removal. *Social Netw. Analys. Mining*, 3(4):829–842, 2013.
6. Paolo Boldi and Sebastiano Vigna. The WebGraph framework I: Compression techniques. In *Proc. of the Thirteenth International World Wide Web Conference (WWW 2004)*, pages 595–601, Manhattan, USA, 2004. ACM Press.
7. Stephen P Borgatti. Identifying sets of key players in a social network. *Computational & Mathematical Organization Theory*, 12(1):21–34, 2006.
8. Stephen P Borgatti, Kathleen M Carley, and David Krackhardt. On the robustness of centrality measures under conditions of imperfect data. *Social networks*, 28(2):124–136, 2006.
9. Ulrik Brandes. A faster algorithm for betweenness centrality. *Journal of Mathematical Sociology*, 25(2):163–177, 2001.
10. Andrei Broder, Ravi Kumar, Farzin Maghoul, Prabhakar Raghavan, Sridhar Rajagopalan, Raymie Stata, Andrew Tomkins, and Janet Wiener. Graph structure in the web. *Comput. Netw.*, 33(1-6):309–320, June 2000.

11. Flavio Chierichetti, Ravi Kumar, Silvio Lattanzi, Michael Mitzenmacher, Alessandro Panconesi, and Prabhakar Raghavan. On compressing social networks. In *Proceedings of the 15th ACM SIGKDD international conference on Knowledge discovery and data mining*, pages 219–228. ACM, 2009.
12. Debora Donato, Stefano Leonardi, Stefano Millozzi, and Panayiotis Tsaparas. Mining the inner structure of the web graph. *Journal of Physics A: Mathematical and Theoretical*, 41(22):224017–12pp, 2008.
13. Donatella Firmani, Loukas Georgiadis, Giuseppe F. Italiano, Luigi Laura, and Federico Santaroni. Strong articulation points and strong bridges in large scale graphs. *Algorithmica*, pages 1–25, 2015.
14. Donatella Firmani, Giuseppe F. Italiano, Luigi Laura, Alessio Orlandi, and Federico Santaroni. Computing strong articulation points and strong bridges in large scale graphs. *Experimental Algorithms*, pages 195–207, 2012.
15. Maksym Gabielkov, Ashwin Rao, and Arnaud Legout. Studying social networks at scale: Macroscopic anatomy of the twitter social graph. In *The 2014 ACM International Conference on Measurement and Modeling of Computer Systems*, SIGMETRICS '14, pages 277–288, New York, NY, USA, 2014. ACM.
16. Loukas Georgiadis, Giuseppe F. Italiano, Luigi Laura, and Nikos Parotsidis. 2-edge connectivity in directed graphs. In *Proceedings of the Twenty-Sixth Annual ACM-SIAM Symposium on Discrete Algorithms*, pages 1988–2005. SIAM, 2015.
17. Monika Henzinger, Sebastian Krinninger, and Veronika Loitzenbauer. Finding 2-edge and 2-vertex strongly connected components in quadratic time. In *Automata, Languages, and Programming - 42nd International Colloquium, ICALP 2015, Kyoto, Japan, July 6-10, 2015, Proceedings, Part I*, pages 713–724, 2015.
18. Giuseppe F. Italiano, Luigi Laura, and Federico Santaroni. Finding strong bridges and strong articulation points in linear time. *Theor. Comput. Sci.*, 447:74–84, 2012.
19. William Di Luigi, Loukas Georgiadis, Giuseppe F. Italiano, Luigi Laura, and Nikos Parotsidis. 2-connectivity in directed graphs: An experimental study. In *Proceedings of the Seventeenth Workshop on Algorithm Engineering and Experiments, ALENEX 2015, San Diego, CA, USA, January 5, 2015*, pages 173–187, 2015.
20. Robert Meusel, Sebastiano Vigna, Oliver Lehmberg, and Christian Bizer. Graph structure in the web — revisited: A trick of the heavy tail. In *Proceedings of the Companion Publication of the 23rd International Conference on World Wide Web Companion*, WWW Companion '14, pages 427–432, 2014.
21. Alan Mislove, Massimiliano Marcon, Krishna P. Gummadi, Peter Druschel, and Bobby Bhattacharjee. Measurement and analysis of online social networks. In *Proceedings of the 7th ACM SIGCOMM Conference on Internet Measurement*, IMC '07, pages 29–42, New York, NY, USA, 2007. ACM.
22. Mark EJ Newman and Juyong Park. Why social networks are different from other types of networks. *Physical Review E*, 68(3):036122, 2003.
23. Usha Nandini Raghavan, Réka Albert, and Soundar Kumara. Near linear time algorithm to detect community structures in large-scale networks. *Physical Review E*, 76(3):036106, 2007.
24. SNAP: Stanford Network Analysis Project. `http://snap.stanford.edu/`.
25. The WebGraph Framework Home Page. `http://webgraph.dsi.unimi.it/`.

Exploratory Computing: Combining Faceted Search with Data Mining

Nicoletta Di Blas[1], Luca Mainetti[2], Paolo Paolini[1], Roberto Vergallo[2]

[1] Dip. Elettronica, Informazione e Bioingegneria, Politecnico di Milano, Milan, Italy
{nicoletta.diblas, paolo.paolini}@polimi.it
[2] Dip. Ingegneria dell'Innovazione, Università del Salento, Lecce, Italy
{luca.mainetti, roberto.vergallo}@unisalento.it

Abstract. This paper is about Exploratory Computing, a novel approach for accessing Rich Data Sets, i.e. sets of objects that can be associated to a complex taxonomy. Exploratory Computing has its own characterization, but it can be better understood as a combination of Faceted Search (with its fast interaction for creating subsets) and Data Mining (with its ability at understanding the properties of a set). The combination is not just a "sum" but it develops also a host of new features. The paper explores concepts, models, novelties, what has been done, what can be done next and what we perceive as challenges. The main point is that this is a new exciting field for research, technical developments and applications.

Keywords: component · exploratory computing · exploratory search · exploratory portals · faceted search · data mining.

1 Introduction

Exploratory Computing is an emerging field that opens new areas of research, new requirements for systems' development and new opportunities for exciting applications. Exploratory Computing can find different interpretations, but has a clear, unique aim: understanding the properties of a Rich Data Set [1,2,3]. The main point of this paper is that a proper way to conceptualize Exploratory Computing is by defining it as a combination of faceted search and data mining. As it is often the case, what starts as a combination of two different paradigms turns out to be not just the sum of the two, but gives vent to new opportunities, not available before. A Rich Data Set, from now on RDS, can be defined as a set of "objects" $\{o_1, o_2, \ldots, o_n\}$ where each object is associated to a set of values belonging to a "taxonomy", i.e. a set of predefined "facets" $[F_1, F_2, \ldots, F_k]$. What we here call "Facet" and "Value" have received in literature different names, but the core idea is that they express the organized "properties" of an object. Let us consider an example (taken, with due simplification, from a real-life application [4]). The RDS of this application consists of a number of experiences with ICT carried on at school. Each experience has some formatted data (location, school level, etc.) some multimedia data (various text files, audio files, video files, etc.) and it is classified according to nearly 60 facets. Examples of facets are: "SL" (School-Level), with values like "primary", "junior", "senior"; "TC" (the Technology used), with values like "Interactive White Board", "Tablet", "Smart-phone", etc.; "BN" (Educational Benefits), with values like "cognitive", "skills", "attitude"; "OR" (Organization used) with values like "group-work", "role-plying", "peer-to-peer", etc. As shown by the example, for some facets only one value can be selected (e.g. for SL), while for other facets, multiple values can be selected (e.g. for TC, BN and OR). Important features to qualify a data set as RDS are the following: a) the number of facets is relatively large; b) facets are semantically relevant, in the sense that they really "describe" the relevant features of each member of the set; and c) the facets are semantically interconnected, i.e. it makes sense for an expert to analyze how they affect each other. In other words, statistical correlations, with no meaning for domain experts, are not considered to be relevant. As an example, for an expert in education, it can be interesting to investigate the relationship between school level, technology used in class and benefits achieved by the students, while an hypothetical correlation between benefits and the children's hair colors would of course be non-relevant. Let us examine now what can be achieved by combining Faceted Search and Data Mining while exploring an RDS. Faceted search applications offer a highly interactive experience, where the user continuously creates new sets of objects, narrowing down the initial set. Interactivity is (in most cases) supported by showing the cardinality of the various facet-values (i.e. how many objects have that value). These numbers provide a "crude" characterization of the current set (see section II). Data mining systems offer instead a means to understanding the properties of a set of objects; the most common approach is (in our terminology) to detect correlations among the values of the facets, combined in couples, triplets, and so on. Exploration, as described in [1], borrows from faceted search the interactive creation of subsets, while deriving from data mining the interest into their properties rather than into their "extension". Exploration can be seen as an interactive process, where the user understands a set of objects, creates subsets, further understands the new sets, etc. with the "mechanics" of faceted search and the "understanding" of data mining. A crucial ingredient (which will not be dealt with further in this paper) is the user interface, where the relevant features of the set are highlighted in order to prompt further action [2,3], [5]. In section 2, we analyze the main concepts and the most challenging research issues. In section 3, we briefly describe some exploratory computing applications already deployed. In section 4, we introduce the basic related works. Finally, in section 5 we draw the conclusions and describe our future research efforts.

2 Main Concepts and Research Challenges

Let us assume an initial RDS called the "Universe", U, with cardinality equal to N_u. A schema S_u for U defines the following: (1) which facets are available in the taxonomy; (2) the set of possible values for each facet; and (3) the rules of consistency for the values of each facet. An example could be: multiple values for a given facet are allowed.

The First Starting Point: Faceted Search. We describe here a typical faceted search application, emphasizing the features that we borrow from this approach.

- At each step, the user can visualize the distribution of facet-values in the set. In other words, the user can visualize how many objects have value x, value y, etc.
- Starting from U (the universe) the user can refine the search, specifying which value(s) for a facet (or a combination of facets) is (are) desired. If for example she selects “x”, within the facet “F”, she restricts the current set to the objects that have that “x” for “F”. The resulting set becomes the current set.
- A “session” amounts to a sequence of sets’ refinements and modifications, through a progressive query.
- Sometimes (seldom) interactively-created sets can be saved with a given name.
- The visualization may combine two components: the cardinality of the various facet-values or/and the current set of objects.

Each faceted search application, in reality, has its own strategy both for operations and visualization. A number of features of the faceted search approach are interesting for exploratory computing:

a) The distribution of facet-values is useful to understand the current set;
b) The distribution of facet-values is used to drive the next selection, since it “inspires” the user;
c) Interactively creating subsets is easy and is a way to better understand the current set.

What we “like less” is the following:

d) Query refinement is a “rough” operation (meaning that no complex selections are allowed, in general);
e) Cardinalities of facet-values provide too little information about a set. Users would like to know more about the current set.

The Second Starting Point: Data Mining. Data Mining systems and applications are meant to understand in depth some interesting features of a dataset. In most cases, correlations (at various levels) are meant to be the interesting features.

In the example discussed in section I, the user could investigate, for example, how technologies are correlated to organization or benefits. In a typical data mining application, the investigation process is carried on in two steps:

- An analysis phase, where correlations are detected (using parameters specified by the user);
- An investigation phase, where the results of the previous phase are investigated (typically through queries).

All the above is very powerful, but not very interactive nor very flexible, nor very “inspiring” for the user. What we find interesting of data mining is the following:

a) The ability to detect powerful properties, without modifying the current set;

b) The possibility of browsing in a sophisticated manner the detected properties of the set.

What we "like less" is the following:

c) The lack of fast interaction;
d) The lack of an "inspiring" visualization (i.e. easy and quick to read, with the most relevant discoveries properly highlighted, etc.);
e) The lack of possibility of a dynamic modification of the set of interest.

For item "e", let us consider again the example of section I. The user may discover (in U, the universe) interesting correlations between technologies and educational benefits. Inspired, s(he) may wonder: do these same correlations hold in all regions of Italy? Does anything change in the case of, for example, the Lombardy region?

Evolution: Faceted Search + Data Mining. Let us put together what we did appreciate of the two paradigms:

1. The distribution of facet-values can be used to understand the current set;
2. The distribution of facet-values can be used to drive the next selection;
3. Interactively creating subsets is a way to understand the current set;
4. The ability to detect properties of a set of objects, without modifying the current set;
5. The possibility of browsing the detected properties of the set of objects.

The above is the initial set of requirements for our approach to exploration. To this list, we add some important additional requirements:

- Users: what we have in mind is an interactive user who a) understands deeply the domain; b) is not a Data Analyst, i.e. not necessarily expert in data mining [1].
- User experiences: first of all, they are highly interactive (as for faceted search), but also organized, systematic and goal-driven. Intermediate results can be used to prompt further explorations. Understanding can take different degrees, from a superficial glance to scientifically-grounded phenomena detection.
- Goals of a session: understanding, sense making, serendipitous discovery, decision-making, research support, etc. Some of these goals are shared with other approaches, but we bundle them together, providing a unique user experience.

Other requirements were discovered after the initial deployments of our portals and observation of the behavior of what real users.

Comparing Properties of Sets. Data mining is good for understanding properties of a set. Faceted search is good at interactively creating new sets. The combination led us to discover that it is often interesting to interactively (and speedily) compare the properties of two sets (or of several pairs of sets). Let us assume, for example, that the user discovers that "tablets" and "smart-phones" have an influence on educational benefits and that s(he) would like to quickly answer the question "does this influence still hold in the case of Lombardy region?". In concrete, s(he) would like to compare the influence detected for the Universe with an analogous influence in a specific region.

A more complex investigation could involve comparing the same influence in all regions with respect to the national properties, or to compare regions in pairs. Comparing properties of sets, interactively created, opens a new host of opportunities.

Interactive Sophisticated Set Creation. Faceted search creates subsets quite roughly (basically binding one facet-value at a time). Data mining systems often allow creating subsets with powerful query languages, but not interactively and not for users who are not experts in query languages. Our aim is to allow selection mechanisms (including multiple values binding, through all logical operators) but in an interactive interface that can be used by anyone, to dynamically create sophisticated definitions of subsets.

Relevance of Facet-values. Facet-values are typically a 0/1 affair; for example, an educational experience either includes tablet (1) or not (0). There are practical reasons for this choice, but in many cases this is an oversimplification of reality. A user, for example, may be interested in investigating the experiences where tablets have been used in a "relevant" manner, not lingering on *all* the experiences with tablets. If the experiences in which tablets have not played a relevant role have been classified with "1", the user will have to spend a lot of time to sort out the ones s(he) really cares for. On the other hand, if these experiences are classified as "0" this can be a problem in the case of users looking for all the experiences where tablets were used, regardless of their relevance.

Our solution is to move toward "fuzzy values", i.e. values between "0" and "1". But then another issue arises: what is the real meaning of "relevance"? How should the fuzzy value be assigned? We have found a host of possible different interpretations [6], with two of them standing out as prominent:

- Quantitative relevance: how long were the tablets used for in the experience? Value "1" can mean that they were used all the time; value "0.1" that they were used only for 10% of the time, etc.
- Qualitative relevance: how important was the use of tablets in the experience? Value "1" means that the usage of tablet was crucial for the success of the experience; value "0.1" means that it was far from decisive, etc.

3 Some Implementations

Our research started in 2009 when the first "exploratory portal" was deployed (in demo version). The portal was about Archeology in Italy: it had three facets only (kind of location – museum, archeo-park, superintendence; geographical location; civilization) with a few values each. In spite of its basicness, it was invaluable to start off our speculations.

We immediately detected "exploratory computing" phenomena when we noted that changing geographical location (e.g. selecting Southern Italy only) the values of "civilizations" dramatically changed with respect to the initial set (the Greeks emerged, while for the whole of Italy "Romans" were of course dominant). This observation was made almost by chance, due to the fact that the values of "civilization" were visualized through a word-cloud instead of through absolute numbers like for the other facet-values. This simple observation opened up to the next developments.

In the years that followed, four more portals were deployed: "COMFIT" illustrates tourism locations in Italy (Como lake area) and Switzerland (hoc5.elet.polimi.it:8080/comfitportal/); "PoliCultura" displays more 1,000 "multimedia stories" done by schools and classified through a taxonomy including categories such as school level, school subject, narrative style (www.policulturaportal.it, [7]); "Built Heritage" hosts the papers submitted to an international conference, classified according to the presentation type, the geographical provenance, the subject dealt with, etc. (www.bh2013.polimi.it/portal.html), while Learning4All (L4All) gathers educational experiences with technology at school (http://193.204.76.235:8080/L4AllPortal/, [8]). L4All is our most sophisticated deployment (Fig.1). It hosts nearly 300 objects describing educational experiences in which the use of technology was relevant. Each object entails several information items: an abstract, some structured data, one or more reports, interviews, documents produced within the experience, etc. All the objects are classified by pedagogy experts according to a complex taxonomy. Based on L4All, a number of scientific investigations by different research groups took place: on the relation between different forms of group-work and inclusion, on digital storytelling and related benefits, etc. [9,10,11]. Let us see an example of investigation. In the case of the research on group-work and inclusion, the main point was examining whether there was any relation between the two. In order to answer this question, the value "inclusion" was selected within the facet "key features"; taking a look at the values related to group-work within the facet "(pedagogical) organization" and comparing them with the Universe (the

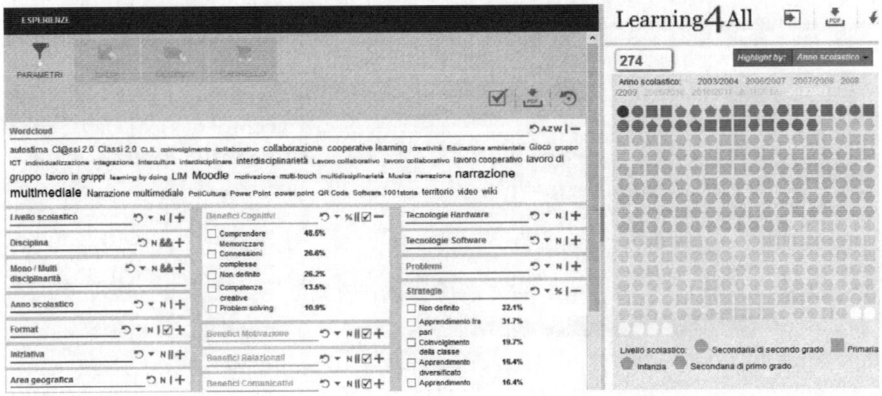

Fig. 1. The L4All portal (in Italian only): on the left, the facets and some values (in percentages); on the right, the "canvas" where datasets are visualized

initial set) it immediately appeared that a strong relation was there: all the values were higher. Thus it was clear that when inclusion issues were at stake, group-work was devised as a popular solution by teachers. The example shows at the same time the power of the approach to answer important questions and the limits of the implementation: the comparison between the subset created by selecting the values "inclusion" & "group work" and the initial set, the "Universe", had to be done "by hand", writing down all the facet-values in the Universe and comparing them with those of the subset: the operation was time-consuming. Thus it was through these studies and trials that the requirements presented in this paper, for a more effective exploratory approach, were derived.

The software architecture of the exploratory technology we are working on (Fig. 2) is an evolution of the faceted search-based applications we described in the previous section. Users access the exploratory portals through a web browser-based rich client. At the server layer, the user interface is provided to web browsers hosting the web application inside an Apache web server instance. The two main business logic building blocks of our technology are available as independent service at the server layer: the faceted search service and the data mining service. This facilitates the system's evolution and the correct intertwining of the two services at the presentation layer. The faceted search service is built upon an Apache Solr [12], [1] search engine instance, which is an open source search platform – written in Java – that provides features as full-text search, faceted search, real-time document indexing, and dynamic clustering. The Solr engine is executed by an Apache Tomcat runtime; the rich clients invoke the faceted search service via a JSON interchange protocol and asynchronous JavaScript. Instead, the data mining service has been released as an instance of Microsoft OLE DB for DM technology [13]. This choice facilitates the establishment of common interface between data mining consumers (the exploratory applications) and data mining providers (Microsoft Decision Trees and Microsoft

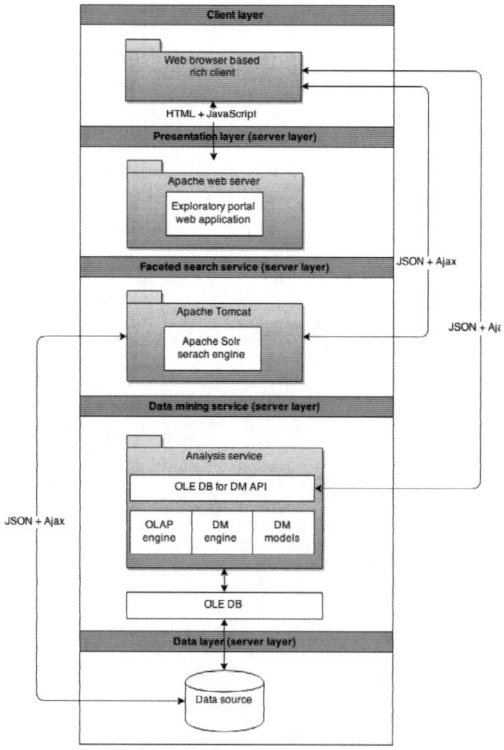

Fig. 2. System architecture and proposed technology.

Clustering), and other services (as the Microsoft OLAP engine). Furthermore the OLE DB for DM allows consumer applications to communicate with different data mining algorithm providers through the same SQL-like query language. As for the faceted search service, the rich clients invoke the analysis service via a JSON protocol and asynchronous JavaScript interface. Both faceted search and analysis components access the same relational data source at the data layer exploiting respectively a JSON communication and an OLE DB API (Application Programming Interface).

4 Related Work

In this section, we report on related work focusing on main components of exploratory computing: faceted search and data mining. Faceted navigation [14] has undergone a major adoption in these last years and thus has become "the" standard for information "exploration". Faceted search is faceted navigation enhanced by the use of retrieval systems making use of keywords; it was put forth for querying documents, databases [15] and semantic data [16] (referred to as semantic faceted search). Faceted search is based on facet taxonomy, according to which the single pieces of information are classified [17]. Each piece of content is classified according to a number of parameters [18,15]; e.g. for archeological "objects" parameters could be "period" or "civilization", etc. Facet browsing systems make use of these same parameters to support dynamic access structures; the user is allowed to refine her queries combing the facets' "values" [19,20]. The outcome can be: (a) the set of items that satisfy the criteria; (b) the set of property values that can be combined with the query to produce a non-empty set of answers. The user's refinements can possibly support a sense-making of the universe of items the system is offering [18], [21,22,23]. The main difference among different implementations consists in the way the structured data and the query are syntactically and semantically modeled. Basic faceted navigation [24], [14] is in fact based on modeling item features as property-value pairs that are usually combined conjunctively only. Dynamic taxonomies [18], [20] and Logical Information Systems (LIS) [25] generalize the faceted navigation model by allowing arbitrary combinations (including conjunctions, distinctions and negations) of concepts belonging to multiple taxonomies. Another stream of research explores the possibility of making sense of semantically structured data, such as RDF graphs [26]. Recent proposals for semantic faceted search include gFacet [27], Visor [28] and Sewelis [25], which is an evolution of the LIS approach for the semantic web. Finally, a number of studies [29,30,31], [19], [25], [21] are focused on the visual feedback provided to the user at each step of navigation, paving the road for a systematic definition of "interestingness" or "relevance" metrics for.

Data mining query languages are clearly related to our work. In this section, we report on six different query languages we analyzed to study the knowledge discovery processes and querying processes they support. DMQL (Data Mining Query Language) [32] is an SQL-like data mining query language designed for mining several kinds of rules in relational databases, such as classification and association rules. A DMQL association rule is a relation between the values of two sets of predicates evaluated on a database. The predicates are of the form P(X, y), where P is a predicate that takes the name of an attribute of the source relation, X is a variable representing the tuples in the source relation that satisfy the rule, and y is a value in the domain of this attribute. DMQL also provides users with the ability to define templates (meta-patterns), which restricts the structure of the rules to be extracted. MSQL [33] is an SQL-like data mining query language that focuses only on mining intra-tuple association rules in relational databases. It extracts association rules that are based on descriptors, each descriptor being an expression of the type (Ai = aij), where Ai is an attribute and aij is a value or a range of values in the domain of Ai. In MSQL, a "conjunctset" is defined as a set containing an arbitrary number of descriptors, such that no two descriptors are formed using the same attribute. So, an association rule is of the form A ⇒ B, where A is a conjunctset and B a single descriptor. MSQL provides specific queries to mine rules (GetRules) and other queries for post-processing purposes over a materialized collection of rules (SelectRules). MINE RULE [34] is an extension of SQL proposed for association rule mining discovery in relational databases. Authors define the operational semantics of MINE RULE by means of an extended relational algebra. Additionally, the same authors specify how MINE RULE can be implemented on top of an SQL server. An interesting aspect of MINE RULE is that it is possible to work on different levels on grouping during the extraction (in a similar way as the GROUP BY clause of SQL). Defining two level of grouping leads to the definition of clusters (sub-groups). In that case, rules components can be taken in two different clusters, eventually ordered, inside a same group. OLE DB for DM [35] is an extension of the OLE DB API to access database systems designed by Microsoft Corporation. It aims at supporting the communication between the data sources and the solvers that can belong to different query evaluation system. It can thus work with many different solvers and types of patterns. To support the manipulation of the objects of the API during a knowledge discovery in database process, OLE DB for DM proposes an extension of SQL called DMX (Microsoft's Data Mining extensions). DMX provides data analysts with data definition language (DDL) statements, data manipulation language (DML) statements, functions and operators. SPQL (Simple Pattern Query Language) [36] is another extension of SQL that was designed for frequent itemset mining. A system called ConQueSt has also been developed, which is equipped with SPQL and a user-friendly interface. SPQL supports a very large set of constraints of different types, such as anti-monotone, monotone, succinct, convertible, and soft constraints. SPQL provides an operator for discretization of numerical values. Another interesting functionality of SPQL is that the result of the queries is stored into the database so that they can be queried using standard SQL. SIQL (Structured Inductive Query Language) [37] is a SQL extension offering new operators for several data mining tasks, such as itemset mining, classification and clustering, and also provides pre-processing facilities, such as discretization and feature selection. A system prototype named SINDBAD (Structured Inductive Database Development) is available to execute mining tasks in SIQL. It is clear that, while all data mining query languages and related systems that we did analyze afford important features (association rules discovery, item-sets analysis with support and confidence constraints) they lack in interactive features typical of the inductive approach of faceted search.

5 Conclusions and Future Work

There are two main issues that we propose to the reader: a) combining faceted search and data mining provides interesting features; b) the combination is not just a "sum" but a fertile field for new research and new challenges. Let us briefly examine our current research directions. On the practical side, we are working at improving performances, since in an interactive environment the user expects fast replies. In an exploration session, the user typically does not know exactly what s(he) is looking for, so s(he) tries this or that in order to get inspiration: fast reaction is therefore mandatory. The tradeoff is that the more we advance with providing features for in-depth analysis, the more performances slow down! The second practical research field is visualization: we need to combine usable interfaces (understandable at a glance) with powerful interaction and operational features. On a more conceptual ground, we are working at improving the way sets of objects can be defined and at better understanding what it means to answer questions like "what's the difference between educational projects in Lombardy and in Apulia?". The issue is far from being simple (and solved). Another conceptual aspect is how to combine advanced set definitions with detection of properties. Questions like "what are the properties of educational projects that use tablet or smartphones, but not both, and not the interactive white boards?" can be difficult for many data mining systems, especially if fast interaction is expected. The introduction of the notion of "relevance", as described in section II, requires changes in modeling, and changes in the interaction paradigms. In addition, the underlying architecture of the system must also be modified. We are working on a specific data-set (musical instruments at the Castello Sforzesco in Milan); preliminary results that "relevance" can be highly important for applications and also highly challenging for a data modelling point of view [6]. The most challenging research directions are about an Exploration Language and Social Exploration. An Exploration Language is for exploration what SQL is for Data Bases. It will provide two advantages: shortening up interaction processes when the same action is repeated several times with few parameters changing; allowing writing "macro" for exploration that can be exploited by more skilled users. "Serious" explorations take time and involve several people. We did use our portal to investigate the influence of technologies over education for under-performing students (inclusion); this research lasted a month and involved 15 researchers working in 3 different locations. In situations like this one, users would need social features, for saving intermediate results, sharing intermediate results, "attaching" comments to objects that can be seen by other people, "customizing" facets, etc. All these social features are not commonly available in Faceted Search and Data Mining systems alike. A similar direction is taken by [38] who put an emphasis into empowering different kinds of users to perform data "explorations". Finally, we keep developing portals as exploratory applications in various domains: education, cultural heritage and tourism.

Acknowledgment. The work was partially supported by the Italian Ministry of Education, University and Research (MIUR) under the PON4a2_B EDOC@WORK3.0 (Education and Work on Cloud) national research project.

References

1. M. Mazuran, E. Quintarelli and L. Tanca, "IQ4EC: Intensional answers as a support to exploratory computing," Data Science and Advanced Analytics (DSAA), 2015. 36678 2015. IEEE International Conference on, Paris, 2015, pp. 1-10.
2. N. Di Blas, P. Paolini, "Exploratory portals. The need for a new generation", In Proceedings of DSAA 2014 (International Conference on Data Science and Advanced Analytics), Shanghai, China, Oct. 30-Nov. 1, 2014.
3. N. Di Blas, M. Mazuran, P. Paolini, E. Quintarelli, L. Tanca, "Exploratory computing: a draft manifesto", In Proceedings of DSAA 2014 (International Conference on Data Science and Advanced Analytics), Shanghai, China, Oct. 30-Nov. 1, 2014.
4. N. Di Blas, A. Fiore, L. Mainetti, P. Paolini, R. Vergallo, "A portal of educational resources: providing evidence for matching pedagogy with technology", In: Research in Learning Technology, vol. 22, ISSN: 2156-7069, UK: Co-Action Publishing, May 2014, pp. 1-26.
5. N. Di Blas, M. Mazuran, P. Paolini, E. Quintarelli, L. Tanca, "Exploratory computing: a challenge for visual interaction", In Proceedings of the 2014 International Working Conference on Advanced Visual Interfaces (AVI '14). ACM, NY, USA, 2014, pp. 361-362.
6. D. Nesi (2015). "The notion of relevance: Modeling for an exploratory approach", master graduation thesis, Dept. of Electronics, Information and Bioengineering, Politecnico di Milano, 2015.
7. N. Di Blas, P. Paolini, L. Spagnolo, "Policultura portal: 15.000 students tell their stories about cultural heritage", In N. Proctor and R. Cherry (Eds.), Museums and the Web 2012, Selected Papers from an International Conference, Archives &Museum Informatics, 2012.
8. L. Ferrari, A. Author, A. Author, A. Arpetti, R. Lanzillotti, F. Falcinelli, R. Vergallo, M.G. Ierardi, E. Pacetti, "Learning for all: is everyone learning?", In Theo Bastiaens & Gary Marks (Eds), Proceedings of World Conference on E-Learning in Corporate, Government, Healthcare, and Higher Education 2012, 2012, pp. 1782-1792.
9. N. Di Blas, P. Paolini, "Technology and group work: inclusion or diversification of talents?", In Parmigiani, D., Pennazio, V., & Traverso, A. (Eds.). Learning & Teaching with Media & Technology. ATEE-SIREM Winter Conference Proceedings. 7-9 March 2013, Genoa (Italy). Brussels: ATEE aisbl, pp. 218-231.
10. F. Falcinelli, "Evidence-based research about the impact of ICT on italian schools: the Cl@ssi2.0 project", Online Educa Berlin, Berlin, 20-30 November 2012.
11. F. Falcinelli, C. Laici, "Teaching with ICT: the policultura and moodle didactic format experimented in schools", IJCEE, Vol. 2, No. 1, January-March 2012.
12. M. Nayrolles, "Mastering Apache Solr: A practical guide to get to grips with Apache Solr", Inkstall Solutions LLC, 1 edition, 2014.
13. Z. Tang, J. Maclennan, P.P. Kim, "Building data mining solutions with OLE DB for DM and XML for analysis", In: SIGMOD Record, Vol. 34, No. 2, June 2005.
14. D. Tunkelang, "Faceted search", Synthesis Lectures on Information Concepts, Retrieval, and Services, Morgan and Claypool Publishers. ISBN 1598299999, 2009.
15. W. Dakka, P.G. Ipeirotis, K.R. Wood, "Automatic construction of multifaceted browsing interfaces", In CIKM, ACM, 2005, pp. 768-775.
16. M. Schraefel, A. Wilson, D. Russell, A. Smith, "Mspace: improving information access to multimedia domains with multimodal exploratory search", Commun. ACM, 49(4), 2006, pp. 47-49.
17. S. Ranganathan, "Colon classification", volume 960. Asia Publishing House, 1964.

18. G. Sacco, "Dynamic taxonomies and guided searches", Journal of the American Society for Information Science and Technology, 57(6), 2006, pp. 792–796.
19. G. Sacco, "The model", In G. M. Series on Information Retrieval, Springer Berlin Heidelberg. ISBN 978-3-642-02359-0, 2009, pp. 113–144.
20. Y. Tzitzikas, " Faceted taxonomy-based sources", Dynamic Taxonomies and Faceted Search, 2009, pp. 19–34.
21. L. Spagnolo, D. Bolchini, A. Author, A. Author, "Beyond findability: search-enhanced information architecture for content-intensive RIAs", Journal of Information Architecture, vol. 2, issue 1, 2010, pp. 19-36.
22. L. Spagnolo, "Exploratory computing: designing discovery-driven user experiences", PhD dissertation, Dept. of Electronics and Information, Politecnico di Milano, 2013.
23. A. Wagner, G. Ladwig, T. Tran, "Browsing-oriented semantic faceted search", In Proceedings of the 22nd international conference on Database and expert systems applications, Volume Part I (DEXA'11), Abdelkader Hameurlain, Stephen W. Liddle, Klaus-Dieter Schewe, and Xiaofang Zhou (Eds.), Springer-Verlag, Berlin, 2011, pp. 303-319.
24. M. Stefaner, B. Muller, "Elastic lists for facet browsers", Database and Expert Systems Applications, DEXA '07, 18th International Workshop on, 3-7 Sept. 2007, pp. 217-221, doi: 10.1109/DEXA.2007.44.
25. S. Ferré, O. Ridoux, "Introduction to logical information systems", Information Processing & Management, 40(3), 2004, pp. 383–419.
26. G. Klyne, J.J. Carroll, "Resource Description Framework (RDF): concepts and abstract syntax", W3C Recommendation, http://www.w3.org/TR/rdf-schema, 2004.
27. P. Heim, T. Ertl, and J. Ziegler, "Facet graphs: complex semantic querying made easy", In ESWC, Springer, 2010, pp. 288–302.
28. I. Popov, M. Schraefel, W. Hall, N. Shadbolt, "Connecting the dots: a multi-pivot approach to data exploration", The Semantic Web, 2011, pp. 553- 568.
29. O. Ben-Yitzhak, N. Golbandi, N. Har'El, R. Lempel, A. Neumann, S. Ofek-Koifman, D. Sheinwald, E. Shekita, B. Sznajder, S. Yogev, "Beyond basic faceted search", In WSDM, ACM, 2008, pp. 33–44.
30. D. Dash, J. Rao, N. Megiddo, A. Ailamaki, G. Lohman, "Dynamic faceted search for discovery-driven analysis", In CIKM, ACM, 2008, pp. 3–12.
31. M. Dörk, S. Carpendale, C. Williamson, "Visualizing explicit and implicit relations of complex information spaces", Information Visualization, 11(1), 2012, pp. 5–21.
32. J. Han, Y. Fu, W. Wang, K. Koperski, O. Zaiane, "DMQL: A data mining query language for relational databases", In: ACM SIGMOD Workshop DMKD, 1996.
33. T. Imielinski, A. Virmani, "Msql: a query language for database mining", Data Mining Knowledge Discovery 3(4), 1999, pp. 373–408.
34. R. Meo, G. Psaila, S. Ceri, "An extension to sql for mining association rules", Data Mining and Knowledge Discovery 2(2), 1998, pp. 195–224.
35. A. Netz, S. Chaudhuri, J. Bernhardt, U. Fayyad, "Integration of data mining and relational databases", In Proc. VLDB'00, Cairo, Egypt. Morgan Kaufmann, 2000, pp. 719–722.
36. F. Bonchi, F. Giannotti, C. Lucchese, S. Orlando, R. Perego, R. Trasarti, "A constraint-based querying system for exploratory pattern discovery information systems", Information System, 2008.
37. J. Wicker, L. Richter, K. Kessler, S. Kramer, "Sinbad and siql: an inductive databse and query language in the relational model", In: Proc. ECML-PKDD, 2008, pp. 690–694.
38. M. Buoncristiano, G. Mecca, E. Quintarelli, M. Roveri, D. Santoro, and L. Tanca. 2015. Database Challenges for Exploratory Computing. SIGMOD Rec. 44, 2 (August 2015), 17-22. doi: 10.1145/2814710.2814714.

Humans Fighting Uncertainty: Crowdsourcing for Top-K Query Processing (Extended abstract)

Eleonora Ciceri, Piero Fraternali, Davide Martinenghi, and Marco Tagliasacchi

Dipartimento di Elettronica, Informazione e Bioingegneria
Politecnico di Milano, Milan, Italy
first.last@polimi.it

Abstract. Querying uncertain data has become a prominent application due to the proliferation of user-generated content from social media and of data streams from sensors. When data ambiguity cannot be reduced algorithmically, crowdsourcing proves a viable approach, which consists in posting tasks to humans and harnessing their judgment for improving the confidence about data values or relationships. This paper tackles the problem of processing top-K queries over uncertain data with the help of crowdsourcing for quickly converging to the real ordering of relevant results. Several offline and online approaches for addressing questions to a crowd are defined and contrasted on both synthetic and real data sets, with the aim of minimizing the crowd interactions necessary to find the real ordering of the result set.

1 Introduction

Both social media and sensing infrastructures are producing an unprecedented mass of data characterized by their uncertain nature, due to either the noise inherent in sensors or the imprecision of human contributions. Therefore query processing over uncertain data has become an active research field. In the well-known class of applications commonly referred to as "top-K queries", the objective is to find the best K objects matching the user's information need, formulated as a scoring function over the objects' attribute values. If both the data and the scoring function are deterministic, the best K objects can be univocally determined and totally ordered so as to produce a single ranked result set (as long as ties are broken by some deterministic rule). However, in application scenarios involving uncertain data and fuzzy information needs, this does not hold: when either the attribute values or the scoring function are nondeterministic, there may be no consensus on a single ordering, but rather a space of possible orderings. To determine the correct ordering, one needs to acquire additional information so as to reduce the amount of uncertainty associated with the queried data and consequently the number of orderings in such a space. An emerging trend in data processing is *crowdsourcing*, defined as the systematic engagement of humans in the resolution of tasks through online distributed work.

In this paper, we present a synthesis of the results described in [2]. Our approach combines human and automatic computation in order to solve complex problems: when data ambiguity can be resolved by human judgment, crowdsourcing becomes a viable tool for converging towards a unique or at least less uncertain query result. The goal of this paper is to define and compare task selection policies for uncertainty reduction via crowdsourcing, with emphasis on the case of top-K queries.

Problem formulation: Given a data set with uncertain values and an allowed budget of posable questions, determine the set of questions (to be posed to a crowd) that minimizes the expected residual uncertainty of the result, possibly leading to a unique ordering of the top K results.

2 Background

We consider the problem of answering a top-K query over a relational database table T containing N tuples. The relevance of a tuple to the query is modeled as a score. Let $t_i \in T$ be a tuple in the database, and $s(t_i)$ be the score of tuple t_i, computed by applying a *scoring function* over t_i's attribute values. When the score $s(t_i)$ is known for each tuple t_i, the tuples in T can be totally ordered in descending order of $s(t_i)$ by breaking ties deterministically. Instead, if the score $s(t_i)$ is uncertain and thus modeled as a random variable (with a probability density function (pdf) f_i), such an uncertainty induces a partial order over the tuples. Indeed, when the pdf's of two tuples overlap, their relative order is undefined (see, e.g., the pfd's shown in Figure 1(a) for three tuples t_1, t_2, t_3). Therefore, we define the *space of possible orderings* as the set of all the total orderings compatible with the given score probability functions. This space can be represented by means of a *tree of possible orderings* $\mathcal{T}$ (henceforth: TPO) [27], in which each node (except the root) represents a tuple t_i, and an edge from t_i to t_j indicates that t_i is ranked higher than t_j (denoted $t_i \prec t_j$). Each path $\omega = t_1 \prec t_2 \prec \ldots \prec t_N$ represents a possible ordering of the underlying set of tuples T, and is associated with a probability $\Pr(\omega)$ [13]. Figure 1(b) shows the TPO corresponding to the pdf's of the tuples shown in Figure 1(a). Since processing a top-K query over uncertain data requires computing the orderings of the first K tuples, in order to answer such a query it suffices to build the subtree $\mathcal{T}_K$ of possible orderings up to depth K, compatibly with the pdf's of the tuple scores, since no other tuple may be relevant to answer the query. Building the complete tree $\mathcal{T}$ of depth N is thus unneeded, as the probabilities $\Pr(\omega_K)$ for each $\omega_K \in \mathcal{T}_K$ can be computed without knowing $\mathcal{T}$ and its probabilities, and thus much more efficiently. Indeed, $|\mathcal{T}|$ can be shown to increase exponentially with the number of tuples N and the score probability distribution spread δ, while $|\mathcal{T}_K|$ is typically slightly larger than K. Figure 2(a) shows an example TPO with 4 tuples; Figure 2(b) shows the same TPO when only the first $K = 2$ levels are considered.

Given a TPO $\mathcal{T}_K$, we propose four measures to quantify its level of uncertainty. These measures are based on the idea that the larger the number of orderings in $\mathcal{T}_K$ and the more similar their probabilities, the higher its uncertainty.

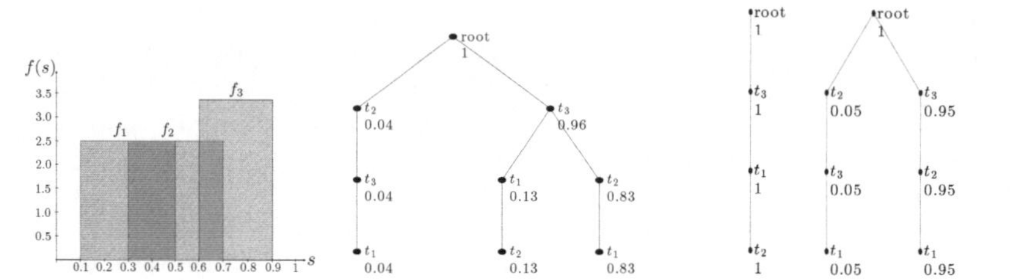

(a) Score pdf's (b) Tree of possible orderings $\mathcal{T}$ (c) Left: $\mathcal{T}^{t_1 \prec t_2}$. Right: $\mathcal{T}^{t_1 \not\prec t_2}$

Fig. 1. (a) Score pdf's for tuples t_1, t_2 and t_3; (b) their TPO $\mathcal{T}$; (c) sub-trees corresponding to the possible relative orders of t_1 and t_2. Each node is labeled with the probability of the corresponding prefix.

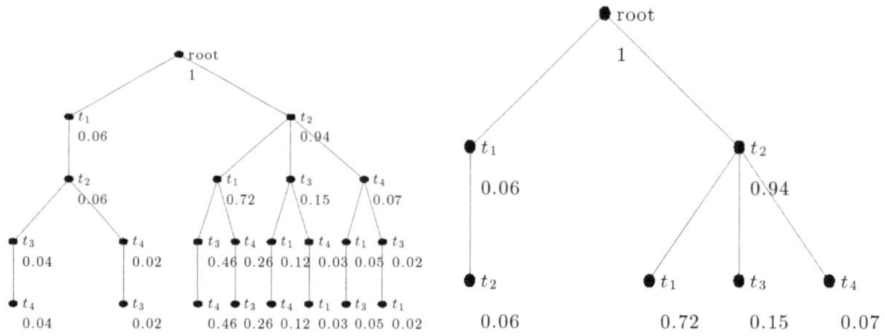

(a) A complete TPO $\mathcal{T}$ with $N = 4$ (b) TPO $\mathcal{T}_2$ cut at $K = 2$

Fig. 2. (a) Tree of possible orderings $\mathcal{T}$; (b) its cut at depth $K = 2$.

- **Entropy.** $U_H(\mathcal{T}_K)$ measures $\mathcal{T}_K$'s uncertainty via Shannon's entropy, based *only* on the probabilities of its leaves.
- **Weighted entropy.** $U_H(\mathcal{T}_K)$ is a weighted combination of entropy values at the first K levels of the TPO.
- **ORA.** $U_{\mathrm{ORA}}(\mathcal{T}_K)$ is based on the idea of comparing all the orderings in $\mathcal{T}_K$ with the Optimal Rank Aggregation (ORA) [26], which is a sort of median ordering in $\mathcal{T}_K$.
- **MPO.** $U_{\mathrm{MPO}}(\mathcal{T}_K)$ refers to another representative ordering, i.e., the Most Probable Ordering (MPO) [26].

We have observed that measures of uncertainty that take into account the structure of the tree in addition to ordering probabilities (i.e., U_{MPO}, U_{H_w} and U_{ORA}) are better suited than state-of-the-art measures (i.e., U_H) when used for our purposes, i.e., finding the best possible criteria to prune irrelevant branches from the tree, thus making it less uncertain so as to converge to a linear ordering.

3 Humans fighting uncertainty

The number of possible orderings in a TPO (i.e., paths from the root to a leaf in $\mathcal{T}$) depends on the number of tuples N and on the overlaps of their pdf's f_i, $i = 1, \ldots, N$, and can be very large even for small values of N.

We have two main ways of reducing uncertainty in $\mathcal{T}$ to quickly converge to the correct ordering: *i)* building only the first K levels of the TPO, thereby focusing on $\mathcal{T}_K$ instead of $\mathcal{T}$, and *ii)* defining crowd tasks for disambiguating the relative order of tuples in order to prune the TPO.

We consider crowd tasks expressed as questions of the form $q = t_i \overset{?}{\prec} t_j$, which compare t_i and t_j to determine which one ranks higher. Given a crowd worker's answer (i.e., either $t_i \prec t_j$ or $t_i \not\prec t_j$), we can prune from $\mathcal{T}_K$ all the paths disagreeing with the answer. As an example, Figure 1(c) shows two sub-trees derived from the tree in Figure 1(b) when either $t_1 \prec t_2$ or $t_1 \not\prec t_2$ (which are the possible answers to the question $t_1 \overset{?}{\prec} t_2$). Note that the leaf probabilities are always normalized so that they sum up to 1, i.e., each probability $\Pr(\omega)$ in a sub-tree $\mathcal{T}' \in \{\mathcal{T}^{t_i \prec t_j}, \mathcal{T}^{t_i \not\prec t_j}\}$ is recomputed as $\frac{\Pr(\omega)}{\sum_{\omega' \in \mathcal{T}'} \Pr(\omega')}$. As soon as the relative order of two objects t_i and t_j is known, the sub-tree that agrees with it becomes the new TPO.

The goal of the *Uncertainty Reduction* (UR) problem is to find a sequence of questions the answers to which allow pruning the TPO $\mathcal{T}_K$ so that a single ordering (the "real" ordering ω_r) remains. A UR algorithm is *optimal* if the sequence it finds is always minimal.

Theorem 1. *No deterministic UR algorithm is optimal.*

We consider two practical classes of algorithms: *i)* offline algorithms, which determine the questions a priori, before obtaining any answer from the crowd, and *ii)* online algorithms, whereby the questions are determined incrementally as the answers to previous questions arrive. These classes reflect two common situations in crowdsourcing markets: one where the interaction is limited to the publication of a batch of tasks, which is evaluated for acceptance as a whole; and one where the employer can inspect the outcome of crowd work as it becomes available and incrementally publish further tasks.

Since optimality is unattainable, we simply aim at maximizing the *expected* uncertainty reduction after pruning $\mathcal{T}_K$. The set $\mathcal{Q}_K$ of relevant questions to ask consists of those that compare tuples with an uncertain relative ordering, i.e., whose pdf's overlap. Let B denote the maximum number of questions (budget) that can be asked to the crowd workers. Our goal is then to select the best sequence of questions $\mathcal{Q}^* = \langle q_1^*, \ldots, q_B^* \rangle$ from $\mathcal{Q}_K$ that causes the largest amount of expected uncertainty reduction (with consequent reduction of the number of orderings in $\mathcal{T}_K$). An offline UR algorithm that always does so is said to be *offline-optimal*.

3.1 Offline question selection strategies

We present an offline-optimal algorithm, and two sub-optimal but faster alternatives.

Best-first search offline algorithm (`A*−off`). This algorithm adapts the well-known A* search algorithm to exhaustively explore the space of question sets.

Theorem 2. `A*−off` *is offline-optimal.*

Top-B offline algorithm (`TB−off`). For each question $q \in \mathcal{Q}_K$, we compute the expected residual uncertainty $\mathcal{R}_q(\mathcal{T}_K)$ (i.e., the uncertainty of the TPO obtained by pruning $\mathcal{T}_K$ according to the answer collected after q is asked). Then, $\mathcal{Q}^*$ is defined as the set of B questions with the highest $\mathcal{R}_q(\mathcal{T}_K)$.

Conditional offline algorithm (`C−off`). This method iteratively selects one question at a time based on the previous selections. Let $\{q_1^*, \ldots, q_i^*\}$ be the first i selected questions ($\emptyset$ when $i = 0$). The $(i+1)$-th question q_{i+1}^* is selected by `C−off` from $\mathcal{Q}_K \setminus \{q_1^*, \ldots, q_i^*\}$ so as to minimize $\mathcal{R}_{\langle q_1^*, \ldots, q_i^*, q_{i+1}^* \rangle}(\mathcal{T}_K)$, i.e., the residual uncertainty conditioned by the choice of the previously selected questions $q_1^*, \ldots, q_i^*$. The final output is thus $\mathcal{Q}^* = \{q_1^*, \ldots, q_B^*\}$.

3.2 Online question selection strategies

An online algorithm can determine the i-th question based on the answers to all the previously asked $i-1$ questions.

Best-first search online algorithm (`A*−on`). An online UR algorithm that iteratively applies `A*−off` B times.

Top-1 online algorithm (`T1−on`). The `T1−on` algorithm builds the sequence of questions $\mathcal{Q}^*$ iteratively: at each iteration, the algorithm selects the question that minimizes the expected residual uncertainty with budget $B = 1$, appends it to $\mathcal{Q}^*$ and asks it to the crowd. The TPO $\mathcal{T}_K$ is then updated to the sub-tree that agrees with the received answer. Early termination may occur if all uncertainty is removed with $|\mathcal{Q}^*| < B$.

3.3 Handling noisy workers

In a crowdsourcing scenario, the collected answers might be noisy. When a crowd worker's accuracy (i.e., the probability that his/her answer is correct) is less than 1, no pruning of $\mathcal{T}_K$ takes place, but the probabilities of the possible orderings are appropriately adjusted so as to reflect the collected answers. Let $\Pr(\omega)$ and $\Pr(\omega | ans_q = t_i \prec t_j)$ denote, respectively, the probability of the same ordering ω before and after the answer $t_i \prec t_j$ is received, respectively. Then, by Bayes' theorem

$$\Pr(\omega | ans_q = t_i \prec t_j) = \frac{\Pr(ans_q = t_i \prec t_j | \omega) \Pr(\omega)}{p \Pr(t_i \prec t_j) + (1-p) \Pr(t_i \not\prec t_j)},$$

where $\Pr(ans_q = t_i \prec t_j | \omega) = p$, if $t_i \prec t_j$ in ω; otherwise, $1-p$; similarly for $t_i \not\prec t_j$.

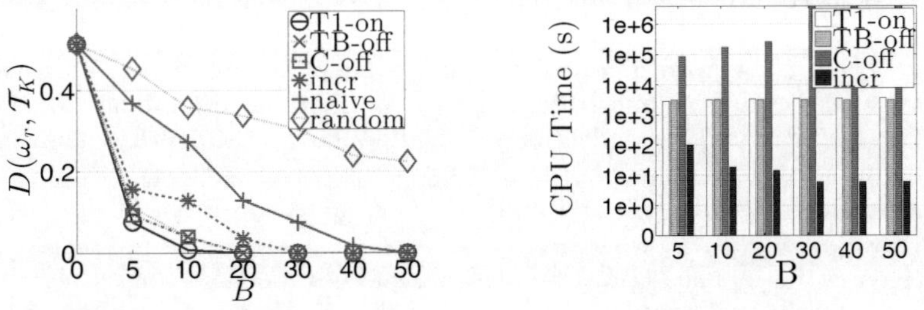

(a) Distance to real ordering ω_r

(b) CPU time

Fig. 3. Performance of faster algorithms as budget B varies.

3.4 Incremental algorithm

The `incr` algorithm, builds the TPO $\mathcal{T}_K$ incrementally, one level at a time, by alternating tree construction with a round of n questions and tree pruning, thereby reducing the time needed to materialize trees containing a large number of orderings. The number n of questions posed at each round is between 1 and B, thus `incr` can be considered a hybrid between an online and an offline algorithm. Each TPO $\mathcal{T}_k$, $1 \leq k \leq K$, is built by adding one level to $\mathcal{T}_{k-1}$. We only build new levels if there are not enough questions to ask. Then, we select the best questions, pose them to the crowd, collect the answers and apply the pruning accordingly, until either the budget B is exhausted or the TPO is entirely built.

4 Experimental evaluation

The proposed algorithms have been evaluated experimentally against baselines that select questions either randomly or focusing on tuples with an ambiguous order: *i)* the `Random` algorithm returns a sequence of B questions chosen at random among all possible tuple comparisons in $\mathcal{T}_K$; *ii)* the `Naive` algorithm avoids irrelevant questions by returning a sequence of B questions chosen randomly from $\mathcal{Q}_K$. We observed that measures of uncertainty that take into account the structure of the tree in addition to ordering probabilities (i.e., U_{MPO}, U_{H_w}, U_{ORA}) perform better than state-of-the-art measures (i.e., U_H). The experiments show that the `T1−on` and `C−off` algorithms offer a good tradeoff between performance (Figure 3(a)) and costs (Figure 3(b)), with significant reductions of the number of questions wrt. the baselines, and nearly as good as with the A*-based algorithms, but at a fraction of the cost. The proposed algorithms have been shown to work also with non-uniform tuple score distributions and with noisy crowds [2]. Much lower CPU times are possible with the `incr` algorithm, with slightly lower quality (which makes `incr` suited for large, highly uncertain datasets).

5 Related work

Many works in the crowdsourcing area have studied how to exploit a crowd to obtain reliable results in uncertain scenarios, both online and offline [20, 21, 16, 7, 22]. However, none of the mentioned works applies to the top-K setting.

The problem of ranking tuples in the presence of uncertainty has been addressed in several works [27, 14, 13, 18], although not regarding the intervention of a crowd.

Recent works on uncertain top-K scenarios where questions comparing tuples in a set are asked to a crowd include [5, 17, 23, 4, 11], but none of these can be compared to our approach because they either assume no prior knowledge on the tuples or offer no guarantee that the extracted objects are the top K tuples.

Finally, we mention that several works [6, 4, 5, 12] use majority voting as a tool for aggregating multiple noisy answers and computing trusted labels, or other approaches [8, 25, 15, 19, 28, 9, 10, 3, 24, 29, 1].

6 Conclusions and future work

In this paper we have introduced Uncertainty Reduction (UR), which is the problem of identifying the minimal set of questions to be submitted to a crowd in order to reduce the uncertainty in the ordering of top-K query results. Since UR does not admit deterministic optimal algorithms, we have introduced two families of heuristics (offline and online, plus a hybrid thereof) capable of reducing the expected residual uncertainty of the result set. The proposed algorithms have been evaluated experimentally on both synthetic and real data sets, against baselines that select questions either randomly or focusing on tuples with an ambiguous order. The experiments show that offline and online best-first search algorithms achieve the best performance, but are computationally impractical. These trends are further validated on the real datasets. Future work will focus on generalizing the UR problem and heuristics to other uncertain data and queries, for example in skill-based expert search, where queries are desired skills and results contain sequences of people sorted based on their topical expertise and skills can be endorsed by community peers.

Acknowledgments. Support is acknowledged from the EC's FP7 "Smart H2O" project (`http://smarth2o-fp7.eu/`) and the "Proactive" project (`http://www.proactiveproject.eu/`), funded by the EU and Regione Lombardia.

References

1. A. Anagnostopoulos et al. The importance of being expert: Efficient max-finding in crowdsourcing. In *SIGMOD*, 2015.
2. E. Ciceri et al. Crowdsourcing for top-k query processing over uncertain data. *IEEE Trans. Knowl. Data Eng.*, 28(1):41–53, 2016.
3. N. N. Dalvi et al. Aggregating crowdsourced binary ratings. In *WWW*, pages 285–294, 2013.

4. A. Das Sarma et al. Crowd-powered find algorithms. In *ICDE*, pages 964–975. IEEE, 2014.
5. S. B. Davidson et al. Top-k and clustering with noisy comparisons. *ACM Trans. Database Syst.*, 39(4):35:1–35:39, 2014.
6. C. Gokhale et al. Corleone: hands-off crowdsourcing for entity matching. In *SIGMOD*, pages 601–612, 2014.
7. S. Guo et al. So who won?: Dynamic max discovery with the crowd. In *SIGMOD '12*, pages 385–396, 2012.
8. F. C. Heilbron and J. C. Niebles. Collecting and annotating human activities in web videos. In *ICMR*, page 377, 2014.
9. P. G. Ipeirotis et al. Quality management on amazon mechanical turk. In *SIGKDD workshop on human computation*, pages 64–67. ACM, 2010.
10. M. Joglekar et al. Comprehensive and reliable crowd assessment algorithms. *ICDE*, 2015.
11. H. Kaplan, I. Lotosh, T. Milo, and S. Novgorodov. Answering planning queries with the crowd. *PVLDB*, 6(9):697–708, 2013.
12. S. K. Kondreddi et al. Combining information extraction and human computing for crowdsourced knowledge acquisition. In *ICDE*, pages 988–999, 2014.
13. J. Li and A. Deshpande. Ranking continuous probabilistic datasets. *PVLDB*, 3(1-2):638–649, 2010.
14. J. Li et al. A unified approach to ranking in probabilistic databases. *PVLDB*, 2(1):502–513, 2009.
15. X. Liu et al. CDAS: A crowdsourcing data analytics system. *PVLDB*, 5(10):1040–1051, 2012.
16. A. Marcus et al. Crowdsourced databases: Query processing with people. In *CIDR '11*, pages 211–214, 2011.
17. A. Marcus et al. Human-powered sorts and joins. *PVLDB*, 5(1):13–24, Sept. 2011.
18. L. Mo et al. Cleaning uncertain data for top-k queries. In *ICDE, 2013*, pages 134–145. IEEE, 2013.
19. Q. V. H. Nguyen et al. Minimizing Efforts in Validating Crowd Answers. In *The 2015 ACM SIGMOD/PODS Conference*, 2015.
20. A. Parameswaran et al. Human-assisted graph search: It's okay to ask questions. *PVLDB*, 4(5):267–278, 2011.
21. A. Parameswaran et al. Crowdscreen: Algorithms for filtering data with humans. In *SIGMOD '12*, pages 361–372, 2012.
22. A. Parameswaran and N. Polyzotis. Answering queries using humans, algorithms and databases. In *CIDR '11*.
23. V. Polychronopoulos et al. Human-powered top-k lists. In *WebDB*, pages 25–30, 2013.
24. V. C. Raykar and S. Yu. Ranking annotators for crowdsourced labeling tasks. In *NIPS*, pages 1809–1817, 2011.
25. J. Redi and I. Povoa. Crowdsourcing for rating image aesthetic appeal: Better a paid or a volunteer crowd? In *ACM MM*, CrowdMM '14, pages 25–30. ACM, 2014.
26. M. Soliman et al. Ranking with uncertain scoring functions: semantics and sensitivity measures. In *SIGMOD '11*, pages 805–816, 2011.
27. M. Soliman and I. Ilyas. Ranking with uncertain scores. In *ICDE '09.*, pages 317 –328, 2009.
28. P. Venetis and H. Garcia-Molina. Quality control for comparison microtasks. In *Int. Workshop on Crowdsourcing and Data Mining*, pages 15–21. ACM, 2012.
29. C. J. Zhang et al. Reducing uncertainty of schema matching via crowdsourcing. *PVLDB*, 6(9):757–768, July 2013.

Towards Exploratory OLAP on Linked Data

S. Rizzi[1], E. Gallinucci[1], M. Golfarelli[1], A. Abelló[2], and O. Romero[2]

[1] DISI, University of Bologna, Italy
[2] ESSI, Universitat Politècnica de Catalunya, Barcelona, Spain

Abstract. In the context of exploratory OLAP, coupling the information wealth of linked data with the precision and detail of corporate data can greatly improve the effectiveness of the decision-making process. In this paper we outline an approach that enables users to extend the hierarchies in their corporate cubes through a user-guided process that explores selected linked data and derives hierarchies from them. This is done by identifying in the linked data the recurring modeling patterns that express roll-up relationships between RDF concepts and translating them into multidimensional knowledge.

Keywords: OLAP, linked data, ontologies

1 Introduction and Overview

Business intelligence (BI) techniques have been enormously accelerating and improving the decision making process in companies for two decades. However, the recent years witness a push towards two directions: on the one hand, enriching the decisional process by including, besides data extracted from the corporate sources, also external data coming for instance from the web; on the other hand, enabling data enthusiasts to build their own reports on-the-fly, without any support from ICT people. The resulting approach is often called *exploratory OLAP* because external data must be discovered and acquired [2].

When accessing external data and integrating them in the decision-making process, knowing the data semantics is important; ontologies may obviously offer a strong contribution in this direction [2]. A relevant role in this context is played by *linked data*, whose shared, structured, and interlinked nature should make them easily accessible and searchable. Unfortunately, linked data are often chaotic and badly organized, especially from the schema point of view, which often prevents users from taking full advantage of the informative wealth expressed by linked data. On the other hand, multidimensional modeling appears to be an effective approach to so-called *small analytics on big data* (essentially, aggregate queries on large volumes of data), because it enables users to get a comprehensive yet synthetic picture of the information of interest.

The work of this paper is inspired by the *fusion cubes* vision [1], where a corporate, stationary data warehouse can be dynamically extended by the users on a self-service basis, by including some external situational data. In particular, the goal of our approach, named *iMOLD* (Interactive Multidimensional Modeling of Linked Data), is to enable users to extend the hierarchies in the corporate cubes through a user-guided process that explores selected linked data, derives hierarchies from them, and populates these hierarchies with data. This is done by identifying in the linked data the recurring modeling patterns that express roll-up relationships between RDF concepts and translating them into multidimensional knowledge, to be stored locally and shared with every user for reuse purposes. The knowledge base built and maintained by the system to store such information is called *Internal Ontology* (IO)[3], whereas any source of linked data will be referred to as an *External Ontology* (EO).

From a functional point of view, the user locates a concept of interest in a selected EO (e.g., the concept of city on DBpedia), then she uses it as a starting point to build her hierarchies. The typical scenario that we envision can be subdivided into three iterative phases.

1. **Assessment:** the user accesses the IO to check whether the concept of interest is already present and which hierarchies have already been built around it, and she can decide to reuse the information previously acquired either by herself or by others.
2. **Acquisition:** if the concept of interest is not present in the IO or it is not satisfactorily modeled, the user can search for aggregation patterns in the EOs, build her own multidimensional schema by selecting the concepts of interest, and integrate the results into the IO.
3. **Integration:** the user launches a set of system-generated queries that create and populate new dimension tables with the data selected; these tables are then integrated with those in the corporate cubes to enable richer analyses.

The first phase is mainly a matter of delivering a smart user interface for effectively browsing the IO. The third phase requires to automatically create and execute some SPARQL queries to extract data, to transform and load them into ad hoc dimension tables, and to establish a correlation between rows in these dimension tables and rows in the corporate dimension tables. The only demanding step in the third phase is the last one, which requires inter-member mappings to be found; though this problem has not been deeply investigated in the literature, some existing approaches could be adapted to implement it (e.g., [4, 9, 6]). The second phase, on which this paper is focused, is the one that raises the most challenging and novel research issues.

Remarkably, while several previous papers address the problem of building multidimensional schemata starting from source data, most of them are meant to be used at design-time in the context of so-called *supply-driven design* and consider well-structured data sources (e.g., Entity/Relationship diagrams and relational schemata) where hierarchies can be easily detected by following functional dependencies (FDs, represented, respectively, by many-to-one relationships and by foreign keys). Conversely, our approach operates at query-time to integrate the corporate cubes with situational data; besides, the modeling heterogeneity

[3] The description of the IO structure is not given here for space reasons; we just mention that it reuses the QB4OLAP model to represent OLAP cubes in the RDF format [5] and the SM4AM metamodel to store metadata on a QB4OLAP cube [11].

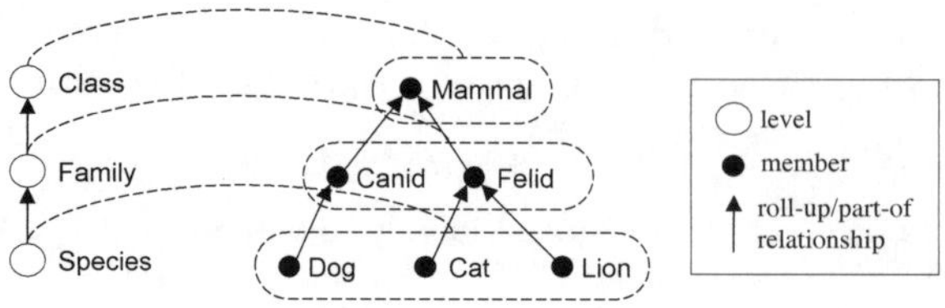

Fig. 1. An example of multidimensional modeling: levels and roll-up relationships (left), members and part-of relationships (right)

of linked data and the impossibility of describing the multiplicity of properties in the RDFS vocabulary make hierarchy detection more complex. Most of the approaches that consider ontologies and semi-structured sources work at the schema level to avoid sampling or querying instances [10]. A solution that stands in the middle is the one proposed in [12], which is based on XML schema but, in some cases, infers many-to-one relationships from instances. Finally, in [11] an instance-based approach is sketched but only basic rules are described and no formal definitions of their expressiveness is provided.

2 Aggregation Patterns in Ontologies

The multidimensional model is the core of data warehouse and OLAP applications. Our specific goal in this work is to detect hierarchies in linked data, for this reason we will focus on the modeling of hierarchies.

Definition 1 (Hierarchy). *An* aggregation hierarchy *(or, briefly, a* hierarchy*) is a directed tree of* levels *rooted in a dimension. Each arc models a* roll-up relationship $u = (l, p, l')$ *between two levels, a* child l *and a* parent l'*, and has semantics* p*. Each level has a domain made by a set of* members*. The roll-up relationship* u *induces a many-to-one* part-of relationship *on the members of* l *and* l'*, such that each member of* l *is part of exactly one member of* l'*.*

Example 1. As a working example we use the hierarchy in Figure 1. Levels are shown as white circles; for instance, Species rolls-up to (i.e., is a child of) Family. Members are shown as black circles; for instance, Canid and Felid (member instances of Family) are part of member Mammal (member instance of Class).

In the remainder of this section we describe the two main aggregation patterns in RDF data that can give rise to roll-up relationships. To this end we assume that, though the EOs may be incomplete and not fully correct, its data are statistically representative.

OLAP aggregation hierarchies express part-whole relationships, which in RDF are commonly modeled using properties. Thus, as exemplified in Figure 2, pattern (a) corresponds to two classes (e.g., ex:Family and ex:Class in Figure 3) whose instances are related by an RDF property (because of the incompleteness

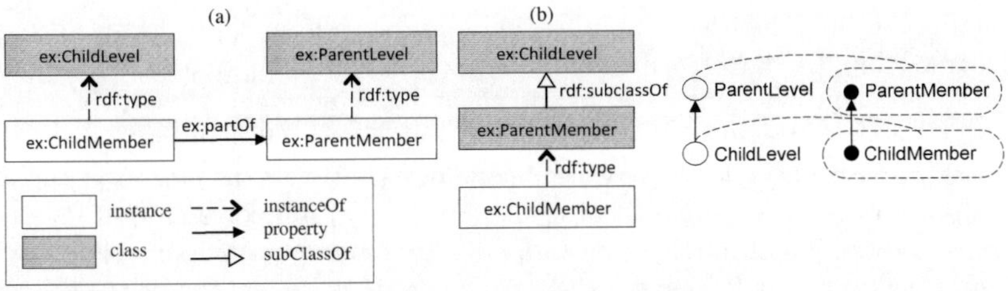

Fig. 2. The two main RDF aggregation patterns (left) and their multidimensional counterpart (right)

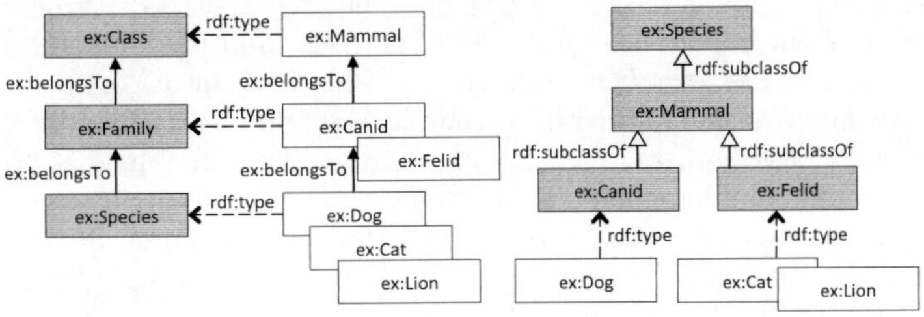

Fig. 3. The hierarchy in Figure 1 modeled in RDF using associations (left) and generalizations (right)

of linked data, we cannot assume that this property also exists at the level of classes). Noticeably, the ontology designer may have modeled the association in one direction or the other. For instance, the aggregation between ex:Family and ex:Class in Figure 3 could also have been modeled with the RDF property ex:hasFamily, where ex:Class is the domain and ex:Family is the range. For this reason, the child and parent roles can be inverted with reference to those shown in Figure 2. Another variant of this pattern arises when the instances are associated to a data type instead of a class (i.e., we have literals instead of objects); in this case there is no class modeling the parent (child) level, so its name must be provided by the user.

Unfortunately, we cannot rely on the existence of multiplicities in RDF; thus, in pattern (a) we have to sample the associated instances to check the proportion of existing many-to-one relationships (e.g., we retrieve from the SPARQL endpoint how many instances of Class are related to each instance of Family). Then, these patterns are identified only if the average cardinality of the association is close to 1 on the side of the parent, i.e., if an *approximate FD* holds [8].

The second possibility for modeling an aggregation hierarchy in RDF is based on generalization. Generalizations express an *is a* semantics that induces a subsumption between sets of instances of related classes; so, for instance, Mammal generalizes Canid and Felid since the set of mammal species is a superset of the set of species instances of Canid and Felid. But then, species can be grouped into mammals (and reptiles), or into canids and felids, and the former grouping is coarser than the latter, which in OLAP terms translates to a part-of relationship between members Canid + Felid and Mammal. This suggests that there is roll-up relationship between two different levels, which we will call Family and Class.

From the example above we can conclude that here the classes in the EO correspond to members instead of levels. So, to find an expression of levels in this case, we must look farther. Indeed, though generalizations are binary relationships between pairs of classes, they can be grouped depending on the criteria used (*powertype* in UML terminology). Thus, in pattern (b), the class corresponding to the child level is specialized into subclasses (i.e., subsets), each corresponding to a parent member, using the parent level as a powertype. For instance, class Species is specialized into Canid and Felid based on powertype Family; these two subclasses give rise to two parent members, and their instances (Dog, Cat, and Lion) to child members. A variant of this pattern arises when child members are modeled as classes rather than instances in the linked data, which may happen because of incompleteness or because of a different level of abstraction chosen by the ontology designer. In this case the different classes corresponding to child members (e.g., Cat and Lion, whose instances could be for instance Felix and Simba) would be generalized into a superclass (Felid) that would be the corresponding parent member.

Powertypes are normally not made explicit in RDF, so the user will have to provide names for the levels corresponding to powertypes.

3 Acquisition

In this section we discuss the core phase of iMOLD, whose goal is to build aggregation hierarchies out of an EO by letting users choose the specific roll-up relationships of interest. As previously stated, the acquisition of multidimensional knowledge is done by detecting aggregation patterns on a selected EO. Exploring an EO in its entirety to find every potential roll-up relationship is clearly unfeasible. Some approaches have been devised for effectively exploring linked data using advanced visualization techniques (e.g., [7, 3]); in this work we adopt a basic approach for supporting the user interaction with the EO, and we simply require the user to first choose a class of interest c in an EO, to be mapped into a level l and used as an entry point for pattern detection.

Every detection is focused, besides on c, on a direction dir, which can be either *outbound* or *inbound*; this means that, given c and dir, we detect the patterns by exploring the triples where c (or its instances) is either the subject (dir = 'outbound') or the object (dir = 'inbound'). Indeed, given a relationship a between subject s and object o, a is equally detected either by starting from s and moving to o in the outbound direction, or by starting from o and moving to s in the inbound direction. Pattern detection relies on a SPARQL query, to be directly submitted to the SPARQL endpoint of a selected EO. Each pattern detected is then mapped into a roll-up relationship. The detection process is done in a breadth-first fashion: this means that c is completely analyzed in its

Algorithm 1 Detect Pattern (a)

Input EO: an external ontology, c: a starting class, dir: a direction (either 'outbound' or 'inbound'); $multTol$: tolerance for giving -to-one multiplicity to an association
Output R: a set of roll-up relationships

$R \leftarrow \emptyset$ ▷ Initialize R
$q \leftarrow Query(c, dir)$ ▷ Create q...
$A \leftarrow Execute(EO, q)$ ▷ ...and execute it against EO
for each $a \in A$ **do** ▷ Find the roll-up relationships in A
  if $rightCard(a) \leq multTol$ **then** ▷ If a is -to-one...
    $R \leftarrow R \cup \{a\}$ ▷ ...add it to R
  else
    if $leftCard(a) \leq multTol$ **then** ▷ If a is one-to-...
      $R \leftarrow R \cup \{a^{-1}\}$ ▷ ...add its inverse to R
return R

relationships with other classes or datatypes but no recursive detection is done to avoid an exponential explosion. The roll-up relationships selected by the user lead to new classes, from which the user can iteratively perform new searches.

A key feature of linked data is that of creating connections between different ontologies, so as to enable the reuse of knowledge. In an ontology, this connection is provided by mentioning objects of a different ontology with their original URIs. An example is the triple <dbpedia:Barcelona rdf:type yago:City108524735>, specified in DBPedia, which reuses a class defined in YAGO, therefore providing a link between the two ontologies. In iMOLD, the connectivity of linked data is exploited to enable users to jump from the currently explored ontology to a different one whenever the application of a pattern detects an external concept (i.e., one whose namespace is different from the one of the starting concept). At this point, if the user wishes to continue the exploration of the external concept, she will be asked by the system whether she wants to jump to the ontology that concept belongs to. If so, the transition can be seamlessly made by launching the next searches for patterns on the SPARQL endpoint of the new ontology.

In the remainder of this section we give a short description of how the two main aggregation patterns seen in Section 2 can be detected on an RDF ontology.

3.1 Acquisition of Pattern (a)

Detecting this pattern means determining whether a property p involving c can be mapped to a roll-up relationship, where the domain and range of p are mapped to a child and a parent level (or vice versa) in the hierarchy.

Definition 2 (Association). *An* association *is a triple* $a = (d, p, r)$ *where* p *is a property,* d *is the domain of* p*, and* r *is the range of* p*. Association* a *has a* right cardinality $rightCard(a)$*, i.e., the average number of distinct instances of* r *linked to an instance of* d *through* p*, and* a left cardinality $leftCard(a)$*, i.e., the average number of distinct instances of* d *linked to an instance of* r *through* p*. Given* $a = (d, p, r)$*, with* $a^{-1} = (r, p, d)$ *we denote its inverse.*

An association a is a roll-up relationship if its multiplicity is either many-to-one or one-to-many; in particular, a corresponds to a roll-up relationship $u = a$ if its multiplicity is many-to-one, to a roll-up relationship $u = a^{-1}$ if its multiplicity is one-to-many. Since the RDFS vocabulary does not provide means to describe the multiplicity of a property, the only way to determine the multiplicity of a is through a statistical analysis at the instance level, which means inspecting the relationships in which the instances of d and r are involved.

The pseudocode for detecting association-based patterns is shown in Algorithm 1. First of all, a SPARQL query q is generated by function *Query* (line 2); given a starting class c and a direction dir, q returns a set A of associations involving c in direction dir, together with the left and right cardinality of each association. The specific form of q depends on dir; for instance, this is the query generated in the outbound direction:

```
SELECT ?prop ?range (?nProp/?nObj AS ?rightCard) (?nProp/?nSubj AS ?leftCard) ?nObj ?nSubj
WHERE
{  SELECT ?prop ?range (COUNT(*) AS ?nProp) (COUNT(DISTINCT(?obj)) AS ?nObj)
          (COUNT(DISTINCT(?subj)) AS ?nSubj)
   WHERE {  ?subj rdf:type ?c .                          ▷ Step 1: select instances of c
            ?subj ?prop ?obj .             ▷ Step 2: retrieve the associations of each subject
            ?obj rdf:type ?range . }       ▷ Step 3: retrieve the classification of each object
   GROUP BY ?prop ?range }          ▷ Step 4: group the instances to get the list of associations
```

Function *Execute* (line 3) submits q to the SPARQL endpoint of the EO. In the lines from 4 to 9, the associations in A are filtered according to their multiplicities and added to R. In lines 5 and 8, threshold $multTol$ is applied to right (left) cardinalities to determine if each association a is -to-one (one-to-).

We close this section by remarking that, due to the huge number of roll-up relationships potentially found, only the most relevant relationships in R should be returned to the user, being the relevance of a relationship defined in function of its support in the EO.

3.2 Acquisition of Pattern (b)

This pattern is cheaper to detect than the previous one because (i) no query at the instance level is required and (ii) the only inter-class property that must be considered is rdfs:subClassOf. On the other hand, it applies less intuitive transformations to classes: whereas distinct classes always correspond to distinct levels in pattern (a), in (b) distinct subclasses that belong to the same superclass can be grouped together to become members of a single level, which corresponds to the powertype of the subclasses.

Consistently with our acquisition approach, the generalizations g involving a given class c are detected by navigating the rdfs:subClassOf properties according to direction dir: the superclasses of c are found by bounding d to c and taking dir = 'outbound', while the subclasses of c are found by bounding r to c and taking dir = 'inbound'. In both cases, an interaction with the user is necessary to filter out non-relevant generalizations; more specifically: (i) when operating inbound, the user must select the subclasses of c of interest; (ii) when operating outbound, the user must select the superclass of interest. In both cases, the user must provide the name of the powertype.

Though the algorithm pseudocode is not shown for space reasons, we mention that, when a generalization taxonomy is iteratively explored by the user, the process of mapping the patterns detected into levels of a hierarchy H is more complex than for pattern (a), because the way the mapping is done depends not only on dir, but also on the previous structure of H.

4 Implementation

The prototype we built to test iMOLD is implemented as a Java web application; we rely on the Jena Library for the communication with SPARQL endpoints and for in-memory manipulation of ontologies. The IO is stored within a simple RDF file. Finally, we used Javascript to implement the user interface. To increase the effectiveness of the user experience, two alternative interaction approaches are proposed to the user in our prototype: an *ontology-driven experience*, oriented to users who have good familiarity with ontologies and semantic web, where the focus is set on the EO and the user intentionally detects one pattern or the other; and an *OLAP-driven experience*, targeted to users who have good familiarity with multidimensional modeling, where patterns are transparent to users and the hierarchy is progressively built using OLAP-inspired operators.

References

1. Abelló, A., et al.: Fusion cubes: Towards self-service business intelligence. IJDWM 9(2), 66–88 (2013)
2. Abelló, A., et al.: Using semantic web technologies for exploratory OLAP: a survey. IEEE Trans. Knowl. Data Eng. 27(2), 571–588 (2015)
3. Castano, S., Ferrara, A., Montanelli, S.: Thematic exploration of linked data. In: Proc. VLDS. pp. 11–16 (2011)
4. Chang, K.C., Garcia-Molina, H.: Mind your vocabulary: Query mapping across heterogeneous information sources. In: Proc. SIGMOD. pp. 335–346 (1999)
5. Etcheverry, L., Vaisman, A.: QB4OLAP: A vocabulary for OLAP cubes on the semantic web. In: Proc. COLD. CEUR-WS.org (2012)
6. Golfarelli, M., Mandreoli, F., Penzo, W., Rizzi, S., Turricchia, E.: OLAP query reformulation in peer-to-peer data warehousing. Inf. Syst. 37(5), 393–411 (2012)
7. Hirsch, C., Hosking, J., Grundy, J.: Interactive visualization tools for exploring the semantic graph of large knowledge spaces. In: Proc. VISSW. vol. 443 (2009)
8. Huhtala, Y., Kärkkäinen, J., Porkka, P., Toivonen, H.: TANE: An efficient algorithm for discovering functional and approximate dependencies. Comput. J. 42(2), 100–111 (1999)
9. Jovanovic, P., Romero, O., Simitsis, A., Abelló, A., Mayorova, D.: A requirement-driven approach to the design and evolution of data warehouses. Information Systems 44, 94–119 (2014)
10. Romero, O., Calvanese, D., Abelló, A., Rodriguez-Muro, M.: Discovering functional dependencies for multidimensional design. In: Proc. DOLAP. pp. 1–8 (2009)
11. Varga, J., Romero, O., Pedersen, T.B., Thomsen, C.: SM4AM: A semantic metamodel for analytical metadata. In: Proc. DOLAP. pp. 57–66 (2014)
12. Vrdoljak, B., Banek, M., Rizzi, S.: Designing web warehouses from XML schemas. In: Proc. DaWaK. pp. 89–98 (2003)

Leveraging Equality Generating Dependencies for Chase Termination

Marco Calautti, Sergio Greco, Cristian Molinaro, and Irina Trubitsyna

DIMES, University of Calabria
87036 Arcavacata di Rende (CS) - Italy
{calautti, greco, cmolinaro, trubitsyna}@dimes.unical.it

Discussion Paper

Abstract. Tuple- and equality-generating dependencies have a wide range of applications in knowledge representation and databases, including ontological reasoning, data exchange, and data cleaning. In such settings, the chase is a central tool for many reasoning tasks. Since the chase evaluation might not terminate and it is undecidable whether it terminates, several termination criteria have been proposed, that is, (decidable) sufficient conditions ensuring termination. One of the main weaknesses of current approaches is the limited analysis they perform on equality-generating dependencies (EGDs).
In this paper, we show that an explicit analysis of EGDs can yield significant benefits and discuss a novel approach along this line.

1 Introduction

Tuple- and equality-generating dependencies (TGDs and EGDs, for short) were introduced for the purpose of database normalization and design, and have seen a revival of interest in the last years, with a wide range of applications in knowledge representation and databases (e.g., ontological reasoning, data exchange, and data cleaning). TGDs (a.k.a. existential rules) and EGDs are the basis of several prominent knowledge representation formalisms, such as Datalog+/− [14], and are closely related to the Horn fragments of the OWL 2 ontology language, as well as to Datalog with function symbols (e.g., see [26, 9, 12, 29, 28, 8, 13, 11, 30]).

In this regard, the chase [5] is a central tool for solving many reasoning tasks. It was originally proposed for classical database problems, such as query optimization, query containment and equivalence, dependency implication, and database schema design [1, 4, 27, 35]. In recent years, it has seen a revival of interest because of a wide range of applications where it plays a central role, such as data exchange, data cleaning and repairing, data integration, and ontological reasoning [19, 6, 3, 2, 15, 16, 21, 20, 25, 31].

The execution of the chase involves inserting tuples possibly with null values to satisfy tuple-generating dependencies, and replacing null values with constants or other null values to satisfy equality-generating dependencies. Specifically, the chase consists of applying a sequence of steps, where each step enforces a dependency that is not satisfied by the current instance. It might well be the case that multiple dependencies can be enforced and, in this case, the chase picks one nondeterministically. Different choices lead to different sequences, some of which might be terminating, while others might not. This aspect is illustrated in the following example.

Example 1. Consider the set of dependencies Σ_1 below:

$$r_1: \ N(x) \rightarrow \exists y \ E(x,y) \qquad r_2: \ E(x,y) \rightarrow N(y) \qquad r_3: \ E(x,y) \rightarrow x = y$$

and the database $D = \{N(a)\}$. All dependencies are satisfied by D, except for r_1. Thus, the chase enforces r_1 by adding $E(a, \eta_1)$ to D, where η_1 is a (labeled) null value. However, this causes both r_2 and r_3 to be violated. Suppose the chase chooses to enforce r_2 by adding $N(\eta_1)$. Now r_1 is not satisfied again, while r_3 continues to be violated. Suppose the chase chooses to enforce r_1. Then, similar to the first step, $E(\eta_1, \eta_2)$ is added to the current instance, and this causes r_2 to become violated again. It is easy to see that repeatedly enforcing first r_1 and then r_2 yields an infinite chase sequence that introduces an infinite number of facts: $N(\eta_2), E(\eta_2, \eta_3), N(\eta_3), \ldots$.

However, by enforcing first r_1 and then r_3, we get a terminating chase sequence. Specifically, enforcing r_1 adds $E(a, \eta_1)$ to D. Then, the application of r_3 updates the null value η_1 to a. At this point, no further dependency needs to be enforced, and the chase terminates with the resulting database being $\{N(a), E(a,a)\}$.

The importance of the chase in many applications is due to the fact that several problems (e.g., checking query containment under dependencies, checking implication of dependencies, computing solutions in data exchange, and computing certain answers in data integration) can be solved by exhibiting a *universal model*, and the chase computes a universal model, when it terminates [17]. Roughy speaking, a *model* for a database and a set of dependencies is a finite instance that includes the database and satisfies the dependencies. A *universal model* is a model that can be "mapped" to every other model—in a sense, it represents the entire space of possible models. Universal models are slight generalizations of universal solutions in data exchange [19], and can be used to compute them. Moreover, the certain answers to a conjunctive query in the presence of dependencies can be computed by evaluating the query over a universal model (rather than considering all models). Answering conjunctive queries over a set of facts extended with existential rules is a prominent problem in ontological reasoning. Other applications of universal models (e.g., dependency implication and query containment under dependencies) can be found in [17].

Thus, finding a universal model is a central problem in many applications and, once again, the chase is a tool to solve it, provided that it terminates. As a consequence, checking whether the chase terminates becomes a central problem, but unfortunately, it is an undecidable one [22]. To cope with this issue, several "termination criteria" have been proposed, that is, (decidable) sufficient conditions ensuring chase termination.

Indeed, as illustrated in Example 1 above, when we talk about chase termination, it is important to distinguish between two problems: checking whether *all* chase sequences are terminating, and checking whether there is *at least one* terminating chase sequence. Most of the work in the literature has focused on the problem of checking if all chase sequences are terminating, independently of the considered database. However, since in many applications the ultimate goal is to compute a universal model, checking for the existence of a terminating chase sequence and constructing it suffices for the purpose.

Furthermore, the weaker requirement of checking for the existence of a terminating chase sequence can be profitably leveraged to identify more sets of dependencies for which we can compute a universal model. For instance, the set of dependencies Σ_1 of Example 1 might be identified by a criterion ensuring termination of at least one chase sequence. However, every criterion requiring all chase sequences to be terminating will not recognize Σ_1, thereby providing no information about whether we can compute a universal model.

Despite the significant body of work in this area, there are still large classes of dependencies for which the chase is not applicable as termination cannot be statically established. One weakness of current approaches is that the analysis of EGDs is limited or absent. In fact, more general approaches, such as *super-weak acyclicity* [36], semi-dynamic approaches *MFA* and *MSA* [24], and rewriting approaches [32–34], were meant to guarantee termination of TGDs only. Other approaches, such as *weak acyclicity* [19] and *safety* [37], guarantee the termination of a set of TGDs and EGDs, but do not analyze EGDs, which leads them to impose strong conditions on TGDs. Firing relations among dependences used in stratification-based approaches [17, 37, 33, 34] consider EGDs in a limited way. To mitigate the aforementioned issues, an "indirect" way of dealing with EGDs was proposed in [23, 36], where a set Σ of TGDs and EGDs is rewritten into a set Σ' containing only TGDs, and termination analysis is carried out on Σ'. The aim is to "simulate" the behavior of the EGDs by means of TGDs. While these preprocessing steps ensure soundness, i.e., if all chase sequences of Σ' are terminating then all chase sequences of Σ are terminating, they are not complete, i.e., the implication in the opposite direction does not hold.

Treating EGDs as first-class citizens is very important, as they are among the most popular classes of dependencies in real applications, playing a critical role in maintaining data integrity, query optimization and indexing, and schema design [18]. For instance, functional dependencies can be expressed by EGDs. In very simple scenarios, such as Example 1 above, current termination criteria are not able to say whether a universal model can be found. As a further scenario, Example 2 shows a simple set of dependencies for which all chase sequences are terminating, but there is no terminating chase sequence for the set of dependencies obtained from the EGD simulation.

In this paper, we show that an explicit analysis of EGDs can yield significant benefits, and discuss a novel approach able to perform this kind of analysis.

2 Dealing with EGDs

In this section, we discuss several issues that arise in the presence of EGDs.

TGDs		TGDs and EGDs		
$\mathsf{CT}^{\mathsf{obl}}_{\forall} = \mathsf{CT}^{\mathsf{obl}}_{\exists}$	$\mathsf{CT}^{\mathsf{sobl}}_{\forall} = \mathsf{CT}^{\mathsf{sobl}}_{\exists}$	$\mathsf{CT}^{\mathsf{obl}}_{\forall} \subsetneq \mathsf{CT}^{\mathsf{obl}}_{\exists}$	$\mathsf{CT}^{\mathsf{sobl}}_{\forall} \subsetneq \mathsf{CT}^{\mathsf{sobl}}_{\exists}$	
$\mathsf{CT}^{\mathsf{obl}}_{\exists} \subsetneq \mathsf{CT}^{\mathsf{sobl}}_{\forall}$	$\mathsf{CT}^{\mathsf{sobl}}_{\exists} \subsetneq \mathsf{CT}^{\mathsf{std}}_{\forall}$	$\mathsf{CT}^{\mathsf{obl}}_{\exists} \nparallel \mathsf{CT}^{\mathsf{sobl}}_{\forall}$	$\mathsf{CT}^{\mathsf{sobl}}_{\exists} \nparallel \mathsf{CT}^{\mathsf{std}}_{\forall}$	$\mathsf{CT}^{\mathsf{obl}}_{\exists} \nparallel \mathsf{CT}^{\mathsf{std}}_{\forall}$
$\mathsf{CT}^{\mathsf{std}}_{\forall} \subsetneq \mathsf{CT}^{\mathsf{std}}_{\exists}$	$\mathsf{CT}^{\mathsf{core}}_{\forall} = \mathsf{CT}^{\mathsf{core}}_{\exists}$	$\mathsf{CT}^{\mathsf{std}}_{\forall} \subsetneq \mathsf{CT}^{\mathsf{std}}_{\exists}$	$\mathsf{CT}^{\mathsf{core}}_{\forall} = \mathsf{CT}^{\mathsf{core}}_{\exists}$	

Table 1: Relationships among the $\mathsf{CT}^{\mathsf{c}}_{\mathsf{q}}$'s classes.

We will denote by $\mathsf{CT}^{\mathsf{c}}_{\forall}$ (resp. $\mathsf{CT}^{\mathsf{c}}_{\exists}$), with $\mathsf{c} \in \{\mathsf{std}, \mathsf{obl}, \mathsf{sobl}, \mathsf{core}\}$, the class of sets of dependencies Σ such that for every database D all (resp. some) c-chase sequences of D with Σ are terminating. Here, std, obl, sobl and core refer to different variants of the chase, namely *standard*, *oblivious*, *semi-oblivious*, and *core*—we refer the reader to [10, 7] for more details on them. In the rest of the paper, given two sets C_1 and C_2, we write $C_1 \nparallel C_2$ iff $C_1 \nsubseteq C_2$ and $C_2 \nsubseteq C_1$.

The relationships between the aforementioned classes have been studied in the presence of TGDs only in [38]. Specifically, it has been shown that:

$$\mathsf{CT}^{\mathsf{obl}}_{\forall} = \mathsf{CT}^{\mathsf{obl}}_{\exists} \subsetneq \mathsf{CT}^{\mathsf{sobl}}_{\forall} = \mathsf{CT}^{\mathsf{sobl}}_{\exists} \subsetneq \mathsf{CT}^{\mathsf{std}}_{\forall} \subsetneq \mathsf{CT}^{\mathsf{std}}_{\exists} \subsetneq \mathsf{CT}^{\mathsf{core}}_{\forall} = \mathsf{CT}^{\mathsf{core}}_{\exists}$$

In the presence of arbitrary sets of dependencies (possibly including both TGDs and EGDs), the relationships between the classes $\mathsf{CT}^{\mathsf{c}}_{\mathsf{q}}$, where $\mathsf{q} \in \{\forall, \exists\}$ and $\mathsf{c} \in \{\mathsf{std}, \mathsf{obl}, \mathsf{sobl}, \mathsf{core}\}$, become those in Table 1, which reports the relationships for the case of TGDs only and when both TGDs and EGDs are allowed.

As already mentioned, chase termination criteria proposed in the literature focus on TGDs considering EGDs in a very limited way. An "indirect" way of dealing with EGDs has been proposed in [23, 36]. Specifically, the analysis of a set of dependencies Σ containing both TGDs and EGDs is performed on a set Σ' derived from Σ and containing only TGDs. The aim is to "simulate" the behavior of the EGDs by means of TGDs only. The first approach of this kind, known as *natural simulation*, has been proposed in [23], and further refined by the *substitution-free simulation* in [36]. Below is an example showing how the substitution-free simulation works.

Example 2. Consider the following set of dependencies Σ_2:

$$\begin{array}{llll} r_1: & A(x) \wedge B(x) \rightarrow C(x) & r_4: & A(x) \wedge A(y) \rightarrow x = y \\ r_2: & C(x) \rightarrow \exists y\, A(x) \wedge B(y) & r_5: & B(x) \wedge B(y) \rightarrow x = y \\ r_3: & C(x) \rightarrow \exists y\, A(y) \wedge B(x) & & \end{array}$$

The substitution-free simulation works as follows:

1. *The TGDs below (equality-axioms) are added to Σ_2:*

$$\begin{array}{ll} a_1: Eq(x,y) \rightarrow Eq(y,x) & a_{3.1}: A(x) \rightarrow Eq(x,x) \\ a_2: Eq(x,y) \wedge Eq(y,z) \rightarrow Eq(x,z) & a_{3.2}: B(x) \rightarrow Eq(x,x) \\ & a_{3.3}: C(x) \rightarrow Eq(x,x) \end{array}$$

2. *Every occurrence of $x = y$ in Σ_2 is replaced with $Eq(x,y)$. In our case, this affects r_4 and r_5 only, which are replaced with:*

$$r'_4: A(x) \wedge A(y) \rightarrow Eq(x,y) \qquad r'_5: B(x) \wedge B(y) \rightarrow Eq(x,y)$$

3. Dependency r_1, which contains multiple occurrences of x in the body, is (non-deterministically) replaced with one of the following two dependencies, where one of the two occurrences of x is replaced with x_2, and the atom $Eq(x, x_2)$ is added to the body:

$$r_1' : A(x_2) \wedge B(x) \wedge Eq(x, x_2) \rightarrow C(x)$$
$$r_1'' : A(x) \wedge B(x_2) \wedge Eq(x, x_2) \rightarrow C(x)$$

Notice that the only dependencies that remain unchanged are r_2 and r_3 and that no EGDs occur in the resulting set of dependencies.

Although somehow left implicit in [23, 36], the natural simulation and the substitution-free simulation ensure the desirable *soundness* property: if $\Sigma' \in \mathsf{CT}^{\mathsf{c}}_{\forall}$, then $\Sigma \in \mathsf{CT}^{\mathsf{c}}_{\forall}$, for $\mathsf{c} \in \{\mathsf{obl}, \mathsf{sobl}, \mathsf{std}\}$. The natural question now is whether these simulations are also *complete*, that is, if the implication in the opposite direction holds. The answer is negative for both approaches.

For example, the set of dependencies Σ_2 of Example 2 above belongs to $\mathsf{CT}^{\mathsf{c}}_{\forall}$ (and thus belongs to $\mathsf{CT}^{\mathsf{c}}_{\exists}$ too), but any of its substitution-free simulations is not even in $\mathsf{CT}^{\mathsf{c}}_{\exists}$, for every $\mathsf{c} \in \{\mathsf{obl}, \mathsf{sobl}, \mathsf{std}\}$. The problem is that the simulation of EGDs by means of TGDs is not able to fully capture the specific behavior of EGDs, which replace null values (with constants and other null values). This aspect is not faithfully modeled by storing the information that a null value is equal to a constant or to another null value.

Dealing with EGDs needs some care. In some cases the presence of EGDs allows us to have a terminating c-chase sequence when the set consisting only of the TGDs does not have one; at the same time, the opposite case can occur, that is, in the presence of EGDs there is no terminating c-chase sequence while the set consisting only of the TGDs does have one, where c can be one of $\{\mathsf{obl}, \mathsf{sobl}, \mathsf{std}\}$. The following two examples show such cases.

Example 3. Consider the set of dependencies Σ_1 of Example 1 and the database $D = \{N(a)\}$. There is no terminating c-chase sequence of D_1 with the set of TGDs $\Sigma_1' = \{r_1, r_2\}$, for every $\mathsf{c} \in \{\mathsf{obl}, \mathsf{sobl}, \mathsf{std}\}$. In fact, it is easy to see that an infinite number of facts is introduced: $E(a, \eta_1)$, $N(\eta_1)$, $E(\eta_1, \eta_2), \ldots$. However, the addition of the EGD r_3 allows us to have a terminating c-chase sequence, obtained by enforcing first r_1 and then r_3, and whose result is the universal model $\{N(a), E(a, a)\}$.

Example 4. Consider the set of dependencies Σ_4 below:

$$r_1 : \; N(x) \rightarrow \exists y \, \exists z \; E(x, y, z)$$
$$r_2 : \; E(x, y, y) \rightarrow N(y)$$
$$r_3 : \; E(x, y, z) \rightarrow y = z$$

For every database D, every c-chase sequence of D with the set of TGDs $\Sigma_4' = \{r_1, r_2\}$ is terminating, for every $\mathsf{c} \in \{\mathsf{obl}, \mathsf{sobl}, \mathsf{std}\}$. On the other hand, there is no terminating c-chase sequence of $D = \{N(a)\}$ with Σ_4, as an infinite number of facts is introduced: $E(a, \eta_1, \eta_1)$, $N(\eta_1), E(\eta_1, \eta_2, \eta_2)$, $N(\eta_2), \ldots$.

3 A Rewriting Approach

In this section, we illustrate a decidable sufficient condition for a set of dependencies to be in $\mathsf{CT}_{\exists}^{\mathsf{std}}$. It is an algorithm which takes as input a set of dependencies, and gives as output a set of adorned dependencies and a boolean value. The aim of the algorithm is twofold: *(i)* it defines a termination criterion on its own—on the basis of the boolean value returned by the algorithm; and *(ii)* it can be combined with other termination criteria to enhance them, in that (strictly) more sets of dependencies in $\mathsf{CT}_{\exists}^{\mathsf{std}}$ can be identified by using our algorithm in conjunction with a termination criterion—this is achieved by analyzing the set of adorned dependencies returned by the algorithm.

Thus, the input is a set of dependencies Σ, while the output is a set of adorned dependencies Σ^{μ} along with a boolean value *Acyc*. More specifically, if *Acyc* is *false*, then a form of cyclicity has been detected; otherwise, for every database D, there is a terminating standard chase sequence of D with Σ. As for the second aim of the algorithm, the adorned set of dependencies Σ^{μ} given as output can be used as follows: a sufficient condition for checking membership in $\mathsf{CT}_{\exists}^{\mathsf{std}}$ is applied to Σ^{μ} rather than Σ. If Σ^{μ} satisfies the condition, then the original set of dependencies Σ is in $\mathsf{CT}_{\exists}^{\mathsf{std}}$.

The basic idea of the algorithm is to produce adorned dependencies from the original ones by keeping track of what facts can be derived by a chase execution and how terms are derived. When adorning dependencies, the algorithm's strategy is to adorn first full dependencies, and to adorn existentially quantified dependencies only when no further full dependency can be adorned. This is iterated as long as new adorned dependencies can be derived. EGDs are leveraged to see if free symbols can be changed.

The algorithm makes use of *adornment definitions*, which are expressions of the form $f_i = f_z^r(\alpha)$, whose intuitive meaning is that z is an existentially quantified variable in the head of the TGD r and α is an adornment for the body of r. Roughly speaking, adornment definitions are some sort of provenance information used to keep track of the "history" of a null.

The following example gives the basic idea of how the technique works.

Example 5. Consider the set of dependencies Σ_1 of Example 1. Initially, the following two adorned dependencies, mapping unadorned atoms to atoms adorned with strings of b's, are added to Σ_1^{μ}:

$$s_1 : N(x) \to N^b(x) \qquad s_2 : E(x, y) \to E^{bb}(x, y)$$

The algorithm then proceeds by adorning full dependencies and adds the following adorned dependencies to Σ_1^{μ}:

$$s_3 : E^{bb}(x, y) \to x = y \qquad s_4 : E^{bb}(x, y) \to N^b(x)$$

Next, the existentially quantified dependency (namely, r_1) is adorned and the following adorned dependency is added to Σ_1^{μ}:

$$s_5 : N^b(x) \to \exists y \; E^{bf_1}(x, y)$$

Moreover, the following adornment definition is derived $f_1 = f_y^{r_1}(b)$. *After that, the algorithm starts considering full dependencies again. By adorning the EGD* r_3, *the following adorned dependency is obtained, which is added to* Σ_1^μ:

$$s_6 : E^{bf_1}(x, y) \rightarrow x = y$$

The adorned EGD s_6 *is analyzed by the algorithm, which replaces* f_1 *with* b *in* Σ_1^μ. *The resulting set of adorned dependencies is* $\Sigma_1^\mu = \{s_1, s_2, s_3, s_4, s_5'\}$, *where* s_5' *is derived from* s_5 *by replacing* f_1 *with* b, *that is,* $s_5' : N^b(x) \rightarrow \exists y\ E^{bb}(x, y)$.

At this point, no further dependencies can be adorned and the algorithm terminates by returning the value $Acyc = true$ *along with* Σ_1^μ.

References

1. S. Abiteboul, R. Hull, and V. Vianu. *Foundations of Databases.* Addison-Wesley, 1995.
2. M. Arenas, P. Barceló, R. Fagin, and L. Libkin. Locally consistent transformations and query answering in data exchange. In *PODS*, pages 229–240, 2004.
3. M. Arenas, L. E. Bertossi, and J. Chomicki. Consistent query answers in inconsistent databases. In *PODS*, pages 68–79, 1999.
4. C. Beeri and M. Y. Vardi. Formal systems for tuple and equality generating dependencies. *SIAM J. Comput.*, 13(1):76–98, 1984.
5. C. Beeri and M. Y. Vardi. A proof procedure for data dependencies. *J. ACM*, 31(4):718–741, 1984.
6. L. E. Bertossi, S. Kolahi, and L. V. S. Lakshmanan. Data cleaning and query answering with matching dependencies and matching functions. In *ICDT*, pages 268–279, 2011.
7. M. Calautti, G. Gottlob, and A. Pieris. Chase termination for guarded existential rules. In *PODS*, pages 91–103, 2015.
8. M. Calautti, S. Greco, C. Molinaro, and I. Trubitsyna. Checking termination of logic programs with function symbols through linear constraints. In *RuleML*, pages 97–111, 2014.
9. M. Calautti, S. Greco, C. Molinaro, and I. Trubitsyna. Logic program termination analysis using atom sizes. In *IJCAI*, pages 2833–2839, 2015.
10. M. Calautti, S. Greco, C. Molinaro, and I. Trubitsyna. Exploiting equality generating dependencies in checking chase termination. *PVLDB*, 9(5):396–407, 2016.
11. M. Calautti, S. Greco, C. Molinaro, and I. Trubitsyna. Using linear constraints for logic program termination analysis. *To appear in TPLP*, 2016.
12. M. Calautti, S. Greco, F. Spezzano, and I. Trubitsyna. Checking termination of bottom-up evaluation of logic programs with function symbols. *TPLP*, 15(6):854–889, 2015.
13. M. Calautti, S. Greco, and I. Trubitsyna. Detecting decidable classes of finitely ground logic programs with function symbols. In *PPDP*, pages 239–250, 2013.
14. A. Calì, G. Gottlob, and T. Lukasiewicz. A general datalog-based framework for tractable query answering over ontologies. *J. Web Sem.*, 14:57–83, 2012.
15. A. Calì, G. Gottlob, and A. Pieris. Advanced processing for ontological queries. *PVLDB*, 3(1):554–565, 2010.
16. G. De Giacomo, D. Lembo, M. Lenzerini, and R. Rosati. On reconciling data exchange, data integration, and peer data management. In *PODS*, pages 133–142, 2007.

17. A. Deutsch, A. Nash, and J. B. Remmel. The chase revisited. In *PODS*, pages 149–158, 2008.
18. R. Fagin. Equality-generating dependencies. In *Encyclopedia of Database Systems*, pages 1009–1010. 2009.
19. R. Fagin, P. G. Kolaitis, R. J. Miller, and L. Popa. Data exchange: semantics and query answering. *Th. Comp. Sc.*, 336(1):89–124, 2005.
20. W. Fan, F. Geerts, X. Jia, and A. Kementsietsidis. Conditional functional dependencies for capturing data inconsistencies. *ACM TODS*, 33(2), 2008.
21. F. Geerts, G. Mecca, P. Papotti, and D. Santoro. The LLUNATIC data-cleaning framework. *PVLDB*, 6(9):625–636, 2013.
22. T. Gogacz and J. Marcinkowski. All-instances termination of chase is undecidable. In *ICALP*, pages 293–304, 2014.
23. G. Gottlob and A. Nash. Efficient core computation in data exchange. *J. ACM*, 55(2), 2008.
24. B. C. Grau, I. Horrocks, M. Krotzsch, C. Kupke, D. Magka, B. Motik, and Z. Wang. Acyclicity notions for existential rules and their application to query answering in ontologies. *JAIR*, 47:741–808, 2013.
25. G. Greco, S. Greco, I. Trubitsyna, and E. Zumpano. Optimization of bound disjunctive queries with constraints. *TPLP*, 5(6):713–745, 2005.
26. S. Greco and C. Molinaro. *Datalog and Logic Databases.* Synthesis Lectures on Data Management. Morgan & Claypool Publishers, 2015.
27. S. Greco, C. Molinaro, and F. Spezzano. *Incomplete Data and Data Dependencies in Relational Databases.* Synthesis Lectures on Data Management. Morgan & Claypool Publishers, 2012.
28. S. Greco, C. Molinaro, and I. Trubitsyna. Bounded programs: A new decidable class of logic programs with function symbols. In *IJCAI*, pages 926–932, 2013.
29. S. Greco, C. Molinaro, and I. Trubitsyna. Logic programming with function symbols: Checking termination of bottom-up evaluation through program adornments. *TPLP*, 13(4-5):737–752, 2013.
30. S. Greco, C. Molinaro, I. Trubitsyna, and E. Zumpano. NP datalog: A logic language for expressing search and optimization problems. *TPLP*, 10(2):125–166, 2010.
31. S. Greco, C. Sirangelo, I. Trubitsyna, and E. Zumpano. Feasibility conditions and preference criteria in querying and repairing inconsistent databases. In *DEXA*, pages 44–55, 2004.
32. S. Greco and F. Spezzano. Chase termination: A constraints rewriting approach. *PVLDB*, 3(1):93–104, 2010.
33. S. Greco, F. Spezzano, and I. Trubitsyna. Stratification criteria and rewriting techniques for checking chase termination. *PVLDB*, 4(11):1158–1168, 2011.
34. S. Greco, F. Spezzano, and I. Trubitsyna. Checking chase termination: Cyclicity analysis and rewriting techniques. *IEEE TKDE*, 27(3):621–635, 2015.
35. D. Maier, A. O. Mendelzon, and Y. Sagiv. Testing implications of data dependencies. *ACM TODS*, 4(4):455–469, 1979.
36. B. Marnette. Generalized schema-mappings: from termination to tractability. In *PODS*, pages 13–22, 2009.
37. M. Meier, M. Schmidt, and G. Lausen. On chase termination beyond stratification. *PVLDB*, 2(1):970–981, 2009.
38. A. Onet. The chase procedure and its applications in data exchange. In *Data Exchange, Integration, and Streams*, pages 1–37. 2013.

Multi-Type Classification from Heterogeneous Networks
(Discussion Paper)

Francesco Serafino, Gianvito Pio, Donato Malerba, and Michelangelo Ceci

University of Bari, Dept. of Computer Science, Via Orabona, 4, 70125 Bari (Italy)

{firstname.surname}@uniba.it

Abstract. Heterogeneous information networks are networks consisting of different types of objects and links, and can be found in several social, economical and scientific fields. In the literature, many clustering and classification algorithms have been proposed which work on networks, but they are usually tailored for homogeneous networks or they make strict assumption on the network structure. In this work we propose a novel algorithm, called HENPC, which is able to work on heterogeneous networks with an arbitrary structure. In particular, it is able to identify possibly overlapping and hierarchically-organized heterogeneous clusters and to exploit them for predictive purposes. Our approach works in the semi-supervised transductive setting and is able to build a different classification model for each level of the hierarchy, giving the possibility to consider either more globally-based or more locally-based predictions. Experiments show that HENPC generates good quality heterogeneous clusters that can be fruitfully exploited for predictive purposes, leading to more accurate prediction with respect to the considered competitors.

1 Introduction

Many objects in the real world can be considered interconnected, forming complex information networks. They can be found in several social, economical and scientific fields, ranging from the Internet to social sciences, including biology, epidemiology, geography, finance, and many others. Current studies about mining networked data focus on homogeneous information networks, i.e., networks consisting of a single type of objects connected by a single type of links.

More recent works have started focusing on heterogeneous information networks since they can more easily represent real-world scenarios. In most of cases, the proposed approaches focus on the clustering task [8, 9] and on the classification task [4, 5]. Methods working in a similar scenario have been proposed in the context of relational data mining. In [2] the authors propose an approach which exploits the Naïve Bayes classification method in the multi-relational setting. More recently, in [10] the authors introduced the methods implemented in the tool RelWEKA, an extension to the multi-relational setting of the tool WEKA.

However, most of existing works do not take into account one of the main issue raised by the task of learning models from network data, i.e. the presence

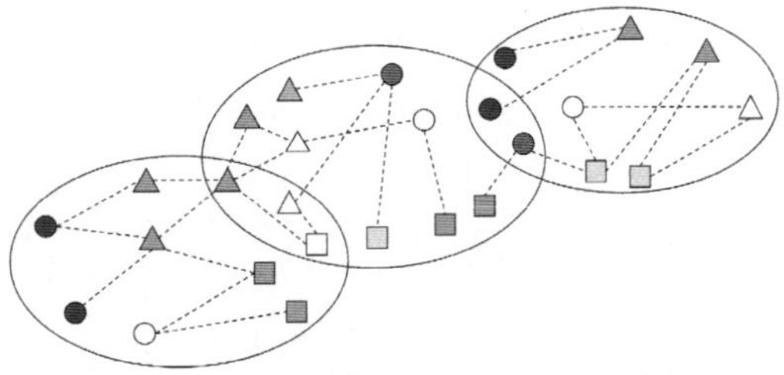

Fig. 1. Multi-type classification from heterogeneous networks. Different shapes indicate different types of objects while different colors indicate different class labels. White colored objects are unclassified objects. Ellipses represent possible clusters.

of some form of autocorrelation [1, 7]. In particular, in a network, this means that the value of an attribute at a given node depends on the values of the same attribute of the nodes it is connected with.

In this paper, we propose a classification method which works on data represented as an heterogeneous network. The way we consider network information conforms to the *within-network* setting: objects for which the class is known are linked to objects for which the class must be estimated. This setting is semi-supervised and differs from the *across-network* setting, where learning is performed from one (labeled) network and prediction is performed on a separate, presumably similar, network. The proposed solution falls in the category of *predictive clustering* methods, since it exploits the results of heterogeneous clustering for predictive purposes, implicitly taking into account autocorrelation. Moreover, our method is able to simultaneously learn a classification model for objects of different types (we call this task *multi-type classification*), according to different classification schemes (in this work, we focus the attention on the single-label case). In particular, heterogeneous clusters of objects are identified, then a cluster description and a predictive model are associated to each cluster. Unlabeled objects are assigned to clusters on the basis of the cluster descriptions, and the corresponding predictive models are considered to provide predictions for the target attribute. In this way, highly connected objects falling in the same clusters will contribute to the learning of the same predictive models. Moreover, the heterogeneity of the clusters is exploited for the simultaneous classification of objects of different types, by assuming that class values of objects of type A are in some way related to class values of objects of type B, when all these objects belong to the same heterogeneous cluster (see Fig. 1).

Note that in the predictive clustering setting, the clustering results strongly influence the prediction phase. For this reason we identify a hierarchy of clusters and build classification models for each hierarchical level, in order to have the possibility of choosing either more globally-based or locally-based predictions.

In the next section we detail the proposed method, while in Section 3 we report the results obtained on some real-world datasets. Finally, in Section 4 we draw some conclusions and introduce possible future work.

2 Multi-type Classification from Heterogeneous networks

In the following, we introduce the notation and some useful definitions.

Def. 1 (Heterogeneous network). An heterogeneous network is a network $G = (V, E)$, where V is the set of nodes and E is the set of edges among nodes, where both nodes and edges can be of different types. Moreover:

- each node $v' \in V$ is associated to a single node type $t_v(v') \in \mathcal{T}$, where $\mathcal{T}$ is the finite set $\{T_p\}$ of all the possible types of nodes in the network;
- each node type T_p implicitly defines a subset of nodes $V_p \subseteq V$;
- a node type T_p defines a set of attributes $\mathcal{X}_p = \{X_{p,1}, X_{p,2}, \ldots, X_{p,m_p}\}$;
- an edge e between two nodes v' and v'' is associated to an edge type $R_j \in \mathcal{R}$, where $\mathcal{R}$ is the finite set $\{R_j\}$ of all the possible edge types in the network. Formally, $e = \langle R_j, \langle v', v'' \rangle \rangle \in E$, where $R_j = t_e(e) \in \mathcal{R}$ is its edge type;
- an edge type R_j defines a subset of edges $E_j \subseteq (V_p \times V_q) \subseteq E$, where $T_p \leq T_q$;
- node types $\mathcal{T}$ are partitioned into $\mathcal{T}_t$ (target), i.e. considered as target of the clustering/classification task, and $\mathcal{T}_{tr}$ (task-relevant). Only nodes of target types are actually clustered and classified, on the basis of all the nodes.

Def. 2 (Heterogeneous cluster). We define a heterogeneous cluster, or multi-type cluster, as $G' = (V', E')$, where: $V' \subseteq V$; $\forall v' \in V', t_v(v') \in \mathcal{T}_t$ (nodes in the clusters are only of target types); $E' \subseteq (E \cup \hat{E})$ is a set of edges (among the nodes in V') belonging either to E or to a set of edges $\hat{E}$ containing *extracted* edges, which relate nodes that are not directly connected in the original network.

Def. 3 (Hierarchical organization of clusters). A hierarchy of heterogeneous clusters is defined as a list of hierarchy levels $\{L_1, L_2, \ldots, L_k\}$, each of which consisting of a set of heterogeneous and possibly overlapping clusters.

Def. 4 (Classification schemes). Each target type $T_p \in \mathcal{T}_t$ can be associated to a different classification scheme. Some target types may have no classification scheme and they could be considered as target only for clustering. We define $\mathcal{T}_t^* \subseteq \mathcal{T}_t$ the set of target types which have an associated classification scheme.

The task consists in the identification of a hierarchy of clusters $\{L_1, L_2, \ldots, L_k\}$ and of a classification function $\psi_p^{(i)} : V_p \rightarrow \mathcal{Y}_p$ for each hierarchy level L_i and for each target type $T_p \in \mathcal{T}_t^*$. In the following, we describe our solution consisting of three steps: identification of the strength of relationships among nodes, hierarchical heterogeneous clustering, and identification of classification models.

2.1 Identification of the strength of the relationship among nodes

The strength of the relationship among nodes of different types corresponds to the weight of an hypergraph link, which is represented as a tuple of nodes.

Def. 5 (Tuple of nodes). A tuple is defined as $\boldsymbol{v_i} \in T_{p_1} \times T_{p_2} \times \ldots \times T_{p_r}$, where $\forall j = 1, \ldots, r$: $T_{p_j} \in \mathcal{T}_t$ and $\mathcal{T}_t - \{T_{p_1}, T_{p_2}, \ldots T_{p_r}\} = \emptyset$. Intuitively, a tuple is represented by all the target types of nodes, taken at least once (i.e., $r \geq |\mathcal{T}_t|$).

For each possible tuple $\boldsymbol{v}_i$, we compute the score s_i which represents the strength of the relationship among all the nodes in the tuple. s_i corresponds to the minimum score obtained from a pairwise evaluation of the nodes of the tuple. The score $pairscore(v_{i,j'}, v_{i,j''})$ of a pair of nodes $v_{i,j'}, v_{i,j''}$ is computed by exploiting c shortest paths among the considered pair of nodes. In particular, for each path P between the nodes in the pair, we compute a score $pathscore(P, v_{i,j'}, v_{i,j''})$ representing the strength between $v_{i,j'}$ and $v_{i,j''}$ with respect to the path P. The score s_i is computed as the maximum score obtained over the considered paths.

Each path P is represented as a finite set of sequences of nodes. If a sequence in P connects $v_{i,j'}$ and $v_{i,j''}$, then $pathscore(P, v_{i,j'}, v_{i,j''}) = 1$. Otherwise, it is computed as the maximum similarity between the sequences which start with $v_{i,j'}$ and the sequences which end with $v_{i,j''}$. The similarity between two sequences $seq_{d'}$ and $seq_{d''}$ is computed as the average between the similarity of target attributes and the similarity of non-target attributes of the nodes in the two sequences. Following [3], the similarity between two values of a numerical attribute x is computed as $1 - \frac{|val_x(seq_{d'}) - val_x(seq_{d''})|}{max_x - min_x}$ (min_x and max_x are the minimum and maximum values, respectively, observed for the attribute x). If x is not numeric, then $s_x(seq_{d'}, seq_{d''}) = 1$ if $val_x(seq_{d'}) = val_x(seq_{d''})$, 0 otherwise.

Nodes belonging to node types that are not involved in any path are aggregated according to the *arithmetic mean* for numeric attributes and the *mode* for attributes of any other type, and are associated to the nodes connected to them.

2.2 Building a hierarchy of heterogeneous clusters

Once all the possible tuples are identified, each associated with its strength score, we first build a set of (possibly overlapping) clusters in the form of cliques to be used in the subsequent step. A cluster is in the form of a clique if all the tuples involving only nodes in the cluster have a score above a given threshold $\beta \in [0, 1]$. The algorithm consists of the following steps:

i) A filtering phase on the set of tuples, which keeps only the tuples with a score greater than (or equal to) β. The result is the subset of tuples $\{\boldsymbol{v_i} \,|s_i \geq \beta\}$.
ii) Building of an initial set of cliques, each consisting of a tuple in $\{\boldsymbol{v_i} \,|s_i \geq \beta\}$.
iii) A process that iteratively merges two clusters G' and G'' into a new cluster G'''. The initial set of clusters is regarded as a list and is sorted according to an ordering relation $<_c$ that reflect the quality of the clusters. Each cluster G' is merged with the first cluster G'' in the list leading to a merged cluster G''' which still is a clique. This step is repeated until no more merging can be performed. The obtained result is the first hierarchy level L_1.

The ordering relation $<_c$ is based on the *multi-type cohesiveness*, which is defined as: $h(G) = \frac{1}{|tuples(G)|} \cdot \sum_{\boldsymbol{v_i} \in tuples(G)} s_i$. Formally, $G' <_c G'' \iff h(G') > h(G'')$.

Once the first level L_1 of the hierarchy has been identified, the other levels are built by evaluating whether some pairs of clusters (cliques, in L_1) can be reasonably merged. The approach is similar to that used to obtain the first level of the hierarchy. The main difference is that, instead of working on cliques, we work on generic clusters, where the strength score associated to each tuple is not necessarily greater than β. Due to this difference, and inspired by [6], two clusters G' and G'' are merged into a cluster G''' if $h(G''') > \alpha$, where α is a user defined threshold. It is noteworthy that low values of α lead to an higher number of mergings at the price of lower quality of clusters.

We repeat the process until no merging is possible and return the obtained hierarchy of heterogeneous clusters $\{L_1, L_2, \ldots, L_k\}$, according to Def. 3.

2.3 Building classification models from clusters

Once the hierarchy of clusters has been identified, we define a classification function $\psi_p^{(i)}$ for each hierarchy level i and each target type $T_p \in T_t^*$. Each unlabeled node is classified according to a variant of the majority voting approach, which considers that the same node may belong to multiple clusters. In particular, we build a predictive model for all the clusters in which the unlabeled node falls, by considering the labels of the nodes of the same type belonging to those clusters. Moreover, since in general we consider more reliable those clusters containing many labeled nodes with respect to unlabeled nodes, we compute a weight for the prediction model associated to each cluster as the percentage of labeled nodes.

Formally, for each hierarchical level L_i, the classification function $\psi_p^{(i)}(v)$ exploits the probability that a given node v belongs to the class Y, computed for each cluster G' containing v. Such probability is estimated as:

$$P(cl(v) = Y | v \in un(G'_p)) = \frac{freq(Y, lab(G'_p))}{|lab(G'_p)|} \tag{1}$$

where $cl(v)$ is a possible label for v; G'_p is the set of nodes of type T_p in G'; $lab(G'_p)$ (resp. $un(G'_p)$) is the set of labeled (resp. unlabeled) nodes of type T_p in G'; $freq(Y, lab(G'_p))$ is the number of nodes of type T_p labeled as Y in G'_p. The function $\psi_p^{(i)}(v)$ returns the class label which maximizes the weighted average of such probabilities over the clusters containing v. Formally:

$$\psi_p^{(i)}(v) = \arg\max_{Y \in \mathcal{Y}_p} \frac{\sum_{\{G' | v \in G' \wedge G' \in L_i\}} \left[w(G'_p) \cdot P(cl(v) = Y | v \in un(G'_p)) \right]}{\sum_{\{G' | v \in G' \wedge G' \in L_i\}} w(G'_p)} \tag{2}$$

where $\{G' | v \in G' \wedge G' \in L_i\}$ is the set of clusters of level L_i containing v, and $w(G'_p) = |lab(G'_p)|/|G'_p|$ is percentage of labeled nodes of type T_p in G'.

Finally, we introduce the possibility to consider homogeneous clusters built from the single target types (we call this clustering *intra-target*, to differentiate it from the *inter-target* approach considered until now). We weight the predictions obtained from both the points of view by means of a parameter $\gamma \in [0, 1]$, such that high values of γ give more importance to the intra-target results.

3 Experiments

The method proposed in this paper has been implemented in the system HENPC (HEretogeneous Network Predictive Clustering). The datasets considered in these preliminary experiments are: WEBKB[1], which contains web-pages collected by the World Wide Knowledge Base project of the CMU text learning group; DBLP, which contains information about the co-authorship of scientific papers in computer science stored in the DBLP bibliographic database; YELP[2], which contains reviews and talks about business activities taken from the YELP website. Some quantitative information about the datasets are reported in Table 1.

Table 1. Quantitative information about the considered datasets.

Dataset	$\mathcal{T}_t$	$\mathcal{T}_t*$	**Node/Edge Types**	**#Nodes**	**#Egdes**
WEBKB	*pages, terms*	*pages*	3/3	1,586	34,359
DBLP	*papers, authors*	*papers*	3/2	1,867	2,494
YELP	*business, users*	*business, users*	7/8	41,006	41,906

We perform a comparison between HENPC and three other classification systems which exploit data organized in the heterogeneous network fashion, i.e. Mr-SBC [2], RelIBk and RelSMO (i.e., the relational extension of k-NN and SMO algorithms implemented in RelWEKA [10]).
Classification results are evaluated according to the micro-accuracy measure, which is defined, for each target type $T_p \in \mathcal{T}_t^*$, as: $m\_acc(T_p) = \frac{\sum_{Y \in \mathcal{Y}_p} TP_Y}{|un(V_p)|}$, where TP_Y is the number of true positive examples for the category Y. We average the results obtained with a stratified 10-fold cross validation and report the weighted (according to the number of distinct class values) average results obtained on multiple targets. For each dataset, we compute the value of β such that we keep a given percentage of tuples. In particular, we compute the values of β which lead to keep 20%, 40% and 60% of tuples, in order to evaluate the influence of β on the classification performances, when the number of tuples in the dataset increases. As for the other parameters, we set the maximum depth of the analysis to 2 (starting from the target types) for all the considered methods, $k \in \{1, 3, 5\}$ for RelIBk and $c = 3$, $\alpha = \beta - 0.2$ and $\gamma \in \{0.7, 0.8, 0.9\}$ for HENPC.

Results are reported in Table 2. As it can be observed, HENPC is able to outperforms all the considered systems in the first level of the hierarchy, when at least 40% of tuples are considered. In the case of WEBKB dataset, all the hierarchical level lead to better results with respect to competitors.

Moreover, in order to evaluate the significance of the results from a statistical viewpoint, we performed a Nemeniy test for each dataset, where samples were built with the micro-accuracy values obtained over the 10 folds with all the considered values of beta. The results are summarized by means of critical distance graphs in Fig. 2, which show the statistically significant differences (i.e., when the difference between the average ranks is greater than the critical distance).

[1] `www.cs.cmu.edu/afs/cs/project/theo-20/www/data/`
[2] `www.yelp.com/dataset_challenge`

Table 2. Micro-accuracy results. Bold indicates that HENPC obtained the best accuracy value among all the considered methods.

System	Params	DBLP			WEBKB			YELP		
RelIBk	$k = 1$	0.416			0.606			0.532		
	$k = 3$	0.433			0.606			0.551		
	$k = 5$	0.422			0.606			0.541		
RelSMO		0.419			0.612			0.557		
MrSBC		0.472			0.585			0.507		
HENPC	γ	β: 20%	β: 40%	β: 60%	β: 20%	β: 40%	β: 60%	β: 20%	β: 40%	β: 60%
Level 1	0.70	0.442	**0.480**	0.460	**0.974**	**0.978**	**0.974**	0.433	**0.635**	**0.592**
	0.80	0.442	**0.478**	0.460	**0.974**	**0.978**	**0.974**	0.429	**0.634**	**0.593**
	0.90	0.447	**0.493**	0.458	**0.974**	**0.976**	**0.974**	0.463	**0.633**	**0.581**
Level 2	0.70	0.382	0.428	0.457	**0.804**	**0.804**	**0.804**	0.332	0.558	0.542
	0.80	0.382	0.430	0.455	**0.804**	**0.804**	**0.806**	0.333	0.562	0.540
	0.90	0.383	0.423	0.455	**0.806**	**0.806**	**0.808**	0.332	0.560	0.522
Level 3	0.70	0.390	0.375	0.432	**0.789**	**0.790**	**0.790**	0.345	0.539	0.518
	0.80	0.390	0.373	0.433	**0.794**	**0.792**	**0.794**	0.342	0.545	0.503
	0.90	0.388	0.359	0.435	**0.794**	**0.798**	**0.802**	0.342	0.544	0.490

From Fig. 2 it is possible to observe that HENPC is able to outperform all the other systems in all of its hierarchical levels on the WEBKB dataset. As regards DBLP, the first hierarchical level significantly outperforms all the other systems except for Mr-SBC. However, the difference between HENPC and Mr-SBC is not statistical significant according to the critical distance.

As for the YELP dataset, whose accuracy values are averaged over the results obtained on two node types, exhibits a more complex situation. Also in this case, the first level of HENPC is able to outperform the other systems, even if there is no statistical difference with respect to RelSMO and RelIBk with $k = 3$ and $k = 4$. However, contrary to what we observed on DBLP, we statistically outperform Mr-SBC. This behavior suggests that, in principle, HENPC is able identify at least one hierarchical level which well fits each specific network structure. Finally, it is noteworthy that the higher hierarchical levels of HENPC often do not lead to results which are statistically better than competitors. This is possibly due to the intrinsic behavior of the hierarchical clustering, which at higher levels can lead to too much large clusters and, thus, to more general classification models which are not able to distinguish well among the classes. This also suggest that the influence of the value of the parameter α deserves a more deep investigation.

4 Conclusion

In this work, we considered the task of multi-type classification in heterogeneous networks organized in an arbitrary structure. We proposed the algorithm HENPC which extracts hierarchically organized, possibly overlapping and heterogeneous clusters and exploit them for predictive purposes. Experiments show that, in some cases, the proposed approach is able to significantly outperform existing approaches. Results also emphasize the need to perform a more deep investigation with respect to the criteria adopted for stopping the construction of the hierarchy. Moreover, future work will include the possibility to introduce a strategy for discarding noisy objects in order to let HENPC focus on most cohesive groups of nodes and possibly increase the classification performance.

Fig. 2. Critical distance graphs obtained from the results of the Nemenyi test.

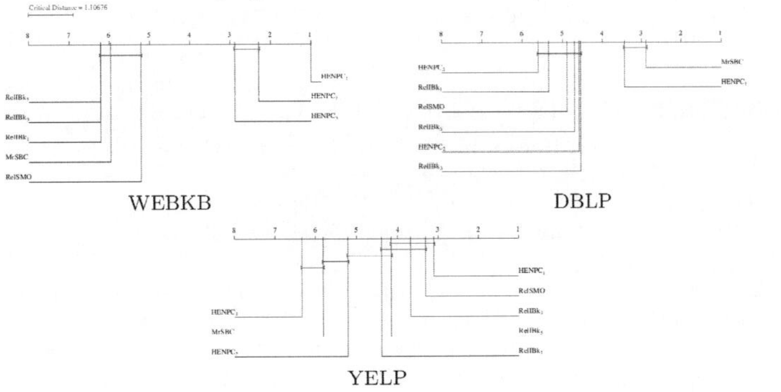

Acknowledgements

We would like to acknowledge the support of the European Commission through the project MAESTRA - Learning from Massive, Incompletely annotated, and Structured Data (Grant number ICT-2013-612944).

References

1. P. Angin and J. Neville. A shrinkage approach for modeling non-stationary relational autocorrelation. In *ICDM*, pages 707–712. IEEE Computer Society, 2008.
2. M. Ceci, A. Appice, and D. Malerba. Mr-SBC: a multi-relational naive bayes classifier. In *PKDD 2003*, pages 95–106. Springer, 2003.
3. J. Han, M. Kamber, and J. Pei. *Data Mining: Concepts and Techniques, Second Edition.* Morgan Kaufmann, 2 edition, Jan. 2006.
4. M. Ji, J. Han, and M. Danilevsky. Ranking-based classification of heterogeneous information networks. SIGKDD '11, pages 1298–1306, NY, USA, 2011. ACM.
5. M. Ji, Y. Sun, M. Danilevsky, J. Han, and J. Gao. Graph regularized transductive classification on heterogeneous information networks. In *ECML PKDD 2010*, volume 6321 of *LNCS*, pages 570–586. Springer Berlin, 2010.
6. G. Pio, M. Ceci, D. D'Elia, C. Loglisci, and D. Malerba. A Novel Biclustering Algorithm for the Discovery of Meaningful Biological Correlations between microRNAs and their Target Genes. *BMC Bioinformatics*, 14(S-7):S8, 2013.
7. D. Stojanova, M. Ceci, A. Appice, and S. Dzeroski. Network regression with predictive clustering trees. *Data Min. Knowl. Discov.*, 25(2):378–413, 2012.
8. Y. Sun, J. Han, P. Zhao, Z. Yin, H. Cheng, and T. Wu. Rankclus: integrating clustering with ranking for heterogeneous information network analysis. EDBT '09, pages 565–576, New York, NY, USA, 2009. ACM.
9. Y. Sun, Y. Yu, and J. Han. Ranking-based clustering of heterogeneous information networks with star network schema. In *ACM SIGKDD*, KDD '09, pages 797–806, New York, NY, USA, 2009. ACM.
10. A. Woznica, A. Kalousis, and M. Hilario. Learning to combine distances for complex representations. In Z. Ghahramani, editor, *ICML 2007*, volume 227, pages 1031–1038. ACM, 2007.

Looking for Similar Patterns in Genomic Sequences*

Piero Montanari[1], Ilaria Bartolini[1], Paolo Ciaccia[1], Marco Patella[1], Stefano Ceri[2], and Marco Masseroli[2]

[1] DISI - Università di Bologna, Italy
[2] DEIB - Politecnico di Milano, Italy

Abstract. Genomics is opening many interesting practical and theoretical computational problems; one of them is the search for a collection of genomic regions at given distances from each other, i.e., a *pattern* of genomic regions. We designed and implemented an optimized pattern-search algorithm able to find efficiently, within a large set of genomic data, genomic region sequences which are similar to a given pattern and present its applicability to the problem of enhancer detection.

1 Introduction

Thanks to Next Generation Sequencing (NGS), huge repositories of genomic sequences are nowadays being collected by large consortia of research laboratories, e.g., ENCODE [2] and TCGA [9]. So far, bio-informatics has been challenged by NGS *primary analysis* (production of sequences in the form of short DNA segments, or "reads") and *secondary analysis* (alignment of reads to a reference genome and extraction of specific genomic features), yet the most important emerging problem is *tertiary analysis*, concerned with multi-sample processing, annotation and filtering of variants, and genome browser-driven exploratory analysis [7]. Tertiary analysis targets data produced by secondary analysis and is responsible of *sense making*, e.g., how genomic regions interact with each other.

The GenData 2020 project addresses this challenge by enabling queries and analysis of processed genomic data. Among the project's results are a *Genometric Data Model* (GDM), which encodes genomic data in terms of their regions and metadata, and a *Genometric Query Language* (GMQL) [4]. According to GDM, a genomic (DNA) *region* is a quadruple $\langle chr, left, right, strand \rangle$, in which *chr* represents the region chromosome, the *strand* (either + or −) can be missing, and the region includes all the DNA nucleotides whose position is between *left* and *right*. Moreover, typically a region is associated by secondary analysis with a *feature vector*, where each feature is extracted by suitable processing.

Several tertiary analysis problems consist of searching for *patterns of regions*, i.e., co-occurrences of certain region configurations, among which the *search for enhancers* (particular regions of the non-coding part of the genome playing the role of enhancing or repressing gene expressions) and the *investigation on 3D*

* This work is supported by the PRIN Project GenData 2020 (`http://www.bioinformatics.deib.polimi.it/gendata/`).

properties of the genome. Informally, a pattern is a collection of regions that are present on one or more *tracks*, where a track is an ordered sequence of regions produced by a specific NGS experiment. All regions of a pattern are placed within the same chromosome, but they need not to be contiguous on the original track.

In this paper we introduce an efficient *pattern-search algorithm* which provides biologists with the ability, once they identify an interesting genomic region pattern, to look for *similar* occurrences of such pattern in the whole genome.[3] Each result of our algorithm is a collection of regions with properties similar to the query pattern, in particular with (approximately) the same spatial configuration (*structural similarity*) and similar feature values (*region similarity*). As Figure 1 suggests, structural similarity ignores absolute coordinate values of regions, focusing on *inter-region distances*.

Fig. 1. Example of search result on target tracks with high structural similarity to the query pattern: inter-region distances of the pattern are (approximately) preserved in the regions of the result, both along the same target track and across different tracks.

2 The Base Problem

In the *base version* of our problem, the pattern to be searched is single-track, regions are reduced to points, and region features are not present. Formally, a track T is a strictly increasing sequence of N elements, $T = \langle t_1, \ldots, t_N \rangle$, where each $t_i \in \mathbb{N}^+$ and $t_i < t_{i+1}$. Given a "query" track $Q = \langle q_1, \ldots, q_M \rangle$ and a "target" track $T = \langle t_1, \ldots, t_N \rangle$, with $N \geq M$, a *matching of* Q *in* T is a strictly increasing function $f : [1, M] \rightarrow [1, N]$ that assigns to each element q_i of Q an element $t_{f(i)}$ of T. We refer to $(q_i, t_{f(i)})$ as a *matched pair*, and to $\langle (i, f(i)) \rangle$ as a *matched index pair*. Notice that, although a matching only requires $N \geq M$, in practice it will be $N \gg M$ (typically $M \leq 10$, while $N = 10^3 \div 10^6$).

In order to search for patterns in the target track that are similar to the query track, we take a cost-based approach, where lower cost implies high similarity.

Definition 1 (Matching Cost). *Given tracks Q and T and a real value τ, the τ-matching cost of a matching f, $C_f(Q, T; \tau)$, is defined as:*

$$C_f(Q, T; \tau) = \sum_{i=1}^{M} \left(t_{f(i)} - q_i - \tau \right)^2 \tag{1}$$

[3] A stand-alone desktop application available at `http://www-db.disi.unibo.it/research/GenData/` and described in [5] enables biologists to define patterns of interest using the Integrated Genome Browser [6].

and the matching cost of f, $C_f(Q,T)$, is the minimum *τ-matching cost of f over all τ values, $C_f(Q,T) = \min_\tau C_f(Q,T;\tau)$.*

Let $\delta_{i,j} = t_j - q_i$ be the *absolute* offset between elements t_j and q_i. The τ parameter in Equation 1 allows us to consider *shifted* $(\delta_{i,j} - \tau)$ rather than absolute $(\delta_{i,j})$ offsets, and is used to translate Q so as to better match elements of T. For any given matching f of Q in T, the matching cost $C_f(Q,T)$ is obtained for $\tau = \sum_{i=1}^{M} \delta_{i,f(i)}/M$, i.e., the matching cost equals M times the variance of absolute offsets $\delta_{i,f(i)}$ of matched elements.

Given tracks Q and T, the best-matching problem (BMP) is to determine the matching f^* with minimum matching cost, i.e., $C_{f^*}(Q,T) \leq C_f(Q,T)\ \forall f$.

Example 1. Let $Q = \langle 1,7,10\rangle$ and $T = \langle 3,5,9,11,13,14,18,\ 21\rangle$. One of the possible matchings of Q in T is $f = \{((1,1)), ((2,3)), ((3,8))\}$ that assigns elements $(3,9,21)$ to corresponding elements of Q. Assuming $\tau = 7$, the τ-matching cost of f is 66, since $C_f(Q,T;7) = (3-1-7)^2 + (9-7-7)^2 + (21-10-7)^2 = 66$. The matching cost of f is obtained for $\tau = ((3-1)+(9-7)+(21-10))/3 = 5$: $C_f(Q,T) = 54$. The solution to the BMP is $f^* = \{((1,2)), ((2,4)), ((3,7))\}$ that matches Q to elements $(5,11,14)$ of T, which yields $\tau = 4$. The matching cost of f^* is $C_{f^*}(Q,T) = (5-1-4)^2 + (11-7-4)^2 + (14-10-4)^2 = 0$.

The best-matching problem, which amounts to finding a *minimum-variance matching*, is a specific case of quadratic assignment problem, which is known to be NP-hard [1]. Although this does not immediately lead to conclude that BMP is NP-hard as well, we strongly suspect this is the case, even because variance-minimization problems are reputed difficult to solve [8].

2.1 The Root-element Approach

An alternative cost definition that leads to a tractable version of the problem is to consider a fixed value of τ. In particular, we take $\tau \equiv \tau^r = t_{f(1)} - q_1$, i.e., a zero-cost for the first pair of matched elements of Q and T, which are therefore called *root (reference) elements*. The *root-element matching cost* $C_f^r(Q,T)$ is:

$$C_f^r(Q,T) = \sum_{i=1}^{M} \left(\delta_{i,f(i)} - \tau^r\right)^2 = \sum_{i=1}^{M} \left(\delta_{i,f(i)} - \delta_{1,f(1)}\right)^2 \quad (2)$$

and the root-element BMP (R-BMP) is finding the matching f^* with minimum root-element matching cost. Notice that, unlike BMP, in R-BMP the contribution of a matched pair $(q_i, t_{f(i)})$ to the overall cost is decoupled from that of the other pairs, since τ^r only depends on the root-elements and not on the whole matched elements. This is the key to develop an efficient dynamic programming (DP) algorithm, WDP-RBMP, where the 'W' stands for "windowed".

Lemma 1. *A matching f is optimal only if the (partial) matching $(f(1), f(2), \ldots, f(\ell))$, $\ell = 1,\ldots,M-1$, has minimum cost among all (partial) matchings*

$f' = (f'(1), f'(2), \ldots, f'(\ell))$ such that $f'(1) = f(1)$ and $f'(\ell) = f(\ell)$, i.e., $\sum_{i=1}^{\ell}(\delta_{i,f(i)} - \delta_{1,f(1)})^2 \leq \sum_{i=1}^{\ell}(\delta_{i,f'(i)} - \delta_{1,f'(1)})^2$. The condition is sufficient when also the last assignment, $\ell = M$, is considered.

The intuition about the proof is that, for given "start" ($f(1)$) and "end" ($f(\ell)$) positions in T, any partial matching f' which also matches q_1 to $t_{f(1)}$ ($f'(1) = f(1)$) and q_ℓ to $t_{f(\ell)}$ ($f'(\ell) = f(\ell)$), yet has a partial cost higher than that of f cannot be completed to yield a matching with minimum cost.

Based on the above lemma, our WDP-RBMP algorithm starts by partitioning the problem into $(N - M + 1)$ subproblems, one for each possible value of $f(1)$ and, consequently, of τ^r.[4] Given $f(1)$, we apply the DP technique by constructing an $M \times N$ matrix $Z_{f(1)}$. The value of cell (i, j) of this matrix, also called the *cell cost*, $Z_{f(1)}(i, j)$, is computed as the minimum cost obtainable by matching the first $i - 1$ elements of Q in the first $j - 1$ elements of T and q_i with t_j, i.e.:

$$Z_{f(1)}(i, j) = \min_{h:h<j} \{Z_{f(1)}(i - 1, h)\} + (\delta_{i,j} - \tau^r)^2 \tag{3}$$

Let h' denote the value of index h yielding the minimum in the above equation. For each cell (i, j) we also maintain a list, $ML_{f(1)}(i, j)$, of the indices of the matched elements of T, which is updated as $ML_{f(1)}(i, j) = ML_{f(1)}(i - 1, h') + (j)$, where '+' denotes list append. The procedure starts by filling a single cell, $(1, f(1))$, in the first row of the matrix, for which it is, by definition, $Z_{f(1)}(1, f(1)) = 0$ and $ML_{f(1)}(1, f(1)) = (f(1))$.

Theorem 1. *When cells of each matrix $Z_{f(1)}$, $1 \leq f(1) \leq (N - M + 1)$, are filled according to Equation 3, it is $C^r_{f^*}(Q, T) = \min_{f(1)} \min_j \{Z_{f(1)}(M, j)\}$.*

Because of the constraint $f(i) < f(i + 1)$, several cells of matrix $Z_{f(1)}$ will remain *unfilled* (their cell cost is assumed to be ∞). Indeed, it is possible to considerably reduce the number of matrix cells to be filled, as follows.

The closest match of q_i in T ($i > 1$) is the element of T, with index $cm(i)$, for which $cost(i, j) \stackrel{\text{def}}{=} (\delta_{i,j} - \tau^r)^2$, that is, the cost of matching q_i and t_j, is minimized.[5] Since both T and Q are strictly increasing sequences, it is $cm(i) \leq cm(i+1)$. In absence of "conflicts" among the closest matches, i.e., when $cm(i) < cm(i + 1)$, the matching $f_{cm} = (f(1), cm(2), \ldots, cm(M))$ would be the best one for the given root element $t_{f(1)}$. However, this breaks down in case of conflicts ($cm(i) = cm(i + 1)$), since f_{cm} would *not* be a matching anymore.

The intuition behind the WDP-RBMP algorithm is that the optimal matching has to be "close" to f_{cm}, thus for each row i of $Z_{f(1)}$ only a *window* of cells of limited size around $cm(i)$ has to be considered.

Theorem 2. *In order to find the best possible matching f^*, for each matrix $Z_{f(1)}$ the only cells to be filled are those in the* DP-window *defined as $W =$*

---

[4] It has to be $f(1) \leq N - M + 1$ in order to respect the constraint $f(i) < f(i + 1)$.

[5] We omit here the very particular case when the closest match is tied among two adjacent elements in T, which would unnecessarily lengthen the description.

$\{W_i : i > 1\}$, *where* $W_i = \{(i,j) : j \in [L_i, H_i]\}$, *and*

$$L_M = cm(M) \quad L_i = \min\{cm(i), L_{i+1} - 1\} \; (i = 2, \ldots, M-1)$$
$$H_2 = cm(2) \quad H_i = \max\{cm(i), H_{i-1} + 1\} \; (i = 3, \ldots, M)$$

Notice that, it is $L_i < L_{i+1}$ and $H_i < H_{i+1}$. Figure 2 shows a sample DP-window for the case $M = 7$ and the worst-case scenario in which all the $M - 1$ closest matches, $cm(i)$, are in conflict.

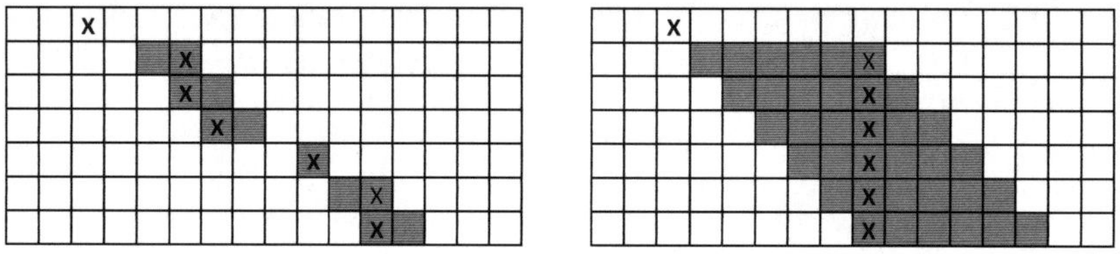

Fig. 2. Examples of DP-windows: closest matches are denoted with a **X**: A possible DP-window for the case $M = 7$ (left) and the worst-case scenario (right).

The complexity of the WDP-RBMP algorithm is $\mathcal{O}(MN(\log N + M))$, which is $\mathcal{O}(N \log N)$ when $M = o(N)$: for each of the $(N - M + 1)$ matrices we execute $M - 1$ binary searches to find the closest matches and then fill, in the worst case, $M - 1$ cells on each row. The cost of filling each cell is $\mathcal{O}(1)$, since for determining h', i.e., the value of index h which yields the minimum in Equation 3, it is sufficient to keep track of the minimum cell cost when filling the cells in a row.[6]

Example 2. Let $Q = \langle 8, 20, 22, 36 \rangle$ and $T = \langle 10, 15, 17, 27, 35, 39, 45, 50, 62, 70 \rangle$, and consider Z_2 (see Figure 3), one of the $(N - M + 1) = 7$ matrices generated by WDP-RBMP, for which it is $\tau^r = 15 - 8 = 7$. It is $cm(2) = 4$, since the closest match for $q_2 + \tau^r = 20 + 7$ is $t_4 = 27$. The same value is obtained for $cm(3)$, whereas $q_4 + \tau^r = 36 + 7 = 43$ yields $cm(4) = 7$. Based on Theorem 2 it is $W_2 = [3, 4]$, $W_3 = [4, 5]$, and $W_4 = [7, 7]$. To see how cells are filled consider cell $(3, 5)$, for which Equation 3 yields $Z_2(3, 5) = \min_{h:h<5}\{Z_2(2, h)\} + (\delta_{3,5} - \tau^r)^2 = 0 + ((35 - 22) - 7)^2 = 36$. It is $h' = 4$, thus $ML_2(3, 5) = ML_2(2, 4) + (5) = (2, 4, 5)$. The best matching f for Z_2 is obtained in cell $(4, 7)$, that is, $f = (((1, 2)), ((2, 4)), ((3, 5)), ((4, 7)))$ that assigns $(15, 27, 35, 45)$ to $(8, 20, 22, 36)$, with cost 40.

Z_2	**1**(10)	**2**(15)	**3**(17)	**4**(27)	**5**(35)	**6**(39)	**7**(45)	**8**(50)	**9**(62)	**10**(70)
1 (8)		0 (2)								
2 (20)			100 (2, 3)	**0** **(2, 4)**						
3 (22)				**104** **(2, 3, 4)**	36 (2, 4, 5)					
4 (36)							**40** **(2, 4, 5, 7)**			

Fig. 3. WDP-RBMP algorithm: the matrix Z_2 of Example 2. Closest matches, $cm(i)$, are in boldface.

[6] Here we apply the identity $\min\{a_1, \ldots, a_{n-1}, a_n\} = \min\{\min\{a_1, \ldots, a_{n-1}\}, a_n\}$.

3 Extending the Base Model

In this section we provide some intuition on how the base model can be extended so as to consider the following aspects:

Interval regions: In actual genomic applications elements t_i and q_j are intervals rather than points. Our solution is to reduce each interval to its *centroid*, which implies no changes to the WDP-RBMP algorithm. If regions' lengths are deemed to be relevant for the specific problem at hand, they can be modeled as region features (see below).

Multi-track patterns: When a query pattern is defined on NT different tracks, i.e., $\mathcal{Q} = (Q^1, \ldots, Q^{NT})$, where $Q^x = \langle q_1^x, \ldots, q_{M_x}^x \rangle$, each pattern track Q^x is searched in a different target track $T^x = \langle t_1^x, \ldots, t_{N_x}^x \rangle$. In order to give the same importance to all the tracks, we use as root-elements the couple $(q_1^y, t_{f^y(1)}^y)$ that introduces the minimal overall cost (defined as the sum of matching costs for each pattern track). WDP-RBMP can be extended by using NT matrices $Z_{f^y(1)}^x$, $x = 1, \ldots, NT$, when the root-element $t_{f^y(1)}^y$ is chosen from T^y. For each of the $N_y - M_y + 1$ possible values of the root-element, we fill matrix $Z_{f^y(1)}^y$ as in the single-track case, whereas for each other matrix $Z_{f^y(1)}^x$, $x \neq y$, we also fill the 1st row, since there is no root-element defined for T^x.

Negative matchings: Negative matching tracks are target tracks in which there must be no regions in the area of a result, thus they are used to limit the space of the solutions. The matrix columns of each element of a target track corresponding to regions in a negative track can therefore be dropped before starting the search process (such cells are given cost $= \infty$).

Partial matchings: The rationale behind partial matchings is that, in some cases, requiring to match all pattern elements might lead to a poor solution. In such cases, it might be preferable to "skip" one or more pattern elements, assigning them a cost $c(\perp)$. In order to apply WDP-RBMP to the partial matching case, a matrix $ZP_{f(1)}^x$ for each partial matching track TP^x is needed. The cost of cell (i, j) of $ZP_{f(1)}^x$ must now consider also the null $(\perp)$ case, and matrix $ZP_{f(1)}^x$ needs to be extended with an additional "0" column, corresponding to an unmatched first element.

Region features: Region features are used to determine the *region distance* of each couple of matched regions, which becomes part of the cost function. Since the region distance is not monotone, it is not possible to limit the search only to a neighborhood of the closest matches of q_i elements.

Top-k queries: The Top-K version of R-BMP aims to discover the K matchings $F = \{f_1, \ldots, f_K\}$ with the smallest overall cost. We further require that resulting patterns have no regions in common, so as to increase the diversity of the result. This is obtained by comparing results produced by all the matrices and keeping the best K disjoint results; note that each matrix can produce at most one result, as all the matchings associated with a matrix share the same root element.

4 Experiments

We applied the WDP-RBMP algorithm to solve the relevant biological problem of *finding enhancer regions*. This involves the search for DNA regions outside of the genes, at a certain distance from a gene's transcription start site (TSS), and associated with the presence or absence of specific regions, where given molecules bound to the DNA, that can be measured through NGS ChIP-seq experiments.

In particular, biologists believe that an *active putative enhancer* (APE) region should be not closer than 20K bases to the closest TSS, and have presence of overlapping peaks of the H3K4me1 and H3K27ac signals, and absence of H3K4me3 signal peaks. Furthermore, an APE could optionally include overlapping peaks of the DHS, CTCF, P300, and/or Pol2 signals. Thus, the search for APE regions can be expressed as a multi-track, interval region matching problem where peak regions of the H3K4me1 and H3K27ac signals constitute two positive matching tracks, TSS regions and peak regions of the H3K4me3 signal constitute two negative matching tracks, and peak regions of the DHS, CTCF, P300 and Pol2 signals constitute four partial matching tracks, respectively.

For TSS regions we used public data from SwitchGear Genomics, provided by the UCSC annotation database. For all other signals, we considered ChIP-seq experiments on specimens of the K562 cell line (Chronic Myeloid Leukemia), which are publicly available in the ENCODE project repository; thus, we extracted all H3K4me1, H3K27ac, H3K4me3, DHS, CTCF, P300 and Pol2 samples of ChIP-seq peaks of the K562 cell line, we merged sample replicates, and created a single dataset with a single sample (track) for each signal, all samples with the same region features. The number of regions in each track is listed in Table 1.

The Top-100 results found by WDP-RBMP were visually inspected by an expert, who evaluated all of them correct. Automatic evaluation of all the 1,651 results found by WDP-RBMP (in less than one minute) is difficult, since there is neither consolidated knowledge of enhancers, nor a consensus on the computational method specifically designed for their discovery. Therefore, we used for comparison a different set of data, about *chromatin*[7] *state segmentation*, generated by the Broad Institute for a few cell lines, including K562, and made publicly available also in the ENCODE repository. These data, denoted as ENCODE HMM, describe a set of chromatin states of the genome using a Hidden Markov Model (HMM); in particular, each 200 base pair (i.e., nucleotide) interval is assigned to its most likely state under the model; one of such state is associated with enhancers.[8] Although ENCODE HMM data were obtained considering a different set of epigenomic signals (with only 3 out of 9 signals overlapping with the signals considered by us), we found a very good matching between the regions denoted as enhancers by ENCODE HMM and the regions determined by WDP-RBMP, as shown in Table 1. This evaluation demonstrates both the correctness of the pattern-matching method and its ability to find interesting regions.

[7] Chromatin is a complex of molecules consisting of DNA, proteins, and RNA.

[8] Detailed information about the method and model parameters can be found in [3].

Table 1. Considered tracks and number of genomic regions, left. Precision of WDP-RBMP wrt. ENCODE HMM dataset (EH), right.

sample	regions
TSS	131,780
H3K4me1	116,503
H3K27ac	45,796
H3K4me3	142,738
DHS	360,648
CTCF	318,982
P300	69,370
Pol2	177,900

top-K results	EH overlapping results	precision
10	9	90.00%
50	45	90.00%
100	86	86.00%
250	215	86.00%
500	415	83.00%
1,000	837	83.70%
(all) 1,651	1,411	85.46%

5 Conclusions

We presented an efficient method to find patterns in genomic region sequences; it has practical applications in revealing interesting and unknown regions of the genome, and therefore it is an important ingredient in supporting biological research. In our future work, we plan to use the method for biological research, in strong connection with biologists of the GenData 2020 project, by using experimental data produced at IEO or by connecting to public data sources.

References

1. R. E. Burkard et al. Assignment problems. SIAM, 2009.
2. ENCODE Project Consortium. An integrated encyclopedia of DNA elements in the human genome. *Nature*, 489(7414):57-74, 2012.
3. J. Ernst et al. Mapping and analysis of chromatin state dynamics in nine human cell types. *Nature*, 473(7345):43-49, 2011.
4. M. Masseroli et al. GenoMetric Query Language: A novel approach to large-scale genomic data management. *Bioinformatics*, 31(12):1881-1888, 2015.
5. P. Montanari et al. An IGB-based application for the search of patterns in a genomic sequence. *GenData 2020 Tech. Rep.*, May 2015.
6. J. W. Nicol et al. The Integrated Genome Browser: free software for distribution and exploration of genome-scale datasets. *Bioinformatics*, 25(20):2730-2731, 2009.
7. Paradigm4, Inc. Accelerating bioinformatics research with new software for Big Data to Knowledge (BD2K). Waltham, MA, 2015 (available at: `http://www.paradigm4.com/`).
8. M. Sniedovich. Solution strategies for variance minimization problems. *Computers & Mathematics with Appl.*, 21(2-3):49-56, 1991.
9. J. N. Weinstein et al. The cancer genome atlas pan-cancer analysis project. *Nat. Genet.*, 45(10):1113-1120, 2013.

Community Detection in Social Networks: Breaking the Taboos*

Alessio Conte[†], Roberto De Virgilio[◇], Antonio Maccioni[◇], Maurizio Patrignani[◇], Riccardo Torlone[◇]

[†] Università di Pisa, Pisa, Italy
conte@di.unipi.it
[◇] Università Roma Tre, Rome, Italy
{dvr,maccioni,patrigna,torlone}@dia.uniroma3.it

Abstract. Current approaches to community detection in social networks usually neglect nodes, which we call *taboo*, whose neighborhood does not fit into main memory. In this paper, we model communities as cliques and present a distributed approach that is able to detect maximal cliques in social networks with taboo nodes. Our technique relies on a two-level decomposition algorithm. The first level aims at recursively identifying and isolating tractable portions of the network. The second level further decomposes the tractable portions into small blocks. This process is able to detect *all* maximal cliques provided that the sparsity of the network is bounded, as it happens in real-world social networks.

1 Introduction

The detection of communities allows us to reveal fundamental properties of networks in a variety of domains such as sociology, bibliography, and biology [7, 12]. A rigorous way to model communities considers maximal cliques, that is, maximal subgraphs in which any pair of nodes is connected by an edge. Maximal clique enumeration (MCE) is a paradigmatic problem in computer science and, due to its known complexity, several solutions have been proposed to deal with real-world scenarios [3, 8, 9, 13, 14].

When very large networks are involved, state-of-the-art strategies consist of decomposing the network into blocks that are independently processed in a distributed and parallel environment [4, 5, 8, 11, 16]. A crucial aspect of this approach is the choice of the size m of the blocks. Clearly, m is bounded by the dimension of the memory, but it has been shown that artificially reducing m to values as low as 1/100 or 1/1000 of the available memory results in a more efficient computation [4, 5]. On the other hand, if the size of the blocks is too small, the effectiveness of the approach is compromised. In fact, consider a node n such that the graph induced by its neighborhood does not fit into a block. We call such a *taboo* node. In any block of the decomposition a portion

* Work partially supported by ESF EuroGIGA GraDR and by the MIUR project AMANDA "Algorithmics for MAssive and Networked DAta".

of the neighborhood of n will be necessarily omitted and, consequently, some maximal cliques involving n may remain undetected and some non-maximal cliques could be erroneously found. Hence, while fixing the size of the blocks, state-of-the-art decomposition approaches also need to find a trade-off between efficiency and effectiveness. Even if efficiency is not an issue, effectiveness can be jeopardized since real-world social networks often contain nodes whose degree (i.e., the number of incident edges) is so high that their neighborhood does not fit into main memory altogether.

Actually, high degree nodes are connatural in *scale-free networks*, where the degree distribution of the nodes follows a power law. This property implies that the number of nodes with h connections to other nodes decreases exponentially as h increases and that the set of nodes with arbitrary high degree is not empty [1]. Several works in literature show that social networks, such as Facebook and Twitter, are scale-free [15]. It has also been shown that scale-freeness is exhibited whenever the network has a growth mechanism based on preferential attachment [2], that is, when new connections are distributed among nodes according to how many connections they already have. Hence, as social networks grow, this property is expected to be exacerbated.

In this paper, we address these limitations by proposing an approach to the problem of maximal clique enumeration in very large social networks that meets both the requirements of completeness and efficiency. The approach leverages on sparsity, another property of real-world networks, which basically means that the network can have very dense areas but, overall, nodes and edges are of the same order of magnitude. Our solution is based on a two-level decomposition of the network. The first-level decomposition aims at recursively identifying and isolating tractable portions involving non-taboo nodes only. Intuitively, this operation allows us to "break" taboo nodes by progressively decreasing their degree. The second-level decomposition suitably splits tractable portions of the network into small blocks that can be handled separately. Within a block, we then select the most promising state-of-the-art algorithm for enumerating its maximal cliques. A suitable procedure allows us to recognize and filter out those that are not maximal for the overall network. We formally show that this process is able to correctly detect *all* maximal cliques, provided that the sparsity of the network is bounded, as it is the case of real-world social networks.

We have performed a large number of experiments over data from real-world social networks showing that our approach is effective, efficient, and scalable [6]. The experimentation confirms that in order to have an efficient computation it is convenient to choose a relatively small size of the blocks, which further increases the number of taboo nodes. The experiments also confirm that, if taboo nodes were neglected, significant cliques would remain undetected.

The rest of the paper is organized as follows. In Section 2 we provide a general overview of our technique whereas, in Section 3, we describe in more detail the decomposition algorithm. Section 4 contains our conclusions. Further details of our study can be found in the full paper [6], which includes the experiments and the formal proofs of the correctness and completeness of the approach.

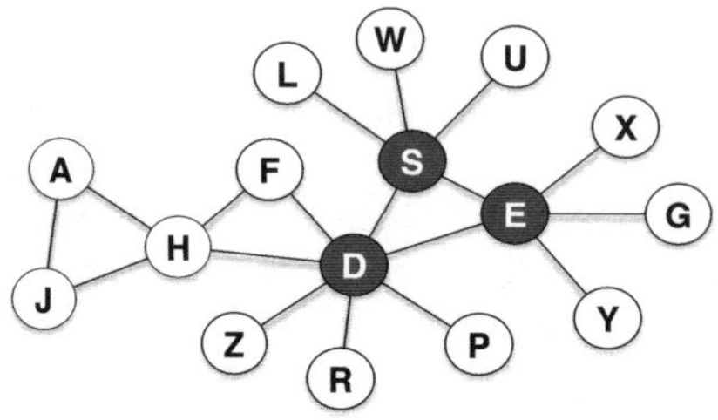

Fig. 1. Feasible nodes (white) and taboo nodes (red) when $m = 5$.

2 Overview and intuition

Our approach is based on a decomposition of the input network in smaller subgraphs called blocks that can partially overlap with each other. As we have discussed in the Introduction, this requires a careful choice of the size of the blocks, depending on hardware limitations and performance issues. Whichever the choice, let m be the maximum number of nodes that can fit in a block. The value of m identifies two types of nodes in the network: (i) the set N_h of *taboo nodes* having degree greater or equal than m (i.e., those nodes that would not fit into a block with all their neighbors) and (ii) the set N_f of *feasible nodes* having degree less than m.

Consider, for example, the network in Figure 1 and suppose $m = 5$. The set N_h consists of the red-coloured nodes D, S, and E of degree 7, 5, and 5 respectively, whereas N_f consists of the remaining white nodes.

Now, let C_f be the set of all maximal cliques of G involving at least one node in N_f and let C_h be the set of all maximal cliques in the network G_h induced[1] by the nodes in N_h. For example, in the network in Figure 1 we have that C_f includes the cliques $\{\mathsf{A}, \mathsf{J}, \mathsf{H}\}$ and $\{\mathsf{H}, \mathsf{F}, \mathsf{D}\}$, as they both involve feasible nodes, while C_h includes the clique $\{\mathsf{D}, \mathsf{S}, \mathsf{E}\}$, since G_h consists only of the nodes D, S, E and of the edges between them.

Our approach is based on the intuition that the set of all maximal cliques of the network G can be obtained from C_f and C_h alone. This is confirmed by a result in [6], which establishes that the set of the maximal cliques of G is the union of C_f and the set C'_h obtained by filtering out from C_h any clique that is contained into a clique of C_f.

This result suggests that if we process separately the nodes in N_f and the nodes in N_h, no clique is left out. We then obtain an effective decomposition strategy which is also efficient since the neighbors of a feasible node fit into a block of size m by definition, while the degree of the nodes in the induced graph G_h is strongly reduced since G_h only involves a limited number of nodes in scale

[1] We recall that the subgraph of $G = (N, E)$ *induced* by a set of nodes $N' \subseteq N$ is the restriction of G to the nodes in N' and the edges between them.

free networks. For instance, in the network of Figure 1, G_h is the cycle $\{\mathsf{D}, \mathsf{S}, \mathsf{E}\}$ and its maximum degree is two.
Regarding the computation of the cliques in C_f and C_h we proceed as follows.

C_f: As in [5], we compute a suitable partition of N_f and add to each set S of the partition the neighborhood in G of the nodes in S. The obtained sets of nodes, together with the edges between them, form the blocks of the decomposition. Observe that a node (including the taboo ones) may be included into several blocks as a neighbor node, together with a subset of its edges. Differently from [5], we allow for blocks of heterogeneous size and high connectivity that can be processed independently in an efficient way. Then, taking advantage of a decision tree, we apply on each block the most promising MCE algorithm based on the block characteristics. For instance, if the block is sparse, we find the maximal cliques with the algorithm in [10], while if the block is dense we adopt the algorithm described in [14].

C_h: We apply the whole approach recursively to G_h by partitioning its nodes N_h into two sets N'_f and N'_h of feasible and taboo nodes, respectively. This is possible since the degree of the nodes in N_h is strongly reduced. The recursion produces a sequence of sets N'_f, N''_f, N'''_f, ... of decreasing size until there are no more taboo nodes remaining.

In [6] we have shown that, under the hypothesis that the input graph is sparse enough, this recursive process converges, in the sense that it ends with a bipartition involving only tractable nodes. Moreover, in all our experiments on real-world data sets the process needed at most a few recursive steps [6].

Summarizing, our approach consists of the following.

1. **First level decomposition:** we identify the set N_f of *feasible* nodes of G, whose degree is less than m, and the set N_h of *taboo* nodes of G, whose degree is greater or equal than m.
2. **Recursive call:** if N_h is not empty, we build the subgraph G_h of G induced by the nodes in N_h and apply recursively the whole process to G_h.
3. **Second level decomposition:** given a set of feasible nodes N_f we compute a set of blocks by partitioning N_f and by adding to each node of a block its neighbors.
4. **Block analysis:** we apply a suitable MCE algorithm to each block generated by the second level decomposition to compute all its maximal cliques. The MCE algorithm is chosen from a collection of alternatives, taken from the literature, based on the properties of the block.
5. **Filtering:** the output is obtained by taking the union of the maximal cliques computed in step 4 and those computed in step 2, filtering out redundant cliques.

3 Network Decomposition

Overall approach. Algorithm 1 (`FIND-MAX-CLIQUES`) is the highest-level recursive procedure for computing maximal cliques. The `CUT` procedure call (line 1)

Algorithm 1: `FIND-MAX-CLIQUES`: Overall algorithm

Input : A graph $G = \langle N, E \rangle$ and a block size m.
Output: The set C of the maximal cliques of G.

1 $\langle N_f, N_h \rangle \leftarrow$ `CUT(`G`,m);` `/*` 1st `level decomp. */`
2 $\mathcal{B} \leftarrow$ `BLOCKS(`G`,` N_f`, m);` `/*` 2nd `level decomp. */`
3 $C_f \leftarrow \emptyset$;
4 **foreach** $b \in \mathcal{B}$ **do**
5 $\quad C_f \leftarrow C_f \cup$ `BLOCK-ANALYSIS(`b`);`
6 $C_h \leftarrow$ `FIND-MAX-CLIQUES(induced(`G`,`N_h`),m);`
7 $C'_h \leftarrow$ `filter(`C_h, C_f`);`
8 **return** $C_f \cup C'_h$;

Algorithm 2: `CUT`: First-level decomposition

Input : A graph $G = \langle N, E \rangle$ and a block size m.
Output: The sets N_f and N_h of feasible and taboo nodes of G, respectively.

1 $N_f \leftarrow \emptyset$;
2 **foreach** $n \in N$ **do**
3 $\quad$ **if** `isfeasible(`$\{n\}$`,`G`,m)` **then**
4 $\quad\quad N_f \leftarrow N_f \cup \{n\}$;
5 $N_h \leftarrow N - N_f$;
6 **return** $\langle N_f, N_h \rangle$;

performs the first-level decomposition while the `BLOCKS` procedure call (line 2) performs the second-level decomposition.

Algorithm `BLOCK-ANALYSIS` (line 5) can be any MCE algorithm. In particular, in order to improve efficiency, we take advantage of a decision tree to select, based on the block characteristics, the most promising MCE algorithm among a collection of algorithms/data-structures alternatives [6]. Procedure `induced` (line 6) accepts as input a graph G and a subset N_h of its nodes and computes the subgraph of G induced by N_h. Procedure `filter` (line 7) accepts as input two sets C_h and C_f of cliques and outputs all cliques in C_h that are not contained into some clique of C_f.

First level decomposition. Algorithm 2 describes the `CUT` procedure that is responsible of identifying the set N_f of feasible nodes and the set N_h of taboo nodes. This is done by means of the procedure `isfeasible` (also called by procedure `BLOCKS`) that takes as input a set of nodes, the graph G and the maximum block size m and checks whether the union of the given nodes and all their neighborhoods in G has less than m elements. The set N_h of taboo nodes is simply obtained, at line 5, as the difference between the nodes of G and N_f.

Second level decomposition. Algorithm 3 describes the `BLOCKS` procedure, responsible of decomposing the input graph G into tractable blocks of maximum size m. The input graph G is assumed to have maximum degree $m - 1$. Here,

Algorithm 3: `BLOCKS`: Second-level decomposition

Input : A graph $G = \langle N, E \rangle$, a set N_f of feasible nodes, and a block size m.
Output: A set of blocks $\mathcal{B}$.

$\bar{K} \leftarrow \emptyset$; $\mathcal{B} \leftarrow \emptyset$;
while $N_f \neq \emptyset$ **do**
    $K, H, V \leftarrow \emptyset$;
    $n \leftarrow$ `select`(N_f);
    while `isfeasible`$(K \cup \{n\}, G,$m$)$ **do**
        $N_f \leftarrow N_f - \{n\}$;
        $\bar{K} \leftarrow \bar{K} \cup \{n\}$;
        $K \leftarrow K \cup \{n\}$;
        $V \leftarrow N(n) \cap \bar{K}$;
        $H \leftarrow N(n) - V$;
        $n \leftarrow$ `select`$(N_f \cap H)$;
    $\mathcal{B} \leftarrow \mathcal{B} \cup$ `induced`$(G, K \cup H \cup V)$;
return $\mathcal{B}$;

we model blocks similarly to [5] but allow for blocks of heterogeneous sizes and leverage the adjacency of the nodes to put dense subgraphs into the same block. Hence, this step, in addition to distributing the computational load into tasks that could be accomplished separately in a distributed environment, also preprocesses the input producing internally homogeneous and compact chunks.

Blocks are defined sequentially in a greedy way. Each block will have *kernel* nodes, *border* nodes, and *visited* nodes. Each node of N_f is kernel node in exactly one block (i.e., kernel nodes form a partition of N_f). All the nodes of G that are adjacent to at least one kernel node of a block B and that are not kernel nodes of B are divided into border nodes and visited nodes of B, where visited nodes are those nodes that have been already used as kernel nodes for some previously defined block. The block is completed with all the edges among its nodes, irrespectively of the type.

For instance, consider again the network in Figure 1. Nodes D, E, and S are identified as taboo nodes by procedure `FIND-MAX-CLIQUES` and will be processed in a subsequent recursive call of the same procedure. Figure 2 shows a possible decomposition of the network in eleven blocks obtained by focusing on the remaining non-taboo nodes. In the figure kernel nodes are white, border nodes are green and visited nodes are double-marked. Note that all feasible nodes (white-filled in Figure 1) occur in exactly one block as kernel nodes (white-filled in Figure 2). Also, observe that each block of Figure 2 includes all the neighborhood of the kernel nodes. However, the taboo nodes (D, E, and S) never occur as kernel nodes in any block. Instead, their neighborhood has been distributed among the various blocks. Finally, note that every maximal clique occurs in at least one block: this is an important property that allows us to independently process each block. If a maximal clique occurs in more than one block, only the occurrence without visited nodes will be considered. This is the case, for in-

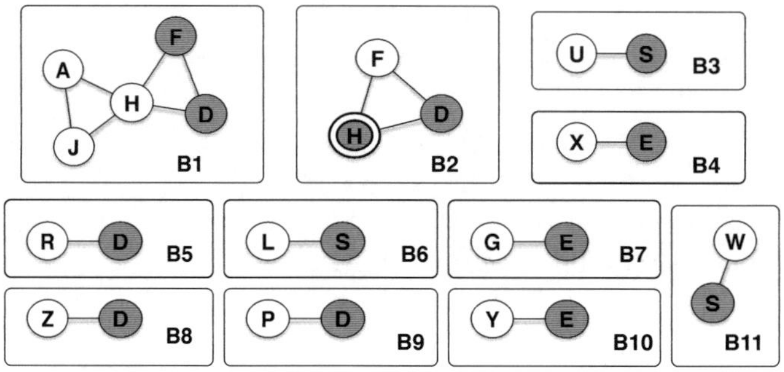

Fig. 2. A graph decomposition obtained by focusing on the feasible nodes of Figure 1.

stance, for the maximal clique {H, F, D} that is detected both when processing $B1$ and when processing $B2$, but is discarded in the latter case since it contains a visited node.

We start to build a block B by picking a node n from N_f (line 4 of Algorithm 3) and adding it to the set K of kernel nodes of B (line 8). We then build: (i) the set V of visited nodes (line 9), composed of neighbors of nodes in K that are already used as kernel nodes in a previously defined block (we maintain these latter nodes in $\bar{K}$, which is updated at line 7), and (ii) the set H of border nodes (line 10), composed of neighbors of K that are not yet visited. Then we proceed by selecting one node of N_f that is a border node of B and transforming it into a kernel node of B (line 10). In order to produce blocks that correspond to dense graphs, we order the candidate border nodes based on the number of their adjacency with kernel nodes, and we stop either if we exceed the limit m by adding further nodes (line 5) or if all candidate border nodes have a number of adjacency with kernel nodes below a specified threshold.

4 Conclusions and future work

In this paper, we have presented a novel technique for computing all the maximal cliques of an arbitrarily large network in a distributed environment. The approach relies on a two-level decomposition strategy that allows us to achieve efficiency by suitably lowering the size of the blocks without jeopardizing completeness. This is confirmed by a number of theoretical results showing the correctness and completeness of the technique over sparse graphs, a natural property of real-world social networks [6].

An extensive campaign of experiments conducted over real-world scenarios has shown the efficiency and scalability of our proposal [6]. We have also demonstrated experimentally that, if our technique was not adopted, a significant portion of the most relevant cliques would have been lost.

In the future, we plan to explore the possibility of extending our approach to relaxed definitions of communities, such as k-cliques, k-clubs, k-clans, and k-plexes. We are also interested in studying an incremental version of our approach that takes into account the evolution of the social network.

References

1. R. Albert and A.-L. Barabási. Statistical mechanics of complex networks. *Rev. Mod. Phys.*, 74:47–97, 2002.
2. A.-L. Barabási and E. Bonabeau. Scale-free networks. *Scientific American*, 288(5):50–59, 2003.
3. C. Bron and J. Kerbosch. Finding all cliques of an undirected graph (algorithm 457). *Commun. ACM*, 16(9):575–576, 1973.
4. J. Cheng, Y. Ke, A. W.-C. Fu, J. X. Yu, and L. Zhu. Finding maximal cliques in massive networks. *ACM Trans. Database Syst.*, 36(4):21, 2011.
5. J. Cheng, L. Zhu, Y. Ke, and S. Chu. Fast algorithms for maximal clique enumeration with limited memory. In *KDD*, pages 1240–1248, 2012.
6. A. Conte, R. D. Virgilio, A. Maccioni, M. Patrignani, and R. Torlone. Finding all maximal cliques in very large social networks. In *EDBT*, pages 173–184, 2016.
7. W. Cui, Y. Xiao, H. Wang, and W. Wang. Local search of communities in large graphs. In *SIGMOD*, pages 991–1002, 2014.
8. N. Du, B. Wu, L. Xu, B. Wang, and X. Pei. A parallel algorithm for enumerating all maximal cliques in complex network. In *ICDM Workshops*, pages 320–324, 2006.
9. D. Eppstein, M. Löffler, and D. Strash. Listing all maximal cliques in sparse graphs in near-optimal time. In *ISAAC*, pages 403–414, 2010.
10. D. Eppstein and D. Strash. Listing all maximal cliques in large sparse real-world graphs. In *SEA*, pages 364–375, 2011.
11. E. Gregori, L. Lenzini, and S. Mainardi. Parallel k-clique community detection on large-scale networks. *Trans. Parallel Distrib. Syst.*, 24(8):1651–1660, 2013.
12. A. Prat-Pérez, D. Dominguez-Sal, and J.-L. Larriba-Pey. High quality, scalable and parallel community detection for large real graphs. In *WWW*, pages 225–236, 2014.
13. E. Tomita and T. Kameda. An efficient branch-and-bound algorithm for finding a maximum clique with computational experiments. *J. Global Optimization*, 44(2):311, 2009.
14. E. Tomita, A. Tanaka, and H. Takahashi. The worst-case time complexity for generating all maximal cliques and computational experiments. *Theor. Comput. Sci.*, 363(1):28–42, 2006.
15. J. Ugander, B. Karrer, L. Backstrom, and C. Marlow. The anatomy of the facebook social graph. *CoRR*, abs/1111.4503, 2011.
16. J. Xiang, C. Guo, and A. Aboulnaga. Scalable maximum clique computation using mapreduce. In *ICDE*, pages 74–85, 2013.

An Interval-based Query Language for High-level Surveillance Event Detection *

Sven Helmer and Fabio Persia

Faculty of Computer Science
Free University of Bozen-Bolzano, Italy
{sven.helmer,fabio.persia}@unibz.it
Discussion Paper

Abstract. We propose a language based on relational algebra extended by intervals for detecting high-level surveillance events from a video stream. The operators we introduce for describing temporal constraints are based on the well-known Allen's interval relationships. The semantics of our language are clearly defined and we illustrate its usefulness by expressing typical events in it and showing the promising results of an experimental evaluation.

Keywords: High-Level Event Detection; Event Query Languages; Intervals

1 Introduction

For the detection of certain behavioral or other patterns in the surveillance context, low-level events are usually not very useful. Thus, in order to fill this semantic gap, we need to derive knowledge on a higher level from low-level events by combining the latter to complex structures. Basically, this is the task of an *event query language* (EQL).

An issue of many current EQLs is the lack of formal semantics [4]. In our approach we propose a language based on relational algebra for detecting high-level events. The relational algebra is clearly defined and forms the basis for many database query languages such as SQL. Using relational algebra as a foundation for an EQL is not a completely new idea [4, 5]. The novelty of our approach is mapping the concepts of event detection to a relational algebra extended by interval operators based on *Allen's interval relationships* [6]. While a few operators, such as the overlap join, have been integrated into database systems, the full range of operators we need is not yet available in temporal or stream databases.

In summary, we make the following contributions: we define an event query language based on relational algebra extended by interval operators, and illustrate how our language can be used to detect high-level events in a video surveil-

* This paper refers to [1], which has just been published in the Tenth IEEE International Conference on Semantic Computing

lance context. A brief experimental study using real-world data sets shows that queries in our language can be evaluated efficiently.

2 Related Work

There is a substantial body of work on searching for specifically defined patterns of activities in a video surveillance context using stochastic automata [7]: Albanese et al. [8] propose an indexing technique for temporal stochastic automaton-based activity models and then go on to find observation sequences that are not sufficiently explained by models within an initial set of predefined innocuous and dangerous activities [9, 10]. Potentially, our technique could be combined with this approach to update and extend the event knowledge base of models.

The major drawbacks of event detection approaches based on *nondeterministic finite automata* (NFA) are the representations of negation and concurrent events, which can be handled by our approach. Also, the evaluation order in the NFA-based approaches is fixed and determined by a state transition diagram. Usually, queries are evaluated by performing *backward search* starting from the final state. In our case, we can exploit well-known database query optimization techniques to make the execution of queries faster.

Moreover, Amato et al. [3] propose an event query language to deal with and express queries on events generated by wireless sensor networks. However, while in [3] an event can be simply recognized by the occurrence of a combination of values measured by appropriate transducers, in our approach we focus on the temporal relationships between the intervals representing lower-level events.

Furthermore, Eckert et al. [4] propose the Complex Event Relational Algebra (CERA), which is able to represent execution plans for complex event queries in an extended version of the relational algebra. They also show how $XChange^{EQ}$ [11], a high-level EQL, can be mapped to CERA. Of all the approaches discussed so far, CERA comes closest to ours. However, whereas our approach offers the full spectrum of Allen's interval relationships extended with (optional) thresholds, CERA only provides generic temporal operators for overlapping events.

3 Overview and Formalization

Before going into details, we present the overall architecture of our proposed system in Fig. 1. The interval action detector aggregates the results from the low-level labeling into medium-level events using medium-level predicates. As we focus on high-level events, we do not go into details here, assuming an approach similar to the one in [12] is utilized. Let Pr be the set of medium-level predicates.

Definition 1 (Interval Labeling) *A* medium-level annotation *is a tuple* $\mu = (pred, s_f, e_f, arg_1, ..., arg_l)$*, where* $\mu.pred \in Pr$ *is the* medium-level predicate *describing a medium-level event,* $\mu.s_f$ *and* $\mu.e_f$ *are the start and end frame delineating the event, and* $\mu.arg_1, \ldots, \mu.arg_l$ *are arguments of the predicate. An*

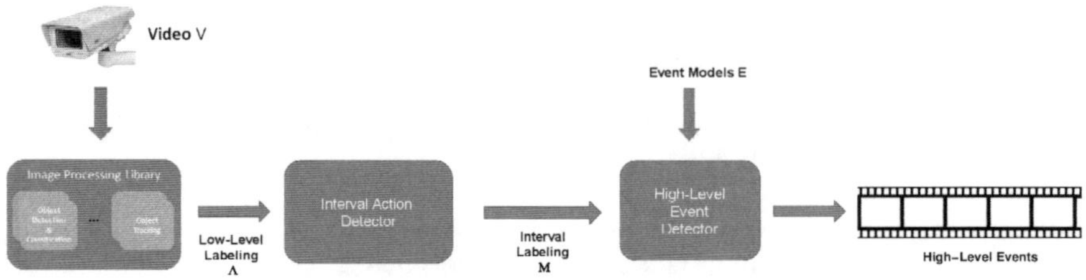

Fig. 1: Overall architecture

interval labeling M *is a finite sequence of medium-level annotations* μ_i. *More specifically,* $\forall \mu \in M, \mu.pred \in Pr, \mu.s_f, \mu.e_f \in \mathbb{N}, \mu.s_f \leq \mu.e_f$.

We give some examples for predicates describing medium-level events; in order to keep them readable, we assume a small set of predicates, here $Pr = \{in, hasPkg, insideCar\}$.

Example 1 (Medium-level Predicates) *Let* $\mu_i \in M, 1 \leq i \leq 3$ *be medium-level annotations with*

- $\mu_1 = (in, 30, 88, p_1, person)$, *meaning that from frame 30 to frame 88, person* p_1 *has been detected*
- $\mu_2 = (hasPkg, 50, 88, p_1, pkg_1)$: *from frame 50 onwards (until* p_1 *leaves in frame 88),* p_1 *is carrying package* pkg_1
- $\mu_3 = (insideCar, 188, 244, p_2, c_1)$: p_2 *is inside car* c_1 *from frame 188 until frame 244*

4 Representing and Processing Interval Data

From the definition of interval labeling in Section 3, it becomes clear that we need a way to represent and process interval data in an efficient manner. In order to address the first issue, we exploit the concept of an *interval relation*, which is simply a relation in which every tuple is associated with the starting and end point of an interval. Clearly, an interval labeling M is an interval relation.

4.1 Relational Algebra Operators

For the examples in this section we use the example relations R and S depicted in Fig. 2 with $r_1.T = [1, 5]$, $r_2.T = [1, 10]$, $r_3.T = [7, 11]$, $r_4.T = [9, 10]$, $s_1.T = [2, 2]$, $s_2.T = [3, 12]$, $s_3.T = [4, 5]$, $s_4.T = [5, 6]$, and $s_5.T = [8, 9]$.

The names for our operators come from Allen's interval relationships [6]. We map them to relational algebra operators and also extend them by allowing constraints defined on distances between endpoints of intervals, similarly to Walzer et al. [13] (however, Walzer et al. did not use relational algebra).

Definition 2 (Left/Right Overlap Join) *Given two interval relations R and S and the tuples $r \in R$, $s \in S$, then r and s satisfy the* left overlap join *predicate, iff $0 \leq s.T_s - r.T_s \leq \delta$ and $0 \leq s.T_e - r.T_e \leq \epsilon$ and $0 \leq \delta \prec size(r)$*[1] *and $0 \leq \epsilon \prec size(s)$.*
When joining R and S via a left overlap join, we use the notation R LOJ S. If we exchange the role of R and S, we derive the reverse counterpart of LOJ, called right overlap join (ROJ).
For a (general) left overlap join between R and S we get the following result: $\langle r_1, s_2\rangle$, $\langle r_1, s_3\rangle$, $\langle r_1, s_4\rangle$, $\langle r_2, s_2\rangle$. If we fix the value of δ to 2, we obtain $\langle r_1, s_2\rangle$, $\langle r_2, s_2\rangle$. The result of the Right Overlap Join between the two relations is $\langle r_4, s_5\rangle$. Assigning 0 to ϵ, the answer set is empty.

If a user omits the threshold values δ and ϵ, we assign the maximum allowed value to them (this is the least restrictive case).

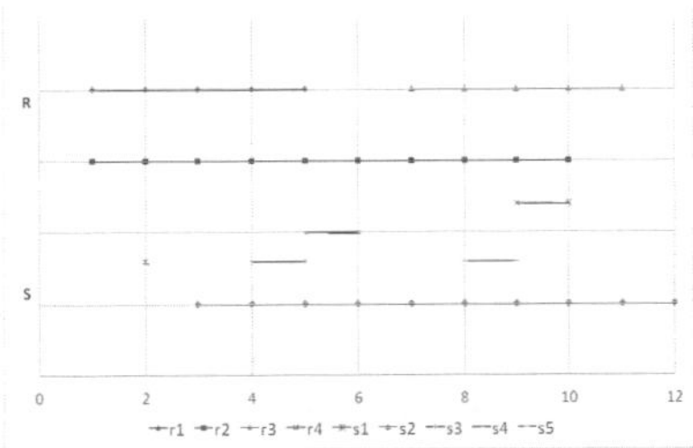

Fig. 2: Interval Relations' Examples

Definition 3 (During/Reverse During Join) *Given two interval relations R and S and the tuples $r \in R$, $s \in S$, then r and s satisfy the* during join *predicate, iff $0 \leq r.T_s - s.T_s \leq \delta$ and $0 \leq s.T_e - r.T_e \leq \epsilon$ and $0 \leq \delta \leq size(r) + \epsilon$ and $0 \leq \epsilon \leq size(r) + \delta$.*
When joining R and S via a during join, we use the notation R DJ S. If we exchange the role of R and S, we derive the reverse counterpart of DJ, called reverse during join (RDJ).
Using the example relations from Fig. 2, the result of R DJ S is: $\langle r_3, s_2\rangle$, $\langle r_4, s_2\rangle$. Assigning a value of 4 to δ results in one pair: $\langle r_3, s_2\rangle$. Joining R and S via a reverse during join gives us the following result: $\langle r_1, s_1\rangle$, $\langle r_1, s_3\rangle$, $\langle r_2, s_1\rangle$, $\langle r_2, s_3\rangle$, $\langle r_2, s_4\rangle$, $\langle r_2, s_5\rangle$, $\langle r_3, s_5\rangle$. R $RDJ_{\delta=4\wedge\epsilon=3}$ S is equal to $\langle r_1, s_1\rangle$, $\langle r_1, s_3\rangle$, $\langle r_3, s_5\rangle$.

As a sidenote, setting δ and ϵ to 0 in Definition 2 and 3 means that two tuples are joined only if their intervals coincide.

Definition 4 (Start Preceding) *Given two interval relations R and S and the tuples $r \in R$, $s \in S$, then r and s satisfy the* start preceding join *predicate, iff $0 \leq s.T_s - r.T_s \leq \delta$ and $r.T_e - s.T_s \geq 0$.*

[1] $size(r) = r.T_e - r.T_s + 1$

The notation for a start preceding join is R SP S.
The result of a start preceding join between R and S is (see Fig. 2 for R and S): $\langle r_1, s_1\rangle$, $\langle r_1, s_2\rangle$, $\langle r_1, s_3\rangle$, $\langle r_1, s_4\rangle$, $\langle r_2, s_1\rangle$, $\langle r_2, s_2\rangle$, $\langle r_2, s_3\rangle$, $\langle r_2, s_4\rangle$, $\langle r_2, s_5\rangle$, $\langle r_3, s_5\rangle$. *Assigning 1 to* δ *gives us* $\langle r_1, s_1\rangle$, $\langle r_2, s_1\rangle$, $\langle r_3, s_5\rangle$.

With this operator we basically check that the intervals overlap and $r.T$ starts not later than $s.T$. We do not care which of the intervals ends first. Strictly speaking, this is not a new operator, but introduced to simplify the formulation of events. It can be expressed using a logical disjunction of the *Left Overlap Join* and *Reverse During Join* operators.

Definition 5 (End Following) *Given two interval relations R and S and the tuples* $r \in R$, $s \in S$, *then r and s satisfy the* end following join *predicate, iff* $0 \leq r.T_e - s.T_e \leq \epsilon$ *and* $s.T_e - r.T_s \geq 0$.
The notation for an end following join is R EF S.
Applying an end following join to R and S from Fig. 2 gives us: $\langle r_1, s_1\rangle$, $\langle r_1, s_3\rangle$, $\langle r_2, s_1\rangle$, $\langle r_2, s_3\rangle$, $\langle r_2, s_4\rangle$, $\langle r_2, s_5\rangle$, $\langle r_3, s_5\rangle$, $\langle r_4, s_5\rangle$. *With* $\epsilon = 1$, *the result would be* $\langle r_1, s_3\rangle$, $\langle r_2, s_5\rangle$, $\langle r_4, s_5\rangle$.

The end following predicate is similar to the start preceding one insofar that this time we want overlapping intervals and $r.T$ to end not before $s.T$. Again, this is a short cut for expressing a logical disjunction between two other operators: a *Right Overlap Join* and a *Reverse During Join.*

The following operators do not check for overlapping intervals, but require one interval to occur before the other one.

Definition 6 (Before/After) *Given two interval relations R and S and the tuples* $r \in R$, $s \in S$, *then r and s satisfy the* before join *predicate, iff* $0 \prec s.T_s - r.T_e \leq \delta$.
The notation for a before join is R Bef S. If we exchange the role of R and S, we derive the reverse counterpart of Bef, called after join *(Aft).*
Applying a before join with $\delta = 3$ *to R and S gives us* $\langle r_1, s_5\rangle$ *(see Fig. 2 for the relations R and S). An after join with* $\delta = 2$, *results in* $\langle r_3, s_3\rangle$, $\langle r_3, s_4\rangle$.

If we set δ to 1 in a before or after join, then the two intervals have to be contiguous. When omitting a value for δ, we use as default the largest possible value, i.e., the overall video length in frames.

5 Finding High-Level Events Via Interval Operators

We now briefly illustrate how to use the operators we have defined in the previous section to detect high-level events. For that purpose, in [1] we defined a number of typical video surveillance scenarios involving different variants of package exchanges and a potential car theft[2]. Because of space constraints, here we just show the *Basic Direct Package Exchange (BDPE)* definition.

The *BDPE* occurs when one person carries a package up to a certain frame f_i and then another person has the same package from frame $f_i + 1$ onwards. Formulating the *BDPE* scenario using our operators then boils down to the following expression (M_1 and M_2 are instances of the *interval labeling* M):

$$\begin{aligned}
&\pi_{M_1.arg_1, M_2.arg1, M_1.arg_2, M_1.s_f, M_2.e_f}(\\
&\sigma_{M_1.arg_1 \neq M_2.arg_1 \wedge M_1.arg_2 = M_2.arg_2}(\\
&\ \sigma_{pred=\text{``}hasPkg\text{''}}(M_1)\\
&\quad Bef_{\delta=1}\\
&\ \sigma_{pred=\text{``}hasPkg\text{''}}(M_2)))
\end{aligned}$$

6 Experimental Evaluation

We implemented our operators in a relational database system[3] and evaluated the retrieval and run-time performance of the approach. For more implementation details, please look at [2].

We used three different video data sets as a basis for our experiments: *ITEA CANDELA*[4], which is a publicly available data set with multiple videos depicting a number of (staged) package exchanges and object drop-offs/pick-ups; a benchmark data set about video surveillance at a *train station*[5]; video shots from monitoring a University *parking lot* [9, 10].

We concatenated multiple videos from these data sets to create a single video of about 50 minutes. The interval labeling M was obtained by extracting the frames from this video and annotating them. In the absence of an image processing library and an interval action detector, this was done manually.

First, we evaluate precision and recall measured against a ground truth provided by human annotators. The annotators were informed about the events to discover by providing them with informal descriptions. Second, we also measure the processing time of executing each of the event queries and illustrate how well this processing scales by using different video lengths.

Evaluating Accuracy Table 3(a) summarizes the results obtained by exploiting the well-known *Precision* (P) and *Recall* (R) metrics.

[2] The defined events are: *Basic Direct Package Exchange (BDPE)*, *Direct Package Exchange, Scenario 2 (DPE_2)*, *Basic Indirect Package Exchange (BIPE)*, *Indirect Package Exchange, Scenario 2 (IPE_2)*, *Potential Car Theft (PCT)* and *Unattended Package (UP)*.

[3] We implemented each operator described in Section 4.1 as a stored procedure in *PL/pgSQL* in *PostgreSQL 9.4* and used them to define the events from Section 5. All experiments were conducted on a 2.4 GHz Intel Core i5 machine with 8 GBytes of RAM running Windows 8.

[4] http://www.multitel.be/image/research-development/research-projects/candela/

[5] http://www.cvg.rdg.ac.uk/PETS2006/data.html

Event	Data Set	Occ. Ret.	Grnd Truth	P	R
BDPE	ITEA C.	3	3	1	1
DPE_2	ITEA C.	3	3	1	1
BIPE	ITEA C.	7	4	0.571	1
IPE_2	ITEA C.	4	4	1	1
UP	Station	5	5	1	1
BDPE	Prkg lot	1	1	1	1
DPE_2	Prkg lot	0	1	0	0
BIPE	Prkg lot	4	4	1	1
IPE_2	Prkg lot	4	4	1	1
PCT	Prkg lot	1	1	1	1

(a) Precision/Recall values

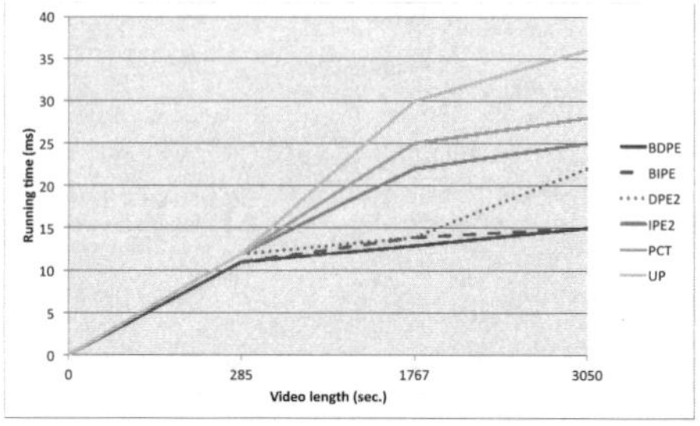

(b) Processing times

Fig. 3: Experimental evaluation

Actually, we checked the reasons for the lower precision value of *BIPE* in *ITEA CANDELA* and found that the false positives were caused by someone dropping off a package and shortly afterwards picking it up again before giving it to another person. Finally, when running the DPE_2 query for the *Parking lot* dataset, we did not get any output, even though there is such an event, i.e., we have a false negative. However, the package exchange took place inside of a car, which made it difficult to detect.

Evaluating Performance For measuring the run-time performance, we have concatenated the three videos, starting with *ITEA CANDELA* (0s - 285s), continuing with the parking lot (285s - 1767s), and ending with the train station (1767s - 3050s), so we could have a longer video and measure run time as a function of video length. The results for running our queries on this long video are shown in Fig. 3(b).

As a final remark we would like to point out that we still see a lot of potential for optimization here. Nevertheless, even a mostly straightforward implementation of the queries already gives us good results: the longest-running query finishes in under 40ms when evaluated for the whole video.

7 Conclusion and Future Work

We propose an event query language based on relational algebra extended by interval relationships. This results in a language with well-defined semantics and powerful, flexible constructs for expressing events, specifically those with temporal constraints often found in applications analyzing video streams.

We have identified two potential areas for improvement, one is on the implementation level, the other is usability. Thus, on the one hand we can increase the performance of our approach by integrating the new operators into the query processing framework of a database management system. On the other hand, we are planning to improve the usability of our approach by adding a layer on top of it. This can be a (declarative) language or a graphical user interface for defining events.

A long-term goal is the realization of the whole framework as shown in Fig. 1. A crucial component here is the image processing library. Nevertheless, we think that an approach based on an interval-extended relational algebra can also be applied to the low-level and interval labeling steps, leading to a fully integrated system for event detection.

References

1. S. Helmer and F. Persia: "High-level Surveillance Event Detection Using an Interval-based Query Language", 2016 IEEE Tenth International Conference on Semantic Computing (ICSC), pp. 39-46, February 2016.
2. S. Helmer and F. Persia: "ISEQL: an Interval-based Surveillance Event Query Language", To appear in International Journal of Multimedia Data Engineering and Management (IJMDEM), 2016.
3. G. Amato, S. Chessa, C. Gennaro, C. Vairo: "Querying moving events in wireless sensor networks", in Pervasive and Mobile Computing, Vol. 16, pp. 51-75, 2015.
4. M. Eckert, F. Bry, S. Brodt, O. Poppe, and S. Hausmann: "Two semantics for CEP, no double talk: Complex event relational algebra (CERA) and its application to XChangeEQ", in Reasoning in Event-Based Distributed Systems (S. Helmer, A. Poulovassilis, and F. Xhafa, eds.), vol. 347 of Studies in Computational Intelligence, pp. 71-97, Springer Berlin Heidelberg, 2011.
5. A. Arasu, S. Babu, and J. Widom: "The CQL continuous query language: Semantic foundations and query execution", The VLDB Journal, vol. 15, pp. 121142, June 2006.
6. J. F. Allen: "Maintaining knowledge about temporal intervals", Commun. ACM, vol. 26, pp. 832843, Nov. 1983.
7. S. Hongeng and R. Nevatia, "Multi-agent event recognition", in Computer Vision, 2001. ICCV 2001. Proceedings. Eighth IEEE International Conference on, vol. 2, pp. 8491 vol.2, 2001.
8. M. Albanese, A. Pugliese, and V. Subrahmanian: "Fast activity detection: Indexing for temporal stochastic automaton-based activity models", Knowledge and Data Engineering, IEEE Transactions on, vol. 25, pp. 360373, Feb 2013.
9. M. Albanese, C. Molinaro, F. Persia, A. Picariello, and V. Subrahmanian: "Discovering the top-k unexplained sequences in time-stamped observation data", Knowledge and Data Engineering, IEEE Transactions on, vol. 26, pp. 577594, March 2014.
10. M. Albanese, C. Molinaro, F. Persia, A. Picariello, and V. S. Subrahmanian: "Finding unexplained activities in video", in IJCAI (T. Walsh, ed.), pp. 16281634, IJCAI/AAAI, 2011.
11. F. Bry and M. Eckert: "Rule-based composite event queries: The language xchange eq and its semantics".
12. M. Albanese, R. Chellappa, N. Cuntoor, V. Moscato, A. Picariello, V. Subrahmanian, and O. Udrea: "Pads: A probabilistic activity detection framework for video data", Pattern Analysis and Machine Intelligence, IEEE Transactions on, vol. 32, pp. 22462261, Dec 2010.
13. K. Walzer, T. Breddin, and M. Groch: "Relative temporal constraints in the rete algorithm for complex event detection", in Proceedings of the Second International Conference on Distributed Event-based Systems, DEBS 08, (New York, NY, USA), pp. 147155, ACM, 2008.

Completeness, Correctness and Freshness of Cloud-Managed Data Streams

Francesco Buccafurri, Gianluca Lax, Serena Nicolazzo, and Antonino Nocera

DIIES, University Mediterranea of Reggio Calabria
Via Graziella, Località Feo di Vito
89122 Reggio Calabria, Italy
E-mail:{bucca,lax,s.nicolazzo,a.nocera}@unirc.it

Discussion Paper

Abstract. Cloud computing provides users with the possibility to store their data in third-party servers. These data centers may be untrusted or susceptible to attacks, hence they could produce incorrect answers to query. This paper presents a new approach allowing users to verify that their query results are complete (no data are omitted), correct (the result values are not corrupted), and fresh (the newest version of the results is returned). The scheme is intended for range selection on ordered attributes of a relational database. Moreover, the proposed technique is computationally affordable and particularly suited for data streams in which the frequency of data insertion is very high.

Keywords Cloud Computing, Range Queries, Integrity.

1 Introduction

Cloud computing has recently emerged as an innovative paradigm leading towards the availability of ubiquitous access to resources and computation capabilities to everyone. This raises significant drawbacks in terms of data security and privacy [12, 3, 1]. Indeed, users cannot have any assurance about the integrity of query results on data saved in the cloud, because servers can be malicious, hacked or lazy [13, 7, 8].

In this work, we propose a new approach to allow the verification of query result integrity in cloud. The term integrity means that results has to be *(i)* complete, i.e., no record satisfying the query conditions is omitted in the response, *(ii)* fresh, i.e., the results refer to the latest version of the database, and *(iii)* correct, i.e., the result records are not corrupted. In our work, we make explicit reference to a scenario with a network of *battery-powered cameras* (such as drones, micro-drones, insect spy drones) that monitor a high size area and store images into a cloud server. Besides allowing data storage, this server provides an interface to access data and to perform query processing on behalf of the data owner, who administrates and analyzes query results in accordance to specific application-related requirements. Due to the *battery-powered* nature of the cameras, the recording is enabled only on request to allow battery saving. As battery saving assumes a very important aspect, excessive computation on recording sensors should be avoided. Typical solutions in this scenario are based on Merkle Hash Tree schemes [11, 9, 16, 5], which impose not negligible overheads and computational efforts for insertion operations. As for this aspect, our proposal reduces from logarithmic to constant the space and time complexity of insertion operations, yet maintaining the same complexity as the approaches of the state of the art for verifying the integrity of query results.

The paper is organized as follows. In the next section, we make the comparison with related works. Then, in Section 3, we describe our approach focusing on the data population protocol and the integrity verification protocol. We present the security analysis of our approach in Section 4. Finally, we draw our conclusions and future directions in Section 5.

2 Related work

Integrity of queries relies on the verification of the correctness, the completeness and the freshness of query results.

In the literature, all the existing solutions mainly belong to two kinds of families: probabilistic and deterministic [12]. The first family is composed of techniques providing probabilistic models to detect integrity violations [15, 4, 14, 2].

As for the deterministic approaches, which our proposal belongs to, they detect integrity violations with certainty relying on some additional data that the server should add to the response. These additional data are called verification objects. To make an example, Pang et. al. [11] use signature chaining schemas to organize tuples in a chain so that each record is signed with the information from two neighboring records in the ordered sequence. Therefore, this scheme allows the user to verify whether the result of selection query is continuous by checking the aggregated signature. A further deterministic scheme, called MAC Chain, is proposed in [6], in which a model based on HMAC to verify query results integrity is adopted. This approach implements the verification process on the TTP (Trusted Third Party); moreover, to support query integrity verification, the data owner has to alter the outsourced relation structure by inserting some verification objects. However, such additional objects are computed by means of a MAC taking all the tuple values into account. These two characteristics make this approach not particularly suitable in our scenario in which insertion in the database is very frequent. Other deterministic approaches are presented in [9, 16, 5, 10]. They are essentially based on Merkle tree and its variation (i.e., MB-Tree). From the computational point of view, we reduce the insertion operation cost to O(1) space and time, from O(log n) obtained by Merkle-tree-based solutions [9, 16, 5, 10]. Observe that, the number of markers is not proportional to the number of tuples, so that the identification of the block involved by a query is done in constant time.

3 Basic Approach

Our approach to verify query-result integrity can be classified as a deterministic technique [12]. This type of approach makes use of authenticated data structure and allows the verification of a query result through verification objects that should be included in the results. In the following of this section, we will present our scheme in detail. We start by introducing some basic definitions.

Definition 1. *Given a camera device s_i, we define the image sequence generated by s_i as: $F^i = \{f^i_{t_1}, f^i_{t_2}, \ldots, f^i_{t_n}\}$, where: (i) $f^i_{t_j}$ is the image captured at the instant t_j for each $1 \leq j \leq n$ and (ii) $t_j < t_{j+1}$ (i.e., the instant t_j comes before t_{j+1} in time) for each $1 \leq j < n$.*

In words, an image sequence represents a track associated with a camera device and independent sequences for different devices are maintained. Each image together with all support attributes (such as timestamp, geographic coordinates, etc.) is stored as a new tuple in the database. Therefore, throughout the paper, we will refer to a tuple as an element of an image sequence.

Definition 2. *Given two instants t_l and t_u with $t_1 \leq t_l \leq t_u \leq t_n$,* a range query *$Q^i(t_l, t_u)$ on F^i asks for all the images $f^i_{t_x}$ such that $t_l \leq t_x \leq t_u$.*

Basically, a range query is defined as a request to obtain all the images recorded by a given device s_i during the interval $[t_l, t_u]$, where t_l and t_u, with $t_l \leq t_u$, are valid timestamps during the device recording lifecycle, i.e., its total recording interval $[t_1, t_n]$.

Given a device image sequence F^i, our approach works by organizing database tuples associated with F^i in a chain. The link between two elements is built so that the owner can always verify the chain validity. Specifically, given a tuple $\hat{f}^i_{t_j} = \langle a_1, \ldots, a_p \rangle$, where $a_1 = t_j$ is the tuple timestamp, and $a_2, \ldots, a_p$ are further attributes, our approach modifies it by adding an attribute encoding a link towards the next tuple in our database according to the timestamp value. Therefore, the modified tuple has now the following structure $\hat{f}^i_{t_j} = \langle t_j, attr_2, \ldots, attr_p, MAC \rangle$, where the attribute MAC is a message authentication code and is computed by means of the function $HMAC(v, K_i)$ implementing the $HMAC$ protocol with SHA-256 as cryptographic hash function, $v = (f^i_{t_j} || e)$, K_i is a secret shared by the s_i camera and the data owner, and e can be either the next tuple $\hat{f}^i_{t_{j+1}}$ of s_i, or a special element defined hereafter. Indeed, the chain is completed with the insertion of dummy entries representing *markers* that are used to both validate the head of the chain and to reduce the integrity verification costs by splitting F^i in time buckets. These elements are pre-added in the database and are known to all the actors involved in our scenario (i.e., they are part of the public scheme of our protocol). Figure 1 shows the structure of the chain where dashed elements $d_{T_w} \ldots d_{T_{w+1}}$ represent *markers*, whereas the grey ones are normal tuples.

Concerning the *markers*, they have the following basic structure: $d_{T_w} = \langle T_w, ID_b \rangle$, where T_w is the *marker* pre-fixed time (i.e., T_w is chosen by the owner during the system initialization phase), and ID_b is the bucket identifier. Clearly, each *marker* has also to maintain different attributes, namely $MAC_1, \ldots, MAC_n$, representing links to devices $s_1, \ldots, s_n$, to complete the in-

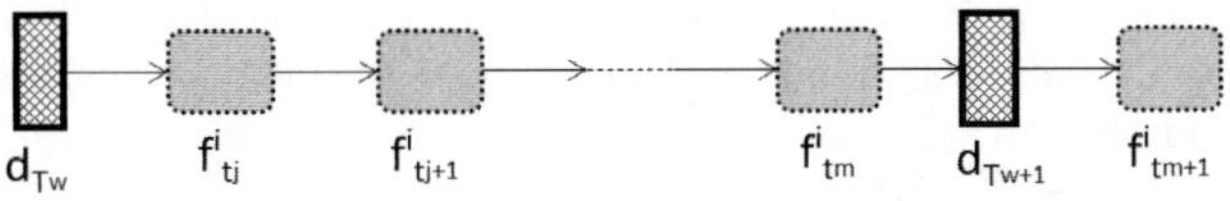

Fig. 1. An example of the chain of a single device image sequence.

tegrity chain described above. Therefore, the complete structure of *markers* will be: $\hat{d}_{T_w} = \langle T_w, ID_b, MAC_1, \ldots, MAC_n \rangle$, where MAC_i is a message authentication code associated with the device s_i and is computed by means of the function $HMAC(v^i, K_i)$ implementing the $HMAC$ protocol with SHA-256 as cryptographic hash function, $v^i = T_w || ID_b || e$, K_i is a secret shared by the s_i camera and the data owner, and e can be either the next s_i tuple $f^i_{t_{j+1}}$ (the first tuple in the corresponding bucket) or the next *marker* $d_{T_{w+1}}$.

According to our scheme, the number of *markers* and their time position (T_w) are established on the basis of the database life period: the *marker* time positions can be simply uniformly distributed in the whole database life period or can follow specific patterns decided by the owner. For instance, he may decide to intensify the number of *markers* during specific time intervals, such as rush hours or critical daily moments. Initial *marker* values are stored in `m_tab`. During this phase, all system entities are informed of the exact position of each *marker*. Observe that, in this initialization phase, the values of each attribute MAC_i is set to *null*.

Now, if the camera s_i wants to insert a new tuple, the procedure is as follows. In the initial phase, no previous tuples have been inserted so the table associated with the camera sequence F^i, say s_i`_tab`, is empty. In this case, s_i has to link the new tuple to the *marker* with the higher time position T_w such that $t_j \geq T_w$, where t_j is the tuple timestamp. Therefore, once the right *marker* has been found, s_i will perform an update on `m_tab` to set the attribute $MAC_i = HMAC(d_{T_w} || f^i_{t_j}, K_i)$ of the *marker* $\hat{d}_{T_w}$. After this, it inserts the new tuple in s_i`_tab` with its MAC attribute set to *null* and also stores it altogether with the time position T_{w+1} of the next *marker* in its local memory. The memorization of these parameters is useful for future insertions as will be clearer in the following. Observe that, we assume that the data owner can always read the device-onboard memory, thus at every moment he can know the timestamp of the last tuple inserted by each device.

Consider now the case in which a device, say s_i, has to insert a new tuple in a non-empty table. Let t_j be the timestamp of the last inserted tuple and t_z be the timestamp of the tuple being inserted. Moreover let T_{w+1} be the *marker* time that s_i stored in its local memory during the previous insertion and T_{w+2} be the next *marker*, we can identify three possibilities:

1. $\mathbf{t_z < T_{w+1}}$. In this case, the new tuple will belong to the existing bucket delimited by *markers* with time position T_w and T_{w+1}. Therefore, to maintain the chain, the tuple will be linked to the previous inserted element. To do so, the device performs an update on s_i`_tab` to change the MAC attribute of the previous inserted tuple from MAC =*null* to $MAC = HMAC(f^i_{t_j}||f^i_{t_z}, K_i)$ and insert the new tuple in the database. Finally, it update the last inserted tuple in its local memory.

2. $\mathbf{T_{w+1} \leq t_z < T_{w+2}}$. The tuple will belong to a new bucket right next the current one; then, s_i will perform an update on s_i`_tab` to change the MAC attribute of the previous inserted tuple from *null* to $HMAC(f^i_{t_j}||d_{T_{w+1}}, K_i)$, an update on `m_tab` to set $MAC_i = HMAC(d_{T_{w+1}}||f^i_{t_z}, K_i)$ for the row corresponding to the *marker* with time position T_{w+1}. Finally, it inserts the new tuple in s_i`_tab` with the MAC attribute set to *null* and also stores it altogether with the time position T_{w+2} of the next *marker* in its local memory.

3. $\mathbf{t_z \geq T_{w+2}}$. In this case, the tuple will belong to a new non-adjacent bucket; therefore, starting from the *marker* with time T_{w+1}, s_i has to find the *marker* with the higher time position T_{w+q} (with $q > 1$) such that $t_z \geq T_{w+q}$. Then, s_i will perform an update on s_i`_tab` to change the MAC attribute of the previous inserted tuple from *null* to $HMAC(f^i_{t_j}||d_{T_{w+1}}, K_i)$, two updates on `m_tab`, the first to set the attribute $MAC_i = HMAC(d_{T_{w+1}}||d_{T_{w+q}}, K_i)$ for the row corresponding to the *marker* $\hat{d}_{T_{w+1}}$ and the second to set the attribute $MAC_i = HMAC(d_{T_{w+q}}||f^i_{t_z}, K_i)$ for the row corresponding to the *marker* $\hat{d}_{T_{w+q}}$. Finally, it inserts the new tuple in s_i`_tab` with the MAC attribute set to *null* and also stores it altogether with the time position T_{w+q+1} of the next *marker* in its local memory.

Our approach implements also an aging mechanism for automatically deleting older tuples to limit the database size. Deletion is carried out only on discrete time intervals, i.e., only the removal of an entire non-empty bucket at a time is allowed. In this mechanism, the *markers* play a key role. Indeed, as only discrete deletion is allowed, each *marker* represents a milestone maintaining device chains when previous elements are removed. Data owner can always compute the first *marker* in the database still valid.

Suppose the data owner submits the range query $Q^i(t_l, t_u)$, meaning that all snapshots recorded by the device s_i in the time interval $[t_l, t_u]$ should be returned intact as result. Our protocol enforces that the query processor module, cloud-side located, returns the tuples belonging to all the buckets involved in the interval $[t_l, t_u]$ along with all the *markers* linked to elements of such buckets. Moreover, as additional information, the data owner knows the time position of each *marker* and, for each device, knows the last tuple inserted in the database. Observe that, this requirement is easy to satisfy because all devices have an internal memory in which this information is stored and we assume that the data owner can access it at every moment. To verify the integrity of the result obtained, the data owner performs the following steps.

(1) First, he verifies the head and tail of the chain. Specifically, as for the head he verifies if the time value of the first *marker*, say T_f, is lower than or equal to t_l. Concerning the tail, instead, we can identify two cases: *(i)* t_u is lower than or equal to the time value of the last *marker* of the query result. In this case the tail is verified and no further checks are required. *(ii)* t_u is greater than

the time value of the last *marker* of the query result. In this case the owner has also to verify if the last tuple stored by s_i is present in the query result.

(2) Then, starting from the first *marker*, he verifies each chain link by iteratively computing the MAC attribute of each element and comparing it with the value returned by the cloud.

4 Security analysis

In this section, we carry out a security analysis of our approach to check if it fulfils its intended purpose also in presence of attacks from the cloud server. Therefore, in the following, we describe the security model and analyze the security properties of our proposal. Concerning this aspect, we may identify the following properties our system has to assure:

SP1. The result of a range query has to be complete, it means that no tuples or attributes are omitted (including *markers*).

SP2. The result of a range query has to be fresh. It means that the data owner can check whether the newest version of the result is returned.

SP3. The result of a range query has to be correct. It means that the data owner can verify that all the values in a query result have not been corrupted, nor have spurious records been introduced.

To analyze the security properties above, our threat model includes the following assumptions:

A1. The camera devices and the data owner are trusted, unbreakable, and dependable.

A2. A secure communication between database and camera devices is established.

A3. Collision, preimage and second preimage attacks on the cryptographic hash function, used by $HMAC$, are infeasible.

Concerning the compliance with SP1, our approach has to resist attacks in which the cloud server may attempt to return incomplete results. We may identify four possible ways the cloud can reach this goal:

The cloud returns an empty set. In this case, the data owner checks whether there exists a last inserted tuple. In the affirmative case, the attack is detected.

The cloud tries to omit some tuples of a query result. In this case, the data owner can check that the result is incomplete by verifying the chain linking all the result elements inside each bucket. Therefore, thanks to Assumption **A3**, this attack is contrasted.

The cloud server does not return a whole internal bucket. Also this attack is not possible because, in the first step of the integrity verification protocol, the data owner identifies the chain header and tail and then, in the second step, verifies the whole chain integrity. Therefore, any missing bucket is detected because the corresponding links in the chain will be missing too, thus causing an interruption in the chain.

The cloud server does not return elements or buckets at the edges of the query result. This attack makes sense only in the case of *unbounded* query, i.e., for query in which one or both interval ends are not fixed. As for the verification of the left-hand bucket, the owner can always identify the first *marker* because this information is part of the public scheme. This is true also in case of deletion, because the owner can always compute the first oldest valid *marker*. In the case of a right unbounded query, the owner can verify the completeness of the result by checking whether the last tuple inserted by the considered device is present.

To be compliant with **SP2**, our approach should resist attacks in which the cloud server tries to return the query result computed on an old complete version of the database. This kind of attack can always be detected by the data owner because he knows the last tuple inserted in the database. Indeed, the MAC attribute of each tuple can be either *null* or assume its final value (i.e., no further updates are allowed after the initialization). Moreover, no *null* MAC attribute value may exist for elements older than the last inserted tuple. Then, an old version of the result can be detected if there exists a tuple older than the last inserted in the database with a *null* MAC attribute.

The compliance with **SP3** requires that our approach guarantees data correctness. We may identify three cases:

The cloud server adds a whole bucket or a single tuple in the query result. However, due to assumptions **A1** and **A3**, no valid MAC attribute can be generated without a secret key stored in the device firmware.

The cloud server compromises some tuples or *markers* in the query result. Also this attack cannot succeed because of the above reasoning on MAC attributes.

The cloud server tries to mix data recorded by different devices. Observe that, each device s_i owns a private key K_i, therefore, due to assumptions **A1** and **A3**, this attack is not possible.

5 Conclusion

In this paper, we presented a scheme for the verification of range queries done on untrusted servers of a cloud computing scenario. Our scheme enables users to have proof of the integrity of query results in terms of completeness, correctness and freshness. In the referred scenario, typical solutions, which are based on digital signature schemes or Merkle Hash Tree, have drawbacks related to to the cost of data insertions, which our proposal overcomes. The security analysis of our approach proved that it guarantees query answer integrity also in presence of attacks from the cloud server.

Acknowledgment

This work has been partially supported by the Program "Programma Operativo Nazionale Ricerca e Competitività" 2007-2013, Distretto Tecnologico CyberSecurity funded by the Italian Ministry of Education, University and Research.

References

1. F. Buccafurri, G. Lax, S. Nicolazzo, and A. Nocera. A Privacy-Preserving Solution for Tracking People in Critical Environments. In *Proc. of the International Workshop on Computers, Software & Applications (COMPSAC'14)*, pages 146–151, Västerås, Sweden, 2014. IEEE Computer Society.
2. F. Buccafurri, G. Lax, S. Nicolazzo, and A. Nocera. Generating k-anonymous logs of people tracing systems in surveilled environments. In *SEBD*, pages 37–44, 2014.
3. F. Buccafurri, G. Lax, S. Nicolazzo, and A. Nocera. Accountability-preserving anonymous delivery of cloud services. In *Trust, Privacy and Security in Digital Business*, pages 124–135. Springer, 2015.
4. S. De Capitani di Vimercati, S. Foresti, S. Jajodia, S. Paraboschi, and P. Samarati. Integrity for join queries in the cloud. *Cloud Computing, IEEE Transactions on*, 1(2):187–200, 2013.
5. P. Devanbu, M. Gertz, C. Martel, and S. G. Stubblebine. Authentic data publication over the internet. *Journal of Computer Security*, 11(3):291–314, 2003.
6. J. Hong, T. Wen, Q. Gu, and G. Sheng. Query integrity verification based-on mac chain in cloud storage. In *Computer and Information Science (ICIS), 2014 IEEE/ACIS 13th International Conference on*, pages 125–129. IEEE, 2014.
7. M. Jensen, J. Schwenk, N. Gruschka, and L. L. Iacono. On technical security issues in cloud computing. In *Cloud Computing, 2009. CLOUD'09. IEEE International Conference on*, pages 109–116. IEEE, 2009.
8. L. M. Kaufman. Data security in the world of cloud computing. *Security & Privacy, IEEE*, 7(4):61–64, 2009.
9. F. Li, M. Hadjieleftheriou, G. Kollios, and L. Reyzin. Authenticated index structures for aggregation queries. *ACM Transactions on Information and System Security (TISSEC)*, 13(4):32, 2010.
10. M. S. Niaz and G. Saake. Merkle hash tree based techniques for data integrity of outsourced data. In *GvD*, pages 66–71, 2015.
11. H. Pang, A. Jain, K. Ramamritham, and K.-L. Tan. Verifying completeness of relational query results in data publishing. In *Proceedings of the 2005 ACM SIGMOD international conference on Management of data*, pages 407–418. ACM, 2005.
12. P. Samarati. Data security and privacy in the cloud. In *ISPEC*, pages 28–41. Springer, 2014.
13. S. Subashini and V. Kavitha. A survey on security issues in service delivery models of cloud computing. *Journal of network and computer applications*, 34(1):1–11, 2011.
14. H. Wang, J. Yin, C.-s. Perng, and P. S. Yu. Dual encryption for query integrity assurance. In *Proceedings of the 17th ACM conference on Information and knowledge management*, pages 863–872. ACM, 2008.
15. M. Xie, H. Wang, J. Yin, and X. Meng. Integrity auditing of outsourced data. In *Proceedings of the 33rd international conference on Very large data bases*, pages 782–793. VLDB Endowment, 2007.
16. Z. Yang, S. Gao, J. Xu, and B. Choi. Authentication of range query results in mapreduce environments. In *Proceedings of the third international workshop on Cloud data management*, pages 25–32. ACM, 2011.

Activity-based Carpooling with ComeWithMe
Discussion Paper

Vinicius Monterio de Lira[1], Salvatore Rinzivillo[2], Valeria Cesario Times[1] , Chiara Renso[2], Raffaele Perego[2]

[1] Universidade Federal de Pernambuco, Recife, Brazil
{vcml, vct}@cin.ufpe.br
[2] ISTI - CNR, Pisa, Italy
{salvatore.rinzivillo, chiara.renso, raffaele.perego}@isti.cnr.it

Abstract. The interest in carpooling is increasing due to the need to reduce traffic and noise pollution. Most of the available approaches and systems are *route oriented*, where driver and passeggers are matched when the destination location is the same. *ComeWithMe* offers a new perspective: the destination is the intended activity instead of a location. This novel matching method is aimed to boost the possibilities of rides if passenger reaches a different location maintaining the activity. We conducted experiments using a real data set of trajectories and our results showed that the proposed matching algorithm improved the traditional carpooling approach in more than 80.0%.

1 Introduction

Carpooling is one of the many travel alternatives promoted by transport policies to reduce the amount of vehicles on the road. The main targets here are the reduction of transport-related pollution, noise nuisance reduction, decrease of congestion levels and minimization of the necessity for parking spaces [1], [2]. It is a broad research area and covers both running carpooling systems and several algorithmic approaches.

In a carpooling system essentially there is a *matching* phase between a driver and a rider in order to get to a destination together. In general, it means that the paths performed by these people have moving stretches of common interest, and therefore they can share a vehicle for a given trip. In most of the cases the destination is fixed and cannot be changed (e.g. go to work).

Among the running systems we can recall CarpoolWorld [3], Djengo [4], Carpooling.com and Carpool.ca. These systems have similar functionalities like search for occasional lifts and regular lifts and matching of rides for groups of users like groups in school, events or companies. Users can have two different roles in the system: *driver* or *passenger* they fill out their profiles providing some personal information.

[3] http://www.carpoolworld.com

[4] http://www.djengo.be

Here we propose a different scenario where the destination is not fixed and it can be changed assuming that the activity to be done (e.g. shopping, eating...) is preserved. Indeed, we noticed that some human activities are not strictly associated with a unique place. For example, if a person wants to have dinner at an Italian restaurant, the user has a wide amount of places to choose to perform this activity. Therefore, for some categories of places, the user can change his destination and he can still perform the same desired activity.

The full version of this work has been presented in [3] where we propose a novel *activity-oriented* carpool method called *ComeWithMe*. We focus on the user's desired activity, rather than than the final destination thus increasing the number of possible rides.

The remainder of this article is organized as follows. Section 2 presents the activity-oriented carpooling method. Section 3 summarizes the results gathered from our experimental evaluation. Section 4 concludes our main findings and lists future works.

2 Methodology

ComeWithMe receives as input a dataset of Points Of Interests (POIs), a set of intervals, a spatial grid, a set of carpooling requests and a dataset of routine trips and produces as output a list of possible matches for carpooling. This process is illustrated in Figure 1 and detailed as follows.

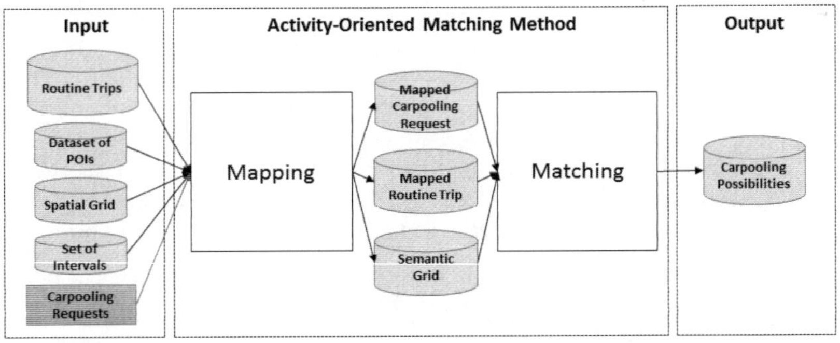

Fig. 1. Schema of the ComeWithMe Process

The *dataset of POIs* provides latitude, longitude, the category and the opening time. The category is mapped to activities while the opening hours indicate when the POI is available. The *set of intervals* corresponds to slices of the day, while the *spatial grid* slices the geographic region of interest into cells corresponding to the area for carpooling pick-up and drop-off. A *carpooling request* represents the need for a ride from a starting point, to a place where to perform the intended activity, and includes a pick-up point, a pick-up time, the destination activity.

The *routine trip* corresponds to a regular trip made by a user like the daily path from home to work. The user who performs a routine trip assumes the role of a potential driver.

Given the input data, the carpooling matching method is composed of two phases: the *Mapping* and the *Matching*. The Mapping phase maps the trips (routine and requests) to the spatial grid, while the Matching phase defines which routine trips can be used for satisfying the users' requests of rides.

The mapping phase is a preparation phase to adapt the Carpooling Requests (CRs) and the routine trips (RTs) for the matching algorithm where both RTs and CRs are mapped into the spatial grid.

We map the POIs location to the corresponding cell in the spatial grid. Then, using the temporal properties and the set of intervals, we also map the availability of the cell according to the business time of the place. Mapping the dataset of POIs to the spatial grid using these two properties gives us a *semantic grid* representing the availability of the POIs for a given category.

The RT is mapped to the semantic grid as a sequence of visited cells associated to the respective visited intervals.

In a Carpooling Request, the desired activity is mapped to the POI categories that are associated to the activity. The departure point is mapped to cell where it is located and the departure and arrival schedule are associated to their corresponding interval from the set of intervals.

The *Spatiotemporal Reallocation Matching* algorithm realizes the matching phase scanning the set of *Mapped Carpooling Requests* that can possibly be supplied using the *Mapped Routine Trips*. The term *Reallocation* indicates the possibility of making spatial and/or temporal changes in the original trip. This is the novel idea of our approach with respect to the classical carpooling. Here we assume that the destination of a request can be "reallocated" to a different destination preserving the activity to be performed. Therefore, if the desired activity category is for example *shopping food*, then the reallocation operation tries to find destinations for the passenger where it is possible to perform *shopping food*. Thus, we assume that the user is able to perform the desired activity even postponing or anticipating the activity execution. The proposed algorithm relies on two assumptions: (1) the CR and the RT are performed by different users; and (2) for a given Mapped Carpooling Request, the departure cell and the arrival cell are always different.

The *Spatiotemporal Reallocation Matching* algorithm is presented in Algorithm 1 while Table 1 details the condition clauses of each function of the algorithm.

The algorithm receives as input one Mapped Carpooling Request (Θ), one Mapped Routine Trip (γ), a Semantic Grid (sg) and a time window (tw) to enable time reallocations. Firstly, in line 1, the function GetPickupCells checks the picking-up possibilities for the passenger. Next, in line 3, the function GetDestinationCells finds the possible destinations for the carpooling request. Finally, in line 5, based on the direction of the Mapped Routine Trip the function checks if the request of carpooling (MCR) can actually be supplied. All steps are eliminatory, in sense that the second step is performed only if the return of the first step is not empty and so on.

Algorithm 1 Spatiotemporal Reallocation Matching

Require: Θ, γ, sg, tw

Ensure: True, if there is matching; False, if there is not.

```
1. pcs = (Θ, γ, sg, tw);
2. if exists (pcs) then
3.    dcs = GetDestinationCells(Θ, γ, sg, tw)
4.    if exists (dcs) then
5.       return CheckOrientation(pcs, dcs);
6.    end if
7. end if
8. return False;
```

1. GetPickupCells: it returns true when there is a spatial possibility to pick up the passenger of the MCR(Θ) using the current MRT (γ). When there is not such possibility it returns false. The departure cell of the ride is always defined by the MCR ($\Theta.dptCell$). The time window (tw) represents a shift of the time anticipating or delaying the departure time of the passenger.
2. GetDestinationCells: this function searches for all available destination cells in the Semantic Grid (sg) of the category (Θ.ctgId) visited by the MRT during the interval between Θ.dptIntv - tw and Θ.arvIntv + tw. Thus, more places and more temporal options are considered as destination of the rides.
3. CheckOrientation: This verification represents the obvious condition that the driver during his trip must first pass into the pickup cell to pickup the passenger and thus next pass into the destination cell to drop off the passenger, of course respecting the visit sequence of the cells.

3 Experimental Evaluation

Intending to corroborate our idea, we propose an evaluation process to prove the efficacy of *ComeWithMe*. The intention is to evaluate the amount of carpool request that could be potentially supplied by exploiting our approach. The basic idea is to analyse an historical trajectories datasets to identify the *Routine trips* and *Occasional trips*. The *Occasional trips* are then mapped to *Carpooling Requests*.

The dataset of real car trajectories has been collected in the city of Florence in Italy. We have 44.278 trips, made by 5.048 users moving during the weekdays for the period from 01/05/2011 to 31/05/2011. This dataset has been provided by

Steps	Conditions
GetPickupCells	γ.Cells *where*(Cell == Θ.dptCell *and* Intv *between* Θ.dptIntv-tw *and* Θ.arvIntv+tw)
GetDestinationCells	γ.Cells *where*(Cell in sg.CellsFor(Θ.ctgId, Θ.dptIntv, Θ.arvIntv) *and* Intv *between* Θ.dptIntv-tw AND Θ.arvIntv+tw)
CheckOrientation	min(γ.(Cells in CellPickUps).Seqn) < max(γ.(Cells in CellDestinations).Seqn)

Table 1. Constraint clauses for each function of the algorithm

OctoTelematics[5] company which installed a GPS device on cars for an insurance company.

Figure 2 shows the instantiation of the *ComeWithMe* approach for the evaluation process. We notice that we have four modules: Input, Pre-Processing, Matching and Output.

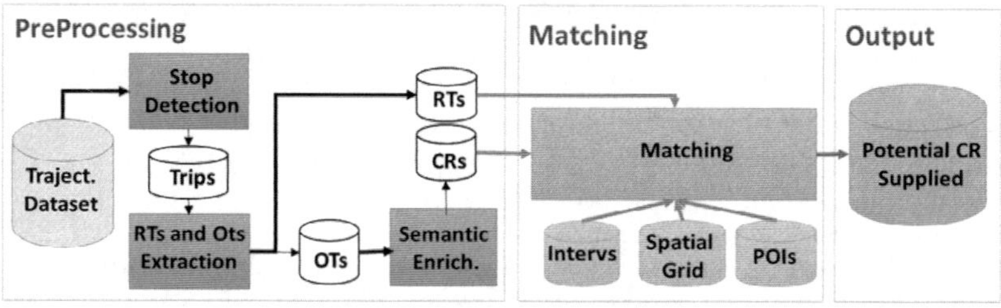

Fig. 2. The *ComeWithMe* Evaluation Process

Starting from a set of raw GPS trajectories, the first step is the pre-processing, where stops are detected: this step splits the data set of trajectories into single trips. The stops were detected using a spatiotemporal threshold $\delta = 50$ meters and time interval i of 20 minutes. The second step aims to separate the routine from the occasional trips. We use the method described in [4] for the extraction of a set of the users routine trips from a set of trajectories. Once we detect the routine trips, we classify all other trips (that do not belong to any similarity cluster) as *occasional* trips. A total of 36.593 trips were classified as occasional trips (OT). The remaining amount of 7.685 trips belong to the clusters of routine trips. From these, a total of 1.122 representative routine trips (RT) were

[5] http://www.octotelematics.com

extracted to summarize these routines. To match an occasional trip OT to a carpooling request CR, we need to infer the intended activity of the OT. Basically, we exploit an heuristics to associate each end point of the trip to a specific POI, thus its associated category can represent the activity. At the end of this step, each occasional trip has an activity destination. We thus convert an occasional trip OT into a carpooling request CR by extracting the departure point, the departure time, the category of the destination POI (associated to an activity) and the arrival time.

We compute from a set of Carpooling Request (Θ) the percentage of requests that could be potentially supplied by exploiting the Routine Trips and by keeping the destination activity of the original Occasional Trip. We performed this evaluation considering different values for the parameters: Spatial grid cell size α and the time window size tw. Using the parameters α and tw, the *match* function checks for each request Θ_t the possibility of ride, if there is at least one ride possibility, the function returns 1, else returns 0. The percentage is the ratio between the sum of supplied carpooling requests and the total amount of request.

The dataset of Points of Interests provides the basic information used to infer the destination activity and the POI temporal availability (opening time). We downloaded a dataset using the API from Foursquare[6]. Since the business hours of some POIs were unknown, we set some default values according to the category.

We used a set of intervals with fixed size of 30 minutes and we performed the experiment with four different sizes of time window tw: 30 minutes, 1 hour, 2 hours and 4 hours.

The Spatial Grid covers an area of 173.49 square kilometers of Florence, 11.790 km height and 14.720 km of width such that all the stops are mapped to the cells. In our experiments we used 3 different combinations of size for the cells (α): 250 meters, 500 meters and 1 kilometer.

We conducted tests to compare our method with a traditional matching for carpooling considered as our baseline. The algorithm BaselineM is described in [3] and keeps the focus on the spatial and temporal aspects disregarding the destination activity. The baseline strictly checks the match between a Mapped Routine Trip (γ) and a Mapped Carpool Request (Θ). In this scenario, the MCR is interpreted as a request for a ride to a specific destination location at specific arrival and departure times.

Figure 3 shows the line graph of the percentage of CRs potentially supplied ($Pot^{CR_{Sup}}$) for each test configuration and reports the main results of the comparison of our algorithm with the baseline BaselineM. As expected, the proposed algorithm, using spatial reallocation, substantially increase the possibilities of carpooling for the tested configurations of α and tw. The potential of supplied requests increases when the values of α and tw are increased, reaching the maximum percentage of potentially supplied requests when these values are the largest. This is understandable since the larger the values of the parame-

[6] www.foursquare.com

ters α and tw are, the less restricting about spatial and temporal aspects the algorithm is. In other words, increasing the parameter tw increases the tolerance of the passenger to change his schedule to perform the desired activity. Also, the more the value of the parameter α is increased, the higher the tolerance to walk. In addition, when the number of grid cells is small, the empty cells tend to disappear replaced by larger cells containing more POIs. As expected, for all investigated test configurations, our algorithm produced the best performance gains, indicating that, in almost all the cases, if the passengers have the flexibility to change the place to go and the time to go, then *ComeWithMe* provides the higher probability of finding an available ride to reach their destinations and perform their intended activities. In our experiments, the maximum gain produced by the Spatiotemporal Reallocation Matching when compared to the Baseline Matching was equals to +83% (92% - 9%) and it was found using $\alpha = 0.5km$ and $tw = 0.5hour$. It shows a significant advantage of our method compared to the baseline approach.

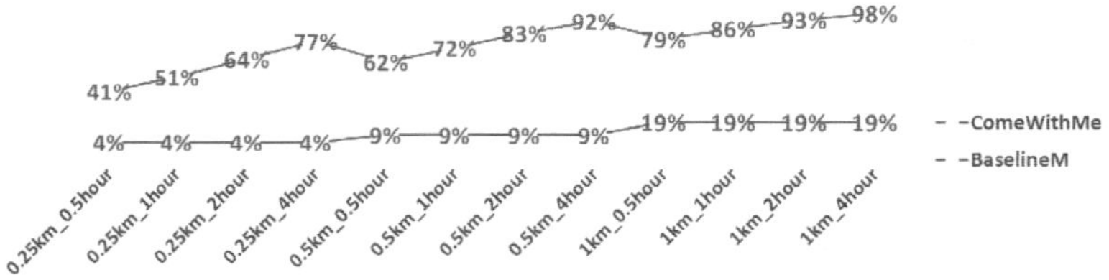

Fig. 3. Percentage of CRs Potentially Supplied ($Pot^{CR_{Sup}}$)

For a more applied practical visualization of the results of our experiments, Table 2 shows the amount in kilometers of occasional trips potentially avoided from the supplied carpooling requests. As expected the values for our proposed algorithm reached values much higher than the baseline approach (BaselineM). These values represent a positive impact for the traffic and the environment. If we consider that using 1 liter of gasoline, a normal car performs about 10 km the lowest result (50.203 km) could save 5.020 liters of gasoline, while the highest (106.786 km), 10.678 liters. These gas savings represent less pollutant for the atmosphere and lower cost for the drivers, since they can share the cost of the trips.

4 Conclusions

The *ComeWithMe* carpool matching method is based on the idea that some activities can be performed at a different number of places, as well as can be postponed or anticipated according to the person convenience. Our matching algorithm works with the possibilities of spatial and temporal reallocation of the trips. We experimented *ComeWithMe* defining first an evaluation process where

Algorithm	*tw*	α = 0.25km	α = 0.5km	α = 1km
BaselineM	0.5hour	5.333 km	10.260 km	18.030 km
	1hour	5.333 km	10.260 km	18.030 km
	2hours	5.333 km	10.260 km	18.030 km
	4hours	5.333 km	10.260 km	18.030 km
ComeWithMe	0.5hour	50.203 km	72.281 km	86.727 km
	1hour	61.101 km	82.716 km	94.353 km
	2hours	75.998 km	94.634 km	101.248 km
	4hours	91.137 km	105.061 km	106.786 km

Table 2. Kilometers of the OTs Potentially Avoided

an historical dataset of trajectories has been used to simulate the carpooling request and the possible rides. As a metric evaluation, we compared the percentage of carpooling requests that could be potentially supplied by our method to a baseline algorithm implementing a traditional carpooling method. The results showed how the carpooling practice can be considerably improved using *ComeWithMe* since we reached a gain of +83% when compared to the baseline method. We are improving the method towards several directions. An interesting point is to refine the evaluation method taking into account the individual willingness to change the destination to take a ride. We also intend to develop a mobile application to provide such carpooling service.

Acknowledgment

This work was partially supported by EU FP7 MarieCurie project SEEK (no. 295179) and also by Conselho Nacional de Desenvolvimento Cientfico e Tecnolgico (CNPq), under the grant 246263/2012-1.

References

1. T. Vanoutrive, E. Van De Vijver, L. Van Malderen, B. Jourquin, I. Thomas, A. Verhetsel, and F. Witlox, "What determines carpooling to workplaces in Belgium: Location, organisation, or promotion?" *Journal of Transport Geography*, vol. 22, pp. 77–86, 2012.
2. A. Dixit, S. Bora, S. Chemate, and N. Kolpekwar, "Real-Time Carpooling System for Android Platform," *International Journal of Engineering and Innovative Technology (IJEIT)*, vol. 2, no. 6, pp. 436–437, 2012.
3. V. Monteiro De Lira, V. C. Times, C. Renso, and S. Rinzivillo, "ComeWithMe: An activity-oriented carpooling approach," in *IEEE 18th International Conference on Intelligent Transportation Systems*, 2015.
4. R. Trasarti, F. Giannotti, and M. Nanni, "Mining Mobility User Profiles for Car-Pooling," in *KDD 2011*, 2011, pp. 1190–1198.

No users no dataspaces! Query-driven dataspace orchestration*
(position paper)

George H. L. Fletcher[1] and Federica Mandreoli[2]

[1] Eindhoven University of Technology
The Netherlands
g.h.l.fletcher@tue.nl
[2] University of Modena and Reggio Emilia
Italy
federica.mandreoli@unimore.it

Abstract. Data analysis in rich spaces of heterogeneous data sources is an increasingly common activity. Examples include querying the web of linked data and personal information management. Such analytics on dataspaces is often iterative and dynamic, in an open-ended interaction between discovery and data orchestration. The current state of the art in integration and orchestration in dataspaces is primarily geared towards close-ended analysis, targeting the discovery of stable data mappings or one-time, pay-as-you-go ad hoc data mappings. The perspective here is dataspace-centric.
In this paper, we propose a shift to a user-centric perspective on dataspace orchestration. We outline basic conceptual and technical challenges in supporting data analytics which is open-ended and always evolving, as users respond to new discoveries and connections.

1 The vision

In many contemporary data management scenarios, users are faced with large collections of independent heterogeneous data sources with which they initially have limited understanding of the structure and semantics. The technical solutions for data sharing are by now quite mature: RESTful API's, linked data standards, and so forth. What remains fundamentally in querying over such spaces of data sources are issues of orchestrating the sources for querying, that is, aligning and exchanging data between sources, towards resolving an information seeking task.

Some example use cases of this scenario are: querying the web of linked data [10], Personal Information Management (PIM) systems [1], and exploratory data analysis [5]. Much of the basic ingredients towards supporting users in these scenarios is by now well understood, coming from the rich literature on data

* This article is based upon work from COST Action KEYSTONE IC1302, supported by COST (European Cooperation in Science and Technology)

integration, (p2p) dataspaces, and data exchange [7, 14, 8, 9]. Of these solutions emerging in the last years, all are aimed at a common objective that is answering to the need of a unified search over the full spectrum of relevant knowledge.

The management of mappings for orchestration of data sources in this context has been almost exclusively from a data-centric perspective. Indeed, in the current state of the art, information and orchestration of dataspaces is primarily geared towards close-ended analysis, targeting the discovery of stable data mappings or one-time, pay-as-you-go data mappings.

A shift in perspective In contrast to this, analytics in the dataspace scenarios discussed above is often iterative and dynamic, where new query results inform and guide further analysis, in an open-ended interaction between discovery and data orchestration. Indeed, the world is always changing, people are all different, people themselves are always changing. Data semantics is in the eye of the consumer. Hence, schemas/ontologies are always idiosyncratic. Furthermore, idiosyncrasies are always evolving. The data engineering community (and, more generally, the computer science research community) has been grappling with this dynamism, this flux in user-driven data usage, since the founding of the field [11].

In this light, close-ended analysis is not the norm, but rather an exceptional activity. In fact, in the absence of users and their information seeking activities, there is no need for orchestrating data sources, and hence no dataspaces. We capture these observations in the slogan *No users no dataspaces!* We are motivated by this to propose a shift of perspective, from data-centric orchestration to user-centric orchestration. This shift of perspective essentially changes the role of mappings that are no longer aimed to support data exchange or data integration application scenarios but rather to contribute to users satisfaction in their information seeking activities. From a data management point of view, the primary visible expression of users are their queries (i.e., the embodiment of a fleeting view and information need in the world). Hence, we start from the perspective of the adhoc query, which we then try to satisfy in the dataspace. In this process of satisfaction, we often need to define and refine *mappings* between data sources and expose the user to the data thereby discovered for their feedback and possibly continued reformulation of their queries. The main novelty thus lies in a different approach to the issue of mapping management that is triggered by the specific user and his/her query and targets to his/her satisfaction. In this way, we perform an important step towards realizing the vision of a fully fledged pay-as-you-go information integration approach for analytics on dataspaces.

Towards realizing this shift And of course, users do not live in isolation, but rather in a diversity of rich overlapping communities. Therefore, all of the effort involved in defining and refining mappings is shared by individuals, within and across communities, across time granularities. Pareto's principle[3] tells us that (1) there are many widely shared commonalities in information needs, and (2) information needs are almost always highly focused and topical, not requiring orchestration at the level of traditional data integration systems. This gives us

[3] `https://en.wikipedia.org/wiki/Pareto_principle`

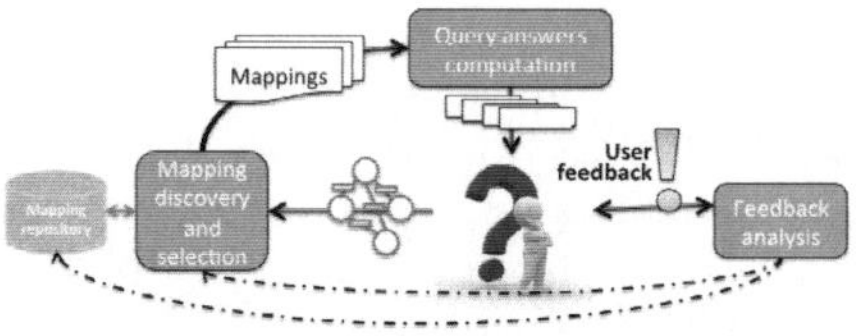

Fig. 1. The QyX query-driven dataspace orchestration process. Solid lines are used to depict the process while dashed lines show the feedback analysis impact.

hope as engineers, towards the design and implementation of effective and efficient user-centric dataspace solutions. Our goal in this paper is to sketch the first steps in this direction by proposing a query-driven dataspace orchestration framework and by discussing the main challenging issues that should be addressed in this context.

2 Query-driven dataspace orchestration

By query-driven dataspace orchestration we mean open-ended dynamic dataspace orchestration, interactively driven by ad-hoc user requests and their interaction with the views induced by past queries and query-refinement and reformulation.

The data modeling abstraction we adopt to represent a dataspace is as lightweight as possible, for the goals of our study. To this end, it is (a) *fully decentralized*, thereby bridging, on the one hand, existing dataspace models that usually rely on a single mediated view [7] and, on the other hand, P2P approaches for data sharing [9]. A dataspace is therefore a collection of autonomous data sources locally connected through an interlinked collection of semantic mappings used to answer past user requests; (b) *schema-flexible*, in the sense that data sources can be schemaless and users do not need to know the complete and exact structure of the data to query it; (c) *based on data exchange*, in that when answering user queries the data source includes data objects that reflects a given set of mappings between the data source and the dataspace [8].

In this context, for the sake of simplicity we assume that an ad-hoc user request is expressed over one data source. The goal of answering the request satisfactorily induces a dataspace orchestration that aims at aligning the dataspace to the specific request through the interactive execution of three steps: mapping discovery and selection, query answer computation, feedback analysis. Figure 1 depicts the process that can stop when the user is satisfied with the delivered answers or when all the alternative answer sets have been already shown to the user. It relies on a mapping repository that stores the mappings used to answer past requests. The update of the repository is part of the process.

In the following, we discuss the key ideas of the process using a running example in a PIM scenario focused on music and composers. We assume that the dataspace is made up of three data sources: a small portion of a social graph containing information about what user's friends like and two knowledge graphs, one focused on composer biographies and the other one on schools of music and art. Data are represented as triples according to the flexible entity-based modeling abstraction typical of dataspaces [7]. In this simplified example we assume that the data sources are aligned in their objects. For instance $(john, likes, mozart)$ and $(likes, type, vote)$ are two triples of the first graph data source G_1 while $(mozart, genre, classical)$ and $(classical, period, 17thCentury)$ belong to the second and third data source, G_2 and G_3, respectively. Let us assume that the first query issued by the user on G_1 asks for the period user's friends are fan of. This query can be expressed in a conjunctive pattern matching form as follows, where $?x$,$?y$, and $?z$ are variables:

$$Q_1 : (?x, periodFanOf, ?z) \leftarrow (?x, likes, ?y), (?y, period, ?z)$$

2.1 Query-driven mapping discovery and selection

Mapping discovery is the core step of the framework and arises many interesting research issues that are discussed in Sec 4. It is query-driven in that it is triggered by the query and aims at discovering mappings in the dataspace and refining existing mappings that are necessary to solve the query itself. For instance, G_1 has not enough information to solve Q_1 or, equivalently, Q_1 can be solved only partially on G_1. Then, the system implements an algorithm that delivers at each step a set of candidate mappings that can be used to totally solve the query.

The algorithm we envision is based on the principle that the match is "partial" by virtue of missing data. For instance for Q_1, $(john, likes, mozart)$ matches $(?x, likes, ?y)$ whereas we assume that there is no triple matching the pattern $(?, period, ?z)$. Therefore, the answer set is not empty if the algorithm finds at least one mapping that generates the missing triple $(mozart, period, w)$ where w is any value. To this end, the algorithm relies on two elements that can be derived from each partial match: the values associated with the bounded query variables, to extract examples from the dataspace under structural indistinguishability [15], and the unmatched query statement, to generate the target of the missing mappings. With reference to the example above, the algorithm extracts the triple $(mozart, genre, classical)$ from G_2 and uses the pattern $(?y, period, ?z)$ to deliver the mapping that define the pattern $(?y, period, ?z)$ on G_1 as the joining of the pattern $(?x, genre, ?y)$ from G_2 with $(?y, period, ?z)$ from G_3:

$$m_a = G_1 : (?x, period, ?z) \leftarrow G_2 : (?x, genre, ?y), G_3 : (?y, period, ?z)$$

This mapping extends G_1 with triples of the form $(w_1, period, w_2)$, where w_1 and w_2 are values, also including $(mozart, period, 17thCentury)$ that is used to compute the answer $(john, periodFanOf, 17thCentury)$ to query Q_1.

During this step, the system capitalizes on past orchestration work by mixing the actual discovery task with a focused selection of mappings from the mapping repository. For instance if m_a is available in the repository and G_1 receive a query asking for the century the user's friends are interested in:

$$Q_2 = (?x, CentOI, ?z) \leftarrow (?x, likes, ?y), (?y, century, ?z)$$

then m_a can be used to build mapping m_b that renames *period* into *century*

$$m_b = G_1(?x, century, ?y) \leftarrow G_1 : (?x, period, ?y)$$

and that would bring the answer $(john, centOI, 17thCentury)$.

2.2 User-oriented strategies for mapping management

The main observation that motivates our proposal is that data semantics is in the eye of the consumer. In our vision different users seeking the same information or the same user seeking the same information at different times are exposed to different satisfaction processes and thus dataspace orchestrations, depending on their backgrounds, interests and current situations.

To this end, the user's profile and situational context are represented as query metadata and exploited for tailored data analysis [12]. At the same time, new query results can inform and guide users for further analysis. We envisage a fruitful interaction with the user that can be involved in query reformulation/refinement tasks and the explorations of intermediate as well as complete query answers. The system then exploits the user behaviour and feedback to annotate mappings with metrics measuring their fitness to user expectations [4].

User-oriented mapping management strategies play a fundamental role in dataspace orchestration for effectiveness and efficiency reasons. As to mapping discovery, it is worth noting that the space of the candidate mappings that can be derived from an issued query is usually very large as it relies on the whole dataspace. User-oriented strategies can guide the scanning of such a wide space toward the mappings that best fit user expectations according to the knowledge the system gained from query metadata and past iterations. As to mapping selection, the mapping collection is indexed over the different user-oriented features of interest such as the queries for which mappings were used and the related fitness metrics, the profiles of the users who submitted such queries and the related contexts. Then, different mapping selection strategies can be adopted.

For instance, if the system follows a strategy that aims to limit mapping discovery efforts, Q_2 can be first evaluated by defining mapping m_b through m_a. Then, if the user is not satisfied with the delivered answers, the system can decide to drive the discovery toward alternative $(?y, century, ?z)$ definitions, e.g. that relate composers with the 20th-century music because, thanks to the interaction with the user, it has understood this is the *century* interpretation user has in mind.

3 Two case studies

In this section we discuss two case studies of data analysis that show different user-system interaction models and give an hint of how the query-driven dataspace orchestration framework we propose can be of support to the user task.

3.1 Case study 1: Exploratory data analysis

Exploratory data analysis helps users to make sense of very big datasets. In [5] it is described as the step-by-step "conversation" of a user and a system that "help each other" to refine the data exploration process, ultimately gathering new knowledge that concretely fulfills the user information needs. Exploratory analysis tools address both data scientists, such as biologists, that have a deep knowledge of the domain of interest and clear and peculiar information needs and data enthusiasts, such as journalists, that want to analyze the data to achieve new and essential knowledge of the domain of interest.

The proposed query-driven dataspace orchestration paradigm can be straightforwardly integrated in the data exploration loop where it allow the system to overcome the logic of one-size-fits all. In this context, the thorough conversation between the user and the system represents the main source for dataspace orchestration to understand the user information needs and purposes. We envision a dataspace orchestration process that, when the conversation starts, leverages the initial knowledge of the user and the user profile for a focused mapping discovery and selection. Then, it will gradually adapt to the new knowledge the user will gain while using the system as well as his/her changes of perspective and interest. For instance, in case of a data enthusiast user, mapping discovery and selection could be initially driven toward jargon-free data objects that would bring easily understandable answers. Then the process will move toward more specialized data sources that could help the user to gain a deeper knowledge of the domain of interest. In this way, each user will have his/her own view of the dataspace that will evolve over time according to his/her level of knowledge and topics of interest.

3.2 Case study 2: Data analysis in dynamic contexts

A significant involvement of the user during the interpretation process is not adequate in dynamic contexts, in which the interaction is often hampered by the communication means and by the need to quickly obtain answers [6]. This is the case, for instance, of a mobile user that would like to find answers to complex requests involving his/her current position.

This kind of requests often concerns geo-referenced and time-variant information as well as crowdsourced data that need to be integrated with strongly correlated and semantically complex data (e.g., Linked Open Data) and unstructured data, or data with a simple and defined structure. The dataspace of interest is therefore made up of highly heterogeneous and dynamic data sources.

In such a dynamic context, standard mapping management approaches could bring to costly and useless integration results because of the rapid changes that characterize the considered scenario.

Catania et al. [6] identify three coordinates relevant in this context: (a) user profile and request context; (b) data and processing quality; (c) similar requests repeated over time. For example, thanks to (a) and (b), it is possible to prefer synthetic and timely answers sacrificing the quality of result in the case of a user on the move or in an emergency situation. The last coordinate, (c), is very common in dynamic contexts and can be used to limit response times and interpretation errors. It occurs, for example, during or after an exceptional event (environmental emergencies or flash mobbing initiatives), in the context of users belonging to the same community or that are in the same place, possibly at different times. The information needs are widespread among different users, because induced by the event, the interests of the community, and the place, respectively.

Our framework for query-driven dataspace orchestration can benefit from these three coordinates to focus mapping management efforts over such information that can contribute to produce satisfactory answers. In particular, profiled query patterns, that is synthetic representations of past requests associated with the corresponding user profiles and contexts, can be used to index the mapping repository for effective mapping searches. Moreover, the dynamism requirements of the submitted request can be exploited both for mapping selection and to drive mapping discovery toward the candidate mappings that best meet the request time.

4 Open challenges and future research directions

Our proposal addresses an old and pressing problem from a new perspective. Although, we can borrow some solutions from past research works there are still several substantial research issues which need to be addressed to complete the picture. We list some of the main issues below.

Although some mapping discovery approaches via data examples have been proposed [2], the non-trivial challenges highlighted by a query-driven perspective on mapping discovery indicates fresh perspectives on research. Indeed, in this case, the discovery is driven by queries, instead of data, and the aim is to find sets of candidate mappings that extend partial matches to total ones. This novel mapping discovery paradigm requires a rigorous in-depth theoretical study: the introduction of a formal notion of candidate mapping followed by a query-driven mapping-discovery algorithm that is sound and complete, i.e. it must deliver all and only the candidate mapping sets for a given request. In this context, it is also interesting to study the impact of different graph query languages on the theoretical framework. To this end, an interesting paper is [3] that studies problems of materializing solutions and query answering for these languages.

The problem of checking the existence of total or partial matches as well as their computation arose in various steps of the process. Although some papers already provide interesting solutions [2], they cannot be adopted as they are because of the relationship between the query to be matched and the network of mappings connecting data sources that has never been addressed before.

Users are not willing to wait query answers for a long time and, then, a system built on the proposed paradigm has strict time constraints that are unknown to standard mapping management systems. As a consequence, both the above research problems need efficient and scalable solutions. From an engineering point of view, the above algorithms can largely benefit from structural indexes and histograms similar to the ones proposed in [16, 15] as well as an effective dataspace representation as an easy-to-navigate graph. Then, specific tasks, such as object alignment, can be faced through on-the-fly techniques [13].

Finally, as to user involvement, we see two core issues that require innovative solutions in the engineering field. Indexing and selection techniques are necessary for the mapping repository. Here, the main questions to be addressed are how to reuse previous mapping collections and to compare/score alternative mappings. As shown in Sec. 3, these issues require solutions specifically tailored to the application scenario. As far as the user feedback is involved, instead, we first need to introduce effective feedback elicitation approaches, similarly to the ones proposed in [4]. Then, we should propose approaches that translate the feedback and behaviour of the user on query results into some kind of mapping annotation useful for mapping selection and discovery.

References

1. Abiteboul, S., Marian, A.: Personal information management systems. In: EDBT Tutorial. Brussels (2015)
2. Alexe, B., ten Cate, B., Kolaitis, P.G., Tan, W.C.: Designing and refining schema mappings via data examples. In: Proc. of SIGMOD. pp. 133–144 (2011)
3. Barceló, P., Pérez, J., Reutter, J.L.: Schema mappings and data exchange for graph databases. In: Proc. of ICDT. pp. 189–200 (2013)
4. Belhajjame, K., et al.: Feedback-based annotation, selection and refinement of schema mappings for dataspaces. In: Proc. of EDBT. pp. 573–584 (2010)
5. Buoncristiano, M., et al.: Database challenges for exploratory computing. SIGMOD Record 44(2), 17–22 (2015)
6. Catania, B., Guerrini, G., Belussi, A., Mandreoli, F., Martoglia, R., Penzo, W.: Wearable queries: adapting common retrieval needs to data and users. In: Proc. of DBRank (co-located with VLDB). pp. 7:1–7:3 (2013)
7. Dong, X., Halevy, A.Y.: Indexing dataspaces. In: Proc. of SIGMOD. pp. 43–54 (2007)
8. Fagin, R., Kolaitis, P.G., Miller, R.J., Popa, L.: Data exchange: semantics and query answering. Theoretical Computer Science 336(1), 89–124 (2005)
9. Halevy, A.Y., Ives, Z.G., Suciu, D., Tatarinov, I.: Schema mediation for large-scale semantic data sharing. VLDB J. 14(1), 68–83 (2005)
10. Heath, T., Bizer, C.: Linked Data: Evolving the Web into a Global Data Space. Synthesis Lectures on the Semantic Web, Morgan & Claypool Publishers (2011)
11. Kent, W.: Data and reality. North Holland, Amsterdam (1978)
12. Koutrika, G., Ioannidis, Y.E.: Personalizing queries based on networks of composite preferences. ACM TODS 35(2) (2010)
13. Papadakis, G., Koutrika, G., Palpanas, T., Nejdl, W.: Meta-blocking: Taking entity resolution to the next level. IEEE TKDE 26(8), 1946–1960 (2014)
14. Penzo, W., Lodi, S., Mandreoli, F., Martoglia, R., Sassatelli, S.: Semantic peer, here are the neighbors you want! In: Proc. of EDBT. pp. 26–37 (2008)
15. Picalausa, F., Fletcher, G.H.L., Hidders, J., Vansummeren, S.: Principles of guarded structural indexing. In: Proc. of ICDT. pp. 245–256 (2014)
16. Scholl, T., et al.: Hisbase: Histogram-based P2P main memory data management. In: Proc. of VLDB. pp. 1394–1397 (2007)

Big Data and Public Administration: a case study for Tuscany Airports

Barbara Furletti[1], Daniele Fadda[1], Leonardo Piccini[2], Mirco Nanni[1], and Patrizia Lattarulo[2]

[1] ISTI - CNR, Via G.Moruzzi,1 Pisa, Italy
{barbara.furletti,mirco.nanni,daniele.fadda}@isti.cnr.it
[2] IRPET, Firenze, Italy
{leonardo.piccini, patrizia.lattarulo}@irpet.it

Abstract. In the last decade, the fast development of Information and Communication Technologies led to the wide diffusion of sensors able to track various aspects of human activity, as well as the storage and computational capabilities needed to record and analyze them. The so-called Big Data promise to improve the effectiveness of businesses, the quality of urban life, as well as many other fields, including the functioning of public administrations. Yet, translating the wealth of potential information hidden in Big Data to consumable intelligence seems to be still a difficult task, with a limited basis of success stories. This paper reports a project activity centered on a public administration – IRPET, the Regional Institute for Economic Planning of Tuscany (Italy). The paper deals, among other topics, with human mobility and public transportation at a regional scale, summarizing the open questions posed by the Public Administration (PA), the envisioned role that Big Data might have in answering them, the actual challenges that emerged in trying to implement them, and finally the results we obtained, the limitations that emerged and the lessons learned.

Keywords: Public Administration, Mobility, Big Data, Data Mining

1 Introduction

Technological evolution and the diffusion of devices that generate and record digital footprints brought along a raising interest in "big data" as a replacement and a supplemental source for more traditional forms of data collection.

PAs have been aware of potential benefits of these instruments, and have been trying to develop and implement tools that use this kind of information to support and evaluate public policies. The city of Chicago, for example, started using text analytics on Twitter and on 311 (the local emergency number) records to detect and prevent phenomena like rat infestations and to track gang and drug-related violence [6]. The Department of Transportation of Florida is using data collected from the Waze app to adjust traffic signaling in real time and prevent traffic jams [7]. In early 2016, the European Statistical System launched a competition[3] to develop nowcasting tools using big data sources on key statistics, such as unemployment, price indexes and tourism. In Italy, the National Institute of Statistics (ISTAT) started few years ago the first experiments in collaboration with universities and research institutions, for the introduction and use of big data to support the traditional statistics, with the aim of understanding the potential of these data and boosting the definition of a legal framework to ensure the safe exploitation of such data sources [10].

Big data sources can help PAs by providing data with better timeliness, reduced costs, improved robustness and applicability in cases where a developed statistical system is still not established. This may support policy makers by providing a more sophisticated depiction of the socio-economic environment, and enabling a more accurate evaluation of needed actions and expected results. Nowcasting can be used to monitor key indicators during the operational phase of the policies, allowing real time adjustment and constant refinement. Finally, big data sources may be used in quasi-experimental design and counterfactual settings, in order to provide better information and services to citizens, and to boost the collaboration with stakeholders and other PAs.

Some of the pros include timeliness, cost effectiveness, spatial and temporal disaggregation, emergence of unexpected and/or unobservable phenomena. On the other hand, since the relative novelty of the methodologies used to deal with these data, extra carefulness needs to be used to acknowledge possible shortcomings in terms of quality, accessibility, applicability, relevance, privacy policy and ownership of the data, all of which may affect the quality of policy evaluation and appraisal[8].

Nonetheless, we believe that big data sources can be successfully used to foster the capabilities of the public institutions to deal with complex problems, to plan effective policies and to evaluate the outcomes of their actions. To this extent, we propose a case study for a methodology that combines a GPS dataset with traditional socio-economic measures to analyze airport choice in a multi-airport region (specifically, Tuscany). The relevance of airport catchment area analysis is testified by the attention reserved, in recent years, to the diversification and growth strategies implemented within the airport system of Tuscany. Even the national strategic documents (ENAC master plan [9]) acknowledges that, in future years, the two main regional airports need to carefully plan their offer to maximize their synergies through an integrated and non-overlapping specialization.

Long range accessibility is a key factor for regional development. Especially for an exporting and tourism-intensive region like Tuscany, ensuring an effective planning of air-side connectivity is crucial to maximize the economic potential of the territory while simultaneously minimizing the environmental impacts and the consumption of public resources. From this situation comes the need for a detailed understanding of the relations that the two airports have established with their territories.

---

[3] BDCOMP: the Big Data for Official Statistics Competition (`http://ec.europa.eu/eurostat/cros/content/bdcomp\_en`)

1.1 Analytical questions

Among the general open issues and interesting questions just discussed, in this paper we focus on the study of airports' attractiveness in Tuscany. The objective is to understand how and how much the two airports attract Tuscany residents, and to identify the main factors that impact on people's choice: how relevant is the geographic distance and/or the travel time? Are such factors significantly discriminant, or is the choice driven by the airports' offer of flights? Is the accessibility by different means of transport a key factor? Is there a competition with neighbor airports outside Tuscany?

Tuscany has two main airports: "G. Galilei" in Pisa and "A. Vespucci" in Florence. The ENAC report about the development of Italian airports [1] tells us that the two airports have different characteristics and history, which are the results of different policy choices along the time, and environmental constraints. "A. Vespucci" has some issues related to its inclusion in a problematic urban context, in addition to small size and flight infrastructure limitations. Situated northwest of Florence, 4 km far from the city center, this airport is connected by highways, but it is not accessible by trains so the public transport consists of only urban and extra-urban buses. In 2011 it registered around 1.9M passengers. "G. Galilei" in 2000 held the role of access door of Tuscany Region, and its importance grew with the introduction of low-cost flights. It is situated South of Pisa, very close to the urban area, and it is connected with highways and motorways, as well as by railway and urban and extra-urban public transports. In 2011, it registered about 4.5M passengers. In 2011, the two airports shared the flights market (in terms of passengers) respecting the following rates: "A. Vespucci" 5.6% for low-cost flights and 94.4% for traditional; "G. Galilei" 83% for low-cost flights and 17% for traditional.

The questions listed above drove our analytical process in collecting information, generating indicators and outlining the attractiveness in order to supply evaluation elements useful for IRPET, as discussed in Sec. 1. In this vision, the residents do not correspond to the formal/administrative ones as reported by the official statistics but, instead, to land users i.e., people who live in the area of interest – in our case, Tuscany municipalities. Resident locations, computed by using the GPS data, correspond to the most frequent locations where vehicles stop [4]. The main idea is to answer to the questions starting from the study of the mobility behaviors of our sample, and enrich the analysis by using other contextual information.
After having introduced in Sec. 2 the main datasets and analytical tools, in Sec. 3 we present the case study and the results, and in Sec. 4 a final discussion and the future developments.

2 Data, sources and analysis tools

For this study we use heterogeneous data coming from both public and private companies (i.e. socio-economic, demographic and geographical data), and GPS data.

GPS data are provided by a leader company in the Insurance Telematics that deals with about the 2% of the total vehicles circulating in Italy. Our dataset counts about 150k private vehicles crossing Tuscany in the month of May 2011, and represents a primary source of information for studying the mobility behaviors. Data on air traffic provided by the Italian Civil Aviation Authority (ENAC)[4] are used to define the theoretical framework and to identify different flights offer, while data of vehicle fleet in Italy provided by the Italian Automobile Club (ACI)[5], and Census data provided by ISTAT[6], are used to re-scale the vehicle sample to the real population. The Observatory of the Real Estate Market dataset provided by the Italian Revenue Agency, is used to enrich the description of the territory and its mobility with an economic indicator derived by real estate values. Trip duration and distances with different transportation means are computed by using a Google service.
As a support to understand the territory we use "GEOscopio"[7] and Open Street Map. GEOscopio is a webgis tool provided by Tuscany Region, through which you can view and query geographic data of the Tuscany Region.
Data mining tasks and statistical computations have been performed by using M-Atlas and Python scripts. M-Atlas is an analytical platform developed at KDD Lab - ISTI, CNR. It is composed of a data mining query language and a mining system centered onto the concept of trajectory. Besides the mechanisms for storing and querying trajectory data, M-Atlas has mechanisms for mining trajectory patterns and models that, in turn, can be stored and queried [2].

3 The attractiveness of the Tuscany airports

To analyze the airports attractiveness, we first concentrate on the identification of the so called access points [2], to understand which roads people use to arrive to the airport by car, and to estimate the impact of the incoming traffic generated by the airports over the total traffic around the city. The more important paths are computed by using the T-Clustering algorithm [3] provided by M-Atlas, adopting a *route similarity* in the clustering phase. Route similarity spatially compares the trajectories and groups those that follow similar routes and have same destination (the airport). By creating a buffer of 5 Km around the airports, we identify the last stretches of the routes shared by the trajectories in the different clusters, and the main access gates in the intersection. The six gates showed in Fig. 1(a) gather the most significant flows. Fig. 1(a) synthesizes the study on Pisa and shows the main access roads and gates. In this case study, by using 500 m as threshold for the route similarity measure, T-Clustering returns 7 significant clusters over 2218 trajectories. Thanks to the clustering results, we can see the contribution of the trajectories belonging to different clusters and

[4] ENAC Open Data website: `https://www.enac.gov.it/canale_di_servizio/open\_data/index.html`
[5] ACI Open Data website: `http://www.aci.it/laci/studi-e-ricerche/dati-e-statistiche/open-data.html`
[6] ISTAT Open Data website: `http://datiopen.istat.it/`
[7] GEOscopio: `http://www.regione.toscana.it/-/geoscopio`

passing through the gates. In the picture we can also appreciate the total volumes of the incoming traffic during the period of observation. It is important to notice that most of the traffic coming from inland of Tuscany is gathered by the SGC *FI-PI-LI* highway. The traffic generated by the airport corresponds to 1.3% to the total traffic passing through the gates. Fig. 1(b) shows instead the flows of vehicles departing from the different municipalities to the two airports. Flows of the sample are re-scaled by using the ACI index of the circulating vehicles in Tuscany [5].

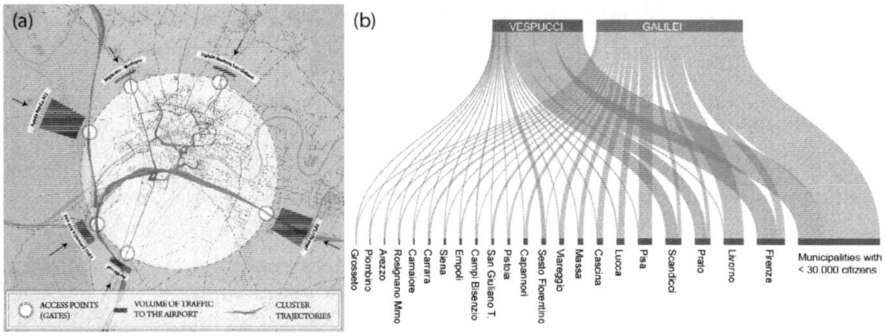

Fig. 1. (a) Access patterns and gates to "G. Galilei". (b) Re-scaled flows of vehicles going to the airports from the different Municipalities.

Then, by reconstructing a Origin/Destination matrix (OD-Matrix), we identify the flows useful for estimating the shares of passengers of the two airports coming from the different Tuscany municipalities. The latter are the origins of the matrix, while the parking areas around the airports are the destinations. For this task, a study of the territory by using GIS tools and GEOscopio was essential to identify the locations where cars typically park, as well as the choice of the parameter "duration of stop" for the reconstruction of the trajectories from raw GPS points. We know, in fact, that the car parks at the airports are free of charges for the firsts 15 minutes, and most of car drivers benefit of this when they give a ride to a departing/arriving person. This habit is confirmed by the distribution of the stops at the airports car parks: Fig. 2 shows, in fact, that the 30 - 35% of the vehicles stop for less than 15 minutes at the toll parking. The percentage rises to the 80% for 1 hour stops. So, we lower the typical 20-minutes threshold for the stop detection used for the trajectory reconstruction, to 5 minutes to maximize the stops around the airports. The increase in terms of car parked is the 108%. The result of this first study is summarized in Fig. 3, that shows the division of the Municipalities towards (a) "G. Galilei", and (b) "A. Vespucci": the higher the color intensity, the higher the attraction. As one might imagine, the two airports have great impact on nearest municipalities, but "G. Galilei" has much more influence on even far municipalities, and on the

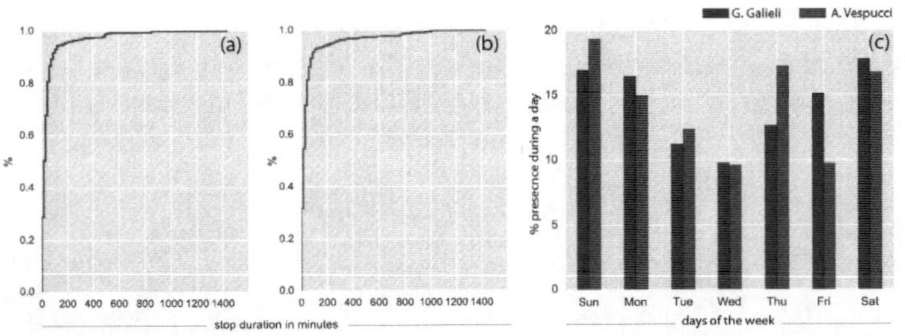

Fig. 2. Distribution of the stop duration at the toll parking near (a) "G. Galilei", and (b) "A. Vespucci". (c) Weekly distribution of the stops at the toll parking near the two airports.

municipality of Florence.

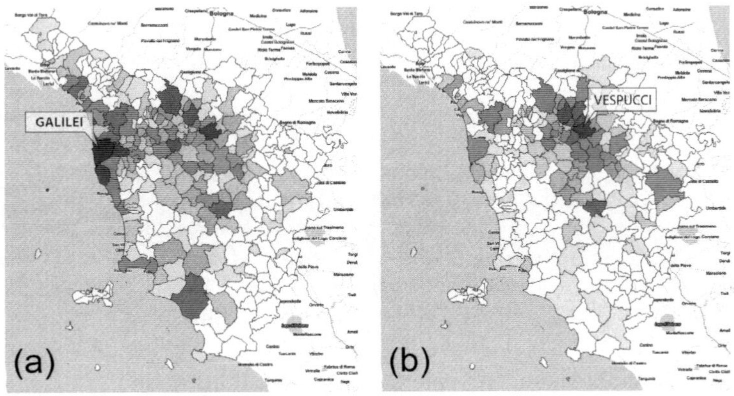

Fig. 3. Representation of the OD-Matrix of how Tuscany Municipalities are attracted by (a) "G. Galilei", and (b) "A. Vespucci".

At this stage of the analysis, adding auxiliary information extracted from other sources was crucial to enrich our analysis and to better characterize the discovered mobility behaviors. By querying Google Maps Distance Matrix API, we extracted the typical travel times based on the recommended route, taken by a car departing from a municipality to an airport. Having 287 municipalities and two airports, we make 574 calls to the APIs. With this information we compute an accessibility index in order to understand the advantage in terms of time-saving of reaching an airport instead of the other. Fig. 4(a) shows the map of the municipalities and the temporal advantage. Municipalities depicted with shades of blue have advantages in going to "A. Vespucci", while the ones depicted with shades of red have advantages in going to "G. Galilei". The ones in white have no temporal advantage so the time taken to reach the two airports is almost the same with a 10 minutes deviation. We are now able to compare the

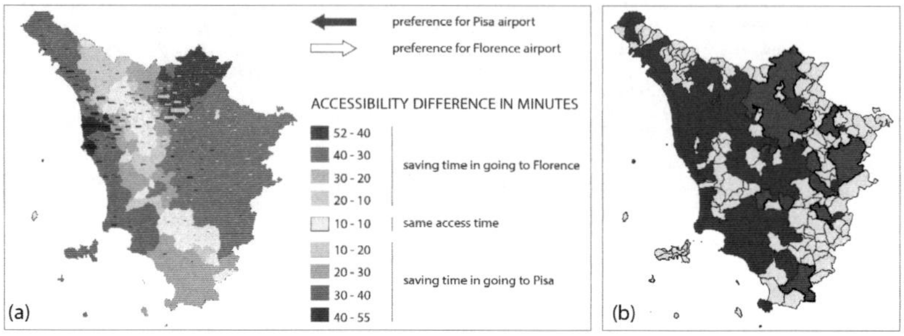

Fig. 4. (a) Accessibility at the two airports in terms of time saving and actual customers' preference. (b) Partition of Tuscany territory on the basis of the airport attractiveness.

potential attractiveness (in term of accessibility) of the airports w.r.t. people's actual choice. To accomplish this task, we overlap the OD-Matrix map to the accessibility map, highlighting the overwhelming choice for each municipality. Fig. 4(a) still merges these information and shows the majority choices with white and blue arrows. People coming from municipalities labeled with a white arrow prefer to go to "G. Galilei", while the other to "A. Vespucci". It is important to notice the areas in light blue, where the real preference is to "G. Galilei" even if the accessibility advantage is to "A. Vespucci". There are also many "neutral" areas in white, where the preference is to "G. Galilei" too.

Fig. 4(b) summarizes how Tuscany can be partitioned on the basis of the airport attractiveness: red area is the set of municipalities under the influence of "G. Galilei", while blue area is under the influence of "A. Vespucci". In white, the municipalities where we did not have a sufficiently representative sample, or for which a clear preference has not been identified.

Finally, to conclude the analysis of the mobility habits, we can see from Fig. 2(c) that the distribution of the stops at the two airports along the week is quite different. This is probably related to the different commercial offer of the two airports. The majority of Low-cost flights at "G. Galilei" tends to concentrate the passengers' turnout close to weekends. At "A. Vespucci" instead, customers of business type, use to the airport also in the middle of the week as described by the peak in Thursday.

4 Discussion and future works

The results showed in this paper allow us to detail the main components of airport choice from a geographical perspective, which can be the basis for predicting future patterns of airport usage in different scenarios. Furthermore, we can spatially evaluate the benefits that the investments undergoing in both analyzed airports can have on the Tuscany residents.

Future developments of the research include the refinement of the airport's choice model with socio-economic variable and mobility indicators. Also, a cross-analysis with other mobility data sources is planned, such as mobile phone traces, which might enable to capture transportation modes other than private vehicles, and therefore complement the results obtained so far. Finally, an in-depth analysis of results will follow, based on contextual information that can help to better characterize the attraction areas of the two airports.

Acknowledgment

This work has been partially funded by the European Union under the FP7-ICT Program: Project Petra n. 609042, and under H2020 Program: Project SoBigData n. 654024.

References

1. Enac: Atlante degli Aeroporti Italiani, `https://www.enac.gov.it/repository/ContentManagement/information/P464245000/CAP_0_Atlante_Aeroporti-PREMESSA.pdf` (2010)
2. Giannotti, F., Nanni, M., Pedreschi, D., et al.: Unveiling the complexity of human mobility by querying and mining massive trajectory data. VLDB Journal 20, 695–719 (2011)
3. Andrienko, G., Andrienko, N., Rinzivillo, S., et al.Toolkit for Cluster-Based Classification of Mobility Data. In: SSTD, 432–435 (2009)
4. Gonzalez, M. C., Cesar, A. H., Barabasi, A-L: Understanding individual human mobility patterns. Nature 453.7196, 779–782 (2008)
5. ACI: Circulating vehicles in 2011, `http://www.aci.it/laci/studi-e-ricerche/dati-e-statistiche/consistenza-parco-veicoli/2011.html`
6. Catlett, Charlie, et al.: Plenario: An Open Data Discovery and Exploration Platform for Urban Science. Bulletin of the IEEE Computer Society Technical Committee on Data Engineering 12/2014; 37(4):27 (2014)
7. Adler, J., Horner, J., Dyer, J., et al. : Estimate Benefits of Crowdsourced Data from Social Media. Technical Report nr. FHWA-JPO-14-165
8. Scannapieco, M., Virgillito, A., Zardetto, D.: Placing Big Data in official statistics: a big challenge. NTTS (2013)
9. ENAC: Piano Nazionale degli aeroporti, `https://www.enac.gov.it/La\_Comunicazione/Pubblicazioni/info-1156450804.html` (2012)
10. Furletti, B., Gabrielli, L., Giannotti, F., et al.: Use of mobile phone data to estimate mobility flows. Measuring urban population and inter-city mobility using big data in an integrated approach. In 47th SIS (2014)

Ranking Documents Efficiently with QuickScorer

Discussion Paper

Domenico Dato[1], Claudio Lucchese[2], Franco Maria Nardini[2], Salvatore Orlando[3], Raffaele Perego[2], Nicola Tonellotto[2], and Rossano Venturini[4]

[1] Tiscali Italia S.p.A.
[2] HPC Lab, ISTI-CNR, Pisa.
[3] Università Ca' Foscari, Venezia.
[4] Università di Pisa

Abstract. This discussion paper presents our recent work on the efficiency of Learning-to-Rank models based on additive ensembles of regression trees. These models, although computationally expensive, have proven to provide a very effective solution to the problem of ranking query results returned by Web search engines, a scenario where quality and efficiency requirements are very demanding. QuickScorer (QS), our novel scoring algorithm, adopts a novel bitvector representation of the tree-based ranking model, and performs an interleaved traversal of the ensemble by means of simple logical bitwise operations. Due to its cache-aware approach, both in terms of data layout and access patterns, and to a control flow that entails very low branch mis-prediction rates, QS performance are impressive, resulting in speedups from 2.4x to 5.9x over the state-of-the-art competitor. The paper proposing QS was awarded best paper at last ACM SIGIR conference.

Keywords: Learning to Rank, Efficiency, Cache-aware Algorithms

1 Introduction

Ranking query results according to a relevance criterion is a fundamental problem in Information Retrieval (IR). Nowadays, an emerging research area named Learning-to-Rank (LtR) [8, 2] has shown that effective solutions to the ranking problem can leverage machine learning techniques. A LtR-based function, which *scores* a set of candidate documents according to their relevance to a given user query, is learned from a *ground-truth* composed of many training examples. The examples are basically a collection of queries $\mathcal{Q}$, where each query $q \in \mathcal{Q}$ is associated with a set of assessed documents $\mathcal{D} = \{d_0, d_1, \ldots\}$. Each pair (q, d_i) is in turn labeled by a *relevance judgment* y_i, usually a positive integer in a fixed range, stating the degree of relevance of the document for the query. These labels induce a partial ordering over the assessed documents, thus defining their *ideal ranking* [7]. The scoring function learned by a LtR algorithm aims to approximate the *ideal ranking* from the examples observed in the training set.

The ranking process is particularly challenging for Web search engines, which, besides the demanding requirements for result pages of high quality in response to user queries, have also to deal with efficiency constraints, which are not so common in other ranking-based applications. Indeed, two of the most effective LtR-based rankers are based on additive ensembles of regression trees, namely GRADIENT-BOOSTED REGRESSION TREES (GBRT) [5], and LAMBDA-MART (λ-MART) [15]. Due to the thousands of trees to be traversed at scoring time for each document, these rankers are also the most expensive in terms of computational time, thus impacting on response time and throughput of query processing. Therefore, devising techniques and strategies to speed-up document ranking without losing in quality is definitely an urgent research topic in Web search [13, 3, 11, 6, 16].

Usually, LtR-based scorers are embedded in complex two-stage ranking architectures [3, 14], which avoid applying them to all the documents possibly matching a user query. The first stage retrieves from the inverted index a sufficiently large set of possibly relevant documents matching the user query. This phase is aimed at optimizing the recall and is usually carried out by using a simple and fast ranking function, e.g., BM25 combined with some document-level scores [10]. LtR-based scorers are used in the second stage to *re-rank* the candidate documents coming from the first stage, and are optimized for high precision. In this two-stage architecture, the time budget available to re-rank the candidate documents is limited, due to the incoming rate of queries and the users' expectations in terms of quality-of-service. Strongly motivated by time budget considerations, the IR community has started to investigate low-level optimizations to reduce the scoring time of the most effective LtR rankers based on ensembles of regression trees, by dealing with features and peculiarities of modern CPUs and memory hierarchies [1, 12].

This discussion paper presents our recent work on the efficiency of Learning-to-Rank models. Our main contribution in this field is QUICKSCORER (QS), a new algorithm advancing the state of the art that allows to efficiently score documents with rankers based on additive ensembles of regression trees. QUICKSCORER adopts a novel representation of the ensemble based on bitvectors, allowing a fast interleaved traversal of the trees to be performed by using fast logical bitwise operations. The performance benefits of the resulting traversal are unprecedented, due to a cache-aware approach, both in terms of data layout and access patterns, and to a program control flow that entails very low branch mis-prediction rates.

The paper is organized as follows. Section 2 provides some background information and discusses the related work, while Section 3 details the QS algorithm and its features. Then, Section 4 details the experimental settings and reports the results of experiments conducted. Finally, we conclude the discussion paper in Section 5 by reporting some conclusions and suggestions for future research.

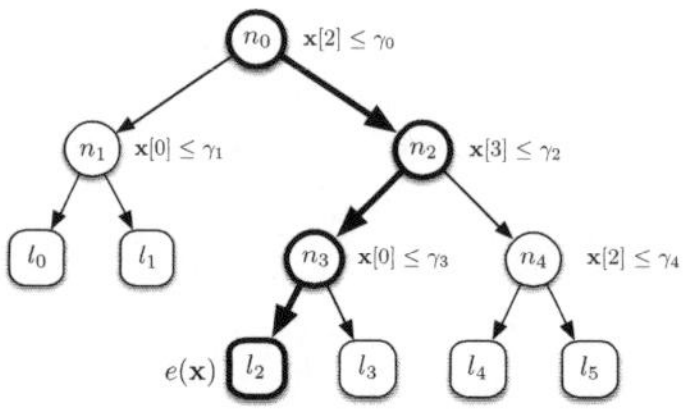

Fig. 1: A decision tree.

2 Background

Each query-document pair (q, d_i) is represented by a real-valued vector $\mathbf{x}$ of *features*, namely $\mathbf{x} \in \mathbb{R}^{|\mathcal{F}|}$ where $\mathcal{F} = \{f_0, f_1, \ldots\}$ is the set of features characterizing the candidate document d_i and the user query q, and $\mathbf{x}[i]$ stores feature f_i. Let $\mathcal{T}$ be an ensemble of trees representing the ranking model. Each tree $T = (N, L)$ in $\mathcal{T}$ is a decision tree composed of a set of internal nodes $N = \{n_0, n_1, \ldots\}$, and a set of leaves $L = \{l_0, l_1, \ldots\}$. Each $n \in N$ is associated with a *Boolean test* over a specific feature with id ϕ, i.e., $f_\phi \in \mathcal{F}$, and a constant threshold $\gamma \in \mathbb{R}$. This test is in the form $\mathbf{x}[\phi] \leq \gamma$. Each leaf $l \in L$ stores the *prediction* $l.\mathtt{val} \in \mathbb{R}$, representing the potential contribution of tree T to the final score of the document.

All the nodes whose Boolean conditions evaluate to FALSE are called *false nodes*, and *true nodes* otherwise. The scoring of a document represented by a feature vector $\mathbf{x}$ requires the traversing of all the trees in the ensemble, starting at their root nodes. If a visited node in N is a false one, then the *right* branch is taken, and the *left* branch otherwise. The visit continues recursively until a leaf node is reached, where the value of the *prediction* is returned. Such leaf node is named *exit leaf* and denoted by $e(\mathbf{x}) \in L$. We omit $\mathbf{x}$ when it is clear from the context.

Hereinafter, we assume that nodes of T are numbered in breadth-first order and leaves from left to right, and let ϕ_i and γ_i be the feature id and threshold associated with i-th internal node, respectively. It is worth noting that the same feature can be involved in multiple nodes of the same tree. For example, in the tree shown in Figure 1, the features f_0 and f_2 are used twice. Assuming that $\mathbf{x}$ is such that $\mathbf{x}[2] > \gamma_0$, $\mathbf{x}[3] \leq \gamma_2$, and $\mathbf{x}[0] \leq \gamma_3$, the exit leaf e of the tree in the Figure 1 is the leaf l_2.

The tree traversal process is repeated for all the trees of the ensemble $\mathcal{T}$, denoted by $\mathcal{T} = \{T_0, T_1, \ldots\}$. The score $s(\mathbf{x})$ of the whole ensemble is finally computed as a *weighted sum* over the contributions of each tree $T_h = (N_h, L_h)$ in $\mathcal{T}$ as:

$$s(\mathbf{x}) = \sum_{h=0}^{|\mathcal{T}|-1} w_h \cdot e_h(\mathbf{x}).\mathtt{val}$$

where $e_h(\mathbf{x}).\mathtt{val}$ is the predicted value of tree T_h, having weight $w_h \in \mathbb{R}$.

Algorithm 1: The QuickScorer Algorithm

QuickScorer($\mathbf{x}$,$\mathcal{T}$):
- **foreach** $T_h \in \mathcal{T}$ **do**
  - `leafindexes[`h`]` $\leftarrow$ `11...11`
- **foreach** $f_\phi \in \mathcal{F}$ **do** `// Mask Computation Step`
  - **foreach** $(\gamma, h, n) \in \mathcal{N}_\phi$ *in ascending order* **do**
    - **if** $\mathbf{x}[\phi] > \gamma$ **then**
      - `leafindexes[`h`]` $\leftarrow$ `leafindexes[`h`]` $\wedge$ `nodemasks[`n`]`
    - **else**
      - **break**
- $score \leftarrow 0$
- **foreach** $T_h \in \mathcal{T}$ **do** `// Score Computation Step`
  - $j \leftarrow$ index of leftmost bit set to 1 of `leafindexes[`h`]`
  - $l \leftarrow h \cdot \Lambda + j$
  - $score \leftarrow score +$ `leafvalues[`l`]`
- **return** $score$

3 QuickScorer

Algorithm 1 illustrates QS. One important result of QS is that to compute $s(\mathbf{x})$ it needs to identify only the *false nodes* [9]. To do so, QS maintains for each tree $T_h \in \mathcal{T}$ a bitvector `leafindexes[`h`]`, made of Λ bits, one per leaf. Initially, every bit in `leafindexes[`h`]` is set to 1. Moreover, each branching node n is associated with a binary mask `nodemasks[`n`]` idendifying the set of unreachable leaves in case the corresponding test evaluates to false. Whenever a false node is visited, the set of unreachable leaves `leafindexes[`h`]` is updated through a *logical and* with `nodemasks[`n`]`. Eventually, the leftmost bit set in `leafindexes[`h`]` identifies the leaf corresponding to the score contribution of T_h, stored in the lookup table `leafvalues`.

To efficiently identify all the *false nodes* in the ensemble, QS processes the branching nodes of all the trees *feature by feature* and in ascending order of their predicate thresholds. Specifically, for each feature f_ϕ, QS builds a list $\mathcal{N}_\phi$ of tuples (γ, h, n), where γ is the predicate threshold of node n occurring in tree T_h. When processing $\mathcal{N}_\phi$ in ascending order by γ, as soon as a test evaluates to true, i.e., $\mathbf{x}[\phi] \leq \gamma$, the remaining occurrences surely evaluate to true as well, and their evaluation is thus safely skipped.

We call *mask computation* the first step of the algorithm during which all the bitvectors `leafindexes[`h`]` are updated, and *score computation* the second step where such bitvectors are used to retrieve tree predictions.

Implementation details A few important remarks concern the bitvectors stored in `leafindexes` and `nodemasks`. The learning algorithm controls the accuracy of each single tree with a parameter Λ, which determines the maximal number of leaves for each $T_h = (N_h, L_h)$ in $\mathcal{T}$, namely $|L_h| \leq \Lambda$. Usually, the value of Λ is kept small (≤ 64). Thus, the length of bitvectors, which have to encode tree leaves, is equal to (or less than) a typical machine word of modern CPUs (64 bits). As a consequence, the bitwise operations performed by Algorithm 1 on them can be realized very efficiently, because they involve machine words (or halfwords, etc). We avoid any possible performance overhead due to shifting operations to align the operands of bitwise logical ANDs by forcing the bitvectors to have uniform length of B bytes. To this end, we pad each bitvector on its right side with a string of 0 bits, if necessary. We always select the minimum number of bytes $B \in \{1, 2, 4, 8\}$ fitting Λ. We first note that `leafindexes` is the only array used in both phases. During the first step `leafindexes` is accessed randomly in read/write to update bitvectors $leaf\_index_h$. During the second step the same array is accessed sequentially in read mode to identify the exit leafs l_h of each tree T_h, and then to access the array `leafvalues` to read the contribution of tree T_h to the document score. Even if the trees and their leaves are accessed sequentially during the second step of QS, the reading access to array `leafvalues` is sequential, but very sparse: only one leaf of each block of $|L_h|$ elements is actually read.

Finally, note that the arrays storing the triples, i.e., `thresholds`, `treeids`, and `nodemasks`, are all sequentially read during the first step, though not completely, since for each feature we stop their inspection at the first test condition that evaluates to TRUE. The cache usage can greatly benefit from the layout and access modes of our data structures, thanks to the increased references locality.

4 Experiments

Experiments reported here are conducted by using a publicly available LtR dataset provided by TISCALI ITALIA S.p.A., used in the past to learn the ranker of Italian web search engine ISTELLA (`http://www.istella.it`). It is composed of 33,018 queries and 10,454,629 query-document pairs. Each query-document pair is represented by a vector of 220 features. The dataset is split in two files: the training set, with 23,319 queries and 7,325,625 vectors for each query-document pair, and the test set, containing 9,799 queries and 3,129,004 vectors. To the best of our knowledge, this dataset is the largest publicly available LtR dataset, particularly useful for large-scale experiments on the efficiency and scalability of LtR solutions.

We use the training set of Istella to train λ-MART [15] ensembles (optimizing NDCG@10) whose maximum number of leaves is equal to 8, 16, 32, or 64. To train these models we use QuickRank[5], our open-source LtR C++11 framework providing efficient implementations of LtR algorithms [4]. In our experiments we compare the scoring efficiency of QS with the following competitors:

- IF-THEN-ELSE. Each decision tree is translated into a sequence of if-then-else blocks, e.g., in C++ language. The resulting code is compiled to generate

[5] `http://quickrank.isti.cnr.it`

an efficient document scorer. IF-THEN-ELSE aims at taking advantage of compiler optimization strategies, which can potentially re-arrange the tree ensemble traversal into a more efficient procedure. The size of the resulting code is proportional to the total number of nodes in the ensemble.

- VPRED. Proposed by Asadi *et al.* [1], VPRED[6] is based on a code optimization transforming *control hazards* into *data hazards*, i.e., data dependencies introduced when one instruction requires the result of another. To reduce *data hazards* the evaluation of a small set of documents (16 was the best setting) is interleaved.

All the algorithms are compiled with GCC 4.9.2 with the highest optimization settings. The tests are performed by using a single core on a machine equipped with an Intel Core i7-4770K clocked at 3.50Ghz, with 32GiB RAM, running Ubuntu Linux 3.13.0. The Intel Core i7-4770K CPU has three levels of cache. Level 1 cache has size 32 KB, one for each of the four cores, level 2 cache has size 256 KB for each core, and at level 3 there is a shared cache of 8 MB. To measure the efficiency of each of the above methods, we run 10 times the scoring code on the test set. We then compute the average per-document scoring cost.

Scoring time analysis The average time (in μs) needed by the different algorithms to score each document are reported in Table 1. In particular, the table reports the per-document scoring time by varying the number of trees and the leaves of the ensemble employed. For each test the table also reports (between parentheses) the gain factor of QS over its competitors. At a first glance, these gains are impressive, with speedups that in many cases are above one order of magnitude. Depending on the number of trees and of leaves, QS outperforms VPRED, the most efficient solution so far, of factors ranging from 2.4x up to 5.9x. For example, the average time required by QS and VPRED to score a document in the Istella test set with a model composed of 10,000 trees and 32 leaves, are 56.0 and 325.7 μs, respectively. The comparison between QS and IF-THEN-ELSE is even more one-sided, with improvements of up to 24.3x. Similar figures can be observed with other settings. These tests confirm the behavior of QS discussed in the original SIGIR paper [9], where different publicly available datasets were used. We invite interested redears to refer to [9] for information about the deep experimental analysis conducted. The reasons of the superior performance of QS over competitor algorithms are manyfold. First, linear arrays are used to store the tree ensemble, while the algorithm exploits cache-friendly access patterns (mainly sequential patterns) to these data structures. Second, the interleaved tree traversal counts on an effective oracle that, with a few branch mis-predictions, is able to detect and return only the internal node in the tree whose conditions evaluate to FALSE. Third, the number of internal nodes visited by QS is in most cases consistently lower than in traditional methods, which recursively visits the small and unbalanced trees of the ensemble from the root to the exit leaf. The deep performance assessment conducted shows that QS

[6] `http://nasadi.github.io/OptTrees/`

exhibits very low cache misses and branch mis-prediction rates, while the instruction count is consistently smaller than the counterparts.

Table 1: Per-document scoring time in μs of QS, VPRED, and IF-THEN-ELSE, on the Istella dataset. Speedups are reported in parentheses.

Method	Λ	Number of trees			
		1,000	5,000	10,000	20,000
QS	8	**2.8** (–)	**12.0** (–)	**33.2** (–)	**41.7** (–)
VPRED		7.6 (2.7x)	39.3 (3.3x)	78.9 (2.4x)	158.3 (3.8x)
IF-THEN-ELSE		9.0 (3.2x)	84.1 (7.0x)	196.1 (5.9x)	585.7 (14.0x)
QS	16	**4.5** (–)	**17.9** (–)	**33.8** (–)	**69.3** (–)
VPRED		14.9 (3.3x)	79.3 (4.4x)	160.5 (4.7x)	326.9 (4.7x)
IF-THEN-ELSE		19.6 (4.4x)	135.5 (7.6x)	401.5 (11.9x)	1696.2 (24.5x)
QS	32	**6.8** (–)	**26.9** (–)	**56.0** (–)	**132.7** (–)
VPRED		28.1 (4.1x)	157.7 (5.9x)	325.7 (5.8x)	678.2 (5.1x)
IF-THEN-ELSE		33.3 (4.9x)	240.6 (8.9x)	1357.1 (24.3x)	2702.8 (20.4x)
QS	64	**11.2** (–)	**57.8** (–)	**146.7** (–)	**289.6** (–)
VPRED		54.3 (4.8x)	326.8 (5.7x)	696.3 (4.7x)	1413.1 (4.9x)
IF-THEN-ELSE		55.0 (4.9x)	911.2 (15.8x)	2334.8 (15.9x)	4678.8 (16.2x)

5 Conclusions

This discussion paper briefly presented a novel algorithm to efficiently score documents by using a machine-learned ranking function modeled by an additive ensemble of regression trees. The algorithm was first presented at ACM SIGIR 2015 where it won the best paper award [9]. The main contribution is a new representation of the tree ensemble based on bitvectors, where the tree traversal, aimed to detect the leaves that contribute to the final scoring of a document, is performed through efficient logical bitwise operations. In addition, the traversal is not performed one tree after another, as one would expect, but it is interleaved, feature by feature, over the whole tree ensemble. Our tests conducted on publicly available LtR datasets confirm unprecedented speedups over the best state-of-the-art competitor.

The QUICKSCORER solution is undergoing an international patent process by TISCALI ITALIA S.p.A. and is used in production by the web search engine ISTELLA (`http://www.istella.it`).

As future work, we plan to apply the same devised algorithm to other contexts, when a tree-based machine learned model must be applied to big data for classification/prediction purposes. Moreover, we aim at investigating whether we can introduce further optimizations in the algorithms, considering that the same tree-based model is applied to a multitude of feature vectors, and thus we could have the chance of partially reusing some work. Finally, we plan to investigate the parallelization of our method, which can involve various dimensions, i.e., the parallelization of the scoring task of each single feature vector, or the parallelization of the simultaneous scoring of many feature vectors.

References

1. N. Asadi, J. Lin, and A. P. de Vries. Runtime optimizations for tree-based machine learning models. *IEEE Trans. Knowl. Data Eng.*, 26(9):2281–2292, 2014.
2. C. J. Burges. From ranknet to lambdarank to lambdamart: An overview. Technical Report MSR-TR-2010-82, 2010.
3. B. B. Cambazoglu, H. Zaragoza, O. Chapelle, J. Chen, C. Liao, Z. Zheng, and J. Degenhardt. Early exit optimizations for additive machine learned ranking systems. In *Proc. ACM WSDM*, pages 411–420. ACM, 2010.
4. G. Capannini, D. Dato, C. Lucchese, M. Mori, F. M. Nardini, S. Orlando, R. Perego, and N. Tonellotto. Quickrank: a C++ suite of learning to rank algorithms. In *Proceedings of the 6th Italian Information Retrieval Workshop (IIR)*, 2015.
5. J. H. Friedman. Greedy function approximation: a gradient boosting machine. *Annals of Statistics*, pages 1189–1232, 2001.
6. Y. Ganjisaffar, R. Caruana, and C. V. Lopes. Bagging gradient-boosted trees for high precision, low variance ranking models. In *Proc. ACM SIGIR*, pages 85–94, New York, NY, USA, 2011. ACM.
7. K. Järvelin and J. Kekäläinen. Cumulated gain-based evaluation of ir techniques. *ACM Trans. Inf. Syst.*, 20(4):422–446, 2002.
8. T.-Y. Liu. Learning to rank for information retrieval. *Foundations and Trends in Information Retrieval*, 3(3):225–331, 2009.
9. C. Lucchese, F. M. Nardini, S. Orlando, R. Perego, N. Tonellotto, and R. Venturini. Quickscorer: A fast algorithm to rank documents with additive ensembles of regression trees. In *Proceedings of the 38th International ACM SIGIR Conference on Research and Development in Information Retrieval (SIGIR)*, pages 73–82. ACM, 2015.
10. S. Robertson and H. Zaragoza. The probabilistic relevance framework: Bm25 and beyond. *Found. Trends Inf. Retr.*, 3(4):333–389, 2009.
11. I. Segalovich. Machine learning in search quality at yandex. ACM SIGIR, Industry track, 2010.
12. X. Tang, X. Jin, and T. Yang. Cache-conscious runtime optimization for ranking ensembles. In *Proc. ACM SIGIR*, pages 1123–1126, 2014.
13. P. Viola and M. J. Jones. Robust real-time face detection. *Int. J. Comput. Vision*, 57(2):137–154, 2004.
14. L. Wang, J. J. Lin, and D. Metzler. A cascade ranking model for efficient ranked retrieval. In *Proc. ACM SIGIR*, pages 105–114, 2011.
15. Q. Wu, C. Burges, K. Svore, and J. Gao. Adapting boosting for information retrieval measures. *Information Retrieval*, 2010.
16. Z. Xu, K. Weinberger, and O. Chapelle. The greedy miser: Learning under test-time budgets. In *Proc. ICML*, pages 1175–1182, New York, NY, USA, 2012. ACM.

Mercurio: predicting financial events from expert knowledge and financial news*

Sara Marchesini[1], Martina Morlacchi Bonfanti[1], Mirjana Mazuran[1], Davide Greco[2], and Letizia Tanca[1]

[1] Politecnico di Milano – Dipartimento di Elettronica, Informazione e Bioingegneria
sara.marchesini@mail.polimi.it, martina.morlacchi@mail.polimi.it,
mirjana.mazuran@polimi.it, letizia.tanca@polimi.it
[2] Accento
d.greco@accento.it

Abstract. Being able to understand the financial market is very important for investors and, given the width and complexity of the topic, tools to support investor decisions are badly needed. In this paper we present Mercurio, the first prototype of a system that supports the decision-making process of financial investors through the automatic extraction and analysis of information coming from financial newspaper articles. Mercurio formalizes the knowledge and reasoning of an expert in financial journalism and uses it to identify relevant financial events inside the financial articles. Then, sequential pattern mining is used to predict the happening of exceptional events given their past occurrences and relationships with other events, and to warn investors about them.

1 Introduction

Neverending amounts of data are daily produced and made available on the Web: their added value resides in the possibility to freely process them to gain insight and competitive advantage. A domain acquiring more and more interest is the financial world, because of its inherent complexity due to the rules governing the financial market and to the internal and external factors that influence it. Investors want to make good investments: they constantly read financial news and analyze financial indexes, using their knowledge and experience to predict market events and make profitable investments. Our research aims at developing Mercurio, a decision support system to help investors during these activities.

Mercurio simulates the behavior of an expert investor; it identifies relevant financial events, understands how they are related to each other and exploits this knowledge to predict future happenings. As a basis, it uses the knowledge of an expert in financial journalism whose understanding of the news are not achievable by sole natural language processing. A domain expert knows "how to" read an article, understand its meaning and interpret the "general mood" of the moment.

* This research is partially supported by the IBM Faculty Award "SOFIA: Semi-autOmatic Financial Information Analytics"

Indeed, the way to communicate a piece of news is never casual, and what is understandable from a literal inspection of the news often does not coincide with the real meaning of what has happened. Financial happenings are all about signals and indications that companies leave behind along their path in the stock-market and that the system must capture and interpret. Investment decisions are still made by human investors, and Mercurio provides them knowledge, possibly hidden to human observers, to improve their decision-making process.

Among the many financial news available on the web, Mercurio looks for those that are "important", i.e., influence and shake the market: we call them *events*. Some of them are more relevant because they represent considerable changes of the financial market: we call them *catastrophes*, and they coincide with extraordinary financial moves, e.g. merger and acquisition or significant stockprice variations. The occurrence of a catastrophe is usually anticipated by "symptoms" that we call *signals*. For example, an investor might observe that, often, before a crash, a company gives an interview stating that profits are increasing; from now on, whenever such an interview is published the expert will expect the related stock to fall in the stock market. Thus, an article containing an interview about increasing profit is a signal, while a stock crash is a catastrophe.

The paper is organized as follows: Section 2 briefly describe some proposals with aims similar as ours, Section 3 gives the details of the Mercurio system, Section 4 provides the first experimental results we achieved and, finally, Section 5 draws the conclusions we have currently reached and future research directions.

2 Related work

Market prediction is the topic that has received the biggest interest in the literature. Mostly, only numerical data are used but some approaches exploit textual information coming from breaking news to increase the quality of input data and improve predictions. The two main research directions so far have been: (i) automatic analysis mostly based on Automated Text Categorization (ATC) and (ii) analysis based on a-priori knowledge usually provided by human operators.

The ATC techniques allow to automatically sort a set of documents into predefined categories. Works in [3–7] use these techniques to predict short-term market reactions to news. Articles are categorized as either good, bad or neutral based on the influence their publication has on financial time indexes. All of these approaches entail correlation of the content of news articles with financial trends, but they adopt different types of classifiers. Our approach differs as (i) we do not use stock market trends but only the textual contents of news and (ii) we use expert knowledge to determine the relevance of articles. Among the examined works, [8] has a similar goal as Mercurio, to find sequences of articles that anticipate a changing trend. Once again the focus is on numerical data, while we are interested in predicting strategically extraordinary financial moves.

Existing works are primarily data driven, however some proposals use a-priori knowledge about the application domain. Works in [9, 10] analyze financial articles and create a handcrafted thesaurus containing words that drive the stock prices and that are later used to predict stock prices. Similarly, [11] uses a-priori domain knowledge to predict interest rates. A cognitive map represents cause-effect relationships among the events in the domain and is used as the basis to retrieve the relevant news; these are then classified as either positive or negative according to the way they influence the rates. A work similar to ours is [12], where the objective is to predict the Tokyo stock exchange price using a-priori knowledge in the form of rules. Domain rules are defined eliciting non-numerical factors that influence the stock price, however, these rules differ from ours as they convey general knowledge about political and international events. On the contrary we focus on financial and economic events typical of a company's life.The latter approaches differ from ours either in the way knowledge is represented or in the kind of knowledge adopted as background; we are currently trying to find a basis for an effective comparison, since the systems are not available and thus an experimental comparison on the same corpus is for the moment impossible.

3 Mercurio

The aim of Mercurio is to predict catastrophes; this goal entails four main phases:

1. *Data acquisition and management*: financial news are extracted from web sources, they are structured and stored into a relational database; their contents are then cleaned and pre-processed;
2. *Event recognition*: articles are analyzed to identify both catastrophes and signals. Mercurio adopts three different approaches for event recognition:
   - *Semantic approach*: events are recognized by means of semantic rules that formalize the knowledge and experience of our domain expert.
   - *Automatic approach*: events are identified by applying clustering algorithms to financial news.
   - *Hybrid approach*: a combination of the previous approaches where catastrophes are recognized with semantic rules and signals by means of clustering.
3. *Model construction*: the events found from the previous step are used in combination with sequential pattern mining to learn a model, represented by means of temporal patterns, to predict the arrival of catastrophes.

3.1 Data acquisition and management

The first thing about data acquisition is choosing the right companies to monitor and the right data sources providing financial news. This choice was guided by our expert's knowledge and resulted in Mercurio currently monitoring 250 Italian mid-cap companies and getting the financial news from important Italian financial and economic web sources such as "Il Sole 24 Ore", "Radiocor", "La Repubblica" and "Il Corriere della Sera". The chosen companies have been selected by our domain expert as neither "too noisy" nor "too silent", i.e., there are neither too many, nor too few news articles about them; noisy companies are difficult to analyze due to an excess of signals while silent companies do not have enough signals to allow an analysis.

Using a Python script, Mercurio extracts articles directly from the newspapers websites and stores them in a MySQL database (our initial data contains about 14,000 articles, from year 2010 to 2015). To avoid incorrect or ambiguous analysis, we keep only articles that are part of financial and economic sections and contain the name of one of the chosen companies in the headline, subheading or abstract. After this phase the article texts are cleaned by tokenization, stopword elimination and word stemming: to this purpose we use NLTK[1] which provides both a list of stopwords and a stemmer.

Mercurio implements two different text pre-processing strategies, one based on the event semantics and the other one based on automatic event recognition. In the first strategy we kept all special characters, symbols, punctuation marks, numbers, words, company names and persons details because they are needed by the expert's rules. In the second strategy these data are not significant, sometimes even misleading when applying clustering algorithms, so much of them were eliminated from the texts.

3.2 Event recognition

Events are detected through text analysis of the contents of the financial news. Mercurio implements three event recognition approaches, and all of them produce as a result a temporal sequence containing the recognized events.

Semantic event recognition. With the guidance of our domain expert, we produced a set of rules that formalize the recognition of relevant events inside financial news. Rules define a relationship between some keywords, regular expressions (in general, sentence structures), and corresponding events (e.g. "take" is a keyword related to an acquisition event). An article that contains the expressions defined in a rule is assigned a label corresponding to the event formalized by the rule. Each article is assigned zero, one or more labels depending on the rules it triggers.

Rules allow us to capture meanings that go beyond the sole natural language processing. For example, financial newspapers, usually, publish interviews when requested by a company. The question is: why would a company want to be interviewed? When this breaks a trend of non communication it must be a signal. Also, an article that mentions the gross profit of a company is not a good sign because this indicator does not provide the amount of real revenue of the company, thus it could hide a negative trend of the company, whereas the net profit is not ambiguous, so this is a positive financial communication.

Using the rules, Mercurio looks for specific sentence structures (possibly containing numbers or percentages related to financial measures) inside articles and labels each of them with the events they convey. The labeled articles are used to build the pattern-based prediction model.

Automatic event recognition. This approach does not use any a-priori knowledge but relies on the detection of events by only applying clustering algorithms to the pre-processed financial news. Articles are represented in the Vector Space Model [1] where the weight of each term is the TF-IDF frequency of its occurrences in the article. Then, articles are clustered using the K-means algorithm and each article is assigned one label, corresponding to the cluster it belongs to.

[1] `http://www.nltk.org/`

The process of article clustering has proven to be quite challenging: we initially tried to perform it on the whole textual contents of each article. This resulted in a huge set of features that made the clustering too time-consuming. More pre-processing was needed to be able to run this approach, in particular: (i) after consulting with our domain expert we decided to perform clustering based only on the features found from the headline, subheading or abstract of each article, thus without considering its body, (ii) among the found features we kept only those which appeared at least twice in the corpus and (iii) we still ended up performing a manual selection of the subset of automatically detected features in order to eliminate those terms that, according to our domain expert, were not significant in the financial context.

At the end of the clustering phase we tried to interpret the results and found it impossible to distinguish between clusters representing signals and those representing catastrophes. This was a big drawback from our point of view since we were not able to understand how to predict catastrophes.

Hybrid event recognition. To overcome the problem exposed above, we "added some semantics" to the automatic approach, obtaining what we called the hybrid one. In this approach, catastrophes are found by using the semantic rules that formalize catastrophic events, while the other signals are obtained by clustering all those articles that were not isolated by the rules defining catastrophic events. This approach also required some tuning, in fact, as a first result, we obtained one huge cluster (more than 50% of articles were grouped in it) whose semantics was hard to comprehend. However, when applying another round of clustering on its elements (this time considering the whole textual content of each article) we noticed that each cluster was in fact describing different "categories" of articles.

3.3 Model construction

The output of the event recognition phase is a sequence of events, each associated with a timestamp that corresponds to the date and time of publishing of the article in which the event was found. Based on this sequence, Mercurio uses Sequential Pattern Mining to find "recurring" temporal patterns in the input data which are then used to predict future catastrophes.

This step is performed by using AIDA[2], a tool that encompasses both the model creation and prediction features. The tool is applied in two phases: (i) given as input a temporal sequence of events, a specific event e from the sequence and a minimum support threshold, it finds all temporal patterns that end with e and whose support is above the threshold; (ii) given the found model and a real-time flow of previously unseen articles, it predicts the happening of the learned events within a certain time span. In particular, during the prediction phase, each incoming new article is processed and labeled according to the events it triggers. Then, the system tries to match each event to the ones in the patterns of the model. If this happens, it waits for another event that would match the next event in the pattern. This process is repeated until a pattern expires because of time constraints or its last but one event is reached. When this happens, we can predict the happening of the next event, which is the one corresponding to the last node of the pattern, which, by construction, is always a catastrophe.

4 Experiments

In this section we briefly relate on the performance of our prototype and compare the results of the semantic approach (SA) and hybrid approach (HA). First of all, let us recall the differences between the two approaches, in terms of article-event relationships: (i) in SA an article might contain both catastrophes and signals, while in HA this is not possible because clustering is computed only on those articles that do not trigger any catastrophe; (ii) in SA an article might not trigger any rules thus not generate any event; in HA all the articles are associated with exactly one event, either a catastrophe or a cluster label; (iii) in SA an article might trigger more than one signal, while in HA each article belong to only one cluster, thus, it is related to only one signal.

These differences make it difficult to qualitatively compare the results of the two approaches, articles that trigger the same events in SA often belong to different clusters in HA. We discuss the two approaches by comparing the models they produce through numerical results about the patterns that were found.

Semantic approach. We considered 2549 instances of events (556 of catastrophes, 1993 of signals) and, for each catastrophe, built a model to predict it. After some initial tuning, we selected 0.3 as the best support threshold, Table 1 gives an overview of the models extracted for 10 different catastrophes (q20, q21,...). For example, the model to predict $q26$ contains 7 patterns, whose lengths vary between 2 and 3 events.

	q20	q21	q33	q19	q29	q26	q30	q36	q34	q13	Total
Number of patterns	1	3	40	11	1	7	9	3	1	12	88
Min pattern length	2	2	2	2	2	2	2	2	2	2	2
Max pattern length	2	2	7	4	2	3	3	2	2	3	7

Table 1. Information about models in the semantic approach

The models, constructed on the training set, were tested on previously unseen data to determine the precision and recall of our predictions (shown in Figure 1 and Figure 2). The test set contains 1077 events extracted from 1796 articles published between 2008 and 2010. We recall that low precision means that there are many wrong predictions, i.e. many times the system predicts a catastrophe which does not actually happen, and a low recall means that there are many missed predictions, i.e. many times the system does not predict a catastrophe and the catastrophe actually happens. Moreover, in the plots, we adopt a conventional value, -1, to denote that no predictions were made at all.

We can see that results vary depending on the catastrophe, e.g., q29 has always both precision and recall equal to -1 because its model has only one pattern which does not appear in the testing set. On the contrary, q20, q21, q36 have always maximum precision because the system makes only right predictions about them. However, q20 and q21 have low recall which means that many times

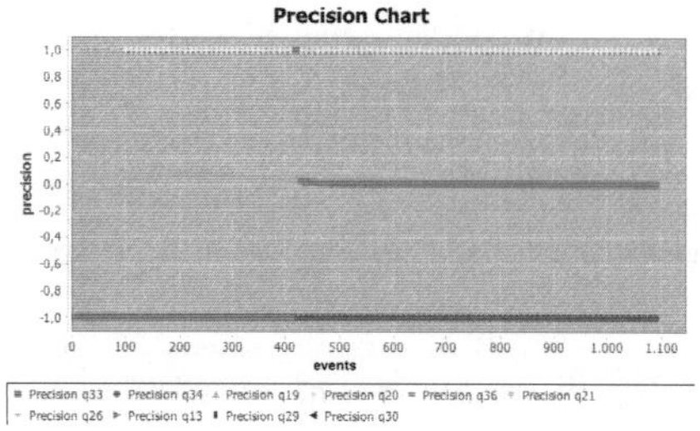

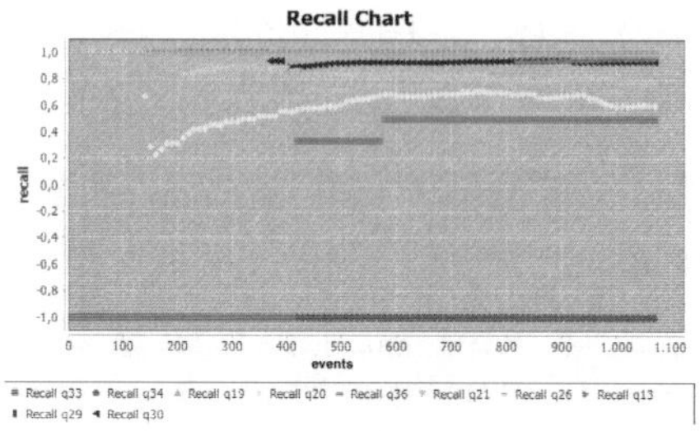

Fig. 1. Precision of the semantic approach **Fig. 2.** Recall of the semantic approach

the catastrophe happens and the system was not able to predict it. These results strongly depend on the minimum support threshold: the higher the support threshold, the higher the precision and the lower the recall; conversely, the lower the support threshold, the lower the precision and the higher the recall.

Hybrid approach. We consider 3283 articles (438 catastrophes, 2845 are clustered). Table 2 gives an overview of 10 extracted models.

	q17	q7	q23	q21	q28	q25	q14	q30	q29	q15	Total
Number of patterns	5	6	21	21	5	21	21	7	4	21	132
Min pattern length	2	2	2	2	2	2	2	2	2	2	2
Max pattern length	3	3	6	3	3	5	5	3	2	5	6

Table 2. Information about models in the hybrid approach

The hybrid approach allows us to obtain a greater number of patterns w.r.t. the semantic approach and results in an increase of the average number of patterns for each catastrophe and also of the maximum pattern length, Figure 3 and Figure 4 show the results in terms of precision and recall. Also in this case results vary depending on the catastrophe: q28 has precision and recall always equal to -1, i.e. the patterns in its model are never found; q21 has both precision and recall equals to 1: these events are perfectly predicted, there are only right predictions and not wrong or missed predictions. Conversely, q29 is very hard to predict: precision equals to -1, recall mostly equals to 0, meaning that there are not right nor wrong predictions, but only missed ones. It can be seen that both approaches offer satisfactory performances, however we are working at making the models more accurate, so that the final prototype will be based on more training data and on an integration the two techniques.

5 Conclusion

In this paper we discussed Mercurio, a system that supports the decision-making process of investors through the automatic extraction and analysis of information coming from financial news articles, with the aim of predicting extraordinary financial moves. Current results are encouraging but leave space for many improvements, especially related to enrichments of the current model, such as introducing weights and polarity to each event and the use of statistical information about the whole financial market, its different sectors and each monitored

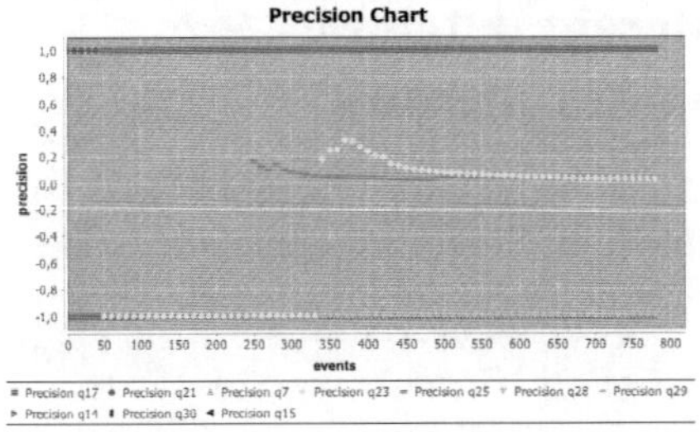

Fig. 3. Precision of the hybrid approach

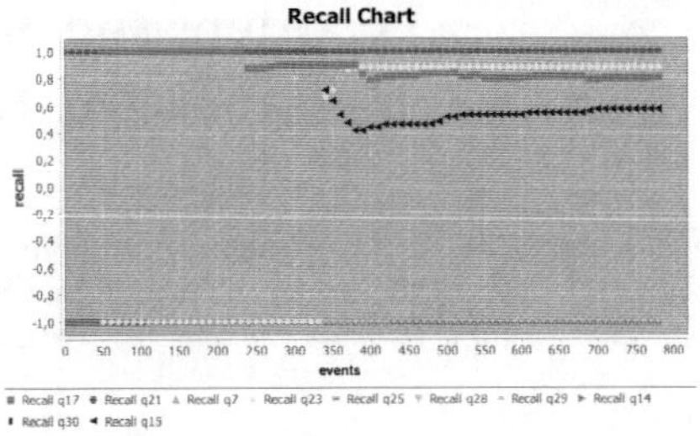

Fig. 4. Recall of the hybrid approach

company. We would like to thank Luca Marconi and all the other students who contributed to this project.

References

1. G. Salton, A. Wong, C. S. Yang. A vector space model for automatic indexing. Commun. ACM 18, 11 (November 1975), 613-620.
2. M. Mazuran, M. Simoni, L. Tanca. AIDA: Automatic Indexing based on DAta mining. SEBD 2015. pp.176-183.
3. S. Bacher. Mining Unstructured Financial News to Forecast Intraday Stock Price Movements. PhD Thesis. University Mannheim. 2012.
4. G.P.C. Fung, J. Xu Yu, W. Lam. News Sensitive Stock Trend Prediction. PAKDD 2002 pp.481-493.
5. G. Gidofalvi. Using News Articles to Predict Stock Price Movements. Department of Computer Science and Engineering, University of California, San Diego. 2001.
6. M.A. Mittermayer. Forecasting Intraday Stock Price Trends with Text Mining Techniques. HICSS 2004.
7. D. Peramunetilleke, R.K. Wong. Currency exchange rate forecasting from news headlines. ADC 2002. pp.131-139.
8. V. Lavrenko, M. Schmill, D. Lawrie, P. Ogilvie, D. Jensen, J. Allan. Language models for financial news recommendation. CIKM 2000. pp.389-396.
9. M.A. Mittermayer, G. F. Knolmayer. NewsCATS: A News Categorization and Trading System. ICDM 2006. pp.1002-1007.
10. B. Wuthrich, V. Cho, S. W. Leung, D. Permunetilleke, K. Sankaran, J. Zhang. Daily stock market forecast from textual web data. ICSMC 1998. pp.2720-2725.
11. T. Hong, I. Han, Knowledge-based data mining of news information on the Internet using cognitive maps and neural networks. Expert Systems with Applications 2002, 23(1):1-8.
12. K. Kohara, T. Ishikawa, Y. Fukuhara, Y. Nakamura. Stock Price Prediction Using Prior Knowledge and Neural Networks. Intelligent Systems in Accounting, Finance and Management 1997, 6(1):11-22.

Persistence on different databases via reflective IoT Middleware

Tommaso Di Noia, Marina Mongiello, Francesco Nocera, Eugenio Di Sciascio

Polytechnic University of Bari, Via Orabona, 4, 70125 Bari, Italy
`{firstname.lastname}@poliba.it`

Abstract. We daily experience the interaction with physical objects which are becoming smarter and smarter with the ability to communicate with each other as well as with diverse information systems. While, on the one hand, we are assisting to the rise of a pervasive Internet of Things (IoT), on the other hand we face the need of a new generation of objects able to adapt to external inputs coming from the environment they are dipped in. Here, we propose a solution allowing a IoT Middleware to conform to Reflective programming paradigm thus giving more flexibility and adaptability to the network behavior which writes data coming from a network of sensors into relational and a non-relational DBMS.

1 Introduction

The Internet of Things (IoT) is for sure one of the most influential technological shift we are facing in the last years. Thanks to the spreading of sensors and to the diffusion of low-cost miniaturized computational resources, we are able to make objects produce data and interact with each other thus producing a network of interconnected things. IoT makes possible to distribute data sources and data consumers in the real world to produce, collect, exchange and consume information usually with a high rate. Elements of the IoT are quite evolved piece of hardware that may be programmed and covered by a software layer implementing complex functionalities. One of the challenges in building a smart IoT-based network is to make it robust with reference to the contextual changes it continually undergoes. We all known that the physical world is not a static environment and it changes accordingly to sometimes unpredictable events. Then, informative objects which are dipped in the physical world should be able to adapt and change their behavior accordingly to the surrounding context. This means that the software they have on board should be able to react in order to change and modify its functions to comply with the new environmental variables. From the point of view of a software architecture, IoT poses many interesting challenges due to its unpredictable yet adaptive requirements. In order to be as effective as possible, in IoT solutions the intelligent objects are usually coordinated by a middleware that acts as a facilitator towards a smoother and homogeneous communication among the various components. A huge work is available in the literature about IoT middleware. Interesting and structured surveys are in [2, 5, 12, 8]. IoT middleware is also facing multiple challenges [4, 1] that are mainly induced by IoT features.

In this paper we propose a reflective extension of an IoT middleware. The approach aims to show a possible solution to make a IoT middleware conforming to the pattern of reflective programming, which allows a software system to dynamically change its logic without internal changes to the code. The remainder of the paper is structured as follows: in the next section we describe the approach we propose and we provide a few details on the implementation. In Section 3 the architecture and the behavior of our adaptable middleware is described. Related works are introduced in Section 4. Conclusion and future work close the paper.

2 Proposed Approach

While designing a IoT solution, the use of traditional methods may lead to excessive complexity of the code that may become slow and/or little maintainable. Among the different patterns available to design a software system, *Reflection* allows the developer to produce an extensible architecture from the beginning. The main concept is the distinction between *base level* and *meta-level*: A base level contains the application logic basic software while the meta-level takes care of all the aspects that can change independently from the base level. A meta-level contains those parts of the application that may vary at run-time, with the goal of creating new applications starting from existing base level classes. Thus, a proper configuration of the base level and meta-objects defines the behavior of an application. In addition, using a programming language that supports reflection, it is possible to change the structure of the objects themselves at run-time and then make the software system more flexible. There is also an additional layer called *MOP* (for *M*eta-*O*bject *P*rotocol), which defines how changes are made to the meta-level. MOP also makes possible the change of connections between the base level and meta-objects.

A IoT middleware can surely benefit from the use of a reflective approach. As an example, we have the possibility of designing a system completely configurable and adaptable to different operating environments. In our implementation, the system will automatically perform actions according to the values received by the sensors of devices by matching a set of formal rules. Our prototype is based on the IoT middleware *DeviceHive*[1]. In order to show the usefulness of reflection we developed a system which writes data coming from a network of sensors into different databases. For illustration purposes we selected a relational and a non-relational DBMS. The hardware used to provide a source of data is based on the *Arduino* platform, a small electronics card equipped with a microcontroller, which is used to quickly achieve hardware prototypes. In addition to the *Arduino* board we have used the *RaspberryPi B+* card to send and receive data from/to the local server which then makes a transition of data to *Cloud DeviceHive* servers.

Hereafter, we describe two components that play an important role in the architecture we are going to present in Section 3.

The DeviceHive middleware. The purpose of a middleware is to act as an intermediary between applications and software components. Our choice for DeviceHive fell on this middleware for ease of installation, the rich documentation and the high integration with a wide range of programming languages and IoT protocols. By using DeviceHive, the set up of a IoT system is made by the following three steps:

[1] http://www.devicehive.com

- Create: the user must create an instance of the *Cloud by DeviceHive*. There are instances of *Microsoft Azure*, *Juju*, *Docker* and *Cloud Playground*. In our implementation, we used the shell instance *Cloud Playground*.
- Connect: using the specific IoT Toolkit, a dedicated gateway is installed. This is the link between the devices and the cloud of DeviceHive. The gateway is written in Go, and in our case communicates with a Python script that is responsible for receiving the data from the sensors within the network.
- Visualize: sent data can be displayed via a Web page.

Redis as a Message Broker. Redis[2] is a NoSQL DBMS built in 2009. It is based on the key-value paradigm but has some characteristics that make it different from other database of its own category: it works in RAM, provides support to the storage of the pair key-value, it offers four data structures: lists, sets, ordered sets and hash. We used Redis as the Message Broker, which allows to translate a message from the messaging protocol of the sender to the recipient's messaging protocol. Through appropriate Pub/-Sub directives Redis implements the mechanism of Publish/Subscribe, whereby senders do not send messages directly to recipients; rather the messages are published and sorted into channels, without knowing who is really writing to the channel. Interested parties express their intention to subscribe to notifications of one or more channels of interest. This decoupling between publishers and subscribers allows for greater scalability and a dynamic network topology.

During the last years there has been a remarkable growth of the techniques and tools used to maintain and optimize the persistence and search on large amounts of data. Besides proven technologies of relational databases, such as MySQL and PostgreSQL, non-relational databases have been established, named **NoSQL** (Not Only SQL). Main features of NoSQL databases is not to use a fixed pattern (schemeless); they can be classified in the following categories: document oriented; graph-based; key-value stored on disk or RAM; ordered key-value; multi value; oject-oriented; tabular; archiving in tuples.

In our project we will only use document-oriented database MongoDB and key-value database stored in RAM Redis.

A Document-Oriented database does not store the data in tables with uniform fields for record but each record is stored as a document with given features (any number of fields with any length). So the fundamental unit is the document. Differences between implementations is determined from details of documents and has a different encoding. More common encodings are XML, YAML, JSON and BSON. Documents are addressed using unique keys; often the key is a simple string, a URI or PATH.

Generally the database maintains a key index to allow quick retrieval of documents. Document-oriented DBMS often provides a query language for content-based retrieval of documents in addition to research based on document key.

MongoDB. We use MongoDB[3] DBMS – a NoSQL document-oriented database, open source written in C ++. MongoDB is designed to be powerful, flexible and scalable; it combines the best features of key-value database; it is easy to use.

[2] http://redis.io/

[3] https://www.mongodb.org/

Databases Key / Value The second category of NoSQL data that we consider in our work is the key-value. This category has a structure based on a dictionary: eash value has a key that enables its retrieval.

The key-value database has a structure based on a dictionary: each value has a key that enables its retrieval.

3 Architecture

In Fig. 3 the architectural scheme of the proposed solution is depicted while in Fig. 2 we show its class diagram. Our component is placed between the devices and the *Cloud DeviceHive*. Within the component, a configuration file will contain the definition of the rules on the data and the actions to take if the rule is checked. The Observer (of the data flow) notifies the Publish/Subscribe about the arrival of new data and the active rule. This is the reflective part that after subscribing will enable the persistence on different databases. The component we developed aims to make reflective the DeviceHive IoT middleware. In order to do this, instead of changing DeviceHive IoT middleware itself, we have created a wrapper to extend its functionalities while remaining almost independent from it. The wrapper is written on top of *Node.js*.

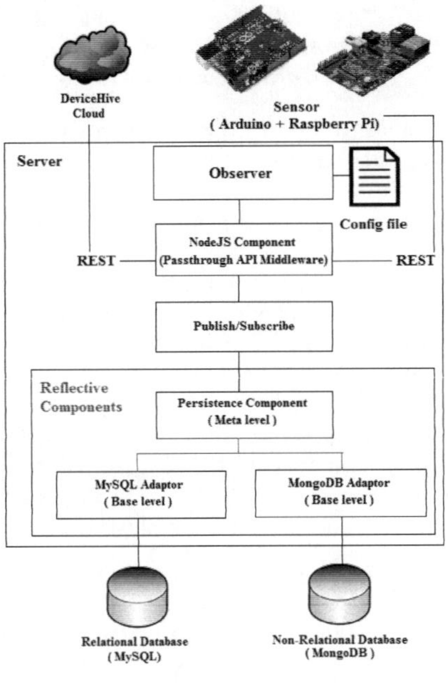

Fig. 1. Architectural schema of proposed solution

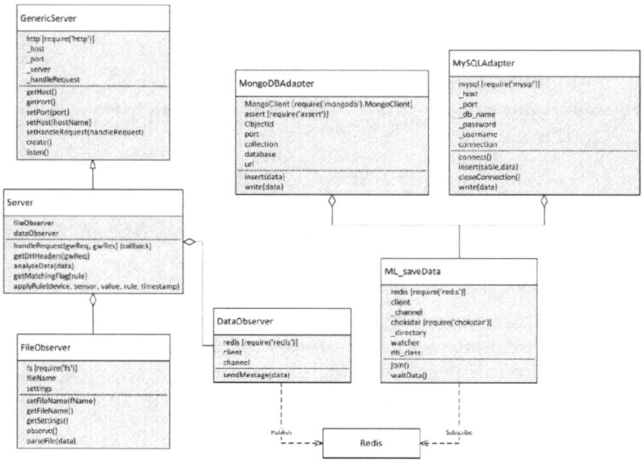

Fig. 2. Class diagram of the proposed architecture

The wrapper replaces the middleware for *passthrough* the requests delivered from devices that will connect to our component, instead of connecting directly to the middleware. This part of the server, implemented by classes `GenericServer` and `Server`, contains a simple HTTP server. Performed steps are:

1. receives the HTTP request from the gateway and analyzes the content;
2. composes a new HTTP request to the server DeviceHive, creating all the headers required by the function `getDHHeaders`;
3. as soon as the server has received the answer from DeviceHive, forwards it to the gateway of the device.

Note that with this approach it may be also possible to implement a set of classes that replace the function `getDHHeaders`, pushing the `Strategy` design pattern, to process requests sent to the middleware always based on a REST approach.

Data sent by the gateway initially directed to the middleware, i.e. DeviceHive in our framework, are intercepted by the server. This latter performs a series of comparisons to evaluate if the appropriate component of base level will be activated. Comparisons are based on checking the rules in the Configuration File, each one related to one or more sensors present on a given device. An example of rules is:

```
"id" : "Arduino_Raspberry_Temp_Hum",
"sensors" : ["temperature_sensor",
"humidity_sensor"],
"rules" : [
{ "sensor": ["humidity_sensor"],
  "action": "write",
  "argument": "mysql",
  "variable_action" : {
  "condition" : "lessThan",
  "value": "20"
```

```
    }
},
{ "sensor": ["temperature_sensor"],
  "action": "write",
  "argument": "mongo",
  "variable_action" : {
  "condition" : "moreThan",
  "value": "10"
  }
}]
```

The class delegated to parsing the configuration file (FileObserver) scans the file and analyzes the rules. In fact, a single rule could be related to several sensors. In this way, given a NOTIFICATION message received by the gateway, it only needs to check if the condition specified in `variable_action` is verified. In case it is verified, the wrapper publishes a message on the Redis Publish/Subscribe server via a DATAOBSERVER class object. FILEOBSERVER parses the configuration file in case of modification while the server is running.

3.1 Reflective Implementation

To implement the reflection mechanism, a component subscribes to the proper channel of the Redis server; the component reads published messages containing information about the specific function to be called, the class the function belongs to and the arguments. The meta-level of the reflective mechanism contains a simple call to a generic function, with the string identifying the function and the class of the function. The function writes data on the database by following the specified rules. According to this mechanism, the logic of the program can be dynamically changed depending on the data got from the sensors and changes are transparent to the internal structure of the software.

Of course, the current implementation related to the persistence component is a toy example to show the potentiality of the software. The meta-level can be extended with the meta-objects to develop considerably more advanced functionality external to the server. In fact, it is sufficient to connect the component to the Redis server for listening to the messages coming from the server.

The meta-level has access to basic levels via the object DBCLASS containing instances of basic objects identified by a particular name which is specified in the configuration file of the base level, that will be eventually analyzed. In the message received by Redis the class name and the name of the function to call are specified in special strings. The data to be written is contained in a separate object, which will be the argument of the function.

In order to determine which are the base levels available at runtime, a system for loading dynamic components within the same meta-level has been implemented. Two files for each basic level are available: a JSON file containing configuration data that the manufacturer will have to accept and a JS file containing the class itself. Objects instantiated with the data in the JSON file will then be stored in an array, and referenced by the name of the same class, specified within each rule.

4 Related work

In this section we present a state of the art of existing approaches for reflective middleware. A survey of reflective middleware for Iot is in [10]. The survey addresses a broad range of techniques, methods, models, functionalities, systems, applications, and middleware solutions related to context awareness and IoT. The paper analyzes, compares and consolidates past research work. One of the first approaches is in [3] that presents an architecture for reflective middleware based on a multi-model approach. Through a number of working examples, they demonstrate that the approach can support introspection, and fine- and coarse- grained adaptation of the resource management framework. More recent relevant approaches of reflective middlewares are in SOAR (SOA with Reflection) [6]. [7] presents a chemical reaction-inspired computational model using the concepts of graphs and reflection, which attempts to address the complexities associated with the visualization, modelling, interaction, analysis and abstraction of information in the IoT. [9] presents Internetware which consists of a set of autonomous software entities distributed over the Internet, together with a set of connectors to enable collaborations among these entities in various ways. To support on-demand collaboration, Internetware middleware employs an RSA and reflection mechanisms on its own application server. [11] extends the Multinetwork INformation Architecture (MINA), a reflective (self-observing and adapting via an embodied Observe-Analyze-Adapt loop) middleware with a layered IoT SDN controller.

5 Conclusion and Future Work

In the recent years, there has been a huge effort to provide an immediate access to information about the physical world through Internet technologies. IoT vision aims to integrate the virtual world of information to the real world of things. The role of a IoT middleware is to provide the connectivity between the virtual world and physical world and an interface between heterogeneous physical devices and applications. We present a reflective extension of an IoT middleware which makes possible the design of a software resulting completely configurable and adaptable to different operating environments. The proposed framework enables to automatically perform actions according to the values received by the sensors by triggering a set of rules. Our current implementation relies on the commercial DeviceHive middleware and wraps it with an adaptable layer thus transforming the whole middleware in a reflective architecture. The approach is general enough and can be extended to deal with diverse functionalities other than the ones currently implemented. We are working to extend the proposed framework with the addition of new Plug and Play actions. Also we are working to extend the framework and enable it for the integration of several middlewares. The idea is to build an "adaptive wrapper" of middlewares able to adapt the reflective middleware to the different clouds.

References

1. Soma Bandyopadhyay, Munmun Sengupta, Souvik Maiti, and Subhajit Dutta. Role of middleware for internet of things: A study. *International Journal of Computer Science & Engineering Survey (IJCSES)*, 2(3):94–105, 2011.

2. Soma Bandyopadhyay, Munmun Sengupta, Souvik Maiti, and Subhajit Dutta. A survey of middleware for internet of things. In *Recent Trends in Wireless and Mobile Networks*, pages 288–296. Springer, 2011.
3. Gordon S Blair, Fábio Costa, Geoff Coulson, Fabien Delpiano, Hector Duran, Bruno Dumant, François Horn, Nikos Parlavantzas, and Jean-Bernard Stefani. The design of a resource-aware reflective middleware architecture. In *Meta-Level Architectures and Reflection*, pages 115–134. Springer, 1999.
4. Moumena Chaqfeh, Nader Mohamed, et al. Challenges in middleware solutions for the internet of things. In *Collaboration Technologies and Systems (CTS), 2012 International Conference on*, pages 21–26. IEEE, 2012.
5. Ghofrane Fersi. Middleware for internet of things: A study. In *Distributed Computing in Sensor Systems (DCOSS), 2015 International Conference on*, pages 230–235. IEEE, 2015.
6. Gang Huang, Xuanzhe Liu, and Hong Mei. Soar: towards dependable service-oriented architecture via reflective middleware. *International Journal of Simulation and Process Modelling*, 3(1-2):55–65, 2007.
7. Ahsan Ikram, Ashiq Anjum, Richard Hill, Nick Antonopoulos, Lu Liu, and Stelios Sotiriadis. Approaching the internet of things (iot): a modelling, analysis and abstraction framework. *Concurrency and Computation: Practice and Experience*, 2013.
8. Valérie Issarny, Nikolaos Georgantas, Sara Hachem, Apostolos Zarras, Panos Vassiliadist, Marco Autili, Marco Aurelio Gerosa, and Amira Ben Hamida. Service-oriented middleware for the future internet: state of the art and research directions. *Journal of Internet Services and Applications*, 2(1):23–45, 2011.
9. Hong Mei, Gang Huang, and Tao Xie. Internetware: A software paradigm for internet computing. *Computer*, 12(6):26–31, 2012.
10. Charith Perera, Arkady Zaslavsky, Peter Christen, and Dimitrios Georgakopoulos. Context aware computing for the internet of things: A survey. *Communications Surveys & Tutorials, IEEE*, 16(1):414–454, 2014.
11. Zhijing Qin, Grit Denker, Carlo Giannelli, Paolo Bellavista, and Nalini Venkatasubramanian. A software defined networking architecture for the internet-of-things. In *Network Operations and Management Symposium (NOMS), 2014 IEEE*, pages 1–9. IEEE, 2014.
12. Mohammad Razzaque, Marija Milojevic-Jevric, Andrei Palade, and Siobhan Clarke. Middleware for internet of things: a survey. *Internet of Things Journal, IEEE*, PP(99), 2015.

Building Data Sources with Linked Open Data to Enrich Mashup Platforms

Giuseppe Desolda, Maria Francesca Costabile

Dipartimento di Informatica, Università degli Studi di Bari Aldo Moro
Via Orabona, 4 – 70125 – Bari, Italy
{giuseppe.desolda,maria.costabile}@uniba.it

Abstract. Nowadays, a huge amount of information is available in the Linked Open Data (LOD) cloud. This paper reports the use of LOD to enrich mashup platforms, which are web tools implementing visual mechanisms to access, compose, modify and use data sources typically available through APIs. Even if many APIs are currently available, it often happens that, due to the specific and diverse end users' information needs, no data source can satisfy such needs. This limitation may be overcome by introducing a *polymorphic data source* built upon the LOD datasets. Implementation in a mashup platform, as well as benefits of the polymorphic data source, are briefly presented. The paper concludes by discussing novel developments of this research.

1 Introduction and motivations

The growing availability of datasets published in the Linked Open Data (LOD) cloud is stimulating researchers to exploit this new source of data in different ways. In the original definition, Linked Data is "a set of best practices for publishing and connecting structured data on the Web" [5]. The goal is to publish data that are readable by a human as well as an automatic agent. LOD are Linked Data distributed under an open license that allows its reuse for free. It is estimated that more than 500 datasets are currently published in the LOD cloud. The main idea is to use the HTTP URIs to denote things (e.g., a person, a city, an organization) and to provide useful information about them by exploiting RDF standard. Thanks to RDF syntax, each thing is coded by a set of triplets in the form *t* = *<subject, predicate, object>*. The *subject* indicates the thing and it is always represented as a URI. The *object* can be a literal or another thing identified by a URI. The *predicate* is represented by a URI, it is contained in ontologies used to provide information about a domain and indicates a semantic relation between the subject and the object.

Before the LOD project, data stored in the Web were simple web pages connected by hyperlinks. Nowadays, one of the biggest datasets in the LOD cloud is DBpedia (the structured version of Wikipedia). The DBpedia English version describes 4.58 million things, out of which 4.22 million are classified in its ontology. In the DBpedia ontology, there are 685 classes.

In this paper, a solution to exploit LOD to enrich mashup platforms is described. Mashup platforms provide end users with graphical notations for combining heterogeneous resources available on Internet through Application Programming Interface (API) [7]. Despite the wide availability of APIs, due to the specific and diverse end users' information needs, often no API can satisfy these needs. This represents a limitation for the spreading of mashup platforms in real contexts and everyday use. To overcome this limitation, this paper presents a *polymorphic data source* that exploits the wide availability of information structured in the LOD cloud. It is called *polymorphic* because, as it will be shown later in this paper, when it is composed with another source *S*, it is capable of modifying its set of attributes depending on the source *S*, in order to better fulfil the users' needs. DBpedia has been chosen as initial LOD cloud thanks to the vast amount of information it provides.

The remainder of this paper is structured as follows. Next section briefly reports some related work. Section 3 describes the polymorphic data source and its use in a mashup platform. Section 4 provides a novel proposal to build a polymorphic data source from scratch. Section 5 concludes the paper.

2 Related work

This work is related to two, so far isolated, research areas: *semantic web* and *mashup*. About the former, a key aspect of the polymorphic data source described in this paper is the semantic annotation of web services available in mashup platforms. Different methods and tools have been already proposed to enrich Web services with semantic annotations, as described in [13]. Typically, these annotations are created to implement features like service recommendation during the composition process [4] or to assist users in finding services that fit their situational needs [15]. Unfortunately, API providers do not offer any semantic information about their APIs but they simply create unstructured web pages as API documentation. An approach that tries to build semantic annotations starting from the provider's documentation has been proposed in [11], where a system called SWEET assists users in building web service semantic information with hRESTS and MicroWSMO. Unfortunately, a significant effort required by users and web page heterogeneity represent an obstacle in adopting this system on a large scale. Other solutions propose semi-automatic approaches for annotating web services. For example, in [14, 16] two similar methods to annotate services with DBpedia classes and web service attributes with DBpedia properties have been reported. However, a lot of effort is still required by users, since low-level API details have to be defined [14] and WSDL service descriptors have to be built for each service. An algorithm to automatically annotate web services has been developed by one of the authors of this paper [8]. In Section 3, it is shown how this algorithm is used to build a polymorphic data source that makes more powerful a mashup platform developed in the last years [2, 3, 9].

About the mashup research area, several mashup methods and tools have been proposed in the last two decades, characterized by different composition paradigms in order to facilitate mashup by non-technical users, i.e. people without expertise in computer programming. One of the pioneers (even if it is not available anymore) was *Yahoo!Pipes* [12] that, in the attempt to better support end users, provided a visual editor to access services and operators visualized as visual modules that could be combined into a canvas pane by means of 'pipes' through drag and drop actions. *NaturalMash* allows users to express in natural language what service(s) they need to use and how to synchronize them [1]. However, problems related to the use of a natural language still remain. A different mashup technique avoids the use of APIs and enables data integration allowing users to act directly on the Web page UI elements, which are considered interactive artefacts that can be combined through a set of mashup operations [6]. The inconvenience of this approach is that it is difficult to generalize due to the heterogeneity of web pages.

The mashup platform we have developed adopts a visual composition paradigm, which is suitable to support non-technical users to create mashup [2, 3, 9]. Other mashup tools and mashup techniques are described in [7]. Moreover, a recent article surveys web service composition techniques and tools [10].

3 A mashup platform and the polymorphic data source

Mashup platforms are web-based tools that allow end users to create data-centric applications (called *mashups*) by composing heterogeneous resources typically available through APIs, databases, files and RSS feeds [7]. These tools are considered a solution for supporting data exploration processes that exceed one-time interactions; indeed, end users are enabled to create new applications and store them for future use. A typical example of mashup is the composition between the very popular Google Maps and SongKick, a service that provides a list of upcoming musical events in a certain location. The composition result is a map that shows the musical events as coloured markers at the specific locations.

One of the results of our research in the last years is a mashup platform called EFESTO [2, 3, 9], characterized by a visual paradigm to support non-technical users in the exploration and composition of heterogeneous data sources. Users can add and compose services into a personal workspace by means of wizard procedures. This approach facilitates the mashup creation since users are guided during the entire composition processes. For example, in Figure 1 a workspace created with EFESTO is depicted. In the middle, it is shown a widget that plots on a map (obtained by Google Maps) musical events gathered by SongKick. This widget has been created by the user (a male) through very simple actions. He first clicks on the gearwheel icon on the top-right corner (circle 1 in Figure 1) and selects the "Create new widget" button. Then, a wizard procedure guides him in selecting both the map and the data source about musical events (SongKick), and in performing a mapping between the SongKick attributes and the map elements. Other wizards have been also implemented to add details to SongKick results by exploiting the *join* operation. A non-technical user, who does not know what a join operation is, implicitly performs a join by adding details about specific data source attribute. For example, referring to Figure 1, a wizard has guided the user to add pictures to concert cities. The system performs this by joining the *city* SongKick attribute with the Google Images data source. More details about these wizard procedures are described in [9].

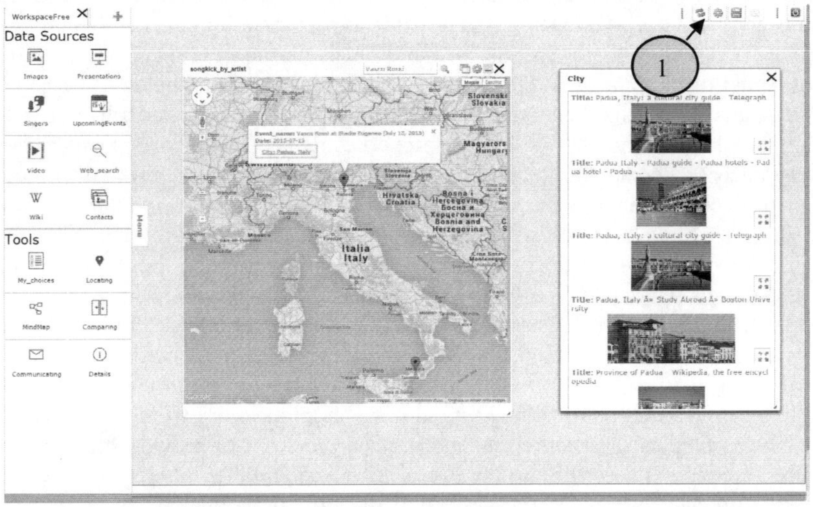

Figure 1. An example of mashup created in the user's workspace of the EFESTO platform.

EFESTO has been validated during two field studies in specific application domains [2, 3]. Besides helping to assess the mashup mechanisms, these studies also highlighted new requirements. Among the most important ones, there is the need to perform join operations with more expressive data sources. Indeed, despite their wide availability, APIs typically describe a portion of a domain and often do not include many details able to satisfy complex information needs. This drawback is overcome by creating a new *polymorphic data source* (PDS) that exploits the LOD cloud; it permits to get information that, with respect to the data sources it is composed of, is represented by attributes that may change depending on the situational needs expressed in the mashup under construction [8], as described in the following section.

3.1 A motivating scenario for the polymorphic data source

To better understand the need for the PDS, let us consider a scenario referring to a situation when a person, Leonard, is using the EFESTO mashup platform to compose services according to his needs. Leonard wants to choose a home to rent during the next holiday in London. First, he adds into his EFESTO workspace the Zoopla service that, starting from a UK city, retrieves a list of homes for rent in that city. He also decides to retrieve for each home, a list of figures related to its location (this is a join between the Zoopla *address* attribute and Google Images). From now on, Leonard has the Zoopla widget in his workspace and, every time a click occurs on an address in the Zoopla widget, a pop-up window shows the Google Images pictures related to the home area. Afterwards, Leonard needs to retrieve, for each home address, details such as coordinates, population density and life expectancy. In both the platform and the overall Web there are no APIs providing such information. Thus, Leonard should go to the Web for a usual (manual) search for the specific information. Luckily, the PDS is now available in EFESTO and it is possible to perform a join of the Zoopla *address* attribute with the PDS. To do this, Leonard clicks on the gearwheel icon at the top-right corner of the Zoopla widget (circle 1 in Figure 2), selects the attribute he wants more details about, and then chooses the PDS to extend the selected attribute. At this point, the platform shows a list of new properties related to the concept *street* (which is the concept associated to the *address* attribute), available in the DBpedia ontology. Leonard decides to create the new data source with *coordinates*, *population density* and *life expectancy* properties. Henceforward, Leonard can find on Zoopla a list of homes to rent and can visualize additional home information on the PDS by clicking on a specific street name (see Figure 2). In this scenario, Leonard keeps composing Zoopla with the same PDS starting from other Zoopla attributes. For each attribute that Leonard decides to extend, the PDS provides different properties related to the semantics of the starting attribute. For example, for the Zoopla *city* attribute, properties like patron Saint, political majority and winter temperature would be shown. This is why this type of data source is said *polymorphic*: it can provide different information (properties) according to the data source attribute that is selected. In contrast, the standard data sources (YouTube, Wikipedia, etc.) provide the same set of properties independently of the selected attribute.

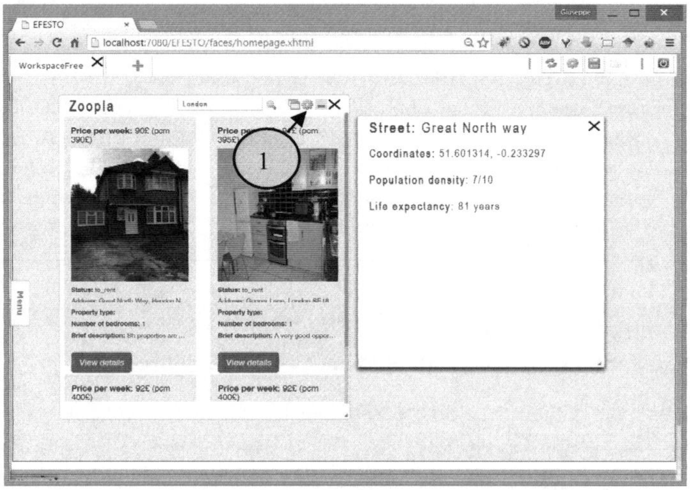

Figure 2. Result of composing the polymorphic data source with Zoopla service.

3.2 LOD for building the polymorphic data source

In order to determine the PDS behavior starting from the DBpedia dataset, a mapping is required between the attributes of all data sources registered in the mashup platform and the DBpedia ontology classes (*db:City* and *db:Street* in the example of Figure 3). The annotation algorithm described in [8] performs this association on the basis of a semantic similarity and creates some annotation files. Thanks to these annotations, a join between data sources (e.g. the Zoopla service in the scenario described in the previous section) and the PDS can be performed. It is the user who selects the PDS attributes he wants to visualize, by choosing among the properties of the class annotating the data source attributes he has chosen. In the example of Figure 2, for the attribute *address,* Leonard has selected to visualize *coordinates*, *population density* and *life expectancy.*

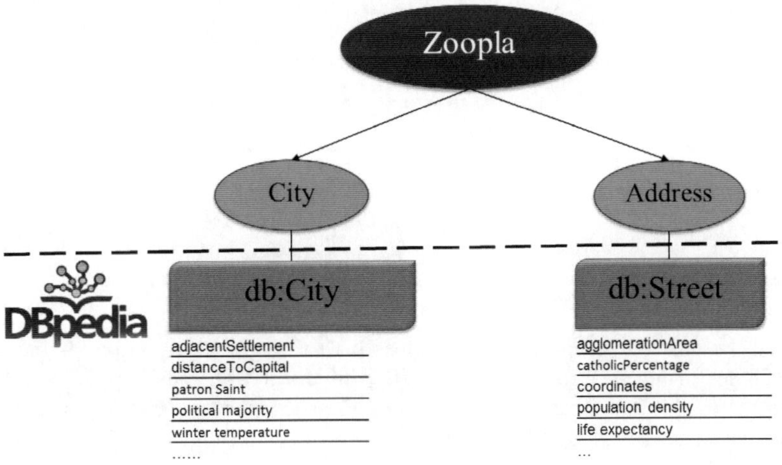

Figure 3. Example of a result of the annotation algorithm: classes db:City and db:Street are associated to some attributes of the Zoopla service.

4 The polymorphic data source 2.0

Until now, the PDS has been created through a join operation of existing data sources, in order to satisfy specific users' requirements, which emerged during the evaluation of the EFESTO platform [2, 3]. We are currently investigating a new solution: instead of creating a PDS starting from the providers' APIs (e.g. YouTube, SongKick), we want to build from scratch a new PDS able to retrieve data about a specific topic. To briefly introduce this new PDS 2.0, let us suppose that the user is interested in creating a data source that retrieves food information. To this aim, he starts the widget creation in his platform workspace in a traditional way but, instead of selecting a specific service, he selects to create a PDS. Thus, he types some keywords (e.g. food) specific for the data source he is interested to build. The platform shows him a list of topics (e.g. Italian Food, General Food, Healthy Food, etc.), which are the DBpedia classes that are semantically related to the typed keywords. From this list, the user chooses the topic that better fits his needs, e.g. Italian Food. He goes on by mapping some of the Italian Food attributes into a visual template provided by the platform. From now on, he can use the created Food data source to retrieve a particular food. For example, in Figure 4 the user typed 'Pizza' in the search field and the food details are visualized according to the visual template he had chosen.

Figure 4. A polymorphic data source created from scratch.

While in the previous proposal the PDS was built through an algorithm associating the attributes of all data sources in a mashup platform with the DBpedia ontology classes, the PDS 2.0 is created starting from a class that the user chooses in order to indicate the semantics of the data source under creation. Because the DBpedia ontology contains hundreds of classes, the user cannot easily find the best class by navigating the entire ontology. To assist the user in selecting the class of interest, we developed an algorithm that retrieves a list of classes based on the keywords the user types to indicate the data that the PDS has to provide (e.g. *food* in the above example). In this reduced list of classes (e.g. *Italian Food, General Food, Healthy Food* in our example), it is easier for the user to select the one to start the PDS 2.0 creation. Selecting the class of interest is a critical aspects to build the PDS 2.0. The algorithm works in three main steps. First, it stems the keywords provided by the user, in order to reduce them to the root form. Second, for each stemmed keyword, It uses the lexical ontology WordNet to find words related to the stemmed keywords on the basis of semantic relationships, e.g. synonyms, homonyms, meronyms, etc. Third, it selects from DBpedia the classes whose names are similar to the words retrieved by WordNet, on the basis of a Levenshtein distance threshold that is empirically defined.

5 Conclusions

A limitation of current mashup platforms is that, despite the wide availability of APIs, often none of them can satisfy the specific information needs of very diverse users. This paper discussed how Linked Open Data can help overcoming this limitation. In

particular, it described the creation of a polymorphic data source, built on top of the Linked Open Data cloud, that users compose with other Web sources, in order to obtain information that traditional sources do not provide.
A novel proposal of the polymorphic data source 2.0 was also presented. It is work in progress, but we are confident that it can, indeed, enrich mashup platforms thanks to the possibility to create from scratch data sources that exploit the vast amount of data available in the Linked Open Data cloud.

References

1. Aghaee, S., Pautasso, C. (2014). End-User Development of Mashups with NaturalMash. In *Journal of Visual Languages & Computing* 25(4), 414-432
2. Ardito, C., Bottoni, P., Costabile, M.F., Desolda, G., Matera, M., Picozzi, M. (2014). Creation and Use of Service-based Distributed Interactive Workspaces. In *Journal of Visual Languages & Computing* 25(6), 717-726
3. Ardito, C., Costabile, M.F., Desolda, G., Lanzilotti, R., Matera, M., Piccinno, A., Picozzi, M. (2014). User-Driven Visual Composition of Service-Based Interactive Spaces. In *Journal of Visual Languages & Computing* 25(4), 278-296
4. Bianchini, D., Antonellis, V.D., Melchiori, M. (2010). A Recommendation System for Semantic Mashup Design. In: *Proc. of DEXA '10*. Porto, Portugal. Aug. 30 - Sept. 3 2010. pp. 159-163
5. Bizer, C., Heath, T., Berners-Lee, T. (2009). Linked data-the story so far. In *Semantic Services, Interoperability and Web Applications: Emerging Concepts* 205-227
6. Daniel, F. (2015). Live, Personal Data Integration Through UI-Oriented Computing. In: *Proc. of ICWE '15*. Rotterdam, the Netherlands. 23 – 26 June 2015. pp. 479-497
7. Daniel, F., Matera, M.: Mashups: Concepts, Models and Architectures. Springer (2014)
8. Desolda, G. (2015). Enhancing Workspace Composition by Exploiting Linked Open Data as a Polymorphic Data Source. In: *Proc. of KES-IIMSS '15*. Sorrento, Italy. 17-19 June 2015. pp. 97-108
9. Desolda, G., Ardito, C., Matera, M. (2015). EFESTO: A platform for the End-User Development of Interactive Workspaces for Data Exploration. In: *Proc. of ICWE '15*. Rotterdam, the Netherlands. 23 – 26 June 2015. pp. 63 - 81
10. Lemos, A.L., Daniel, F., Benatallah, B. (2015). Web Service Composition: A Survey of Techniques and Tools. In *ACM Comput. Survey* 48(3), 1-41
11. Maleshkova, M., Kopecký, J., Pedrinaci, C. (2009). Adapting SAWSDL for Semantic Annotations of RESTful Services. In: *Proc. of OTM '09*. Vilamoura, Portugal. 1-6 November 2009. pp. 917-926
12. Pruett, M.: Yahoo! pipes. O'Reilly (2007)
13. Reeve, L., Han, H. (2005). Survey of semantic annotation platforms. In: *Proc. of SAC '05*. Santa Fe, New Mexico. 13 -17 March 2010. pp. 1634-1638
14. Saquicela, V., Vilches-Blázquez, L.M., Corcho, Ó. (2010). Semantic Annotation of RESTful Services Using External Resources. In: *Proc. of ICWE '10*. Vienna, Austria. 5 - 9 July 2010. pp. 266-276
15. Talantikite, H.N., Aissani, D., Boudjlida, N. (2009). Semantic annotations for web services discovery and composition. In *Computer Standards & Interfaces* 31(6), 1108-1117
16. Zhang, Z., Chen, S., Feng, Z. (2013). Semantic Annotation for Web Services Based on DBpedia. In: *Proc. of SOSE '13*. San Francisco, USA. 25-28 March 2013. pp. 280-285

Semi-Supervised Multi-View Learning for Gene Network Reconstruction
(Discussion Paper)

Michelangelo Ceci[1], Gianvito Pio[1], Vladimir Kuzmanovski[2,3] and Sašo Džeroski[2,3]

[1]University of Bari, Computer Science Dept, Via Orabona, 4, 70125 Bari (IT)
[2]Jožef Stefan Institute, Knowledge Technologies Dept, Jamova 39, 1000 Ljubljana (SI)
[3]Jožef Stefan International Postgraduate School, Jamova 39, 1000 Ljubljana (SI)
michelangelo.ceci@uniba.it, gianvito.pio@uniba.it
vladimir.kuzmanovski@ijs.si, saso.dzeroski@ijs.si

Abstract. The task of gene regulatory network reconstruction is receiving increasing attention in recent years. As a consequence, many inference methods for solving this task have been proposed in the literature. It has been recently observed, however, that no single inference method performs optimally across all datasets. It has also been shown that the integration of predictions from multiple inference methods is more robust and shows high performance across diverse datasets. In this paper, we present a solution which *learns to combine* predictions from multiple inference methods by exploiting multi-view, semi-supervised and ensemble-based learning techniques. In particular, it automatically adapts to patterns on the outputs of individual inference methods, in order identify regulatory interactions more reliably when these patterns occur.
Experiment on a prokaryotic organism (E. coli) and on a eukaryotic organism (S. cerevisiae) clearly shows improved performance over the state of the art methods. The software, the datasets and the results are available at: http://figshare.com/articles/Semi_supervised_Multi_View_Learning_for_Gene_Network_Reconstruction/1604827.

1 Introduction

Recent developments in systems biology led to an improved understanding of the mechanisms of organisms, which are described as a complex and dynamical system with multiple levels of regulation. Such levels of regulation are typically represented via biological networks (i.e., Gene-Regulatory Networks - GRNs) that model the interactions (edges) among the components (nodes) in a cell. Identifying the structure of GRNs helps in the biological understanding of disease mechanisms and raises possibilities for better clinical care [9].

In the literature, a wide range of approaches for inferring GRNs have been proposed. Moreover, several network reconstruction methods have been evaluated and compared within the DREAM5 challenge. In a follow-up study [7], the authors show that combining, by averaging ranks, prediction scores of the presented methods leads to a more accurate network reconstruction. An alternative solution for combining the output of several methods has been proposed in [6]. In such work, the predictions of each method are ranked according to their scores and the "combined rank" of each interaction is computed as the k-th highest rank among all the considered methods, where k is an input parameter.

Following this stream of research, in [3] we proposed a machine learning-based approach which automatically combines methods' outcomes to improve the reconstruction of the network. In particular, the solution we propose is to build a (stronger) predictive model by considering as input features the scores returned by several algorithms for network reconstruction (henceforth "base methods"), resorting to a solution which is borrowed from meta-learning [10]. However, the application of existing meta-learning techniques requires to take into account several specific issues: ***i)*** Considering many base methods can lead to construct a highly redundant set of input features, especially when the considered base methods are based on the same main principle; ***ii)*** The set of known regulatory interactions to exploit for building the predictive model consists of very few examples of interactions (or even none). Moreover, their labels are generally only positive (i.e., existing regulatory interactions), whereas no examples labeled as negative (i.e., non-existing regulatory interactions) are usually available. ***iii)*** The number of interactions for which the label is known is strongly *imbalanced* with respect to the number of interactions for which the label is unknown.

Concerning *i)*, instead of straightforwardly remove redundant features, we consider the adoption of the multi-view learning framework, a variant of the co-training framework [1]. The basic idea is to learn classifiers on different views (typically, different feature sets) of the same dataset and iteratively use predictions of one classifier as training instances for the other classifiers. In order to satisfy the assumptions of the co-training framework (see [1] for details), we build the views by partitioning the feature set into subsets, such that correlated features fall in the same view and uncorrelated features fall in different views.

Concerning *ii)*, the multi-view learning framework is able to exploit unlabeled examples to boost classification iteratively. This is important when few labeled examples are available. Moreover, the classifier we consider is able to build a classification model from only positive examples and from unlabeled examples.

Concerning *iii)*, the imbalance between labeled and unlabeled examples is attacked by resorting to an ensemble-based approach: the same approach is used to build a different model for each different view. This means that, for each view, instead of learning a single classifier, we learn an ensemble of classifiers.

In [3],we performed experiments on synthetic data and on the DREAM5 challenge datasets [7]. In the first case, we combined the output of several methods based on the *relevance networks* approach [2]. In the second case we considered a more heterogeneous set of inference methods, based on regression, mutual information, correlation, Bayesian networks and other (hybrid) approaches.

2 Methods

Before describing our approach for learning to combine the predictions of several algorithms for network reconstruction, we introduce some notions and formally define the task we solve. Let:

- E be the set of genes, which represent the nodes of the network;
- $x = \langle e', e'' \rangle \in (E \times E)$ be a (possible) link between the genes e' and e'';
- $p_k(x)$ be the score of the link x, returned by the k-th base method, $1 \leq k \leq s$;
- $p(x) = [p_1(x), p_2(x), \ldots, p_s(x)]$ be the vector of scores associated with x;
- $l(x) = 1$ if x exists, 0 if it is unknown (regardless of whether x exists or not);
- $L = \{x \in (E \times E) | l(x) = 1\}$ be the initial set of labeled interactions;
- $U = (E \times E) \setminus L$ be the set of (initially) unlabeled interactions;
- $f(x)$ be an ideal function which returns 1 if x exists , 0 otherwise.

The task we solve is then defined as follows:

Given: a set of training examples $\{\langle p(x), l(x) \rangle\}_x$. *Find:* a function $f' : \mathbb{R}^s \rightarrow \mathbb{R}$ which takes as input a vector of scores $p(x)$ and returns the probability that the interaction x exists. We have that $f'(p(x)) \approx \mathcal{P}(f(x) = 1)$.

Our approach, called GENERE (GEne NEtwork REconstruction) solves this task in three phases, which are summerized in Fig. 1 and detailed in the following.

2.1 Phase 1 - Assigning labels and identifying multiple views

Once the vector of prediction scores $p(x)$ is initialized and $l(x)$ is defined for each interaction x, GENERE constructs V different views of the same dataset. Each view consists of the whole set of examples and one subset of the original set of features, where each feature is the score returned by one base method.

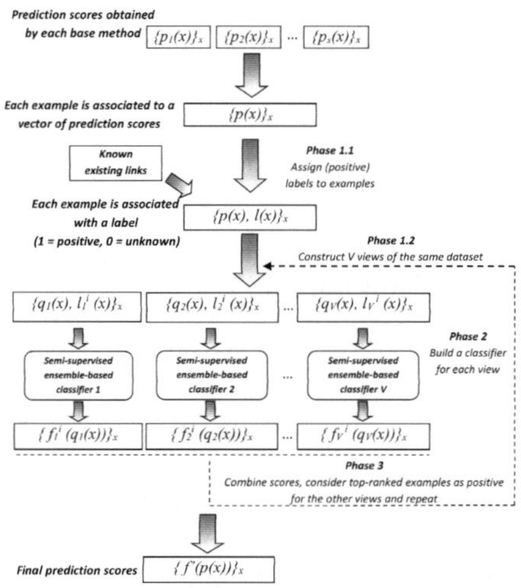

Fig. 1. General workflow of GENERE approach.

According to the original co-training setting [1] and works on multi-view learning [5], such views should be as independent as possible. For this reason, we apply a clustering algorithm to the features in order to obtain a partitioning which minimizes the inter-cluster similarity and, thus, the correlation between features belonging to different views. Although almost all the clustering algorithms can, in principle, be applied for this task, in [3] we considered two well-know algorithms: Principal Component Analysis (PCA) and K-means. In both cases, each feature is associated with one of the V clusters. Formally, given the vectors of prediction scores $\{p(x)\}_x$, we partition the features into V subsets. Each example is then represented by V (disjoint) vectors of prediction scores $q_1(x), q_2(x), \ldots, q_V(x)$, each of which corresponds to a subset of features and contributes to build a different view (see Fig. 1).

At the beginning, each example x in the view v is associated with the vector $q_v(x)$ and with the label $l(x)$. During the process shown in Fig. 1, the labeled interactions are iteratively extended with new (positive) examples. Given the initial labeled interactions $L = \{x \in (E \times E) | l(x) = 1\}$, we indicate as $L_v^i \supseteq L$ the labeled interactions for the view v, at the i-th iteration. Formally, $L_v^i = \{x \in (E \times E) | l_v^i(x) = 1\}$, where $l_v^i(x) = 1$ if the interaction x is labeled at the iteration i for the view v, 0 otherwise. Accordingly, we indicate as $U_v^i \subseteq U$ the unlabeled interactions at the iteration i for the view v. Formally, $U_v^i = (E \times E) \setminus L_v^i$.

Note that $L = L_1^0 = \ldots = L_V^0$ and $U = U_1^0 = \ldots = U_V^0$. For the subsequent iterations ($i > 0$), L_v^i and U_v^i can contain different examples, since they are iteratively updated according to the output of the other views (see Section 2.3).

2.2 Phase 2 - Building a classifier for each view

In Phase 2, we build a different classifier from each view, by exploiting information conveyed by both known (existing) and unknown interactions.

The goal of the v-th classifier at the i-th iteration is to identify a function $f_v^i(q_v(x))$ which approximates the probability that $f(x) = 1$, that is, $f_v^i(q_v(x)) \approx \mathcal{P}(f(x) = 1)$. In [4], the authors suggest to exploit the fact that only known existing interactions are labeled (i.e., $\mathcal{P}(f(x) = 1 | l(x) = 1) = 1$), and the Bayes' rule, in order to compute $f_v^i(q_v(x))$ as:

$$f_v^i(q_v(x)) \approx \mathcal{P}(f(x) = 1) = \frac{\mathcal{P}\left(l_v^i(x) = 1\right)}{\mathcal{P}\left(l_v^i(x) = 1 | f(x) = 1\right)} \tag{1}$$

where the numerator and the denominator can be estimated by means of a so-called "non-traditional" classifier, whose definition is explained in the following.

Estimating $\mathcal{P}(l_v^i(x) = 1)$ and $\mathcal{P}(l_v^i(x) = 1 | f(x) = 1)$. We build a so-called "non-traditional" classifier for each view v at the iteration i, whose output is the probability that an example is labeled, i.e., $\mathcal{P}(l_v^i(x) = 1)$. For this purpose, in this work, we adopt an SVM-based classifier with Platt Scaling.

Each non-traditional classifier v at iteration i identifies a function $g_v^i(q_v(x))$ which returns the probability that x is labeled, i.e. $g_v^i(q_v(x)) \approx \mathcal{P}(l_v^i(x) = 1)$.

By assuming that all the labeled examples are taken completely randomly from the positive examples (see [4]), we exploit $g_v^i(q_v(x))$ to estimate Equation (1):

$$f_v^i(q_i(x)) \approx \frac{g_v^i(q_v(x))}{\frac{1}{|L_v^i|}\sum_{x' \in L_v^i} g_v^i(q_v(x'))} \tag{2}$$

Differently from [4], we also have to deal with the problem of imbalanced class distributions. This issue is considered in the next subsection.

Ensemble learning of $\mathbf{g_v^i(\cdot)}$. In order to deal with the imbalance between the number of labeled and unlabeled examples, following [8], we exploit a sampling procedure similar to that used in bootstrap estimation and bagging. In particular, for each view v at a given iteration i, we learn a set of W non-traditional classifiers $\{g_{vj}^i(q_v(x))\}_{j=1,2,\dots,W}$ whose outputs are combined to obtain $g_v^i(q_v(x))$. Each classifier is built from the set of examples $L_v^i \cup U_{vj}^i$, that is, from all the labeled examples L_v^i and from the set U_{vj}^i, with $j = 1, 2, \dots, W$. U_{vj}^i is a subset of the unlabeled examples U_v^i, obtained by a random sampling, with replacement, of n examples from U_v^i. The proportion of unlabeled examples in each U_{vj}^i is $\frac{n}{|U_v^i|}$, where n is a user-defined parameter. Differently from data partitioning, which is affected by only one parameter W (the number of subsets), the data sampling procedure used in this work is controlled by two parameters: n and γ. The first represents the number of unlabeled examples in each sample and is chosen reasonably on the basis of the number of labeled examples. The second represents the percentage of unlabeled examples we intend to take into account (i.e., to cover) and influences the number of samples W.

Once the W classifiers are learned, each function $g_{vj}^i(q_v(x))$ is applied to estimate of $\mathcal{P}(l_v^i(x) = 1)$ for all the examples in U_{vj}^i. Since the same unlabeled example can belong to more than one sample, we average the outputs as follows:

$$g_v^i(q_v(x)) = \underset{\{j \mid U_{vj}^i \text{ contains } x\}}{average} g_{vj}^i(q_v(x)) \tag{3}$$

2.3 Phase 3 - Combining the output of views

Once all the functions $f_v^i(q_v(x))$ for the iteration i are computed, we combine their outputs in order to update the set of (positively) labeled examples for the next iteration (i.e., the $(i+1)$-th iteration). In the original co-training framework, the examples are chosen on the basis of their classification reliability. In our case, since we only learn from positive examples of interactions, we simply choose those for which we have, on average over the views, the highest scores. In particular, to update the set of labeled examples of the view v at the iteration $i+1$, we average the outputs $f_z^i(q_z(x))$ over all the views $z \neq v$, for each interaction x:

$$f_{comb_v}^i(x) = \frac{1}{W-1} \sum_{z=1,2,\dots W;\ z \neq v} f_z^i(q_z(x)) \tag{4}$$

The set of labeled examples of the view v at the iteration $i+1$, i.e. L_v^{i+1}, is built by taking a percentage $\delta\%$ of the top-ranked examples according to $f_{comb_v}^i(x)$.

3 Experimental evaluation

In this section, we describe the considered competitor approaches, the datasets and the experimental setting. We compare GENERE with the strategies proposed in [7] (that we call **Borda**) and in [6] (that we call **TopK**, with $k \in [1, 20]$ which leads to better results according to [6]), as well as with an adapted version of the algorithm proposed in [8] (that we call **1VI**) which is a simplified version of GENERE, with one view (i.e., $V = 1$) and one iteration (i.e., $max\_iter = 1$).

In [3], experiments have been performed on a set of synthetic datasets and on the datasets of the DREAM5 challenge [7]. Here, for space constraints, we report only the results obtained on the DREAM5 datasets. In details, we consider Network1 (a synthetic dataset of 1,643 genes, that we call *D5InSilico*), Network3 (a real dataset of 4,511 genes of the E.Coli organism, that we call *D5EColi*) and Network4 (a real dataset of 5,950 genes of the S. Cerevisiae organism, that we call *D5Yeast*). As input features for GENERE we consider the scores obtained by the 35 methods of the competition (see [7]).

After preliminary experiments (see [3]), we considered the following sets of parameter values: $\gamma = 0.99$, $max\_iter = 5$, $n = |L_v^i|$, $\delta \in \{0.5\%, 1.0\%\}$ and $V \in \{1, 2, 3, 4, 5\}$. Moreover, in order to guarantee a fair comparison with Borda and TopK, which are unsupervised, we forced our system and 1VI to work in the scenario in which there is no known interaction. For this aim, at the beginning we label as positive the top $\delta\%$ examples, ranked according to the average score.

In [3], we performed experiments with both PCA and K-means and evaluated the results in terms of AUROC and AUPRC. Here, for space constraint, we report only the results obtained with K-Means, in terms of AUROC.

4 Results and discussion

Results are presented in Fig. 2 by means of boxplots, by considering the AUROC values obtained with different iterations for GENERE, and with different values of k for TopK. By observing the results, we can draw several conclusions. First, the best values are generally obtained when the number of views is 3, 4 or 5. This means that values of $V \in \{3, 4, 5\}$ lead to better groups of base methods that allow us to distinguish better among their properties. This result is in line with [7], where the authors identified four clusters of base methods.

Second, by comparing the results obtained for the three datasets, we note that gene network reconstruction from the *D5Yeast* dataset produces the worst results (this is true also for competitors). This is possibly due to the base methods used. Indeed, as observed in [7], in *D5Yeast* dataset, the dependency distributions of interacting and non-interacting gene pairs are almost identical, suggesting that it is much more difficult to detect interactions from this dataset.

Third, concerning the sensitivity of GENERE to the number of iterations, in Fig. 3 we report a summary of the average AUROC and the number of wins, i.e., the number of cases for which the considered configuration shows the best AUROC. By observing the figure, we can conclude that the best number of iterations is generally 1-2. This means that the algorithm converges fast to its

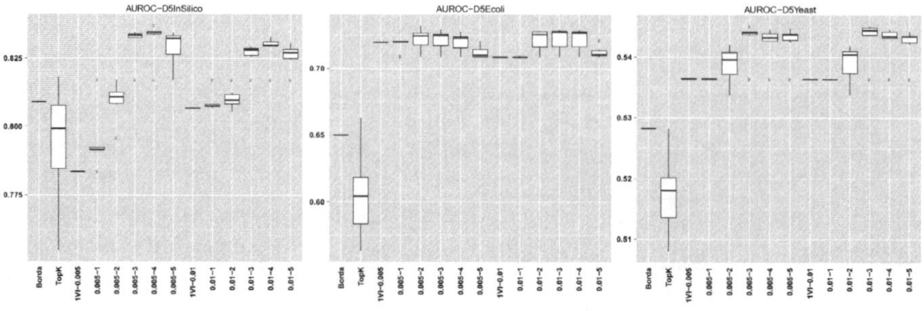

Fig. 2. AUROC boxplots for the DREAM5 datasets.

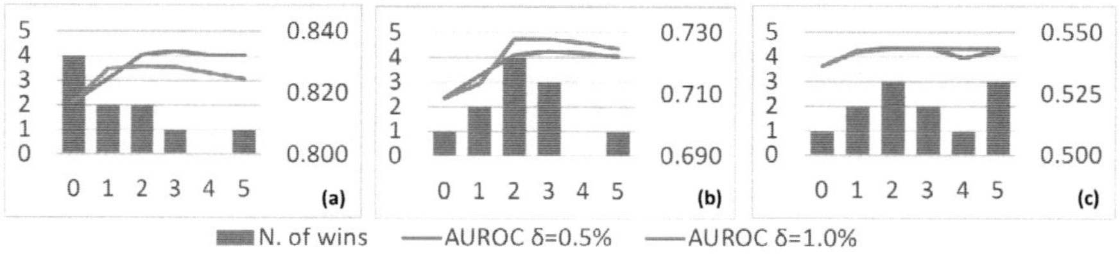

Fig. 3. Number of wins, in terms of AUROC (blue histograms) and average AUROC (red and grey lines), obtained for *D5InSilico* (a), *D5Ecoli* (b) and *D5Yeast* (c).

best performance for each dataset. Moreover, the average AUROC generally do not deteriorate when the number of iterations increases beyond the best choice.

Furthermore, we applied the Wilcoxon signed rank test with the False Discovery Rate (FDR) correction for multiple tests. Looking at the results in Table 1, we can observe that GENERE significantly outperforms the competitors in terms of median AUROC values. A closer analysis confirms that the best number of views are generally 3, 4 and 5. Moreover, the fact that GENERE significantly outperforms 1VI (this is evident when $V = 5$) confirms the advantage of the multi-view learning framework, which can fully exploit the differences among the base methods falling in the same view (i.e., among similar base methods).

Finally, results do not show significant changes for different values of δ. However, including only more reliable values at each iteration ($\delta = 0.5\%$) leads to better results (see Table 1, lines Borda and TopK). Using a lower value of δ is thus advisable. For 1VI, whose results also depend on δ, there is no consistent difference for the different values of δ across the different number of views.

GENERE vs	δ	**1 View**	**2 Views**	**3 Views**	**4 Views**	**5 Views**
Borda	**0.5%**	**0.00019**	**0.00025**	**0.00017**	**0.00017**	**0.00017**
	1.0%	**0.00020**	**0.00032**	**0.00017**	**0.00017**	**0.00017**
TopK	**0.5%**	**0.00075**	**0.00330**	**0.00030**	**0.00017**	**0.00017**
	1.0%	**0.00350**	**0.02129**	**0.00034**	**0.00018**	**0.00017**
1VI	**0.5%**	0.13085	0.18772	0.05697	**0.00415**	**0.00103**
	1.0%	*0.09432*	0.18772	**0.02129**	**0.00125**	**0.00042**

Table 1. Adjusted *p*-values of the Wilcoxon signed rank test. Significant values (< 0.05) are shown in bold. Italic values indicates that the competitor outperforms GENERE.

5 Conclusion

In this work, we addressed the problem of gene regulatory network reconstruction. Our method combines the scores returned by several algorithms for predicting interactions among genes. Contrary to existing approaches, which use simple combination strategies, our solution learns to combine the predictions by exploiting multi-view, semi-supervised and ensemble-based learning techniques.

Experiments proved that GENERE significantly outperforms state of the art approaches in the reconstruction of well-known gene interaction networks such as those in *E. coli* and *S. cerevisiae*, from both synthetic and real data.

In further work, we will consider gene interactions as inter-dependent and exploit the autocorrelation among interactions involving similar genes. Moreover, we will investigate new "transfer learning" techniques which exploit GRNs reconstructed from some organisms in the reconstruction of GRNs of other organisms.

Acknowledgments

We acknowledge the support of the Slovenian Research Agency - grant P2-0103, the European Commission - grants ICT-2013-612944 MAESTRA and ICT-2013-604102 HBP, as well as the grant CCI2007SI051PO001 through the European Social Fund for co-financing postgraduate studies in the context of the Operational Programme for Human Resources Development for the period 2007-2013.

References

1. Blum, A., Mitchell, T.: Combining labeled and unlabeled data with co-training. In: COLT '98. pp. 92–100. ACM, NY, USA (1998)
2. Butte, A.J., Tamayo, P., Slonim, D., Golub, T.R., Kohane, I.S.: Discovering functional relationships between RNA expression and chemotherapeutic susceptibility using relevance networks. Nat. Academy of Sciences 97(22), 12182–12186 (2000)
3. Ceci, M., Pio, G., Kuzmanovski, V., Dzeroski, S.: Semi-supervised multi-view learning for gene network reconstruction. PLoS ONE 10(12), e0144031 (12 2015)
4. Elkan, C., Noto, K.: Learning classifiers from only positive and unlabeled data. In: ACM SIGKDD. pp. 213–220. ACM, USA (2008)
5. Guo, H., Viktor, H.L.: Multirelational classification: A multiple view approach. Knowledge and Information Systems 17(3), 287–312 (2008)
6. Hase, T., Ghosh, S., Yamanaka, R., Kitano, H.: Harnessing diversity towards the reconstructing of large scale gene regulatory networks. PLoS Computational Biology 9(11), e1003361 (11 2013)
7. Marbach, D., Costello, J.C., Küffner, R., Vega, N.M., Prill, R.J., Camacho, D.M., Allison, K.R., Kellis, M., Collins, J.J., Stolovitzky, G.: Wisdom of crowds for robust gene network inference. Nature Methods 9, 796–804 (2012)
8. Pio, G., Malerba, D., D'Elia, D., Ceci, M.: Integrating microRNA target predictions for the discovery of gene regulatory networks: A semi-supervised ensemble learning approach. BMC Bioinformatics 15(S-1), S4 (2014)
9. Smith, V.A., Jarvis, E.D., Hartemink, A.J.: Evaluating functional network inference using simulations of complex biological systems. Bioinformatics 18(suppl 1), S216–S224 (2002)
10. Vilalta, R., Drissi, Y.: A perspective view and survey of meta-learning. Artificial Intelligence Review 18(2), 77–95 (2002)

Enhanced User Search Activity by Big Data Tools (Discussion Paper)

Nunziato Cassavia[2], Elio Masciari[2], Chiara Pulice[1], and Domenico Saccà[1]

[1] DIMES, University of Calabria, Italy
[2] ICAR-CNR, Italy
{cpulice, sacca}@dimes.unical.it
{cassavia, masciari}@icar.cnr.it

Abstract. Due to the emerging Big Data paradigm, traditional data management techniques result inadequate in many real life scenarios. In particular, the availability of huge amounts of data pertaining to social interactions among users calls for advanced analysis strategies. Furthermore, heterogeneity and high speed of this data require suitable data storage and management tools to be designed from scratch. In this paper, we describe a framework tailored for analyzing user interactions with intelligent systems while seeking for some domain specific information (e.g., choosing a good restaurant in a visited area). The framework enhances user quest for information by exploiting previous knowledge about their social environment, the extent of influence the users are potentially subject to and the influence they may exert on other users. It is worth noting that, gathering information about user preferences, is crucial in several scenarios like viral marketing, tourism promotion and food education.

Keywords: Big Data, User Search, Influence Spread

1 Introduction

The impressive progress and development of Internet and on-line technologies has led to an increasing availability of a huge volume of data generated by heterogeneous sources at high production rates [1]. These massive data, referred as *Big Data*[5], exhibit a great variety and may be exploited to gather information about people, things, services and their interactions. In this respect, a great deal of attention has been devoted to the design of novel algorithms for analyzing information available from Twitter, Google, Facebook, and Wikipedia, to cite a few of the main big data producers.

It turns out that the issue of devising novel solutions for analyzing big data, coming both from heterogeneous information sources and from logs of user interactions and behaviors, is becoming more and more compelling in the construction of *Intelligent Information Systems* (IIS) to assist end user in the search of relevant information and in the interaction with services in the net. To this end, several research issues need to be dealt with.

First of all, data gathered by social network and search engines available on the web are inherently non structured; therefore, a data exchange task has to be performed for moving source data into a target "structured" database enabling an effective analysis of user behavior.

A second relevant issue is to adapt the content of target data to the strategy followed by the users when seeking for useful information. In particular, the user may be driven by some predefined faceted features (*browsing*) or may simply formulate a query using "free" keywords (*searching*). Most of the present systems mainly follow one of the two mentioned paradigms and only few systems offer a mix of the two of them. A new frontier for IIS is to combine searching and browsing by using features that are not a-priori predefined but selected for and adapted to the search context. The challenge explored in this paper is: *detecting on-the-fly features that are relevant in the search context and tailored to the user behavior.* As an example, consider the case of a user expressing an enthusiastic comment on a recently visited city (e.g., by a Facebook "like" and/or post). Most likely, his/her friends could be interested to utilize the positive feedback on that city when deciding their next travel destination. In this respect, enabling users to exploit some useful information in the search for a specific destination can be done by suggesting some categorized high level information (e.g., "funny cities for young people"), which can be eventually further refined (e.g., by adding specific search keywords).

The relevance of user behavioral features prompted us to investigate the following two additional issues: *How to allow relevant information about user search preferences propagate over the network? How to measure the possible information spread*? The two issues are preliminary to the activity of discovering new dimensions to be added to the information sources and to be later used to support a search mixed with tailored browsing.

In sum, in this paper we focus on (i) the analysis of user's searching and comment posting activities in order to identify potentially interesting suggestions about user searches, (ii) the proposal of a novel data exchange setting that exploits them for enhancing the information contents of the source databases and (iii) the definition of a search strategy based on tailored faceted features. Our approach is motivated by the observation that both performed searches and posted comments define a quite accurate profiling of user wishes and feedbacks that can be exploited to construct background information and knowledge in an application domain for supporting advanced further searches. The final result of our work is a user behavior oriented search framework for implementing new generation IIS.

2 System Architecture

The underlying idea. In this section, we describe the overall architecture of our system for big data search exploiting. Our goal is to provide users a flexible tool for assisted text search, that is interactive, scalable and dynamic. To this end, we exploited several indexing and data management strategies that allow us to cope with high volume, heterogenous and burst information.

In the following, we first introduce a running example to ease the understanding of our proposal and, later on, we provide a detailed description of our overall technologic framework. Our application scenario is tourism recommendation. The ratio behind the choice of this scenario is that, users (i.e., tourists) do an extensive search activity when traveling and they post comments and suggestions, thus contributing to the definition of their behavior and needs and to the construction of a background knowledge ground to assist them in further searches.

Example 1. Consider the scenario depicted in Figure 1. Each node of the network represents a user interacting with a social network[3]. When interacting with the social network, users usually issue several queries, post comments and upload (tagged) files. For example a user may pose the following query: *Find a restaurant in Milan*. Traditional search engines will provide user results ranked on the basis of their default criteria. However, this ranking could be ineffective as users may not be satisfied by query answers as they are mainly based on

[3] In our prototype we used Facebook, Yelp and Twitter but the same reasoning applies to every social network

proximity search and some fixed categorization (e.g. stars, price). In order to overcome this limitation, we perform a data pre-processing by clustering user comments stored in our system. As a result, we obtain a set of comment groups that may contain some new possible search categories (referred in the following as search *dimensions*) previously hidden in the data. It could therefore happen that the clustering algorithm suggests to add a new dimension to the source information that classifies the quality of dishes served at each restaurant, while matching the user query for a restaurant located in Milan area. The new dimension could be *Food Quality*. As users interact with the system and new enquiries and comments are made, some other additional dimensions could arise. For instance, the *Food Quality* could be refined by an additional dimension *fresh fish* with suitable values: *bad/good/excellent*.

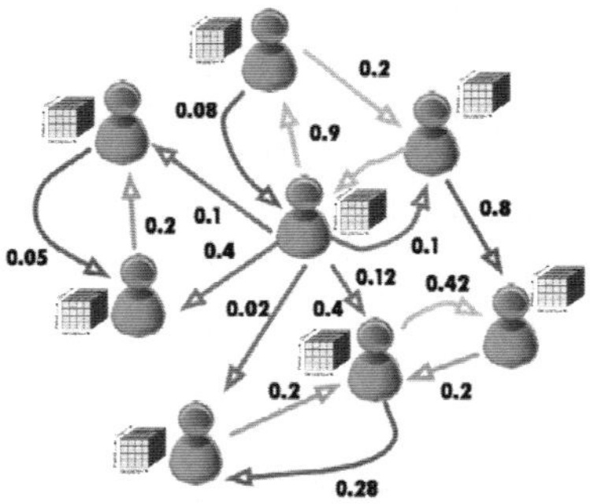

Fig. 1: Our influence model for user search

Furthermore, as users may be *influenced* by their social contacts, the new dimensions might spread in the network so that an increasing number of queries include them. Therefore, to understand how the discovered dimensions spread over the network, we need to take into account the probability that a user could be influenced by her/his social contacts. By simply considering how the new dimensions spread in the network, we can eventually detect the influence spreading on the network and update the user connection graph consequently. More in detail, by analyzing the social environment of each user and her/his search activity log over time, we label each edge with a value representing the influence currently exerted by a user to its connections – see the labeled edges in Figure 1. The influence plays a crucial role for filtering dimensions that the clustering algorithm will suggest for a tailored search.

Moreover, Data posting [7] is used both to enrich the source raw data with the discovered dimensions and to personalize them for the current user so that the enriched information may be added to the search toolbar as soon as search keywords (e.g., "starters" or "main courses") are typed for which the dimensions are pertinent, thus enabling a faceted browsing – this functionality is represented as a cube aside the user symbol in Figure 1.

Due to space limitations, we describe the overall system in the following section and we discuss in more detail only the influence evaluation model (see Section 3). □

Our system at work In this paragraph, we provide an high-level description of our framework for implementing user search task described in the example above. In Figure 2 we depict the overall process of information analysis, enrichment and delivery to the final user.

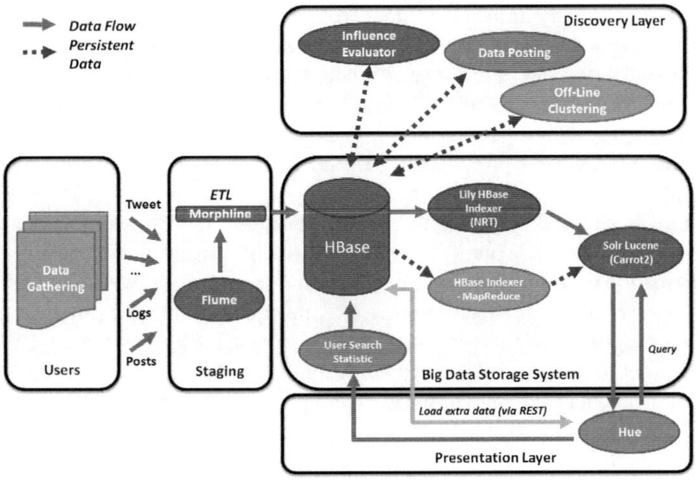

Fig. 2: System Architecture for Big Data search

In order to guarantee maximum implementation flexibility, we exploited several open source tools as Apache Hadoop [4], Flume [5], HBase [6], Solr [7], Lily HBase Indexer [8] and Hue [9]. They have been used for implementing our Data Posting and Influence Evaluation strategies.

Data about user activities and interactions with a social network are collected by our **Big Data Storage System**, which performs the following preliminary operations: i) it first computes some high level statistics about user search (e.g. most frequent search keywords) that will be refined during the information analysis and enrichment steps; ii) it stores all the collected data in a staging area to overcome potential problems due to different speed, size and format of incoming data; iii) it performs the proper extraction, transformation and loading operations for making data well suited for efficient storage (space saving) and analysis (fast execution time); iv) finally, it stores the pre-processed data in a structure tailored for Big Data. We choose *HBase* as our big data storage because it is a column family based data store [6], thus it is tailored for supporting fast execution of the kind of queries supported by our system. More in detail, as data have been collected and cleansed, two kind of analysis can be performed: 1) *static* analysis of consolidated data and 2) *dynamic* analysis of data flows. In our system we provide both features, in order to meet different user needs that could arise in a real life scenario. More in detail, the overall architecture offers two interaction models for either domain experts or end-users. Indeed, end-users (e.g. tourists searching for information about a restaurant) are interested in *(Near) Real Time* searches, i.e., dynamic analysis, while domain experts are interested in static analysis consisting in a more refined study that must be performed in *Batch* mode. We point out that, guaranteeing both static and dynamic analysis cause different indexing strategies to be implemented. If static analysis has to be performed,

[4] http://hadoop.apache.org
[5] https://flume.apache.org/
[6] https://hbase.apache.org/
[7] http://lucene.apache.org/solr/
[8] http://ngdata.github.io/hbase-indexer/
[9] http://gethue.com/

then we exploit *Map Reduce Indexer* module (represented as a green ellipse in Fig 2). This module performs a quick *Map* operation that creates the pairs $< key, value >$ that will be used by subsequent *reduce* step, in order to create the objects to be queried by *Solr*. On the contrary, dynamic analysis refers to fresh data materialized into the data store, and it needs *near real time indexing* which is provided by *Lily* framework. *Lily* detects the most recent data (by exploiting the trigger provided by Hbase) and indexes them in *Solr* allowing their on-line querying.

After data pre-elaboration takes place, we go through the **Discovery Layer**, which includes three modules. The first one is based on a suite of clustering algorithms that are devoted to the extraction of unsupervised information hidden in the collected data. The obtained clusters, are filtered by the influence evaluator module that identifies the dimensions that have the potential to spread across the network. After this filtering step, high level information will be used by the data posting module to enrich information sources. We stress that data posting differs from classical data exchange because, while moving data, the contents are enriched by supplying additional pieces of information. To this end, a source database is linked with additional tables, called *domain relations*, that store the dimensions to be added into the target database and aggregate data dependencies (in particular, count constraints) are used to select dimension values that better characterize user behaviors. We observe that the dimension-based structure of a target database can be effectively supported by a column-based Big Data storage system such as HBase.

Finally the **Presentation Layer** is used to personalize the enriched information for the current user query and to present portions of it (dimensions) into the search toolbar that are pertinent with entered keywords for enabling a faceted browsing. In order to properly display search results, we exploit *Hue* features. The latter, is a software offering a customizable user friendly interface. In our system, we provide two customized views tailored for different user categories, i.e. *end-users* and *domain experts*. In particular, end-users are able to search only data indexed by *Solr*, while domain experts can also view/query data available in the data warehouse (including those automatically detected by the system and suggested by the influence diffusion and data posting tasks) and (eventually) add new dimensions. The rationale behind this choice is the following: end-users are interested to data pertaining their own search, thus they are not interested in additional details. On the opposite side, domain experts need a comprehensive view of the interactions taking place among users. We recall that, as end-users interact with the system, we collect usage statistics that are stored for better evaluating how dimensions spread among users.

3 Modeling discovered dimensions diffusion

Social network users links each other in several ways. They can simply establish a friendship relation (e.g., Facebook friends) or they can follow other users (e.g., Twitter followers). As user interactions take place, some users could become more influential than others, i.e. they are able to drive their friends (or followers) choices in many context such as food, entertainment and travels. Users influence can be also exploited for providing personalized search suggestions to their social connection. As explained above we derive new knowledge about user search preferences by clustering. However, only a subset of the obtained dimensions can be actually considered in order to provide useful suggestions. To this end, we define an influence evaluation model tailored for dimension ranking such that only the most promising ones will be suggested to the network users. This ranking can be computed by exploiting the possible *influence* exerted by users to their social links. The ratio behind this choice is that, when users need to take a decision, they are largely influenced by their social environment. Moreover, users performing complex searches are usually sensitive to suggestions about related searches performed by other users.

As a result, identifying for each user his/her most influential friends and ranking the dimensions in decreasing order of their diffusion probability will allow us to improve both users interaction with the (specialized) search engine and their query experience. To this end, in the following, we describe the model exploited to emulate the dimensions diffusion across the network and the heuristic we have proposed to compute their diffusion probability. Moreover, we introduce the mathematical basis of influence evaluation that have been exploited for updating the influence weight associated to each edge of the social graph.

3.1 Our Algorithm for Influence Evaluation

In this section, we describe our algorithm for modeling the diffusion of dimensions across the network. Let $G = (V, E)$ be a directed graph representing a social network, where V is the set of nodes (i.e., users) and E the set of edges (i.e., social links between users). We denote with $N^{in}(v)$ (resp. $N^{out}(v)$) the set of in-neighbors (resp. out-neighbors) of an user v, i.e., $N^{in}(v) = \{u \in V | \exists (u, v) \in E\}$ (resp. $N^{out}(v) = \{u \in V | \exists (v, u) \in E\}$). Let D^v be the set of dimensions exploited by user v for issuing his/her last query, and let $\mathbf{D} = \{D^1, \cdots, D^n\}$, with $n = |V|$, be the current assignment of search dimensions for each user in the graph. In order to evaluate the spread of a set of dimensions $\mathcal{D}^*$ catching their diffusion process, we consider the *Linear Threshold* model (LT), one of the most widely-studied diffusion models [4]. In the LT model, the diffusion process evolves in discrete time and involves a set S of initial active users (e.g., users who have exploited some suggested dimensions). Moreover, a node v is influenced by its neighbor u according to the weight $b_{u,v}$ labeling the edge between u and v. More in detail, at the beginning of the process, each node v chooses a threshold ϑ_v uniformly at random from the interval $[0, 1]$. Then, starting from the set S, each inactive node v is activated if the total weight of its active neighbors is at least ϑ_v. As the sum of in-neighbors weights for each node must not exceed 1, ϑ_v represents the weighted fraction of v's in-neighbors that must become active[10] in order to activate v. The process runs until no more activations are possible.

In order to simulate the diffusion process of $\mathcal{D}^*$ through the LT model, we need to learn its parameters. To this end, we initialize $b_{u,v}$ by applying the Bernoulli model proposed in [2] to the available social network activity logs. Thus, for each edge $(u, v) \in E$, the weight $b_{u,v}$ is computed as the ratio between the number of actions performed by both u and v if v's actions took place after u's, and the total number of actions performed by v. This weight is next updated by our influence evaluator every time v poses a new query as follows:

$$b_{u,v} = \begin{cases} \dfrac{|D^u \cap D^v| + b_{u,v}}{|D^u \cup D^v| + 1} & if\ |D^u| \neq 0 \\ b_{u,v} & otherwise \end{cases} \tag{1}$$

According to Eq.1, $b_{u,v}$ will be updated only in the case that u exploits some of the dimensions suggested by the system. Clearly enough, the higher is the number of dimensions shared by u and v, the greater will be the increase of $b_{u,v}$. The same reasoning applies if the number of shared dimensions decrease thus causing a lower value for $b_{u,v}$ to be set. As the

[10] In our application scenario, we say that a user u is active for a given dimension d if u has exploited d for issuing its last query, i.e., $d \in D^u$

sum of the in-weights for a node could exceed 1, we perform a normalization of these values dividing each $b_{u,v}$ by their sum. The latter allows to accomplish the constraint imposed by the LT model.

Once assigned the weights to graph edges, we exploit the solution proposed in [3] to estimate the diffusion probabilities of $\mathcal{D}^*$. In the LT model, the probability of a path $\pi = [v_0, v_1, \ldots, v_l]$ $(l > 0)$ is defined as $Pr[\pi] = \sum_{i=0}^{l-1} b_{v_i,v_{i+1}}$. In [3], it has been shown that the overall activation probability of a node u in the LT model, given a set of initial spreader S, can be computed by summing up, for each node $s \in S$, the path probability of each path from s to u that does not cross any other node in S.

Inspired by the study presented in [3] we designed our algorithm for influence diffusion analysis. Algorithm 1 shows our proposed heuristic, namely *DIM-DIFF*, that, given a dimensions assignment **D**, computes the diffusion probabilities **A** of a set of dimensions $\mathcal{D}^*$ by considering the possible paths along which they can spread across the network.

Algorithm 1 *DIM-DIFF*

Require: Weighted graph $G = (V, E, b)$, dimensions assignment $\mathbf{D} = \{D^1, \cdots, D^n\}$ with $n = |V|$, set $\mathcal{D}^*$ of dimensions to spread, pruning threshold δ
Ensure: Diffusion probability **A** for $\mathcal{D}^*$
1: $S \leftarrow \emptyset$; $\mathbf{A} \leftarrow \emptyset$
2: **for** $u \in V$ **do**
3:   **if** $\mathcal{D}^* \cap D^u \neq \emptyset$ **then**
4:     $S \leftarrow \langle u, \mathcal{D}^* \cap D^u \rangle$ {*identifies nodes that are active for at least one dimension in* $\mathcal{D}^*$}
5: **while** $S \neq \emptyset$ **do**
6:   $\langle u, d^* \rangle \leftarrow S.extract()$
7:   $visited[u] = true$
8:   $computeProbability(u, d^*, 1, visited)$ {*starts the depth first visit from each active node*}
9: **return A**;

10: **Function** ***computeProbability***$(u, d^*, pp, visited)$
11: **for** $v \in N^{out}(u) \wedge !visited[v]$ **do**
12:   $pp \leftarrow pp \times b_{u,v}$ {*updates the path probability*}
13:   $d^* \leftarrow d^* \setminus D^v$ {*removes the dimensions node* v *is currently activated for*}
14:   **if** $d^* \neq \emptyset \wedge pp \geq \delta$ **then**
15:     $A^v \leftarrow \mathbf{A}[v]$
16:     **for** $d \in d^*$ **do**
17:       $A^v(d) = A^v(d) + pp$ {*updates the diffusion probability of dimension* d *for node* v}
18:     $visited[v] = true$
19:     $computeProbability(v, d^*, pp, visited)$
20:     $visited[v] = false$

DIM-DIFF first computes the set S of initial active nodes for $\mathcal{D}^*$. Since a user can be active only for a subset d^* of dimensions in $\mathcal{D}^*$, we need to keep track of this subset during the diffusion process (steps 2-6). Once built the set S, our algorithm proceeds by considering all the paths whose source nodes belongs to S and computing the path probability by multiplying the weight of the edges which compose the path. To this end, a recursive implementation of the depth first visit from an active node at a time is provided by the function *computeProbability*. The latter takes as input the last node u of the path currently considered, the set d^* of dimensions that u might propagate to its neighbors, the path probability pp

and a vector which keeps track of the nodes already visited, and tries to extend the path by considering u's out-neighbors (line 14). Once the probability of the new path which includes edge (u, v) is obtained (step 15), *DIM-DIFF* updates the set of dimensions that can spread through node v by removing those for which v is already active (step 16). By step 20 we update the diffusion probability of the dimensions not yet used by node v. Clearly, since the path probability rapidly diminishes as the path gets longer, a threshold δ is used to consider only the contributions of paths with a reasonable probability (step 17).

The algorithm described above can be used for defining a strategy for dimension recommendation based on the potential influence that can be excerpted by a user. We recall that, in our system, dimensions can arise, disappear and/or reappear according to the users needs. Thus, we are not interested in maximizing the spread of a dimension in the network. However, our system can be easily exploited to detect the most influential users, as it allows to keep track of users who lead to the largest cascade of dimension diffusion. In the experimental sections, we will show that the algorithm exhibits good performances in real scenarios.

4 Conclusion and Future Work

The impressive progress and development of Internet and on-line technologies has led to an increasing availability of a huge volume of data generated by heterogeneous sources at high production rates. The availability of such unprecedented large amount of information sources represents an opportunity for the analysis of human behavior, and their evolution when influenced by other people's opinion/suggestion. Therefore, the issue of devising novel solutions for analyzing big data, coming both from various information sources and from logs of user interactions and behaviors, is becoming more and more compelling in the construction of Intelligent Information Systems (IIS) to assist end users in the search of relevant information and in the interaction with services in the net. In this paper, we have presented a user behavior oriented search framework for implementing new generation IIS that offers advanced search functionalities.

Further research lines include: 1) testing the approach on a wider set of social networks and application contexts; 2) applying more sophisticated diffusion models and influence evaluation algorithms.

References

1. Economist, T.: Data, data everywhere. The Economist (Feb 2010)
2. Goyal, A., Bonchi, F., Lakshmanan, L.V.S.: Learning influence probabilities in social networks. In: Proceedings of the Third International Conference on Web Search and Web Data Mining, WSDM 2010, New York, NY, USA, February 4-6, 2010. pp. 241–250 (2010)
3. Goyal, A., Lu, W., Lakshmanan, L.V.S.: SIMPATH: an efficient algorithm for influence maximization under the linear threshold model. In: 11th IEEE International Conference on Data Mining, ICDM 2011, Vancouver, BC, Canada, December 11-14, 2011. pp. 211–220 (2011)
4. Kempe, D., Kleinberg, J.M., Tardos, É.: Maximizing the spread of influence through a social network. In: KDD. pp. 137–146 (2003)
5. Nature: Big data. Nature (Sep 2008)
6. Redmond, E., Wilson, J.R.: Seven Databases in Seven Weeks: A Guide to Modern Databases and the NoSQL Movement. Pragmatic Bookshelf (2012)
7. Saccà, D., Serra, E.: Data posting: a new frontier for data exchange in the big data era. In: Bravo, L., Lenzerini, M. (eds.) Proceedings of the 7th Alberto Mendelzon International Workshop on Foundations of Data Management, Puebla/Cholula, Mexico, May 21-23, 2013. CEUR Workshop Proceedings, vol. 1087. CEUR-WS.org (2013), http://ceur-ws.org/Vol-1087

Efficient Analysis of Process Logs
(Discussion Paper)

Bettina Fazzinga[2], Sergio Flesca[1], Filippo Furfaro[1], Elio Masciari[2], Luigi Pontieri[2], and Chiara Pulice[1]

[1] DIMES, University of Calabria, Italy
[2] ICAR-CNR, Italy
{flesca, furfaro, cpulice}@dimes.unical.it
{fazzinga, masciari, pontieri}@icar.cnr.it

Abstract. The issue of devising efficient and effective solutions for supporting the analysis of process logs has recently received great attention from the research community, as effectively accomplishing any business process management task requires understanding the behavior of the processes. In this paper, we propose a new framework supporting the analysis of process logs, exhibiting two main features: a flexible data model (enabling an exhaustive representation of the facets of the business processes that are typically of interest for the analysis) and a graphical query language, providing a user-friendly tool for easily expressing both selection and aggregate queries over the business processes and the activities they are composed of. The framework has been implemented, and different physical organizations of the data have been tried: in particular, both the "traditional" technology of two relational DBMSs and the "innovative" Big-Data-oriented technology of the NoSQL DBMS *Neo4J* have been considered. The comparative analysis between these implementations is a contribution of independent interest: besides assessing the capability of the framework to be a support for evaluating queries over process logs, it gives an insight on the differences between the relational and the graph-based models in terms of efficiency of evaluation of the typical queries posed during business process analysis.

Keywords: Business Process logs, NoSQL, RDBMS

1 Introduction

The increasing diffusion of powerful storage, computing and collaboration technologies has caused a deep change in the way business processes take place. This forced many organizations to deal with an unprecedented amount of process data (in particular, of execution logs), which have become a common kind of organizational asset [8], representing a rich source of knowledge on the behavior of business processes.

From a business company point of view, these data need to be used intelligently in order to compete with other organizations in terms of efficiency, prompt reaction to the market and quality of service. In this respect, the challenge is shifting from the efficient storage of large process data volumes to a new intriguing goal: *How gather actionable information from (big) process data?* Answering this question is rather complex and implies detecting and analyzing typical execution patterns, and evaluating how well a process is aligned to business objectives. Obviously, as process logs are essentially composed of time-related events, one could think of adopting data analysis paradigms defined for non process-aware logs, such as web access logs, search query logs, transaction logs, and several other kinds of event-centered repositories [2, 5]. However, these paradigms are not suitable for analyzing process logs, as they disregard the information that some events happened during the execution of the same process instance, which are useful for understanding process logs.

Traditionally, analyzing process data has been the main objective of *Business Process Analysis* approaches, which can be roughly grouped in two main categories: *process discovery methods*, allowing for automatically extracting some kind of process model [1] from log data; and *deductive techniques*, allowing for formulating and evaluating queries [4, 6, 7, 3] against log contents.

In this work, we specifically focus on the second flavor of analysis, that can help test hypotheses on the behavior of a business process, and retrieve or aggregate process instances that follow a pattern of interest (involving, e.g., inefficient or forbidden execution flows), and may deserve further fine-grain investigation/diagnoses. Unfortunately, none of the currently available log querying tools represents an optimal solution, ensuring satisfactory levels for easiness of use, flexibility/expressiveness, and efficiency of query evaluation.

In order to overcome this drawback, we propose a framework for supporting the analysis of business process logs that, taking into account the very nature of business processes, allows (even non-expert) users to query the logs intuitively and efficiently. Our proposal bases on a general data model for a process log, viewed as a set of process instances (*p-instances*). In turn, any p-instance consists of activity instances (*a-instances*), each referring to a process activity (i.e., a well-defined task, performed for the p-instance).

In order to ease the analysis tasks for non expert users, we propose a novel expressive graph-based query language, that allows the analyst to query process data at different levels of detail. A query is based on the notion of *Precedence Graph Pattern* (*PGP*), that allows selection conditions to be expressed on both the structure of a p-instance (both in terms of involved activities/executors and of order relationships among a-instances), and on properties of its a-instances (e.g., starting/ending time, executor, etc). Besides returning the p-instances that match a pattern, the language allows aggregate statistics to be computed.

2 Storing Log Data

Retrieving actionable information from log data requires to represent information about both process instances and their associated activity instances. Specifically, for each process instance the analyst may be interested in knowing aggregate information, such as the overall elapsed time. Moreover, for each activity executed in a process instance the analyst may be interested in knowing detailed information about its execution, such as its starting and ending times, the executor that performed the activity and the activity execution context (e.g., the place where the activity is performed). In this section, we first introduce the logical model of log data which is adopted in this work, and next define two distinct physical models, which can be used to store and efficiently query log data represented in the introduced logical model.

2.1 A logical model for Log Data

Process instances and activity executions are logically represented in two separate tables: P-INSTANCES and A-INSTANCES. Each tuple in P-INSTANCES (called *p-instance*) stores high level information about an *overall* process instance, and has the form $\langle id, type, n_A, n_e, n_c, n_s, t_{tot}\rangle$, where:

- id is a process instance identifier;
- $type$ is a process instance category. This attribute is intended to allow analysts to define a taxonomy (such as *Urgent* or *Not Urgent*) over process instances.

– n_A is the number of distinct activities pertaining the p-instance;
– n_e is the number of different executors involved in the p-instance;
– n_c is the number of different contexts where the process activities took place;
– n_s is the number of a-instances performed within the p-instance;
– t_{tot} is the overall duration of the process instance.

Each tuple in A-INSTANCES (referred as *a-instance*) describes an activity instance (i.e. an activity execution), and takes the form $\langle id, p, A, e, c, \tau_s, \tau_d \rangle$, where:
– id is an a-instance identifier;
– p is a p-instance identifier;
– A is an activity;
– e is an executor;
– c is an execution context, i.e. this attribute can model either a physical device devoted to the activity execution (e.g. a specific server within the organization) or a place where the activity was executed (e.g. a dock);
– τ_s, τ_d are the starting time and the duration of the activity execution.

Basically, an a-instance $\langle id, p, A, e, c, \tau_s, \tau_d \rangle$ describes a "step" of the p-instance p, as it says that this p-instance contains an execution of the activity A, performed by e within the context c starting at time τ_s, and ending at time $\tau_s + \tau_d$. In the following, given a log-tuple t, we will say that t has been "*performed*" (or, equivalently, "*executed*") referring to the execution of the process step represented by t.

2.2 Physical Organization of Log Data

We investigated different physical organizations of log data, trying both relational and graph-based (NOSQL) DBMSs.

A Relational-based Architecture for Log Data. In this section, we describe the physical organization of the log data exploited to store them into two relational DBMSs, namely *Oracle 12c* and *MySQL*. Besides materializing the tables P-INSTANCES and A-INSTANCES defined in the previous section, we also created a table, named PREC used to store precedence relationships between activity instances. In more detail, if two activity executions a_1 and a_2 appeared in the same process instance p, we say that a_2 was performed *sequentially after* a_1 if: $i)$ a_2 started after the end of a_1, and $ii)$ there is no other activity execution in the same p-instance that both started and ended between the end of a_1 and the beginning of a_2. Table PREC stores a triple $\langle a_2, a_1, p \rangle$ for each pair of activities a_1, a_2 such that a_2 was performed sequentially after a_1, both within p. The above defined relational schema is shown in Fig. 1.

Intuitively enough, materializing PREC avoids the usage of SQL queries with negation in order to check whether two activities are executed one sequentially after the other. As a matter of fact, this kind of conditions are commonly used in queries supporting process log analysis. In the following section, we will see that our query language supports the expression of such conditions.

As regards specific physical organization issues, in the *Oracle 12c* implementation, we exploited the clustering features provided by the DBMS in order to reduce query answering times. In more detail, a cluster is a schema object that contains data (from one or more tables) sharing some columns. *Oracle 12c* stores together all the rows (possibly from different tables) that share the same cluster key, thus speeding up the query process whenever the tuples associated with that cluster need to be processed together. In our relational representation of log data using *Oracle 12c*, we clustered tables P-INSTANCES, A-INSTANCES and PREC using the p-instance identifier as clustering key. We also defined indexes over p-instance types and time coordinates of the activities.

In the *MySQL* implementation, we used *MyISAM* engine (which is known to support faster query evaluation than the other engines), and we exploited the horizontal partitioning mechanism allowed by MySQL (in fact, MySQL has not the clustering features provided by *Oracle 12c*). In particular, we defined a horizontal partition over A-INSTANCES and PREC, using the p-instance identifier as partitioning key. The same indexes as those defined over *Oracle 12c* were used.

A Graph-Based architecture for Process Data. As an alternative physical organization of the log data, we considered a NOSQL database adopting a graph-based data model. More specifically, we used *Neo4J*, an open source graph database system. A suitable graph-based organization of the process instances is naturally suggested by the characteristics of the processes and their activities. The schema that we used to represent the log data in *Neo4J* is reported in Fig. 2(a). Specifically, we used five different types of nodes:

- *Process Instance* nodes, that represent p-instances and are characterized by the attributes *type*, *#activities*, *#executors*, *#contexts*, *#steps* and *duration*;
- *Activity Instance* nodes, that represent a-instances and are characterized by the attributes *start* and *duration*;
- *Executor* nodes, that represent executors;
- *Context* nodes, that represent execution contexts;
- *Activity* nodes, that represent activities.

Moreover, each Activity Instance node is associated with a Process Instance node, an Executor node, a Context node, an Activity node and an arbitrary number of Activity Instance nodes, representing activity instances executed sequentially after the current one. An example of p-instance represented in *Neo4J* is shown in Fig. 2(b).

3 Querying Log Data

In order to extract actionable information from log data an analyst should be able to pose queries at different levels of detail. In this section, we first introduce a new query language allowing users to pose queries over log data easily and effectively. Next, we describe query rewriting mechanisms for translating queries expressed in this language into the native query language of the underlying DBMSs.

3.1 Log Activity Queries

We first introduce the notion of *Activity Query Graph* (AQG). An AQG is a pair $\langle V, E\rangle$ where V is a set of nodes and E is a set of edges. A node $v \in V$ represents an activity

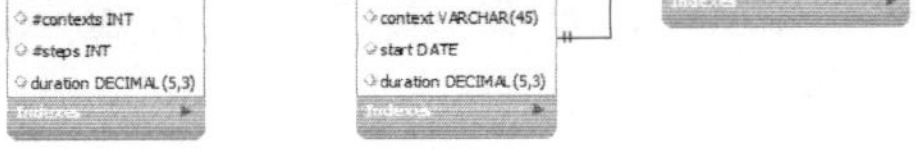

Fig. 1: A Relational Schema For Activities and Processes

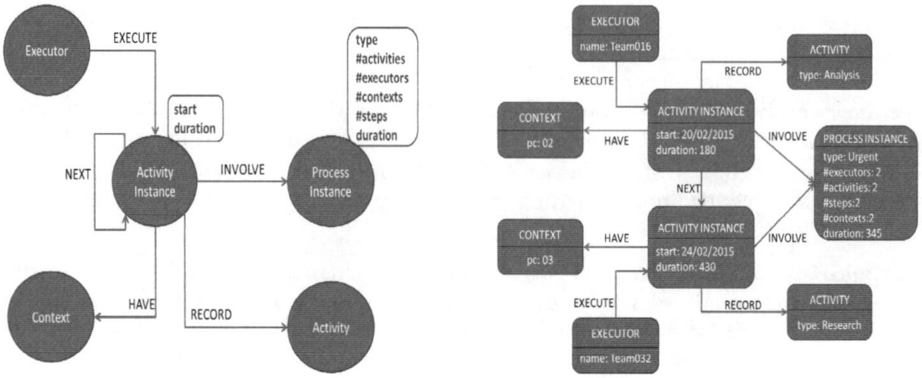

(a) (b)

Fig. 2: (a) Graph schema and (b) its instance

instance. Moreover, $v.A$, $v.e$, $v.c$, $v.\tau_s$ and $v.\tau_d$ represent the activity type, executor, context, starting time and duration of the activity instance v, respectively. Edges in E can be either *solid* or *dashed*. A *solid* edge is a pair $\langle v_i, v_j \rangle$, and it specifies that v_i and v_j represent activities *sequentially* executed one after the other. Analogously, a *dashed* edge is a pair $[v_i, v_j]$, and expresses the condition that the activity instance v_j is executed after v_i, but not necessarily sequentially after v_i. Moreover, we point out that all the nodes in V refer to a-instances belonging to the same p-instance.

We can now introduce the notion of *precedence graph pattern - PGP*. A *PGP* π is a triple $\langle AQG, p, \varphi_\pi \rangle$ where AQG is an Activity Query Graph, p is a variable denoting the p-instance including the a-instances onto which the nodes of AQG are mapped and φ_π is a boolean formula whose terms are of the form $\phi\theta k$, where θ is a comparison operator, k is a constant, and ϕ is linear combination of terms of the form $x.y$, with $x \in V_{AQG} \cup \{p\}$ and either (i) $y \in \{A, e, c, \tau_s, \tau_d\}$, in the case that $x \neq p$, or (ii) $y \in \{type, n_A, n_e, n_c, n_s, t_{tot}\}$, in the case that $x = p$.

We can now define *Log Activity Queries* exploited in our framework.

Definition 1 (Log Activity Query). *A log activity query is a pair* $\langle \mathcal{F}, \pi \rangle$*, where* π *is a PGP and* $\mathcal{F}$ *is either:*

1. *a linear combination of terms of the form* $x.y$*, with* $x \in V_{AQG} \cup \{p\}$ *and either (i)* $y \in \{A, e, c, \tau_s, \tau_d\}$*, in the case that* $x \neq p$*, or (ii)* $y \in \{id, type, n_A, n_e, n_c, n_s, t_{tot}\}$*, in the case that* $x = p$*;*
2. `COUNT`
3. *an aggregation function* $\gamma(\psi)$*, where* $\gamma \in \{\text{MIN, MAX, AVG}\}$ *and* ψ *is a linear combination of terms of the form* $x.y$*, with* $x \in V_{AQG} \cup \{p\}$ *and either (i)* $y \in \{A, e, c, \tau_s, \tau_d\}$*, in the case that* $x \neq p$*, or (ii)* $y \in \{type, n_A, n_e, n_c, n_s, t_{tot}\}$*, in the case that* $x = p$*.*

We refer to these kind of queries as log activity queries as they represent a general form of queries that can be instantiated as:

1. *Process queries* if at least a term of the form $p.y$ appears in $\mathcal{F}$ or φ_π, or
2. *Instance Queries*, otherwise.

Log activity queries can be expressed graphically using our querying interface.

Example 1. Consider two log activity queries Q_1 and Q_2 defined as follows. Q_1 asks for the identifiers of the p-instances containing three activity executions of the same activity $A1$, performed by three different executors and one sequentially after the other, and Q_2 counts the p-instances whose identifiers are returned by Q_1. Query Q_1 can be expressed as a pair $\langle p.id, \pi\rangle$, such that $\pi = \langle AQG, p, \varphi_\pi\rangle$, where: *(i)* $AQG = \langle\{v_1, v_2, v_3\}, \{\langle v_1, v_2\rangle\ \langle v_2, v_3\rangle\}\rangle$, and *(ii)* $\varphi_\pi = v_1.A = A1 \wedge v_2.A = A1 \wedge v_2.A = A1 \wedge v_1.e \neq v_2.e \wedge v_2.e \neq v_3.e \wedge v_1.e \neq v_3.e$. Query Q_2 can be written as $\langle COUNT, \pi\rangle$.

As regard the semantics of log activity queries, it can be easily given in terms of homomorphisms from nodes of the AQG to a-instances. For the sake of brevity of presentation here we do not report the formal definition of the semantics, but the interested reader can have a hint about it from the query rewritings provided in the next section.

3.2 Query Rewriting

The different architectures we used to store log data exploit different query languages. Thus, in order to properly issue queries on specific DBMSs, we need to reformulate log activity queries both in SQL (for query against relational databases) and in Cypher (for query against NEO4J). This task is automatically accomplished in our prototype, according to the rewriting rules described next. Let us first discuss SQL translation.

1. *Process Translation*: in the case that a process query is to be translated, the P-INSTANCE table is included in the FROM CLAUSE.
2. *Node Translation*: For each node appearing in the PGP of the log activity query to be translated, an occurrence of the A-INSTANCE table is included in the FROM clause. If the query is a process query, a join condition between the occurrence of A-INSTANCE and the P-INSTANCE table is included in the WHERE clause.
3. *Edge Translation*:
   (a) for each solid edge $\langle v_i, v_j\rangle$, we insert an occurrence of table PREC in the FROM clause, and two join conditions (linking PREC to the A-INSTANCE occurrences referring to v_i and v_j, resp.) in the WHERE clause.
   (b) for each dashed edge $[v_i, v_j]$, we insert an SQL condition encoding $v_i.\tau_s < v_j.\tau_s$ in the WHERE clause.
4. *Conditions and Output Translation*: The formula φ_π is translated by adding the corresponding SQL conditions to the WHERE clause. Moreover, an SQL expression corresponding to $\mathcal{F}$ is inserted in the SELECT clause. In the case that $\mathcal{F}$ is `COUNT` a query of the form "`SELECT COUNT(*) FROM (SELECT DISTINCT idProcess FROM ... WHERE ...)`" is used, where the subquery is the query obtained by applying the translation rules.

For Log Data stored in *Neo4J*, we translate a query into Cypher as described below.

1. *Process Translation*: in the case that a process query is to be translated, a Process node is mentioned in the MATCH clause.
2. *Node Translation*: For each node appearing in the PGP an *ActivityInstance* node is mentioned in the MATCH clause. In the case that the query is a process query, an edge between the *ActivityInstance* and the *Process* node labeled with *INVOLVE* is specified in the MATCH clause.
3. *Edge Translation*:

(a) for each solid edge $\langle v_i, v_j \rangle$, we connect the two ActivityInstance nodes n_i and n_j (corresponding to v_i and v_j, respectively) in the MATCH clause, with an edge labeled with *NEXT*.
(b) for each dashed edge $[v_i, v_j]$, we insert in the WHERE clause a condition encoding $v_i.\tau_s < v_j.\tau_s$.

4. *Conditions and Output Translation*: φ_π is translated by adding the corresponding conditions on node attributes in the WHERE clause. Moreover, for each condition mentioning a term $v.A$, $v.e$ or $v.c$ a node labeled with "Activity", "Executor" or "Context", respectively, is included in the MATCH clause connected with a proper edge to the node corresponding to v.
Finally, an expression corresponding to $\mathcal{F}$ is inserted in the RETURN clause. Note that, similarly to the case of condition translation, we include "Activity", "Executor" or "Context" nodes in the MATCH clause if mentioned in the RETURN clause.

4 Experimental Evaluation

Dataset features. We considered a dataset coming from a real Service Management System, provided by Rabobank Group ICT as a benchmark for *BPI challenge 2014*. Specifically, the log used in the tests was extracted from the tables "Detail Incident" and "Detail Incident Activities", concerning instances of Incident Management processes ran between October 1st, 2013 and March 31st, 2014. The dataset mentions about 20 process types and about 40 activity types. The original data were translated into our data model (in particular, the duration of each activity was randomly generated, since this information was missing in original log). However, since the size of the original dataset was too small, we replicated every p-instance 300 and 600 times while varying the timestamps and durations of the associated a-instances, thus obtaining two datasets consisting of a 10GB and 20GB A-INSTANCES tables and a 1GB and 2GB P-INSTANCES tables, respectively.

Hardware Settings and Query Workload. All the tests were performed with a typical client machine available for decision makers: a desktop with 12 GB of RAM (referred to as *Client* hereinafter). The query workload Q considered in the analysis consisted of 500 queries, obtained as follows. First, for each $N \in \{5, 10, 15, 20, 25\}$, we considered 2 different $AQGs = \langle V, E \rangle$ such that $|V| = N$, one using solid edges only and the other using dashed edge only, obtaining 10 $AQGs$. Secondly, from each of these 10 $AQGs$, we generated 50 log activity queries $\langle \mathcal{F}, \pi \rangle$, where $\pi = \langle AQG, p, \phi \rangle$ and ϕ was a (possibly empty) conjunction of randomly generated conditions on the starting/ending times of the activities. As regards $\mathcal{F}$, for each query, we randomly chose $\mathcal{F} \in \{$COUNT, MIN(α),MAX(α),AVG(α)$\}$, where α was randomly generated in the set $\{p.n_A, p.n_e, p.n_c, p.n_s, p.t_{tot}, x.\tau_s, x.\tau_d\}$, where x was a node randomly drawn from V.

In more detail, Q was partitioned into 4 subsets of queries:
Q_1: only solid edges, and no condition on the starting/ending times of the activities;
Q_2: only dashed edges, and no condition on the starting/ending times of the activities;
Q_3: only solid edges, and conditions on the starting/ending times of some activities;
Q_4: only dashed edges, and conditions on the starting/ending times of some activities.

Results and Discussion. Table 1 summarizes the execution times vs. the number of nodes of the PGP for each class of queries, dataset and DBMS. The meaning of NA in a cell of Table 1 is that no answer was obtained within 2 hours of execution for at least one half of the queries in the portion of the query workload corresponding to the cell.

# Nodes	***MySQL***								***Oracle 12c***								***Neo4J***							
	$10GB$				$20GB$				$10GB$				$20GB$				$10GB$				$20GB$			
	Q_1	Q_2	Q_3	Q_4	Q_1	Q_2	Q_3	Q_4	Q_1	Q_2	Q_3	Q_4	Q_1	Q_2	Q_3	Q_4	Q_1	Q_2	Q_3	Q_4	Q_1	Q_2	Q_3	Q_4
5	2	NA	<1	NA	54	NA	2	NA	55	2	41	1	132	17	104	11	206	284	151	221	NA	NA	NA	NA
10	68	NA	2	NA	4261	NA	20	NA	59	2	41	1	225	26	197	21	220	276	156	215	NA	NA	NA	NA
15	78	NA	36	NA	NA	NA	68	NA	61	2	42	1	202	19	186	11	225	273	160	215	NA	NA	NA	NA
20	NA	NA	NA	NA	NA	NA	NA	NA	68	2	52	1	195	41	126	11	228	290	166	227	NA	NA	NA	NA
25	NA	NA	NA	NA	NA	NA	NA	NA	59	3	51	1	210	27	176	21	232	292	169	235	NA	NA	NA	NA

Table 1: Execution Times (sec) for different dataset sizes, query sizes, DBMS and class of queries

Results shown above allow us to draw a quite interesting pictures of the business process querying scenario. First of all, it is worth noting that *Neo4J* was able to provide answers only over the 10GB dataset. This is due to the low amount of RAM available in our hardware setting. *MySQL* did not provide answers within the specified timeout for most of the queries, especially over the 20GB dataset. Moreover, *MySQL* never returned answers for queries containing dashed edges only ($Q2$ and $Q4$). *Oracle 12c* always returned query answers within the specified timeout. Interestingly enough, *Oracle 12c* outperformed both *MySQL* and *Neo4J* in most cases. In fact, *MySQL* was much faster than *Oracle 12c* only on $Q1$ queries with 5 nodes and $Q3$ queries with less than 20 nodes over both the datasets. Moreover, both *Oracle 12c* and *Neo4J* were insensitive to the query size (measured as number of nodes), while the performances of *MySQL* got worse when the query size increases.

5 Conclusions and future works

In this paper, we described a framework for querying process log data relying on an expressive graph-based query language. It gives to end users the opportunity to analyze process logs using an intuitive graphical language. A prototype has been implemented, trying different physical infrastructures, based on relational and NoSQL DBMSs. As a future improvement, we will work on making our approach deal with the streaming scenario as to fully catch the Big Data features of process data.

References

1. van der Aalst, W.M.P., van Dongen, B.F., Herbst, J., Maruster, L., Schimm, G., Weijters, A.J.M.M.: Workflow mining: a survey of issues and approaches. Data & Knowledge Engineering 47(2), 237–267 (2003)
2. Aalst, W.M.V.D.: A decade of business process management conferences: Personal reflections on a developing discipline. In: Business Process Management. pp. 1–16 (2012)
3. van der Aalst, W.M.P., de Beer, H.T., van Dongen, B.F.: Process mining and verification of properties: An approach based on temporal logic. In: Proc. of OTM Confederated Intl Conferences. pp. 130–147 (2005)
4. Deutch, D., Milo, T.: Type inference and type checking for queries over execution traces. The VLDB Journal 21(1), 51–68 (2012)
5. Gao, X.: Towards the next generation intelligent bpm in the era of big data. In: Business Process Management. pp. 4–9 (2013)
6. Grigori, D., Casati, F., Castellanos, M., Dayal, U., Sayal, M., Shan, M.C.: Business process intelligence. Comput. Ind. 53(3), 321–343 (Apr 2004)
7. Schiefer, J., List, B., Bruckner, R.M.: Process data store: A real-time data store for monitoring business processes. In: Proc. of DEXA. pp. 760–770 (2003)
8. Wang, S., Lv, C., Wen, L., Wang, J.: Managing massive business process models and instances with process space. In: Business Process Management Demos. p. 91 (2014)

Computing Skylines over Encrypted Data in Cloud Environments

Suvarna Bothe[1], Alfredo Cuzzocrea[2], Panagiotis Karras[3], and Akrivi Vlachou[4]

[1] Rutgers University, NJ, USA
suvarnabothe@gmail.com
[2] University of Trieste and ICAR-CNR, Italy
alfredo.cuzzocrea@dia.units.it
[3] Skolkovo Institute of Science and Technology, Russia
P.Karras@skoltech.ru
[4] Norwegian University of Science and Technology,Norway
vlachou@isi.ntnu.no

Abstract. Making co-existent and convergent the need for *efficiency of relational query processing* over *Clouds* and the *security of data* themselves is figuring-out how one of the most challenging research problems in the *Big Data* era. Indeed, in actual analytics-oriented engines, such as *Google Analytics* and *Amazon S3*, where *key-value* storage-representation and efficient-management models are employed as to cope with the simultaneous processing of billions of transactions, *querying encrypted data* is becoming one of the most annoying problem, which has also attracted a great deal of attention from the research community. While this issue has been applied to a large variety of data formats, e.g. relational, RDF and multidimensional data, very few initiatives have pointed-out *skyline query processing over encrypted data*, which is, indeed, relevant for database analytics. In order to fulfill this methodological and technological gap, in this paper we present *eSkyline*, a prototype system and query interface that enables the processing of skyline queries over encrypted data, even *without* preserving the order on each attribute as order-preserving encryption would do. Our system comprises of an encryption scheme that facilitates the evaluation of domination relationships, hence allows for state-of-the-art skyline processing algorithms to be used. In order to prove the effectiveness and the reliability of our system, we also provide the details of the underlying encryption scheme, plus a suitable GUI that allows a user to interact with a server, and showcases the efficiency of computing skyline queries and decrypting the results.

1 Introduction

A critical trade-off is arising in the *Big Data* era (e.g., [1]): making co-existent and convergent the need for *efficiency of relational query processing* over *Clouds* (e.g., [18]) and the need for *security of data* themselves (e.g., [2]). The latter is a critical requirement when data stored in remote Cloud-enabled DBMS are distributed and queried for analytics purposes (e.g., [9, 6]), according to the well-known *DaaS* (*Database as a Service*) paradigm [14].

An illustrative example demonstrating the relevance of the research challenge above is clearly reported by actual analytics-oriented engines, such as *Google Analytics*, *Amazon S3*, and so forth, which, in order to cope with the simultaneous processing of billions of transactions, employ *key-value* storage-representation and efficient-management models which represent the "natural humus" for *MapReduce* [10] tasks. Here, data are distributed over Clouds and are accessed during query processing, hence *security and privacy risks* arise (e.g., [15]). A solution is then exploiting solid *data encryption mechanisms* (e.g., [12]) in order to further secure sensitive data sets, but this can introduce relevant drawbacks affecting the efficiency of the query processing itself.

Figure 1 shows a reference case study of the problem we investigate. Here, Alice and Bob are accessing a Cloud infrastructure populated by Cloud-enabled DBMS on top of which DaaS services are running. Relational data in the Cloud-enabled DBMS are encrypted based on a given encryption mechanism. Alice and Bob edit proper data-intensive analytical workflows that allow them to extract suitable analytics based on proper business goals. Ad-hoc GUI interfaces offer to both Alice and Bob with visual metaphors and components capable of editing the target workflow easily and get the (graphical) results accordingly. The database research challenge thus concerns the second step, which is the main goal of our research.

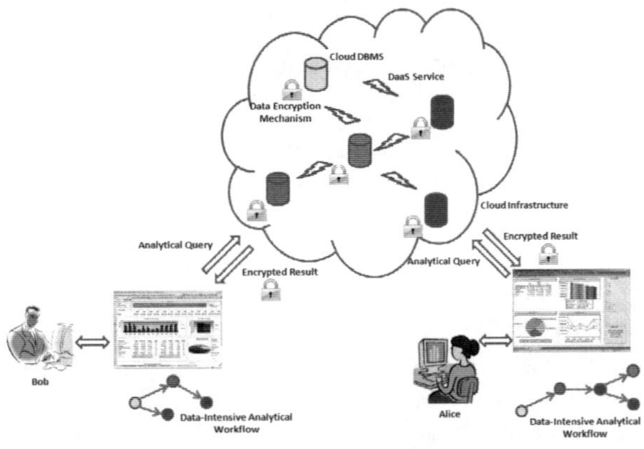

Fig. 1. Querying encrypted data application scenario.

As a result, recently a great deal of attention has been devoted by the research community in the annoying issue falling under the term *querying encrypted data* (e.g., [4, 16]), by focusing on a large variety of data formats, e.g. relational [13], RDF [11], multidimensional [17] data, and so forth, but very few initiatives have pointed-out *skyline query processing over encrypted data*, which is, indeed, relevant for database analytics.

Indeed, the advent of Cloud Computing redefines the traditional query processing paradigm. Whereas computational overhead and memory constraints become less prohibitive, data privacy, security, and *confidentiality* concerns become top priorities, as highlighted above. In particular, as data owners outsource the management of their data to service providers, query processing over such data has more resources to tap into, yet the data oftentimes has to be encrypted so as to prevent unauthorized access, like in the Cloud application scenario described in Figure 1.

From a genuine research point-of-view, the challenge that arises in such a setting is to devise an encryption scheme that still allows for query results to be efficiently computed using the encrypted data values. An important type of query that raises unconventional requirements in terms of the operator that has to be evaluated is the skyline query, which returns a set of objects in a data set whose values are not dominated by any other object therein. Following this main intuition, in this paper we present *eSkyline*, a prototype system and query interface that enables the processing of skyline queries over encrypted data, even *without* preserving the order on each attribute as order-preserving encryption would do. Our system comprises of an encryption scheme that facilitates the evaluation of domination relationships, hence allows for state-of-the-art skyline processing algorithms to be used. The actual data values are reconstructed only at the client side, where the encryption key is known. In order to prove the effectiveness and the reliability of our system, we also provide the details of the underlying encryption scheme, plus a suitable GUI that allows a user to interact with a server

2 *eSkyline*: System Overview

In this Section, we discuss the main building blocks of our system. We start out by presenting skyline computation techniques, which we adopt from previous research for our purposes. Then we outline the novel encryption scheme we employ. Last, we present the architecture of the prototype system we have implemented for use in the assessment of the effectiveness and reliability of our system. We emphasize that an analysis of the security features of our encryption scheme with regards to the computational power of an adversary falls outside the scope of this paper and is relegated to a more extensive research effort.

Symbol	Description
m	Dimensionality
$\mathcal{DB}$	Dataset
t, s	Tuples of $\mathcal{DB}$
$\mathcal{S}_{sky}$	Skyline tuples

Table 1. Notation overview.

We are given a data set $\mathcal{DB}$ on a data space defined by a set of m attributes (dimensions) $\{d_1, ..., d_m\}$. A tuple $t \in \mathcal{DB}$ is represented as $t = \{t_1, ..., t_m\}$ where t_i is the value on dimension d_i. Without loss of generality, we assume that $\forall d_i : t_i \geq 0$, and that larger values of each attribute are preferable to smaller ones. Table 1 provides an overview of the notation we employ.

DEFINITION 1 **Skyline Query** *We say that a tuple $t \in \mathcal{DB}$* dominates *another tuple $s \in \mathcal{DB}$, as relationship denoted as $t \prec s$, if (1) on every dimension d_i, $t_i \geq s_i$; and (2) on at least one dimension d_j, $t_j > s_j$. The* skyline *is the set of points $\mathcal{S}_{sky}$ that are not dominated by any other point in $\mathcal{DB}$.*

Regardless whether the data set $\mathcal{DB}$ is encrypted or not, the computation of a skyline requires a capacity to determine one fundamental relationship among any pair of tuples $\{s, t\}$: to ascertain whether one dominates the other. In addition, it is useful to possess the values of any function $f(t)$ that is *monotonic* on each attribute t_i of t, i.e., non-decreasing as the value of t_i changes in the direction of higher preferability. Under the assumption that larger values are preferable to smaller ones, we can simply use the *aggregate* function over all attribute values as our $f(t)$. We can then efficiently compute the skyline set using the Sort-Filter-Skyline (SFS) algorithm of previous research [5], shown in Algorithm 1.

3 The Encryption Mechanism

To our knowledge, the only extant solution for secure skyline querying over some form of encrypted data is provided in [19]. This solution uses OPES, the Order-Preserving Encryption scheme proposed in [3]. Unfortunately, OPES, built on an encoding that preserves the order of the numerical data in each column, is not sufficiently secure; an adversary who observes the encrypted data effectively learns the order of tuples on each attribute, which is a significant amount of information by itself.

Nevertheless, as we show, order preservation per se is not a necessary condition to enable the processing of skyline queries over encrypted data. After all, the fundamental operation we have to perform in order to answer a skyline query is the operation that decides whether a tuple t dominates or is dominated by another tuple s. In other words, given a pair of tuples in $\mathcal{DB}$, (t, s), we need to

Algorithm 1 Sort-Filter-Skyline

```
1: Input: data set DB sorted by f(t)
2: Output: skyline set of DB
3: S_sky ← ∅
4: for (each tuple t in DB) do
5:     dominant = TRUE;
6:     s = first point in S_sky;
7:     while ((dominant) ∧ (s ≠ NULL)) do
8:         if s dominates t then
9:             dominant = FALSE;
10:        end if
11:        s = next point in S_sky;
12:    end while
13:    if dominant then
14:        S_sky = S_sky ∪ {t};
15:    end if
16: end for
17: return S_sky
```

decide whether there is a *domination relationship* among them, as in Line 8 of Algorithm 1. Furthermore, the problem of determining domination, as a decision problem, does not need to specify whether it is t that dominates s or s that dominates t; it suffices to ascertain whether a domination exists among them. The specification of the dominant and dominated tuples can be easily performed as an auxiliary operation, provided that the values of monotonic function f for both tuples are available; the tuple of higher f values is the dominant one. Thus, without loss of generality, for each tuple t we can always compute such a function as the *sum* of all attribute values, and treat it as attribute t_0.

Then, assuming each tuple has m (original) attributes, and using "$\cdot$" to denote the scalar product of vectors, the existence of a domination relationship between s and t can be expressed as follows:

$$(t_i - s_i) \cdot (t_{i+1} - s_{i+1}) > 0, \quad 0 \leq i \leq m-1 \tag{1}$$

For the sake of conciseness, we use $>$ in our inequalities, without prejudice to the fact that the strict domination definition requires a $>$ inequality along at least one dimension, while it suffices to have a $\geq$ inequality along other dimensions. In our implementation, we take care of the strict definition of domination. For each tuple vector $t =< t_0, t_2, \ldots, t_m >$, we construct a set of sub-vectors:

$$t^j =< t_0, t_2, \ldots, t_j >, \quad {}^j t =< t_1, ..., t_{j+1} >, \quad 0 \leq j \leq m{-}1$$

Then the set of Inequalities (1) can be also expressed as:

$$\begin{aligned} &(t^0 - s^0) \cdot ({}^0 t - {}^0 s) > 0 \\ &(t^j - s^j) \cdot ({}^j t - {}^j s) - (t^{j-1} - s^{j-1}) \cdot ({}^{j-1} t - {}^{j-1} s) > 0 \end{aligned} \tag{2}$$

For $1 \leq j \leq m-1$. Following the exact definition of domination, we can express the condition as follows: The series of terms

$$(t^j - s^j) \cdot ({}^j t - {}^j s), \quad 0 \leq j \leq m-1 \tag{3}$$

should be an *non-descending series* of non-negative terms, with at least one pair of consecutive terms being strictly *ascending*.

In effect, the problem of determining domination between two tuples is mapped to a problem of computing scalar products among the sub-vectors of tuples, as well as comparing their f values, in case domination exists. We can then deal directly with the differences among these sub-vectors and the scalar products of those. Let $p = t - s$. Then it suffices to compute terms of the form:

$$p^j \cdot {}^j p \tag{4}$$

We should then have a method for computing scalar products of this form, where p may have been computed from any two tuples in $\mathcal{DB}$. Such scalar products can in turn be expressed as:

$$\left((p^j)^T \times M_j\right) \times (M_j^{-1} \times {}^j p) \tag{5}$$

Where p^j and ${}^j p$ are represented as column vectors, M_j is any invertible $(j+1) \times (j+1)$ matrix, "$\times$" denotes matrix multiplication, and a^T denotes the transpose of a. Based on the above analysis, if we have a set of $m-1$ invertible matrices $M_1, M_2, ..., M_{m-1}$, we can encrypt all the sub-vectors we need as follows:

$$E(t^j) = M_j^T \times t^j, \quad E({}^j t) = M_j^{-1} \times {}^j t \tag{6}$$

where $E()$ is our encryption function. Then, for any t, s, with p calculated as $p = t - s$, and for any $j \in [0, m-1]$, it holds that $E(p^j) \cdot E({}^j p) = (M_j^T \times p^j)^T \times M_j^{-1} \times {}^j p = (p^j)^T \times {}^j p = p^j \cdot {}^j p$. Thus, all scalar product calculations we need can be effectively performed by working solely over encrypted sub-vectors and their differences. At same time, given the encrypted sub-vectors of a tuple t, $E(t^j)$ and $E({}^j t)$, it is not possible for an adversary to determine the value of t_j or any other metric of t without knowing M_j. In other words, the set of invertible matrices is the key of our encryption scheme.

We emphasize that the attribute t_0 of any tuple t undergoes a relatively trivial encryption, as matrix M_0 is only a scalar value. However, this feature does *not* constitute a weakness of our scheme. On the contrary, we intentionally design our scheme this way so that values of attribute t_0, namely the monotonic function $f(t)$, allow their *order* relationships to be recovered after being encrypted. That is, as long as M_0 is positive, their order remains unchanged. On the other hand, it takes significantly more effort to recover the order, or, for that matter, the values of other attributes, apart from the extent to which those can be inferred from domination relationships.[5]

Using the encryption scheme, we can safely compute whether there is a tuple s dominates another tuples t. In more detail, given a data set $\mathcal{DB}$ of m-dimensional tuples and a set of m invertible matrices $M_0, M_2, ..., M_{m-1}$, as described above, and a monotonic function $f(t)$, the *encrypted* from of $\mathcal{DB}$, $\mathcal{DB}'$, is created by mapping each tuple $t \in \mathcal{DB}$ to a $m^2 + m$-dimensional tuple t' formed by concatenating the contents of t^j and ${}^j t$ for $0 \leq j \leq m-1$. In our framework, this task is implemented by algorithm `Skyline-DB-Encryption` (see Algorithm 2).

Thereafter, a service provider holding the encrypted data applies the SFS algorithm directly on encrypted tuples in order to answer skyline queries. The only modification required is that now domination is ascertained by computing a sequence of scalar products. For each domination check, this sequence of scalar products is aborted as soon as a product gives negative result, which indicates that domination does not hold. In our framework, this is the main task, which is implemented by algorithm `AOPF-SFS` (see Algorithm 3).

[5] An adversary could launch a known plaintext attack in order to determine that contents of matrices M_j; still, a complete security analysis of our scheme is outside the scope of this paper.

Algorithm 2 `Skyline-DB-Encryption`

blue

Input: database $\mathcal{DB}$ sorted by $f(t)$; m invertible matrices $M_0, M_1, ..., M_{m-1}$
Output: encrypted database $\mathcal{DB}'$, $\mathcal{S}_{sky}$
$\mathcal{DB}' \leftarrow \emptyset$;
for (each tuple t in $\mathcal{DB}$) **do**
  $f(t) = \sum_{i=0}^{m-1} t_i$;
  for (each j in $\{0, \ldots, m-1\}$) **do**
    $t^j = < t_0, t_2, \ldots, t_j >$;
    ${}^j t = < t_1, ..., t_{j+1} >$;
    $E(t^j) = M_j^T \times t^j$;
    $E({}^j t) = M_j^{-1} \times {}^j t$;
    $t' = E(t^j) \cdot E({}^j t)$;
    $\mathcal{DB}' \leftarrow \langle t', f(t) \rangle$;
  end for
end for
return $\mathcal{DB}'$

After all calculations, the server returns the encrypted form of tuples to the client. An encrypted sub-vector $E({}^{m-1}t)$ of t suffices to decrypt all of t's attributes' values at the client side by the matrix-vector multiplication $t = M_j \times^{m-1} t$. In our framework, this task is implemented by algorithm `Skyline-Q-Decryption` (see Algorithm 4).

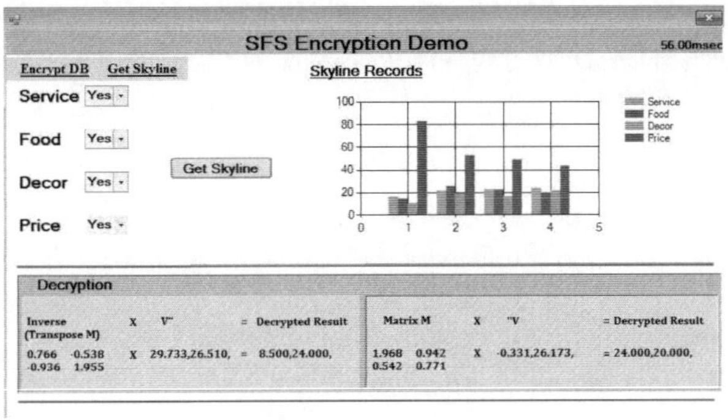

Fig. 2. eSkyline interface.

4 *eSkyline*: System Architecture

We have implemented a prototype system that performs the tasks of both server and client. A database $\mathcal{DB}$ is encrypted using a series of randomly generated matrices M_j and uploaded to the server module, while observing user preferences during encryption. Thereafter, the server processes user-issued skyline queries over the encrypted data and return the results. These results are decrypted at the client side and the final result presented to the user. Figure 2 presents a screenshot of the user interface during the final result decryption, along with a visualization of the final skyline tuples via a colored bar-gram, with one bar per attribute per tuple.

Algorithm 3 `Attribute-Order-Preserving-Free-SFS`

blue

Input: encrypted database $\mathcal{DB}'$
Output: skyline set of $\mathcal{DB}'$
$\mathcal{S}_{sky} \leftarrow \emptyset$;
for (each tuple t' in $\mathcal{DB}'$) **do**
  $dominant = \text{TRUE}$;
  $s =$ first point in $\mathcal{S}_{sky}$;
  while $((dominant) \wedge (s \neq \text{NULL}))$ **do**
    $p = t' - s$;
    for ((each j in $\{0, \ldots, m-1\}$) $\wedge$ $(dominant == \text{TRUE})$) **do**
      if $(p^j \cdot^j p < 0)$ **then**
        $dominant = \text{FALSE}$;
      end if
    end for
    $s =$ next point in $\mathcal{S}_{sky}$;
  end while
  if $dominant$ **then**
    $\mathcal{S}_{sky} = \mathcal{S}_{sky} \cup \{t'\}$;
  end if
end for
return $\mathcal{S}_{sky}$

Algorithm 4 `Skyline-Q-Decryption`

blue

Input: skyline $\mathcal{S}'_{sky}$ computed over encrypted data; m invertible matrices $M_0, M_1, \ldots, M_{m-1}$
Output: decrypted skyline $\mathcal{S}_{sky}$
$\mathcal{S}_{sky} \leftarrow \emptyset$;
for (each tuple t' in $\mathcal{S}'_{sky}$) **do**
  for (each j in $\{0, \ldots, m-1\}$) **do**
    $t = M_j \times^{m-1} t'$;
    $\mathcal{S}_{sky} \leftarrow t$;
  end for
end for
return $\mathcal{S}_{sky}$

5 Conclusions and Future Work

This paper presented *eSkyline*, a novel system architecture for processing skyline queries over encrypted data. Our system allows for a service provider to answer queries posed by clients without having the actual data values disclosed. This functionality is enabled by a novel encryption scheme we proposed, with allows for the domination among two tuples to be efficiently determined, yet does *not* use any form of order-preserving encryption. In the future, we plan the following extensions: (*i*) validating our results with very large data sets following diverse value distributions; (*ii*) expanding our solution to the case where the data distributed among several servers; (*iii*) making our solution capable of dealing with *OLAP queries* (e.g., [7, 8]), which are extremely useful within database analytics engines.

References

1. Divyakant Agrawal, Sudipto Das, and Amr El Abbadi. Big data and cloud computing: current state and future opportunities. In *EDBT 2011, 14th International Conference on Extending Database Technology, Uppsala, Sweden, March 21-24, 2011, Proceedings*, pages 530–533, 2011.
2. Divyakant Agrawal, Amr El Abbadi, and Shiyuan Wang. Secure and privacy-preserving database services in the cloud. In *29th IEEE International Conference on Data Engineering, ICDE 2013, Brisbane, Australia, April 8-12, 2013*, pages 1268–1271, 2013.
3. Rakesh Agrawal, Jerry Kiernan, Ramakrishnan Srikant, and Yirong Xu. Order-preserving encryption for numeric data. In *SIGMOD*, pages 563–574, 2004.
4. Arvind Arasu, Ken Eguro, Raghav Kaushik, and Ravishankar Ramamurthy. Querying encrypted data. In *International Conference on Management of Data, SIGMOD 2014, Snowbird, UT, USA, June 22-27, 2014*, pages 1259–1261, 2014.
5. Jan Chomicki, Parke Godfrey, Jarek Gryz, and Dongming Liang. Skyline with presorting. In *ICDE*, pages 717–719, 2003.
6. Alfredo Cuzzocrea. Analytics over big data: Exploring the convergence of datawarehousing, OLAP and data-intensive cloud infrastructures. In *37th Annual IEEE Computer Software and Applications Conference, COMPSAC 2013, Kyoto, Japan, July 22-26, 2013*, pages 481–483, 2013.
7. Alfredo Cuzzocrea, Vincenzo Russo, and Domenico Saccà. A robust sampling-based framework for privacy preserving OLAP. In *Data Warehousing and Knowledge Discovery, 10th International Conference, DaWaK 2008, Turin, Italy, September 2-5, 2008, Proceedings*, pages 97–114, 2008.
8. Alfredo Cuzzocrea and Domenico Saccà. Balancing accuracy and privacy of OLAP aggregations on data cubes. In *DOLAP 2010, ACM 13th International Workshop on Data Warehousing and OLAP, Toronto, Ontario, Canada, October 30, 2010, Proceedings*, pages 93–98, 2010.
9. Alfredo Cuzzocrea, Il-Yeol Song, and Karen C. Davis. Analytics over large-scale multidimensional data: the big data revolution! In *DOLAP 2011, ACM 14th International Workshop on Data Warehousing and OLAP, Glasgow, United Kingdom, October 28, 2011, Proceedings*, pages 101–104, 2011.
10. Jeffrey Dean and Sanjay Ghemawat. Mapreduce: simplified data processing on large clusters. *Commun. ACM*, 51(1):107–113, 2008.
11. Mark Giereth. On partial encryption of rdf-graphs. In *The Semantic Web - ISWC 2005, 4th International Semantic Web Conference, ISWC 2005, Galway, Ireland, November 6-10, 2005, Proceedings*, pages 308–322, 2005.
12. Oded Goldreich, editor. *The Foundations of Cryptography - Volume 2*. Cambridge University Press, 2004.
13. Hakan Hacigümüs, Balakrishna R. Iyer, and Sharad Mehrotra. Efficient execution of aggregation queries over encrypted relational databases. In *Database Systems for Advances Applications, 9th International Conference, DASFAA 2004, Jeju Island, Korea, March 17-19, 2004, Proceedings*, pages 125–136, 2004.
14. Hakan Hacigümüs, Sharad Mehrotra, and Balakrishna R. Iyer. Providing database as a service. In *Proceedings of the 18th International Conference on Data Engineering, San Jose, CA, USA, February 26 - March 1, 2002*, pages 29–38, 2002.
15. Meiko Jensen. Challenges of privacy protection in big data analytics. In *IEEE International Congress on Big Data, BigData Congress 2013, June 27 2013-July 2, 2013*, pages 235–238, 2013.
16. Ruixuan Li, Zhiyong Xu, Wanshang Kang, Kinchoong Yow, and Cheng-Zhong Xu. Efficient multi-keyword ranked query over encrypted data in cloud computing. *Future Generation Comp. Syst.*, 30:179–190, 2014.
17. Claudivan Cruz Lopes, Valéria Cesário Times, Stan Matwin, Ricardo Rodrigues Ciferri, and Cristina Dutra de Aguiar Ciferri. Processing OLAP queries over an encrypted data warehouse stored in the cloud. In *Data Warehousing and Knowledge Discovery - 16th International Conference, DaWaK 2014, Munich, Germany, September 2-4, 2014. Proceedings*, pages 195–207, 2014.
18. Yingjie Shi, Xiaofeng Meng, Fusheng Wang, and Yantao Gan. HEDC: a histogram estimator for data in the cloud. In *Proceedings of the Fourth International Workshop on Cloud Data Management, CloudDB 2012, Maui, HI, USA, October 29, 2012*, pages 51–58, 2012.
19. Tansel Zenginler. Secure skyline querying. Master's thesis, Boğaziçi University, 2007.

Adaptive Intrusion Detection in Distributed Environments: An Ensemble-Based Approach

Alfredo Cuzzocrea[1], Gianluigi Folino[2], and Pietro Sabatino[2]

[1] University of Trieste and ICAR-CNR, Italy
alfredo.cuzzocrea@dia.units.it
[2] ICAR-CNR, Italy
folino@icar.cnr.it, pietro.sabatino@icar.cnr.it

Abstract. This paper describes *a distributed framework for supporting adaptive ensemble-based intrusion detection*. Open issues and limitations of actual state-of-the-art proposals, are analyzed and the main functionalities of a suitable architecture that, based on actual, emerging research trends, finally defines *an innovative ensemble-based network intrusion detection system*.

1 Introduction

Intrusion Detection Systems (IDS) (e.g., [32]) are devoted to the issue of detecting *unauthorized accesses* to computer systems and computer networks. An *intrusion* can be defined as an attempt by an outsider to gain access to the target system (local or network system). *Network Intrusion Detection Systems* (NIDS) (e.g., [5]) are IDS that preeminently operate in network environments, the most probing environment for security aspects, and are specifically classified in three main classes: (*i*) *anomaly-based* (e.g., [3]), (*ii*) *signature-based* (e.g., [26]), and (*iii*) *hybrid* intrusion detection systems (e.g., [27]).

A specific category of NIDS and, more specifically, their underlying *intrusion detection techniques*, is represented by approaches that make use of *Data Mining methods and algorithms* to support the detection phase. From this research trend, a plethora of proposals appeared in recent years. Despite this, classical *sequential algorithms* are not suitable to capture in real time new trends and changes in *streaming data*, which may denote a network intrusion, as they assume that data are static and not changing due to external modifications. In this specific application scenario, *ensemble-based algorithms* (e.g., [28]) expose some specific characteristics of great interest in the context of intrusion detection, and, as a consequence, several *ensemble-based intrusion detection techniques* have been proposed recently (e.g., [20,23,25]). Among well-recognized characteristics of such class of Data Mining algorithms, some that make them particularly suitable to support intrusion detection are the following ones: (*i*) they can be easily implemented in *parallel/distributed architectures*; (*ii*) they can improve the accuracy of a *weak learner*; (*iii*) they can be specialized for the detection of *a particular class*; (*iv*) they are particularly suitable to the special case of *unbalanced datasets*.

In this area, *Collaborative Intrusion Detection Systems* (e.g., [37]) are also particularly interesting due to the fact that, by correlating information coming from different nodes, they permit the discovery of more complex attacks and generally present a lower number of false positive alarms. In fact, they share information with the other nodes in a sub-network, either in the form of correlated alarms or in the form of models for detecting the attacks and therefore they minimize the rate of false positive alarms and are able to detect complex attacks that spread across entire sub-networks.

Following these main considerations, in this paper we provide the anatomy of a general architecture for supporting ensemble-based NIDS that combines the highlighted requirements, namely: *distribution*, *cooperativeness*, *scalability*, *multi-scale network traffic analysis*, *feature selection and extraction*.

2 Anatomy of the Proposed Architecture

The upper level of the proposed architecture is made up (see Figure 1) of a set of nodes interconnected by using a P2P network. In order to guarantee maximum scalability, nodes can be of two types; Local Node (LN) strictly integrated in the architecture and a number of heterogeneous systems that can include commercial IDSs as well as open source solutions such as Snort and BroIDS. The totality of the nodes interact by sharing alerts through the P2P network. Indeed, on each node is present a module, called *Alert Generation/Alert Correlation* module, (AG/AC) for short, that collects alerts generated locally; then the shared alerts are subject to an analysis in order to correlate them.

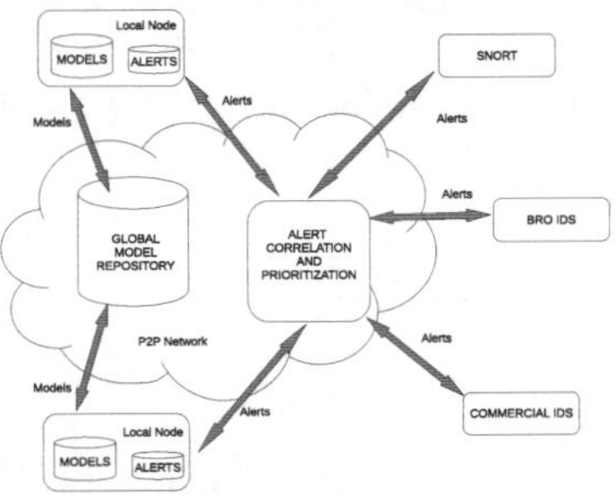

Fig. 1. Ensemble-Based NIDS General Architecture

Output format for the alerts generated by IDSs does not follow in general a standard, as a consequence AG/AC has the capacity to process alerts and encode them following a common protocol, for instance that proposed in the (RFC) of the Internet Engineering Task Force (IETF), [17], the so called Intrusion Detection Message Exchange Format (IDMEF). For the sake of scalability, alert correlation is not implemented in a centralized way but by a distributed mechanism that involves each single node as active part. The nodes integrated in the architecture (LNs), interacts with the rest of the nodes by using the AG/AC unit as outlined above. Moreover, LNs share through the P2P network interesting information, i.e. data stream models, network traffic models and in particular, vulnerabilities. In the rest of this paragraph, we go more in detail on the way in which the single LN works, see Figure 2.

The data stream in input come from different sources: network traffic coming from a particular interface or coming from a router, system logs, application logs concerning the software installed on the system, etc. After the preprocessing phase, the features are extracted and the data stream is ready for further analysis. The next stage of the elaboration is performed by the module called *Change Detector*. The function of the Change Detector is to perform a large scale analysis of the data stream in search of qualitative deviations from the normal behavior. Indeed, as it must perform a real time analysis, it subdivides the data stream in time windows of prefixed duration and then suitable functions are computed on the values of aggregated features coming from the window considered. The set of the values of these functions, that we call "concept" are chosen in such a way to capture qualitative characteristics of the data stream; if an anomaly is detected in these sequences, or in the initial training phase of the system, the module *Model Generator* is activated in order to generate new models for the fine grained analysis of the data stream, performed by the *Distributed Ensemble* module. These module employs different techniques to perform the analysis, i.e., classification, clustering and statistical analysis. Moreover, the meta data in form of concepts, as described above, are stored in the new models, and then this information is employed by the Update Ensemble module in order to activate them.

Then, the models are temporarily stored in a local database, *Model Repository*, see Figure 2 and shared trough the P2P network. They are then stored in the various local Model Repositories, and they are available to the module *Update Ensemble*. The module *Distributed Ensemble* is meant as the principal mechanism for the analysis of incoming data stream and the identification of suspicious activities. Models inside the ensemble are constantly updated by the *Update Ensemble* by analysing information coming from various sources, among which the principal one is provided by the Change Detector, for instance concepts stored in the models as meta-information are compared with that coming from the current data stream in order to activate/deactivate models in the ensemble. Finally, the result of the analysis performed by the Distributed Ensemble made up the basis for the generation of raw alerts subsequently elaborated by the *Alert Generation/Correlation* unit in order to correlate them globally and generate more sophisticated alerts.

In the following, we provide detailed description on structure and functionalities of the internal components of the proposed architecture.

3 Local Node Structure and Functionalities

3.1 Raw Data and Preprocessing

At the level *Raw Data*, the data stream is captured from different sources: network interfaces, routers, system logs and application logs. In the case of network traffic, it can be acquired with the aid of software based on `libpcap`, such as `tcpdumpb` or more apt to an high performance environment such as `Gulp`. Naturally, system logs and application logs are acquired following the specification of the various systems and applications involved and subsequently converted in a common format.

Then, data streams acquired in the previous phase are preprocessed in order to extract features needed in the subsequent analysis. Network traffic can be modeled at the level of flows, in which suitable features are extracted and aggregated in the so called IP-flows. Moreover, data streams coming from network traffic can be analyzed by *deep packet inspection* (DPI) or in other words by an analysis that focuses on the packet payload. For instance, payload of HTTP packets is made up of textual content and then it can be analyzed by using the technique of *n*-grams. Analogously, also system logs and application logs acquired in a textual format can be modeled by using the same technique. It is worth to notice that the choice of techniques used to analyze the data streams depends clearly on the type of analysis performed in the subsequent stages.

3.2 Change Detector

More in general, the works present in the literature can be subdivided into two types. The first type considers the systems that inspect the traffic at the level of the packets payload. They usually concentrate on textual-based protocols, i.e. whose content is represented in plain text, such as for instance HTTP. In these cases the analysis of the payload is based on the technique of *n*-grams. The second type made up of systems that model the traffic at the level of network flow. The two types of approach have their weaknesses and strengths. First of all, the most computational intensive is generally the one that inspects package payload. It turns out that solutions based on the network flow are more adequate to modern environments involving high speed traffic and a consequent higher volume of data [35]. On the other hand, packet inspection-based methods are particularly efficient in the detection of attacks that present anomalous requests, i.e., cross-site scripting. Network flow analysis is particularly useful when applied to complex attacks as the case of DDos. For the reasons explained above, it should be interesting to try and implement a hybrid solution taking the best

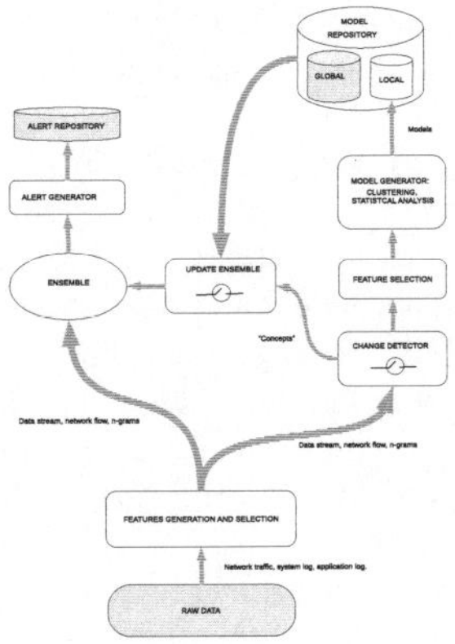

Fig. 2. Local Node (LN) Architecture

of the two approaches. It is worth noticing that in any case both the approaches require a high computational load, especially if the analysis stage is based on the anomaly detection paradigm.

In view of the above considerations, it is desirable to set up an anomaly detection mechanism based on aggregate features and, in the proposed architecture, this task is accomplished by the module called *Change Detector* (or CD for short). Indeed, only the time windows, in which the change detector individuates an anomaly should be analyzed at a deeper level. As this mechanism should act in real time, a tradeoff between accuracy and speed should be reached. In particular, for each time window of a prefixed length, the CD computes the values of a number of suitable functions dependent from aggregated features extracted from the data flow, the set of these values form what we call, in analogy with [1], a *concept*. For instances aggregated features that could be considered are the number of bytes, the number of packets and the number of flows in a time window. For the above-described functions, we have again a number of choices such as fractal dimensions, Liapunov exponent, see for instance [34], [22], [**?**]. Moreover another possible approach is the use of techniques inspired by statistical mechanic and thermodynamics to detect anomalies in the distribution of the packets due to malicious activities, see [24, 31]. Independently from the aggregated features and the functions employed, the concepts have to provide a large-scale, qualitative characterization of the data flow captured in a determinate time window, and their computation have to involve computational complexity so that real time analysis is possible. for instance, in order to detect windows presenting anomalies, time series can be computed on the values that made up the concepts, then suitable algorithms apt to detect anomalies in time series can be employed to analyze these time series and consequently the windows can be flagged as anomalous. Compare for instance the approach used in [6, 33].

3.3 Model Generator

Data stream, after preprocessing, and in the initial operative phase of a node, is forwarded to the module called *Model Generator* (MG). This module, as the name suggests, is responsible for the analysis of the data stream by classification and clustering and the generation of models employed by the module Distributed Ensemble to classify instances in data stream. Moreover, the MG is activated by the change detector in case it detects qualitative change in a particular time window.

The first stage of the analysis performed by the MG consists in feature selection and extraction. It is well known that preprocessing steps and feature selection and extraction are key points in designing an efficient NIDS and the other part of the algorithm could benefit from an opportune design of these phases, see [16]. For instance, employing the technique of *n*-grams has the drawback of an exponential grow of the dimension of the feature space, feature selection seems then mandatory in order to avoid the problem known as "curse of dimensionality". For the problem of feature selections various options are available such as solutions based on statistical, data-mining and information theoretic techniques. Moreover, we identified current trends in the literature that employ sophisticated techniques such as manifold learning, and in particular diffusion maps ([7–9]), laplacian eigenmap([4]), isomaps ([36]) and Hessian eigenmaps [19]. Particularly apt to operate in the environment is the technique known as Power Iteration Clustering [30].

After the feature selection stage, data stream are analyzed by various techniques such as statistical based ones, for instance Hidden Markov Models, and data mining based techniques. In case of analysis based on data mining, an approach of type "clustering ensemble" can be employed, see for instance [6]. First of all, data set in the feature space is projected on a number of low dimensional subspaces, for instance of dimension 2 or 3, each subspace is then analysed by a clustering algorithm that can vary from one subspace to the other. The final result is then obtained by combining the various analysis by a suitable ensemble.

Clustering results can be subject to a stability analysis, see [2]. After stability analysis, result of the clustering are employed in order to identify outliers, following [6, 15], this can be accomplished by considerations taking into account density of the regions of the feature space involved, moreover models are built by decision trees subsequently employed in module Distributed Ensemble.

4 Distributed Ensemble

The increase in the volume of data to be processed makes it really hard for an NIDS to work in real-time using sequential hardware. Finally, a modern NIDS needs to be capable of dealing with new undocumented attacks, for which a signature is not available (0-day attacks).

In view of the above remarks, solutions based on algorithms that can be implemented in parallel/distributed environment should be preferred.

By analyzing the data mining algorithms present in the literature for the intrusion detection task, though generally the authors note that their solutions are suitable to be implemented in parallel environments, there is usually a lack of experiments that test the proposed solutions on real parallel hardware and on real network traffic. Ensemble-based techniques or Multiple Classifier Systems (MCS) permit one to combine multiple (heterogeneous or homogeneous) models in order to classify new unseen instances. In practice, after a number of classifiers are built usually using some parts of the original dataset, the predictions of the different classifiers are combined and a common decision is taken. Different schemas can be considered to generate the classifiers and to combine them in an ensemble, i.e. the same learning algorithm can be trained on different datasets or/and different algorithms can be trained on the same dataset. IDSs benefit from using these kinds of algorithm for a number of reasons. First, MCSs perform well both when data are very scarce and when we have a huge amount of data; furthermore, they can be easily implemented in efficient computing environments such as parallel, multi-core, and GPGPU architectures and also on P2P and Cloud computing environments. In addition, they can easily model different abstractions or parts of a network, i.e., some models can be trained on some parts or on some levels of the network and finally combined together, to assure a better prediction.

The module *Distributed Ensemble* (DE) is responsible for the classification of the incoming stream of data. As was pointed out above, one of the advantages of the ensemble approach is its flexibility, permitting to use heterogeneous classifiers in the ensemble. In particular, in order to boost performance and efficiency, DE will contain a component that analyze the data stream, and in particular that coming from the network traffic, based on the misuse paradigm. Signatures for this component are constantly updated by the Update Ensemble module of each node. In order to accomplish this task the Update Ensemble component keeps track of newly discovered vulnerabilities and relative signature available on online data bases. Finally, this component can be implemented with the aid of either open source solutions such as Snort, BroIDS, or a new module implementing similar characteristics. Other components of the ensemble are based on the models coming from the local Model Repository maintained on each node. This repository stores non only models generated locally after analyzing local data streams, but also models coming from different nodes and shared through the P2P network.

Thanks to the ensemble approach, other components can be easily added, for instance specialized components for particular types of attacks such as port scan, DDos and so on. Each component is made up of an ensemble and the various analysis can be combined together by a meta ensemble approach. The choice of combining functions can be implemented employing techniques coming from genetic programming, see for instance Folino e Pisani [21]. Genetic programming could in principle provide a way to combine and evolve models. For instance, the fitting function can be obtained taking into account feedbacks provided by domain expert inspecting the alerts generated.

4.1 Model Repository

The module called *Model Repository* stores models generated locally by the Model Generator module on the local node and moreover models that come from other nodes shared through the global P2P network. Generation of new models is triggered by the Change Detector upon detection of a qualitative change in the traffic characteristics in a particular time window, characteristics that are encoded in what we call "concepts". Concepts are encoded in the models as meta information that are employed in order to activate them.

Models imported from external nodes keep track of vulnerabilities that are not observed locally yet. Once imported a model is not activated immediately; in practice, it is not inserted in the Distributed Ensemble module and do not take part to the classification of the data stream. For this reason, we distinguish between *active models* and *proactive models*, and the activation of the models is performed by the Update Ensemble module, see the next section for further details.

4.2 Update Ensemble

The Distributed Ensemble module stores two type of models: *active models* and *passive models* or *proactive models*. Active models are imported in the Distributed Ensemble as soon as the Change Detector module activates the Model Generator because it detects a change in the traffic characteristics. Passive models or proactive models, are the result of importing models coming from the external nodes that made up the system.

In a similar way as in [1] proactive models are activated by a mechanism based on the notion of *"concept"*, see Section relative to Change Detector. Namely, in the generation stage of the model, information coming from the Change Detector are encoded in it in the form of concept. These information are compared by the UE module to those provided by the Change Detector and, on the basis of this comparison the model could become active. In any case, proactive models are employed for the analysis of the current data stream, but this analysis is not integrated in the final output. A measure of the efficiency of the model, i.e., a feedback provided by domain experts, can be encoded in a weight associated to the model. Based on these weight, it can be implemented another mechanism to activate proactive models, see [18]. Clearly, is not feasible to import models in the system indefinitely and the above described mechanism provide a way to deactivate an active model and moreover to eventually remove it from the local model repository.

5 Conclusions and Future Work

The architecture and the main functionalities of a distributed ensemble-based network intrusion detection system have been defined starting from a detailed analysis of the open issues and limitations of the actual state-of-the-art proposals. In addition, benefits and limitations of our architecture have been remarked.

Future work is mainly oriented to make our proposed framework capable of dealing with innovative requirements posed by *big data processing* (e.g., [14]), which heavily impact on privacy and security issues (e.g., [10, 11, 13]). Among these, coping with *efficiency* (e.g., [12]) and *uncertainty* (e.g., [29]) seem promising directions.

References

1. C. Alippi, G. Boracchi, and M. Roveri. Just-in-time classifiers for recurrent concepts. *Neural Networks and Learning Systems, IEEE Transactions on*, 24(4):620–634, April 2013.
2. Monowar H. Bhuyan, D. K. Bhattacharyya, and J. K. Kalita. An effective unsupervised network anomaly detection method. In *Proceedings of the International Conference on Advances in Computing, Communications and Informatics*, ICACCI '12, pages 533–539, New York, NY, USA, 2012. ACM.
3. Monowar H. Bhuyan, D. K. Bhattacharyya, and Jugal K. Kalita. Network anomaly detection: Methods, systems and tools. *IEEE Communications Surveys and Tutorials*, 16(1):303–336, 2014.
4. Christopher JC Burges. Geometric methods for feature extraction and dimensional reduction-a guided tour. In *Data mining and knowledge discovery handbook*, pages 53–82. Springer, 2010.
5. Ismail Butun, Salvatore D. Morgera, and Ravi Sankar. A survey of intrusion detection systems in wireless sensor networks. *IEEE Communications Surveys and Tutorials*, 16(1):266–282, 2014.
6. Pedro Casas, Johan Mazel, and Philippe Owezarski. Unsupervised network intrusion detection systems: Detecting the unknown without knowledge. *Computer Communications*, 35(7):772 – 783, 2012.
7. R. R. Coifman, S. Lafon, A. B. Lee, M. Maggioni, B. Nadler, F. Warner, and S. W. Zucker. Geometric diffusions as a tool for harmonic analysis and structure definition of data: Diffusion maps. *Proceedings of the National Academy of Sciences of the United States of America*, 102(21):7426–7431, 2005.
8. R. R. Coifman, S. Lafon, A. B. Lee, M. Maggioni, B. Nadler, F. Warner, and S. W. Zucker. Geometric diffusions as a tool for harmonic analysis and structure definition of data: Multiscale methods. *Proceedings of the National Academy of Sciences of the United States of America*, 102(21):7432–7437, 2005.
9. Ronald R. Coifman and Stéphane Lafon. Diffusion maps. *Applied and Computational Harmonic Analysis*, 21(1):5 – 30, 2006. Special Issue: Diffusion Maps and Wavelets.
10. Alfredo Cuzzocrea and Elisa Bertino. A secure multiparty computation privacy preserving OLAP framework over distributed XML data. In *Proceedings of the 2010 ACM Symposium on Applied Computing (SAC), Sierre, Switzerland, March 22-26, 2010*, pages 1666–1673, 2010.
11. Alfredo Cuzzocrea and Elisa Bertino. Privacy preserving OLAP over distributed XML data: A theoretically-sound secure-multiparty-computation approach. *J. Comput. Syst. Sci.*, 77(6):965–987, 2011.
12. Alfredo Cuzzocrea, Jérôme Darmont, and Hadj Mahboubi. Fragmenting very large XML data warehouses via k-means clustering algorithm. *IJBIDM*, 4(3/4):301–328, 2009.
13. Alfredo Cuzzocrea and Vincenzo Russo. Privacy preserving OLAP and OLAP security. In *Encyclopedia of Data Warehousing and Mining, Second Edition (4 Volumes)*, pages 1575–1581. 2009.
14. Alfredo Cuzzocrea, Domenico Saccà, and Jeffrey D. Ullman. Big data: a research agenda. In *17th International Database Engineering & Applications Symposium, IDEAS '13, Barcelona, Spain - October 09 - 11, 2013*, pages 198–203, 2013.
15. G. David. *Anomaly Detection and Classification Via Diffusion Processes in Hyper-networks.* Tel Aviv University, 2009.
16. Jonathan J. Davis and Andrew J. Clark. Data preprocessing for anomaly based network intrusion detection: A review. *Computers & Security*, 30(6-7):353 – 375, 2011.
17. H. Debar, D. Curry, and Feinstein B. The intrusion detection message exchange format (idmef). `https://www.ietf.org/rfc/rfc4765.txt`. RFC 4765 (Proposed Standard), Accessed: 2015-06-04.

18. Gregory Ditzler and Robi Polikar. Incremental learning of concept drift from streaming imbalanced data. *Knowledge and Data Engineering, IEEE Transactions on*, 25(10):2283–2301, Oct 2013.
19. David L. Donoho and Carrie Grimes. Hessian eigenmaps: Locally linear embedding techniques for high-dimensional data. *Proceedings of the National Academy of Sciences*, 100(10):5591–5596, 2003.
20. G. Folino and P. Sabatino. Ensemble based collaborative and distributed intrusion detection systems: A survey. *Journal of Network and Computer Applications*, 2016. to appear.
21. Gianluigi Folino and Francesco Sergio Pisani. Combining ensemble of classifiers by using genetic programming for cyber security applications. In Antonio M. Mora and Giovanni Squillero, editors, *Applications of Evolutionary Computation*, volume 9028 of *Lecture Notes in Computer Science*, pages 54–66. Springer International Publishing, 2015.
22. Gianluigi Folino, Clara Pizzuti, and Giandomenico Spezzano. Mining distributed evolving data streams using fractal gp ensembles. In Marc Ebner, Michael ONeill, Anik Ekrt, Leonardo Vanneschi, and AnnaIsabel Esparcia-Alczar, editors, *Genetic Programming*, volume 4445 of *Lecture Notes in Computer Science*, pages 160–169. Springer Berlin Heidelberg, 2007.
23. Gianluigi Folino, Clara Pizzuti, and Giandomenico Spezzano. An ensemble-based evolutionary framework for coping with distributed intrusion detection. *Genetic Programming and Evolvable Machines*, 11(2):131–146, 2010.
24. David Ford. Application of thermodynamics to the reduction of data generated by a non-standard system. *arXiv preprint cond-mat/0402325*, 2004.
25. Giorgio Giacinto, Roberto Perdisci, Mauro Del Rio, and Fabio Roli. Intrusion detection in computer networks by a modular ensemble of one-class classifiers. *Information Fusion*, 9(1):69–82, 2008.
26. Neminath Hubballi and Vinoth Suryanarayanan. False alarm minimization techniques in signature-based intrusion detection systems: A survey. *Computer Communications*, 49:1–17, 2014.
27. P. Arun Raj Kumar and S. Selvakumar. Detection of distributed denial of service attacks using an ensemble of adaptive and hybrid neuro-fuzzy systems. *Computer Communications*, 36(3):303–319, 2013.
28. Ludmila Kuncheva. Combining pattern classifiers: methods and algorithms, 2004.
29. Carson Kai-Sang Leung, Alfredo Cuzzocrea, and Fan Jiang. Discovering frequent patterns from uncertain data streams with time-fading and landmark models. *T. Large-Scale Data- and Knowledge-Centered Systems*, 8:174–196, 2013.
30. Frank Lin and William W Cohen. Power iteration clustering. In *Proceedings of the 27th International Conference on Machine Learning (ICML-10), June 21-24, 2010, Haifa, Israel*, pages 655–662, 2010.
31. John C. McEachen and Cheng Wai Kah. An analysis of distributed sensor data aggregation for network intrusion detection. *Microprocessors and Microsystems*, 31(4):263 – 272, 2007. Special Issue with selected papers from the 11th IEEE Symposium on Computers and Communications (ISCC06).
32. Rob Mitchell and Ing-Ray Chen. A survey of intrusion detection techniques for cyber-physical systems. *ACM Comput. Surv.*, 46(4):55:1–55:29, 2013.
33. J.O. Nehinbe. Time series analyses for forecasting network intrusions. In *Cybernetic Intelligent Systems (CIS), 2011 IEEE 10th International Conference on*, pages 111–116, Sept 2011.
34. Xun-Yi Ren, Hai-Shan Wan, Yu Yang, and Xin Xie. Fractal lyapunov exponent based anomaly detection of network traffic. *International Journal of Advancements in Computing Technology(IJACT)*, 4(11):275 – 282, 2011.
35. A. Sperotto, G. Schaffrath, R. Sadre, C. Morariu, A. Pras, and B. Stiller. An overview of ip flow-based intrusion detection. *Communications Surveys Tutorials, IEEE*, 12(3):343–356, Third 2010.
36. Joshua B. Tenenbaum, Vin de Silva, and John C. Langford. A global geometric framework for nonlinear dimensionality reduction. *Science*, 290(5500):2319–2323, 2000.
37. Emmanouil Vasilomanolakis, Shankar Karuppayah, Max Mühlhäuser, and Mathias Fischer. Taxonomy and survey of collaborative intrusion detection. *ACM Comput. Surv.*, 47(4):55, 2015.

Querying NoSQL-based Crowdsourcing Systems Efficiently

Alfredo Cuzzocrea[1], Marcello Di Stefano[2], Paolo Fosci[3], and Giuseppe Psaila[3]

[1] University of Trieste and ICAR-CNR, Italy
alfredo.cuzzocrea@dia.units.it
[2] University of Palermo, Italy
marcello.distefano@unipa.it
[3] University of Bergamo, Italy
paolo.fosci@unibg.it, psaila@unibg.it

Abstract. In this paper, we provide *a novel approach for effectively and efficiently support query processing tasks in novel NoSQL crowdsourcing systems*. The idea of our method is to exploit the *social knowledge* available from reviews about products of any kind, freely provided by customers through specialized web sites. We thus define a *NoSQL* database system for large collections of product reviews, where queries can be expressed in terms of natural language sentences whose answers are modeled as lists of products ranked based on the relevance of reviews w.r.t. the natural language sentences. The best ranked products in the result list can be seen as the best *hints* for the user based on crowd opinions (the reviews). By exploiting the well-known IMDb dataset, which comprises more than 2 million reviews for more than 100,000 movies, we experimentally shows that our prototype obtains good performance in terms of execution time, demonstrating that our approach is feasible.

1 Introduction

Novel *NoSQL database systems* are playing a leading role in latest research, due to their well-understood characteristics that well-marry with actual trends laying under the terms *Cloud Computing* and *Big Data*. On the other hand, *Crowdsourcing* is becoming a very attractive research area (e.g. [7]), particularly in the context of Web search scenarios. In this paper, we try to cross-layering these two leading contexts, by providing *a novel approach for effectively and efficiently support query processing tasks in novel NoSQL crowdsourcing systems*. The idea of our method is to exploit the *social knowledge* available from reviews about products of any kind, freely provided by customers through specialized web sites. We thus define a *NoSQL* database system for large collections of product reviews, where queries can be expressed in terms of natural language sentences whose answers are modeled as lists of products ranked based on the relevance of reviews w.r.t. the natural language sentences. The best ranked products in the result list can be seen as the best *hints* for the user based on crowd opinions (the reviews).

Reviews about products that customers can freely write on specialized web sites constitute an incredible source of information, by means of which users would like to get useful *hints*. But how could a user obtain them? Typically, the user has some wishes and would like to find products that match those wishes, based on opinions of other users. But to do that, a specialized system is necessary.

Looking at the problem from a database technology point of view, product reviews constitute a text database that has a given structure; user's wishes can be seen as natural language queries over the set of reviews and the user wants to obtain the products whose set of reviews matches the query at the highest degree; the ideal solution, is to get a ranked list, where the best ranked products can be seen as the best hints for the user based on crowd opinions (the reviews). We focus only on reviews, since every single review is a mine of unstructured information that are hard to be queried by classical techniques. In other words, such a system is a *NoSQL* database system, where queries are natural language sentences.

Thus, our prototype is a *NoSQL* database system for large collections of product reviews; the database is queried by expressing a natural language sentence; the result is a list of products ranked based on the relevance of reviews w.r.t. the natural language sentence. Semantic tagging and term expansion (by means of WordNet) are performed, both indexing reviews and querying them. Figure 1 shows system architecture and, in more detail, data structures underlying the *Query Engine*. The proposed system is composed by several components, each one devoted to perform a specific task.

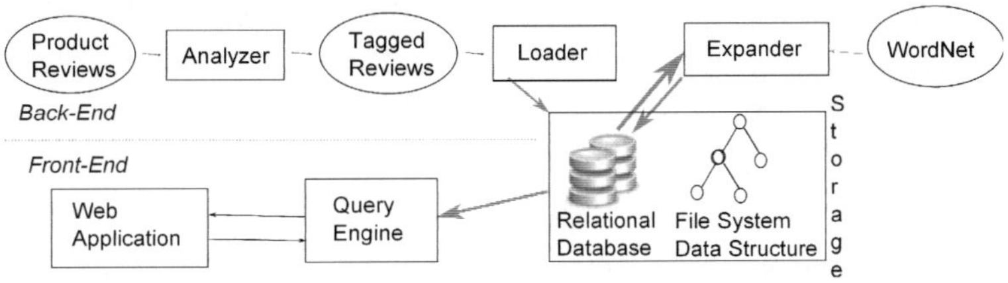

Fig. 1. Architecture of the Proposed System.

In particular, we distinguish between the *back-end* and the *front-end*: the former is responsible for collecting, analyzing and indexing data from product reviews; the latter is the actual user interface accessed by users, that is built on top of the *Query Engine*. In the back-end of the system, we find the components (rectangles) that prepares the data structure on which queries are executed. These components operate on source data and intermediate results (ovals) and upload data structures in the *Storage* box. In particular, the *Analyzer* is responsible for analyzing product reviews, identifying words and their grammar category (noun, verb, adjective or adverb). This *pos-tagging* operation is performed by the *Stanford Parser*[4]. As a result, reviews are transformed into tagged sentences, composed of *tagged terms*, i.e., a term associated to a tag that denotes the grammar category. The *Loader* loads *Tagged Reviews* into the data structures on which queries are performed. The *Expander*, After the loading phase has ended, expands tagged terms are on the basis of an ontology (in our case, *WordNet*), so that the *Query Engine* can exploit semantic relationships in order to capture a wider set of results related with the query. As regards the front-end of the system, from the architectural point of view, the key component of the front-end is the *Query Engine*: it exploits the preliminary work performed by back-end components, and works on data structures describing occurrences of terms in product reviews. The *Web Application* component has been developed to give end users the capability to exploit the system.

In our experimental analysis provided in Section 4, we aim at demonstrating that it is possible to obtain an answer to a query in acceptable time on a large set of reviews. Therefore, we tested the prototype on reviews about movies downloaded from the IMDb.com web site, that includes more than 2 million reviews for more than 100,000 movies. The study about execution times at query time is presented.

[4] from the *Stanford NLP Group*: http://nlp.stanford.edu/index.shtml

2 Related Work

Research in the database area is more and more addressing the concept of NoSQL database. Several attempts to define the concept can be found. Referring to [10], three categories of data stores are considered: *Key-Value stores*, *Document stores* and *Column Family stores*. The first category deals with datasets similar to maps or dictionaries where data are addressed by a unique key. The second category deals with sets of text documents, and our work falls into this category. The third category encompasses column oriented stores, extensible record stores and wide columnar stores. *Graph databases* can be considered as well belonging to the world of NoSQL databases [9].

One important aspect of NoSQL data stores is performance. Often, NoSQL databases are necessary due to the implicit limitation of relational databases in given application contexts, where the relational structure of data is an obstacle to obtain fast execution times. The work in [1] tries to address this perspective and presents six features of NoSQL data stores. The are: (1) the ability to horizontally scale simple operation throughput over many servers; (2) the ability to replicate and to distribute (partition) data over many servers; (3) a simple call level interface or protocol (in contrast to a SQL binding); (4) a weaker concurrency model than the ACID transactions of most relational (SQL) database systems; (5) efficient use of distributed indexes and RAM for data storage; (6) the ability to dynamically add new attributes to data records.

The ranking metrics we defined as the basis of the proposed system is inspired to the concept of itemset, developed in the area of data mining for mining frequent itemsets and association rules. Several works [6, 8] adopt association rule mining for analyzing customer reviews and extract opinions from them. In [6], association rule mining is used to extract, from within customer reviews, relevant features the characterize opinions of users about products. In [8], a system to compare opinions about products is presented, where product reviews reports PROs and CONs; in particular, association rule mining is exploited to assign a positive or negative polarity to words (namely, adjectives) in product reviews, and use this polarity to rank the opinion about products. The work in [5] extracts, by means of an association rule mining technique, relevant features that summarize product reviews.

3 Query Processing Support

We now describe the key component, i.e., the query engine. Based on a natural language sentence (the query) it extracts those products whose reviews are mostly relevant for the query. Relevance is evaluated by means of a *ranking metric*; retrieved products are returned as a list sorted in reverse order of relevance. Hereafter, we describe how the ranking metric is defined.

3.1 Termsets

In this paper we consider a query q as a *set of terms* (or briefly, a *termset*). Thus, we describe a query containing a number n of terms as $q = \{t_1, \ldots, t_n\}$[5], and we investigate only those queries where $n > 1$ or, in other words, $|q| > 1$. With I, we denote a generic termset that is a subset of q for which applies $|I| > 1$. With D_q, we denote the set of termsets I derived from q. Notice that the cardinality of D_q is $|D_q| = 2^n - (n+1)$, i.e. D_q is the power set of q without the empty set and the n single terms that compose q. With I_l we denote an l-termset of q, that is a termset composed by l terms, i.e. $|I_l| = l$. With $D_{q,l}$ we denote the set of l-termsets I_l. Notice that the cardinality of $D_{g,l}$ is $|D_{q,l}| = \binom{n}{l}$.

[5] At moment, in this stage of the project we do not consider word order or repetitions

3.2 Termset Weight

We now define the concept of *weight* for a termset.
Definition 1: The weight of a $l-$termset is a function of its length and the length of the query q ($|q| = n$) and it is denoted as $w_q(l)$.
For $n = 2$ there is only one 2-termset and its weight is $w_q(2) = 1$ by definition.
For $n > 2$ the weight of the single $n-$termset q is, by definition, $w_q(n) = 0.5$, while for $2 < l < n$ it is $w_q(l) = w_q(l+1)/(\binom{n}{l}+1)$ and for $l = 2$ it is $w_q(2) = w_q(3)/\binom{n}{2}$. □

The rationale behind Definition 1 is the following. The topmost termset, corresponding to the whole query, is the most important one, and its weight is equal to the overall weight of all the shorter termsets. The same principle is valid for any generic termset I_l (with $2 < l < n$), whose weight is equal to the overall weight of all lower levels termsets (even those that are not subset of I_l). In this way, reducing the size of termsets, the contribution of each level quickly decreases. Notice, that the overall weight of all termsets is exactly 1 ($\sum_{I \in D_q} w_q(|I|) = 1$). Figure 2 shows the termsets levels with an example query.

l	$\#I_l$	*weight*	*termsets (I)*
4	1	0.5000	{funny, great, hilarious, jokes}
3	4	0.1000	{funny, great, hilarious}
			{funny, great, jokes}
			{funny, hilarious, jokes}
			{great, hilarious, jokes}
2	6	0.0167	{funny, great} {funny, hilarious}
			{great, hilarious} {great, jokes}
			{funny, jokes} {hilarious, jokes}

Fig. 2. Termsets levels for query *great funny hilarious jokes* and corresponding weights.

3.3 Query Expansion and Semantic Coefficient

As stated above, reviews are processed performing several operations. Similar operations are performed on a user query in natural language as well.
Pos-Tagging. By means of *Stanford Parser*, each word of a user query is tagged with an attribute that denotes its grammar role (*verb*, *noun*, *adjective* to name a few) in the query.
Stopwords Filtering. Stopwords are those words that are too common in reviews (such as *articles*, *conjunctions*); furthermore, common verbal forms like *is* or *have* (just to name a few) are treated as stopwords. Stopwords include also some very context-dependent words such as the word *actor* in a movie context. These words hold a small semantic meaning, so after pos-tagging operation *stopwords* are discarded from the query. Thus, denoting with SW the set of possible stopwords, in the rest of the paper the notation:

$$q = \{t_1, \ldots, t_n\}$$

includes only those terms $t_i \notin SW$, and, as stated in Section 3.1, we consider only those queries q such that $|q| > 1$ (actual length without stopwords).
Term Expansion. By means of *WordNet* ontology, each tagged term $t_i \in q$ is expanded with all those terms directly associated to t_i depending by its grammar tag. Thus, for example a *noun* is expanded with all its *synonyms*, *hypernyms* or *hyponyms* and so on, while a *verb* is expanded with all its *synonyms* or *meronyms*, to name a few. There are actually a total of 15 possible different relations between a tagged term and its expanded words. We denote with t_i^* the generic expanded term of t_i, and with $ET(t_i)$ the set of all expanded terms of t_i.

By definition, $t_i \in ET(t_i)$ with an *identity* relation, thus, $|ET(t_i)| \geq 1$. Notice that, given a generic expanded term t^*, it can happen that $t^* \in ET(t_i)$ and $t^* \in ET(t_j)$ with $i \neq j$. In other words, we cannot state a-priori that $ET(t_i) \cap ET(t_j) = \oslash$ with $i \neq j$. As an example, the term *colour* can be an *hypernym* expansion for both terms *red* and *black*.

Query Expansion. An *expanded query* q^* is each combination of $\{t_1^*, \ldots, t_n^*\}$. We consider *valid* a combination $q^* = \{t_1^*, \ldots, t_n^*\}$ only if $t_i^* \neq t_j^*$ $\forall i \neq j$ Notice that the original query q is a particular q^* itself, and it is *valid* by definition.

Expanded Termsets. Previous considerations about query q and its expansions, are applicable to each termset I_l. With I_l^* we denote an *expanded termset* $I_l^* = \{t_1^*, \ldots, t_l^*\}$, and similarly I_l^* is *valid* only if $t_i^* \neq t_j^*$ $\forall i \neq j$. With $EI(I)$ we denote the set of all possible expanded termset I^* that can be derived from I. The cardinality of $EI(I) = \prod_{t \in I} |ET(t)|$, that is the number of all possible combinations of the expanded terms of those terms that compose I. Finally, with D_q^*, we denote the set of all valid expanded termsets that are included in q and all its valid expansions q^*.

Semantic Coefficient. Each $t^* \in ET(t)$ has a *semantic coefficient* $sc_t(t^*)$, with $0 < sc_t(t^*) \leq 1$, that depends on the cardinality of $ET(t_i)$.

Definition 2: For each $t^* \in ET(t)$ except t, $sc_t(t^*) = 0.5/|ET(t)|$, and $sc_t(t) = 0.5 + 0.5/|ET(t)|$. □

The rationale of semantic coefficient, is the following. A term describes a semantic concept that is mostly expressed by the term itself, but receives a small contribution from expanded terms: the greater the number of expansion, the smaller the semantic contribution of a single expanded term. Notice that $\sum_{t^* \in ET(t)} sc_t(t^*) = 1$. Table 1.a shows how sc_t varies with $ET(t)$ cardinality.

$\|ET(t)\|$	$sc_t(t)$ (not expanded)	$sc_t(t^*)$ ($t^* \neq t$)
1	1.0000	—
2	0.7500	0.2500
3	0.6667	0.1667
5	0.6000	0.1000
10	0.5500	0.0500

a)

I^* (structure)	#	$sc_t(I^*)$
$\{t_1, t_2\}$	1	0.4444
$\{t_1^*, t_2\} or \{t_1, t_2^*\}$	4	0.1111
$\{t_1^*, t_2^*\}$	4	0.0278

b)

Table 1. a) Trend of Semantic coefficient w.r.t. the cardinality of $ET(t)$. b) Semantic coefficient for a generic 2-termset where each term has two expansions.

With $sc_I(I^*)$ we denote the semantic coefficient for an expanded termset I^* derived from I.

Definition 3: Given an expanded termset $I^* = \{t_1^* \ldots t_l^*\}$ derived for a termset $I = \{t_1 \ldots t_l\}$, it is $sc_I(I^*) = \prod_{t_i^* \in I_l^*} sc_{t_i}(t_i^*)$. □

This way, a termset that contains only original terms gives the highest semantic contribution, while augmenting the number of expanded terms in the termset, the semantic contribution decreases. Table 1.b shows the trend of the semantic coefficient for a 2-termset where each original term has two expansions. Notice that, according to the above definition, $\sum_{I^* \in EI(I)} sc_I(I^*) = 1$.

3.4 Product Reviews and Termsets

Consider a product p (a movie, a camera, etc.), its set of reviews is denoted by $R(p) = \{r_1, \ldots, r_k\}$. Each review is a text, i.e., a sequence of term occurrences $r_i =<$

$t_1, \ldots, t_s >$. With $T(R(p))$ we denote the set of terms appearing in reviews for product p, and with $T(r_i)$ the set of terms appearing in review $r_i \in R(p)$.

Definition 4: A termset I is said *relevant* for product p if $\exists r_i | I \subseteq T(r_i)$. □

The set of relevant termsets for product p is denoted as $RD_{p,q}$. In an analogous way, $RD^*_{p,q}$ is the set of all relevant expanded termsets for product p. Notice that $RD_{p,q} \subseteq D_q$, and also $RD^*_{p,q} \subseteq D^*_q$.

3.5 Termset Average Density

In a preliminary work [4], we assumed that every termset occurrence in product reviews contribute to the *support* of the termset with the same weight, i.e. 1, since the support, by definition, is the number of reviews containing the termset on the total amount of reviews. Given a termset I, in a single review, terms in I can be very dense or, on the opposite case, very sparse. We consider a review in which the occurrences of terms in I are dense being more relevant for the query than a review where occurrences are sparse. Thus, we introduce the concept of *Termset Density* of an termset I for a single review.

Definition 5: Consider a product p, a review $r \in R(p)$, and a termset I_l. The *Termset Review Density* $d_r(I_l)$ is defined as

$$d_r(I_l) = l/minWin_r(I_l)$$

where $minWin_r(I_l)$ is the size of the minimal window in review r that includes all the terms of termset I_l. □

Notice that for *Termset Review Density*, it holds that $0 < d(I_l, r) \leq 1$. The next step is to define a *Termset Average Density* for a generic termset I (we omit the subscript l not to burden notation) w.r.t. a product p.

Definition 6: Consider a product p and its set of reviews $R(p)$. With $R_I(p)$ we call the subset of $R(p)$ of those reviews containing termset I. The *Termset Average Density* for product p, denoted as $ad_p(I)$, is defined as:

$$ad_p(I) = (\textstyle\sum_{r \in R_I(p)} d_r(I))/|R(p)|$$

□

The Termset Average Density is analogous to termset support, with the difference that the contribution of the occurrence of a termset I in a review r is not 1 but its density $d_r(I)$. Notice, thus, that $ad_p(I) \leq s_p(I) \leq 1$, where with $s_p(I)$ we denote the support of a termset I for a product p.

3.6 Product Ranking Metric

Finally, we can now define the *Product Ranking Metric PRM.*

Definition 7: Consider a query q, the set of termsets D^*_q derived from q, the system of the weights $w_q(|I^*|)$ and semantic coefficients $sc_q(I^*)$ for each expanded termset $I^* \in D^*_q$. Consider a product p, the set of reviews $R(p)$ and the set of relevant expanded termsets $RD^*_{p,q}$ that can be actually extracted from $R(p)$. Given for each $I^* \in RD^*_{p,q}$ the average termset density $ad_p(I^*)$, the *Product Relevance Value* for product p is defined as

$$PRM_q(p) = \textstyle\sum_{I^* \in RD^*_{p,q}} (w_q(|I^*|) \times ad_p(I^*) \times sc_q(I^*))$$

□

The rationale of the above definition is the following. For each termset I^* included in the query q and actually relevant in the reviews, its contribution to the overall relevance value is given by its weight $w_q(|I^*|)$ (that depends on its size) multiplied by its *average density* $ad_{p,q}(I^*)$ and its semantic coefficient $sc_q(I^*)$. The system of weights and semantic coefficients has been designed to obtain a $PRM_q(p) = 1$ for an *ideal* set of reviews for product p, where each review contains every expanded termset I^* that can be derived from q with a density $d_r(I^*) = 1$, and every expanded termset I^* is *valid*.

4 Experimental Assessment and Analysis

Our dataset is composed by a total of *2,207,678* user reviews for *109,221* movies downloaded from the IMDb.com web site[6]. The size of the text we downloaded is approximatively *3,091Mb*. Each movie has a number of reviews included between *1* and *4,876*, and the average number of reviews per movie is *20*. Experiments has been run on a PC with two Intel Xeon Quad-core 2.0GHz/L3-4MB processors, 12GB RAM, four 1-Tbyte disks and Linux operating system.

Schema	A	B	Diff %
Pos-Tagger	active	inactive	
Distinct tagged terms	1,151,827	776,852	-32.55%
Occurrences	216,345,522	216,345,522	0.00%
Analysis Time (A = Ps+Pt)	2226.80h	3.82h	-99.83%
Parsing Time (Ps)	2.11h	2.42h	+14.74%
Pos-tagging Time (Pt)	2224.69h	1.40h	-99.94%
Db Loading Time (D)	56.05h	49.76h	-11.23%
Term Expansion Time (E)	3.73h	2.67h	-28.49%
Total Time (T = A+D+E)	2286.58h	56.25h	-97.54%

Table 2. Indexed schemes

While indexing our data set, as described in the *back-end* side of proposed architecture in Section 1, we figured out how *pos-tagging* affects the proposed system. Disabling pos-tagging means tagging each term with a unique trivial tag, and considering for each term every possible expansion regardless of its role inside the query; in other words, disabling pos-tagging means a significant reduction of the number of managed terms because words are distinguished on the basis of their grammar category (for instance word *colour* could be both a noun and a verb); however, the counter effect is that the possible number of expansions for a termset combinatorially increases.

Table 2 reports data collected during dataset indexing. Column *A* shows data regarding indexing with pos-tagging activated (*Schema A*), while Column *B* shows data regarding indexing with pos-tagging deactivated (*Schema B*). Column *Diff %* shows the percentage variation from data of Schema A to data of Schema B (where applicable).

For our query performance tests we prepared a set of 25 standard user queries like *I want to know more about the history of Greece and the Persian wars*, or *All those moments will be lost in time, like tears in rain*[7]. Our test compares the variation of performance of the query engine working on *Schema A* (ad described in Section 4) in a *single-searching-thread* version versus a *5-searching-threads* version. Table 3 shows the average results of the test performed on the set of 25 standard queries mentioned before. Column *Single-thread* shows performance of the single-thread search engine, while Column *5-threads* shows performance of the 5-threads search engine, and column *Diff %* shows the percentage variation from

[6] we focus on *movies* as Imdb data-set as been the first freely accesible big-data set we've found. Anyway the same approach is suitable for any set of product reviews.

[7] from *Blade Runner* movie

	Single-thread	5-threads	Diff %
Average Time (T=QE+TG+TE+TM+S)	2,501.12 ms	1,994.66 ms	-20.25%
Query Expansion (QE	286.44 ms	286.40 ms	-0.01%
Thread generation (TG)	0.40 ms	1.88 ms	370.00%
Thread execution (TE $\leq$ O+R)	2,199.64 ms	1,691.60 ms	-23.10%
Occurrences Loading (O)	1,962.52 ms	1,639.84 ms	-16.44%
Ranking (R)	237.12 ms	75.12 ms	-68.32%
Thread merging (TM)	1.64 ms	1.80 ms	9.76%
Sorting (S)	13.00 ms	12.98 ms	-0.17%

Table 3. Single-thread search engine Vs 5-threads search engine

single-thread w.r.t. 5-threads search engine. For each search engine version, the average execution time per query is provided in row *Average Time*.

5 Conclusions and Future Work

The scope of this paper was to present the architecture and the query engine of a *NoSQL* database system. In future work, we intend to integrate term expansion with *linked-data* as a source for semantic ontology about terms, and also considering *word order* and *word repetition* of queries in our ranking model, as well as advanced semantic issues such as *negative sentences*. On another side, we aim at integrating in our architecture innovative paradigms such as *distributed big data compression* (e.g., [3]) and *big data analytics* (e.g., [2]).

References

1. R. Cattell. Scalable sql and nosql data stores. *SIGMOD Record*, 39 (4):12–27, 2011.
2. Alfredo Cuzzocrea, Ladjel Bellatreche, and Il-Yeol Song. Data warehousing and OLAP over big data: current challenges and future research directions. In *Proceedings of the sixteenth international workshop on Data warehousing and OLAP, DOLAP 2013, San Francisco, CA, USA, October 28, 2013*, pages 67–70, 2013.
3. Alfredo Cuzzocrea, Filippo Furfaro, and Domenico Saccà. Hand-olap: A system for delivering OLAP services on handheld devices. In *6th International Symposium on Autonomous Decentralized Systems (ISADS 2003), 9-11 April 2003, Pisa, Italy*, pages 80–87, 2003.
4. Paolo Fosci and Giuseppe Psaila. Toward a product search engine based on user reviews. In *DATA-2012 Int. Conf. on Data Technologies and Applications, Rome (Italy)*, July 2012.
5. Minqing Hu and Bing Liu. Mining and summarizing customer reviews. In Won Kim, Ron Kohavi, Johannes Gehrke, and William DuMouchel, editors, *KDD*, pages 168–177. ACM, 2004.
6. Minqing Hu and Bing Liu. Mining opinion features in customer reviews. In Deborah L. McGuinness and George Ferguson, editors, *AAAI*, pages 755–760. AAAI Press / The MIT Press, 2004.
7. Joongheon Kim and Wonjun Lee. Stochastic decision making for adaptive crowdsourcing in medical big-data platforms. *IEEE Trans. Systems, Man, and Cybernetics: Systems*, 45(11):1471–1476, 2015.
8. Bing Liu, Minqing Hu, and Junsheng Cheng. Opinion observer: analyzing and comparing opinions on the web. In Allan Ellis and Tatsuya Hagino, editors, *WWW*, pages 342–351. ACM, 2005.
9. Hecht Robin and Stefan Jablonski. Nosql evaluation: A use case oriented survey. In *CSC-2011 International Conference on Cloud and Service Computing, Hong Kong, China*, pages 336–341, December 2011.
10. C. Strauch. Nosql databases. *http://www.christof-strauch.de/nosqldbs.pdf*, 2011.

Collaborative Building of a Shared Library of Performance Indicators

[DISCUSSION PAPER]

Claudia Diamantini, Domenico Potena, and Emanuele Storti

Dipartimento di Ingegneria dell'Informazione
Università Politecnica delle Marche
via Brecce Bianche, 60131 Ancona, Italy
{c.diamantini,d.potena,e.storti}@univpm.it

Abstract. In this paper, which is an extended abstract of [1], we introduce a semantic framework for representing Performance Indicators, that supports the construction and maintenance of a minimal and consistent dictionary. We discuss how the logical representation of the formulas used for the calculation of PIs enables automatic reasoning capable to check equivalence of PIs and consistency of the dictionary. Upon these services, a web application has been implemented for collaborative construction and maintenance of the dictionary.

1 Introduction

Modern networked business paradigms require models offering a common ground for interoperability and collaboration. Reference models have been established for supply chains and other networked organizations, that include the description of business processes structure and performances as described in a library of Performance Indicators (PIs), like the Supply Chain Operations Reference model (SCOR)[1] or the Value Reference Model (VRM)[2]. These models are typically built as a "consensus view" over the partners' own views, which is reached mostly by human interaction.

In the present paper, that is an extended abstract of [1], we propose a logic model for the representation of PIs that supports the construction of a valid reference model (or PI ontology) by enabling the integration of definitions proposed by different engineers in a minimal and consistent system. The approach is characterised by the representation of what we call the *compositional* semantics of PIs, i.e. the meaning of PIs is composed from the meaning of their subparts. As a matter of fact, PIs are measures generated by means of operations like aggregation and algebraic composition. The aggregative structure of PIs is captured by the multidimensional model, whose formalization is well studied in the Literature. The composite structure of PIs refers to the *calculation formula* by which an indicator is calculated as a function of other indicators, for instance

[1] http://www.apics.org/sites/apics-supply-chain-council/frameworks/scor
[2] http://www.value-chain.org/en/cms/1960

in the form of a ratio (e.g. the ratio between income and investments, known as Return On Investment). Moreover, it is at least as fundamental as aggregation to capture PI semantics, especially when a shared dictionary of indicators is collaboratively managed, e.g. in networked organizations collecting PI definitions for reference use or for interoperability purposes. Here, each autonomous entity proposes PI terms, definitions and properties, and a consensus is needed in order to decide the dictionary entries. Some typical use cases can be recognised in this process: check of identity for a PI to establish if it already exists in the dictionary, considering the semantics of the indicator as given by its calculation formula; introduction of a new PI for the incremental building of the dictionary; update and deletion of existing PIs including proper mechanisms for consistency management; browsing and searching; consensus management and versioning. Unfortunately, traditional libraries include neither a formal representation of indicators nor consistency management mechanisms.

Composite indicators are anyway represented in some work (e.g., [2]), and their calculation with full or partial specification of the formula linking the indicator to its components is also discussed. In such work formula representation does not however rely on logic-based languages, and no inference mechanism and formula manipulation is enabled. In the data warehouse field, while the ontological representation of the aggregation structure of PIs is largely studied, the compound nature and consequent dependency among indicators is much less explored [3,4]. Despite the increasing interest in collaboration and networking there is still a lack of work in addressing data cubes in distributed and collaborative contexts. A proposal in this respect is [5], where interoperability of heterogeneous and autonomous data warehouses is taken into account. Again, although a preliminary attempt to include formulas in the framework, the compositional semantics of PIs is missed.

In a distributed networking scenario, the proposal of the present paper is to provide advanced support for the above mentioned use cases by leveraging on the representation and manipulation of the formula defining a PI. In particular, (i) we define KPIOnto, an ontology introducing a logical representation of PIs and their formulas, allowing to make the algebraic relationships among indicators explicit; (ii) we discuss a framework for reasoning over formulas, for PI identity, equivalence and consistency checking, formula and dependencies inference; (iii) we show through a web application how semantic reasoning supports the flexible management of a shared ontology of PI definitions. The rest of the paper is organised as follows: Sections 2 and 3 introduce the model and related reasoning services respectively. Section 4 is devoted to briefly show a web application implementing the framework. Section 5 provides some concluding remarks and discusses future work.

2 KPIOnto: an Ontology of Key Performance Indicators

From the analysis of PI dictionaries and the multidimensional model, we derived the main properties for the development of KPIOnto, an ontology devoted to formally describe indicators. The core of the ontology is composed by a set of disjoint classes, that are detailed in the following: `Indicator`, `Dimension` and `Formula`. The full specifications of KPIOnto are available at *http://w3id.org/kpionto.*

Indicator It is the key class of KPIOnto, and its instances (i.e., indicators) describe the metrics enabling performance monitoring. Properties of an indicator include name, identifier, acronym, definition (i.e., a plain text giving a detailed description of its meaning and usage), compatible dimensions (see next paragraph), formula, unit of measurement chosen for the indicator (i.e., both the symbol and the description, given by referring to the Measurement Units Ontology[3]), business object and aggregation function:

$$\begin{aligned} \texttt{Indicator} \equiv\ & \forall\ \texttt{hasDimension.Dimension} \sqcap \\ & \forall\ \texttt{hasFormula.Formula} \sqcap \texttt{(=1 hasFormula)} \sqcap \\ & \forall\ \texttt{hasUnitOfMeasure.UoM} \sqcap \texttt{(=1 hasUnitOfMeasure)} \sqcap \\ & \forall\ \texttt{hasBusObj.BusinessObject} \sqcap \texttt{(=1 hasBusObj)} \sqcap \\ & \forall\ \texttt{hasAggrFunction.AggrFun} \sqcap \texttt{(=1 hasAggrFunction)} \end{aligned}$$

As an example, Figure 1 shows the main properties of a PI *PersonnelTrainingCosts*, calculated as `HourlyCost*PersonnelTrainingTime`.

Dimension A dimension is the coordinate/perspective along which a metric is computed. Following the multidimensional model, a dimension is usually structured into a hierarchy of levels, where each level represents a different way of grouping elements of the same dimension. For instance, Organization can be grouped by virtual enterprise, enterprise, department, business unit, project team and person, while the Time dimension can be arranged in years, semesters, quarters, months and weeks. Each level is instantiated in a set of elements known as members of the level, e.g. the company "ACME" or the month "2013-01". In order to describe dimensions in KPIOnto, our approach is similar to the one proposed in [6]. In particular, the top class is *Dimension*, which is composed of a set of subclasses, one for each specific dimension, like Organization Dimension, Time Dimension, and so forth. Levels are represented as disjoint primitive subclasses of the dimension (or the set of dimensions) they belong to, whereas each member is an instance of these classes, and the dimension's hierarchy is represented by a transitive $\texttt{partOf}^{+}$ relation. An example is shown in the following:

$$\begin{aligned} & \texttt{VE} \sqsubseteq \texttt{OrganizationDimension} \\ & \texttt{Enterprise} \sqsubseteq \texttt{OrganizationDimension} \sqcap \forall \texttt{partOf.VE} \sqcap \texttt{(=1 partOf)} \\ & \texttt{Department} \sqsubseteq \texttt{OrganizationDimension} \sqcap \forall \texttt{partOf.Enterprise} \sqcap \texttt{(=1 partOf)} \\ & \texttt{VirEnt1:VE},\ \texttt{ACME:Enterprise},\ \texttt{R\&D:Department} \\ & \texttt{partOf(R\&D,ACME)},\ \texttt{partOf(ACME,VirtEnt1)} \end{aligned}$$

from which the reasoner can infer `partOf(R&D,VirEnt1)`. See also Figure 1,

[3] Measurement Units Ontology: http://idi.fundacionctic.org/muo/muo-vocab.

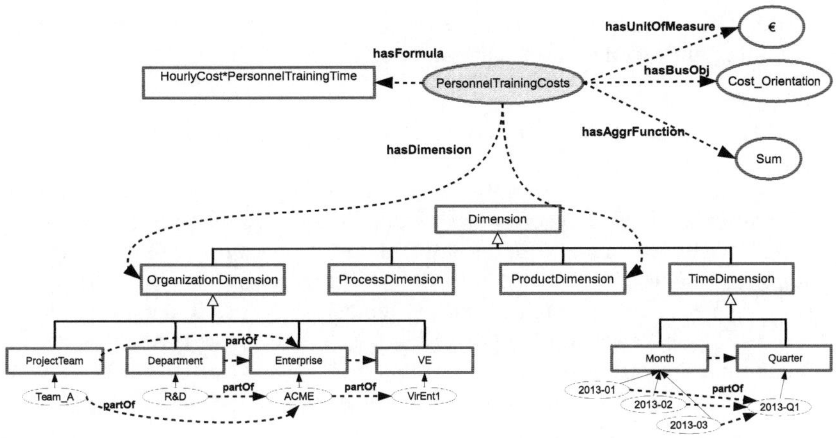

Fig. 1. KPIOnto: properties of indicator PersonnelTrainingCosts.

where an excerpt of the hierarchies for Organization and Time dimensions is shown. This ontological description enables usual OLAP operations over PIs, namely roll-up and drill-down. The roll-up has a direct correspondence with the partOf relationship, while the drill-down implies an opposite path. Due to the existence of possible branched dimensions (e.g. `Person→Department→Enterprise` and `Person→BusinessUnit→ Enterprise`), the derivation of this path is not straightforward. In our proposal, the drill-down of a member M at level L_1 is the set of instances of the lower level (L_2), which belongs to the class described by the following expression: ∃ `partof.M` ⊓ `L_2`. Referring to the example, we have that ∃ `partof.{ACME}={R&D,Team_A}`, so ∃ `partof.{ACME}`⊓ `Department ={R&D}` is the drill-down of ACME along the branch `Person→Department→Enterprise`.

Formula A PI can be either an atomic or a compound datum, built by combining several lower-level indicators. Dependencies of compound PIs on its building elements are defined by means of algebraic operations, that is a *Formula* capable to express the semantics of an indicator. A formula describes the way the indicator is computed, and is characterised by the aggregation function, the way the formula is presented, the semantics (i.e., the mathematical meaning) of the formula, and references to its components, which are in turn (formulas of) indicators. If we refer to algebraic operators like $\{+, -, *, /, \hat{}\}$ then well-formed indicators can be represented by mathematical expressions in prefix notation, like $+(-(A, B), *(C, D))$. Formulas can be graphically represented by a forest of disjoint lattices, where each node is a PI and its children are the operands of its formula, while leaves are atomic PIs. The formal representation and manipulation of the structure of a formula is essential in collaborative networked organizations to check inconsistencies among independent indicator definitions, reconcile indicators values coming from different sources, and provide the necessary flexibility to indicators management.

3 Reasoning-based Support Functionalities

Reasoning about PIs is mainly based on the capability to manipulate formulas according to strict mathematical axioms, like commutativity, associativity and distributivity of binary operators, and properties of equality needed to solve equations. Therefore, in order to define PI reasoning functionalities we represent both KPIOnto formulas and mathematical axioms in a common logic-based layer in Logic Programming (LP). While the descriptive properties of indicators and dimension are represented in OWL2-RL (based on a subset of OWL-DL) that can be directly mapped to LP, indicator formulas are represented through a fact `formula(indicator, expression, type)`, where *type* distinguishes between an atomic (leaf_node) and a compound (branch_node) indicator.

The main functionalities for reasoning about PIs include *Formula manipulation* and *Consistency Check*, as explained in the following.

Manipulation of mathematical expressions is performed by specific predicates from PRESS (PRolog Equation Solving System) [7], which is a formalization of algebra in Logic Programming for solving symbolic, transcendental and non-differential equations. Its code can be represented as axioms of a first order mathematical theory and the running of the program can be regarded as inference in such a theory. More in detail, given that predicates and functions in PRESS represent relationships among expressions of algebra, it can be interpreted as a Meta-Theory of algebra. The predicates in which it is organised (more than 900) can manipulate an equation to achieve a specific syntactic effect (e.g. to reduce the occurrences of a given variable in an equation) through a set of rewriting rules. The most interesting are predicates for the `simplification` and for the `resolution` of equations, on which all the other reasoning functionalities are built. The former are used both to compact and to improve the rendering of a formula, while the latter enables the symbolic resolution of equations by applying mathematical properties (e.g., commutativity, factorization), and properties of equality.

As for consistency check, an indicator is consistent with the ontology if three conditions are satisfied: its definition must be unique in the ontology (uniqueness), its formula must not be equivalent to a formula already in KPIOnto (equivalence)[4] and its formula must not contradict any other already defined formulas (coherence). The approach we adopt is such that after every insertion of an indicator, the ontology is guaranteed to be consistent. In this way, enterprises always have available an ontology containing valid and usable information. These characteristic is very important considering the domain of the ontology, as indicators are used to make decisions, often strategic.

[4] In case of equivalence, possible policies include merging the duplicates by leaving only one definition for each PI in the ontology or allowing multiple definitions by introducing a *sameAs* property among them.

4 Web Application

To support end-users in the management of KPIOnto, we developed a web application named *KPIOnto Editor*[5]. The application provides users with a graphical interface devoted to search for indicators, formulas and dimension's members previously stored in KPIOnto as well as to create, modify and delete indicators and members, according to user privileges.

Introduction of a new PI A new PI can be introduced only if it is consistent with the ontology, as explained in the previous Section. To this end, the formula of the new PI is checked by using consistency predicates: `identical`, `equivalence` and `incoherent`. Only if these three are false the new PI can be introduced. To give an example, let us consider an ontology with three formulas about investments for employees:

`PersonnelTrainingCosts=HourlyCost*PersonnelTrainingTime`
`TeachCosts=PersonnelTrainingTime*HourRate`
`InvestmentInEmployees=PersonnelTrainingCosts+TeachCosts`

A user introduces a new indicator, currently not defined, which is aimed to measure the total internal costs invested for training of employees:

`TotCostsEmpTrain=TeachCosts+PersonnelTrainingTime*HourlyCost`.

Since there is no formula for `TotCostsEmpTrain` in the ontology, the `identical` predicate returns false and the first step of consistency check is passed. As concerns `equivalence`, by using the formula about `PersonnelTrainingCosts` and after some formula manipulation, the reasoner discovers that `TotCostsEmpTrain` is structurally equivalent to `InvestmentInEmployees`. Hence, either the user refer to this last one to annotate her data without introducing a new indicator, or a `sameAs` relation linking the two PIs can be defined. Finally, the `incoherence` returns false.

Figure 2 shows the interface used to define a new PI. The form allows to insert both the descriptive and the structural definition of a PI.

Update of an existing PI The formula of the PI to update is temporarily removed from the ontology, then the procedure for introducing a new PI is executed. If the ontology with the updated formula remains consistent then we proceed with the update, otherwise the old formula is restored. For instance, let us consider that an user requires to update `PersonnelTrainingTime`, committing a manifest error when typing the formula (inserting a sum instead of a division): `PersonnelTrainingTime=PersonnelTrainingCosts+HourlyCost`. The new formula directly contradicts the definition of `PersonnelTrainingCost` together with every other higher-level indicators depending on it, i.e. in this case it is incoherent with `InvestmentInEmployees`.

Deletion of a PI A PI can be deleted only if it does not make the ontology inconsistent. Hence, either the PI is a root-node, so it is not part of any other

[5] http://boole.dii.univpm.it/kpieditor

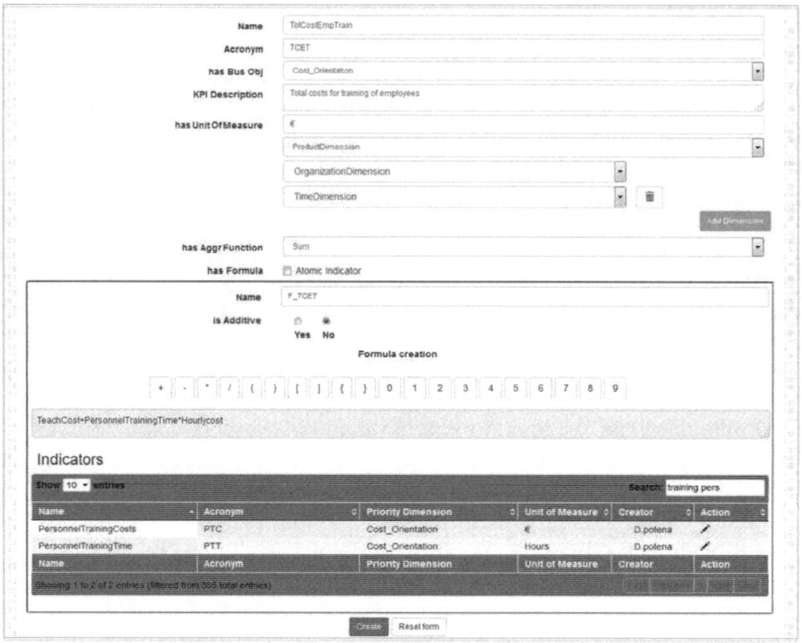

Fig. 2. KPIOnto Editor: form for definition of a new indicator.

formulas, or for each formula in which the PI appears we can infer at least a new formula which does not contain the PI. Since all inferable formulas of an indicator are equivalent, we replace formulas containing the PI to delete with one of the inferred formulas not containing the PI. Then, the indicator is removed from the ontology.

Other functionalities The *search by term* is implemented by querying the descriptive part of the ontology, while the *search by formula* is enabled by unification of the requested pattern with all formulas in the ontology. For instance, searching for the pattern `PersonnelTrainingTime*X`, where `X` is a variable, the system will return the formulas of `PersonnelTrainingCosts` and `TeachCosts`. In order to obtain details of a specific indicator, formula or member, the *KPI-Onto Editor* provides dynamically generated views with information retrieved from the ontology. The formula reported in the indicator panel can be interactively browsed: clicking on a PI, this is replaced with its formula; moving on the name of the PI, a tooltip with its description is also shown. As for members, together with descriptive information, a graphical representation of the inferred `partOf` hierarchy is provided.

5 Conclusions

In this work, we presented a model for the formalization of PI properties, which focuses on the characterisation of formulas and reasoning over them, and supports most of the activities foreseen in a scenario of collaborative creation and management of a PI ontology. At present, a Wiki collaborative model is assumed for consensus management and versioning, which is proven to be a powerful model to leverage collective intelligence and effectively integrate diverse points of view in networked environments. A study of the actual appropriateness of this model in the context of business and performance managers can be in order. Much work can be made to empower and extend the present proposal, e.g. the model can be exploited to support novel types of data exploration (an example can be found in a recent work [8]), or analysis of similarities among formulas in order to explain differences among a set of indicators or define similarities classes.

References

1. Diamantini, C., Potena, D., Storti, E.: SemPI: A semantic framework for the collaborative construction and maintenance of a shared dictionary of performance indicators. Future Generation Computer Systems **54** (2016) 352–365
2. Horkoff, J., Barone, D., Jiang, L., Yu, E., Amyot, D., Borgida, A., Mylopoulos, J.: Strategic business modeling: representation and reasoning. Software & Systems Modeling (2012)
3. Xie, G., Yang, Y., Liu, S., Qiu, Z., Pan, Y., Zhou, X.: EIAW: Towards a Business-Friendly Data Warehouse Using Semantic Web Technologies. In: The Semantic Web. Volume 4825 of Lecture Notes in Computer Science. Springer Berlin Heidelberg (2007) 857–870
4. Kehlenbeck, M., Breitner, M.H.: Ontology-based exchange and immediate application of business calculation definitions for online analytical processing. In: Proc. of the 11th International Conference on Data Warehousing and Knowledge Discovery. DaWaK '09, Berlin, Heidelberg, Springer-Verlag (2009) 298–311
5. Golfarelli, M., Mandreoli, F., Penzo, W., Rizzi, S., Turricchia, E.: OLAP Query Reformulation in Peer-to-peer Data Warehousing. Information Systems **37** (2012) 393–411
6. Neumayr, B., Schrefl, M.: Multi-level conceptual modeling and owl. In: Proceedings of the ER 2009 Workshops on Advances in Conceptual Modeling - Challenging Perspectives, Berlin, Heidelberg, Springer-Verlag (2009) 189–199
7. Sterling, L., Bundy, A., Byrd, L., O'Keefe, R., Silver, B.: Solving symbolic equations with press. J. Symb. Comput. **7** (1989) 71–84
8. Diamantini, C., Potena, D., Storti, E.: Extended drill-down operator: Digging into the structure of performance indicators. Concurrency and Computation: Practice and Experience (2016) cpe.3726.

Towards a Fair VQR with the Aid of Database (and Game) Theory

Gianluigi Greco, Francesco Lupia, and Francesco Scarcello

University of Calabria, 87036, Rende, Italy
ggreco@mat.unical.it, {lupia, scarcello}@dimes.unical.it

Abstract. In a great number of applications, it is necessary to distribute resources or tasks to agents collaborating with each other in a network in order to maximize the overall social welfare. The question in these cases is how to divide in a fair way the outcome that the network eventually earns, say money, to the participating agents. The paper faces this issue by focusing on a real-world application: the distribution of funds to Italian research structures and substructures, after a research assessment program (known as VQR) that is currently evaluating the Italian research production over years 2011–2014. In fact, we report our recent results in [1], for allocation problems that find application to the VQR. In particular, we describe a number of desirable properties for any reasonable fair division rule, we identify a division rule satisfying all such properties, as well as algorithms for its computation. The proposed solution is based on the game-theoretic notion of Shapley value, and the algorithms for its computation exploit recent advances in the problem of counting solutions to conjunctive queries.

1 Introduction

In 2015, the National Agency for the Evaluation of Universities and Research Institutes (ANVUR) promoted the second 'VQR' program to evaluate the quality of the Italian research production in the period 2011-2014. Every research structure R has to select some research products, and submit them to ANVUR. While doing so, the structure R is in competition with all other Italian research structures, as the outcome of the evaluation will be used to proportionally transfer the funds allocated by the Ministry to support research activities in the next years (until the subsequent evaluation process). Every structure R is then interested in selecting and submitting its *best* research products.

The program is articulated in three phases: (1) Authors affiliated to R are asked to self-evaluate their products, according to some evaluation criteria defined by groups of experts chosen by ANVUR. Here, it is assumed that, having such criteria, every author is able to equip each product with a quality score.(2) Based on the self-evaluations being collected, R selects and submits to ANVUR (at most) two products for each one of its authors[1] in such a way that any product is formally associated with one author at most. (3) ANVUR formulates its independent quality judgment about the submitted publications, and the sum of their "true" scores (i.e., those resulting by ANVUR actual evaluation) is then the VQR score of R. Eventually, R will receive funds in the next

[1] The number of publications is not always two, in some specific exceptions. To our ends, this detail is immaterial.

years proportionally to this score. Furthermore, by using such products scores, ANVUR evaluates all substructures, too (e.g., all departments, if R is a University). Finally, the scores are also used for evaluating individual researchers that are recently hired by R (this also greatly influences R's funds in the next years), as well as those researchers that are members of PhD committees.

As far as the latter point is concerned, it is then natural for the structure R to exploit the VQR scores of its substructures to divide funds among them. However, it is not clear how the evaluation of the research products, designed for the evaluation of the whole structure, may be extended for the evaluation of substructures and, possibly, of single researchers. It is easy to see that the rule used by ANVUR is highly unsatisfactory for a number of reasons, so that in [2,4] we model the problem as a coalitional game and define a *fair division rule* based on the game-theoretic notion of Shapley value [11]. The proposed rule enjoys a number of desirable properties, such as the independence of the specific allocation of research products, the independence of the preliminary (optimal) products selection, the guarantee of the actual (marginal) contribution, and so on. In fact, computing the Shapley value of such games is #P-hard-hard in general [1], and there exists an efficient fully polynomial-time randomized approximation scheme [5]. Here, we illustrate a tractability result for the exact (deterministic) computation of this solution concept for those instances whose agents' interaction-graph has bounded treewidth [1]. The result is based on recent advances on counting solutions of conjunctive queries with existential variables [3], and the method exploited for its derivation can be useful in further contexts, such as in social networks analysis.

2 Allocation Games and Division Rules

Let R be a research structure, and let $\mathcal{R}$ be the set of researchers affiliated with R. For each researcher $r \in \mathcal{R}$, let $products(r, R)$ (or just $products(r)$, if R is understood from the context) be the set of the research products of r in the given period 2011-2014.

An *allocation* for a set of researchers $\mathcal{S} \subseteq \mathcal{R}$ is a function ψ mapping each researcher $r \in \mathcal{S}$ to a set of publications $\psi(r) \subseteq products(r)$ with $|\psi(r)| \leq 2$ and with $\psi(r) \cap \psi(r') = \emptyset$, for each $r' \in \mathcal{S} \setminus \{r\}$. An allocation for R is an allocation for all researchers $\mathcal{R}$, while an allocation for a substructure S of R is an allocation for the researchers affiliated to S. In the VQR program, every research structure R has to submit to ANVUR for its evaluation a set of products $\mathcal{P}_\psi$ such that $\mathcal{P}_\psi = \bigcup_{r \in \mathcal{R}} \psi(r)$, for some allocation ψ for all researchers $\mathcal{R}$ affiliated to R. Then, for each $p \in \mathcal{P}_\psi$, ANVUR calculates a quality score $score_{\text{VQR}}(p)$, so that R will receive funds proportionally to its overall score $score_{\text{VQR}}(\psi) = \sum_{p \in \mathcal{P}_\psi} score_{\text{VQR}}(p)$.

Example 1. Let us consider the simple scenario that is illustrated in Figure 1, by exploiting an intuitive graphical notation based on a weighted bipartite graph, whose vertices are the researchers and the products, and whose weights are the VQR scores of the products. Assume that there are just three researchers, r_1, r_2, and r_3, affiliated to R. Moreover, consider the allocation ψ such that $\psi(r_1) = \{p_1, p_3\}$, $\psi(r_2) = \{p_2, p_4\}$, and $\psi(r_3) = \{p_6, p_7\}$. Thus, we have that $\mathcal{P}_\psi = \{p_1, p_2, p_3, p_4, p_6, p_7\}$ is the set of publications submitted for the evaluation. Note that p_2 is co-authored by r_1, r_2, and r_3, while p_3 is co-authored by r_1 and r_2. According to the VQR score assigned to each product (i.e., the weight of the corresponding vertex in Figure 1), we get that $score_{\text{VQR}}(\psi) = 45$.

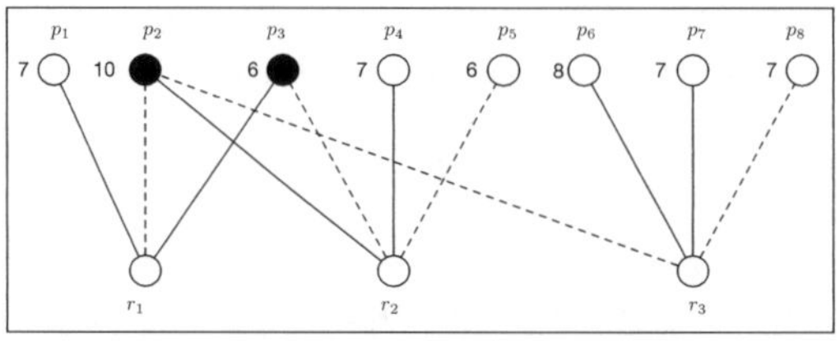

Fig. 1. Running example in Section 2.

Definition 1. *A* division rule γ *for R is a real-valued function that, given a researcher $r \in \mathcal{R}$ and an allocation ψ for R, returns its score $\gamma_\psi(r, R) \geq 0$ with respect to the allocation ψ. By slightly abusing notation, for any substructure $\mathcal{S} \subseteq \mathcal{R}$ (here just viewed as the set of its members), we denote by $\gamma_\psi(\mathcal{S}, R)$ the value $\sum_{r \in \mathcal{S}} \gamma_\psi(r, R)$. Whenever R is understood from the context, we just write $\gamma_\psi(r)$ and $\gamma_\psi(\mathcal{S})$, in place of $\gamma_\psi(r, R)$ and $\gamma_\psi(\mathcal{S}, R)$, respectively.* □

Currently, ANVUR's score is based on the naive $proj$ rule where, for any researcher r, $proj_\psi(r)$ is the sum of the VQR scores of the products allocated to r in ψ. In fact, the rule has been used up to the level of the individuals, besides substructures (the researchers that have been recently hired, the members of PhD committees, and who knows in the future). We therefore discuss all fairness properties with reference to individual researchers, even because all issues about individuals immediately extend to the substructures they belong to. We start by observing that, in the setting of Example 1, $\texttt{proj}_\psi(r_1) = 13$, $\texttt{proj}_\psi(r_2) = 17$, and $\texttt{proj}_\psi(r_3) = 15$. More generally, this rule satisfies a very basic requirement for every division rule, which we state below.

Budget-balance. *A division rule γ must precisely distribute the VQR score of R over all its members, i.e., $\sum_{r \in \mathcal{R}} \gamma_\psi(r) = score_{\text{VQR}}(R)$.*

In fact, the rule designed by ANVUR is hardly perceivable as a fair one. Indeed, $proj$ might lead to scenarios where some researcher r (and in turn her/his substructure) has reasonable arguments against her/his structure because of possible alternative allocations where r would get higher scores. This is next exemplified.

Example 2. Consider again the allocation ψ depicted in Figure 1. Consider now the different allocation $\bar{\psi}$ where r_1 and r_2 just swap the allocation of the two publications they have co-authored. That is, $\bar{\psi}$ is such that $\bar{\psi}(r_1) = \{p_1, p_2\}$, $\bar{\psi}(r_2) = \{p_3, p_4\}$, and $\bar{\psi}(r_3) = \{p_6, p_7\}$. Of course, we have $\mathcal{P}_\psi = \mathcal{P}_{\bar{\psi}}$ and $score_{\text{VQR}}(\psi) = score_{\text{VQR}}(\bar{\psi})$. Therefore, from the perspective of R the choice of $\bar{\psi}$ in place of ψ is completely immaterial. However, we now would have $\texttt{proj}_{\bar{\psi}}(r_1) = 17$ and $\texttt{proj}_{\bar{\psi}}(r_2) = 13$. Thus, r_2 may well complain to her/his structure, if $\bar{\psi}$ is selected in place of ψ. Symmetrically, r_1 is not happy with ψ, knowing the existence of the alternative allocation $\bar{\psi}$. ◁

Indeed, $proj$ fails to satisfy basic and intuitive requirements of fairness, which we formalize as follows.

Fairness. *Assume that ψ and $\bar{\psi}$ are two allocations of the same research products, i.e., $\mathcal{P}_\psi = \mathcal{P}_{\bar{\psi}}$. A division rule γ must be indifferent w.r.t. the optimal allocation being selected, i.e., for each researcher $r \in \mathcal{R}$, $\gamma_\psi(r) = \gamma_{\bar{\psi}}(r)$. In fact, this implies that, for each substructure $\mathcal{S}_i$, $\gamma_\psi(\mathcal{S}_i) = \gamma_{\bar{\psi}}(\mathcal{S}_i)$ also holds.*

We are now ready to define a property that takes care of the actual contribution of individuals and groups. Let ψ be an allocation and $\mathcal{R}$ a set of researchers (e.g., some substructure). The marginal contribution $marg_{\psi}(\mathcal{S}, \mathcal{R})$ of a subset of these researchers $\mathcal{S}$ to $\mathcal{R}$ is given by the difference between the best outcome that can be obtained by the full group $\mathcal{R}$ and the best outcome that can be obtained without $\mathcal{S}$, that is, by $\mathcal{R} \setminus \mathcal{S}$.

Marginality. *A division rule γ must be such that, for any such a group of researchers $\mathcal{S} \subseteq \mathcal{R}$, $\gamma_{\psi}(\mathcal{S}) \geq marg_{\psi}(\mathcal{S}, \mathcal{R})$. Therefore, every group is granted at least its marginal contribution to the performance of the R.*

In particular, the above property entails that groups without interactions with other researchers, e.g., departments without collaborations with other departments of the same university, are granted precisely the total scores of the products assigned to them according to ψ. Finally, note that in general several alternative optimal allocations can be selected by the structure R. The choice of a specific optimal allocation is immaterial for R but, depending on the division rule being adopted, can be rather sensible to the researchers (or the substructures). A good division rule should be indifferent w.r.t. the optimal allocation being selected by R and submitted to ANVUR.

Independence of the products selection. *Let ψ_1, ψ_2 be any pair of optimal allocations for R. A division rule γ must be such that, for each $r \in \mathcal{R}$, $\gamma_{\psi_1}(r) = \gamma_{\psi_2}(r)$.*

2.1 The division rule

We can show that not only ANVUR's rule but also all the simple division rules that have been proposed until now (e.g., taking the average of the products, or taking the best products considering the coauthors, and so on) miss the above fairness properties. However, by using game theory, we can find what we need. In particular, we next consider the class of *allocation games*, which provides a framework to analyze fair division problems where monetary compensations are allowed and utilities are quasi-linear [8].

Allocation games naturally arise in various application domains, ranging from house allocation to room assignment-rent division, to (cooperative) scheduling and task allocation, to protocols for wireless communication networks, and to queuing problems (see, e.g., [8,6,7,4] and the references therein). Here, it is quite natural to formalize the considered application as an allocation game $\mathcal{G}_{\psi} = \langle \mathcal{R}, \mathtt{best}_{\psi} \rangle$ where the agents in $\mathcal{R}$ are the researchers, and the function $\mathtt{best}_{\psi}$ provides a value to each coalition of researchers as the best value of any allocation assuming they were alone in the structure.

Then, we propose the following division rule, which is easily seen to be precisely the Shapley value of $\mathcal{G}_{\psi}$:

$$\gamma^*_{\psi}(r) = \sum_{\mathcal{S} \subseteq \mathcal{R}} \frac{(|\mathcal{R}| - |\mathcal{S}|)!(|\mathcal{S}| - 1)!}{|N|!} marg_{\psi}(\{r\}, \mathcal{S}), \text{ for each } r \in \mathcal{R}.$$

In our running example, we have $\gamma^*_{\psi}(r_1) = \frac{29}{2}$, $\gamma^*_{\psi}(r_2) = \frac{29}{2}$, and $\gamma^*_{\psi}(r_3) = 16$. This division rule satisfies all fairness properties defined in the previous section [2].

3 Computing the Shapley value of Allocation Problems

In [1] large islands of tractability for the Shapley value of allocation games are identified, by exploiting the structure of the interactions among agents. We next overview these results, by focusing on the classical allocation games where each agent gets one good. With respect to the fairness issues described in the previous section, nothing changes from the case of two (or more) goods that are used in the VQR program. However, the polynomial-time algorithm that we describe next is instead sensible to the number of goods and needs to be extended properly to deal with the case of allocating two or more goods to each agent. This can be done by using our technique, but it is outside the scope of the present paper.

The idea for getting the tractability result is that the marginal contribution can be characterized via the existence of an allocation with certain properties and this problem reduces to counting the number of coalitions whose properties depend on the existence of that allocation. This problem can be modeled as the problem of counting the solutions of a big conjunctive query (or, equivalently, as a constraint satisfaction problem).

Allocation Scenario. Assume that a set $\mathbb{G}$ of goods have to be allocated to a set $N = \{1, ..., n\}$ of agents. Each good $g \in \mathbb{G}$ is associated with a real value $\mathtt{val}(g) \in \mathbb{R}$, and each agent $i \in N$ can receive at most one good taken from her set of interest $\Omega(i) \subseteq \mathbb{G}$. The tuple $\mathcal{A} = \langle N, \mathbb{G}, \Omega, \mathtt{val}\rangle$, with $\Omega : N \rightarrow 2^{\mathbb{G}}$ and $\mathtt{val} : \mathbb{G} \rightarrow \mathbb{R}$, is an *allocation scenario*. Goods are indivisible and unsharable. Hence, an *allocation* for $\mathcal{A}$ is a function $\pi : N \rightarrow \mathbb{G} \cup \{\emptyset\}$ such that: (1) for each agent $i \in N$, $\pi(i) \neq \emptyset$ implies $\pi(i) \in \Omega(i)$; and (2) for each pair $i, i' \in N$ with $i \neq i'$, $\pi(i) \cap \pi(i') = \emptyset$ holds. We denote by $\mathtt{img}(\pi)$ the set of all goods in the image of π, i.e., $\mathtt{img}(\pi) = \{\pi(i) \mid i \in N \wedge \pi(i) \neq \emptyset\}$. By slightly abusing of notation, if $S \subseteq \mathbb{G}$ is a set of goods, then $\mathtt{val}(S)$ denotes the sum of their values. Moreover, if π is an allocation, then $\mathtt{val}(\pi)$ denotes the value of $\mathtt{img}(\pi)$. An allocation π is *optimal* (w.r.t. $\mathcal{A}$) if $\mathtt{val}(\pi) \geq \mathtt{val}(\pi')$ holds, for each allocation π'. The value of any optimal allocation w.r.t. $\mathcal{A}$ is denoted as $\mathtt{opt}(\mathcal{A})$.

Allocation Games. Let $\mathcal{A} = \langle N, \mathbb{G}, \Omega, \mathtt{val}\rangle$ be an allocation scenario and let $C \subseteq N$ be a set of agents. The *restriction of* $\mathcal{A}$ *to* C is the *sub*-scenario $\mathcal{A}[C] = \langle C, \mathbb{G}, \Omega_C, \mathtt{val}\rangle$ where Ω_C is the restriction of Ω over C. The *allocation game* induced by $\mathcal{A}$ is the tuple $\mathsf{G}_{\mathcal{A}} = \langle N, v_{\mathcal{A}}\rangle$, where $v_{\mathcal{A}} : 2^N \rightarrow \mathbb{R}$ is such that $v_{\mathcal{A}}(C) = \mathtt{opt}(\mathcal{A}[C])$, for each $C \subseteq N$. The value of an empty set of goods is 0. Then, the definition trivializes for $C = \emptyset$, with $v_{\mathcal{A}}(\emptyset) = 0$. Moreover, note that $v_{\mathcal{A}}(C) \geq 0$ holds, for each $C \subseteq N$, since the allocation where no agent receives some good is a feasible one.

3.1 From Games to Counting Problems

The first ingredient to establish the result is to move from the usual definition of the Shapley value to a characterization that is useful for our computational purposes. First observe that the Shapley value $\phi_i(\mathsf{G}_{\mathcal{A}})$ of any player i in an allocation game $\mathsf{G}_{\mathcal{A}}$ over the set of agents N can be written as follows:

$$\phi_i(\mathsf{G}_{\mathcal{A}}) = \sum_{h=0}^{n-1} \frac{h!(n-h-1)!}{n!} \beta_i(\mathsf{G}_{\mathcal{A}}, h), \qquad (1)$$

where $\beta_i(\mathsf{G}_{\mathcal{A}}, h) = \sum_{C \subseteq N \setminus \{i\}, |C|=h} (v(C \cup \{i\}) - v(C))$.

Thus, the critical step is the computation of $\beta_i(\mathsf{G}_{\mathcal{A}}, h)$. Now, observe that the difference $v(C \cup \{i\}) - v(C)$ corresponds precisely to the value of the worst good among those associated with the coalition of agents $C \cup \{i\}$. Such a value was needed to provide one good (in our case study, one research product) to all agents in $C \cup \{i\}$, but is no longer necessary if only players in C are considered. We can thus focus on one possible level of worth w_ℓ at a time, so that we can solve the problem efficiently if we are able to compute in polynomial time the value $\xi_i(\mathsf{G}_{\mathcal{A}}, h, w_\ell)$, defined as the cardinality of the set of all coalitions $\{C \mid v(C \cup \{i\}) - v(C) \geq w_\ell \text{ and } |C| = h\}$.

Indeed, having such a value $\xi_i(\mathsf{G}_{\mathcal{A}}, h, w_\ell)$, we can compute the number of coalitions having each possible admissible value w_ℓ (starting from the largest one) for each cardinality (ranging from 0 to the number of players minus 1, because $i \notin C$). From these values, we easily get $\beta_i(\mathsf{G}_{\mathcal{A}}, h)$, and then $\phi_i(\mathsf{G}_{\mathcal{A}})$. Therefore, we have to find an efficient way to count the number of distinct coalitions to which i provides a certain marginal contribution, of course without computing them, because there exponentially many such coalitions in general. We define next some useful notions.

For each "level" ℓ over the possible values, an agent $i \in N$ is said to be *dependent at level* ℓ (short: ℓ-dependent) if for each $g \in \Omega(i)$ with $\texttt{val}(g) \geq w_\ell$, there is an agent $j \in N \setminus \{i\}$ such that $g \in \Omega(j)$. In particular, note that any agent having goods with value at least w_ℓ and which are not shared with any other agent is not dependent at level ℓ; in fact, all her marginal contributions are at least w_ℓ, independently of the coalition to be considered. Let $G_\ell = (N_\ell, E_\ell)$ be the undirected graph where N_ℓ is the set of all ℓ-dependent agents and where $\{i, j\} \in E_\ell$ if, and only if, there is a good $g \in \Omega(i) \cap \Omega(j)$ with $\texttt{val}(g) \geq w_\ell$. Then, a coalition $R \subseteq N_\ell$ of agents is called a *component at level* ℓ (short: ℓ-component) if the subgraph of G_ℓ induced by the nodes in R is connected. As a special case, if there is no good $g \in \Omega(i)$ with $\texttt{val}(g) \geq w_\ell$, then $\{i\}$ is an ℓ-component. If $C \subseteq N$ is a coalition and $i \notin C$ is an agent, then we denote by $\mathbf{p}_\ell^i(C)$ the *ℓ-part* of C w.r.t. i. This is defined as the emptyset if $i \notin N_\ell$; otherwise, $\mathbf{p}_\ell^i(C)$ is the subset-maximal (in fact, unique) ℓ-component $R \subseteq C \cup \{i\}$ with $i \in R$.

Theorem 1. *Let $C \subseteq N$ be a coalition and let $i \in N \setminus C$ be an agent. Then, the following statements are equivalent: (1) $v_{\mathcal{A}}(C \cup \{i\}) - v_{\mathcal{A}}(C) \geq w_\ell$; (2) there is an allocation $\bar{\pi}$ for $\mathcal{A}[\mathbf{p}_\ell^i(C)]$ such that $\texttt{val}(\bar{\pi}(j)) \geq w_\ell$, for each $j \in \mathbf{p}_\ell^i(C)$.*

This is a crucial result for the paper, because it allows us to focus on any allocation satisfying certain properties, instead of using optimal allocations, which occur in the definition of the worth function of the game.

3.2 Making the right Query

For any scenario $\mathcal{A} = \langle N, \mathbb{G}, \Omega, \texttt{val}\rangle$, its *interaction graph* is the undirected graph $G(\mathcal{A}) = (N, E)$ such that $\{i, j\} \in E$ if, and only if, there is a good $g \in \Omega(i) \cap \Omega(j)$.

Recall that a *tree decomposition* of a graph $G = (N, E)$ is a pair $\langle T, \chi\rangle$, where $T = (V, F)$ is a tree, and χ is a function assigning to each vertex $p \in V$ a set of nodes $\chi(p) \subseteq N$, such that the following conditions are satisfied: (1) $\forall b \in N, \exists p \in V$ such that $b \in \chi(p)$; (2) $\forall \{b, d\} \in E, \exists p \in V$ such that $\{b, d\} \subseteq \chi(p)$; (3) $\forall b \in N$, the set $\{p \in V \mid b \in \chi(p)\}$ induces a connected subtree of T. The *width* of $\langle T, \chi\rangle$ is $\max_{p \in V} |\chi(p) - 1|$, and the *treewidth* of G (short: $tw(G)$) is the minimum width over all its tree decompositions (see, e.g., [10]).

X_j^v	X_j	
0	0	
$\odot$	1	if v is a vertex of the form v_g, for some good g with $\mathtt{val}(g) \geq w_\ell$
$\swarrow$	1	if v is not a leaf, v_1 is its left child, and $j \in \chi(v_1)$
$\searrow$	1	if v is not a leaf, v_2 is its right child, and $j \in \chi(v_2)$
$\uparrow$	1	if v is not the root, p is its parent, and $j \in \chi(p)$

$X_j^{v_g}$
0
$\odot$
$\uparrow$

Y_j	X_j	
1	1	
1	0	if $j \neq i$
0	0	if $j \neq i$

Y_j	X_j	$X_{j'}$
1	1	1
0	0	0
0	0	1
1	0	0
1	1	0

X_j^v	$X_j^{v_1}$	$X_j^{v_2}$
0	0	0
$\odot$	$\uparrow$	$\uparrow$
$\uparrow$	$\uparrow$	$\uparrow$
$\swarrow$	$\swarrow$	$\uparrow$
$\swarrow$	$\searrow$	$\uparrow$
$\swarrow$	$\odot$	$\uparrow$
$\searrow$	$\uparrow$	$\swarrow$
$\searrow$	$\uparrow$	$\searrow$
$\searrow$	$\uparrow$	$\odot$

$X_j^{v_g}$	$X_{j'}^{v_g}$
$\forall u \in \{0, \uparrow\}$	$\odot$
$\forall u \in \{0, \uparrow\}$	$\odot$
$\forall u \in \{0, \uparrow\}$	$\odot$
$\forall u \in \{0, \uparrow\}$	$\odot$
$\odot$	$\forall u \in \{0, \uparrow\}$
$\odot$	$\forall u \in \{0, \uparrow\}$
$\odot$	$\forall u \in \{0, \uparrow\}$
$\odot$	$\forall u \in \{0, \uparrow\}$
$\forall u \in \{0, \uparrow\}$	$\forall u \in \{0, \uparrow\}$

Fig. 2. The encoding in Section 3.2.

Now, we show that using Theorem 1 we can compute in polynomial-time the Shapley value over allocation games whose interaction graphs have bounded treewidth. We use the following result on conjunctive queries with existential variables.

Theorem 2 (cf. [9,3]). *Counting the number of answers of conjunctive queries with existential variables is feasible in polynomial time, on classes of conjunctive queries $\mathcal{Q}$ such that the treewidth of the primal graph $G(\mathcal{Q})$ is bounded by a constant, and the size of the domain of each existential variable is bounded by some constant, too.*

We next define a query whose "output" (i.e., free) variables encode the coalitions that we want to count, while the existential variables are auxiliary ones used in the query atom to enforce the desired properties for such coalitions. The challenge to be faced is to use a constant number of possible values for the existential variables occurring in the query. For instance, the natural encoding where some variable X_j (associated with an agent $j \in N$) can take as values the goods in $\Omega(j)$ is not useful here. In fact, we propose an encoding that uses both the given allocation scenario $\mathcal{A}$ and a tree decomposition $\mathtt{TD} = \langle T, \chi \rangle$ of $G(\mathcal{A})$. The idea is that each good is associated with some distinguished vertex of T, while suitable variables in the labels of the tree encode the roadmaps to reach such goods. In particular, their domain just contains the needed road signs (five values are enough). This is detailed below.

We start by building a tree decomposition with certain desirable properties. Let $\langle T', \chi' \rangle$ be a tree decomposition of $G(\mathcal{A})$ whose width is $k > 0$. Note that, for each good $g \in \mathbb{G}$, we are guaranteed about the existence of a vertex v'_g in T' such that $\chi(v'_g) \supseteq \{j \mid g \in \Omega(j)\}$. Indeed, the agents in $\{j \mid g \in \Omega(j)\}$ form a clique in $G(\mathcal{A})$.

In a pre-processing step, we modify $\langle T', \chi' \rangle$ by adding a fresh vertex v_g as a child of v'_g, whose label is $\chi(v_g) = \chi(v'_g) \cap \{j \mid g \in \Omega(j)\}$. By iterating over all goods, we get the desired tree where each good g is associated with a distinguished vertex (in fact, leaf) v_g labeled by the agents to whom g can be allocated. Of course, the transformation is feasible in polynomial time. Eventually, we transform the decomposition by making it binary: For each vertex v with children $v_1, ..., v_n$, we can create a novel vertex $\bar{v}$ as a child of v and with its label, by appending under it all these children but v_1. Let $\mathtt{TD} = \langle T, \chi \rangle$ be the resulting tree decomposition, having the same width as $\langle T', \chi' \rangle$.

The input to our encoding is the allocation scenario $\mathcal{A}$, the agent $i \in N$, the natural number ℓ, and the tree decomposition $\mathtt{TD} = \langle T, \chi \rangle$. Note that, for the moment, we do not consider the size h. Dealing with the cardinality of the coalition needs a further elaboration of the query, which can be found on the full paper. Then, we define the encoding ξ such that $\xi(\mathcal{A}, i, \ell, \mathtt{TD})$ is the conjunctive query instance such that: the set of variables *Var* is $\{\bigcup_{j \in N}\{X_j, Y_j\} \cup \{X_j^v \mid v \text{ is in } T \wedge j \in \chi(v)\}$; the universe of the database is $U = \{0, 1, \odot, \swarrow, \searrow, \uparrow\}$; the database relations are reported in tabular form in Figure 2; and the set of query atoms is defined as follows:

1. For each agent $j \in N$ and vertex v in T with $j \in \chi(v)$, there is an atom $r_{v,j}(X_j^v, X_j)$;
2. For each good g with $\mathtt{val}(g) \geq w_\ell$ and each $j \in \chi(v_g)$, there is an atom $r_{g,j}(X_j^{v_g})$;
3. For each agent $j \in N$, there is an atom $r_j(Y_j, X_j)$;
4. For each pair of agents $j \in N$ and $j' \in N$ that are adjacent in G_ℓ, there is an atom $r_{j,j'}(Y_j, X_j, X_{j'})$;
5. For each non-leaf vertex v whose left (resp., right) child is v_1 (resp., v_2), and for each $j \in \chi(v)$, there is an atom constraint $r'_{v,j}(X_j^v, X_j^{v_1}, X_j^{v_2})$;
6. For each good g with $\mathtt{val}(g) \geq w_\ell$ and for each pair $j, j' \in \chi(v_g)$ with $g \in \Omega(j) \cap \Omega(j')$, there is an atom $r_{g,j,j'}(X_j^{v_g}, X_{j'}^{v_g})$;

Eventually, the output variables are the Boolean variables $\mathcal{W} = \{Y_1, \ldots Y_n\}$, that is, all other variables are existentially quantified. Note that each assignment to these variables encodes a different coalition C, and the query atoms enforce the properties stated in Theorem 1. Therefore, counting the distinct answers of $\xi(\mathcal{A}, i, \ell, \mathtt{TD})$ over the output variables $\mathcal{W}$ gives to us an important information to computed the desired Shapley value. Actually, to obtain the number $\xi_i(\mathsf{G}_\mathcal{A}, h, w_\ell)$ we have to modify a little bit the query to restrict the solutions to those assignments to $\mathcal{W}$ having precisely h variables with value 1. Then, by using the results in [3], we get the following.

Theorem 3. *The Shapley value of allocation games can be computed in polynomial time on all allocation scenarios whose interaction graphs have bounded treewidth.*

References

1. G. Greco, F. Lupia, and F. Scarcello. Structural tractability of shapley and banzhaf values in allocation games. In *Proc. of IJCAI'15*, pages 547–553, 2015.
2. G. Greco and F. Scarcello. Fair division rules for funds distribution: The case of the italian research assessment program (vqr 2004-2010). *Intelligenza Artificiale*, 7(1):45–56, 2013.
3. G. Greco and F. Scarcello. Counting solutions to conjunctive queries: structural and hybrid tractability. In *Proc. of PODS'14*, pages 132–143, 2014.
4. G. Greco and F. Scarcello. Mechanisms for fair allocation problems: No-punishment payment rules in verifiable settings. *J. Artif. Intell. Res. (JAIR)*, 49:403–449, 2014.
5. D. Liben-Nowell, A. Sharp, T. Wexler, and K. Woods. Computing Shapley value in supermodular coalitional games. In *Proc. of COCOON'12*, pages 568–579. 2012.
6. F. Maniquet. A characterization of the Shapley value in queueing problems. *Journal of Economic Theory*, 109(1):90–103, 2003.
7. D. Mishra and B. Rangarajan. Cost sharing in a job scheduling problem. *Social Choice and Welfare*, 29(3):369–382, October 2007.
8. H. Moulin. An application of the Shapley value to fair division with money. *Econometrica*, 60(6):1331–49, November 1992.
9. R. Pichler and S. Skritek. Tractable counting of the answers to conjunctive queries. *Journal of Computer and System Sciences*, 79(6):984–1001, 2013.
10. N. Robertson and P. Seymour. Graph minors iii: Planar tree-width. *Journal of Combinatorial Theory, Series B*, 36(1):49–64, February 1984.
11. L. S. Shapley. A value for n-person games. *Contributions to the theory of games*, 2, 1953.

Greedy Strategies and Larger Islands of Tractability for Conjunctive Queries

Gianluigi Greco, Francesco Lupia, and Francesco Scarcello

University of Calabria, 87036, Rende, Italy
ggreco@mat.unical.it, {lupia, scarcello}@dimes.unical.it

Abstract. Structural decomposition methods have been developed for identifying tractable classes of instances of fundamental problems in databases, such as conjunctive queries and query containment. Most structural decomposition methods can be characterized through hypergraph games that are variations of the *Robber and Cops* graph game that characterizes the notion of treewidth. In particular, decomposition trees somehow correspond to *monotone winning strategies*, where the escape space of the robber on the hypergraph is shrunk monotonically by the cops. The paper overviews some recent results (to appear on the Information and Computation journal) about a general way to exploit the greater power of non-monotonic strategies, by allowing a "disciplined" form of non-monotonicity, characteristic of cops playing in a *greedy* way. It is shown that deciding the existence of a (non-monotone) greedy winning strategy (and compute one, if any) is tractable. Moreover, despite their non-monotonicity, such strategies always induce valid decomposition trees, which can be computed efficiently based on them. As a consequence, greedy strategies allow us to define new islands of tractability for the considered problems properly including all previously known classes of tractable instances.

1 Introduction

Conjunctive queries are defined through conjunctions of atoms (without negation), and are known to be equivalent to Select-Project-Join queries. The problem of evaluating such queries is NP-hard in general, but it is feasible in polynomial time on the class of acyclic queries (we omit "conjunctive," hereafter), which was the subject of many seminal research works since the early ages of database theory (see, e.g., [1]). This class contains all queries Q whose associated query hypergraph $\mathcal{H}_Q$ is acyclic, where $\mathcal{H}_Q$ is a hypergraph having the variables of Q as its nodes, and the (sets of variables occurring in the) atoms of Q as its hyperedges.

In fact, queries arising from real applications are hardly precisely acyclic. Yet, they are often not very intricate and, in fact, tend to exhibit some limited degree of cyclicity, which suffices to retain most of the nice properties of acyclic ones. Therefore, several efforts have been spent to investigate invariants that are best suited to identify nearly-acyclic hypergraphs, leading to the definition of a number of so-called *(purely) structural decomposition-methods*, such as the *(generalized) hypertree* [5], *fractional hypertree* [10], *spread-cut* [3], and *component hypertree* [7] decompositions. These methods aim at transforming a given cyclic hypergraph into an acyclic one, by organizing its edges (or its nodes) into a polynomial number of clusters, and by suitably arranging

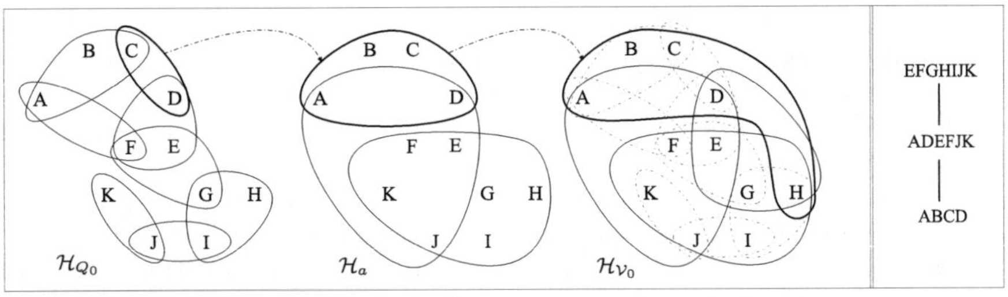

Fig. 1. A tree projection $\mathcal{H}_a$ of $\mathcal{H}_{Q_0}$ w.r.t. $\mathcal{H}_{\mathcal{V}_0}$; On the right: A join tree JT_a for $\mathcal{H}_a$.

these clusters as a tree, called decomposition tree. The original problem instance can then be evaluated over such a tree of subproblems, with a cost that is exponential in the cardinality of the largest cluster, also called *width* of the decomposition, and polynomial if this width is bounded by some constant.

Despite their different technical definitions, there is a simple mathematical framework that encompasses all the above decomposition methods, which is the framework of the *tree projections* [8]. In this setting, a query Q is given together with a set $\mathcal{V}$ of atoms, called views, which are defined over the variables in Q. The question is whether (parts of) the views can be arranged as to form a tree projection (playing the role of a decomposition tree), i.e., a novel acyclic query that still "covers" Q. By representing Q and $\mathcal{V}$ via the hypergraphs $\mathcal{H}_Q$ and $\mathcal{H}_\mathcal{V}$, where hyperedges one-to-one correspond with query atoms and views, respectively, the tree projection problem reveals its graph-theoretic nature. For a pair of hypergraphs $\mathcal{H}_1, \mathcal{H}_2$, let $\mathcal{H}_1 \leq \mathcal{H}_2$ denote that each hyperedge of $\mathcal{H}_1$ is contained in some hyperedge of $\mathcal{H}_2$. Then, a tree projection of $\mathcal{H}_Q$ w.r.t. $\mathcal{H}_\mathcal{V}$ is any acyclic hypergraph $\mathcal{H}_a$ such that $\mathcal{H}_Q \leq \mathcal{H}_a \leq \mathcal{H}_\mathcal{V}$. If such a hypergraph exists, then we say that the pair of hypergraphs $(\mathcal{H}_Q, \mathcal{H}_\mathcal{V})$ has a tree projection

Example 1. Consider the following conjunctive query whose associated hypergraph $\mathcal{H}_{Q_0}$ is depicted in Figure 1, together with other hypergraphs that are discussed next:

$$Q_0 : r_1(A, B, C) \wedge r_2(A, F) \wedge r_3(C, D) \wedge r_4(D, E, F) \wedge \\ r_5(E, F, G) \wedge r_6(G, H, I) \wedge r_7(I, J) \wedge r_8(J, K),$$

To answer Q_0, assume that a set $\mathcal{V}_0$ of views is available comprising some views, called *query views*, playing the role of query atoms, plus four additional views.[1] The set of variables of each view is a hyperedge in the hypergraph $\mathcal{H}_{\mathcal{V}_0}$ (query views are depicted as dashed hyperedges). In the middle between $\mathcal{H}_{Q_0}$ and $\mathcal{H}_{\mathcal{V}_0}$, Figure 1 reports the hypergraph $\mathcal{H}_a$ which covers $\mathcal{H}_{Q_0}$, and which is in its turn covered by $\mathcal{H}_{\mathcal{V}_0}$—e.g., $\{C, D\} \subseteq \{A, B, C, D\} \subseteq \{A, B, C, D, H\}$. Since $\mathcal{H}_a$ is in addition acyclic, $\mathcal{H}_a$ is a tree projection of $\mathcal{H}_{Q_0}$ w.r.t. $\mathcal{H}_{\mathcal{V}_0}$. $\lhd$

An *island of tractability* (cf. [11]) in the tree projection framework is a class $\mathcal{C}$ of pairs $(Q, \mathcal{V})$ that can be efficiently recognized, i.e., we can check in polynomial time whether a given pair actually belongs to $\mathcal{C}$, and such that Q can be efficiently evaluated on every database, by possibly exploiting the views that are available in $\mathcal{V}$.

[1] In the framework, views can be arbitrary, i.e, they do not depend on the given query, and can be reused to answer different queries. In particular, views may be the materialized output of any procedure over the database, possibly more powerful than conjunctive queries.

Many specializations of tree projections, such as *tree decompositions* [14] and *hypertree decompositions* [5], define islands of tractability whenever some fixed bound is imposed on their widths. This is also the case for *fractional hypertree decompositions* [10], whenever the resources sufficient for computing their $O(w^3)$ approximation [12] are used as available views. However, this is not the case for general tree projections. Indeed, while Goodman and Shmueli [8] observed that queries that admit a tree projection can be evaluated in polynomial time, Gottlob et al. [7] proved that checking whether a tree projection exists or not is an NP-hard problem. Hence, the class $\mathcal{C}_{tp} = \{(Q, \mathcal{V}) \mid \mathcal{H}_Q$ has a tree projection w.r.t. $\mathcal{H}_\mathcal{V}\}$ is not an island of tractability in its turn. A natural question is, therefore, whether there is any subclass of $\mathcal{C}_{tp}$, at least including all the tractable classes mentioned above, which identifies an actual island of tractability where tree projections can be computed efficiently.

In the paper, we address the above question. The starting point of our analysis is the game-theoretic characterization of tree projections in terms of the *Robber and Captain* game [9]. The game is played on a pair of hypergraphs $(\mathcal{H}_1, \mathcal{H}_2)$ by a Captain controlling, at each move, a squads of cops encoded as the nodes in a hyperedge $h \in edges(\mathcal{H}_2)$, and by a Robber who stands on a node and can run at great speed along the edges of $\mathcal{H}_1$, while being not permitted to run trough a node that is controlled by a cop. In particular, the Captain may ask any cops in the squad h to run in action, as long as they occupy nodes that are currently reachable by the Robber, thereby blocking an escape path for the Robber. While cops move, the Robber may run trough those positions that are left by cops or not yet occupied. The goal of the Captain is to place a cop on the node occupied by the Robber, while the Robber tries to avoid her capture. The Captain has a winning strategy if, and only if, there is a tree projection of $\mathcal{H}_1$ w.r.t. $\mathcal{H}_2$.

Based on the above characterization, we proceed as follows:

- ► We define the notion of *greedy strategies*, which are winning strategies for the Captain, possibly non-monotone, where it is required that *all* cops available at the current squad h and reachable by the Robber enter in action. If all of them are in action, then a new squad h' is selected, again requiring that all the active cops, i.e., those in the frontier, enter in action. In the Robber and Captain game, it is known that there is no incentive for the Captain to play a strategy that is not monotone [9]. Instead, by focusing on greedy strategies, we can exhibit examples where there exists non-monotone winning strategies but no monotone winning one.
- ► We show that *greedy strategies* can be computed in polynomial time, and that based on them (even on non-monotone ones) it is possible to construct, again in polynomial time, tree projections, which are called *greedy*. Therefore, the class $\mathcal{C}_{gtp} \subset \mathcal{C}_{tp}$ of all greedy tree projections turns out to be an island of tractability.
- ► We show that $\mathcal{C}_{gtp}$ properly includes most previously known islands of tractability, because of the power of non-monotonic strategies. Indeed, (arbitrary) non-monotone strategies do not correspond in general to valid decompositions in the games characterizing such islands of tractability, which are defined in terms of monotone strategies only. In particular, greedy tree projections allow us to define new islands of tractability from any known structural decomposition method, such as the *greedy (generalized) hypertree decomposition* or the *greedy component decomposition*, which are tractable and more powerful than their original versions.

2 Greedy Strategies in Robber and Captain Games

In this section, we define the concept of greedy strategies in the game-theoretic characterization of tree projections proposed in [9], and we show that, unlike arbitrary strategies, greedy ones can be efficiently computed.

To formalize our results, we need to introduce some additional definitions and notations, which will be intensively used in the following.

Assume that a hypergraph $\mathcal{H}$ is given. Let V, W, and $\{X, Y\}$ be sets of nodes. Then, X is said $[V]$-adjacent (in $\mathcal{H}$) to Y if there exists a hyperedge $h \in \mathit{edges}(\mathcal{H})$ such that $\{X, Y\} \subseteq (h - V)$. A $[V]$-path from X to Y is a sequence $X = X_0, \ldots, X_\ell = Y$ of nodes such that X_i is $[V]$-adjacent to X_{i+1}, for each $i \in [0...\ell\text{-}1]$. We say that X $[V]$-touches Y if X is $[\emptyset]$-adjacent to $Z \in \mathit{nodes}(\mathcal{H})$, and there is a $[V]$-path from Z to Y; similarly, X $[V]$-touches the set W if X $[V]$-touches some node $Y \in W$. We say that W is $[V]$-connected if $\forall X, Y \in W$ there is a $[V]$-path from X to Y. A $[V]$-component (of $\mathcal{H}$) is a maximal $[V]$-connected non-empty set of nodes $W \subseteq (\mathit{nodes}(\mathcal{H}) - V)$. For any $[V]$-component C, let $\mathit{edges}(C) = \{h \in \mathit{edges}(\mathcal{H}) \mid h \cap C \neq \emptyset\}$, and for a set of hyperedges $H \subseteq \mathit{edges}(\mathcal{H})$, let $\mathit{nodes}(H)$ denote the set of nodes occurring in H, that is $\mathit{nodes}(H) = \bigcup_{h \in H} h$. For any component C of $\mathcal{H}$, we denote by $\mathrm{Fr}(C, \mathcal{H})$ the *frontier* of C (in $\mathcal{H}$), i.e., the set $\mathit{nodes}(\mathit{edges}(C))$. Moreover, $\partial(C, \mathcal{H})$ denote the *border* of C (in $\mathcal{H}$), i.e., the set $\mathrm{Fr}(C, \mathcal{H}) \setminus C$. Note that $C_1 \subseteq C_2$ entails $\mathrm{Fr}(C_1, \mathcal{H}) \subseteq \mathrm{Fr}(C_2, \mathcal{H})$. In the following sections, given any pair of hypergraphs $(\mathcal{H}_1, \mathcal{H}_2)$ and a set of nodes $C \subseteq \mathcal{H}_1$, we write for short $\mathrm{Fr}(C)$ and ∂C to denote $\mathrm{Fr}(C, \mathcal{H}_1)$ and $\partial(C, \mathcal{H}_1)$, respectively.

2.1 Game-Theoretic Characterization

The *Robber and Captain* game is played on a pair of hypergraphs $(\mathcal{H}_1, \mathcal{H}_2)$ by a Robber and a Captain controlling some squads of cops, in charge of the surveillance of a number of strategic targets. The Robber stands on a node and can run at great speed along the edges of $\mathcal{H}_1$. However, (s)he is not permitted to run trough a node that is controlled by a cop. Each move of the Captain involves one squad of cops, which is encoded as a hyperedge $h \in \mathit{edges}(\mathcal{H}_2)$. The Captain may ask some cops in the squad h to run in action, as long as they occupy nodes that are currently reachable by the Robber, thereby blocking an escape path for the Robber. Thus, "second-lines" cops cannot be activated by the Captain. Note that the Robber is fast and may see cops that are entering in action. Therefore, while cops move, the Robber may run trough those positions that are left by cops or not yet occupied. The goal of the Captain is to place a cop on the node occupied by the Robber, while the Robber tries to avoid her/his capture.

Definition 1. Let $\mathcal{H}_1$ and $\mathcal{H}_2$ be two hypergraphs. The Robber and Captain game on $(\mathcal{H}_1, \mathcal{H}_2)$ is formalized as follows. A *position* for the Captain is a pair (h, M) where h is a hyperedge of $\mathcal{H}_2$ and $M \subseteq h$. A *configuration* is a triple (h, M, C), where (h, M) is a position for the Captain, and C is the $[M]$-component where the Robber stands.[2] The initial configuration is $(\emptyset, \emptyset, \mathit{nodes}(\mathcal{H}_1))$.

[2] It is easy to see that in such games, being the robber arbitrarily fast, what matters is not the precise node where the robber stands, but just the $[M]$-component where (s)he is free to move.

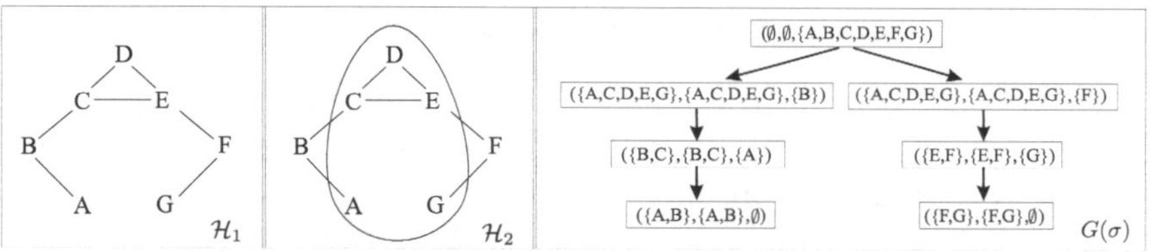

Fig. 2. The hypergraphs $\mathcal{H}_1$ and $\mathcal{H}_2$, plus the graph $G(\sigma)$ in Example 2.

A *strategy* σ is a function that encodes the *moves* of the Captain. Its domain includes the initial configuration. For each configuration $v_p = (h_p, M_p, C_p)$ in the domain of σ, $\sigma(v_p) = (h_r, M_r)$, with $M_r \subseteq h_r \cap \text{Fr}(C_p)$, is the novel position for the Captain. After this move, the Robber can select any $[v_p, M_r]$-*option*, i.e., any $[M_r]$-component C_r such that $C_p \cup C_r$ is $[M_p \cap M_r]$-connected. If there is no $[v_p, M_r]$-option, then $(h_r, M_r, \emptyset)$ is said a *capture* configuration induced by σ. The move of the Captain is *monotone* if, for each $[v_p, M_r]$-option C_r, $C_r \subseteq C_p$. The domain of σ includes the configuration (h_r, M_r, C_r), for each $[v_p, M_r]$-option C_r. No other configuration is in the domain of σ. The strategy σ is monotone if it encodes only monotone moves over the configurations in its domain.

A strategy σ can be represented as a directed graph $G(\sigma) = (N, A)$, called *strategy graph*, as follows. The set N of nodes is the set of all configurations in the domain of σ plus all capture configurations induced by σ. If $v_p = (h_p, M_p, C_p)$ is a configuration and $\sigma(v_p) = (h_r, M_r)$, then A contains an arc from v_p to (h_r, M_r, C_r) for each $[v_p, M_r]$-option C_r, and to $(h_r, M_r, \emptyset)$ if there is no $[v_p, M_r]$-option. We say that σ is a winning strategy (for the Captain) if $G(\sigma)$ is acyclic. Otherwise, i.e., if $G(\sigma)$ contains a cycle, then the Robber can avoid her/his capture forever. □

Example 2. Consider the hypergraphs $\mathcal{H}_1$ and $\mathcal{H}_2$ in Figure 2, with the strategy graph $G(\sigma)$. The graph encodes a winning strategy σ for the Captain. From the initial configuration $(\emptyset, \emptyset, nodes(\mathcal{H}_1))$, the Captain activates all the cops in $\{A, C, D, E, G\}$, so that the Robber has two available options, i.e., $\{B\}$ and $\{F\}$. In the former (resp., latter) case, the Captain activates all the cops in the hyperedge $\{B, C\}$ (resp., $\{E, F\}$), so that the Robber has necessarily to occupy the node A (resp., G). Finally, the Captain activates the cops in $\{A, B\}$ (resp., $\{F, G\}$) and captures the Robber. ◁

In the example, the hyperedge $\{A, C, D, E, G\}$ of $\mathcal{H}_2$ "absorbs" the cycle in $\mathcal{H}_1$, so that it is easily seen that there is a tree projection $\mathcal{H}_a$ of $\mathcal{H}_1$ w.r.t. $\mathcal{H}_2$ (see Figure 3). Below, we stress that the fact that on this pair the Captain has a winning strategy is not by chance. Moreover, observe that winning strategy in Example 2 is not monotone, because the Robber is allowed to return on A and G. However, another important property of this game is that there is no incentive to play a strategy that is not monotone.

Theorem 1 ([9]). *There is a tree projection of $\mathcal{H}_1$ w.r.t. $\mathcal{H}_2$ if, and and only if, there is a winning strategy in the game played on $(\mathcal{H}_1, \mathcal{H}_2)$. Moreover, a winning strategy exists if, and only if, a monotone winning strategy exists; and, from any monotone winning strategy, a tree projection of $\mathcal{H}_1$ w.r.t. $\mathcal{H}_2$ can be computed in polynomial time.*

Example 3. Consider again the setting of Example 2, and the strategy graph $G(\bar{\sigma})$ shown in Figure 3. Note that the strategy $\bar{\sigma}$ is monotone, and in fact the moves of the Captain one-to-one correspond with the hyperedges in the tree projection $\mathcal{H}_a$. ◁

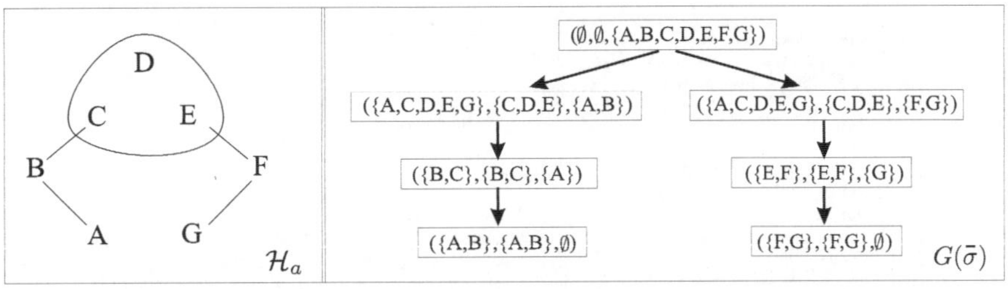

Fig. 3. A tree projection $\mathcal{H}_a$ for the pair in Example 2, plus the graph $G(\bar{\sigma})$.

2.2 Greedy Strategies and Larger Islands of Tractability

Since winning strategies correspond to tree projections, there is no efficient algorithm for their computation. Indeed, just recall that deciding the existence of a tree projection is not feasible in polynomial time, unless P $=$ NP [7]. Our goal is then to focus on certain "greedy" strategies that are easy to compute. Intuitively, in greedy strategies it is required that *all* cops available at the current squad h_p and reachable by the Robber enter in action. If all of them are in action, then a new squad h_r is selected, again requiring that all the active cops, i.e., those in the frontier, enter in action.

Definition 2. On the Robber and Captain game played on $(\mathcal{H}_1, \mathcal{H}_2)$, a strategy σ is *greedy* if, for any configuration $v_p = (h_p, M_p, C_p)$ in the domain of σ, the next position $\sigma(v_p) = (h_r, M_r)$ is such that $M_r = h_r \cap \mathrm{Fr}(C_p)$, where $h_r = h_p$ if $h_p \cap C_p \neq \emptyset$, and h_r is any squad in $edges(\mathcal{H}_2)$ if $h_p \cap C_p = \emptyset$. □

Given such a greedy way to select cops at each step, observe that the former case ($h_p \cap C_p \neq \emptyset$) may only occur if the Robber is able to come back to some position previously controlled by the Captain. Greedy winning strategies are indeed non-monotone in general, and for some pair of hypergraphs it is possible that there is no monotone winning greedy strategy, although monotone winning strategies (non-greedy) exist. For instance, consider again the hypergraphs $\mathcal{H}_1$ and $\mathcal{H}_2$ shown in Figure 2, and recall that the strategy graph of a monotone winning strategy $\bar{\sigma}$ is depicted in Figure 3. However, the reader can check that there is no monotone greedy strategy in this case.

Now, we can show that, differently from arbitrary strategies, the existence of greedy winning strategies can be decided in polynomial time: Consider the GREEDYWINNINGSTRATEGY algorithm illustrated in Figure 4, which receives as input a configuration (h_p, M_p, C_p) for the Robber and Captain game, plus a "level" i. This algorithm is a high-level specification of an alternating Turing machine, say $\mathcal{M}_G$, which can be simulated by a standard machine in polynomial time.

After the first step, where we check that the number of recursive calls has not exceeded the number of all distinct configurations, the algorithm suddenly evidences its *non-deterministic* nature. Indeed, it guesses a hyperedge h_r corresponding to the next move of the Captain (existential step of $\mathcal{M}_G$). Eventually, it returns TRUE if, and only if, the recursive calls GREEDYWINNINGSTRATEGY$(h_r, M_r, C_r, i+1)$ with $M_r = h_r \cap \mathrm{Fr}(C_p)$ succeed on each $[(h_p, M_p, C_p), M_r]$-option (universal step of $\mathcal{M}_G$).

Theorem 2. *Deciding the existence of a greedy winning strategy in the Robber and Captain game, as well as computing the strategy graph of a greedy winning strategy (if any), is feasible in polynomial time.*

Boolean function GREEDYWINNINGSTRATEGY(h_p, M_p, C_p, i);
/* (h_p, M_p, C_p) is an extended configuration over $(\mathcal{H}_1, \mathcal{H}_2)$,
$i \geq 0$ is a natural number */

1) **if** $i >$ `MaxGreedyStrat`$(\mathcal{H}_1, \mathcal{H}_2)$, then **return** FALSE;
2) **if** $h_p \cap C_p \neq \emptyset$, then **let** $h_r = h_p$;
   else guess a hyperedge $h_r \in edges(\mathcal{H}_2)$;
3) **let** $M_r = h_r \cap \mathrm{Fr}(C_p)$;
4) **for each** $[(h_p, M_p, C_p), M_r]$-option C_r **do**
   if *not* GREEDYWINNINGSTRATEGY$(h_r, M_r, C_r, i+1)$, then **return** FALSE;
5) **return** TRUE;

Fig. 4. GREEDYWINNINGSTRATEGY.

Now, we can show that from *any* (possibly non-monotone) greedy winning strategy a tree projection can be still computed in polynomial time.

Theorem 3. *A tree projection of $\mathcal{H}_1$ w.r.t. $\mathcal{H}_2$ can be computed in polynomial time if the Captain has a greedy winning strategy on $(\mathcal{H}_1, \mathcal{H}_2)$.*

The key ingredient of the proof is that any non-monotone greedy strategy can be converted into a monotone one, though not a greedy one in general; with the resulting strategy, a tree projection can be associated as usual (cf. Theorem1), which we now call *greedy tree projection*. With the above result in place, if $\mathcal{C}_{gtp}$ denotes the class of all pairs $(Q, \mathcal{V})$ such that there exists a greedy winning strategy σ for the Captain in the Robber and Captain game on $(\mathcal{H}_Q, \mathcal{H}_\mathcal{V})$, then we get that $\mathcal{C}_{gtp}$ is an island of tractability.

3 Applications to Decomposition Methods

The tractability result about greedy tree projections can be applied to every structural decomposition method, in order to get new tractable variants of these methods. Indeed, any structural decomposition method `DM` can be viewed as a method associating a set $\mathcal{V}$ of views to any given query Q, and the decompositions of Q according to `DM` are precisely tree projections of $\mathcal{H}_Q$ w.r.t. $\mathcal{H}_\mathcal{V}$. Given this correspondence, it is then natural to consider the greedy variant of any structural decomposition method `DM`, denoted by *greedy*-`DM`, whose associated decompositions are the *greedy* tree projections of $\mathcal{H}_Q$ w.r.t. $\mathcal{H}_\mathcal{V}$. The following is then immediate after Theorem3.

Fact 4 *Let* `DM` *be a structural decomposition method. Then, the class of all queries having a greedy-*`DM` *decomposition is recognizable in polynomial time, and every query in the class may be evaluated in polynomial time over any given database.*

For a notable example, consider the method based on generalized hypertree decompositions. It is well-known that, for $k \geq 1$, the width-k generalized hypertree decompositions of a query Q are the tree projections of $(\mathcal{H}_Q, \mathcal{H}_Q^k)$. Indeed, we are considering one distinct view over each set of variables that can be covered by at most k query-atoms. Then, the width-k *greedy hypertree-decompositions* (we omit "generalized", for short) of Q are the greedy tree projections of $(\mathcal{H}_Q, \mathcal{H}_Q^k)$. Accordingly, the *greedy (generalized) hypertree-width* of Q, denoted by *gr-hw*, is the smallest k such that Q has a greedy hypertree decomposition. In fact, this greedy variant provides a new tractable approximation of the (intractable) notion of generalized hypertree decomposition, which is better than (standard) hypertree decompositions—see also Figure 5.

Corollary 1. *For any query Q, $ghw(Q) \leq gr\text{-}hw(Q) \leq hw(Q)$ holds.*

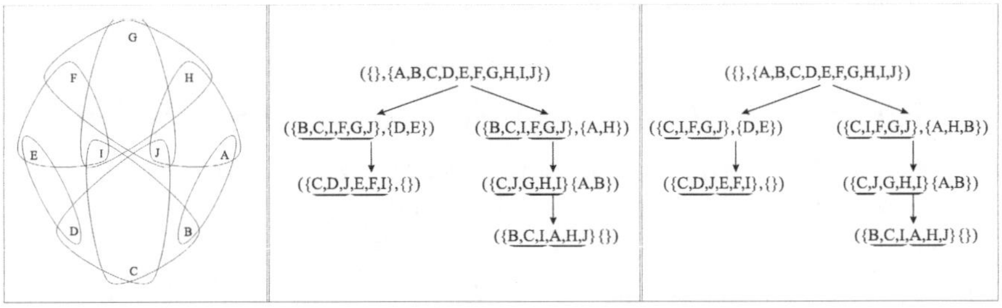

Fig. 5. Example of a query Q for which $gr\text{-}hw(Q) < hw(Q)$.

4 Conclusion

By exploiting a recent game characterization of tree projections, we identified new islands of (structural) tractability based on a greedy version of the powerful non-monotonic strategies in hypergraph games. We are currently working on direct implementations of the proposed techniques in open-source database management systems. In fact, our results find applications in all those problems that can be solved efficiently on acyclic and quasi-acyclic instances, even outside the Database area we focused on. In particular, our results can be exploited immediately for solving Constraint Satisfaction Problems (CSPs) where constraints are represented as finite relations (see, e.g., [4]).

References

1. C. Beeri, R. Fagin, D. Maier, and M. Yannakakis. On the Desirability of Acyclic Database Schemes. *Journal of the ACM*, 30(3), pp. 479–513, 1983.
2. P.A. Bernstein and N. Goodman. The power of natural semijoins. *SIAM Journal on Computing*, 10(4), pp. 751–771, 1981.
3. D. A. Cohen, P. Jeavons, and M. Gyssens. A unified theory of structural tractability for constraint satisfaction problems. *JCSS*, 74(5), pp. 721-743, 2008.
4. G. Gottlob, N. Leone, and F. Scarcello. A Comparison of Structural CSP Decomposition Methods. *Artificial Intelligence*, 124(2), 243–282, 2000.
5. G. Gottlob, N. Leone, and F. Scarcello. Hypertree decompositions and tractable queries. *JCSS*, 64(3), pp. 579–627, 2002.
6. G. Gottlob, N. Leone, and F. Scarcello. Robbers, marshals, and guards: game theoretic and logical characterizations of hypertree width. *JCSS*, 66(4), pp. 775–808, 2003.
7. G. Gottlob, Z. Miklós, and T. Schwentick. Generalized hypertree decompositions: NP-hardness and tractable variants. *Journal of the ACM*, 56(6), 2009.
8. N. Goodman and O. Shmueli. The tree projection theorem and relational query processing. *Journal of Computer and System Sciences*, 29(3), pp. 767–786, 1984.
9. G. Greco and F. Scarcello. Tree projections and structural decomposition methods: Minimality and game-theoretic characterization. *Theoretical Computer Science*, pp. 95-114, 2014.
10. M. Grohe and D. Marx. Constraint solving via fractional edge covers. In *Proc. of SODA '06*, pp. 289–298, 2006.
11. Ph.G. Kolaitis. Constraint Satisfaction, Databases, and Logic. In *Proc. of IJCAI'03*, pp. 1587–1595, 2003.
12. D. Marx. Approximating fractional hypertree width. *ACM Trans. on Algorithms*, 6(2), 2010.
13. D. Marx. Tractable Hypergraph Properties for Constraint Satisfaction and Conjunctive Queries. *Journal of the ACM*, 60(6), 2013.
14. N. Robertson and P.D. Seymour. Graph minors III: Planar tree-width. *Journal of Combinatorial Theory, Series B*, 36, pp. 49–64, 1984.

Enhancing Entity Resolution Efficiency with Loosely Schema-aware Techniques – Discussion Paper –

Giovanni Simonini and Sonia Bergamaschi

Dipartimento di Ingegneria "Enzo Ferrari"
Università di Modena e Reggio Emilia - Italy
firstname.lastname@unimore.it

Abstract. Entity Resolution, the task of identifying records that refer to the same real-world entity, is a fundamental step in data integration. Blocking is a widely employed technique to avoid the comparison of all possible record pairs in a dataset (an inefficient approach). Renouncing to exploit schema information for blocking has been proved to limit the chance of missing matches (i.e., it guarantees high recall), at the cost of a low precision. Meta-blocking alleviates this issue by restructuring a block collection, removing redundant and superfluous comparisons.
Yet, existing meta-blocking techniques exclusively rely on schema-agnostic features. In this paper, we investigate how loose schema information, induced directly from the data, can be exploited in an holistic loosely schema-aware (meta-)blocking approach that outperforms the state-of-the-art meta-blocking in terms of precision, without renouncing high level of recall. We implemented our idea in a system called Blast, and experimentally evaluated it on real-world datasets.

1 Introduction

Entity Resolution (ER), i.e., to identify *entity profiles* (e.g., records of data sources) that refer to the same real-work entity, is a crucial task in data integration. The naive solution, i.e., comparing all possible pairs of records, is an highly inefficient process. *Blockgin* techniques are typically employed to group similar records and limit the actual resolution among those records that appear in the same *blocks* together [4]. To identify blocking criteria (the *blocking keys*) yielding high recall and precision is a difficult and critical task. (For the definition of *recall* and *precision* see Table 1.)
Blocking Background. Blocking techniques relying on schema information (*schema-aware*) often require domain experts to determine good blocking keys, or to have labeled data to train machine algorithms that identify those keys [4, 10]. For example, consider the collection of entity profiles depicted in Figure 1a. A good blocking key may be the concatenation of the first 3 letters of the name and surname. They are directly available as distinct attributes for p_2, and can be extracted splitting the tokens of the attribute `name` for profiles p_1, p_3 and p_4.

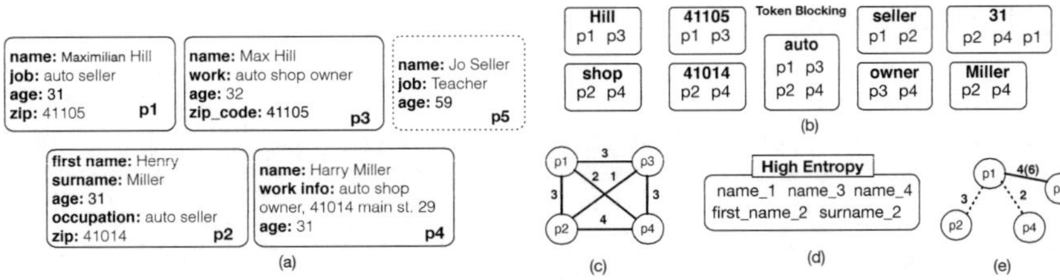

Fig. 1: Blocking example

With this key, the matching pair p_1-p_3 is not indexed; thus, a better blocking key might be the concatenation of the first 3 letters of the surname and the zip code. These techniques require a schema-alignment among the data sources in order to select the blocking key (e.g., a common attribute).

Conversely, techniques that renounce to exploit schema-information (*schema-agnostic*) [11, 13, 10, 12] guarantee high recall in an unsupervised setting, but at the expense of the precision. For instance, in Token Blocking [11] each token appearing in the value of a record is a blocking key, regardless of the attribute in which it appears (example in Figure 1). This allows to minimize the number of false negative due to the mismatches of schema attributes or blocking key extraction. For instance: in the example of Figure 1a, a schema-aware blocking technique might not be able to extract the `zip code` of p_4 from the attribute `work info`, failing to index the pair p_3-p_4, while Token Blocking (Figure 1b) succeeds. Moreover, the schema-agnostic approach has been proved to be the only applicable one to highly heterogeneous and noisy datasets typical of the Web of Data. In fact, with such data, traditional schema-alignment techniques (indispensable for schema-aware blocking) are often inapplicable [9, 11].

Schema-agnostic *meta-blocking* [12, 13, 6] has been proposed to alleviate the efficiency issue of schema-agnostic blocking, aiming to restructure a blocking collection by removing least promising comparisons. Nevertheless, we see significant room for improvement:

Our Approach. We argue that a holistic approach combining blocking, meta-blocking, and *loosely schema-aware* techniques should be attempted. We propose a novel technique to automatically collect significant statistics (e.g. co-occurrences and entropies of values in the attributes) that approximately describe the data sources schemas, and able to exploit such *loose* schema information for both *loosely schema-aware* blocking and meta-blocking. We call it BLAST (Blocking with Loosely-Aware Schema Techniques). In this paper we present the preliminary results achieved by BLAST, demonstrating how it outperforms the state-of-the-art meta-blocking approaches on real datasets.

The reminder of the paper is organized as follows: Section 2 gives the background; Sections 3 presents our approach; Section 4 shows the preliminary experimental results; finally, Section 5 concludes the paper.

2 Preliminaries

Attribute-match Induction. Attribute-match induction, originally introduced in [11] with the *Attribute Clustering* (AC) algorithm, is the task to induce groups of "similar" attributes between two datasets from the distribution of the attribute values, without exploiting the semantic of the attribute names. It differentiates from schema-alignment because its goal is to produce a loose matching among the attributes; in fact its goal is not to identifying semantically matching attributes or hierarchies of properties, but rather produce useful information to support blocking to enhance the precision, without affecting the recall.

Meta-blocking. *Meta-blocking* is the task of restructuring a set of blocks to retain only most promising comparisons [12]. Existing meta-blocking techniques leverage exclusively on schema-agnostic features extracted from the target block collection. *Unsupervised graph-based* meta-blocking [12, 6] represents a block collection as a weighted graph, called *blocking graph* (example in Figure 1c), where each entity profile is a node and an edge exists between two nodes if the corresponding profiles appear at least in one block together. The edges are weighted to capture the likelihood of a match. For instance, in Figure 1c the weight is the number of co-occurrence of profiles in the blocks. Then, an edge pruning threshold is applied to retain only those more promising (Figure 1e). The threshold can be either local and changing for each adjacent edges on a node, or global and unique for all the edges in the graph. The former is typically more expensive to compute, but leads to higher recall than the latter. *Weight-based* thresholds are selected analyzing the weights of the edges; while *Cardinality-based* ones are determined on the basis of a fixed number of edges to be retained. The former generally guarantee higher recall, while the latter are more suitable for applications with time constraints (e.g., running on cloud infrastructures). In all the cases, at the end of the pruning step, each pair of nodes connected by an edge forms a new block. Differently, *supervised graph-based* meta-blocking [13] associates to each edge a vector of schema-agnostic features (e.g. graph topological measures), and treats the problem of identifying promising edge as a *classification* problem. As depending on a labeled training sample, supervised meta-blocking is not always practicable (e.g. it may requires domain experts or crowdsourcing to produce the training sample). Therefore, unsupervised meta-blocking remain a valuable alternative.

3 The Blast Approach

Blast, our novel unsupervised (meta-)blocking approach, consists of the holistic combination of loosely schema-aware blocking and meta-blocking. It is composed of three main steps: (i) the loose schema information extraction, (ii) the blocking, and (iii) the meta-blocking.

Loose Schema Information Extraction In the first step, while an attribute-match induction techniques is employed to obtain information about the attribute similarities, the *entropies* of the attribute values are collected in order to be exploited at a later stage for loosely schema-aware meta-blocking. BLAST can employ as attribute-match induction both AC [11] and LMI[1].

Loosely Schema-aware Blocking. In the second phase, a schema-agnostic blocking is applied in conjunction with an attribute-match induction approach. This allows to disambiguate blocking keys according to the attribute group from which they are derived. For instance, say an entity profile p_5 is added to the collection of Figure 1. If we can disambiguate the token "Seller" (appearing in `name` and `job`), then we avoid two superfluous comparisons (profiles with "Seller" in their names are not indexed together with those that have "Seller" in their job attribute).

Loosely Schema-aware Meta-blocking. In the third phase, meta-blocking is performed exploiting the loose schema information: the blocking graph corresponding to the resulting block collection is generated, weighted taking into account the co-occurrences of the entity profiles and the entropies of the attributes previously computed. In particular, the χ^2 test [5] is employed to measure the strength of co-occurrences. Then, each edge weight is re-weighted according to the *aggregate entropy* associated to it. To give an intuition of the benefits yielded by this latest step, consider the example in in Figure 1 d-e. Without considering the entropies, applying a node-centric pruning (e.g., selecting as weight threshold the average of the local weights) on the p_4 *node-centric* view of the blocking graph (Figure 1e), entails the retention of the non-matching edge (i.e., a superfluous comparison) between p_4 and p_6. A way to avoid this, is to assign increase the score of the edges derived from blocking keys associated to attributes with high entropy. For instance, considering the classification listed in Figure 1d (listing an high entropy attribute cluster), and assigning *bonus* equals to +2 to each edge associated to attributes with high entropy.

Finally, the blocking graph is processed applying a weighted-based threshold. In BLAST, in particular, we combine the described weighting approach to a weighted node-centric pruning (WNP). The alternative would be to select a unique threshold for all the nodes (i.e., *global* and not *node-centric*). WNP is the best choice to yield block collections with high recall [12], while the BLAST loosely schema-aware based wighting focuses on enhancing PQ.

4 Experimental Evaluation

Datasets: For the experimental evaluation we employ established benchmarks [7, 3, 2, 14] composed of real-world datasets with different characteristics and volume. We perform six different comparisons. Each comparison consists of a pair of record sets extracted from on-line data sources of different domain (bibliographic, e-commerce, movies, and general): `ar1` matches article profiles from DBLP (dblp.org) and ACM (dl.acm.org); `ar2` matches article profiles from DBLP and Google Scholar (scholar.google.com); `pr1` matches product profiles

[1] *Loose attribute-Matching Induction* (LMI) is a variation of AC introduced with BLAST; we omit here the description of AC and LMI for sake of brevity, but further details, and the implementation, can be found in the page of the BLAST project [1].

Table 1: Metrics.

$\mathcal{E}$	a collection of entity profiles
$\mathcal{B}$	a block collection for $\mathcal{E}$
$\|\|\mathcal{B}\|\|$	n. of comparisons entailed by $\mathcal{B}$
$\mathcal{D}$	set of duplicate profiles in $\mathcal{E}$
$\mathcal{D}'$	set of duplicate profiles indexed in $\mathcal{B}$
t_o	overhead time
t_r	resolution time

(*recall*) $PC(\mathcal{B})$	$\frac{\|\mathcal{D}'\|}{\|\mathcal{D}\|}$
(*precision*) $PQ(\mathcal{B})$	$\frac{\|\mathcal{D}'\|}{\|\|\mathcal{B}\|\|}$
$\Delta PC(\mathcal{B}, \mathcal{B}')$	$\frac{PC(\mathcal{B})-PC(\mathcal{B}')}{PC(\mathcal{B})}$
$\Delta PQ(\mathcal{B}, \mathcal{B}')$	$\frac{PQ(\mathcal{B})-PQ(\mathcal{B}')}{PQ(\mathcal{B})}$
F_1-score	$2 \cdot \frac{PC(\mathcal{B}') \cdot PQ(\mathcal{B}')}{PC(\mathcal{B}')+PQ(\mathcal{B}')}$

Table 2: Datasets characteristics.

	ar1	ar2	pr1	pr2	mov	dbp
$\mid \mathcal{E}_1 \mid - \mid \mathcal{E}_2 \mid$	$2.6k$–$2.3k$	$2.5k$–$61k$	$1.4k$–$3.0k$	$1.1k$–$1.1k$	$28k$–$23k$	$1.2M$–$2.2M$
n. distinct attr.	4	4	4	4	11	70k
$\|\|\mathcal{B}_{TB}\|\|$	$6.7 \cdot 10^6$	$8.7 \cdot 10^7$	$1.8 \cdot 10^7$	$7.8 \cdot 10^5$	$3.0 \cdot 10^8$	$6.5 \cdot 10^{12}$

from Amazon.com products and Google products (Extracted with the Google Base Data API); `pr2` matches product profiles from Abt.com and Buy.com; `mv` matches movie profiles from IMDB (imdb.com and DBpedia[2]); `dbp` matches entity profiles from two different snapshots of DBpedia (2007 and 2009) – it is important to notice that only the 25% of the name-value pairs is shared among the two snapshots, due to the constant changes in DBpedia, therefore the ER is not trivial. Table 2 lists the characteristics of the datasets. In the first line are listed the number of entity profiles for the two matched data source. In the second line is listed the number of different attributes of the datasources. The third line indicates the number of comparison entailed by the block collection produced with schema-agnostic Token Blocking.

Evaluation Metrics: We evaluate the quality of the produced block collections in terms of precision and recall, through their surrogates *PC* and *PQ* respectively (see Table 1 for all the metrics). PC indicates the number of matching profiles (duplicates) correctly indexed; PC the number the duplicates correctly indexed divided by the number of all the comparison entailed by the collection. Notice that the goal of the evaluation is to assess the quality of the block collection; we are not employing any matching algorithm to perform an actual comparison of the profiles. Therefore, as in [12, 13, 11, 8, 7], we exploit the ground truth of the datasets to determinate is two matching profiles are correctly indexed.

To compare the scalability of the analyzed approaches we consider the overhead time t_o and the resolution time t_r, namely, the time to produce the final block collection and the time to execute the actual comparison respectively. Once the final block collection is built, entity profiles are compared with the Jaccard similarity to assess t_r, as in [12]; even though t_r tightly depends on the technique employed to perform the actual comparison, and its choice is an orthogonal problem not tackled here. In fact, it is important to notice that

[2] dbpedia.org

Table 3: BLAST vs. standard meta-blocking techniques.

	ar1					ar2				
	PC(%)	PQ(%)	F_1	t_o(s)	t_e(s)	PC(%)	PQ(%)	F_1	t_o(s)	t_e(s)
Unsupervised MB	97.30	7.55	0.139	1.52	0.56	96.29	0.41	0.008	2.85	8.18
LMI+Unsupervised MB	97.33	8.39	0.154	0.88	0.35	96.16	0.41	0.008	4.93	4.41
Supervised MB	92.40	49.42	0.644	5.65	0.10	90.30	11.09	0.198	9.09	0.53
BLAST	96.40	31.68	0.477	0.87	0.11	94.06	1.41	0.028	5.51	1.83

	pr1					pr2				
	PC(%)	PQ(%)	F_1	t_o(s)	t_e(s)	PC(%)	PQ(%)	F_1	t_o(s)	t_e(s)
Unsupervised MB	76.07	1.66	0.033	0.76	5.45	78.14	6.48	0.119	0.19	0.19
LMI+Unsupervised MB	89.91	1.77	0.035	1.85	7.95	78.33	6.45	0.119	0.31	0.21
Supervised MB	67.87	39.06	0.495	4.75	0.09	71.55	22.09	0.338	3.35	0.06
BLAST	79.26	7.76	0.142	1.71	0.58	76.30	20.78	0.327	0.28	0.07

	mv					dbp				
	PC(%)	PQ(%)	F_1	t_o(m)	t_e(m)	PC(%)	PQ(%)	F_1	t_o(h)	t_e(h)
Unsupervised MB	96.10	0.33	0.007	1.05	3.90	97.47	0.06	0.001	16	60
LMI+Unsupervised MB	96.41	0.35	0.007	0.95	3.65	98.67	<0.01	<0.001	21	>100
Supervised MB	92.82	4.24	0.081	3.8	0.83	97.30	0.19	0.004	33	39
BLAST	93.37	14.34	0.249	1.3	0.09	96.27	0.83	0.016	51	20

the high t_o of meta-blocking approaches becomes insignificant, when advanced, time-consuming entity matching methods are employed [13].

Our open-source implementation of BLAST [1] is written in `Java 8` as extension[3] of the open source framework presented in [11]. The experiments have been performed under `Ubuntu 14.04`, with 40GB of ram, and `Intel Xeon E5-2670v2` 2.50 GHz.

Results. In Table 3 we present the performance of BLAST compared with traditional meta-blocking. The baseline is Token Blocking in combination with traditional meta-blocking [12] (first line). To demonstrate that traditional meta-blocking cannot fully take advantage of loosely schema-aware blocking, we also compare the naïve combination of LMI and unsupervised meta-blocking (second row). We also compare BLAST against supervised meta-blocking [13], using as training set the 10% of the entity profiles matched in the ground truth (third line). For unsupervised meta-blocking, we choose WNP as pruning schema; PC and PQ are obtained as the average of the PC and PQ values generated with all possible weighting schema of traditional meta-blocking [12].

For supervised meta-blocking we employ WEP schema in combination with Support Vector Machine (SVM), since it is the classification algorithm that, in average, has the best F_1 score. The choice of WEP is due to incompatibility of WNP with supervised meta-blocking, since it always selects a global optimum threshold [13]; nevertheless weight-based pruning remain the best choice to maximize PC.

BLAST needs no configuration. Finally, for all the experiments, Token Blocking is applied in conjunction to block purging [11], a post-processing step that given a block collection remove oversized block, that correspond to highly frequent

[3] github.com/Stravanni/blast

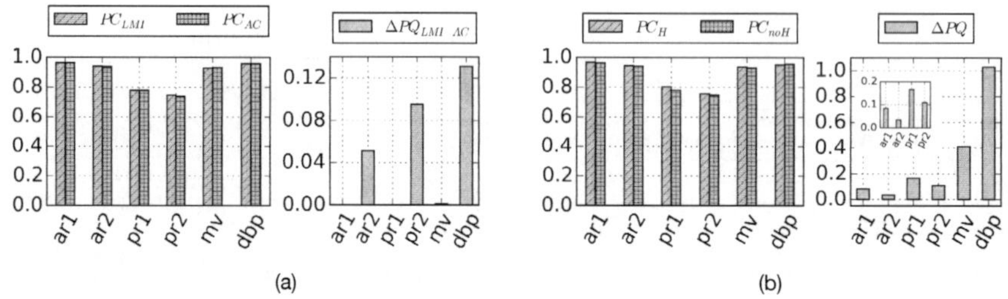

Fig. 2: *PC* comparison and ΔPQ: (a) BLAST with AC vs. BLAST with LMI; (b) BLAST with and without considering cluster entropies.

terms[4]. For all the approaches that require a attribute-match induction phase, t_o includes both the time of LMI (or AC) and Token Blocking.

PC and PQ analysis: Compared to the baseline, BLAST can achieve significantly higher PQ, barely affecting PC. In fact, the $\Delta PC(\mathcal{B}, \mathcal{B}')$ is above -5% for all the datasets; in the case of `pr1` PC is even enhanced. Interestingly, partially mappable comparisons can benefit the most: for `mv` and `dbp` PQ increases of an order of magnitude, with respect to the baseline method, and compared with the supervised meta-blocking, the increase is of 120% and 80% respectively, maintaining almost the same PC.
Another observation is about the inefficacy of LMI as preprocessing step for Token Blocking and meta-blocking (line 2 of Table 3). In fact, for all the comparisons the values of PC and PQ results almost unchanged compared to the baseline. The only exceptions are `pr1`, where PC is significantly increased, and `dbp`, where PC is slightly better than the other techniques, but comes with an extremely low PQ.

Entropy Experiments. The results in Table 3 show how BLAST can actually take full advantage of attribute-match induction techniques. To deeply analize the contribution of the aggregate entropy employed, we compare our technique running BLAST with and without considering the entropy contribution. The result of this comparison is shown in Figure 2b. *PC* remains almost the same, while *PQ* significantly increases for datasets with an high number of attributes, and less markedly for the other ones.

Attribute-match Induction: LMI vs. AC. BLAST supports both LMI (introduced with BLAST, see [1] for details) and AC [11] as attribute-match induction techniques. Figure 2a reports the comparison of BLAST with LMI and BLAST with AC. For the datasets `ar1`, `pr1` and `mv` LMI and AC identify the same clusters, therefore the resulting *PC* and *PQ* are identical; but for the other datasets

[4] This step require a parameter setting to retain blocks; we tune block purging to achieve the best F_1 score for the baseline approach, guaranteeing a $\Delta PC < 3\%$; due to this step results can be slightly different, though not worse, from those presented in [13].

LMI performs better. The reason behind this is that LMI tries to produce cohesive cluster of attributes (i.e., all attribute in the cluster are all highly similar to each other); while AC aims to group together attributes similar to other similar attributes (i.e., each grouped attribute has at least one highly similar attribute in its cluster).

5 Conclusion and Future Work

In this paper, we investigated how *loose schema information*, extracted directly from the data, can be exploited to significantly increase the quality of blocking. In particular we presented our new approach, BLAST, that holistically merge loosely schema-aware blocking and meta-blocking. Experimental results show how BLAST can outperform the state-of-the-art schema-agnostic techniques, without renouncing to the scalability. We released BLAST as open-source, available at [1].

References

1. www.github.com/stravanni/blast.
2. S. Bergamaschi, D. Ferrari, F. Guerra, and G. Simonini. Discovering the topics of a data source: a statistical approach. In *SDSW @ISWC*, 2014.
3. S. Bergamaschi, D. Ferrari, F. Guerra, G. Simonini, and Y. Velegrakis. A statistical approach for discovering the topics of a data source. In *Journal of Data Semantics.*
4. P. Christen. A survey of indexing techniques for scalable record linkage and deduplication. *IEEE TKDE*, 24(9):1537–1555, 2012.
5. T. Dunning. Accurate methods for the statistics of surprise and coincidence. *Computational Linguistics*, 19(1):61–74, 1993.
6. V. Efthymiou, G. Papadakis, G. Papastefanatos, K. Stefanidis, and T. Palpanas. Parallel meta-blocking: Realizing scalable entity resolution over large, heterogeneous data. In *2015 IEEE Big Data 2015.*
7. H. Köpcke, A. Thor, and E. Rahm. Evaluation of entity resolution approaches on real-world match problems. *PVLDB*, 3(1):484–493, 2010.
8. Y. Ma and T. Tran. Typimatch: type-specific unsupervised learning of keys and key values for heterogeneous web data integration. In *Sixth ACM WSDM 2013.*
9. J. Madhavan, S. Cohen, X. L. Dong, A. Y. Halevy, S. R. Jeffery, D. Ko, and C. Yu. Web-scale data integration: You can afford to pay as you go. In *CIDR 2007.*
10. G. Papadakis, G. Alexiou, G. Papastefanatos, and G. Koutrika. Schema-agnostic vs schema-based configurations for blocking methods on homogeneous data. *PVLDB*, 9(4):312–323, 2015.
11. G. Papadakis, E. Ioannou, T. Palpanas, C. Niederée, and W. Nejdl. A blocking framework for entity resolution in highly heterogeneous information spaces. *IEEE TKDE*, 25(12):2665–2682, 2013.
12. G. Papadakis, G. Koutrika, T. Palpanas, and W. Nejdl. Meta-blocking: Taking entity resolutionto the next level. *IEEE TKDE*, 26(8):1946–1960, 2014.
13. G. Papadakis, G. Papastefanatos, and G. Koutrika. Supervised meta-blocking. *PVLDB*, 7(14):1929–1940, 2014.
14. G. Simonini and S. Zhu. Big data exploration with faceted browsing. In *2015 International Conference on High Performance Computing & Simulation, HPCS 2015, Amsterdam, Netherlands, July 20-24, 2015*, pages 541–544, 2015.

Patient wellness: geoanalysis of biological and environmental data
Extended Abstract

Giovanni Canino †, Pietro H Guzzi †, Mariagrazia Scarpino †, Giuseppe Tradigo ‡, Pierangelo Veltri †.

†University of Catanzaro,
Department of Medical and Surgical Sciences
canino,scarpino,hguzzi,veltri@unicz.it
‡DIMES, University of Calabria
tradigo@dimes.unical.it

Abstract. Citizens' health status is usually stored in clinical records (a.k.a. Electronic Medical Records, EMRs) storing data related to hospitalization. More recently, EMRs have been extended to store also wellness data (e.g. fitness, blood analysis, lifestyle) filling larger time windows on the stay in clinical structures. Thus, EMRs are electronic citizen health records which may host information regarding lifestyle, activities, habits, environment (e.g. water sources, air quality) as well as routine health screening. Data production increased dramatically with personal smart devices (e.g. smartphones and sensors) and the cloud. These data can often be related to a geographic context. We report the design, development, and testing of a geo-based web system storing and analyzing biological data with a geographic information system. We use clinical anonymized data extracted from a biological department of University Magna Graecia Hospital. We show that, by associating geographic operators to statistical methods, the analysis of health and environmental data may improve citizen habits and wellness. [1]

1 Introduction

Clinical records (also known as electronic medical records or EMRs) are the collection point for information relating citizens health. Formally, EMR is a systematic collection of electronic health information about individual patients or populations [1]. Thus, from a computer science perspective, an EMR is a record storing data about patients able to improve patient-data sharing among healthcare providers.

Data stored into EMRs usually contain a broad range of data going from personal (e.g. demographic data, personal history of patients) to clinical (e.g. laboratory analyses results, medical images, healthcare insurances). Data is mainly generated by doctors, health specialists and by instruments [2]. Patients may

[1] An extended version of this paper has been submitted to ICCS 2016 conference

as well interact with clinical health records and produce data. For instance, in [23] Patient Clinical Information System (PatCIS) interfaces with the clinical data repository at New York Presbyterian Hospital (NYPH) and allows patients to add information on their medical records. More recently, there is growing interest in extended EMRs, storing health data as well as wellness related information [3]. Wellness is a broader context representing patients' health status and healthcare providers attention grows in taking care of it.

Consequently, health data regards not only the (usually limited) hospitalization period, i.e. the period spent by patients in a health structure, but larger time windows in which the citizen's *wellness* status is being monitoring. We recently participated in a research project, funded by the European community, focused on patient records enrichment by mean of personal habits and environmental information in what we call *e*lectronic citizen health records (ECHR).

Examples of data related to wellness are: life style activities, (e.g., time spent in sports activities), habits (e.g. smoking or non smoking, good alimentary habits), environments (e.g., water sources or air quality). Consequently such set of heterogeneous data may be stored in an extension of the classical EMRs defined as *e*lectronic citizen health record. The production of such wellness-related data has been significantly improved by the rise of smart personal technological devices coupled with smartphones as well as data produced by devices (internet of things data). After their production, the collection of data has been enabled by the development of high performance and distributed databases based on cloud infrastructure.

Gathering and storing data from available devices allow monitoring the health status as well as information coming from the environment. For example, [22] developed an application for mobile devices to acquire vocal signal, calculates the fundamental frequency and thus monitoring voice health status.

The generation and availability of data got the interest of scientific community through the application of advanced data analysis framework to study habits and phenomenon from a novel perspective [4]. In this scenario, an interesting trend is represented by reading healthy related data through a geographic lens. The interest is currently through epidemiological patterns or in pathology studies.

Despite this, there is a lack of experiences about using geographic information as pivot element for reading information from different data sources. Reading information from clinical data, from environmental data as well as from behavior related data can help in furnishing useful information.

The idea is to define a framework for the integration of clinical, environment, health and wellness data. We designed Geoblood, a system able to store and analyze biological data. It is based on a web infrastructure and the use of geographical information. We tested the system in collaboration with the University Magna Græcia hospital.

2 Related Work

EMR data can be used for conducting extensive research studies in the medical, biomedical or epidemiological research fields [6], including epidemiological investigations to determine associations between exposure and disease, health services research involving patient outcomes and observational comparative effectiveness studies to weight the effectiveness of one therapy against another. For example, the values of EMR data on child birth date, visit date, sex, height, and weight can be used to provide information on patient BMI or to identify the prevalence of pediatric obesity in a given population. There exist many data extraction techniques, one of which is pattern matching, which aims in searching known or common patterns (e.g. text strings, dictionary entries) in a data corpus.

Other approaches involve the analysis of the surface of a language. The latter present some problems because, considering the English for instance, *general English* is different from *medical English* and, therefore, models need to be adapted to correctly retrieve the desired information contents. The disadvantage of this approach is its limited portability to new domains. The ontology-driven approach uses an ontology to extract information from free text, thus combining syntax and semantics. Machine learning techniques gained remarkable consensus in the clinical field but have proven to be very expensive both regarding economy and time. Many research efforts have been done in recent years providing standard knowledge representations to create semantic information systems for health care. Excellent results have been achieved as Unified Medical Language System medical ontologies (UMLS),[7].

The MedLEE, for instance, has been used to extract codes in the field of neuroradiology and to extract SNOMED codes [8]. Medication data, in electronic medical records, is often recorded in clinical notes as free-text.

Many studies describe the relation of health information with geographic data. In [18], a study on HIV care in Rural Rwanda is presented. In [19] clinical data, in particular, ICD-10 codes that identifies the disease, are used to determine correlations between the different diseases, patient stratification and how it can be mapped to the underlying systems biology revealing possible causes for the observed correlations. Demographic information and co-morbidities extracted from EMRs of asthma patients can be used to create a predictive model of COPD. In this model, it has been demonstrated that age, sex, race, smoking history, and eight co-morbidities modulate the risk of COPD[21].

3 System Architecture

Figure 1 reports the web-based architecture of GeoBlood. Blood Panel is the module deputed to the interface with the user and communicates with the back-end server through a secure socket. The back end is constituted by two cloud databases storing clinical information (EMRs datasets), hospital information (DRGs Datasets) and geographic information.

The web system has been implemented using the following technologies: PHP Server Side Language, MySQL as the database management system (DBMS),

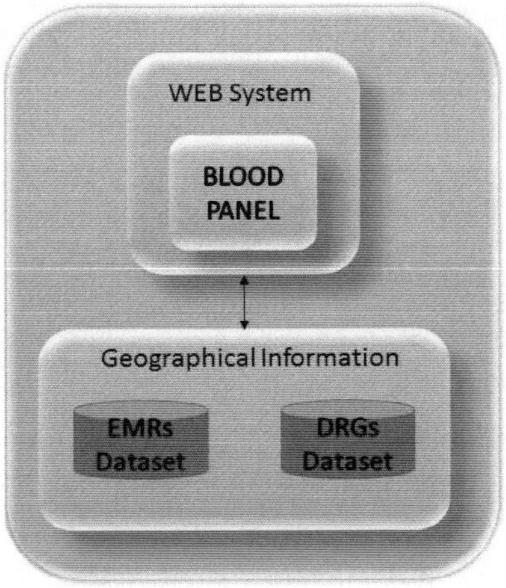

Fig. 1. Functional architecture

Javascript, JQuery client-side language, Twitter Bootstrap framework as the front-end. The PHP5 scripting language has been used for the implementation of the server-side scripts. Moreover, the system is structured according to the MVC design pattern (Model View Controller). In particular, the PDO (PHP Data Objects) extension has been used as the sole interface to access the database. JQuery has been used for client-side scripts (i.e. auto-completion, managing Ajax requests, dynamic manipulation of Domain Object Model). To implement the system front-end, we decided to use the Bootstrap framework, which facilitates the development and maintenance of websites by offering ready-to-use Responsive Web Designs primitives. Finally, an import/export interface has been implemented to import daily analytes from medical laboratories as well as to export analytes anonymized from personal data.

Thanks to a web interface, users can access and analyze biological analytes data, navigate through them by using statistics and export relevant data.By using the system, biologists and physicians can have a more precise idea of: (*i*) how analytes change over time in a single patient, and (*ii*) what are the statistics of blood values by sex and age.Furthermore, geographic data can be used to map results into a geographic readable format.

4 Case Study

This section describes a case study related the analysis of a real dataset of the University Hospital using Geoblood. After the description of the dataset, we report main steps required to analyze data and finally we show some example queries. A web-based system has been implemented which allows biologists and physicians to access data and perform statistics both on analytes, as well as

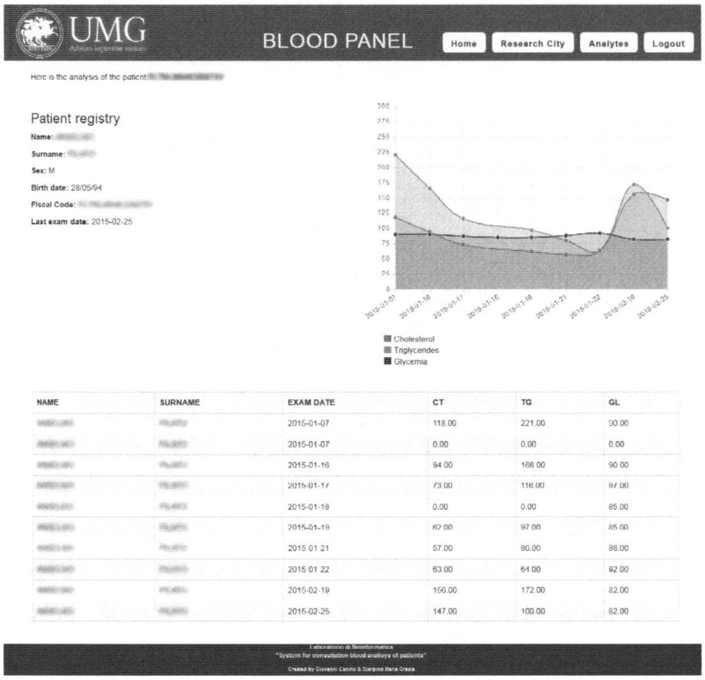

Fig. 2. GUI of Geoblood showing the trend of the analytes of a patient over a given time window.

on specific patients information. The web system has been implemented using Java, MySQL as the DBMS and JQuery as the client-side language (i.e. auto-completion, managing Ajax requests, dynamic manipulation of Domain Object Model) Moreover, the system is structured according to the MVC design pattern (Model View Controller). An I/O module has been implemented to import daily analytes from medical laboratories as well as to export analytes anonymized from personal data.

We used two datasets of EMRs and DRG data:
(*i*) A dataset containing EMRs of patients. The EMRs dataset has been used as a reference model to identify average values and normal distribution of blood analytes (patient-anonymized) in the region of interest;
(*ii*) A dataset containing information about citizens, such as demographic data, personal history of patients (e.g. medication, immunization, results of laboratory test), medical images, as well as information about insurances (by healthcare system). Dismissing diagnosis are mapped into a category code, each including classes of pathologies. Consequently, data are heterogeneous regarding formats (textual, images, time-series, biomedical signals) and representations.

For each patient, in our dataset we have blood analysis and information disease and geographical.

For this test, we used analytes related to blood analysis of 2015, for which we have 20000 tests, of which 9735 unique patients (for some of them more than one blood test is present). Analyses contain 120 analytes, selected by the physician (usually we have 10 or 15 analytes for each blood test). To create the dataset, we anonymized patient information and assigned each patient a unique code.

The DRGs dataset contains 9375 tuples, each identifying a patient. The dataset schema contains: patient code, geographical information, MDC, hospitalized time, code diagnosis and surgical operation code. Geographical information is in text format (address, zip code, city) and we created a software module which converts it in latitude and longitude.

Thanks to a web interface, users can access biological analytes data, analyze them, visualize statistics and export relevant data in some formats. By using the system it is possible to study (*i*) how analytes change over time in a single patient, and (*ii*) what are the statistics of blood values by sex and age. For example, one of our case studies has been extracting patient analytes like Cholesterol CT, Triglycerides TG and Glycemia GL to verify and understand the evolution of data value in patient hospitalization. An example of the result is reported in Figure 2.

The Geoblood system allows to map blood analysis information and correlate diseases with geographic features. Geo data is mapped in standard WGS84 latitude and longitude format. Figure 3 depicts an example of areas with higher concentration of TSH value (Hyperthyroidism patients).

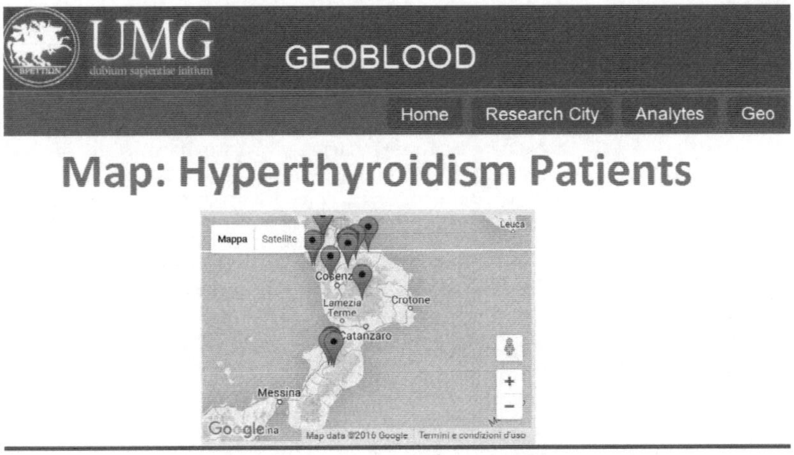

Fig. 3. Geoblood result of an analysis on the map.

5 Conclusion

The paper presented Geoblood, a web-based system able to store and analyze biological data from a geographical perspective. It is based on a web infrastructure and on the use of geographical information. We tested the system in a collaboration with the University Magna Græcia hospital that shared clinical data about patients. After the anonymization of data, we provided geographical information as well as habits of each patient. We demonstrated that it is possible to extract it is possible to extract and produce useful information. In the future we will design algorithms to extract relevant knowledge from available datasets.

Acknowledgment

This paper has been partially funded by regional funds of PIA GIDAH project.

References

1. Gunter, T. D., Terry, N. P. (2005). The emergence of national electronic health record architectures in the United States and Australia: models, costs, and questions. Journal of Medical Internet Research, 7(1), e3.
2. Yang, C. C., Veltri, P. (2015). Intelligent healthcare informatics in big data era. Artificial intelligence in medicine, 65(2), 75-77.
3. Macri, M., Mastratisi, M. A., Mirarchi, D., De Francesco, E., Granata, L., Tradigo, G., Veltri, P. (2015, October). LiSE: a personal booklet for Health care annotation. In Healthcare Informatics (ICHI), 2015 International Conference on (pp. 362-367). IEEE.
4. Vizza, P., Curcio, A., Tradigo, G., Indolfi, C., Veltri, P. (2015). A framework for the atrial fibrillation prediction in electrophysiological studies. Computer methods and programs in biomedicine, 120(2), 65-76.
5. Roque, F. S., Jensen, P. B., Schmock, H., Dalgaard, M., Andreatta, M., Hansen, T., Jensen, L. J. (2011). Using electronic patient records to discover disease correlations and stratify patient cohorts. PLoS Comput Biol, 7(8), e1002141.
6. Verde, L., De Pietro, G., Veltri, P., Sannino, G. (2015, June). An m-health system for the estimation of voice disorders. In Multimedia Expo Workshops (ICMEW), 2015 IEEE International Conference on (pp. 1-6). IEEE.
7. Bodenreider, O. (2004). The unified medical language system (UMLS): integrating biomedical terminology. Nucleic acids research, 32(suppl 1), D267-D270.
8. Meystre, S. M., Savova, G. K., Kipper-Schuler, K. C., Hurdle, J. F. (2008). Extracting information from textual documents in the electronic health record: a review of recent research. Yearb Med Inform, 35, 128-44.
9. Xu, H., Stenner, S. P., Doan, S., Johnson, K. B., Waitman, L. R., Denny, J. C. (2010). MedEx: a medication information extraction system for clinical narratives. Journal of the American Medical Informatics Association, 17(1), 19-24.
10. Savova, G., Kipper-Schuler, K., Buntrock, J., Chute, C. (2008). UIMA-based clinical information extraction system. Towards enhanced interoperability for large HLT systems: UIMA for NLP, 39.

11. Savova, G. K., Masanz, J. J., Ogren, P. V., Zheng, J., Sohn, S., Kipper-Schuler, K. C., Chute, C. G. (2010). Mayo clinical Text Analysis and Knowledge Extraction System (cTAKES): architecture, component evaluation and applications. Journal of the American Medical Informatics Association, 17(5), 507-513.
12. Pakhomov, S., Weston, S. A., Jacobsen, S. J., Chute, C. G., Meverden, R.,Roger, V. L. (2007). Electronic medical records for clinical research: application to the identification of heart failure. American Journal of Managed Care, 13(6), 281-289.
13. Pollard, C., Bailey, K. A., Petitte, T., Baus, A., Swim, M., Hendryx, M. (2009). Electronic patient registries improve diabetes care and clinical outcomes in rural community health centers. The Journal of Rural Health, 25(1), 77-84.
14. Brownstein, J. S., Murphy, S. N., Goldfine, A. B., Grant, R. W., Sordo, M., Gainer, V., Kohane, I. S. (2010). Rapid identification of myocardial infarction risk associated with diabetes medications using electronic medical records. Diabetes care, 33(3), 526-531.
15. Feldstein, A., Elmer, P. J., Smith, D. H., Herson, M., Orwoll, E., Chen, C., Swain, M. C. (2006). Electronic medical record reminder improves osteoporosis management after a fracture: a randomized, controlled trial. Journal of the American Geriatrics Society, 54(3), 450-457.
16. Kho, A. N., Pacheco, J. A., Peissig, P. L., Rasmussen, L., Newton, K. M., Weston, N., Kullo, I. J. (2011). Electronic medical records for genetic research: results of the eMERGE consortium. Science translational medicine, 3(79), 79re1-79re1.
17. Kullo, I. J., Ding, K., Jouni, H., Smith, C. Y., Chute, C. G. (2010). A genome-wide association study of red blood cell traits using the electronic medical record. PloS one, 5(9), e13011.
18. Amoroso, C. L., Akimana, B., Wise, B., Fraser, H. S. (2010). Using electronic medical records for HIV care in rural Rwanda. Stud Health Technol Inform, 160(Pt 1), 337-341.
19. Roque, F. S., Jensen, P. B., Schmock, H., Dalgaard, M., Andreatta, M., Hansen, T., Jensen, L. J. (2011). Using electronic patient records to discover disease correlations and stratify patient cohorts. PLoS Comput Biol, 7(8), e1002141.
20. Geraghty, E. M., Balsbaugh, T., Nuovo, J., Tandon, S. (2010). Using Geographic Information Systems (GIS) to assess outcome disparities in patients with type 2 diabetes and hyperlipidemia. The Journal of the American Board of Family Medicine, 23(1), 88-96.
21. Himes, B. E., Dai, Y., Kohane, I. S., Weiss, S. T., Ramoni, M. F. (2009). Prediction of chronic obstructive pulmonary disease (COPD) in asthma patients using electronic medical records. Journal of the American Medical Informatics Association, 16(3), 371-379.
22. Verde, L., De Pietro, G., Veltri, P., Sannino, G. (2015, June). An m-health system for the estimation of voice disorders. In Multimedia Expo Workshops (ICMEW), 2015 IEEE International Conference on (pp. 1-6). IEEE.
23. Cimino, J. J., Patel, V. L., Kushniruk, A. W. (2002). The patient clinical information system (PatCIS): technical solutions for and experience with giving patients access to their electronic medical records. International journal of medical informatics, 68(1), 113-127.

Fast Access to XML Data: A Set-Based Approach*

Nicola Ferro and Gianmaria Silvello

Department of Information Engineering, University of Padua, Italy
silvello@dei.unipd.it

Abstract. XML is a pervasive technology for representing and accessing semi-structured data. XPath is the standard language for navigational queries on XML documents and there is a growing demand for its efficient processing.
In order to increase the efficiency in executing four navigational XML query primitives, namely descendants, ancestors, children and parent, we introduce a new paradigm where traditional approaches based on the efficient traversing of nodes and edges to reconstruct the requested subtrees are replaced by a brand new one based on basic set operations which allow us to directly return the desired subtree, avoiding to create it passing through nodes and edges.
Our solution stems from the *NEsted SeTs for Object hieRarchies (NESTOR)* formal model, which makes use of set-inclusion relations for representing and providing access to hierarchical data. We define in-memory efficient data structures to implement NESTOR, we develop algorithms to perform the descendants, ancestors, children and parent query primitives and we study their computational complexity.

1 Introduction

The *eXtensible Markup Language (XML)* is the standard technology for semi-structured data representation, processing, and exchange and it has been widely used and studied in several fields of computer science, such as databases, information retrieval, digital libraries, and the Web.

An XML document is a hierarchy which contains elements nested one inside another and it is naturally modeled as a tree, where elements are nodes and parent-child relations are edges among them. When it comes to process and access XML, fundamental operations rely on the retrieval of a subset of the XML nodes or the data contained in them by satisfying path constraints which are typically expressed in the *XML Path Language (XPath)* [6].

In this paper we propose a paradigm shift for XPath querying by departing from the above mentioned navigational-like approaches and introducing a brand new one, relying on basic set operations. Instead of using edges between nodes or adjacency matrices for representing a tree, we represent a hierarchy as a family

* Extended Abstract [5]

of nested sets where the inclusion relationship among sets allows us to express parent/child relations and each set contains the elements belonging to a specific sub-hierarchy. In this way, rather than navigating in a tree and reconstructing sub-hierarchies by traversing nodes and edges, we answer queries by serving the correct subset(s) which already contain all the requested elements (sub-hierarchy) just in one shot or may request minimal intersection/union operations to obtain the desired elements, thus avoiding the need to collect them one-by-one as it happens in the other approaches. This method provides a sizeable improvement in the time requested for answering a navigational query and it is competitive in terms of space occupation and pre-processing time.

More in detail, the proposed solution is based on the *NEsted SeTs for Object hieRarchies (NESTOR)* formal model [4] which is an alternative way, based on the notion of set-inclusion, for representing and dealing with hierarchical data, as XML is. Since XPath supports a number of powerful modalities and many applications do not need to use the full language but exploit only some fragments, we focused this work only on those XPath fragments which, according to [2]: (i) support both *downward* and *upward* navigation; (ii) are *recursive*, thus allowing navigation also along the ancestor and descendant axes and not only parent and child axes; and (iii) are *non-qualified*, i.e. without predicates testing properties of another expression. Therefore, we focus on efficient in-memory execution of four kinds of navigational queries over hierarchical data – *descendants*, *ancestors*, *children*, and *parent* of a given element – which represent a basic means for accessing and retrieving data from XML.

We present three alternative in-memory dictionary-based data structures instantiating the NESTOR model: *Direct Data Structure (DDS)*, *Inverse Data Structure (IDS)*, and *Hybrid Data Structure (HDS)*. For each query primitive we have two different modalities: the *set-wise modality* where we access the structure of the XML tree and the *element-wise modality* where we access the content of the XML tree. These data structures are defined with no assumption on document characteristics and underlying physical storage and they could be employed by any existing solutions for speeding-up XPath primitives execution. For each data structure and modality, we define algorithms for performing the *descendants*, *ancestors*, *children*, and *parent* operations and we study their computational complexity.

We compare the four target query primitives against state-of-the-art in-memory implementations of XPath – three java-based solutions (i.e., Xalan, Jaxen and JXPath) based on in-memory DOM navigation and a highly-efficient native XML database management system based on node labeling (i.e., BaseX)– in order to assess the benefits in terms of faster execution times.

The experimental findings show that the NESTOR-based data structures and query primitives consistently outperform state-of-the-art XPath solutions at query time and are competitive also from the pre-processing time and main memory occupation viewpoints. From the results achieved the set-based approach proves to be highly efficient and can represent a valid alternative to tree navigation for fast XML querying.

2 Background

The NESTOR model is defined by two set-based data models: The *Nested Set Model (NS-M)* and the *Inverse Set Data Model (INS-M)*. These models are defined in the context of set theory as a collection of subsets, their properties are formally proved as well as their equivalence to the tree in terms of expressive power [3,4,1].

The most intuitive way to understand how these models work is to relate them to the tree. In Figure 1b we can see how a sample XML snippet can be represented through a tree and how this tree can be mapped into the NS-M and the INS-M. The XML elements are represented by nodes in the tree and by sets in the NS-M and the INS-M; the text data within each XML node are represented as lists of elements within each tree node and as elements belonging to sets in the NS-M and the INS-M.

In the NS-M each node of the tree is mapped into a set, where child nodes become *proper subsets* of the set created from the parent node. Every set is subset of at least of one set; the set corresponding to the tree root is the only set without any supersets and every set in the hierarchy is subset of the root set. The external nodes are sets with no subsets. The tree structure is maintained thanks to the nested organization and the relationships between the sets are expressed by the set inclusion order. Even the disjunction between two sets brings information; indeed, the disjunction of two sets means that these belong to two different branches of the same tree.

The second data model is the INS-M and we can see that each node of the tree is mapped into a set, where each parent node becomes a subset of the sets created from its children. The set created from the tree's root is the only set with no subsets and the root set is a proper subset of all the sets in the hierarchy. The leaves are the sets with no supersets and they are sets containing all the sets created from the nodes composing tree path from a leaf to the root. An important aspect of INS-M is that the intersection of every couple of sets obtained from two nodes is always a set representing a node in the tree. The intersection of all the sets in the INS-M is the set mapped from the root of the tree.

3 Data Structures and Primitives for Fast XML Access

Let us consider a collection of subsets $\mathcal{C}$ which can be defined according to the NS-M as well as the INS-M – refer to Figure 1 for a graphical example. The data structures for producing $\mathcal{C}$ have to take into account the structural and the content components of such a collection of subsets. From the structural point-of-view, the information that has to be stored regards the inclusion dependencies between the sets; whereas, from the content point-of-view, we need to store the materialization of the sets (i.e. the elements belonging to each set).

For a collection of subsets $\mathcal{C}$ we consider the following three main dictionaries:

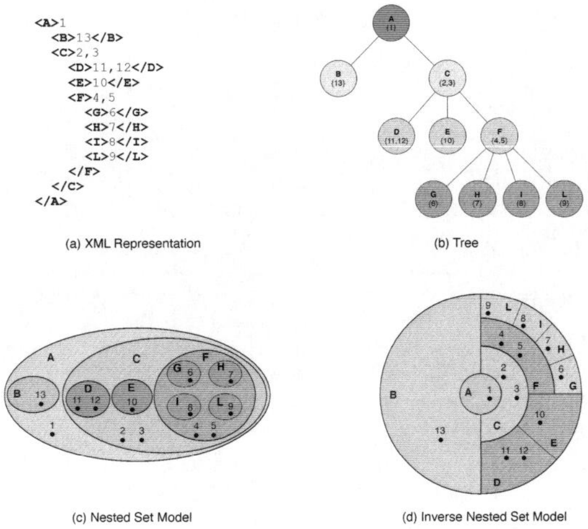

Fig. 1. (a) A sample XML representation; (b) Tree representation of the XML; (c) NS-M representation; (d) INS-M representation.

- **Materialized Dictionary** (MD), containing the materialization of the sets in $\mathcal{C}$.
- **Direct-Subsets Dictionary** (DD), containing the direct subsets of each set in $\mathcal{C}$.
- **Supersets Dictionary** (SD), containing the supersets of each set in $\mathcal{C}$.

These three dictionaries are employed in all the three proposed data structures – i.e. *Direct Data Structure (DDS)*, *Inverse Data Structure (IDS)* and *Hybrid Data Structure (HDS)*. DDS is a structure built around the constraints defined by the NS-M as depicted in Figure 2a. If we consider the tree shown in Figure 1a and modeled with the NS-M reported in Figure 1b, we can see that the materialized sets (MD) report the integer values corresponding to all the elements belonging to each set; we know that in the NS-M the set corresponding to the root of the tree contains all the elements of the tree. Indeed, we can see in Figure 2a that A contains all the elements in the collection. Furthermore, for each set, DD contains all its direct subsets – e.g. set C contains the sets D, E, F which are its direct subsets as shown in Figure 1b. SD contains the supersets of each set – e.g. D contains the sets C, A.

IDS is a structure built around the constraints of INS-M as reported in Figure 2b. In this case we can see that the materialized sets MD contain the elements belonging to the sets. As we can see in the DDS the set cardinality in MD decreases while going from the top – i.e. set A – to the bottom – i.e. sets G, H, I, L – whereas in IDS the cardinality increases. Furthermore, for each entry in DD there is just one set; indeed, in the INS-M each set has at most one direct subset with the sole exception of the set representing the root of the tree which has no subsets.

MD	DD	SD
A [1,2,3,4,5,6,7,8,9,10,11,12,13]	A [B,C]	A []
B [13]	B []	B [A]
C [2,3,4,5,6,7,8,9,10,11,12]	C [D,E,F]	C [A]
D [11,12]	D []	D [C,A]
E [10]	E []	E [C,A]
F [4,5,6,7,8,9]	F [G,H,I,L]	F [C,A]
G [6]	G []	G [F,C,A]
H [7]	H []	H [F,C,A]
I [8]	I []	I [F,C,A]
L [9]	L []	L [F,C,A]

(a) The dictionary-based Direct Data Structure (DDS)

MD	DD	SD
A [1]	A []	A [B,C,D,E,F,G,H,I,L]
B [1,13]	B [A]	B []
C [1,2,3]	C [A]	C [D,E,F,G,H,I,L]
D [1,2,3,11,12]	D [C]	D []
E [1,2,3,10]	E [C]	E []
F [1,2,3,4,5]	F [C]	F [G,H,I,L]
G [1,2,3,4,5,6]	G [F]	G []
H [1,2,3,4,5,7]	H [F]	H []
I [1,2,3,4,5,8]	I [F]	I []
L [1,2,3,4,5,9]	L [F]	L []

(b) The dictionary-based Inverse Data Structure (IDS)

MD	DD	SD
A [1]	A [B,C]	A []
B [13]	B []	B [A]
C [2,3]	C [D,E,F]	C [A]
D [11,12]	D []	D [C]
E [10]	E []	E [C]
F [4,5]	F [G,H,I,L]	F [C]
G [6]	G []	G [F]
H [7]	H []	H [F]
I [8]	I []	I [F]
L [9]	L []	L [F]

(c) The dictionary-based Hybrid Data Structure (HDS)

Fig. 2. NESTOR data structure instances of the tree shown in Figure 1.

`SD` reports for each set all its supersets – e.g. `F` contains `G`, `H`, `I`, `L` which are its supersets as shown in Figure 1c.

HDS can be seen as a mixture between DDS and IDS; indeed, its `DD` corresponds to the `DD` dictionary of DDS and its `SD` corresponds to the `DD` of IDS. Each set in `MD` is the result of the set difference between a set and its direct superset in the `MD` of IDS – e.g. in the `MD` of IDS the set $\texttt{A} = [\texttt{1}]$ is the direct superset of $\texttt{C} = [\texttt{1}, \texttt{2}, \texttt{3}]$, thus in the `MD` of HDS it is $\texttt{C} = [2, 3]$.

3.1 NESTOR Primitives

When we deal with a collection of sets defined by the NESTOR model, we can distinguish between *set-wise* and *element-wise* primitives. As above, let us consider a general collection of sets $\mathcal{C}$ with a total number of $m \in \mathbb{N}$ sets, $n \in \mathbb{N}$ elements and where H is a set in the collection; then in the NESTOR model we define five set-wise primitives, and six element-wise primitives. In the following we add the suffix DDS, IDS or HDS to the name of the primitives when we refer to a specific data structure implementation of that primitive – e.g. the descendant primitive is indicated as DESCENDANTS-DDS when we refer to its DDS

Table 1. Set-wise primitives and their computational complexities where m is the total number of sets in the collection of subsets.

Set-wise Primitive Algorithms			
	DDS	**IDS**	**HDS**
	Cost	Cost	Cost
Descendants(H)	$O(m)$	$O(1)$	$O(m)$
Ancestors(H)	$O(1)$	$O(m)$	$O(m)$
Children(H)	$O(1)$	$O(m)$	$O(1)$
Parent(H)	$O(1)$	$O(1)$	$O(1)$

Table 2. Element-wise primitives and their computational complexities where m is the total number of sets and n is the total number of elements in the collection of subsets.

Element-wise Primitive Algorithms			
	DDS	**IDS**	**HDS**
	Cost	Cost	Cost
Elements(H)	$O(1)$	$O(1)$	$O(1)$
Descendants(H)	$O(1)$	$O(m+n)$	$O(m+n)$
Ancestors(H)	$O(m+n)$	$O(1)$	$O(m+n)$
Childrens(H)	$O(n)$	$O(m+n)$	$O(n)$
Parent(H)	$O(n)$	$O(n)$	$O(1)$

implementation, as DESCENDANTS-IDS when we refer to its IDS implementation and as DESCENDANTS-HDS when we refer to its HDS implementation.

In Table 1 we present the computational complexity of the algorithms implementing the set-wise primitives in the three data structures.

In Table 2 we present the references to the algorithms implementing the element-wise primitives in the DDS, IDS and HDS along with their computational complexities.

4 Experiments

NESTOR query primitives on the three proposed in-memory data structures have been implemented in the Java programming language[1]. As anticipated in Section 2, we compare NESTOR against the Xalan 2.7.1, Jaxen 1.1.6, and JX-path 1.3 libraries and the BaseX 7.9 in-memory XML database. The analysis was conducted by choosing the worst possible input set for each primitive, thus if a query performs well in this case it is guaranteed that it performs in the same way or better in the other cases.

Table 3 reports the statistics about the two synthetic datasets we selected for the experiments.

In Figure 3 we report the evaluation times for the XPath operations we are analysing.

As a summary, as general trends we see that NESTOR data structures always outperform the other solutions, even if the specific data structure – DDS, IDS, HDS – may change from case to case. The second best approach is almost always BaseX followed by either Jaxen or JXPath, depending on the cases.

[1] `http://nestor.dei.unipd.it`

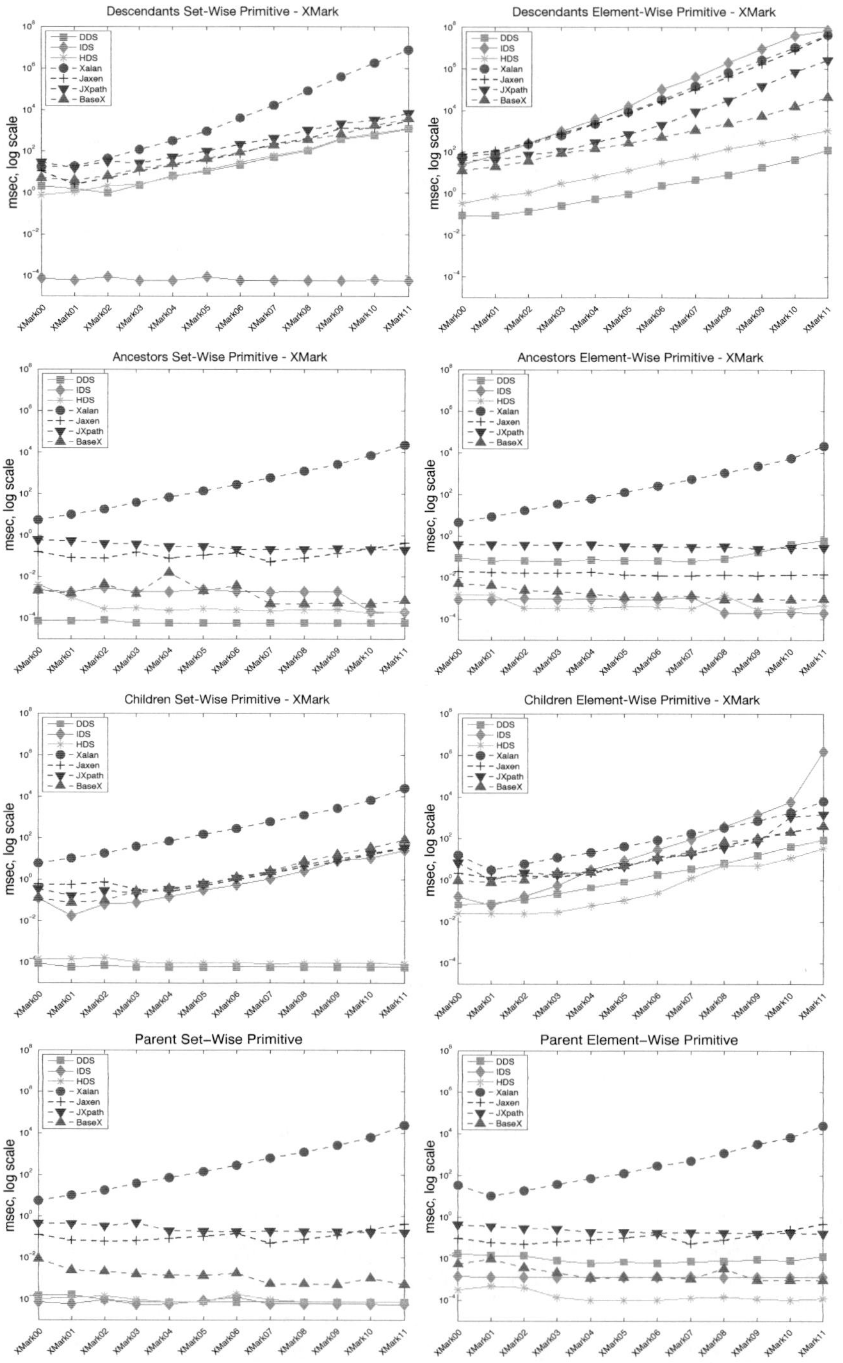

Fig. 3. Evaluation time for the XPath operations under evaluation.

Table 3. Statistics of the twelve selected XMark synthetic files.

	Size (MB)	# nodes	depth	max fan-out	average fan-out
XMark-01	0.581	8,518	12	127	3.69
XMark-02	1.182	17,132	12	255	3.70
XMark-03	2.385	33,140	12	510	3.60
XMark-04	4.840	67,902	12	1,020	3.65
XMark-05	9.595	134,831	12	2,040	3.65
XMark-06	18.855	265,975	12	4,080	3.66
XMark-07	38.145	533,750	12	8,160	3.66
XMark-08	76.016	1,066,768	12	16,320	3.66
XMark-08	152.350	2,140,644	12	32,640	3.66
XMark-10	305.191	4,276,108	12	65,280	3.67
XMark-11	610.043	8,554,409	12	130,560	3.67
XMark-12	1,221.750	17,107,471	12	261,120	3.66

5 Final Remarks

In this paper we presented a brand new approach to address XML query primitives relying on basic set operations. This represents a paradigm shift with respect to the navigational-like approaches widely studied and employed in the past. In particular, we have experimentally shown that NESTOR data structures allow us to outperform state-of-the-art solutions. The evaluation conducted on the XMark dataset allows us to pinpoint that NESTOR primitives scale up well when the size, the depth, the max fan-out and the total number of nodes of an XML document grow.

As future work we plan to explore the efficiency of NESTOR data structures with respect to the full set of XPath operations, such as XPath predicates, in order to address the whole classification of XPath fragments of [2]. Furthermore, we will study how NESTOR can be used with different levels of memory and extended to disk-oriented XML querying.

References

1. M. Agosti, N. Ferro, and G. Silvello. The NESTOR Framework: Manage, Access and Exchange Hierarchical Data Structures. In*Proc. 18th Italian Symposium on Advanced Database Systems (SEBD 2010)*, pages 242–253. Esculapio, 2010.
2. M. Benedikt, W. Fan, and G. M. Kuper. Structural Properties of XPath Fragments. *Theor. Comput. Sci.*, 336(1):3–31, 2005.
3. N. Ferro and G. Silvello. The NESTOR Framework: How to Handle Hierarchical Data Structures. In *Proc. 13th European Conference on Research and Advanced Technology for Digital Libraries (ECDL 2009)*, pages 215–226. LNCS 5714, Springer, Heidelberg, Germany, 2009.
4. N. Ferro and G. Silvello. NESTOR: A Formal Model for Digital Archives. *Inf. Process. Manage.*, 49(6):1206–1240, 2013.
5. N. Ferro and G. Silvello. Descendants, Ancestors, Children and Parent: A Set-Based Approach to Efficiently Address XPath Primitives. *Inf. Process. Manage.*, 52(3):399–429, 2016.
6. W3C. XML Path Language (XPath) 2.0 (Second Edition) – W3C Recommendation 14 December 2010. `http://www.w3.org/TR/xpath20/`, December 2010.

A hypergraph-based model for Multimedia Social Network

F.Amato, V.Moscato, A.Picariello, and G. Sperlì

Dip. di Ingegneria Elettrica e Tecnologie dell'Informazione,
University of Naples Federico II
via Claudio 21, 80125, Naples, Italy
{flora.amato,vmoscato,picus,giancarlo.sperli}@unina.it
Extended Abstract

Abstract. This paper represents an extended abstract of a recent publication where we have defined a novel data model for *Multimedia Social Networks* (MSNs), i.e. networks that combine information on users belonging to one or more social communities together with the multimedia content that is generated and used within the related environments. The proposed model relies on the *hypergraph* data structure to capture and represent in a simple way all the different kinds of relationships of social networks and multimedia sharing systems. Different applications (e.g. multimedia recommendation, influence analysis) can be then built on the top of the introduce data model thanks to the introduction of proper user and multimedia *ranking* functions. Finally, some preliminary experiments concerning effectiveness of the proposed approach for analysis of social and multimedia data are reported and discussed.

Keywords: Multimedia Social Network, Social Network Analysis

1 Introduction

Nowadays, Multimedia Sharing Systems (MSSs) and some On-line Social Networks (OSNs) provide users an interactive platform to create and share multimedia content such as text, image, video, audio, and so on: as an example, each minute, thousands of tweets are sent on Twitter, several hundreds of hours of videos are uploaded to YouTube, and a huge quantity of photos are shared on Instagram or uploaded to Flickr. In such "interest-based" social networks, each user interacts with the others through a certain multimedia content and such interactions create social links that well characterize the behaviors of involved users in the networks.

Indeed, multimedia data play a key-role in a network and several important questions arise in the Social Network Analysis (SNA) domain: Is it possible to exploit multimedia features and the notion of *similarity* in order to discover more links? Are such links useful? Can all the different types of user annotations and interactions with multimedia objects provide a further support for SNA?

Is it possible to integrate and efficiently manage in a unique network the information coming from OSNs and that is related to MSSs (for example, a Twitter user has usually an account also on Instagram or Flickr)? How can we deal with a very large volume of data? In this context, how is possible to model all the various relationships among users and multimedia objects? Are the "graph-based" strategies still the most suitable solutions?

The preliminary step to provide an answer for the above questions lies in the introduction of a model for the introduced interest-based social networks, where their multimedia component plays a funamental role. In particular, we have decided to adopt the term "Multimedia Social Networks" (MSNs) to indicate integrated networks that combine the information on users, belonging to one or more social communities, with all the multimedia contents that can be generated and used within the related environments.

In the literature, the term MSN have been used over the last years together with *Social Multimedia Network* or *Social Media Network* to indicate information networks that leverage multimedia data in a social environment for different purposes: distributed resource allocation for multimedia content sharing in cloud-based systems [1], generation of personalized multimedia information recommendations in response to specific targets of interests [2], evaluation of the trust relationship among users [3], high dimensional video data distribution in social multimedia applications [4], characterization of user behavior and information propagation on the base of multimedia sharing [5], representation of a social collaboration network of archeologists for cultural heritage applications [6], just to cite some of the most recent proposals. As we can notice such proposals face only in part the discussed problems, rather focusing their efforts on specific applications.

The first proposals for social information network modeling take into account only *user* as basic entity and her/his interactions without explicitly considering multimedia content. Successively, more complex models, embedding multimedia data, have been introduced and it is possible to classify them on the base of four main categories. In the first kind of approaches, a social network is defined as a *graph* composed by heterogeneous vertices, such as users, tags, multimedia objects: multimedia annotation [7] and image similarity [8] issues are faced. The second type of models is in turn based on *bipartite graphs* and used to solve influence diffusion [9] and consensus maximization [10] problems. The third category of approaches exploits *tripartite graphs* for clustering multimedia data [11] or to provide personalized video recommendations [12]. Eventually, the last group contains the approaches based on *hypergraph* theory, essentially used for recommendation [13] or influence mining [14] goals.

This paper represents an extended abstract of a recent paper [15] where we have defined a novel and general data model for MSNs that leverage the *hypergraph* structure. In particular, inspired by hypergraph based approaches, our model proposes a solution for representing MSNs sufficiently general with respect to: i) a particular social information network, ii) the different kinds of entities, iii) the different types of relationships, iv) the different applications.

Exploiting hypergraphs, the model allows us to represent in a simple way all the different kinds of relationships that are typical of a MSN (among multimedia contents, among users and multimedia content and among users themselves) and to enable several kinds of analytics and applications by means of the introduction of some *ranking* functions. In addition, we provide a strategy for hypergraph learning from data coming from different OSNs (e.g. Facebook, Twitter) and MSSs (e.g Flickr, Instagram, Last.fm, Youtube).

2 The hypergraph-based Model

In our vision, a MSN is basically composed by three different kinds of entities:

- *Users* - the set of persons and organizations constituting the particular social community: several information concerning their profile, interests, preferences, etc. can eventually be considered and exploited by our model;
- *Multimedia Objects* - the set of multimedia resources (i.e. images, video, audio, etc.) that can be shared within a MSN community: high level (*metadata*) and low level information (*features*) can be properly used in our model;
- *Annotation Assets* - each set of symbols (e.g., keyword, tag, textual comment etc.) exploited by users to annotate multimedia resources within a MSN; we explicitly note that it is possible to associate to a given asset the related semantics by a specific *topic* (the most significant terms or named entities of a given domain) which definition can be found into dictionaries, ontologies and so on.

The model relies on several concepts, *Multimedia Social Network* (seen as particular a weighted and directed hypergraph) and *social paths* (i.e. hyperpaths), which basic definitions are provided in the following.

Definition 1 (Multimedia Social Network) *A* Multimedia Social Network *MSN is a triple* $(V; H_e, = e_i : i \in I\}; \omega)$, *$V$ being a finite set of* vertices, *H_e a set of* hyperedges *with a finite set of indexes I and* $\omega : H_e \to [0, 1]$ *a weight function. The set of vertices is defined as* $V = U \cup M \cup A$, U *being the set of MSN users,* M *the set of multimedia objects and* A *the set of annotation assets. Each hyperedge* $e_i \in H_e$ *is in turn defined by a ordered pair* $e_i = (e_i^+ = (V_{e_i}^+, i); e_i^- = (i, V_{e_i}^-))$. *The element e_i^+ is called the* tail *of the hyperarc e_i whereas e_i^- is its* head, $V_{e_i}^+ \subseteq V$ *being the set of vertices of* e_i^+, $V_{e_i}^- \subseteq V$ *the set of vertices of* e_i^- *and* $V_{e_i} = V_{e_i}^+ \cup V_{e_i}^-$ *the subset of vertices constituting the whole hyperedge. The* degree of a hyperedge *e is defined by the related number of vertices, while the* degree of a vertex *v is* $\sum_{v \in e} \omega(e)$, *$\omega(e)$ being the weight of the hyperedge e.*

Actually, vertices and hyperedge of a MSN are particular *abstract data types* with a set of properties (attributes and methods), which can be obtained using dot notation (see [15] for more details). In particular, in our model each hyperedge has to be characterized at least by the following attributes: *id* (a unique identifier that is automatically assigned), ii) *name* (a generic name that can be assigned to describe the hyperedge), iii) *timestamp* (the given time in which the relationship has been instantiated), iv) *type* (the particular class which hyperedge belongs to). In addition, the weight function can be used to define the confidence or uncertainty of a given relationship in terms of probability, fuzzy membership and so on.

Analyzing the different types of relationships that can be established in the main MSNs, we have identified the following three categories: i) *User to User* relationships, describing user actions towards other users; ii) *Similarity* relationships, describing a relatedness between two multimedia objects, users or annotation assets; iii) *User to Multimedia* relationships, describing user interactions wih multimedia objects, eventually involving some annotation assets or other users. Social paths between two nodes leverage the different kinds of relationships.

Definition 2 (Social path) *A* social path *between vertices v_1 and v_k of a MSN is an alternative sequence of distinct vertices and hyperedges $v_1, e_1, v_2, e_2, v_3, e_3, .., e_{k-1}, v_k$ such that $\{v_i, v_{i+1}\} \subseteq V_{e_i}$ for $1 \leq i \leq k-1$. The* length *of the hyperpath is $\alpha \cdot \sum_{i=1}^{k-1} \cdot \frac{1}{\omega(e_i)}$, where α is a normalizing factor. We say that a social path* contains *a vertex v_h if $\exists e_i : v_h \in e_i$. In turn, we define a* constrained social path *as an hyperpath containing a specific set of hyperedges.*

2.1 Relationships

Definition 3 (User to User relationship) *Let $\widehat{U} \subseteq U \subseteq V$ a set of users in a MSN, we define* user to user relationship *a hyperedge $e_k = (e_k^+ = (V_{e_k}^+, k); e_k^- = (k, V_{e_k}^-))$ with the following properties: i) $V_{e_k}^+ = \{u_i\}$ such that $u_i \in \widehat{U}$, ii) $V_{e_k}^- = \widehat{U} - \{u_i\}$. The weight function for such relationship returns as value $\frac{\hat{H}_{ij}}{H_i}$, $\hat{H}_{ij}$ being the average number of distinct social paths related to relationships between u_i and u_j for each $u_j \in \widehat{U} - \{u_i\}$, and H_i the number of user to user paths having as initial vertex u_i.*

Several examples of user to user relationships that characterize our model are provided by the "friendship" relationship (typical of the Facebook OSN) or the "following" relationship (typical of the Twitter OSN).

Definition 4 (Similarity relationship) *Let $v_i, v_j \in V$ $(i \neq j)$ two vertices of the same type of a MSN, we define* similarity relationship *a hyperedge e_k with the following properties: i) $V_{e_k}^+ = \{v_i\}$, ii) $V_{e_k}^- = \{v_j\}$. The weight function for this relationship returns similarity value between the two vertices.*

In our model, the similarity relationships are defined on the top of a *similarity function* $f_{sim} : V \times V \to R$.

It is possible to compute a similarity value: i) between two users by considering different types of features (interests, profile information, preferences, etc.); ii) between two multimedia objects using the well-know (high and low level) features and metrics proposed in the literature; iii) between two annotation assets exploiting the related concepts and the well-know metrics on vocabularies or ontologies (see [15] for more details).

Definition 5 (User to Multimedia relationship) *Let* $\widehat{U} \subseteq U \subseteq V$ *a set of users in a MSN and* $\widehat{M} \subseteq M \subseteq V$ *a set of multimedia objects, we define* user to multimedia relationship *an hyperarc* $e_k = (e_k^+ = (V_{e_k}^+, k); e_k^- = (k, V_{e_k}^-))$ *with the following properties: i)* $V_{e_k}^+ = \{u_i\}$ *such that* $u_i \in \widehat{U}$, *ii)* $V_{e_k}^- \supseteq \widehat{M}$. *The weight function for such relationship reurns as value* $\frac{\hat{H}_{ij}}{H_i}$, $\hat{H}_{ij}$ *being the average number of distinct social paths related to relationships between* u_i *and* m_j *for each* $m_j \in \widehat{M}$, *and* H_i *the number of user to multimedia paths having as initial vertex* u_i.

Several examples of user to multimedia relationships that characterize our model are provided by the "publishing" or the "annotation" relationships (typical of several OSNs and MSSs). Figure 1 shows as the introduced relationships can be easily represented in our model (see [15] for more details).

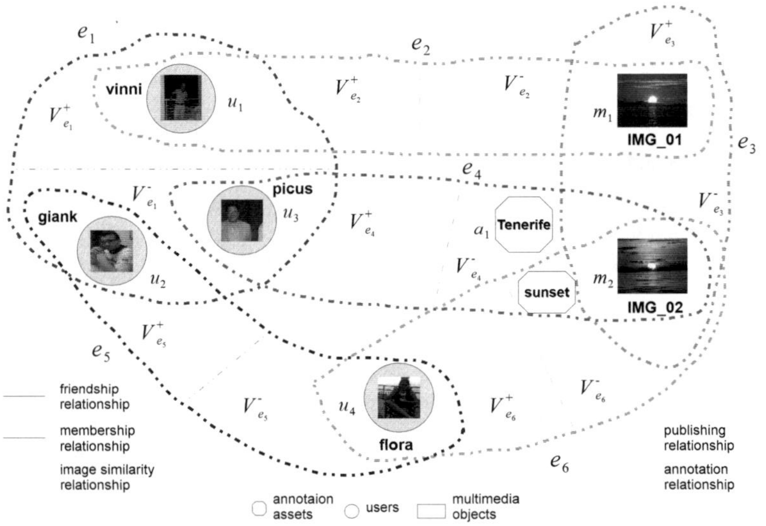

Fig. 1: Example of MSN.

2.2 Ranking functions

In this subsection, we introduce some functions can be profitably used to "rank" users (or multimedia objects) in a MSN in absolute way or with respect to a given topic of interest. Let us first introduce some preliminary definitions.

Definition 6 (Distances) *We define* minimum distance *($d_{min}(v_i, v_j)$),* maximum distance *($d_{max}(v_i, v_j)$) and* average distance *(($d_{avg}(v_i, v_j)$)) between two vertices of a MSN the length of the shortest hyperpath, the lenght of the longest hyperpath and the average length of the hyperpaths between v_i and v_j, respectively. In a similar manner, we define the* minimum distance *($d_{min}(v_i, v_j | v_k)$),* maximum distance *($d_{max}(v_i, v_j | v_k)$) and* average distance *(($d_{avg}(v_i, v_j | v_k)$)) between two vertices v_i and v_j, for which there exists a hyperpath containing v_k.*

Definition 7 (λ-Nearest Neighbors Set) *Given a vertex $v_i \in V$ of a MSN, we define the* λ-Nearest Neighbors Set *of v_i the subset of vertices NN_i^{λ} such that $\forall v_j \in NN_i^{\lambda}$ we have $d_{min}(v_i, v_j) \leq \lambda$ with $v_j \in U$. Considering only the constrained hyperpaths containing a vertex v_k, we denote with NN_{ik}^{λ} the set of nearest neighbors of v_i such that $\forall v_j \in NN_{ik}^{\lambda}$ we have $d_{min}(v_i, v_j | v_k) \leq \lambda$*

If as neighbors we consider only vertices of user type, the NN^{λ} set is called *λ-Nearest Users Set* and denoted as NNU^{λ}, similarly in case of multimedia objects we define the *λ-Nearest Objects Set* as NNO^{λ}. On the top of such definitions, we are able to introduce some users' *ranking* functions for our model.

Definition 8 (User Ranking function) *Given a user $u_i \in U \subseteq V$ and a subset of users $\widehat{U} \subseteq U \subseteq V (u_i \notin \widehat{U})$ of a MSN, a* user ranking function *is a particular function $\rho : U \rightarrow [0, 1]$ able to associate a specific* rank *to the user u_i with respect to the community $\widehat{U}$ that is computed as in the following:*

$$\rho_{u_i}\left(\widehat{U}\right) = \frac{\left|NNU_i^{\lambda} \cap \widehat{U}\right|}{\left|\widehat{U}\right|} \tag{1}$$

NNU_i^{λ} being the λ-Nearest Users Set of u_i.

Definition 9 (Topic-User Ranking function) *Let $u_i \in U \subseteq V$ a user, $\widehat{U} \subseteq U \subseteq V (u_i \notin \widehat{U})$ a subset of users and $a_j \in A \subseteq V$ an annotation asset of a MSN, a* topic-user ranking function *is a particular function $\rho : U \times A \rightarrow [0, 1]$ able to associate a specific* rank *to the user u_i with respect to the community $\widehat{U}$ given the topic a_j that is computed as in the following:*

$$\rho_{u_i}^{a_j}\left(\widehat{U}\right) = \frac{\left|NNU_{ij}^{\lambda} \cap \widehat{U}\right|}{\left|\widehat{U}\right|} \tag{2}$$

NNU_{ij}^{λ} being the λ-Nearest Users Set of u_i.

In a similar way, we have defined the *multimedia ranking function* and the *topic-multimedia ranking function*, considering hyperpaths starting from multimedia objects (see [15] for more details)

In our model the concept of *rank* of a given node is related to the concept of *influence*, and in our vision it can be measured by the number of user nodes that are "reachable" within a certain number of steps using any hyperpath, with respect to a social community of users, and eventually to a given topic of interest.

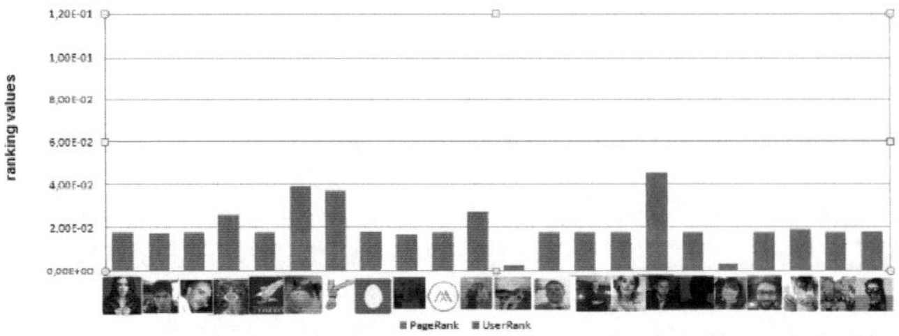

Fig. 2: User ranking.

3 Preliminary Experiments and Results

We report some preliminary experiments concerning the effectiveness of the introduced ranking functions using Twitter[1] and Last.fm[2] data.

We implemented the related information networks as particular hypergraphs leveraging facilities provided by HypergraphDB (a native hypergraph database).

Figure 2 shows a comparison between our user ranking function and the *PageRank* algorithm with respect to the topic "Sport" for the most influencer Twitter users. In turn, Table 1 reports the most "important" songs (with highest values of multimedia rank) of Last.fm considering "pop" and "rap" communities.

Table 1: Multimedia Top-5 for Pop, Rap and Pop-Rap communities

Pop	Rap	Pop-Rap
Lady Gaga - I like it rough	Eminem - We made you	Madonna - Hung up
Klimt 1918 - Snow of '85	Jay-z - U dont know	Britney spears - Piece of me
Rihanna - Umbrella [feat. jay-z]	Dr. dre - Big,ego's	Mariah carey - Reflections
Estelle feat. Kanye West - American boy	Eminem - Forgot about dre	Eminem - Mockingbird
Michael Jackson - Don't stop 'til you get enough	Snoop dogg - Pass it pass it	Eminem - My fault

4 Conclusions and Future Work

In this paper we described a data model for *Multimedia Social Networks*, combining information on users together with the multimedia content. Future work will be devoted to exploit the proposed model for supporting multimedia recommendation and influence analysis applications.

[1] We exploited a subset containing information about 10,000 user accounts.
[2] http://carl.cs.indiana.edu/data/last.fm/, containing a set of data extracted from the Last.fm in the first half of 2009.

References

1. G. Nan, C. Zang, R. Dou, and M. Li, "Pricing and resource allocation for multimedia social network in cloud environments," *Knowledge-Based Systems*, vol. 88, pp. 1 – 11, 2015.
2. D. Liu, G. Ye, C.-T. Chen, S. Yan, and S.-F. Chang, "Hybrid social media network," in *Proceedings of the 20th ACM international conference on Multimedia.* ACM, 2012, pp. 659–668.
3. Z. Zhang and K. Wang, "A trust model for multimedia social networks," *Social Network Analysis and Mining*, vol. 3, no. 4, pp. 969–979, 2013.
4. X. Ji, Q. Wang, B.-W. Chen, S. Rho, C. J. Kuo, and Q. Dai, "Online distribution and interaction of video data in social multimedia network," *Multimedia Tools and Applications*, pp. 1–14, 2014.
5. F. T. O'Donovan, C. Fournelle, S. Gaffigan, O. Brdiczka, J. Shen, J. Liu, and K. E. Moore, "Characterizing user behavior and information propagation on a social multimedia network," in *Multimedia and Expo Workshops (ICMEW), 2013 IEEE International Conference on.* IEEE, 2013, pp. 1–6.
6. V. Moscato, A. Picariello, and V. Subrahmanian, "Multimedia social networks for cultural heritage applications: the givas project," in *Data Management in Pervasive Systems.* Springer, 2015, pp. 169–182.
7. G.-J. Qi, C. Aggarwal, Q. Tian, H. Ji, and T. S. Huang, "Exploring context and content links in social media: A latent space method," *Pattern Analysis and Machine Intelligence, IEEE Transactions on*, vol. 34, no. 5, pp. 850–862, 2012.
8. X. Jin, J. Luo, J. Yu, G. Wang, D. Joshi, and J. Han, "Reinforced similarity integration in image-rich information networks," *Knowledge and Data Engineering, IEEE Transactions on*, vol. 25, no. 2, pp. 448–460, Feb 2013.
9. Z. Zhu, J. Su, and L. Kong, "Measuring influence in online social network based on the user-content bipartite graph," *Computers in Human Behavior*, vol. 52, pp. 184 – 189, 2015.
10. J. Gao, F. Liang, W. Fan, Y. Sun, and J. Han, "A graph-based consensus maximization approach for combining multiple supervised and unsupervised models," *Knowledge and Data Engineering, IEEE Transactions on*, vol. 25, no. 1, pp. 15–28, Jan 2013.
11. G.-J. Qi, C. C. Aggarwal, and T. S. Huang, "On clustering heterogeneous social media objects with outlier links," in *Proceedings of the fifth ACM international conference on Web search and data mining.* ACM, 2012, pp. 553–562.
12. B. Chen, J. Wang, Q. Huang, and T. Mei, "Personalized video recommendation through tripartite graph propagation," in *Proceedings of the 20th ACM international conference on Multimedia.* ACM, 2012, pp. 1133–1136.
13. J. Bu, S. Tan, C. Chen, C. Wang, H. Wu, L. Zhang, and X. He, "Music recommendation by unified hypergraph: combining social media information and music content," in *Proceedings of the international conference on Multimedia.* ACM, 2010, pp. 391–400.
14. Q. Fang, J. Sang, C. Xu, and Y. Rui, "Topic-sensitive influencer mining in interest-based social media networks via hypergraph learning," *IEEE Transactions on Multimedia*, vol. 16, no. 3, pp. 796–812, April 2014.
15. F. Amato, V. Moscato, A. Picariello, and G. Sperli', "Multimedia social network modeling: a proposal," *Fifth IEEE International Workshop on Semantic Multimedia (ICSC-SMM'16)*, 2016.

Exposing Open Street Map in the Linked Data cloud

Vito Walter Anelli[1], Andrea Calì[2], Tommaso Di Noia[1], Andrea Maurino[3], Matteo Palmonari[3], Azzurra Ragone[3]

[1] Polytechnic University of Bari, Via Orabona, 4, 70125 Bari, Italy
v.anelli@studenti.poliba.it, tommaso.dinoia@poliba.it
[2] Birkbeck, University of London, Malet Street, London WC1E 7HX, UK
andrea@dcs.bbk.ac.uk
[3] University of Milano-Bicocca, Piazza dell'Ateneo Nuovo, 1, 20126 Milano, Italy
lastname@disco.unimib.it

Abstract. Nowadays, the pervasive and mobile nature of information paves the way to a new family of location-aware services and tools. Geographical data are gaining momentum and this reflects in the growing of dedicated datasets in the Linked Data (LD) cloud. The very last version of the LD cloud diagram shows Geonames competing with DBpedia not just in terms of amount of data but also with reference to the number of links coming from/going to other datasets. Among the different Web projects, one the most important players in the geo-arena, is for sure Open Street Map (OSM). It exposes a huge amount of data which is continually updated in a crowdsourced fashion. In order to make all this knowledge available as Linked Data, we developed LOSM: a SPARQL endpoint able to query the data available in OSM by an on-line translation form SPARQL syntax to a sequence of calls to the OSM `overpass` API.

1 Introduction

In the last years we are witnessing the spread of knowledge intensive applications that relies on the flourishing of the datasets available in the Linked Data (LD) Cloud [4]. The richness of semantic data they expose is an enabling factor for a new generation of services and tools exploiting the ontological knowledge they encode as well as the possibility to easily mash up data coming from different sources. Among them, geographical datasets are becoming more and more important to deliver location-aware services. The availability of a common query interface *i.e.*, SPARQL, and the crowd-driven standardization of ontological vocabularies allows an intelligent application to grab data from diverse datasets and join them. We may imagine different scenarios where such a feature can be an important asset to provide a high quality service such as context-aware recommendation systems [12], on-line shopping, etc. or public services needed in situations of disaster management where the quality and timeliness of the data is of crucial importance.

In many application scenarios, geographical information is a key factor to enhance system answers to user request, *e.g.,*in a movie recommendation scenario in order to suggests not only a movie according to user preferences, but also with reference to the

[4] `http://lod-cloud.net`

closeness of the cinema. Other examples may refer to transportation planning or emergency management. As an example, while organizing a trip, the user could combine information about the cultural heritage sites and means of transport with hotel accommodations, taking into account their proximity. Analogously, in emergency response situations, data can be combined to obtain a helpful and timely response. In an emergency scenario, *e.g.,*an earthquake, the user should be able to query a knowledge base to look for collection camps, hospitals, rescue places, areas for helicopter landing as well as informal camps where the homeless have set up tent camps. In this paper we present LOSM (Linked Open Street Map), a service that acts as a SPARQL endpoint on top of OSM. LOSM allows one to query Open Street Map data via a SPARQL query as it takes care to translate the query into a set of calls to OSM APIs. This results in exposing all the information contained in the Open Street Map geographical database as Linked Data thus making OSM a first class citizen in the Linked Data Cloud. While LOSM supports an on-the-fly integration of OSM data with data coming from other sources, differently from similar projects (see `LinkedGeoData`[5] [2] for example) LOSM does not rely on a periodical dump of the data, but it always exposes fresh and up-to-date data.

The remainder of this paper proceeds as follows. In Section 2 we start by briefly describing Open Street Map and the reason why we chose it as a provider of linked geo-spatial data, then we describe the system architecture and the query language implemented in LOSM. In Section 3 we review related works relying on the use of geo-spatial data. Conclusion and future work close the paper.

2 LOSM: Linked Open Street Map

In the "geo-data" arena, the crowd sourced project Open Street Map [7] is currently playing a primary role due to its openness, easy of use and of integration in third party applications. OSM is a geographical database maintained by Web users containing a huge amount of data that can also be displayed on a map. Its database is updated every 15 minutes and as of today it contains 5,027,330,590 GPS points and 2,445,598 users who contribute to the project. All this data is either available via weekly dumps or it is queryable through a public API. In particular, `overpass`[6] is a read-only API which allows the user to query Open Street Map by means of at least two different languages: XML or Overpass QL. By means of an `overpass` query, the API is able to retrieve nodes within an area, recognize streets or relations. The query language is very expressive and makes possible to perform spatial reasoning by imposing constraints within the query. For instance, the user may impose relationships among nodes through filters such as `around`, `bounding box` and the `poly` function. It is easy to see that having such data available in the Linked Open Data cloud would surely enrich the amount and quality of the information available within the so called Web of Data.

This is the rationale behind the `LinkedGeoData` project [2]. It aims at triplifying Open Street Map dumps every six months by mapping OSM tags and sourceKey properties with reference to a publicly available ontology. This is a very useful resource because it makes available classes that map keys and tags used in Open Street Map nodes.

[5] `http://linkedgeodata.org/`

[6] `http://wiki.openstreetmap.org/wiki/Overpass_API`

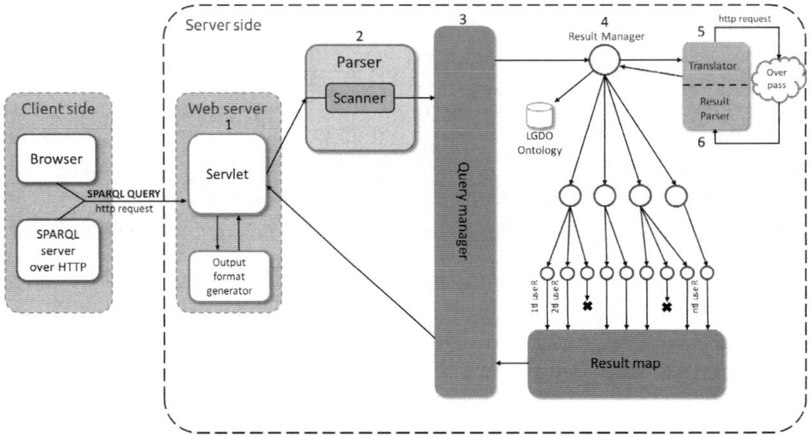

Fig. 1: Overall representation of the system architecture

Although the big effort and work in developing and maintaining the datasets behind the project, LinkedGeoData suffers from the misalignment between the data available via the SPARQL endpoint (based on a dump) and the one available in Open Street Map. Indeed, the updates made by the users are available as RDF triples only when the dump is processed and loaded in the LinkedGeoData triple-store. Despite the considerable effort, LinkedGeoData approach cannot be used for all those scenarios where timeliness and freshness of information is a must have. A flagship example is that of disaster recovery where information about collection camps, rescue places, temporary hospitals, passable roads, etc. needs to be available as soon as possible. Starting from this observation we developed LOSM, a SPARQL endpoint that acts as a translator from a SPARQL query to a set of overpass API calls. In such a way we are sure that the data we retrieve is always fresh and up-to-date as they come directly from the OSM database, which is constantly updated by a crowd of volunteer all around the world.

The scheme in Figure 1 shows an overview of the service architecture. In a few words, the systems is able to translate a SPARQL query to a sequence of (iterative) overpass API calls, collect the data, join and return it to the client. We currently support SPARQL queries via HTTP GET. The **Parser** uses a scanner for the recognition of lexemes in a SPARQL query and creates the data-structures needed by the **Query Manager**. This module is in charge of breaking the query into sub-queries according to the remote functions available in the overpass API. The **Result Manage**r handles the sub-queries and the results they generate to create the final Result map. The Result Manager breaks the graph pattern described in the SPARQL query into a set of connected sub-graphs by identifying their mutual relations. Each sub-query goes through the **Translator** which is in charge of creating the overpass calls.

The system also exposes a Web page with a query editor with autocomplete facilities with respect to the LinkedGeoData ontology classes. LOSM is available at http://sisinflab.poliba.it/semanticweb/lod/losm/.

2.1 The SPARQL sublanguage implemented in LOSM.

In its current version, LOSM implements a subset of the full specification of SPARQL 1.0 plus some non-standard features[7] that results very useful when querying geographical data. We currently support only the `SELECT` query form and the Jena Spatial[8] extension also available in GeoSPARQL [3]. We support simple graph patterns that we anyway consider representative of a large number of queries over geographical data. As for the implemented spatial functions, we may list:

- `spatial:nearby (latitude longitude radius [units])`[9] returns URIs nodes (Open Street Map URIs) within the radius distance of the location of the specified latitude and longitude.
- `spatial:withinCircle (latitude longitude radius [units])` computes a circle centered in specified latitude and longitude and given radius and returns the OSM nodes within the circle.
- `spatial:withinBox (latitude_min longitude_min latitude_max longitude_max)` calculates a rectangle by specifying the list of coordinates for the edges that has to follow the order provided in the function.
- `spatial:within("POLYGON((Point1_lat Point1_lon,...,PointN_lat PointN_lon))")` calculates the polygon area expressed by Well Known Text (WKT) literals and returns OSM nodes available within it.

Regarding the URIs of classes and properties used in the graph pattern for SPARQL queries, LOSM may refer to the LinkedGeoData Ontology controlled vocabulary as well as to an ontological one which is a one-to-one mapping with OSM system of tags[10]. The rationale behind the introduction of this new vocabulary is driven by the main goal we had in mind while developing LOSM: to have a SPARQL endpoint able to timely expose all the changes that continually happen in Open Street Map even at the semantic level (represented by the tags).

Although very useful and structured, a static ontology as the one modelled within the LinkedGeoData project, cannot follow continuous data variations due to users' freedom in inserting new tags and values. In each community a lot of linguistic phenomenons happen in time that change the frequency of a term occurrence and then its importance and adoption by the community itself. To address this problem we introduced a LOSM prefix `<http://sisinflab.poliba.it/semanticweb/lod/losm/ontology/>` (shortened in `losm`) based on the same crowdsourcing concept. The **Parser** recognizes the use of this prefix and prepares the overpass query in the proper way. This lets the user to use any term she considers reasonable and the evaluation of the existence of the term is based only on the real data coming from Open Street Map. As an example, if the user wants to retrieve information classified with the key-value pair `key="refugee" value="yes"` she will refer to the corresponding property represented by the URI `<http://sisinflab.poliba.it/`

---

7 Details on the implemented subset is available at `http://sisinflab.poliba.it/semanticweb/lod/losm/losm_grammar.html`

8 `https://jena.apache.org/documentation/query/spatial-query.html`

9 [units] can be meters ('`m`' or '`M`'), kilometers ('`km`' or '`KM`') or miles ('`mi`' or '`MI`').

10 `http://wiki.openstreetmap.org/wiki/Tags`

semanticweb/lod/losm/ontology/refugee> or equivalently by the CURIE losm:refugee. Some keys are reserved to provide advanced features in LOSM that makes easy the integration with other external knowledge graphs exposing a SPARQL endpoint such as DBpedia[11] or Wikidata[12]. The losm:dbpedia property acts as a converter from the Wikipedia page or Wikipedia id associated to an Open Street Map node to the corresponding DBpedia resource. Analogously, losm:wikipedia returns the complete URI of the corresponding Wikipedia page. In both cases, the output may refer to the main English version of DBpedia/Wikipedia or to a local version depending on the value of the OSM key wikipedia.

2.2 Use case

In the following use case we present how LOSM works, showing the steps performed by the **Query Manager** (see Figure 1). Suppose the following situation: *the day is over in our laboratory and the crew wants to find restaurants nearby (within 200 meters) together with the cinemas which are at most one km far from each restaurant. They want to know the names of restaurants and cinemas together with the URIs of the latter*. The above use case can be modeled by the SPARQL query:

```
PREFIX rdfs: <http://www.w3.org/2000/01/rdf-schema#>
PREFIX lgdo: <http://linkedgeodata.org/ontology/>
PREFIX spatial: <http://jena.apache.org/spatial#>
PREFIX geo: <http://www.w3.org/2003/01/geo/wgs84_pos#>
SELECT ?cinema ?nameC ?nameR
WHERE  {
    ?link rdfs:label "Sisinf Lab" .
    ?link geo:lat ?lat .
    ?link geo:long ?lon.
    ?object spatial:nearby(?lat ?lon 200 'm') .
    ?object a lgdo:Restaurant  .
    ?object rdfs:label ?nameR .
    ?object geo:lat ?lat2 .
    ?object geo:long ?lon2.
    ?cinema spatial:nearby(?lat2 ?lon2 1000 'm') .
    ?cinema a lgdo:Cinema .
    ?cinema rdfs:label ?nameC .
}
```

The query is processed based on a priority system relying on a weighted dependency graph. The triples composing the graph pattern are analysed and grouped into the corresponding sub-graphs by looking at their subject. The system attaches to each triple a value depending on the degree of connection with other groups measured by taking into account shared variables and predicates. Then each group is labeled with a weight proportional to its triples values. The group with the lowest value is the first sent to the Translator component. The **Translator** converts the set of sub-queries to its overpass equivalent starting with the triple with the lowest value. Once the results from overpass API are returned, they are used to update the initial query so new weights are computed. The process iterates on triples groups until the last sub-query has been translated.

?link `[?link rdfs:label "Sisinf Lab", ?link geo:lat ?lat, ?link geo:long ?lon]`

[11] http://dbpedia.org/sparql
[12] https://query.wikidata.org

?object `[?object spatial:nearby ?lat ?lon 200 'm' , ?object a lgdo:Restaurant , ?object rdfs:label ?nameR , ?object geo:lat ?lat2 , ?object geo:long ?lon2 ]`

?cinema `[?cinema spatial:nearby ?lat2 ?lon2 1000 'm' , ?cinema a lgdo:Cinema , ?cinema rdfs:label ?nameC ]`

Based on the above grouping, the Query Manager selects first the **?link** group and generates the Overpass QL expression representing the first query to the `overpass` API:

```
node["name"="Sisinf Lab"];
out body;
```

Then the system executes the `overpass` query related to the **?object** group which is composed by taking into account the results of the previous one.

```
node(around:200,41.1095222,16.8778234)
["amenity"="restaurant"]
["name"];
out body;
```

The final sub-graph is converted into a set of `overpass` API calls; one for each node returned by the previous query. As an example we have:

```
node (around: 1000,41.1085645,16.8768552)
["amenity" = "cinema"]
["name"];
out body;
```

3 Related Work

In recent years several ontologies and languages have been proposed to model and query dataset related to geo-spatial knowledge and to extract information from these knowledge bases. Basic Geo Vocabulary [6] is a simple RDF Schema vocabulary able to represent latitude, longitude and altitude information in the WGS84 reference system. A more structured and ontological representation of the GeoRSS vocabulary is available in the GeoOWL ontology [13]. GeoSPARQL [3] from the Open Geospatial Consortium (OGC) is a standard that has the aim to provide a way to represent and query geospatial data in the Semantic Web. GeoSPARQL addresses this task providing a small ontology to represent features and geometries and a number of SPARQL query predicates and functions. GeoSPARQL standards are supported by the triple-store Parliament [4] to query spatial data via RDF properties, which is able to answer queries like "*find all items located with a region X*". Parliament does not support Basic Geo Vocabulary, differently from OWLIM-SE (now GraphDB) triple store [1] which however supports only points for storage, thus allowing queries to find points within ad-hoc polygons and circles and to compute distances between points. GraphDB data types and queries are not compliant with GeoSPARQL[13]. Strabon[9] is a semantic spatiotemporal RDF store, that can be used to store linked geospatial data and to query them using an extension of SPARQL named *stSPARQL*. *stSPARQL* can be used to query data represented in an extension of RDF called *stRDF* that model geospatial data that changes over time (e.g., the growth of

[13] `http://www.w3.org/2005/Incubator/geo/XGR-geo-20071023/W3C_XGR_Geo_files/geo_2007.owl`

a city over the years). Strabon supports spatial datatypes enabling the serialization of geometric objects in OGC standards WKT and GML, as well as a subset of GeoSPARQL. USeekM[14] is an extension library for semantic databases that adds efficient geospatial support. The module supports OpenGIS geometry types (such as Point, Line, Polygon) and functions (such as Within, Intersects, Overlaps, Crosses) as standardized in the OGC GeoSPARQL standard. Among database engines, Virtuoso Universal Server [14] can handle 2-dimensional points expressed with WGS84 coordinates, as well as storage of geometric shapes (lines, polygons, etc.). In order to check if two geometries are related, Virtuoso uses some built-in predicates (*e.g.,*`ST_contains`, `ST_within`, `ST_intersect`) and supports some geometric functions (*e.g.,* `ST_distance`, `ST_x`, `ST_y`, `ST_z`). At the moment Virtuoso is not fully compliant with GeoSPARQL. Oracle Spatial and Graph[11] supports, among others, RDF Semantic Graph data management and analysis, its applications ranging from semantic data integration to linked open data and network graphs used in transportation, utilities, energy and telcos. Oracle Spatial and Graph uses GeoSPARQL for representing and querying spatial data, even if it is not fully compliant with it. A native RDF triple store implementation with spatial query functionality is described by Brodt et al. [5]. They model spatial features in RDF as typed complex literals and define spatial predicates as filter functions in SPARQL. However, their approach is optimized for storing and querying static RDF data with rare updates, as changes and updates in the location data can have an impact on their indexing and data processing. Then, there are works that show how to expose dynamic data sources as Linked Data. Harth et al. [8] present an approach to expose data coming from information services as Linked Data to support their integration. Mapping is performed by using a tool to map RESTfull services to a reference ontology[16]. Although OSM is considered as one source, only queries based on bounding box have been supported. Thus this work does not proposes a general approach to expose OSM data as Linked Data. Speiser et al.[15] and Norton et al.[10] present in their papers general approaches to expose data provided by services as Linked Data when invoked with a proper input, with [15] providing a more complete approach compared to [10].

4 Conclusion and Future Work

We presented LOSM, a service that acts as a SPARQL endpoint on top of Open Street Map data. Differently from `LinkedGeoData`, it does not work by using dumps of the OSM datasets but it queries directly the OSM database by means of a translation from SPARQL to `overpass` API calls. The implementation currently works on a subset of the SPARQL language plus the geographical query constructs from the Jena Spatial extension. We show how fresh and timely geographical data exposed via a SPARQL endpoint in combination with information coming from multilingual knowledge graphs can affect the search for information in a disaster recovery scenario. We are currently working to extend the expressiveness of the SPARQL sub-language supported by LOSM.

Acknowledgements The authors acknowledge partial support of PON03PE_00136_1 Digital Services Ecosystem: DSE and Progetto Corvallis.

[14] `https://dev.opensahara.com/projects/useekm`

References

1. Ontotext AD. Graphdb (formerly owlim) triple store, 2015. http://ontotext.com/products/graphdb/.
2. Sören Auer, Jens Lehmann, and Sebastian Hellmann. Linkedgeodata: Adding a spatial dimension to the web of data. In *Proceedings of the 8th International Semantic Web Conference*, ISWC '09, pages 731–746, 2009.
3. Robert Battle and Dave Kolas. Geosparql: enabling a geospatial semantic web. *Semantic Web Journal*, 3(4):355–370, 2011.
4. Robert Battle and Dave Kolas. Enabling the geospatial semantic web with parliament and geosparql. *Semantic Web*, 3(4):355–370, 2012.
5. Andreas Brodt, Daniela Nicklas, and Bernhard Mitschang. Deep integration of spatial query processing into native rdf triple stores. In *Proceedings of the 18th SIGSPATIAL International Conference on Advances in Geographic Information Systems*, pages 33–42. ACM, 2010.
6. W3C Semantic Web Interest Group. Basic geo (wgs84 lat/long) vocabulary, 2006. http://www.w3.org/2003/01/geo/.
7. Mordechai Haklay and Patrick Weber. Openstreetmap: User-generated street maps. *Pervasive Computing, IEEE*, 7(4):12–18, 2008.
8. Andreas Harth, Craig A Knoblock, Steffen Stadtmüller, Rudi Studer, and Pedro Szekely. On-the-fly integration of static and dynamic linked data. In *Proceedings of the Fourth International Workshop on Consuming Linked Data co-located with the 12th International Semantic Web Conference*, pages 1613–0073.
9. Kostis Kyzirakos, Manos Karpathiotakis, and Manolis Koubarakis. Strabon: a semantic geospatial dbms. In *The Semantic Web–ISWC 2012*, pages 295–311. Springer, 2012.
10. Barry Norton, Reto Krummenacher, Adrian Marte, and Dieter Fensel. Dynamic linked data via linked open services. In *Workshop on Linked Data in the Future Internet at the Future Internet Assembly*, pages 1–10, 2010.
11. Oracle. Oracle spatial and graph. http://bit.ly/1lvCtWi.
12. Vito Claudio Ostuni, Giosia Gentile, Tommaso Di Noia, Roberto Mirizzi, Davide Romito, and Eugenio Di Sciascio. Mobile movie recommendations with linked data. In *Availability, Reliability, and Security in Information Systems and HCI - IFIP WG 8.4, 8.9, TC 5 International Cross-Domain Conference, CD-ARES*, pages 400–415, 2013.
13. Kostas Patroumpas, Giorgos Giannopoulos, and Spiros Athanasiou. Towards geospatial semantic data management: strengths, weaknesses, and challenges ahead. In *Proceedings of the 22nd ACM SIGSPATIAL International Conference on Advances in Geographic Information Systems*, pages 301–310. ACM, 2014.
14. OpenLink Software. Virtuoso universal server. http://ontotext.com/products/graphdb/.
15. Sebastian Speiser and Andreas Harth. Integrating linked data and services with linked data services. In *The Semantic Web: Research and Applications*, pages 170–184. Springer, 2011.
16. Mohsen Taheriyan, Craig A Knoblock, Pedro Szekely, and José Luis Ambite. Rapidly integrating services into the linked data cloud. In *The Semantic Web–ISWC 2012*, pages 559–574. Springer, 2012.

SINSE+: a software for the acquisition and analysis of open data in health and social area
(Discussion Paper)

Lidia Federico[1], Pasquale Franco[1], Antonio Minelli[2], Alessandra Perri[3], Luciano Caroprese[4], Rocco Picarelli[4], Giuseppe Tradigo[4], Eugenio Vocaturo[4], Francesco Dattola[1], Alfredo Fortunato[3], Pasquale Lambardi[5], Sara Laurita[3], Ivana Pellegrino[1], Alfredo Garro[4], Andrea Pugliese[4], Andrea Tagarelli[4], Pierangelo Veltri[5], and Ester Zumpano[4]

[1] e way Enterprise Business Solutions S.r.l {surname}@eway-solutions.it
[2] Ithea S.r.l. {surname}@ithea.it
[3] Contesti S.r.l. {surname}@contesti.info
[4] University of Calabria, DIMES Dept. {surname}@dimes.unical.it
[5] University of Catanzaro {surname}@unicz.it

Abstract. The paper presents a business intelligence platform, called SINSE+, able to acquire and analyze open data to define and analyze indicators. SINSE+ has been designed and tested to analyse data regarding the context of health and social information, but it can be used for any application area. The aim is to produce dashboards able to combine information from different open data sources regarding social and health information, able to improve citizen wellness. The system is composed by: (i) a data extraction module (web scraping); (ii) an ETL module; (iii) a storage and querying module and (iv) an indicators representation module able to display information according to indicators of interest (dashboard). It has been tested with information regarding social health topics, with particular attention to the BES report (Socio-Economic Welfare). SINSE+ is one of the results of an industrial project, funded by the Calabria Region and coordinated by ICT-SUD consortium.

1 The SINSE+ Prototype

SINSE+ is one of the results of a research project, aiming to develop an Open Data platform to crawl, store and represent heterogeneous data obtained from open data sources. We focus on open data regarding social and government services about social and health related services. The purpose is to support both public and private companies as well as citizens. SINSE+ allows to define a single model, which incorporates advanced technologies for the treatment and handling information related to geographic areas. Heterogeneous data sources are linked and made available to citizens, including data regarding health care, habits, behaviour, environment, social services and so on. The prototype system developed as a result of the project SINSE+, allows you to extract data from open sources, represent and analyze data through analytics tools. The system architecture is reported in Figure 1, and is composed mainly by: (i) a crawling module; (ii) an ETL module; (iii) a storage and querying module; (iv) an analytical module.

The data context regards the generation of indicators related to wellness. This theme plays a crucial role in economic and social analysis as it is of great interest to define and identify indicators able to relate environmental information, geographical information, health related services and pathologies (e.g., chronic pathologies diffusions and prevention actions) and, more general the definition of indicators able to measure status and progress of geographic areas. This theme plays a crucial role in economic and social analysis as it joins a line of international studies aimed at defining and identifying indicators beyond wellness [1]. For instance, SINSE+ has been tested with available open data published by Italian local and regional administrations and by evaluating the following indicators also defined by the Italian Institute for Statistics (Istat)[2, 3]: environmental, health, economic well-being, education and training, work and reconciling life times, social relationships, politics and institutions, security, citizen wellness, landscape and cultural heritage, research and innovation, quality of services.

2 The ETL Module: Alarico

The ETL module, called *Alarico*, aims to manage the data acquisition obtained by crawling open data sources. It is designed to map and elaborate data thus to produce and upload relevant information into a single and reconciled data structure. The architecture is shown in Figure 2. Alarico has been developed in Java by following the following functional requirements: (i) extraction and acquisition from open data (ii) data preprocessing (iii) metadata generation by following user requirements (semi-automatic method); (iv) data export into data warehouse platform; (v) data integration (i.e., a single data file has to be exported).

Alarico accepts as input CSV as well as spreadsheet files (e.g., XLS ones). It allows the user to process one or multiple files and offers all the functions needed to manage metadata and attributes associated with them. It also allows to define matching rules to relate metadata and information extracted from sources.

Alarico preliminarily performs a preprocessing phase (validation and cleaning) of raw data; it then extracts data and loads it in the application allowing the user to refine data and to define transformation rules. Data is loaded into a unique file based on the key-value pairs paradigm. Moreover, it is possible to save and reuse a template with previously defined extraction rules. Alarico also allows the user to define indicators of interest with respect to defined application fields. Metadata files are also defined and can be stored as template; e.g., as a table, where columns represent the fields and rows correspond to a defined indicator.

Starting from metadata files data is extracted from open data sources and associated with files containing the corresponding indicators. This phase is per-

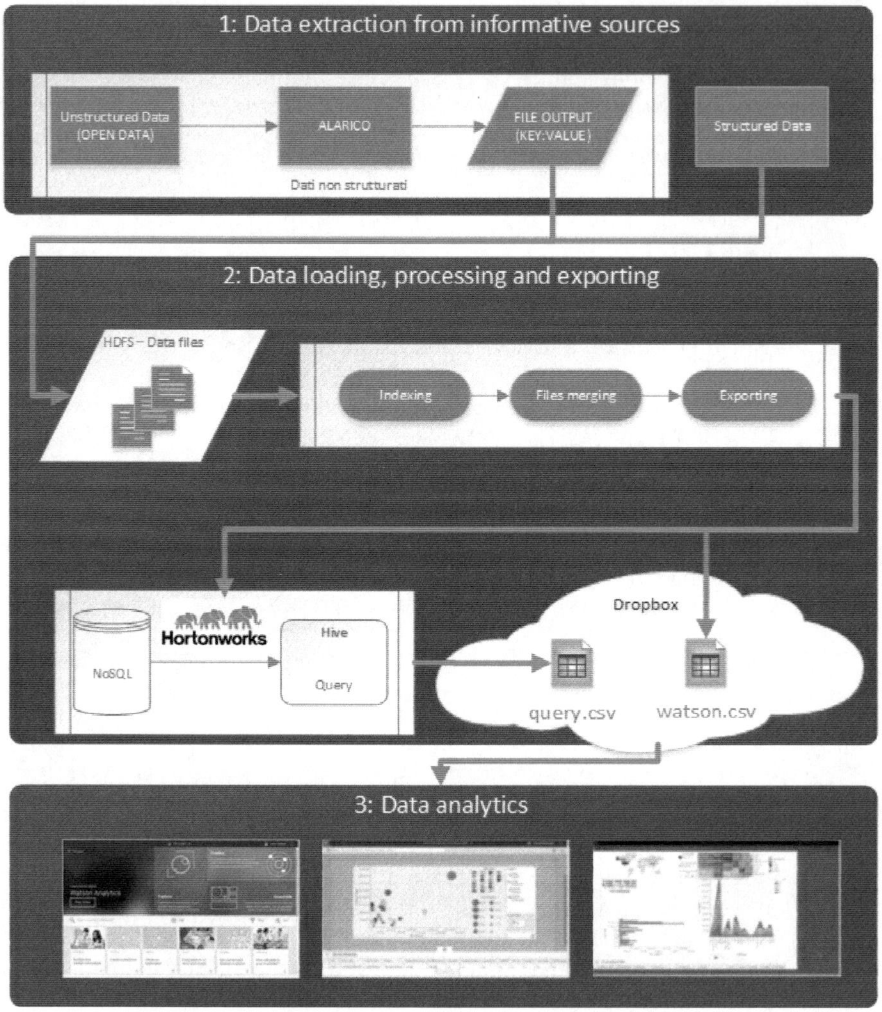

Fig. 1. SINSE+ Logical Architecture

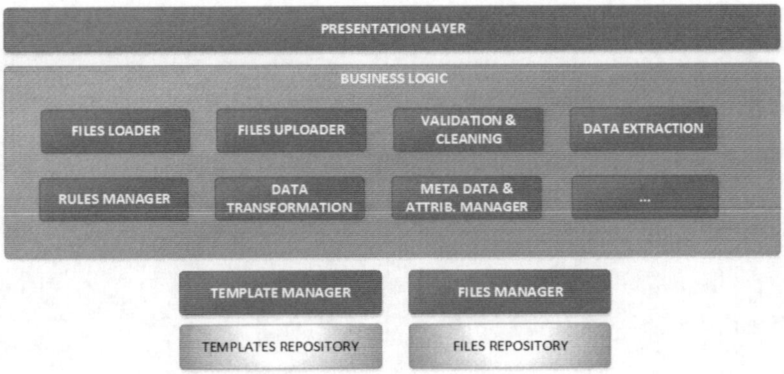

Fig. 2. Alarico ETL Module Architecture

formed in a semi-automatic phase, i.e., domain experts may verify the mapping operation.

Data is mapped into a key-value based file and stored in an Hadoop Distributed File System instance. Then, files are combined to create a single file that is passed to the analysis module for the definition of analytics step. The analitycs module provides advanced reporting tools. Figure 5 reports an analytics result example showing the effects of defining an indicator of interest in a give context.

3 Storage and Combination Module

The *Storage and Combination Module* of SINSE+ combines the produced files with data extracted by Alarico and is based on *Hortonworks*.[6]

Hortonworks is an Hadoop Open Source distribution, a framework designed to easily write applications that can deal with a large amount of data in parallel on large clusters consisting of thousands of nodes. It ensures high reliability and availability. The NoSQL database *HBase*[7] is used, and the structure is well suited to the type of data to be processed. Its tables are characterized by rows having a variable number of columns so that data extracted from different files, having an heterogeneous structure in terms of number and name of fields, can be stored. The Hadoop Distributed File System, HDFS, is a portable and scalable distributed file system written in Java for the Hadoop framework. Each node in Hadoop typically has a single-node data and a cluster of data nodes forms a HDFS cluster. The file system is at the basis of all applications for Hadoop, such as the distributed NoSQL databases and processing operations of Map-Reduce that are performed in parallel on all nodes in the cluster. The Hortonworks

[6] http://hortonworks.com/products/hdp/

[7] https://hbase.apache.org/

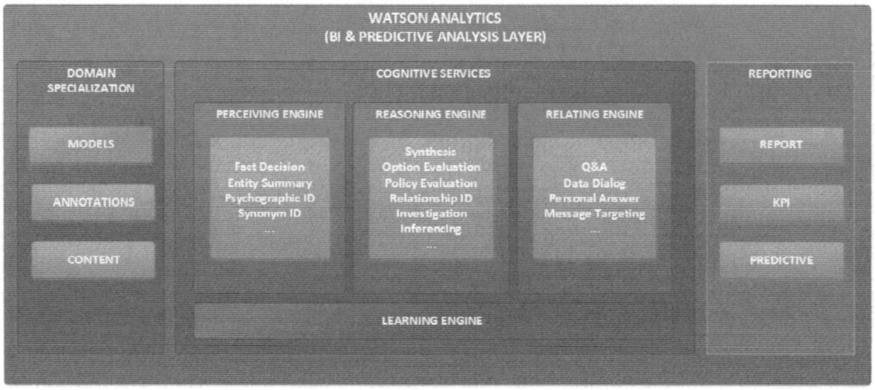

Fig. 3. IBM Watson Analytics architecture

server which Hadoop, HBase and many other services are installed on, for the analysis and management of big data, offers a web interface allowing to access and interact with data. The system can be accessed via username and password, and allows to configure privileges for each user. The current status of the cluster can be verified in real time using a special dashboard for the management of all the platform modules. On the Hortonworks server a Java application, that processes all files uploaded in HDFS using Alarico and combines them in a single file (in key-value format), has been implemented. It also creates a table in the database containing all the data, which can be accessed and queried directly through the tools provided by the server. The obtained files can be exported and submitted to the analysis stage, implemented in the next module.

4 Analysis Module

The SINSE+ Analysis Module is based on *IBM Watson Analytics*,[8] whose structure is reported in Figure 3.

IBM Watson Analytics is a tool allowing to create in a very simply way different types of visual representations to facilitate the analysis of data and predictions. It is accessible through an intuitive platform and does not require a particular prior training. It requires data to match a certain and well-defined scheme. Accepted file formats (e.g., csv and xls), have to be in a tabular form and cannot have completely blank rows or columns. From the main screen of IBM Watson Analytics, it is possible to choose one of the following features:

- **Refine**: It performs a sort of finishing and cleaning of the dataset before submitting it to any other processing stage. It is possible, for example, to add new fields, view the quality of the data for each column, create hierarchies, filters, etc.

[8] http://www.ibm.com/analytics/watson-analytics/us-en/

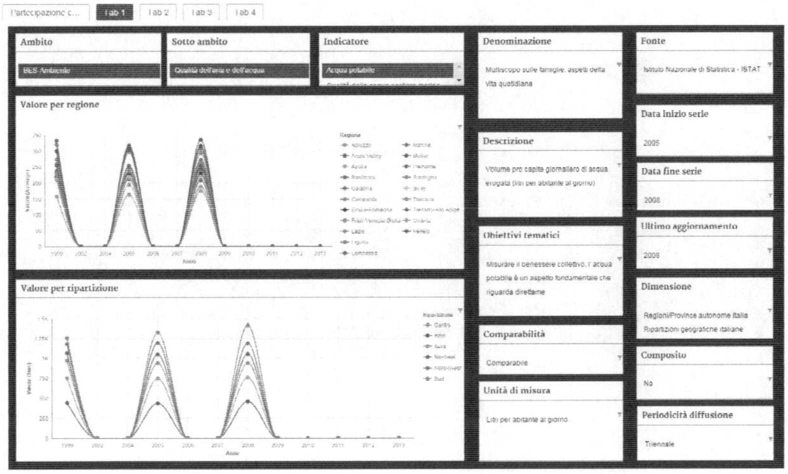

(a)

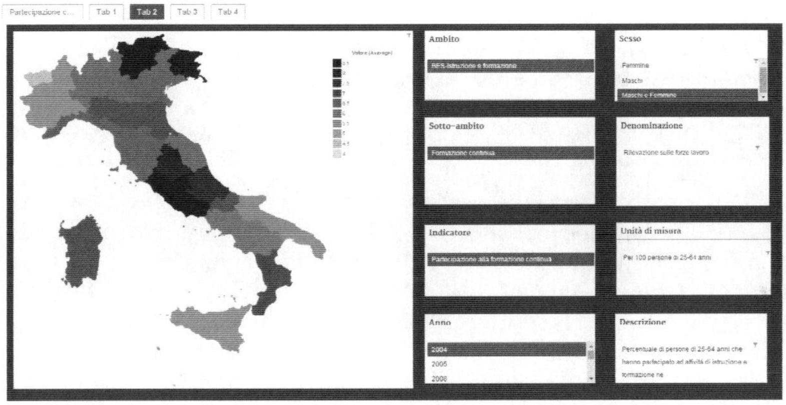

(b)

Fig. 4. Dashboards created with Assemble

- **Explore**: It submits queries to the system over an imported dataset. The application suggests some default queries and allows to create new ones in natural language. IBM Watson Analytics answers to the queries by means of easily understandable charts.
- **Predict**: It can be used to make predictions using uploaded data and by applying special algorithms that look for patterns that will be used to find the fields influencing a given value.
- **Assemble**: It builds informative and interactive dashboard used by the user to analyze the obtained output.

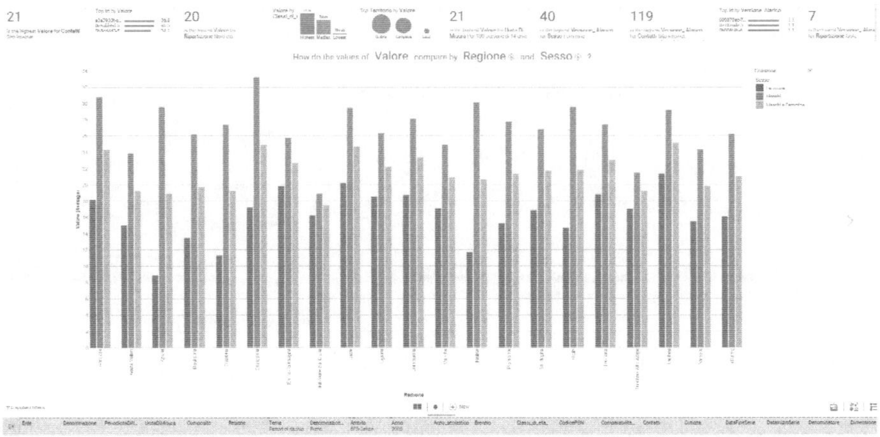

Fig. 5. Graph created with the Explore function

By using the *Assemble* functions, the Analytics module allows the creation of interactive dashboards through which the end users are able to explore data contained in the data warehouse. Users can also choose among different templates composed by functional blocks inside which a number of object can be located (e.g., images, videos, text) as shown in Figure 4.

Particularly, inside the dashboard depicted in Figure 4(b) we can see two graphs: the upper being a line graph representing values by region and the lower a graph showing the same value re-partitioned according to the fields *Ambito* (scope), *Sotto Ambito* (sub-scope) and *Indicatore* (indicator). Given this choice, all of the other fields, e.g., *Denominazione* (name), *Descrizione* (description), *Fonte* (source), will assume the values associated with that indicator.

The Alarico module also allows the extraction of information related to a certain topic form data sources. Files can be presented in a tabular form, whose columns represent fields and rows, each corresponding to an indicator, contain metadata associated to them. Starting from such a file, Alarico is able to extract information contained in it and to associate them with files containing corresponding indicators, in a fully automated fashion.

Data is the extracted and transformed in a common format which will allow it to be combined with other data already contained in the system repository. During this phase the domain expert is required to interactively select fields and dimension contained in data.

Data loaded and stored in the storage module are processed and analyzed in the next phases. The result is represented in a key-value format file loaded in the Hadoop distributed file-system. When all of the files are loaded on the file-system, Alarico is able to combine them in a unique file which will be analyzed in the analytics phase. The Analytics module allows the user for advanced reporting features via the Explore function. In Figure 5, an example graph is depicted showing, in the lower part, the column names of the table containing data. The user can choose one or more columns to generate a graph (e.g., in the example reported, *Tema*, *DenominazioneIndicatore*, *Ambito* and *Anno* columns were selected).

Acknowledgements

This paper has been partly supported by Progetto POR Calabria FESR 2007-2013 "*Sistema di reasoning e tutoring su grandi moli di dati* (SINSE+)", CUP: J84E07000530005, delivered by: e way Enterprise Business Solutions S.r.l (leading partner), Contesti S.r.l., Ithea S.r.l., DIMES - University of Calabria.

References

[1] R. Boarini, A. Johansson, M. Mira d'Ercole, Alternative Measures of Well Being, 2006

[2] Comitato CNEL/Istat sugli indicatori di progresso e benessere, La misurazione del Benessere equo e sostenibile, 2012

[3] S. Bruni, M. Zupi, Gli indicatori integrativi del PIL, 2014

[4] Mecca, Giansalvatore, Paolo Papotti, and Donatello Santoro. "A Short History of Schema Mapping Systems." SEBD. 2012.

[5] Duan, Lian, and Li Da Xu. "Business intelligence for enterprise systems: a survey." Industrial Informatics, IEEE Transactions on 8.3 (2012): 679-687.

[6] Chen, Hsinchun, Roger HL Chiang, and Veda C. Storey. "Business Intelligence and Analytics: From Big Data to Big Impact." MIS quarterly 36.4 (2012): 1165-1188.

[7] Assuno, M. D., Calheiros, R. N., Bianchi, S., Netto, M. A., Buyya, R. "Big Data computing and clouds: Trends and future directions." Journal of Parallel and Distributed Computing 79 (2015): 3-15.

Food Recommendation based on Semantic Annotations and Reference Prescriptions: the SMART BREAK project

Devis Bianchini, Valeria De Antonellis, Michele Melchiori

Dept. of Information Engineering University of Brescia
Via Branze, 38 - 25123 Brescia (Italy)
{devis.bianchini|valeria.deantonellis|michele.melchiori}@unibs.it

Abstract. Food recommendation, as well as searching for health-related information, presents specific characteristics if compared with conventional recommender systems, since it often has educational purposes, to improve behavioural habits of users. In this paper, we presents a Food Recommendation System that aims at addressing some of the above mentioned issues, using a recipe dataset and annotations to propose menus according to user's preferences. Reference prescription schemes, e.g., compliant with nutritional guidelines, are defined to prepare suggested choices. The recommender system has been developed in the context of the SMART BREAK project, supported by a grant from Regione Lombardia in the field of "smart cities and communities" and related to the main topics of the 2015 World Exposition (EXPO2015, Milan, Italy), where the University of Brescia aimed at promoting healthy behavioural habits in nutrition.

1 Introduction

Nutrition habits and their effects on health, on the metabolism and on performance at school, during sports or at work, are becoming more and more important. Existing approaches for recommending food and health-related information consider several aspects, namely personal and cultural preferences, health and religion constraints [1, 2]. Other approaches integrate Semantic Web technologies, namely ontologies [3] and medical vocabularies [4], to reason about different kinds of constraints. Indeed, food recommendation, as well as searching for health-related information, presents specific characteristics if compared with conventional recommender systems, since it often has educational purposes, to improve behavioural habits of users. To this purposes, people are more and more calling on nutritionists and food experts. Motivations are not only related to the treatment of eating disorders or to aesthetic reasons, but people also want to be ensured well-being and healthiness.

In this paper, we presents a Food Recommendation System developed in the context of the SMART BREAK project - an acronym for SMART adaptive Bialetti REestorAtion Kit. The SMART BREAK project has been supported by a grant from Regione Lombardia in the field of "smart cities and communities" and was related to the main topics of the 2015 World Exposition (EXPO2015, Milan, Italy), where the University of Brescia aimed at promoting healthy behavioural habits in nutrition. The food recommender system uses a recipe dataset and annotations to propose menus according to user's preferences. Reference prescription schemes, e.g., compliant with nutritional guidelines, are defined to prepare suggested choices. In a more general way, the recommender is finalized to the improvement of the nutrition habits of the individuals, thanks to an increased awareness of food and drinks ingestion.

Project motivations. The modular system SMART BREAK integrates into a single "object" the features of several appliances, which are today available as stand-alone devices such as coffee machine, kettle, (slow) juicer and (microwave) oven. The SMART BREAK appliance not only integrates them from a mechanical point of view, but the different components are also supported by a (smart) digital communication infrastructure, e.g. in order to minimize power consumption or automatically infer information about appliance usage. In particular, the introduction of a food diary to be filled in a semi-automatic way is one of the most innovative aspects of the project. The diary can be filled: (a) on the SMART BREAK appliance, that is equipped with a component that is able to automatically recognize ingested food and drinks, e.g. by reading the bar codes; (b) through a smartphone APP, to track the ingestion of food and drinks in every moment and everywhere. Moreover, additional data about the physical activity of the individual can be collected using other kinds of wearable devices, such as step counters and smart wristband, in order to balance the individual calorie count. In this way, the user has at disposal information about nutrition facts on food and drinks assumed in every moment. Daily, according to the amount of ingested calories, the SMART BREAK system provides advertisements about recipes to prepare for a healthy nutrition. This has been made possible by integrating data coming from the food diary with other data sources, such as a database of recipes, that contains nutrition facts and calories, as well as guidelines and prescriptions on healthy nutrition habits. Recommended recipes are identified taking into account the user who is advised, considering his/her lifestyle (in terms of nutrition habits, level of physical activity, daily workload), thus enhancing long-term quality of life, in particular for young and old people. As an evolution of this project, our aim is at integrating the food recommender system described in the present paper.

2 Recommendation model

Let's consider, for example, Jasmine, who is looking for recipe suggestions to have lunch during her working hours. Jasmine is registered within a food recommender system, where she has an associated profile. Jasmine declared a preference for having meat during lunches. She suffers from long-term diseases, such as diabetes and high-blood-pressure, therefore white meat is more advisable. She belongs to the Islamic religion, so recommendations about any food that contains alcohol or pork are not acceptable, since this food is prohibited to Muslims. Other characteristics emerge if she is looking for recipes to cook at home, for which ingredients and cooking procedures assume a specific relevance. Each factor may be represented through a feature, that in turn might assume different values. Features can be used both to characterize the recommended items (e.g., recipes, dishes) and to represent users' profiles. Moreover, feature matching can be based either on the feature values contained in a request for suggestions by the user (short-term feature matching), or on the relative frequency of feature values contained within the history of past choices made by the user (long-term feature matching, aiming at considering long-term user's preferences). The underlying recommendation model presents the following distinguishing features, as shown in Figure 1.

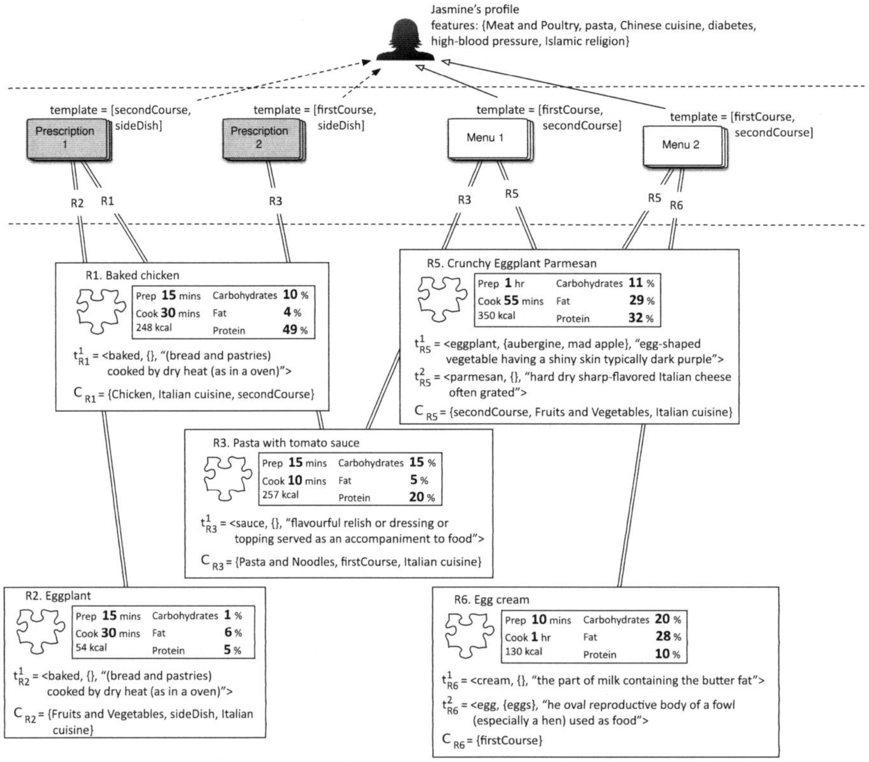

Fig. 1. Recommendation model (recipes, menus and prescriptions) instantiated on the running example.

Multiple levels of aggregations. Recipes represent the most fine-grained items to be recommended. Nevertheless, recipes are suggested in the form of aggregations as menus. For example, in Figure 1 `R3`, `R5` and `R6` are aggregated into two menus, denoted with `Menu 1` and `Menu 2` in figure. Therefore, their relationships with other recipes and variety of suggestions have to be considered for recommendation purposes. Moreover, not all aggregations are suitable. Specific combinations of recipes might be due to particular menu configurations (e.g., appetizer, first course, second course, dessert). According to our general model, a recipe is described as $r_i = \langle ID_i, n_i, \mathcal{C}_i, \mathcal{T}_i \rangle$, where: ID_i ($\forall i = 1, \ldots N$) is the unique identifier of the recipe (we denote with $\mathcal{R}$ the overall set of N recipes available within the dataset); n_i is the name of the recipe; $\mathcal{C}_i$ and $\mathcal{T}_i$ are sets of features used to characterize the recipe. We distinguish among: (i) categories ($\mathcal{C}_i$), that classify the recipe and are taken from a top-down ontology that extends the `food.owl` ontology[1]; (ii) semantic tags, that is, bottom-up keywords assigned to the recipes by users to annotate them and semantically disambiguated using a general-purpose lexical system or thesaurus (WordNet), to face polisemy and synonymy, that affect traditional tagging. For example, in our approach each recipe is classified through categories directly related to food, such as the `RecipeType` (e.g., appetizer, first course, second course, fruits, dessert), the `CookingStyle` (e.g., Asian cuisine), the ingredients used in the recipe (e.g., chicken, beef, rice), and other categories such as the `Religion` (e.g., Islamic) for which the recipe is meant, or the `Pathology` (e.g., diabetes, high-blood pressure), for which the recipe is advised (see [5] for details). Semantic tagging is supported using the semantic disambiguation system extensively described in [5], where a semantic tag $t \in \mathcal{T}_i$ is a triplet, composed of: (i) the tag itself extracted from WordNet; (ii) the set of all the terms in the synset; (iii) the human readable definition associated with the synset. For example, in Figure 1 semantic tag t^1_{R5} defines `eggplant` through its synonyms `aubergine` and `mad apple` and its human readable definition.

Menus and prescriptions. In the context of our food recommendation approach, we distinguish two kinds of aggregations: (a) available *menus*, that is, combinations of recipes chosen in the past by the users of the system; (b) *prescriptions*, that is, proper combinations of recipes that are advisable for specific kinds of users. For instance, some Jasmine's preferences (e.g., having meat during lunches, all the days throughout the week) may contrast with best habits, according to up-to-date medical prescriptions. Moreover, recent medical prescriptions recommend variety and balancing of different ingredients and nutrients, which recipes are composed of. This means that reference prescriptions might be used as first class citizens in recommending recipes to users who present particular profiles. Nevertheless, prescriptions cannot be totally imposed to users, disregarding their own preferences. Lifestyle improvements should gradually guide users towards better choices. Formally, we define an aggregation (either a menu or a prescription) $a_j \in \mathcal{A}$ as $a_j = \langle n_{a_j}, \mathcal{R}[a_j], \tau_{a_j} \rangle$, where: $\mathcal{A}$ denotes the overall set of aggregations; n_{a_j} is the name of the aggregation; $\mathcal{R}[a_j] \subseteq \mathcal{R}$ is the set of recipes aggregated in a_j; τ_{a_j} is the template of the aggregation, expressed in terms of specific categories. In our approach, given an aggregation a_j, τ_{a_j} is identified considering the `RecipeType` category. Examples of templates may be [appetizer, first course, second course, dessert] or [first course, fruit]. The way prescriptions

[1] `http://krono.act.uji.es/Links/ontologies/food.owl/view`.

are associated with users depends on the features used to describe users' profiles.

Long-term and short-term preferences. Users are profiled according to their preferences and past menu choices, that are collected to represent the history of recipe and menu selections made by the user. Formally, we define the profile $p(u)$ of a user $u \in \mathcal{U}$ as $p(u) = \langle ID_u, \mathcal{C}[u], \mathcal{T}[u], \mathcal{M}[u], \mathcal{P}[u] \rangle$, where: $\mathcal{U}$ denotes the overall set of users; ID_u is used to identify the user u; $\mathcal{C}[u]$ and $\mathcal{T}[u]$ are the sets of features (namely, categories and tags) used to denote the preferences of u; $\mathcal{M}[u]$ is the set of menus chosen by the user in the past, that in turn may represent the preferences of the user u about recipes to be recommended; $\mathcal{P}[u]$ is the set of prescriptions assigned to the user in the system. When Jasmine is looking for menu suggestions, she generates a request $r_r(u)$ formulated as $r_r(u) = \langle \mathcal{C}_r, \mathcal{T}_r, \tau_r \rangle$, where: $\mathcal{C}_r$ is a set of categories that represent immediate, *short-term preferences* of Jasmine; similarly, $\mathcal{T}_r$ is a set of (semantic) tags, specified by issuing the request; τ_r is the menu template Jasmine is searching for. The recommender system takes into account the profile $p(u)$ of the user u (Jasmine), who is looking for suggestions. To this aim, the request $r_r(u)$ is expanded with the categories and semantic tags that are present within the profile $p(u)$, that represent *long-term preferences of the user*. We denote with $\widehat{r}_r(u)$ the expanded version of the request, where $\widehat{r}_r(u) = \langle \widehat{\mathcal{C}}_r, \widehat{\mathcal{T}}_r, \tau_r \rangle$. The set $\widehat{\mathcal{C}}_r$ contains both the categories specified in $\mathcal{C}_r$ and the categories within $p(u)$. The set $\mathcal{C}_r$ might also be empty, thus denoting that the system should exclusively rely on the preferences contained within $p(u)$. Each category $c_r \in \widehat{\mathcal{C}}_r$ is weighted by means of a coefficient $\omega_r \in [0, 1]$ such that: (a) $\omega_r = 1$ if $c_r \in \mathcal{C}_r$, (b) $\omega_r = freq(c_r) \in [0, 1]$ otherwise. The value of ω_r means that a category explicitly specified in the request will be considered the most for identifying candidate recipes. The term $freq(c_r)$ computes the relative frequency of category c_r among all the categories that annotate the recipes contained in the menus $\mathcal{M}[u]$ of the profile $p(u)$. Less frequent categories will be considered as less important for identifying candidate recipes. If a category c_r is present both in $\mathcal{C}_r$ and in the profile, then $\omega_r = 1$. The same applies for (semantic) tags. If u is a new user, without a history of past choices, then $\widehat{r}_r(u) = r_r(u)$ (no expansion). In this case, prescriptions will be used to differentiate the user's choices. Frequencies are computed on a menu basis, since recipes are recommended only within menus. For instance, let's consider the recipes and Jasmine's profile shown in Figure 1, and the following request, issued to search for menus and recipes containing `baked poultry`, according to [`firstCourse`, `secondCourse`] template: $r_r(u) = \langle \{\texttt{poultry}\}, \{\texttt{baked}\}, [\texttt{firstCourse}, \texttt{secondCourse}] \rangle$. The following expanded version of the request is generated (relative frequency values are specified among parenthesis):

$$\widehat{\mathcal{C}}_r = \{\texttt{poultry}(1.0), \texttt{secondCourse}(1.0), \texttt{PastaandNoodles}(0.5), \texttt{firstCourse}(1.0), \texttt{Italiancuisine}(1.0), \texttt{FruitsandVegetables}(1.0)\}$$

$$\widehat{\mathcal{T}}_r = \{\texttt{baked}(1.0), \texttt{cream}(0.5), \texttt{egg}(0.5), \texttt{eggplant}(1.0), \texttt{parmesan}(1.0)\}$$

where, for example, `eggplant` is present in all the menus associated with Jasmine's profile.

3 Menu recommendation system

The recommendation steps based on the model described above have been identified as *filter-aggregate-rank* (see Figure 2). The input of the *filter* step is the set $\mathcal{R}$ of all the available recipes and the request $\widehat{r}_r(u)$. First, τ_r element specified in the request is considered. Those recipes such that their `RecipeType` is not included within τ_r will not pass the filtering step. In the running example, only `R2` will not be further considered, because it is neither a first course nor a second course recipe.

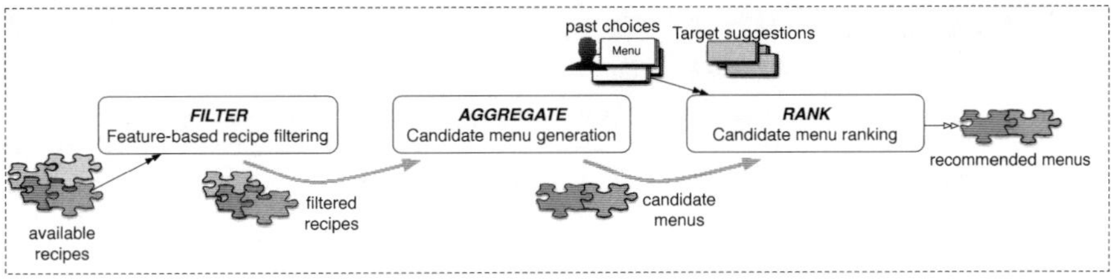

Fig. 2. Menu recommendation steps.

Not all features can be exploited in the same way to filter out not relevant recipes. For instance, let's consider some constraints imposed by the Islamic religion or by some allergies. Recipes that do not respect these constraints must be excluded before any other kind of comparison. These constraints, to keep our model as more general as possible, are defined within the domain ontology and are expressed in terms of other features. For example, the Islamic religion within the Jasmine's profile excludes all recipes that are annotated with `pork` or `alcohol` as contained ingredients. After τ_r and ontological constraints have been used to pre-select recipes, the filtering based on remaining features is applied, according to the *category-based* and *tag-based relevance* metrics summarised in Table 1.

In the *aggregate* step, recipes are aggregated into menus that must be compliant with the template τ_r specified in the request $\widehat{r}_r(u)$. This significantly reduces the number of menu configurations to be generated: in fact, a candidate menu can not contain two recipes r_i and r_j annotated with the same `RecipeType`. Generated menus are *ranked* according to their similarity with: (i) past menu choices made by the user u who is issuing the request for suggestions, represented by the set $\mathcal{M}[u]$; (ii) prescriptions prepared for the user u according to his/her profile, represented by the set $\mathcal{P}[u]$. Since both menus and prescriptions are formally defined as sets of recipes, the building block in this step is the similarity measure between items aggregations (*item aggregation similarity*), that is computed as follows:

$$Sim_{agg}(a_i, a_j) = \frac{2 \cdot \sum_{r_i, r_j} Sim(r_i, r_j)}{|a_i| + |a_j|} \in [0, 1] \tag{3}$$

where a_i and a_j represent the two compared aggregations, r_i (resp., r_j) is an item (i.e., a recipe) included within a_i (resp., within a_j), $|a_i|$ (resp., $|a_j|$) denotes the number of recipes included within a_i (resp., within a_j). Therefore, we consider

Category-based relevance
$$Sim_{cat}(\widehat{r}_r, r_i) = \frac{2 \cdot \sum_{c_r \in \widehat{\mathcal{C}}_r, c_i \in \mathcal{C}_i} \omega_r \cdot CatSim(c_r, c_i)}{\lvert \mathcal{C}_i \rvert} \in [0,1] \quad (1)$$ where $r_i = \langle ID_i, n_i, \mathcal{C}_i, \mathcal{T}_i \rangle$; $\widehat{r}_r(u) = \langle \widehat{\mathcal{C}}_r, \widehat{\mathcal{T}}_r, \tau_r \rangle$ (request); $CatSim(c_r, c_i)$ is the *category similarity* between c_r and c_i (two categories c_r and c_i are more similar as the number of recipes that have been annotated with both the categories increases with respect to the overall number of recipes annotated with c_r and with c_i). The domain ontology is also considered in this case.
Tag-based relevance
$$Sim_{tag}(\widehat{r}_r, r_i) = \frac{2 \cdot \sum_{t_1 \in \widehat{\mathcal{T}}_r, t_2 \in \mathcal{T}_i} TermAff(t_1, t_2)}{\lvert \mathcal{T}_i \rvert} \in [0,1] \quad (2)$$ where: $TermAff(t_1, t_2)$ is the terminological affinity between pairs of tags, one from the first set ($\widehat{\mathcal{T}}_r$) and one from the second set ($\mathcal{T}_i$). The computation of $TermAff(t_1, t_2) \in [0,1]$ takes into account both semantic and traditional tags. See [5] for details.

Table 1. Relevance metrics for feature-based recipe filtering.

two aggregations as more similar as the number of similar items in the two aggregations increases.

The final ranking of a generated menu $a_k \in A^*$, recommended to the user u who issued a request for suggestions, is performed through a ranking function $\rho : A^* \mapsto [0,1]$, computed as follows:

$$\rho(a_i) = \omega_m \cdot \frac{\sum_{a[u] \in \mathcal{M}[u]} Sim_{agg}(a_i, a[u])}{\lvert \mathcal{M}[u] \rvert} + \omega_p \cdot \frac{\sum_{\widehat{a}[u] \in \mathcal{P}[u]} Sim_{agg}(a_i, \widehat{a}[u])}{\lvert \mathcal{P}[u] \rvert} \quad (4)$$

where $\omega_m, \omega_p \in [0,1]$, $\omega_m + \omega_p = 1.0$, are weights used to balance the impact of past menu choices and prescriptions on the ranking of recommended menus. We have chosen $\omega_m < \omega_p$ (i.e., $\omega_m \cong 0.4$ and $\omega_p \cong 0.6$) in order to stimulate users on improving their food and nutrition habits, without recommending menus and recipes that are too much distant from users' preferences. This is the most innovative aspect of the approach presented here, compared to recent food recommendation literature.

Implementation and experimental issues. We implemented the food recommendation approach as a web application called PREFer (**P**rescriptions for **RE**commending **F**ood). The *PREFer Web Interface* guides the user through the registration process, the menu recommendation, the publication of new recipes, also supporting semantic disambiguation of tags. Experiments on our food recommendation approach have been carried on a dataset obtained by extending an existing one[2], containing about 220k recipes, randomly aggregated into about

[2] `http://mslab.csie.ntu.edu.tw/~tim/recipe.zip`.

100k menus. Performance tests have been performed , where the PREFer system is presenting comparable average precision with respect to recent approaches. To verify the impact of the approach in improving the users' habits, further experiments will be performed on a population of about two hundreds users, equally distributed among males and females. The compliance of users' choices with reference prescriptions, in order to quantify how much the system is able to improve their behaviour, is quantified through the average aggregation similarity between users' choices and reference prescriptions, starting from Equation (3).

4 Conclusions

In this paper, we presented a food recommendation approach, related to the topics of the SMART BREAK project. This paper has been meant as a complementary approach to recent food recommendation efforts, in order to take into account reference prescriptions schemes for food recommendation that aim at improving users' nutritional habits. One of the major extensions of the approach concerns its application to support users to compile food diaries and to help medical doctors in implementing remote surveillance on their patients' nutrition habits. Further experiments will be carried on, in order to check how much the proposed approach is able to effectively improve nutritional habits and lifestyles.

Acknowledgments. This paper is an extended abstract of the work presented in [5].

References

1. A. Al Nazer, T. Helmy, M. Al Mulhem, User's Profile Ontology-Based Semantic Framework for Personalized Food and Nutrition Recommendation, Procedia Computer Science (32) (2014) 101–108.
2. Y. Wang, Z. Liu, Personalized health information retrieval system, in: AMIA Annual Symposium Proceedings, 2005, p. 1149.
3. S. Abidi, H. Chen, Adaptable personalized care planning via a semantic web framework, in: 20th Int. Conf. of the European Federation for Medical Informatics, 2006.
4. O. Suominen, E. Hyvonen, K. Viljanen, E. Hukka, HealthFinland - A national semantic publishing network and portal for health information, in: Web Semantics: Science, Services and Agents on the World Wide Web, 2009, pp. 287–297.
5. D. Bianchini, V. De Antonellis, M. Melchiori, A Web-based Application for Semantic-driven Food Recommendation with Reference Prescriptions, in: Web Information Systems Engineering (WISE), 2015, LNCS 9419, pp. 32–46.
6. T. Rankinen, C. Bouchard, Genetics of food intake and eating behavior phenotypes in humans, Annual Review of Nutrition 26 (2006) 413–434.

Government Interoperability Frameworks: Middleware Tools for the Italian SPCoop

Donatello Santoro , Michele Santomauro, and Enzo Veltri

Università della Basilicata – Potenza, Italy

(Discussion Paper)

Abstract. We discuss deployment solutions for e-Government Interoperability Frameworks (GIFs). We concentrate on the italian SPCoop, a prominent example of a middleware-oriented architectures, where middleware modules act as intermediaries among information systems. We review the SPCoop architecture, and two popular open-source implementations, called OpenSPCoop and freESBee. The two solutions follow radically different philosophies in terms of their internal architectures, which we call "container-bound" and "container-independent". We compare the two systems with respect to one of the main problems in large-scale deployment of SPCooop-like GIFs, namely the need to quickly deploy a large number of middleware instances over a relatively small number of servers. We report a number of experiments to discuss how the different design choices impact performance.

1 Introduction

The development of an electronic Public Administration is a priority for the majority of governments in the world. This is related to the goal of promoting a new paradigm of society known as the *information society*, with the aim of making the PA more efficient, effective and citizen-centred [13]. This goal imposes a fundamental and non-trivial technical requirement to PAs, namely the ability to work in a cooperative way, and therefore requires the existence of interoperability frameworks for their information systems (IS). *Interoperability* can be defined as the ability to exchange data and services by different computing systems. A possible way to achieve interoperability is by adopting a *Service-Oriented Architecture* (SOA) [8], where a *service consumer* requires data or applications (also called services) offered by a *service provider*, with an exchange of messages through Web Services organized according to a common format.

Typically, SOA solutions are based on *point-to-point architectures*, in which each consumer is responsible of discovering the relevant services, and to communicate with their providers in a direct way. This paradigm shows a number of limitations in complex organizations or Governments that need to coordinate all agencies within one country. These problems are usually solved adopting *Government Interoperability Frameworks* (GIFs). Some of these frameworks rely on *middleware-oriented solutions*, where systems do not interact directly with each other, but rather with intermediate layers of software. These middleware components are responsible for various services, among which message-format standardization, transparent routing, enhanced security, reliability, and quality-of-service monitoring [11]. Many countries of the world have adopted their own GIFs. In general, we may classify SOA-oriented GIFs in two main categories:

(i) *lightweight* GIFs: frameworks based on a point-to-point architecture, in which a service consumer and a service provider directly exchange messages with one another through Web services organized according to a common format. Lightweight GIFs represent the majority in Europe [5].

(ii) *heavyweight* GIFs frameworks: they typically adopt a more involved architecture, in which service providers and service consumers are decoupled by means of middleware services; in a middleware-oriented framework, systems do not interact directly with each other, but rather communicate with intermediate layers of software that are responsible for various services(message-format standardization, transparent routing, enhanced security, reliability, and quality-of-service monitoring). Examples of heavyweight GIFs are the Italian SPCoop infrastructure [2], and the European Interoperability Standard IDA eLink [4].

In this paper we discuss heavyweight GIFs, and more specifically the implementations of the Italian SPCoop standard. After quickly reviewing the SPCoop architecture, we concentrate on the large-scale deployment of the middleware services, also called *domain gateways*. In this respect, we compare two open source implementations of the SPCoop standard: freESBee [10] and OpenSPCoop [3]. We show how these systems are based on different philosophies in terms of internal design choices, which we call *container-bound architecture* and *container-independent architecture*.

One of the main technical challenges to reach a wide-spread availability of middleware-oriented GIFs is the possibility of effectively deploying a large number of instances of the middleware modules over small-size server farms. In the paper, we report a number of experimental results that show how the inner architecture of the chosen middleware solution deeply impacts deployment policies. In fact, we discuss two different deployment solutions. The first uses a single middleware instance per server and the second solution deploys multiple middleware instances per server.

2 An Overview of SPCoop

SPCoop is the Italian e-government interoperability infrastructure, aimed at enabling the seamless exchange of application services among information systems of Public Administrations. It is based on a set of standards and guidelines [1], and a middleware architecture that has the following goals: (a) to standardize the format of messages; (b) to provide automatic routing; (c) to provide advanced services, like identity management and single sign-on, service level agreements, and publish and subscribe. In this respect, we can say that the SPCoop standard shares a number of similarities with the goals of *Enterprise Service Buses* [14]. However, differently from ESBs, that are typically centralized middleware components for the various information systems, SPCoop is inherently distributed, since it assumes that information systems of Public Administrations are organized in independent domains that need to cooperate while maintaining their autonomy. In this respect, SPCoop can be considered as a large *distributed ESB* for the Italian e-Government.

The three main components of the SPCoop architecture are the *domain gateway*, the *e-Gov envelope*, and the *service agreement*.

The Domain Gateway. In the typical SPCoop scenario, two local information systems belonging to different administrations (either local or central), and therefore to different domains and networks, may exchange messages through the respective domain gateways. In essence, a domain gateway is the unique access point for all information systems of a given domain to exchange services with systems of other administrations. It is composed of two main components, one for outbound and the other for inbound messages, called the *delegate gateway* and the *application gateway* respectively. For example, assume a local information system S1 from domain A intends to request services from a local information system S2 belonging to domain B. SPCoop disallows direct point-to-point communication between S1 and S2. On the contrary, an SPCoop request message originating from S1 goes first to the delegate gateway of domain A. Based on the recipient specified in the message, the domain gateway is responsible for locating and contacting the appropriate domain gateway, the one of domain B, to transfer the message. When the message is received by the domain gateway at domain B the application gateway contacts the intended recipient S2, and delivers the message. The opposite path is followed to return the answer.

The e-Gov Envelope. The SPCoop rules are quite strict with respect to the format of messages that domain gateways exchange with each other. These messages, called *SPCoop messages*, must adopt the SOAP 1.1 standard, and use HTTPS as a communication protocol. In addition, the SOAP envelope must obey to a fixed grammar in terms of structure and headers, that goes under the name of *e-Gov envelope*. Domain gateways are responsible of properly translating the original application messages into well-formed e-Gov envelopes, enriched with the needed headers.

Registry Services and Service Agreements. As it is common, registry services are provided to allow for service identification and location, security management, and quality of services. Domain gateways contact the centralized registries in order to gain information about the list of subjects that are authorized to exchange messages using the infrastructure, and the so called *service agreements*. Service agreements are XML documents stored in the appropriate registry that specify all the rules according to which service requesters and service providers are supposed to exchange services. More specifically, they describe in detail: (a) all subjects that are authorized requesters or providers for a given service; (b) all service interfaces (in essence, fragments of WSDL code); (c) a specification of the cooperation profile for each service, either synchronous, asynchronous or one-way; (d) security policies for the service; (e) service level agreements; (f) additional semantic annotations to further enrich the description of the service.

3 Open-Source Domain Gateways

In this section we discuss two certified implementations of the SPCoop domain gateway: OpenSPCoop and freESBee.

3.1 OpenSPCoop

OpenSPCoop (http://www.openspcoop.org) has been historically the first open-source implementation of the domain gateway. Besides the domain gateway it offers a registry service and an event manager to support publish and subscribe applications. It is a J2EE Web application developed for the JBoss application server.

To understand the relationship between OpenSPCoop and JBoss it is useful to recall that domain gateways are message-oriented applications, i.e., they are conceived to be listening on appropriate network endpoints for incoming messages, receive the messages, process them, and then forward the result to the appropriate network endpoint. In this respect, a crucial component of the overall application is the adoption of an appropriate *messaging service*, i.e., an infrastructure to receive, store, process and exchange messages among components. OpenSPCoop relies on the Java Message Service (JMS) specification [6] and more specifically on its implementation as part of the JBoss application server. In essence, a JMS implementation is a set of queues, each with an appropriate network endpoint, that can be used to receive, store, and pull out messages that have been sent to the associated endpoint. An OpenSPCoop domain gateway is deployed as a Web application within a JBoss installation. As part of the deployment, users need to specify the endpoints of the JMS queues that OpenSPCoop will use as an underlying infrastructure to process SPCoop messages. In this respect, the JBoss integration is quite tight, so that we may say that OpenSPCoop adopts a *container-bound architecture*. This choice has advantages and disadvantages. On one side, it somehow reduces portability and generates a limited form of platform lock-in, since it is not easy to deploy an OpenSPCoop gateway outside of JBoss. On the other side, it guarantees very good performance, given the strong integration with the J2EE container and the excellent JMS implementation provided as part of JBoss.

3.2 freESBee

freESBee (http://www.freesbee.unibas.it) is an alternative implementation of the SPCoop standard, that was developed at University of Basilicata. The development originated by two main observations. First, despite the consolidated nature of the SPCoop standard, the technical documents describe the domain gateway essentially by a set of use-cases, and there is no shared conceptualization of the internal architecture and behavior of the gateway. Second, while the technical specification is rather prescriptive with respect to the core components, there are other components of the middleware, and more specifically the federated identity management system, the service-level agreement management service, and the event manager, for which the specification leaves wide margins of freedom, to the point that the few existing implementations are often quite ad-hoc. The freESBee project provides a number of modules that cover all functional aspects of the SPCoop platform, and it is composed by the following sub-project: (a) freESBee itself is the domain gateway, and offers support for registry services; (b) freESBee-SP[12] is the identity management module; it is conceived to act as a middleware layer between the local information system and the domain gateway on one end, and the identity/attribute provider like, for example, Shibboleth, used to authenticate and authorize message exchanges in the SPCoop domain; (c) freESBee-SLA is the service-level agreement management module; it interacts with the domain gateway to log all metadata that are needed in order to monitor quality of service; (d) freESBee-GE is the event manager, that can be used to implement event-driven applications based on publish and subscribe. In addition to this, freESBee makes two main advancements with respect to other implementations, as discussed in the following paragraphs.

Enterprise Integration Patterns. freESBee using a well-known conceptual model for messaging services, namely *Enterprise Integration Patterns (EIPs)*[7]. These are an application of the design pattern approach to messaging services. They allow one to describe the processing and pathways of a message within a system in terms of a few elementary components, like "channels", "endpoint", "router", "message enricher" and so on. Differently from other pattern languages, EIPs have the nice feature that is it typically possible to design or describe a complete message-oriented application simply by means of the composition of a number of patterns. In this way, they provide an elegant formalism to conceptualize and document the internals of a complex software system, leaving alone the benefits in terms of development and maintenance. There are in fact, various open-source libraries that support the development of EIP-based applications. In essence, these libraries provide ready-made building blocks that an application developer can easily customize and compose. freESBee is implemented on top of Apache Camel (http://camel.apache.org), a well-known implementation of EIPs.

A Container-Independent Architecture. A second, major advancement made by freESBee is its *container-independent architecture*. In fact, the EIP-based design, and the Camel-based implementation are such that the freESBee domain gateway does not rely in any way on the messaging services of the underlying J2EE. Guaranteeing this independence has been a precise design guideline throughout the development of freESBee. In fact installation starts its own set of endpoints for delegate and application gateways, based on a Jetty internal engine. This has two main consequences: (a) each freESBee instance is fully independent from the container, since it does not rely on any of its services; (b) freESBee can be freely used in conjunction with any of the major J2EE containers (Apache Tomcat, JBoss, Glassfish) or can also be deployed as a stand-alone application outside of any J2EE container.

4 Massive Deployment of Domain Gateways

SPCoop was conceived as a nation-wide effort, and therefore aims at supporting interoperability among a very large number of subjects. Besides central Public Administrations, these include also local Public Administrations, like Regions and municipalities, hospitals, and other local agencies. Since each of these administrations typically represents an application domain by itself, and each domain needs a domain gateway in order to interoperate with other parties, a complete deployment of the framework requires to deploy a large number of middleware instances. It was soon realized that only a few administrations have the skills and resources to manage autonomously their SPCoop platform, especially at the local level. On the contrary, for many smaller realities the actual management of the middleware platform turned out to be a major technological and organizational problem.

To solve this problem, it was natural to explore hosting solutions in which larger administrations acted as technology facilitators for smaller ones, offering hosting services for their domain gateways. To give an example, Regions were soon identified as natural intermediaries for smaller municipalities within their territories. This, in turn, generated a significant technical problem: IT departments of Italian Regions were requested to host within their server farms hundreds of different instances of SPCoop domain gateways. There are three main solutions to host multiple instances of a middleware module within a single server-farm. The first one consists in having a dedicate server for each domain gateway instance; in fact, this is closer to a housing solution, and guarantees the highest level of independence for the local administration, since its SPCoop transactions are handled by a separate host; however, when the number of instances is in the order of the thousands, this solution becomes clearly unfeasible. To reduce the number of servers to deploy, several domain gateway instances need to be deployed within a single server. There are two main strategies to do this: (i) *the single-container strategy*, according to which a single server offers a single J2EE container, and all instances are deployed as Web applications within the same container; this is possible only if the gateway implementation adopts a container-independent architecture, otherwise the different instances would collide with each other when using the messaging service infrastructure offered by the container (messaging queues and endpoints); (ii) *the multiple-container strategy*, in which several instances of the J2EE container are installed within a single server, i.e., several JBoss or Tomcat installations listening on different ports of the same server, each with a single instance of the domain gateway; this is the only viable option for container-bound gateways like OpenSPCoop. We compare these two solutions in the next section.

5 Experiments

We conducted a number of experiments using both freESBee and OpenSPCoop. The main goals were to test the scalability of the two solutions, under two main perspectives: (i) first, we measured the throughput achieved by the domain gateway, i.e., the average number of messages per second handled during a test section; (ii) second, we investigated how the throughput varies when the number of instances of the domain gateway per server increases.

For the purpose of our tests we set-up a typical interoperability scenario, with one service provider, one domain gateway, and a number of service requesters. This scenario was conceived to test the scalability of the domain gateway in isolation. Since we are not interested in testing the actual performance of the service provider, nor that of the service requesters, but rather the one of the domain gateway, we chose as a service provider a simple *echo* Web service developed for this test, with messages of 1Kbyte each. To simulate the traffic originated by an increasing number of clients, we used Apache JMeter v. 2.7, configured to simulate variable numbers of concurrent clients, ranging from 10 to 100, each one issuing repeated requests to the service provider through the domain gateway, for a total of 10.000 messages sent for each test session. All components run on the same machine, which was deliberately chosen with a high-end profile, a MacBook Pro with a quad-core Intel i7 2.6 GHz, a 512 GB SSD, and 8 GB of RAM. The DBMS used by the domain gateways to log transactions was PostgreSQL 9.1.

We ran scalability tests both for single-instance-per-server and multiple-instance-per-server configurations of the middleware. Proper care was needed in multiple-instance tests in order to prevent that the DBMS connection pool was saturated. Since

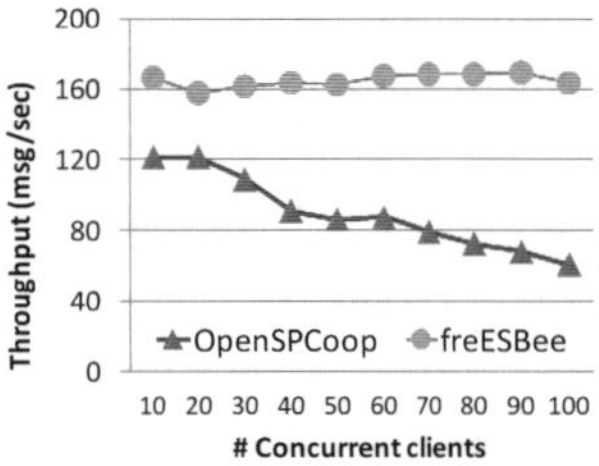

(a) Single Instance

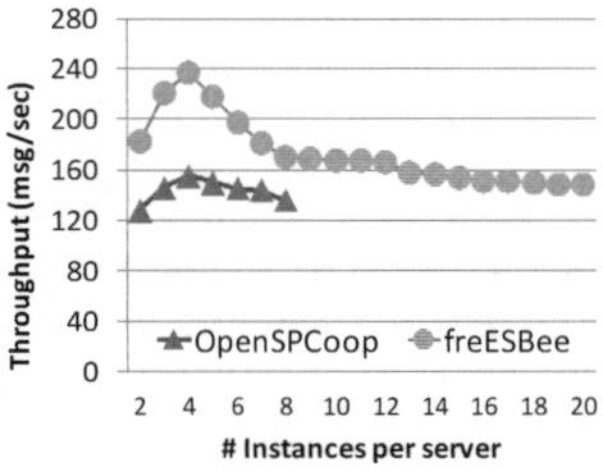

(b) Multiple Instance

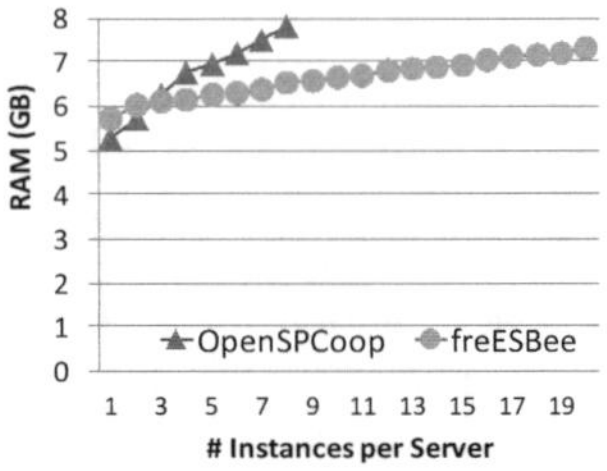

(c) Multiple Instance RAM usage

Fig. 1. Experimental Results

PostgreSQL accepts a maximum of 120 concurrent connections, to execute a test with X instances of the domain gateway we configured each instance to ask for a maximum of 120/X connections.

We tested OpenSPCoop (v. 1.4.1), configured according to the standard set of configuration parameters suggested on their website under JBoss. As suggested, we used JBoss v. 4.2.3, although this is not the most recent version of JBoss available at the moment. Due to its container-bound architecture, multiple-instance tests were run by installing several instances of JBoss on the server, each with a single copy of OpenSPCoop. For some of our experiments, we also ran additional tests using the version of OpenSPCoop (v. 2.0) under Tomcat.

We also tested the latest available version of freESBee (v. 2.2.6), deployed according to the standard set of configuration parameters. We selected Tomcat 7 as a container for freESBee, due to its wide adoption and ease of configuration. Multiple-instance tests were run by deploying different copies of freESBee inside the same Tomcat instance.

Throughput values are the average number of requests completed per second during a test session, computed by JMeter. In addition, we used the operating system built-in profiler to measure RAM occupation and CPU workload. We repeated each experiment 5 times, and took the average result for each output value. A test was successful if we were able to complete the expected number of messages with less that 1% of errors, and none of the domain gateway instances stalled. It was considered as failed otherwise. The two main causes of failures were out-of-memory errors on the server side, and inability to obtain connections within a given timeout from the DBMS

Fig. 1(a) reports scalability results for single-instance tests. A single instance of the domain gateway was installed, and throughput was recorded for increasing numbers of concurrent clients, ranging from 10 to 100. It can be seen that OpenSPCoop v.1.4.1 under JBoss reaches a throughput of 120 messages per second for 10-20 concurrent clients. Then, performance decreases as soon as the PostgreSQL connection pool becomes the bottleneck. We ran the same tests also using OpenSPCoop v.2.0 under Tomcat to confirm the results, and no noticeable change of performance was recorded. These experiments show also how freESBee outperforms OpenSPCoop, reaching a maximum of approximately 150 messages per second.

Figures 1(b-c) report results for multi-instance tests on the loopback scenario. As it was expected, freESBee had better performance in multi-instance tests. Fig. 1(c) reports RAM occupation for multiple-instance tests ranging from 2 to 20 domain gateway instances per server. Tests were run for 10 concurrent clients per instance, i.e., the 20-

instance test with 10 clients per instance simulated the load of 200 concurrent clients. It can be seen that, memory-wise, the container-independent architecture of freESBee guarantees better performance, so that it is possible to run up to 20 instances of the domain gateway inside a single server.

On the contrary, several of the OpenSPCoop tests failed. In the 10-client configuration, the maximum number of OpenSPCoop instances for which the test succeeded was 8. Above those numbers some of the instances stall, and high numbers of errors are observed. This is due to the nasty interaction between excessive memory usage and aggressive requests for connections by the multiple JBoss instances to the DBMS. Fig. 1(b) report throughput results for multiple-instance tests. It can be seen how the throughput of freESBee improved as the number of instance increased, as long as the CPU of the server machine was not saturated. In fact, given the less aggressive thread management policy of Camel, the presence of multiple instances, and therefore of multiple Camel contexts, brings an increase in parallelism.

References

1. AGID. Servizi di interoperabilità evoluta. http://www.agid.gov.it/agenda-digitale/infrastrutture-architetture/sistema-pubblico-connettivita, 2014.
2. R. Baldoni, S. Fuligni, M. Mecella, and F. Tortorelli. The italian e-government enterprise architecture: a comprehensive introduction with focus on the sla issue. In *Service Availability*, pages 1–12. Springer, 2008.
3. A. Corradini and T. Flagella. Openspcoop: un progetto open source per la cooperazione applicativa nella pubblica amministrazione. *Atti del Convegno Italiano AICA*, 2007.
4. E. Dynamics. Ida elink specification. http://ec.europa.eu/idabc/servlets/Doc1a78.pdf?id=18685.
5. L. Guijarro. Interoperability frameworks and enterprise architectures in e-government initiatives in europe and the united states. *Government Information Quarterly*, 24(1), 2007.
6. M. Hapner, R. Burridge, R. Sharma, J. Fialli, and K. Stout. Java message service. *Sun Microsystems Inc., Santa Clara, CA*, 2002.
7. G. Hohpe and B. Woolf. *Enterprise integration patterns: Designing, building, and deploying messaging solutions*. Addison-Wesley Professional, 2004.
8. D. Krafzig, K. Banke, and D. Slama. *Enterprise SOA: service-oriented architecture best practices*. Prentice Hall Professional, 2005.
9. G. Lodi, A. Maccioni, and F. Tortorelli. Spcdata: the italian public administration data cloud. *Information and Communication Technologies in Public Administration: Innovations from Developed Countries*, 195:255, 2015.
10. G. Mecca, A. Pappalardo, and S. Raunich. Soluzioni infrastrutturali open source per il sistema pubblico di cooperazione applicativa. In *SEBD*, pages 156–167, 2008.
11. G. Mecca, M. Santomauro, D. Santoro, and E. Veltri. Middleware-oriented government interoperability frameworks: A comparison. *Journal of Universal Computer Science*, 20(11):1543–1563, 2014.
12. G. Mecca, M. Santomauro, D. Santoro, and E. Veltri. On federated single sign-on in e-government interoperability frameworks. *To Appear in International Journal of Electronic Governance, Special Issue on MeTTeG 2015*, 2016.
13. D. Soares and L. Amaral. Information systems interoperability in public administration: Identifying the major acting forces through a Delphi study. *Journal of Theoretical and Applied Electronic Commerce Research*, 6:61–94, 2011.
14. B. Woolf. Esb-oriented architecture: The wrong approach to adopting soa. *IBM Developerworks Technical Library, September*, 2007.

Improving Opinion Target Identification through Twitter Using Public Conversations

Rania Othman[1], Rami Belkaroui[1] and Rim Faiz[2]

[1] Institut Supérieur de Gestion de Tunis, LARODEC, Université de Tunis, Tunisia
[2] IHEC Carthage, LARODEC, Université de Carthage, Tunisia
rania.othman@gmx.com, rami.belkaroui@gmail.com, rim.faiz@ihec.rnu.tn

Abstract. In this paper, we propose a new method for opinion target identification based on twitter conversations rather than simple individual tweets. We employ conversation interactions to effectively extract the different target features using a product review corpus involving smartphones and other electronics products. Experimental evaluations show that our proposed method is efficient and contributes to improving system performance.

Keywords: Twitter, Conversations, Opinion targets, Anaphora, User interactions.

1 Introduction

Twitter is currently one of the most popular micro-blogs which has grown at an unprecedented rate to reach over 320 million monthly active users[3]. Twitter is both a micro-blogging service and a conversational environment that enables people to interact, engage in daily chatter, join conversations, report news and share information. Conversations are key element in such service. Almost a quarter of Twitter users hold conversations with other users through this platform [8] and huge percentage of Twitter posts are conversational [14]. The huge volume of conversations produced everyday makes them an interesting information source and valuable tool to discover new trends and exchange opinions and feedbacks towards products, news and stories. A large number of the messages are carriers of opinions and feelings [9]. One major field that took advantage of this potential is e-reputation. It has become a common practice for business owners to allow their customers to review their products through public web sites (e.g. epinions.com, amazon.com). This enables businesses to have general overview on their consumer satisfaction and attitudes about the product or the service offered. While conversations are very rich source of information, retrieving relevant information remains challenging. The large number of messages involved in these conversations makes it hard for users to cope with rate of messages involving a lot of noise and redundancy. Thus, applying automated systems that aim to retrieve individual opinion words or phrases and what they are about, referred to as the opinion target or opinion topic, could be quite useful for business owners.

[3] https://about.twitter.com/company

In this paper, we propose a new method for opinion target identification based on Twitter conversations. To date, little research has been adressed to tackle conversations despite their prevalence in social streams. Most existing works on opinion analysis through Twitter, have so far focused on handling simple individual tweets rather than considering the whole conversations [12, 4, 1]. As tweets are limited to 140 characters and usually written in an informal way involving a lot of abbreviations, typos and slangs, it is frequently hard to detect the exact meaning of a tweet when taken separately. Also, a large number of features are generally referenced by anaphoric pronouns in major succeeding replies of a conversation message. Anaphora can be defined as the use of an expression the interpretation of which depends specifically upon a previous expression [15]. Consider this example sentence: "It is fantastic.". If one wants to extract what the opinion in this sentence is about, previous replies must be analysed. Frequently, while handling conversations, a large amount of messages are left unnoticed due to their vague and unclear aspect. Therefore, we adopt a conversation-based method that employs conversation interactions, notably reply links, to effectively extract the target product features involved in the messages. To the best of our knowledge, this is the first research employing twitter conversations in the opinion target identification task.

The rest of this paper is organized as follows. Section 2 overviews the related work on opinion target identification. In section 3, we introduce our new approach for opinion target identification on Twitter conversations. Section 4 reports the experiment results. Finally, Section 5 concludes this paper with some perspectives.

2 RELATED WORK

Opinion target extraction is crucial for opinion mining (OM) and summarization especially given that this task provides the foundation for opinion summarization [5]. Opinion target can be defined as the entity (i.e., person, object, feature, event or topic) about which the user expresses his opinion. Extensive approaches and techniques have been addressed to mine opinion components or targets from unstructured reviews. These works can be very broadly divided into two main categories supervised and unsupervised. Other works have also employed the semi-supervised approach. In the supervised learning approaches, a machine-learning model is trained on manually labeled data to extract and classify the feature set in the reviews. Although these techniques provide good results for opinion target extraction, they require extensive manual work for the training set preparation, they are also time consuming, and sometimes domain dependent. The most common techniques employed in supervised approaches are decision tree, support vector machine (SVM), K-nearest neighbor (KNN), nave Bayesian classifier and neural network [7, 11, 17]. On the other hand, unsupervised approaches automatically extract product features using syntactic and contextual patterns without the need of labeled data [6, 9]. A challenge which is frequently encountered in the opinion target extraction task is, that entities can be sometimes implicit and therefore hard to find. In the case of explicit target identification, we generally employ noun phrases with syntactic rules [6, 13] . While for implicit targets, context dependency or distribution similarity are employed. To the best of our knowledge, there is currently only two systems that integrate coreference information and apply anaphora resolution (AR) in OM. Stoyanov and Cardie [16] develop an algorithm that identifies coreferring targets in newspaper articles. They rely on manually annotated targets thus, a candidate selection phase for the opinion targets is not required. The authors focus only on the coreference resolution but they do not resolve pronominal anaphora in order to achieve this purpose. For their part, [7] adapt the rule based AR algorithm CogNIAC to extract opinion targets on a movie review corpus. They have shown that extending an OM algorithm with AR for opinion target extraction can achieve significant improvements. In this paper, we apply AR to extract opinion targets (i.e., product features) from Twitter conversations. To the best of our knowledge, this is the first research employing twitter conversations and AR for the feature extraction task.

3 PROPOSED APPROACH

In our work, we aim to extract product features reviewed by users in our tweet collection based on Twitter conversations. Our approach is based on three main modules namely, pre-processing, conversation retrieval and opinion target identification. Figure 1 presents an overview of the proposed approach. Given a tweet

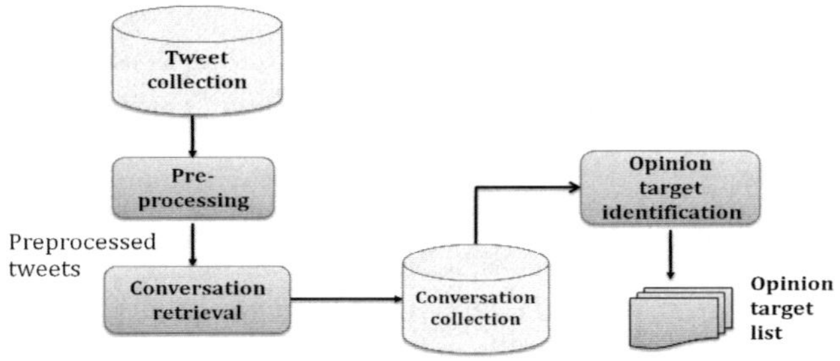

Fig. 1. Overview of our proposed approach

corpus on electronic products, we clean our collection via the pre-processing phase, than we proceed to retrieve conversations from the collection of separate tweets. The final step consists on extracting opinion targets commented by users through the conversation collection. The three modules are illustrated in details in the following subsections.

3.1 Pre-processing

The collection of tweets is preprocessed before the conversation retrieval module. First of all, the URL in each message is analyzed. While different shortened URLs might redirect to the same end URL, it is necessary to replace them with the real URLs they redirect. Thereafter, we employ an API service [4] for HTML text extraction which removes comments, links, ads, and other unrelated parts of a web page and returns key contents in plain text. Then, we proceed to the second step of the processing involving the text analysis. In this step,

[4] http://www.alchemyapi.com/

both the text content of the tweet and the text retrieved from the URLs are taken into account. We cleaned the text by removing ASCII characters, numbers, punctuation, and stop words. In the end, we convert the text to lower case and we tokenize it. The remaining tweet features such as the ID of the author and other social information are also extracted from the API and stored. We indexed the collection of tweets with Apache Lucene [5] which is full-featured text search engine library written entirely in Java.

3.2 Conversation Retrieval Module

In this section, we describe the process of constructing conversations from a collection of tweets. We consider the conversation definition presented by [3]. They defined a conversation as a set of short text messages posted by a set of users at specific timestamps on the same topic. This messages can be directly replied to other users by using "@username" or indirectly by liking, retweeting, commenting and other possible interactions. We apply the same method developed by [3] who proposed a user-based tree model for retrieving conversations from microblogs. They do not only retrieve direct messages based on reply links but also consider indirect messages that can be related to the conversation via other links such as retweet and mention interactions. To avoid bias related to features existing with a very small number, we cleaned our collection of conversations by filtering out the conversations that involve less than 3 participants and containing less than 7 tweets.

3.3 Opinion Target Identification Module

In this stage, we aim to extract the opinion targets or features customers expressed their opinions on. For example, if we want to generate an OM about iPod, some of the common features are "battery life", "sound quality" and "ease of use". Given a conversation collection, our system splits the reviews into sentences, then, it converts them to lower case and remove the non literal characters at the beginning and the end of each word (e.g. "#IPhone#" becomes "iphone"). Steinberger et al.[15] reveal that noun and noun phrases in the sentence are likely to be the features customers expressed their opinions on. We therefore perform the Part-of-Speech (POS) tagging of the whole document to identify the grammatical class of each word using TreeTagger [6]. We extract nouns from the reviews and we move on to the feature decider step. We construct our stop word list and we filter out the extracted nouns existing in the stop word list. Then, we construct noun phrases which are composed of two successive nouns (e.g. Click wheel, Battery Life). We extract all noun phrases but we only keep those appearing together at least 3 times in the reviews. We remove sentence redundancy, if a noun appears more than one time in the same sentence, we consider as if it appears one time. We then compute frequency of occurrences in the reviews for the whole set of extracted nouns and we only keep those whose frequency is greater than 0.02.

To decide if the noun phrases we collected are meaningful, we apply a similarity measure called point-wise mutual information (PMI-IR) [18] that uses

[5] https://lucene.apache.org/

[6] http://www.cis.uni-muenchen.de/ schmid/tools/TreeTagger/

page counts returned by a web search engine to recognize synonyms. Like [9], we detect the compactness of a noun phrase using the number of tweets concerning a given product instead of the search engine page counts. We prune noun phrases having PMI < 0.

Having our feature list, we proceed to the next step which aims to affect each review (or post/message) in our corpus to the feature the author comment on in his post. To do so, we apply our proposed Target Identification Algorithm based on conversation interactions notably the reply-links. Indeed, a large number of features appearing as noun phrases and even simple nouns in reviews are generally referenced by anaphoric pronouns in major succeeding sentences of a review document [10, 7]. The anaphoric term is called an anaphor. For example, in the sentence: "I'm so glad with my new iPhone 5, it's just amazing", the pronoun "it" is an anaphor, referring back to the antecedent "my new iPhone 5". Actually, the overwhelming majority of the opinion targets (i.e., product features) are pronouns in the datasets [10]. Thus, AR is crucial for binding feature-review pairs, otherwise a very big number of opinion reviews will be left unnoticed due to their ambiguous aspect. In order to identify the associations of such reviews with correct features, a conversation-interactions based algorithm has been developed. To the best of our knowledge, this is the first such algorithm that employs conversation interactions notably reply-links for effective binding of feature-review pairs. Our algorithm proceeds as follows, for a tweet $t_{i,l}$, that does not contain any feature words existing in the feature list but involves opinionated words (i.e., adjectives and adverbs) along with some pronouns, all anaphora pronouns present in this sentence that require mapping are extracted, and a set of anaphora P=$\{p_1, p_2, p_3, ..., p_n\}$ is compiled for proper context determination. We employ a backtracking mechanism in which review documents are accessed in reverse order based on reply-links to extract precedent sentences $t_{i-1,j}$ that $t_{i,l}$ replies on. For each anaphora pronoun $p_i \in$ P, proper context is determined to compile a set A=$\{a_{k,1}, a_{k,2}, a_{k,3}, ..., a_{q,m}\}$ consisting of candidate antecedents. The best antecedent $a_{k,t} \in$ A is selected for binding with a_o using CogNIAC algorithm [2], a publically available algorithm for AR that employs a rule based approach for antecedent identification. This approach can be an adequate strategy for our OM task, since in our corpus, a small pourcentage of the total number of pronouns are actual product features (only 6%). We denote the lth tweet at iteration i $t_{i,l}$ while the jth tweet at iteration i is denoted $t_{i,j}$. As each anaphora pronoun is replaced by the selected antecedent, backtracking process terminates with the iteration i-1 for each sentence. At the end of this phase, we obtain a set of opinionated sentences and each sentence is associated to the corresponding target feature that the user commented on.

4 EXPERIMENTS AND RESULTS

4.1 Dataset Description

Due to the lack of test collections for Twitter conversations, we have created our own collection. We crawled 221 663 English tweets using Twitter Application Programmable Interface (API) [7]. The Twitter API allows developers around the

[7] https://dev.twitter.com/overview/api

world to have free and open access to Twitter's database. The tweet collection was crawled over a period of 4 months from April 25th 2015 to July 25th 2015.

We only search popular tweets talking about a given product involving character description, promotion information and comments about new products. After removing the repeated ones, 211 350 tweets remained. From our collection of tweets, we have constructed 8 720 conversations involving 64 370 tweets and 13 827 bloggers. We employ statuses/lookup.json files accessed through Twitter API, which contain all information related to the tweets. Table 1 outlines some statistics on our Conversation collection. As shown, there exist over 120K pronouns and roughly 11.13 % of the opinion targets are referred to by pronouns.

Table 1. Corpus size statistics

Tweets	64 370
Tokens	2 568 160
Target + Opinion Pairs	7 960
Targets which are Pronouns	886
Pronouns	> 120 350

4.2 Evaluation Results

We implement our approach using java language and we conducted our experiments using the Twitter conversations of five electronics products: 2 digital cameras and 3 smartphones. As our work evaluation requires substantial human effort to identify product features and subjective reviews, we reduced the set of 8K conversations to just 4K. For each product, we extract the first 800 conversations. After preprocessing, our system is applied to perform opinion summarization. For evaluation, we manually read all the extracted conversations. For each tweet, if it involves user opinions, all the features on which the author has expressed his opinion are tagged. For each product, we manually produced a feature list. Column "Nbr of features" in Table 2 shows the number of manual features for each product. The features generated by our system are compared with the manually tagged results. In this subtask, we used precision and recall which are among the main evaluation measures employed in the feature selection task. In our case, TP is the number of relevant features identified, TP+TN represent the number of relevant features and TP+FP gives the number of features identified. Table 2 shows the evaluation results for the 5 products obtained in the feature identification phase. The highest values reached by our system are 77.81% precision and 82.62% recall. Our system presents high precision and recall scores. The recall value is higher than precision indicating that the majority of correct features were correctly recognized by the system. This can show the efficacity of the use of converation interactions in extracting product features that have been commented by users. The precision value is lower than recall indicating that some identified features are not correct. This can be justified since most of the reviewers do not follow grammatical rules strictly while writing tweets due to which the parser fails to assign correct POS tag and thereby correct dependency relations between words. On analysis, we observed that, when a pronoun to be

Table 2. Evaluation results for the feature detection phase

Product	Nbr of features	Feature identification on individual tweets		Feature identification on conversations (this research)	
		Precision(%)	Recall(%)	Precision(%)	Recall(%)
Digital camera 1	27	68.33	62.13	75.26	79.61
Digital camera 2	31	63.52	**64.40**	76.78	77.98
Smartphone 1	52	55.97	51.83	75.22	78.23
Smartphone 2	25	**71.54**	57.74	69.46	**82.62**
Smartphone 3	43	57.88	53.73	**77.81**	81.73
Average		63.44	57.96	74.90	80.03

resolved has more than two or three candidate antecedents, the occurrence of noisy anaphora-antecedent pairs increases. This leaves scope for enhancing our method for detecting features to reach better precision level. To further illustrate the effectiveness of our feature identification phase, we compared the features generated using our method with features found by the same method applied to the same set of tweets taken separately rather than extracting conversations and without the use of AR between messages. This method is closely similar to the feature detection process employed by [9] which extract product features from customer reviews based on product reviews collected via electronic commerce websites and Twitter. The average recall of opinion sentence extraction is nearly 63% while the average precision is around 57%. We observe that both the average recall and precision of the second method are significantly lower than those of our method. On analysis, we observed that, in testing dataset, a total of 13 824 anaphoric pronouns are present, in which 886 pronouns correctly refer to product features. By applying the second method, almost 60% of pronouns are left unnoticed or erroneously extracted. Comparing the results in Table 2, we can clearly see that the proposed method is much more effective for our task.

5 Conclusion

In this paper, we proposed a new method for opinion target identification that handles twitter conversations rather than single tweets. We employ conversation interactions, notably reply links, to effectively extract the target product features from customer reviews. Our experimental results indicate that the proposed method is very promising in performing its task. In particular, we have proved that incorporating conversation structure in the opinion target identification task contributes to improving system performance.

In our future work, we plan to further experiment it with other entities not only products. We will also look into employing our approach on other customer opinion ressources rather than Twitter. We also intend to enhance the AR process.

References

1. Bahrainian, S.A., Dengel, A.: Sentiment analysis and summarization of twitter data. In: Computational Science and Engineering (CSE), 2013 IEEE 16th Interna-

tional Conference on. pp. 227–234. IEEE (2013)
2. Baldwin, B.: Cogniac: high precision coreference with limited knowledge and linguistic resources. In: Proceedings of a Workshop on Operational Factors in Practical, Robust Anaphora Resolution for Unrestricted Texts. pp. 38–45. Association for Computational Linguistics (1997)
3. Belkaroui, R., Faiz, R., Elkhlifi, A.: Conversation analysis on social networking sites. In: Signal-Image Technology and Internet-Based Systems (SITIS), 2014 Tenth International Conference on. pp. 172–178. IEEE (2014)
4. Bora, N.N.: Summarizing public opinions in tweets. International Journal of Computational Linguistics and Applications 3(1), 41–55 (2012)
5. Feldman, R., Fresko, M., Goldenberg, J., Netzer, O., Ungar, L.: Extracting product comparisons from discussion boards. In: Data Mining, 2007. ICDM 2007. Seventh IEEE International Conference on. pp. 469–474. IEEE (2007)
6. Hu, M., Liu, B.: Mining and summarizing customer reviews. In: Proceedings of the tenth ACM SIGKDD international conference on Knowledge discovery and data mining. pp. 168–177. ACM (2004)
7. Jakob, N., Gurevych, I.: Using anaphora resolution to improve opinion target identification in movie reviews. In: Proceedings of the ACL 2010 Conference Short Papers. pp. 263–268. Association for Computational Linguistics (2010)
8. Java, A., Song, X., Finin, T., Tseng, B.: Why we twitter: understanding microblogging usage and communities. In: Proceedings of the 9th WebKDD and 1st SNA-KDD. pp. 56–65. ACM (2007)
9. Jmal, J., Faiz, R.: Customer review summarization approach using twitter and sentiwordnet. In: Proceedings of the 3rd International Conference on Web Intelligence, Mining and Semantics. p. 33. ACM (2013)
10. Kamal, A., Abulaish, M.: Statistical features identification for sentiment analysis using machine learning techniques. In: Computational and Business Intelligence (ISCBI), 2013 International Symposium on. pp. 178–181. IEEE (2013)
11. Kessler, J.S., Nicolov, N.: Targeting sentiment expressions through supervised ranking of linguistic configurations. In: ICWSM. AAAI Press (2009)
12. Meng, X., Wei, F., Liu, X., Zhou, M., Li, S., Wang, H.: Entity-centric topic-oriented opinion summarization in twitter. In: Proceedings of the 18th ACM SIGKDD international conference on Knowledge discovery and data mining. pp. 379–387. ACM (2012)
13. Popescu, A.M., Etzioni, O.: Extracting product features and opinions from reviews. In: Natural language processing and text mining, pp. 9–28. Springer (2007)
14. Ritter, A., Cherry, C., Dolan, B.: Unsupervised modeling of twitter conversations. In: HLT-NAACL. pp. 172–180. The Association for Computational Linguistics (2010)
15. Steinberger, J., Poesio, M., Kabadjov, M.A., Ježek, K.: Two uses of anaphora resolution in summarization. Information Processing & Management 43(6), 1663–1680 (2007)
16. Stoyanov, V., Cardie, C.: Topic identification for fine-grained opinion analysis. In: Proceedings of the 22nd International Conference on Computational Linguistics-Volume 1. pp. 817–824. Association for Computational Linguistics (2008)
17. Toh, Z., Su, J.: Nlangp: Supervised machine learning system for aspect category classification and opinion target extraction. In: Proceedings of the 9th International Workshop on SemEval. pp. 719–724 (2015)
18. Turney, P.: Mining the web for synonyms: PMI-IR versus LSA on TOEFL. In: Machine Learning: ECML. pp. 491–502 (2001)

Mining User Habits in Smart Spaces through Process Mining Techniques (Extended abstract)*

Marcella Dimaggio[1], Francesco Leotta[1], Massimo Mecella[1], and Daniele Sora[1]

Sapienza Università di Roma
dimaggio.1569169@studenti.uniroma1.it,
{leotta,mecella,sora}@dis.uniroma1.it

Abstract. Independently of the specific task to be enacted in a smart space, it is always crucial to mine a set of models representing environmental dynamics and, noteworthy, user habits and desires. Many different formalisms have been proposed to model human habits, but the vast majority of them are either difficult to read and evaluate or their definition requires a huge amount of work from either experts or users. In this paper we propose to employ process mining techniques in order to model human habits, and we experimentally evaluate such an approach on a dataset built adopting the Smart-Home-in-a-Box toolkit with real users.

1 Introduction

The main goal of a smart space is to employ raw data coming from *sensors* deployed into the environment to make decisions about the environment itself [1]; these decisions are then applied through *actuators*, either virtual or physical, or proposed to the final user in the form of suggestions or alerts. Specific tasks can have many different goals, but they are mainly performed according to a set of models representing environmental dynamics and, noteworthy, user habits and desires. These models can be either hand-made by experts or automatically extracted (through learning and mining techniques) from previously acquired *sensor logs*. In the latter case, the amount of labeling work in charge to the final user strongly influences how much applicable a specific technique is in a real setting. From this point of view, automatic learning techniques can be classified as supervised, semi-supervised and unsupervised. The latter ones are particularly interesting in a smart space scenario as they (potentially strongly) reduce the burden on the final users to manually label the dataset fed as input. Semi-supervised learning is often associated with active learning approaches, whereas unsupervised techniques are

* Results in this paper have been obtained with an academic license of Disco freely provided by Fluxicon. The work of Daniele Sora has been partly supported by the Italian project NEPTIS, other authors have been partly supported by the Italian projects NEPTIS, SM&ST and RoMA, and the Sapienza grant ICE. We also thank prof. Diane Cook and the CASAS project of Washington State University for providing the Smart-Home-in-a-Box kit. This extended abstract is a reduced version of the paper *M. Dimaggio, F. Leotta, M. Mecella, D. Sora: Process-Based Habit Mining: Experiments and Techniques. Proc. 13th IEEE International Conference on Ubiquitous Intelligence and Computing (UIC 2016).*

the main tools employed for data mining. If we focus our attention on models of human habits, many attempts have been made to represent human behavior through different kinds of state-based modeling techniques. Recently, approaches that model human habits as workflows have been proposed, thus opening to the possibility of applying process mining [4] techniques to obtain, in a semi or unsupervised manner, human-readable models that can be easily validated by end-users. Still, many new challenges have to be addressed [3]. Human habits are flexible in their nature. Humans do not follow a precise workflow while performing their daily activities; they instead follow a series of best practices that are difficult to be described using a precise sequence of tasks. Additionally, process mining techniques need a log segmented in traces, which is not a reasonable assumption in many application scenarios. This problem is made even harder by the presence of multiple users performing different habits at the same time, thus producing interleaving sensor measurements from unrelated activities.

In this paper we propose a methodology to apply process discovery techniques to a dataset and we discuss the performance of such an approach and possible future works.

2 Preliminaries and case study

We can abstract a smart space as producing, at runtime, a sensor log containing raw measurements from available sensors. Given a set S of sensors, a sensor log $\mathscr{S}$ is an ordered sequence of measurements of the kind $\langle ts, s, v \rangle$ where ts is the timestamp of the measurement, $s \in S$ is the source sensor and v the measured value, which belongs to a domain D_s that can be either categorical or quantitative. Measurements can be produced on a periodic base (e.g., temperature) or whenever a particular event is detected (e.g., a door opening). Many solutions expect as input an *event log* instead.

Sensor logs can be used to automatically discover models of human habits. Such models can take many different forms, but the fundamental idea is to describe constraints between events onset and their relationships with the state of the house. There are many different ways these models can be used including anomaly detection, automatic adaptation, recommender systems. The granularity of the obtained model strongly influences the possible applications for smart space automation. In this paper we show how models can be represented by using an established business process modeling technique and extracted using process discovery as proposed in [3].

We leverage on a typical approach to deal with unstructured processes, i.e., fuzzy mining [2]; it borrows concepts from the world of maps and cartography and apply them to zoom in and out on a process model highlighting the importance of certain tasks and connection between tasks just like they were points and paths on a map. In this paper we will show how fuzzy mining can be used to cluster events into classes correspondent to habits and to show how the onsets of these events are related one each other.

If no filtering is applied, the output of fuzzy mining is a weighted directed graph where nodes are tasks and an arc from task T_1 to T_2 with weight w states that T_2 follows T_1 (respectively T_1 precedes T_2) w times. By tuning the parameters of fuzzy mining it is possible to zoom in and out the model by highlighting path that are significant with respect to the zoom level. This allows to focus only on the important aspects of the

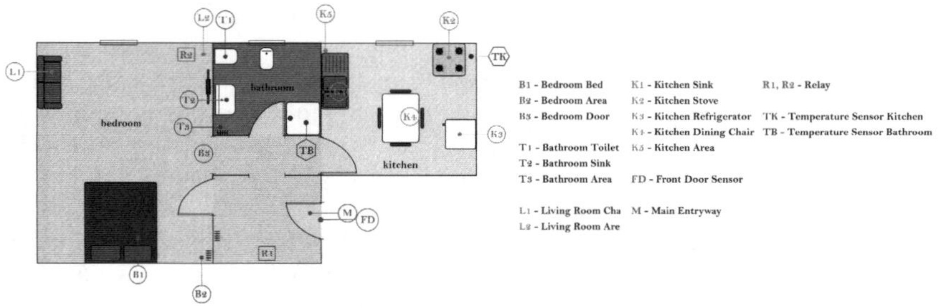

Fig. 1: SHiB kit installation layout.

model. Implementations of the fuzzy miner are available as either open source (e.g., as plugin of the ProM framework) or commercial (e.g., Disco).

The zooming operation is performed according to two fundamental metrics: *(i)* significance and *(ii)* correlation. Significance, which can be determined both for event classes (i.e., activities) and binary precedence relations over them (i.e., edges), measures the relative importance of behavior. As such, it specifies the level of interest we have in events, or their occurring after one another. Correlation is instead relevant for precedence relations over events, i.e., how closely related two events are.

In order to show the suitability of fuzzy mining to model human habits we will refer to a dataset gathered using the kit provided by the Smart Home in a Box (SHiB) project of Washington State University through the CASAS laboratory. Sensors provided with the kit include Presence Infrared (PIR) sensors, switch sensors attached to the main entry door and temperature sensors. All the sensors are powered by batteries and connected wireless to a gateway. Figure 1 shows a map of the SHiB installation we used during our experiments. Vast majority of sensors are PIR ones with the exception of temperature sensors TK and TB and the switch sensor FD that is connected to the front door. PIR sensors represent a typical example of sensing units provided by freely available datasets. Usually these sensors are installed on the ceiling following a grid layout; they trigger upon the detection of an object entering their field of view and automatically reset after a fixed amount of time. The main distinctive feature of a PIR, is the detection area that can be modulated to cover different area sizes ranging from a tile on the floor to an entire room. Our installation included 4 area level PIR sensors (namely B2, T3, L2, K5) corresponding to the rooms of the house, and 10 object level PIR sensors. The map also shows the location of the relay, which is used to ensure that the wireless signals from the sensors are actually received by the gateway.

3 The proposed approach

In this paper we will assume that only discrete output sensors are available. In particular, among the sensors provided with the SHiB installation we will only employ PIR sensors. We will also assume that the granularity of available PIR sensors is enough detailed for the kind human processes we want to extract, e.g., if the sensor on top of the basin triggers we are only interested in the fact that somebody is using the basin without getting into the details of the action he is performing (e.g., washing hands, washing face, cleaning teeth). With these assumptions, the only step needed to translate the sensor log $\mathscr{S}$ into the event log $\mathscr{E}$ is a filtering step removing useless measurements. In particular, only activation measurements are kept and analyzed.

Differently from the common process mining scenario, event logs do not contain any information about which user/s caused a certain sensor to trigger or to provide a specific measurement. Thus, mining habits in a multi-user scenario is significantly harder than a single user scenario. Our use case, based on PIRs, is particularly challenging from this point of view as, even though multiple users can be identified by the spatial distance between PIRs triggering close in time, when trajectories intersect, tracking techniques must be employed to keep following users.

A common prerequisite of process mining techniques is to have a trace log explicitly segmented in traces (process instances). This assumption is usually not met by sensor logs as labeling is generally an expensive task to be performed by humans. This problem can be translated into a precise question: what is a habit? Is that a specific routine (e.g., cleaning the kitchen) or is it more generally what happens in a specific time frame of the day (e.g., between 8:00am and 9:00am). On the one hand, choosing the second solution makes it easier to segment the log as we cannot assume that a user will not perform different routines at the same time and there is no way, from the log solely, to identify such a situation. On the other hand, according to what criteria should we choose the time ranges? The trivial solution of segmenting the day in fixed length stints of time fails if something anomalous happens (e.g., holidays). Possible solutions are:

- Associating specific combinations of sensor measurements to the beginning and to the end of a time range. E.g., the morning habit starts whenever a movement sensor different than the ones mounted over the bed triggers and ends whenever the movement sensor in correspondence of the exit door triggers.
- Active learning. In order to let the system learn his habits, the user explicitly signals to the system the beginning and the end of a specific habit.

In this paper we uses as traces the different segments provided by the multiple user detection algorithm. This way every single trace represents a sequence of actions performed by a single user, and we leave the task of choosing the granularity of a habit to the fine-tuning of the parameters of the fuzzy miner as we will see in Section 4.

Separating multiple users through tracking. The separation of traces performed by different users is obtained by a combination of topological information about sensors and the "status" of involved users. At the end of this task, the event log $\mathscr{E}$ results split into n portions $\{A_1,\ldots,A_n\}$, each representing a sequence of events generated by a single user. Noteworthy, each portion can include events from different habits though.

At any given moment, the algorithm keeps a set of "open" portions, i.e., portions that it is possible to add new events to. A portion is closed when the status of the correspondent user is set to sleep. When the event e_i in $\mathscr{E}$ is read, it is appended to at most one open portion that respects the topological compatibility matrix and minimize the difference in velocity with respect to the previous events. If such a portion does not exists a new portion is created and is put to the "open" status.

	B2	B1	K1	K2	K5	K4	T3	L2	T1	L1	K3	T2
B2	✓	✓					✓	✓				
B1	✓	✓										
K1			✓	✓	✓	✓					✓	
K2			✓	✓	✓	✓					✓	
K5			✓	✓	✓	✓	✓				✓	
K4			✓	✓	✓	✓					✓	
T3	✓				✓		✓	✓	✓			✓
L2	✓						✓	✓		✓		
T1							✓		✓			✓
L1								✓		✓		
K3			✓	✓	✓	✓					✓	
T2							✓		✓			✓

Table 1: Topological compatibility matrix

The first step consists of building the topological compatibility matrix, which considers all the installed sensors and couples (✓) a couple $\langle s_i, s_j \rangle$ of sensors when effectively s_i could follow s_j. Table 1 shows the matrix for our case study.

Users in the house environment can be in one of two different statuses in every moment: acting or resting. The status of an inhabitant depends on the *velocity vector* v_i which is calculated referring to the previously inserted action for the log portion $\mathscr{E}_i$ that is considered for the user (i.e., the sensor that is involved in the measurement with the related timestamp) and a *distance policy* representing *logical* distances between couples of sensors. The *distance policy* takes into account the relations described in the compatibility matrix. If we denote *(i)* with s_i a generic sensor, *(ii)* with S_r the area sensor for room r, *(iii)* with s_i^r one position sensor for room i, and *(iv)* with $s_i \longleftrightarrow s_j$ the logical distance between sensors s_i and s_j, distances are ordered in ascendant order as in Table 2 where the minimum distance is assigned to a sensor with respect to itself whereas the maximum one is assigned to an area sensor for a room r with respect to a position sensor in another room. Table 2 shows between parenthesis the values that have been used during our experiments. Whenever the velocity v_i falls under a prefixed threshold, the user for whom v_i is calculated is intended to be still, thus the action we were analyzing should belong to some other person who is instead in an "acting" status.

Identifying habits. The different portions obtained following the methodology introduced in Section 3 and representing sequences of actions performed by a single user are fed into the fuzzy miner. If no filtering is applied, the fuzzy miner produces a weighted graph (with weighted nodes) that is difficult to analyze and where single habits cannot be distinguished one each other. In order to identify habits, we use the tuning parameters of fuzzy mining algorithm. In particular, if we focus only on filtering by the significance

Table 2: Distances between sensors

$s_i \longleftrightarrow s_i$ (0.4)
$S_r \longleftrightarrow s_i^r$ (10)
$s_i^r \longleftrightarrow s_j^r$ (500)
$S_r \longleftrightarrow S_t$ (1500)
$s_i^r \longleftrightarrow s_j^t$ (2000)
$S_r \longleftrightarrow s_i^t$ (4000)

Table 3: Numerical results of evaluation.

Habit	Habit name	Similarity
H_1	Morning routine	0.63206
H_2	Relax	0.99278
H_3	Washing Dishes	0.74736
H_4	Cooking/Eating	0.72549

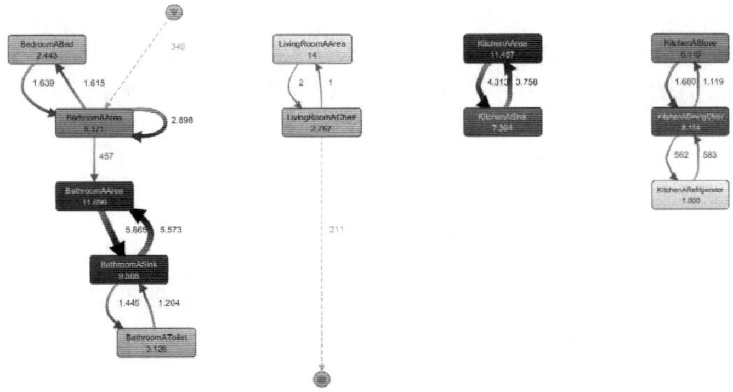

Fig. 2: The result of the application of fuzzy mining to the dataset – filtered results

of paths we are able to separate habits as group of events that are strongly connected one each other as we will see in the next section.

4 Evaluation

We evaluated the proposed technique on a dataset covering 4 months of the house previously described containing 2 permanent inhabitants with the sporadic presence of guests. In order to have a ground truth for the evaluation, we asked users to manually label a period of 20 days. Noteworthy low level activities allow a human to aggregate into higher level habits according to the results provided by the proposed technique.

The application of the fuzzy mining to the whole dataset using the approach described in Section 3 returned the habit models shown in Figures 3 (the results without applying any filter to the fuzzy miner output) and 2 (the results by only showing the most important paths). As it can be noticed, fuzzy miner filtering clearly identifies four habit models we can give a representative name to by looking at the kind of events they contain, namely H_1 - morning, H_2 - relax, H_3 - washing dishes, and H_4 - cooking/eating.

In order to evaluate the performance, we exploited manual labeling to segment the event log from the 20 labeled days in 4 different logs (each one corresponding to a H_i habit) divided into traces (i.e., repetitions of the habit). We then applied fuzzy mining to these four logs and compare the obtained graphs with the ones in Figure 2 by using a Jaccard similarity between arcs and nodes. Given, two graphs G_1 and G_2 with the same nodes (i.e., the same event types), the Jaccard similarity $J(G_1, G_2)$ is:

$$J(G_1,G_2) = \frac{\sum_i \sum_j min(G_1(n_i,n_j),G_2(n_i,n_j)) + \sum_i min(G_1(n_i),G_2(n_i))}{\sum_i \sum_j max(G_1(n_i,n_j),G_2(n_i,n_j)) + \sum_i max(G_1(n_i),G_2(n_i))} \quad (1)$$

where $G_k(n_i, n_j)$ is the weight assigned to the arc from n_i to n_j in G_k (if the arc is absent the weight is 0), $G_k(n_i)$ is the weight assigned to node n_i in graph G_k, and *min* (resp. *max*) are binary operators returning the minimum (resp. the maximum) between two operands. The Jaccard measure is always a positive real number minor or equal to 1.

The weights in the graph have been normalized prior to the Jaccard similarity calculation. Numerical results of evaluation are shown in Table 3 confirming how the method proposed can identify habits models as those extracted for the manually segmented habit are very similar to those automatically extracted by fuzzy mining after user separation.

5 Conclusions

In this paper, we proposed a methodology to employ an established process discovery technique to mine human behavior. To obtain this result a technique to separate multiple user behaviors has been devised. The experimental evaluation shows promising results that will be further investigated in future works. Our approach was able to identify four different habits whose models resemble with an high confidence the behavior of users.

Future investigations will include more sophisticated techniques to turn the sensor log into an event log to be used for process discovery. With respect to fuzzy mining, in particular, event logs can contain many other valuable information that have not been exploited in this work. Additionally, future studies will cover methodologies to exploit discovered models at runtime in order to provide valuable services to end users. An application example is smart space automation. Usually variables in a smart environment can be classified as either controllable or non-controllable from the point of view of the smart space system. If an event corresponds to the change of state of a controllable variable, the smart space system, once recognized that a user is performing a specific habit, may decide to anticipate user decisions.

References

1. Aztiria, A., Izaguirre, A., Augusto, J.C.: Learning patterns in ambient intelligence environments: A survey. Artificial Intelligence Review 34(1), 35–51 (2010)
2. Günther, C.W., Van Der Aalst, W.M.: Fuzzy mining–adaptive process simplification based on multi-perspective metrics. In: Business Process Management, pp. 328–343. Springer (2007)
3. Leotta, F., Mecella, M., Mendling, J.: Applying process mining to smart spaces: Perspectives and research challenges. In: Advanced Information Systems Engineering Workshops. pp. 298–304. Springer (2015)
4. Van Der Aalst, W.: Process mining: Discovery, conformance and enhancement of business processes. Springer Science & Business Media (2011)

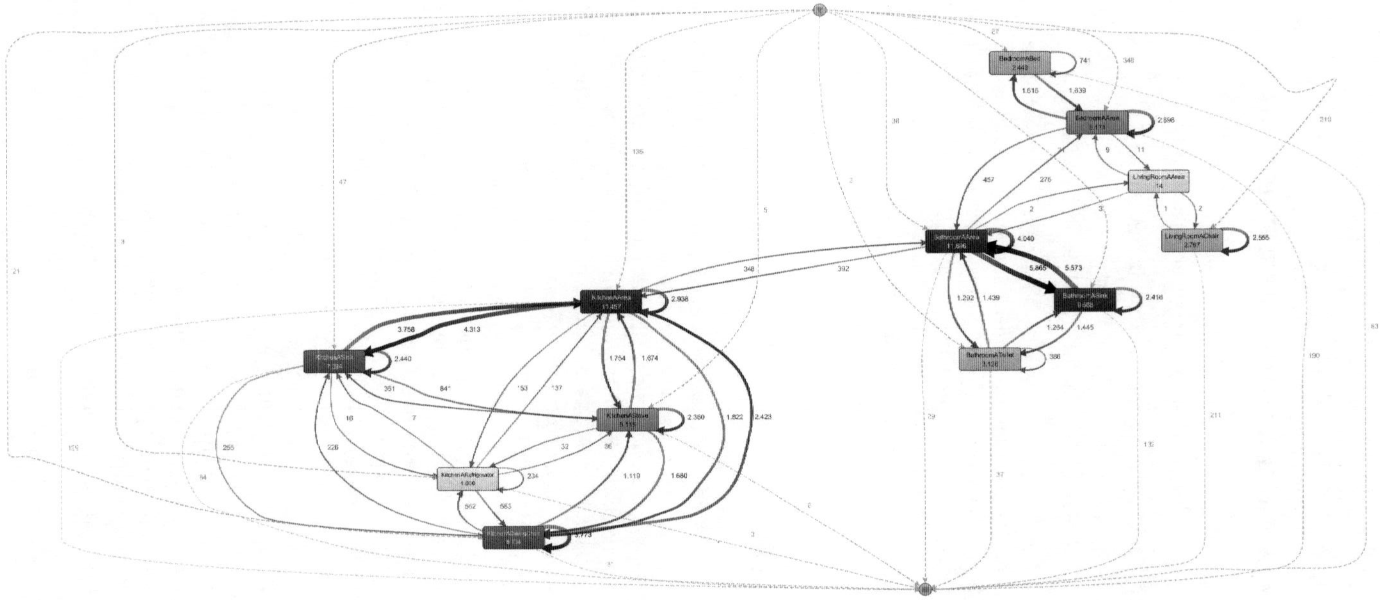

Fig. 3: The result of the application of fuzzy mining to the dataset – unfiltered results

On the Reification of Relationships

Nicola Guarino[1], Giancarlo Guizzardi[1,2]

[1]ISTC-CNR Laboratory for Applied Ontology (LOA), Trento, Italy
[1,2]Computer Science Department, Federal University of Espírito Santo (UFES), Brazil
guarino@loa.istc.cnr.it, gguizzardi@inf.ufes.br

Abstract. In this paper we propose a novel ontological analysis of relations and relationships based on a re-visitation of a classic problem in the practice of conceptual modeling, namely *relationship reification*. Despite the two terms 'relation' and 'relationship' are often used interchangeably, we shall assume a radical difference between the two: a relation *holds* in virtue of the *existence* of a relationship. We see therefore relationships as *truthmakers*, accounting not only for the *fact* that a relation holds, but also for the *way* it develops in time.

1 Introduction

In a seminal paper [1], Chen describes relationships in E-R diagrams in the following manner: *"a relationship is an association among entities.* [However,] *it is possible that some people may view something (e.g., marriage) as an entity while other people may view it as a relationship. We think that this is a decision which should be made by the Enterprise Administrator"*. In the same passage, Chen defines an Entity as a "thing" and claims that *"a specific person, a company, or an event is an example of an entity"*. Further in the paper, he defines a *relationship type* as a *"mathematical relation"*, that is, a set of tuples, and a relationship as one of such tuples. Chen also admits that relationships can bear properties. In one of his original examples, he illustrates how a *project-worker* relationship can have the attribute *percentage-of-time* representing an intrinsic property of the relationship itself.

We here subscribe to many of Chen's original intuitions. In particular, we agree with him on admitting that relationships can bear properties. However, in his paper Chen does not take an explicit ontological stance on the very nature of relationships and, as a consequence, the real-world semantics of this construct –a fundamental one– is left underspecified. In a subsequent paper [2], Chen elaborates on some of these ontological aspects while analysing the English sentence structure of textual descriptions. He states that entity types are the E-R counterpart of common nouns and that relationships are normally expressed by transitive verb phrases (e.g., *owns*, *belongs to*, *loves*). In addition, he recognizes that "nouns converted from a verb" (i.e., *verb nominalizations*) correspond to relationships (e.g., the *shipping* of the product to a customer or the *assigning* of an employee to a machine). Now, since verbs are typically the language proxy for events (including actions), it seems at first that Chen is committed to the view that relationships are events. Yet, in the very same paper he brings examples of relationship names such as *location of* or *part of*, which may not obviously correspond to events.

In any case, events are ontologically very different from tuples, so a question-begging issue that seems to be present since these early seminal papers on Conceptual Modeling is: what is a *relationship* after all? Is it just a tuple? Is it an event? Or is it something else? Moreover, is the difference between Entities and Relationships only a matter of a pragmatic modeling, as Chen seems to suggest, or are there deep ontological reasons for such distinction? In this paper we shall address the issues above by revisiting a classic problem in the practice of conceptual modeling, namely *relationship reification*. Despite the two terms 'relation' and 'relationship' are sometimes used interchangeably, we shall assume a radical difference between the two: a relation *holds*, while a relationship *exists*. Indeed, our idea is that the relation holds *in virtue of* the relationship's existence. As we shall see, we see therefore relationships as *truthmakers*, accounting not only for the *fact* that a relation holds, but also for the *way it develops in time*. In practice, we assume that, when a worker works in a project as a result of job assignment, there is something more fine-grained than just the two *relata* (the worker and the project) that is responsible for the relation to hold. This new entity –the relationship– includes specific *aspects* of the two relata, such as the *obligation* the worker has, but also the actual effort invested, the degree of satisfaction or stress, and so on. Together, all these aspects contribute to describe the *nature* of the relation, and the *way* it develops.

Our main claim is that relationships are objects (*endurants*). The basic intuitions behind this claim were already present in Guizzardi's early works [4,5], later advanced in [6] and with an alternative version in [7]. In such works, reified relationships are conceptualized as *relators,* which are endurants of a special kind, with the power of *mediating* other endurants. In a recent paper [Caise], we revisited the foundations of this early work, investigating and clarifying the very nature of relators in the light of the notion of truthmaking, and ultimately identifying them with reified relationships. We limited ourselves however to a particular class or relations that deserve reification of their relationships, namely what we called *extrinsic relations*. In the following, we present a general theory of reification and truthmaking that overcomes such limitation, covering all relations, including comparative relations and also unary relations.

The paper is structured as follows. In section 2, we first characterise the class of relations that deserve being reified, while clarifying and revising Guizzardi's earlier distinction between *formal relations* and *material relations*. We re-define the latter as *descriptive relations,* that hold in virtue of some qualities of their relata, and analyze the nature of their truthmakers, focusing first on unary descriptive relations (descriptive properties). In section 3, we discuss the crucial case of comparative relations, which was problematic in earlier Guizzardi's work, and generalize our results to extrinsic relations, discussing the differences with respect to previous approaches. In section 4 we present our conclusions.

2 Reification and Truthmaking

Before illustrating our theory, let us briefly clarify some terminological issues concerning reification and relationships. In general, reification is the process of including a certain entity in the domain of discourse. For example, when we ascribe metaproperties like symmetry to a binary relation such as *married with*, we are reifying the whole relation (intended as a set of tuples). This is different from reifying a single *instance* of a relation, say the single tuple <*John, Mary*>, and is also different from reifying the result of a *nominalization* process of the relation's predicate holding for that tuple, namely the *marriage* between John and Mary. The latter, *and not the tuple*, is what we call a *relationship*.

It is important to stress that such understanding of a relationship deviates from the mainstream, since Chen defines a *relationship type* as a mathematical relation (that is, a set of tuples), and a relationship as one of such tuples. So, relations and relationships are *extensional* notions. Yet, he admits that different relationships (say, *friend of* and *colleague of*) may involve the same tuples, so each relationship seems to have a unique "meaning" (its *intension*) conveyed by its *name*. We believe that it is exactly this intensional aspect of a relationship (and not the relationship itself, which is extensional) that people reify, when they talk of relationship reification. This is why, for the sake of clarity, we prefer to use the term 'relationship' only in its intensional meaning, adopting 'tuple' to refer to the extension. The rest of the paper will be devoted to understanding when it is useful and legitimate to consider such 'intensional meaning' as an element of our domain of discourse, and, if so, what its ontological nature is.

2.1 Which relations deserve reification?

In the past, a problem we encountered while developing our approach to relationships reification concerned the kinds of relation that deserve reification. In the early Guizzardi's work, a crisp distinction was assumed between *formal relations*, which "hold between two or more entities directly without any further intervening individual", and *material relations*, which require the existence of an intervening individual. The modeling proposal was to systematically introduce –for all material relations– a specific construct, called the *relator*, standing for such intervening individual. Note that *comparative relations* such as *taller than* were considered by Guizzardi as formal, based on the fact that they hold just in virtue of nothing else but the intrinsic properties of the relata.

However, in some cases the *mere existence* of the relata is enough to entail that a comparative relation holds, but in other cases this is not enough. For example, the existence of an electron *e* and a proton *p* is enough to conclude that *heavier(p, e)* holds (since both of them have that particular mass *essentially*), but the existence of John and Mary is not enough to conclude that *taller(John, Mary)* holds, since they don't have that particular height essentially, so something else is required. So, the picture is rather complicated, and this is the reason why, in a previous paper [9], we decided to abandon the formal/material distinction and just focus on a relevant class of relations that certainly deserve reification, those we called *extrinsic* relations, without taking a position on the reification of *intrinsic* relations, to which comparative relations belong.

In short, an intrinsic relation is a relation that can be derived from the intrinsic properties of its relata. This clearly applies to all comparative relations (whether or not they depend on the mere existence of their relata), as well as to all relations that just depend on the mere existence of their relata. Extrinsic relations are just the relations that are not intrinsic: for example, you can't decide whether *married(John, Mary)* holds just on the basis of the intrinsic properties of John and Mary.

Now, no doubt that *extrinsic* relations (i.e., those Guizzardi labeled *material* relations) deserve reification. But are we sure that comparative relations don't deserve reification? For instance, one may want to keep track of the difference in height between him and his son, or may measure the extent of a temperature difference between two bodies. In general, we may be interested in talking of *qualitative relationships* among things: we can have temperature relationships, size relationships, mass relationships... For instance, we can say that the mass relationship between the Earth and the Moon is responsible of the way they move around.

In the light of these examples, our position is that, besides extrinsic relations, also comparative relations may deserve reification. But what do they have in common? Our answer is that, together, they form the broad class of what we call *descriptive relations*. In short, a descriptive relation holds in virtue of *some particular aspect* (some *individual qualities*) of its relata. On the contrary, a non-descriptive relation holds in virtue of the nature of its relata, considered as wholes. So, for instance, an existential dependence or a part-of relation would count as non-descriptive, while a *taller than* or a *being in love with* relation would count as descriptive.

In sum, to decide whether a relation deserves or not reification we need to check whether it is a descriptive relation or not, i.e., whether it holds in virtue of some individual qualities of its relata. Individual qualities, originally introduced in the DOLCE ontology [8], are now a common feature (with minor differences) of top-level ontologies such as DOLCE, UFO [4], and BFO [13]. In the following, we shall see how individual qualities capture the notion of truthmaking, accounting not only for the truth of a relational predication, but also for the way a relationship behaves in time. In short, we shall see how *individual qualities constitute relationships*.

2.2 Weak truthmaking.

In our earlier paper [9], we based our re-visitation of Guizzardi's original idea of *relators* on the philosophical notion of *truthmaking*. In that paper, we did not take a position concerning the specific nature of such notion, just assuming that truthmaking is a primitive, fundamental relation linking what is true to what exists. More in general, a shared intuition is that a truthmaker for a property or a relation is an entity *in virtue of* which that property of relation holds. Several attempts have been made by philosophers to formally capture such intuition [10], i.e., to account for what '*in virtue of*' means. According to the mainstream doctrine, the truthmaker of a proposition is something *whose very existence* entails that the proposition is true. This means that the truthmaking relation holds *necessarily*. There is, however, a weaker notion of truthmaking, introduced by Josh Parsons [11], according to which the truthmaker of a proposition is something that makes the proposition true not just because of its existence (i.e., because of its *essential* nature), but because *of the way it contingently is* (i.e., because of its *actual* nature). The truthmaking relation does therefore hold *contingently*. This notion of *weak truthmaking* is the one we shall adopt here, since –as we shall see– it seems to be the most apt to support our view of (descriptive) relationships as entities that can change in time, accounting not only for the *fact* that a relation holds, but also for the *way* it holds and develops in time.

In the following, we shall illustrate such a view by considering separately three main cases of descriptive relations: descriptive properties (i.e., descriptive unary relations), comparative relations, and extrinsic relations. While in our previous paper we only focused on the third case, we believe that considering the former two cases is illuminating in developing a general theory of truthmaking and reification.

2.3 Descriptive properties and weak truthmaking.

Consider a simple proposition involving a descriptive property (i.e., a descriptive unary relation), such as *this rose is red*. What is its truthmaker? According to the mainstream theory, an answer is that it is the specific redness the rose exhibits. Such specific redness is what is called a *particularized property*, or a *trope*. It is an entity that *inheres* in the rose, in the sense that it is existentially dependent on the rose, and only on the rose. The very existence of such entity entails that the proposition is true.

Suppose now that the rose is red at time *t1*, and becomes brown after several days, at time *t2*. According to the mainstream theory, the truthmaker at *t2* will be a different one, namely a specific brownness. According to Parsons' theory, instead, the *weak truthmaker* at both times is the rose itself: it is the very same rose, because of the way it is at *t1* and at *t2*, that is a truthmaker of '*this rose is red*' at *t1* and a truthmaker of '*this rose is brown*' at *t2*. In other words, a weak truthmaker is something such, because of the way it is, makes a proposition true.

The rose is not however the *minimal* weak truthmaker of these propositions. There is something smaller –so to speak– than the whole rose: the rose's *color*. Indeed, it is exactly because of the rose's color that the rose is red at *t1* and brown at *t2*. As we mentioned above, this color is modeled as an *individual quality* in the DOLCE, UFO and BFO ontologies. A peculiar characteristic of individual qualities is that they are *endurants*, i.e., they can qualitatively change in time (e.g., change their "value" from red to brown) while maintaining their identity.

In sum, we can conclude that individual qualities are the minimal weak truthmakers of (unary) descriptive propositions. So to speak, they are *responsible* for the truth of such propositions, in the precise sense –as explained by Parsons– that the proposition can't become false without an intrinsic change of an individual quality, i.e., without a movement in a space of possible values that quality can assume. Note that, as we have seen, the same quality can be responsible for the truth of different propositions holding at different times.

Let us see now how the weak truthmaking mechanism described above can be used to establish an ontological foundation for *reification* choices in the practice of conceptual modeling: whenever you have a descriptive property holding for an individual, typically represented by an instance attribute of a class, consider the possibility of introducing the corresponding weak truthmaker in your domain of discourse. Suppose for example that, in an employment scenario, you have the attribute *mood* for the *Employee* class, with possible values *happy* or *sad*; reifying the *mood* quality as a separate class (whose instances inhere to the instance of *Employee*) would allow you the possibility to express:

1. Further *details* on the quality itself;
2. Information on the quality's *temporal behavior*;

3. Information on *causal interactions* of the quality with the world.

The above are, in general, the main reasons for relation reification (including property reification as in this case). Note that, strictly speaking, we cannot say that in this way we are reifying, the *happy* and the *sad* properties, since the same *mood* quality may "reify" both of them at different times. A strict reification would result in the explicit introduction of a specific happiness and a specific sadness, intended as *completely determined* particularized properties, which would be tropes and not qualities. In this case, however, as discussed by Moltmann [12] and in our earlier paper, we would loose the flexibility of expressing the additional information described above. In conclusion, we may consider the strategy of introducing *weak truthmakers* of descriptive relations in the domain of discourse as a *weak reification* strategy, which turns out, however, to be more effective in practice than a strict reification strategy (which we shall label *strong reification* just to contrast it with the former one).

3 Descriptive relations and weak truthmaking

3.1 Comparative relations

Let us consider now the case of comparative relations. Take for example *taller(John, Mary)*. In the light of the previous discussion, it is easy to see that its minimal weak truthmaker is the *mereological sum*[1] of two individual qualities, namely John's height and Mary's height. Similarly to what noted above, should the *height relationship* between John and Mary change, this would be also the weak truthmaker of *as-tall-as(John, Mary)* and *taller(Mary, John)*. In our view, this means that there is a single entity in our ontology, namely a *height relationship*, consisting of a *quality complex* having the two individual heights as proper parts. Such a relationship is an *endurant*, whose internal configuration may be such that one of the three possible propositions above is true at a given time.

In conclusion, we can say that comparative relationships are the weak truthmakers of comparative relations. Reifying them has the same advantages we have seen above in terms of the possibility to add further details: for instance, we can express the actual *height-distance* between the two relata as a property of the relationship (which in principle may itself be reified, originating a height-distance individual quality inhering in the quality complex).

Note that the approach described above can be generalized to the case of relations expressing arbitrary configurations of intrinsic qualities, such as weights or colors. Considering spatial position also an intrinsic quality (as done in DOLCE, although debatable), relations describing spatial configurations (patterns) may be also be reified in terms of quality complexes.

---

[1] The mereological sum of x and y is an entity z such that whatever overlaps z also overlaps x or y

3.2 Extrinsic relations

The case of extrinsic relations has been discussed in detail in our earlier paper. Their main difference with respect to comparative relations and descriptive properties is that their weak truthmakers are constituted of *relational* qualities, which inhere in one relatum but are *existentially dependent* on another one.

Let us comment here the novelties with respect to that work. A major difference concerns the adoption of the weak truthmaking notion, which allows for a homogenous theory of reification and truthmaking that includes descriptive properties and comparative relations. This also results in significant simplifications of our previous technical framework. For example, consider the case of the *married-to* relation, and assume it is a genuine descriptive relation, in the sense that it holds in virtue of a mutual pattern of commitments and obligations that inhere in the two partners. In our earlier paper, we took such pattern of commitments and obligations as the truthmaker, but –at least in the institutional case where the marriage is the result of a wedding event– we were forced to acknowledge the presence of another (minimal) truthmaker, namely the wedding event. Then we eliminated such historical truthmakers by assuming that only *synchronous* truthmakers should be considered while analyzing the notion of extrinsic relationship. By assuming weak truthmaking this problem disappears, since although such patterns of commitments and obligations depend for their existence on the occurrence of a previous wedding event, still they are such that the relation holds, and this is enough for the notion of weak truthmaking.

A further difference is related to the fact that, as we have seen, the same *relationship* (i.e., the same weak truthmaker) may make different kinds of *relational propositions* true. Consider for instance a love relationship between John and Mary. At different times, we can describe it in different ways: as a mutual love, as a non-mutual-love, as a passionate love, as a mostly inexistent love, etc. All the corresponding propositions would share the same weak truthmaker, i.e., the same love relationship (of course, exhibiting qualitative changes in time).

4 Conclusions

In this paper, we believe we made a substantial step forward towards in understanding the nature of a fundamental construct in conceptual modeling, namely, *relationships*. Space does not allow to discuss here the practical implications of the theory presented here, which have been however discussed extensively in other papers. What was still lacking was a general ontological analysis of reification and truthmaking, which explains why and how a relation holds. We believe we have such a theory now.

As a next step in our research, we intend to re-engineer the OntoUML metamodel to accommodate the proposal put forth here. This shall have an impact not only in the language, but also in its supporting methodological and computational tools [14]. Moreover, in order to allow these distinctions to be formally reflected in the ontological semantics of the language, we need to extend its underlying foundational ontology (UFO).

References

1. Chen. P., The entity-relationship model: Towards a unified view of data, ACM Transactions on Database Systems 1(1), 1976.
2. Chen, P., English Sentence Structure and Entity-Relationship Diagrams, Information Sciences, Volume 29, Issues 2–3, May–June 1983, pp. 127–149
3. Moltmann, F., Events, Tropes and Truthmaking, Philosophical Studies (2007).
4. Guizzardi, G., Ontological Foundations for Structural Conceptual Models, Telematics Instituut Fundamental Research Series, No. 015, ISSN 1388-1795, The Netherlands, 2005.
5. Guizzardi, G., Wagner, G., What's in a relationship: an ontological analysis, Conceptual Modeling (ER 2008), Barcelona, Spain, in: LNCS 5231, 2008, pp. 83–97.
6. Costal, D., Goméz, C., Guizzardi, G., Formal Semantics and Ontological Analysis for Understanding Subsetting, Specialization and Redefinition of Associations in UML, 30th Int. Conf. on Conceptual Modeling (ER 2011), Brussels, Belgium, 2011.
7. Guizzardi, G., Zamborlini, V., Using a Trope-Based Foundational Ontology for Bridging different areas of concern in Ontology-Driven Conceptual Modeling, Science of Computer Programming, 2014.
8. Masolo, C., Borgo, S., Foundational Choices in DOLCE, in S. Staab and R. Studer (eds.), Handbook on Ontologies, Springer-Verlag, Berlin, p. 361-381, 2009.
9. N. Guarino and G. Guizzardi, "'We Need to Discuss the Relationship': Revisiting Relationships as Modeling Constructs.," *CAiSE*, vol. 9097, no. 18, pp. 279–294, 2015.
10. F. MacBride, "Truthmakers," in *Stanford Encyclopedia of Philosohy*, 2014, pp. 1–69.
11. J. Parsons, "There is no 'truthmaker' argument against nominalism," *Australasian Journal of Philosophy*, vol. 77, no. 3, pp. 325–334, 1999.
12. F. Moltmann. Abstract Objects and the Semantics of Natural Language. Oxford University Press 2013
13. R. Arp, B. Smith, A. D. Spear. Building Ontologies with Basic Formal Ontology. MIT Press 2015.
14. Guizzardi, G., Ontological Patterns, Anti-Patterns and Pattern Languages for Next-Generation Conceptual Modeling, Conceptual Modeling (ER 2014), Atlanta, USA.

Author Index

Matematicamente.It
Corso Umberto, 39
73010 San Donato (Lecce)
Italy

ISBN 978-1-5108-3690-7